CIMA Official
Learning System

Relevant for
Computer-Based Assessments

C03 – Fundamentals of Business Mathematics

CIMA Certificate in Business Accounting

Graham Eaton

ELSEVIER

AMSTERDAM   BOSTON   HEIDELBERG   LONDON   NEW YORK   OXFORD
PARIS   SAN DIEGO   SAN FRANCISCO   SINGAPORE   SYDNEY   TOKYO

CIMA Publishing is an imprint of Elsevier
The Boulevard, Langford Lane, Kidlington, Oxford, OX5 1GB
30 Corporate Drive, Suite 400, Burlington, MA 01803, USA

First edition 2008
Reprinted 2011

Copyright © 2009 Elsevier Ltd. All rights reserved

No part of this publication may be reproduced, stored in a retrieval system
or transmitted in any form or by any means electronic, mechanical, photocopying,
recording or otherwise without the prior written permission of the publisher

Permissions may be sought directly from Elsevier's Science & Technology Rights
Department in Oxford, UK: phone (+44) (0) 1865 843830; fax (+44) (0) 1865 853333;
email: permissions@elsevier.com. Alternatively you can visit the Science and Technology
books website at www.elsevierdirect.com/rights for further information.

Notice
No responsibility is assumed by the publisher for any injury and/or damage to persons
or property as a matter of products liability, negligence or otherwise, or from any use
or operation of any methods, products, instructions or ideas contained in the material
herein.

British Library Cataloguing in Publication Data
A catalogue record for this book is available from the British Library

Library of Congress Cataloguing in Publication Data
A catalogue record for this book is available from the Library of Congress

ISBN: 978-1-85617-783-2

For information on all CIMA publications
visit our website at www.elsevierdirect.com

Typeset by Macmillan Publishing Solutions
(www.macmillansolutions.com)

Printed and bound in China

11 12 13 14 15   7 6 5 4 3 2

**Working together to grow
libraries in developing countries**

www.elsevier.com | www.bookaid.org | www.sabre.org

ELSEVIER   BOOK AID International   Sabre Foundation

Contents

The CIMA *Learning system*	ix
How to use your CIMA *Learning System*	ix
Study technique	xi
Computer-Based Assessments	xii
Fundamentals of Business Mathematics and Computer-Based Assessments	xiii
Learning outcomes and indicative syllabus content	xiv
Mathematical Tables	xix

1 Basic Mathematics — 1

	Learning Outcomes	3
1.1	Introduction	3
1.2	Mathematical operations and brackets	3
1.3	Different types of numbers	4
1.4	Rounding	5
	1.4.1 Rounding to the nearest whole number	5
	1.4.2 Significant figures	5
	1.4.3 Decimal places	6
	1.4.4 Rounding up or rounding down	6
1.5	Powers and roots	7
	1.5.1 Definitions	7
1.6	Mathematical operations in Excel	8
	1.6.1 Rounding numbers in Excel	8
1.7	Variables and functions	10
1.8	Formulae	11
1.9	Exponential numbers	13
1.10	Solving equations	14
	1.10.1 Linear equations with only one variable	14
	1.10.2 Quadratic equations with only one variable	15
	1.10.3 Simultaneous linear equations	16
1.11	Manipulating inequalities	18
1.12	Percentages and ratios	19
1.13	Accuracy and approximation	20
1.14	Errors from rounding	21
1.15	Using Excel to produce graphs of Linear and Quadratic Equations	21
	1.15.1 Producing a single linear equation in Excel	21
	1.15.2 Drawing multiple equations on a single graph	22
	1.15.3 Single quadratic equation	23
	1.15.4 Two quadratic equations on one graph	24
1.16	Using Excel to produce the graph of a hyperbola	25
1.17	Summary	26
	Revision Questions	27
	Solutions to Revision Questions	33

2 Obtaining Data — 39

Learning Outcomes — 41
2.1 Introduction — 41
    2.1.1 The difference between information and data — 42
2.2 Primary data: sampling — 43
2.3 Probability sampling methods — 44
    2.3.1 Simple random sampling — 44
    2.3.2 Stratified random sampling — 44
2.4 Other sampling methods — 46
2.5 Multistage sampling — 47
2.6 Secondary data: sources — 48
2.7 Questionnaires — 48
2.8 Contact with respondents — 49
2.9 Importing data to Excel — 50
    2.9.1 Importing data from Word — 50
    2.9.2 Using the Excel Text to Columns feature — 51
2.10 Summary — 52

Revision Questions — 53

Solutions to Revision Questions — 59

3 Presentation of Data — 63

Learning Outcomes — 65
3.1 Introduction — 65
3.2 Linear graphs — 65
3.3 Solving simultaneous linear equations using graphs — 70
3.4 Quadratic graphs — 71
3.5 Tallying frequency distributions — 72
3.6 Discrete and continuous variables — 75
3.7 Cumulative frequency distribution — 76
3.8 Histograms and ogives — 78
3.9 Pie charts — 85
3.10 Bar charts — 87
    3.10.1 Creating Bar charts using Excel — 90
3.11 Tabulation — 95
3.12 Pareto analysis – The 80-20 rule — 96
3.13 Using spreadsheets to produce histograms, ogives and pie charts — 98
    3.13.1 Creating a histogram in Excel — 98
    3.13.2 Creating an ogive in Excel — 101
    3.13.3 Creating a Pie chart in Excel — 102
3.14 Summary — 103

Readings — 105

Revision Questions — 109

Solutions to Revision Questions — 117

4 Descriptive Statistics — 125

    Learning Outcomes — 127
- 4.1 Introduction — 127
- 4.2 The arithmetic mean — 127
- 4.3 The median — 131
- 4.4 The mode — 135
- 4.5 A comparison of the three averages — 137
- 4.6 Measures of spread — 139
- 4.7 The range — 139
- 4.8 The interquartile range; the quartile deviation — 140
- 4.9 Deciles — 142
- 4.10 The mean absolute deviation — 144
- 4.11 The standard deviation — 145
- 4.12 The coefficient of variation — 148
- 4.13 A comparison of the measures of spread — 150
- 4.14 Descriptive statistics using Excel — 150
- 4.15 A practical example of descriptive statistical analysis using Excel — 152
  - 4.15.1 The questionnaire — 153
  - 4.15.2 Data capture — 153
  - 4.15.3 Preliminary analysis — 155
  - 4.15.4 Descriptive statistics — 157
  - 4.15.5 Worked Example Conclusions — 161
- 4.16 Summary — 162

    Readings — 165

    Revision Questions — 169

    Solutions to Revision Questions — 179

5 Index Numbers — 185

    Learning Outcomes — 187
- 5.1 Introduction — 187
- 5.2 Definitions — 187
- 5.3 Interpretation of index numbers — 188
- 5.4 Choice of base year — 189
- 5.5 Change of base year — 190
- 5.6 Combining series of index numbers — 191
- 5.7 Chain-base index numbers — 192
- 5.8 Composite index numbers — 194
- 5.9 Relative price indices — 196
- 5.10 Aggregative price indices — 198
- 5.11 Choice of base weighting or current weighting — 199
- 5.12 Quantity indices — 200
- 5.13 The construction of the UK retail price index — 202
- 5.14 Using the RPI — 202
- 5.15 Summary — 206

    Readings — 207

    Revision Questions — 209

    Solutions to Revision Questions — 217

6 Financial Mathematics — 223

    Learning Outcomes — 225
- 6.1 Introduction — 225
- 6.2 Simple interest — 225
- 6.3 Compound interest — 227
- 6.4 Equivalent rates of interest — 228
- 6.5 Depreciation — 230
- 6.6 More complex investments — 231
- 6.7 Geometric progressions — 233
- 6.8 Present values — 234
- 6.9 Net present values – practical examples — 236
- 6.10 Problems using NPV in practice — 239
- 6.11 Annuities — 239
- 6.12 PV of a perpetuity — 241
- 6.13 Loans and mortgages — 242
- 6.14 Internal rate of return — 243
- 6.15 Financial functions in Excel — 246
  - 6.15.1 The investment reports — 246
- 6.16 Summary — 248

    Readings — 251
    Revision Questions — 253
    Solutions to Revision Questions — 263

7 Correlation and Regression — 271

    Learning Outcomes — 273
- 7.1 Introduction — 273
- 7.2 Correlation — 274
- 7.3 Pearson's correlation coefficient — 278
- 7.4 Interpreting correlation coefficients — 279
- 7.5 Rank correlation: Spearman's coefficient — 280
- 7.6 Which correlation coefficient to use — 282
- 7.7 Regression — 282
- 7.8 The least-squares criterion — 283
- 7.9 Interpreting a and b — 286
- 7.10 Forecasting — 287
- 7.11 Which variable to denote by y — 289
- 7.12 Judging the validity of forecasts — 290
- 7.13 Summary — 292

    Revision Questions — 293
    Solutions to Revision Questions — 301

8 Time Series — 307

    Learning Outcomes — 309
- 8.1 Introduction — 309
- 8.2 Components and models of time series — 309

8.3	Forecasting linear trends	312
8.4	Forecasting seasonal components	314
8.5	Producing the final forecast	317
8.6	Seasonal adjustment	318
8.7	Moving average trends	319
8.8	Other types of data	322
8.9	Judging the validity of forecasts	324
8.10	Computations involving the additive model	325
8.11	Summary	328
	Readings	329
	Revision Questions	331
	Solutions to Revision Questions	339

9 Probability — 345

	Learning Outcomes	347
9.1	Introduction	347
9.2	Definitions of probability	348
9.3	Addition rules of probability	349
9.4	The probability of opposites	351
9.5	The multiplication rules of probability	351
9.6	More conditional probabilities	355
9.7	Discrete probability distributions; expectations	356
9.8	Expectation and decision-making	358
9.9	Limitations of this approach	361
9.10	Characteristics of the normal distribution	362
9.11	Use of the tables of normal distribution	363
9.12	Further normal distribution examples	368
9.13	Venn diagrams	370
	9.13.1 Using Venn diagrams to assist with probability	371
9.14	Uncertainty and risk	372
9.15	Summary	375
	Revision Questions	377
	Solutions to Revision Questions	385

10 Spreadsheet Skills using Excel — 393

	Learning Outcomes	395
10.1	Introduction	395
10.2	Spreadsheet terminology	396
	10.2.1 Workbooks and Worksheets	396
	10.2.2 Cells	396
10.3	A note on macros and application development	396
10.4	Getting started with Excel	397
	10.4.1 Workbooks of files	397
	10.4.2 Worksheets	397
	10.4.3 Scroll bars	398

	10.4.4	Status bar	398
	10.4.5	Toolbars	398
10.5	Good spreadsheet design		398
10.6	Getting started		399
	10.6.1	Problems with this spreadsheet	399
	10.6.2	Positive aspects of this spreadsheet	399
10.7	Ownership and version		399
	10.7.1	Problems with this spreadsheet	400
	10.7.2	Positive aspects of this spreadsheet	400
10.8	Formatting		400
	10.8.1	Problems with this spreadsheet	400
	10.8.2	Positive aspects of this spreadsheet	401
10.9	Documentation		402
10.10	Minimising absolute values		403
	10.10.1	Problems with this spreadsheet	404
10.11	Control checks for auditing		405
10.12	Charts		406
10.13	Tips for larger plans		406
10.14	Templates		407
	10.14.1	Data input forms	408
10.15	The use of spreadsheets by management accountants		409
10.16	Summary		410

Preparing for the Assessment — 411

Revision technique — 413
Format of the assessment — 414

Revision Questions — 417

Solutions to Revision Questions — 453

Mock Assessment 1 — 481

Mock Assessment 2 — 505

Index — 535

The CIMA Learning System

How to use your CIMA *Learning System*

This *Fundamentals of Business Mathematics Learning System* has been devised as a resource for students attempting to pass their CIMA computer-based assessments, and provides:

- a detailed explanation of all syllabus areas;
- extensive 'practical' materials;
- generous question practice, together with full solutions;
- a computer-based assessments preparation section, complete with computer-based assessments standard questions and solutions.

This Learning System has been designed with the needs of home-study and distance-learning candidates in mind. Such students require very full coverage of the syllabus topics, and also the facility to undertake extensive question practice. However, the Learning System is also ideal for fully taught courses.

This main body of the text is divided into a number of chapters, each of which is organised on the following pattern:

- *Detailed learning outcomes* expected after your studies of the chapter are complete. You should assimilate these before beginning detailed work on the chapter, so that you can appreciate where your studies are leading.
- *Step-by-step topic coverage.* This is the heart of each chapter, containing detailed explanatory text supported where appropriate by worked examples and exercises. You should work carefully through this section, ensuring that you understand the material being explained and can tackle the examples and exercises successfully. Remember that in many cases knowledge is cumulative: if you fail to digest earlier material thoroughly, you may struggle to understand later chapters.
- *Activities.* Some chapters are illustrated by more practical elements, such as comments and questions designed to stimulate discussion.
- *Question practice.* The test of how well you have learned the material is your ability to tackle exam-standard questions. Make a serious attempt at producing your own answers, but at this stage do not be too concerned about attempting the questions in computer-based assessments conditions. In particular, it is more important to absorb the material thoroughly by completing a full solution than to observe the time limits that would apply in the actual computer-based assessments.

- *Solutions.* Avoid the temptation merely to 'audit' the solutions provided. It is an illusion to think that this provides the same benefits as you would gain from a serious attempt of your own. However, if you are struggling to get started on a question you should read the introductory guidance provided at the beginning of the solution, where provided, and then make your own attempt before referring back to the full solution.

Having worked through the chapters you are ready to begin your final preparations for the computer-based assessments. The final section of the CIMA *Learning System* provides you with the guidance you need. It includes the following features:

- A brief guide to revision technique.
- A note on the format of the computer-based assessments. You should know what to expect when you tackle the real computer-based assessments, and in particular the number of questions to attempt.
- Guidance on how to tackle the computer-based assessments itself.
- A table mapping revision questions to the syllabus learning outcomes allowing you to quickly identify questions by subject area.
- Revision questions. These are of computer-based assessments standard and should be tackled in computer-based assessments conditions, especially as regards the time allocation.
- Solutions to the revision questions.

Two mock computer-based assessments. You should plan to attempt these just before the date of the real computer-based assessments. By this stage your revision should be complete and you should be able to attempt the mock computer-based assessments within the time constraints of the real computer based assessments.

If you work conscientiously through the CIMA *Learning System* according to the guidelines above you will be giving yourself an excellent chance of success in your computer-based assessments. Good luck with your studies!

Guide to the Icons used within this Text

Key term or definition

Exam tip or topic likely to appear in the computer-based assessments

Exercise

Question

Solution

Comment or Note

Discussion points

Equations to learn

Study technique

Passing exams is partly a matter of intellectual ability, but however accomplished you are in that respect you can improve your chances significantly by the use of appropriate study and revision techniques. In this section we briefly outline some tips for effective study during the earlier stages of your approach to the computer-based assessments. Later in the text we mention some techniques that you will find useful at the revision stage.

Planning

To begin with, formal planning is essential to get the best return from the time you spend studying. Estimate how much time in total you are going to need for each paper you are studying for the Certificate in Business Accounting. Remember that you need to allow time for revision as well as for initial study of the material. The amount of notional study time for any paper is the minimum estimated time that students will need to achieve the specified learning outcomes set out below. This time includes all appropriate learning activities, for example, face-to-face tuition, private study, directed home study, learning in the workplace, revision time, etc. You may find it helpful to read *Better Exam Results: a Guide for Business and Accounting Students* by S. A. Malone, Elsevier, ISBN: 075066357X. This book will provide you with proven study techniques. Chapter by chapter it covers the building blocks of successful learning and examination techniques.

The notional study time for the Certificate in Business Accounting paper *Fundamentals of Business Mathematics* is 130 hours. Note that the standard amount of notional learning hours attributed to one full-time academic year of approximately 30 weeks is 1,200 hours.

By way of example, the notional study time might be made up as follows:

	Hours
Face-to-face study: up to	40
Personal study: up to	65
'Other' study – e.g. learning in the workplace, revision, etc.: up to	25
	130

Note that all study and learning-time recommendations should be used only as a guideline and are intended as minimum amounts. The amount of time recommended for face-to-face tuition, personal study and/or additional learning will vary according to the type of course undertaken, prior learning of the student, and the pace at which different students learn.

Now split your total time requirement over the weeks between now and the exam. This will give you an idea of how much time you need to devote to study each week. Remember to allow for holidays or other periods during which you will not be able to study (e.g. because of seasonal workloads).

With your study material before you, decide which chapters you are going to study in each week, and which weeks you will devote to revision and final question practice.

Prepare a written schedule summarising the above – and stick to it!

The amount of space allocated to a topic in the Learning System is not a very good guide as to how long it will take you. For example, the material relating to Section A 'Basic Mathematics' and Section C 'Summarising and Analysing Data' both account or 15% of the syllabus, but the latter has more pages because there are more illustrations, which take up more space. The syllabus weighting is the better guide as to how long you should spend on a syllabus topic. It is essential to know your syllabus. As your course progresses you will become more familiar with how long it takes to cover topics in sufficient depth. Your timetable may need to be adapted to allocate enough time for the whole syllabus.

Tips for effective studying

1. Aim to find a quiet and undisturbed location for your study, and plan as far as possible to use the same period of time each day. Getting into a routine helps to avoid wasting time. Make sure that you have all the materials you need before you begin so as to minimise interruptions.
2. Store all your materials in one place, so that you do not waste time searching for items around your accommodation. If you have to pack everything away after each study period, keep them in a box, or even a suitcase, which will not be disturbed until the next time.
3. Limit distractions. To make the most effective use of your study periods you should be able to apply total concentration, so turn off all entertainment equipment, set your phones to message mode, and put up your 'do not disturb' sign.
4. Your timetable will tell you which topic to study. However, before diving in and becoming engrossed in the finer points, make sure you have an overall picture of all the areas that need to be covered by the end of that session. After an hour, allow yourself a short break and move away from your Learning System. With experience, you will learn to assess the pace you need to work at.
5. Work carefully through a chapter, making notes as you go. When you have covered a suitable amount of material, vary the pattern by attempting a practice question. When you have finished your attempt, make notes of any mistakes you made, or any areas that you failed to cover or covered only skimpily.
6. Make notes as you study, and discover the techniques that work best for you. Your notes may be in the form of lists, bullet points, diagrams, summaries, 'mind maps', or the written word, but remember that you will need to refer back to them at a later date, so they must be intelligible. If you are on a taught course, make sure you highlight any issues you would like to follow up with your lecturer.
7. Organise your notes. Make sure that all your notes, calculations etc can be effectively filed and easily retrieved later.

Computer-Based Assessments

CIMA uses computer-based assessments (CBAs) for all subjects for the Certificate in Business Accounting. The website says

Objective questions are used. The most common type is 'multiple choice', where you have to choose the correct answer from a list of possible answers, but there are a variety of other objective question types that can be used within the system. These include true/false questions, matching pairs of text and graphic, sequencing and ranking, labelling diagrams and single and multiple numeric entry.

Candidates answer the questions by either pointing and clicking the mouse, moving objects around the screen, typing numbers, or a combination of these responses. Try the online demo at http://www.cimaglobal.com to see how the technology works.

The CBA system can ensure that a wide range of the syllabus is assessed, as a pre-determined number of questions from each syllabus area (dependent upon the syllabus weighting for that particular area) are selected in each assessment.

In every chapter of this Learning System we have introduced these types of questions but obviously we have to label answers A, B, C etc. rather than using click boxes. For convenience, we have retained quite a lot of questions where an initial scenario leads to a number of sub-questions. There will be questions of this type in the CBA but they will rarely have more than three sub-questions. In all such cases the answer to one part does not hinge upon a prior answer.

Fundamentals of Business Mathematics and Computer-Based Assessments

The computer-based assessments for Fundamentals Business Mathematics is a 2-hour computer-based assessments comprising 45 compulsory questions, with one or more parts. Single part questions are generally worth 1–2 marks each, but two and three part questions may be worth 4 or 6 marks. There will be no choice and all questions should be attempted if time permits. CIMA are continuously developing the question styles within the CBA system and you are advised to try the on-line website demo at www.cimaglobal.com, to both gain familiarity with assessment software and examine the latest style of questions being used.

Fundamentals of Business Mathematics

Syllabus outline

The Syllabus comprises:
Topic and study weighting

A	Basic Mathematics	15%
B	Probability	15%
C	Summarising and Analysing Data	15%
D	Inter-relationships between variables	15%
E	Forecasting	15%
F	Financial Mathematics	15%
G	Spreadsheets	10%

Learning Aims

This syllabus aims to test the candidate's ability to:

- demonstrate the use of basic mathematics, including formulae and ratios;
- identify reasonableness in the calculation of answers;
- demonstrate the use of probability where risk and uncertainty exist;
- apply techniques for summarising and analysing data;
- calculate correlation coefficients for bivariate data and apply the technique of simple regression analysis;

- demonstrate techniques used for forecasting;
- apply financial mathematical techniques;
- apply spreadsheets to facilitate the presentation of data, analysis of univariate and bivariate data and use of formulae.

Assessment strategy

There will be a computer-based assessments of 2 hours duration, comprising 45 compulsory questions, each with one or more parts.

A variety of objective test question styles and types will be used within the assessment.

Learning outcomes and indicative syllabus content

A Basic Mathematics – 15%

Learning Outcomes

On completion of their studies students should be able to:

(i) demonstrate the order of operations in formulae, including brackets, powers and roots;
(ii) calculate percentages and proportions;
(iii) calculate answers to appropriate number of decimal places or significant figures;
(iv) solve simple equations, including two variable simultaneous equations and quadratic equations;
(v) prepare graphs of linear and quadratic equations.

Indicative syllabus content

- Use of formulae, including negative powers as in the formula for the learning curve.
- Percentages and ratios.
- Rounding of numbers.
- Basic algebraic techniques and solution of equations, including simultaneous equations and quadratic equations.
- Manipulation of inequalities.

B Probability – 15%

Learning outcomes

On completion of their studies students should be able to:

(i) calculate a simple probability;
(ii) demonstrate the addition and multiplication rules of probability;
(iii) calculate a simple conditional probability;
(iv) calculate an expected value;
(v) demonstrate the use of expected value tables in decision making;

(vi) explain the limitations of expected values;
(vii) explain the concepts of risk and uncertainty.

Indicative syllabus content

- The relationship between probability, proportion and percent.
- Addition and multiplication rules in probability theory.
- Venn diagrams.
- Expected values and expected value tables.
- Risk and uncertainty.

C Summarising and Analysing Data – 15%
Learning Outcomes

On completion of their studies students should be able to:

(i) explain the difference between data and information;
(ii) identify the characteristics of good information;
(iii) tabulate data and prepare histograms;
(iv) calculate for both ungrouped and grouped data: arithmetic mean, median, mode, range, variance, standard deviation and coefficient of variation;
(v) explain the concept of a frequency distribution;
(vi) prepare graphs/diagrams of normal distribution, explain its properties and use tables of normal distribution;
(vii) apply the Pareto distribution and the '80:20 rule';
(viii) explain how and why indices are used;
(ix) calculate indices using either base or current weights;
(x) apply indices to deflate a series.

Indicative syllabus content

- Data and information.
- Tabulation of data.
- Graphs and diagrams: scatter diagrams, histograms, bar charts and ogives.
- Summary measures of central tendency and dispersion for both grouped and ungrouped data.
- Frequency distributions.
- Normal distribution, the Pareto distribution and '80:20 rule'.
- Index numbers.

D Inter-relationships between Variables – 15%
Learning outcomes

On completion of their studies students should be able to:

(i) prepare a scatter diagram;
(ii) calculate the correlation coefficient and the coefficient of determination between two variables;

(iii) calculate the regression equation between two variables;
(iv) apply the regression equation to predict the dependent variable, given a value of the independent variable.

Indicative syllabus content

- Scatter diagrams and the correlation coefficient
- Simple linear regression

E Forecasting – 15%

Learning outcomes

On completion of their studies students should be able to:

(i) prepare a time series graph;
(ii) identify trends and patterns using an appropriate moving average;
(iii) identify the components of a time series model;
(iv) prepare a trend equation using either graphical means or regression analysis;
(v) calculate seasonal factors for both additive and multiplicative models and explain when each is appropriate;
(vi) calculate predicted values, given a time series model;
(vii) identify the limitations of forecasting models.

Indicative syllabus content

- Time series analysis – graphical analysis.
- Trends in time series – graphs, moving averages and linear regression.
- Seasonal variations using both additive and multiplicative models.
- Forecasting and its limitations.

F Financial Mathematics – 15%

Learning Outcomes

On completion of their studies students should be able to:

(i) calculate future values of an investment using both simple and compound interest;
(ii) calculate an annual percentage rate of interest given a monthly or quarterly rate;
(iii) calculate the present value of a future cash sum using formula and CIMA Tables;
(iv) calculate the present value of an annuity and a perpetuity using formula and CIMA Tables;
(v) calculate loan/mortgage repayments and the value of the loan/mortgage outstanding;
(vi) calculate the future value of regular savings and/or the regular investment needed to generate a required future sum using the formula for the sum of a geometric progression;
(vii) calculate the net present value (NPV) and internal rate of return (IRR) of a project and explain whether and why it should be accepted.

Indicative syllabus content

- Simple and compound interest.
- Annuities and perpetuities.
- Loans and mortgages.
- Sinking funds and savings funds.
- Discounting to find NPV and IRR and interpretation of NPV and IRR.

G Spreadsheets – 10%

Learning Outcomes

On completion of their studies students should be able to:

- explain the features and functions of spreadsheet software;
- explain the use and limitations of spreadsheet software in business;
- apply spreadsheet software to the normal work of a Chartered Management Accountant.

Indicative syllabus content

- Features and functions of commonly used spreadsheet software: workbook, worksheet, rows, columns, cells, data, text, formulae, formatting, printing, graphics and macros. Note: Knowledge of Microsoft Excel type spreadsheet vocabulary/formulae syntax is required. Formulae tested will be that which is constructed by users rather than preprogrammed formulae.
- Advantages and disadvantages of spreadsheet software, when compared to manual analysis and other types of software application packages.
- Use of spreadsheet software in the day-to-day work of the Chartered Management Accountant: budgeting, forecasting, reporting performance, variance analysis, what-if analysis and discounted cashflow calculations.

Mathematical Tables

PROBABILITY
$A \cup B = A$ or B. $A \cap B = A$ **and** B (overlap).
$P(B \mid A)$ = probability of B, **given** A.

Rules of Addition
If A and B are *mutually exclusive*: $P(A \cup B) = P(A) + P(B)$
If A and B are not mutually exclusive: $P(A \cup B) = P(A) + P(B) - P(A \cap B)$

Rules of Multiplication
If A and B are *independent*: $P(A \cap B) = P(A) * P(B)$
If A and B are **not** independent: $P(A \cap B) = P(A) * P(B \mid A)$

$E(X)$ = expected value = probability * payoff

Quadratic Equations
If $aX^2 + bX + c = 0$ is the general quadratic equation, then the two solutions (roots) are given by:

$$X = \frac{-b \pm \sqrt{b^2 - 4ac}}{2a}$$

DESCRIPTIVE STATISTICS
Arithmetic Mean

$$\bar{x} = \frac{\sum x}{n} \qquad \bar{x} = \frac{\sum fx}{\sum f} \quad \text{(frequency distribution)}$$

Standard Deviation

$$SD = \sqrt{\frac{\sum (x - \bar{x})^2}{n}} \qquad SD = \sqrt{\frac{\sum fx^2}{\sum f} - \bar{x}^2} \quad \text{(frequency distribution)}$$

INDEX NUMBERS
Price relative = $100 * P_1/P_0$ Quantity relative = $100 * Q_1/Q_0$

Price: $\sum W * P_1/P_0 / \sum W * 100$,   where W denotes weights
Quantity: $\sum W * Q_1/Q_0 / \sum W * 100$,   where W denotes weights

TIME SERIES
Additive Model
$$\text{Series} = \text{Trend} + \text{Seasonal} + \text{Random}$$

Multiplicative Model
$$\text{Series} = \text{Trend} * \text{Seasonal} * \text{Random}$$

LINEAR REGRESSION AND CORRELATION
The linear regression equation of y on x is given by:
$$Y = a + bX \quad \text{or} \quad Y - \bar{Y} = b(X - \bar{X})$$

where
$$b = \frac{\text{Covariance}(XY)}{\text{Variance}(X)} = \frac{n\Sigma XY - (\Sigma X)(\Sigma Y)}{n\Sigma X^2 - (\Sigma X)^2}$$

and
$$a = \bar{Y} - b\bar{X}$$

or solve
$$\sum Y = na + b\sum X$$
$$\sum XY = a\sum X + b\sum X^2$$

Coefficient of Correlation
$$r = \frac{\text{covariance }(XY)}{\sqrt{\text{var}(OX) \cdot \text{var}(Y)}} = \frac{n\sum XY - (\sum X)(\sum Y)}{\sqrt{(n\sum X^2 - (\sum X)^2)(n\sum Y^2 - (\sum Y)^2)}}$$

$$R(\text{rank}) = 1 - \frac{6\sum d^2}{n(n^2 - 1)}$$

FINANCIAL MATHEMATICS
Compound Interest (Values and Sums)
Future Value of S, of a sum X, invested for n periods, compounded at r% interest
$$S = X[1 + r]^n$$

Annuity
Present value of an annuity of £1 per annum receivable or payable for n years, commencing in one year, discounted at r% per annum.
$$\text{PV} = \frac{1}{r}\left[1 - \frac{1}{[1 + r]^n}\right]$$

Perpetuity
Present value of £1 per annum, payable or receivable in perpetuity, commencing in one year, discounted at r% per annum.
$$\text{PV} = \frac{1}{r}$$

Note that logarithm tables are also available when you sit your assessment.

LOGARITHMS

	0	1	2	3	4	5	6	7	8	9	1	2	3	4	5	6	7	8	9
10	0000	0043	0086	0128	0170	0212	0253	0294	0334	0374	4 4	9 8	13 12	17 16	21 20	26 24	30 28	34 32	38 37
11	0414	0453	0492	0531	0569	0607	0645	0682	0719	0755	4 4	8 7	12 11	15 15	19 19	23 22	27 26	31 30	35 33
12	0792	0828	0864	0899	0934	0969	1004	1038	1072	1106	3 3	7 7	11 10	14 14	18 17	21 20	25 24	28 27	32 31
13	1139	1173	1206	1239	1271	1303	1335	1367	1399	1430	3 3	7 7	10 10	13 12	16 16	20 19	23 22	26 25	30 29
14	1461	1492	1523	1553	1584	1614	1644	1673	1703	1732	3 3	6 6	9 9	12 12	15 15	18 17	21 20	24 23	28 26
15	1761	1790	1818	1847	1875	1903	1931	1959	1987	2014	3 3	6 5	9 8	11 11	14 14	17 16	20 19	23 22	26 25
16	2041	2068	2095	2122	2148	2175	2201	2227	2253	2279	3 3	5 5	8 8	11 10	14 13	16 15	19 18	22 21	24 23
17	2304	2330	2355	2380	2405	2430	2455	2480	2504	2529	3 2	5 5	8 7	10 10	13 12	15 15	18 17	20 19	23 22
18	2553	2577	2601	2625	2648	2672	2695	2718	2742	2765	2 2	5 5	7 7	9 9	12 11	14 14	16 16	19 18	21 21
19	2788	2810	2833	2856	2878	2900	2923	2945	2967	2989	2 2	4 4	7 6	9 8	11 11	13 13	16 15	18 17	20 19
20	3010	3032	3054	3075	3096	3118	3139	3160	3181	3201	2	4	6	8	11	13	15	17	19
21	3222	3243	3263	3284	3304	3324	3345	3365	3385	3404	2	4	6	8	10	12	14	16	18
22	3424	3444	3464	3483	3502	3522	3541	3560	3579	3598	2	4	6	8	10	12	14	15	17
23	3617	3636	3655	3674	3692	3711	3729	3747	3766	3784	2	4	6	7	9	11	13	15	17
24	3802	3820	3838	3856	3874	3892	3909	3927	3945	3962	2	4	5	7	9	11	12	14	16
25	3979	3997	4014	4031	4048	4065	4082	4099	4116	4133	2	3	5	7	9	10	12	14	15
26	4150	4166	4183	4200	4216	4232	4249	4265	4281	4298	2	3	5	7	8	10	11	13	15
27	4314	4330	4346	4362	4378	4393	4409	4425	4440	4456	2	3	5	6	8	9	11	13	14
28	4472	4487	4502	4518	4533	4548	4564	4579	4594	4609	2	3	5	6	8	9	11	12	14
29	4624	4639	4654	4669	4683	4698	4713	4728	4742	4757	1	3	4	6	7	9	10	12	13
30	4771	4786	4800	4814	4829	4843	4857	4871	4886	4900	1	3	4	6	7	9	10	11	13
31	4914	4928	4942	4955	4969	4983	4997	5011	5024	5038	1	3	4	6	7	8	10	11	12
32	5051	5065	5079	5092	5105	5119	5132	5145	5159	5172	1	3	4	5	7	8	9	11	12
33	5185	5198	5211	5224	5237	5250	5263	5276	5289	5302	1	3	4	5	6	8	9	10	12
34	5315	5328	5340	5353	5366	5378	5391	5403	5416	5428	1	3	4	5	6	8	9	10	11
35	5441	5453	5465	5478	5490	5502	5514	5527	5539	5551	1	2	4	5	6	7	9	10	11
36	5563	5575	5587	5599	5611	5623	5635	5647	5658	5670	1	2	4	5	6	7	8	10	11
37	5682	5694	5705	5717	5729	5740	5752	5763	5775	5786	1	2	3	5	6	7	8	9	10
38	5798	5809	5821	5832	5843	5855	5866	5877	5888	5899	1	2	3	5	6	7	8	9	10
39	5911	5922	5933	5944	5955	5966	5977	5988	5999	6010	1	2	3	4	5	7	8	9	10
40	6021	6031	6042	6053	6064	6075	6085	6096	6107	6117	1	2	3	4	5	6	8	9	10
41	6128	6138	6149	6160	6170	6180	6191	6201	6212	6222	1	2	3	4	5	6	7	8	9
42	6232	6243	6253	6263	6274	6284	6294	6304	6314	6325	1	2	3	4	5	6	7	8	9
43	6335	6345	6355	6365	6375	6385	6395	6405	6415	6425	1	2	3	4	5	6	7	8	9
44	6435	6444	6454	6464	6474	6484	6493	6503	6513	6522	1	2	3	4	5	6	7	8	9
45	6532	6542	6551	6561	6571	6580	6590	6599	6609	6618	1	2	3	4	5	6	7	8	9
46	6628	6637	6646	6656	6665	6675	6684	6693	6702	6712	1	2	3	4	5	6	7	7	8
47	6721	6730	6739	6749	6758	6767	6776	6785	6794	6803	1	2	3	4	5	5	6	7	8
48	6812	6821	6830	6839	6848	6857	6866	6875	6884	6893	1	2	3	4	4	5	6	7	8
49	6902	6911	6920	6928	6937	6946	6955	6964	6972	6981	1	2	3	4	4	5	6	7	8

LOGARITHMS

	0	1	2	3	4	5	6	7	8	9	1	2	3	4	5	6	7	8	9
50	6990	6998	7007	7016	7024	7033	7042	7050	7059	7067	1	2	3	3	4	5	6	7	8
51	7076	7084	7093	7101	7110	7118	7126	7135	7143	7152	1	2	3	3	4	5	6	7	8
52	7160	7168	7177	7185	7193	7202	7210	7218	7226	7235	1	2	2	3	4	5	6	7	7
53	7243	7251	7259	7267	7275	7284	7292	7300	7308	7316	1	2	2	3	4	5	6	6	7
54	7324	7332	7340	7348	7356	7364	7372	7380	7388	7396	1	2	2	3	4	5	6	6	7
55	7404	7412	7419	7427	7435	7443	7451	7459	7466	7474	1	2	2	3	4	5	5	6	7
56	7482	7490	7497	7505	7513	7520	7528	7536	7543	7551	1	2	2	3	4	5	5	6	7
57	7559	7566	7574	7582	7589	7597	7604	7612	7619	7627	1	2	2	3	4	5	5	6	7
58	7634	7642	7649	7657	7664	7672	7679	7686	7694	7701	1	1	2	3	4	4	5	6	7
59	7709	7716	7723	7731	7738	7745	7752	7760	7767	7774	1	1	2	3	4	4	5	6	7
60	7782	7789	7796	7803	7810	7818	7825	7832	7839	7846	1	1	2	3	4	4	5	6	6
61	7853	7860	7868	7875	7882	7889	7896	7903	7910	7917	1	1	2	3	4	4	5	6	6
62	7924	7931	7938	7945	7952	7959	7966	7973	7980	7987	1	1	2	3	3	4	5	6	6
63	7993	8000	8007	8014	8021	8028	8035	8041	8048	8055	1	1	2	3	3	4	5	5	6
64	8062	8069	8075	8082	8089	8096	8102	8109	8116	8122	1	1	2	3	3	4	5	5	6
65	8129	8136	8142	8149	8156	8162	8169	8176	8182	8189	1	1	2	3	3	4	5	5	6
66	8195	8202	8209	8215	8222	8228	8235	8241	8248	8254	1	1	2	3	3	4	5	5	6
67	8261	8267	8274	8280	8287	8293	8299	8306	8312	8319	1	1	2	3	3	4	5	5	6
68	8325	8331	8338	8344	8351	8357	8363	8370	8376	8382	1	1	2	3	3	4	4	5	6
69	8388	8395	8401	8407	8414	8420	8426	8432	8439	8445	1	1	2	2	3	4	4	5	6
70	8451	8457	8463	8470	8476	8482	8488	8494	8500	8506	1	1	2	2	3	4	4	5	6
71	8513	8519	8525	8531	8537	8543	8549	8555	8561	8567	1	1	2	2	3	4	4	5	5
72	8573	8579	8585	8591	8597	8603	8609	8615	8621	8627	1	1	2	2	3	4	4	5	5
73	8633	8639	8645	8651	8657	8663	8669	8675	8681	8686	1	1	2	2	3	4	4	5	5
74	8692	8698	8704	8710	8716	8722	8727	8733	8739	8745	1	1	2	2	3	4	4	5	5
75	8751	8756	8762	8768	8774	8779	8785	8791	8797	8802	1	1	2	2	3	3	4	5	5
76	8808	8814	8820	8825	8831	8837	8842	8848	8854	8859	1	1	2	2	3	3	4	5	5
77	8865	8871	8876	8882	8887	8893	8899	8904	8910	8915	1	1	2	2	3	3	4	4	5
78	8921	8927	8932	8938	8943	8949	8954	8960	8965	8971	1	1	2	2	3	3	4	4	5
79	8976	8982	8987	8993	8998	9004	9009	9015	9020	9025	1	1	2	2	3	3	4	4	5
80	9031	9036	9042	9047	9053	9058	9063	9069	9074	9079	1	1	2	2	3	3	4	4	5
81	9085	9090	9096	9101	9106	9112	9117	9122	9128	9133	1	1	2	2	3	3	4	4	5
82	9138	9143	9149	9154	9159	9165	9170	9175	9180	9186	1	1	2	2	3	3	4	4	5
83	9191	9196	9201	9206	9212	9217	9222	9227	9232	9238	1	1	2	2	3	3	4	4	5
84	9243	9248	9253	9258	9263	9269	9274	9279	9284	9289	1	1	2	2	3	3	4	4	5
85	9294	9299	9304	9309	9315	9320	9325	9330	9335	9340	1	1	2	2	3	3	4	4	5
86	9345	9350	9355	9360	9365	9370	9375	9380	9385	9390	1	1	2	2	3	3	4	4	5
87	9395	9400	9405	9410	9415	9420	9425	9430	9435	9440	0	1	1	2	2	3	3	4	4
88	9445	9450	9455	9460	9465	9469	9474	9479	9484	9489	0	1	1	2	2	3	3	4	4
89	9494	9499	9504	9509	9513	9518	9523	9528	9533	9538	0	1	1	2	2	3	3	4	4
90	9542	9547	9552	9557	9562	9566	9571	9576	9581	9586	0	1	1	2	2	3	3	4	4
91	9590	9595	9600	9605	9609	9614	9619	9624	9628	9633	0	1	1	2	2	3	3	4	4
92	9638	9643	9647	9652	9657	9661	9666	9671	9675	9680	0	1	1	2	2	3	3	4	4
93	9685	9689	9694	9699	9703	9708	9713	9717	9722	9727	0	1	1	2	2	3	3	4	4
94	9731	9736	9741	9745	9750	9754	9759	9763	9768	9773	0	1	1	2	2	3	3	4	4
95	9777	9782	9786	9791	9795	9800	9805	9809	9814	9818	0	1	1	2	2	3	3	4	4
96	9823	0827	9832	0836	9841	9845	9850	9854	9859	9863	0	1	1	2	2	3	3	4	4
97	9868	9872	9877	9881	9886	9890	9894	9899	9903	9908	0	1	1	2	2	3	3	4	4
98	9912	9917	9921	9926	9930	9934	9939	9943	9948	9952	0	1	1	2	2	3	3	4	4
99	9956	9961	9965	9969	9974	9978	9983	9987	9991	9996	0	1	1	2	2	3	3	3	4

AREA UNDER THE NORMAL CURVE

This table gives the area under the normal curve between the mean and a point Z standard deviations above the mean. The corresponding area for deviations below the mean can be found by symmetry.

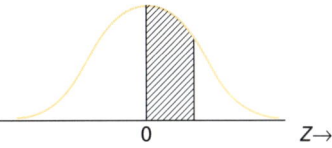

$Z = \frac{(x - \mu)}{\sigma}$	0.00	0.01	0.02	0.03	0.04	0.05	0.06	0.07	0.08	0.09
0.0	.0000	.0040	.0080	.0120	.0159	.0199	.0239	.0279	.0319	.0359
0.1	.0398	.0438	.0478	.0517	.0557	.1596	.0636	.0675	.0714	.0753
0.2	.0793	.0832	.0871	.0910	.0948	.0987	.1026	.1064	.1103	.1141
0.3	.1179	.1217	.1255	.1293	.1331	.1368	.1406	.1443	.1480	.1517
0.4	.1554	.1591	.1628	.1664	.1700	.1736	.1772	.1808	.1844	.1879
0.5	.1915	.1950	.1985	.2019	.2054	.2088	.2123	.2157	.2190	.2224
0.6	.2257	.2291	.2324	.2357	.2389	.2422	.2454	.2486	.2518	.2549
0.7	.2580	.2611	.2642	.2673	.2704	.2734	.2764	.2794	.2823	.2852
0.8	.2881	.2910	.2939	.2967	.2995	.3023	.3051	.3078	.3106	.3133
0.9	.3159	.3186	.3212	.3238	.3264	.3289	.3315	.3340	.3365	.3389
1.0	.3413	.3438	.3461	.3485	.3508	.3531	.3554	.3577	.3599	.3621
1.1	.3643	.3665	.3686	.3708	.3729	.3749	.3770	.3790	.3810	.3830
1.2	.3849	.3869	.3888	.3907	.3925	.3944	.3962	.3980	.3997	.4015
1.3	.4032	.4049	.4066	.4082	.4099	.4115	.4131	.4147	.4162	.4177
1.4	.4192	.4207	.4222	.4236	.4251	.4265	.4279	.4292	.4306	.4319
1.5	.4332	.4345	.4357	.4370	.4382	.4394	.4406	.4418	.4430	.4441
1.6	.4452	.4463	.4474	.4485	.4495	.4505	.4515	.4525	.4535	.4545
1.7	.4554	.4564	.4573	.4582	.4591	.4599	.4608	.4616	.4625	.4633
1.8	.4641	.4649	.4656	.4664	.4671	.4678	.4686	.4693	.4699	.4706
1.9	.4713	.4719	.4726	.4732	.4738	.4744	.4750	.4756	.4762	.4767
2.0	.4772	.4778	.4783	.4788	.4793	.4798	.4803	.4808	.4812	.4817
2.1	.4821	.4826	.4830	.4834	.4838	.4842	.4846	.4850	.4854	.4857
2.2	.4861	.4865	.4868	.4871	.4875	.4878	.4881	.4884	.4887	.4890
2.3	.4893	.4896	.4898	.4901	.4904	.4906	.4909	.4911	.4913	.4916
2.4	.4918	.4920	.4972	.4925	.4927	.4929	.4931	.4932	.4934	.4936
2.5	.4938	.4940	.4941	.4943	.4945	.4946	.4948	.4949	.4951	.4952
2.6	.4953	.4955	.4956	.4957	.4959	.4960	.4961	.4962	.4963	.4964
2.7	.4965	.4966	.4967	.4968	.4969	.4970	.4971	.4972	.4973	.4974
2.8	.4974	.4975	.4976	.4977	.4977	.4978	.4979	.4980	.4980	.4981
2.9	.4981	.4982	.4983	.4983	.4984	.4984	.4985	.4985	.4986	.4986
3.0	.49865	.4987	.4987	.4988	.4988	.4989	.4989	.4989	.4990	.4990
3.1	.49903	.4991	.4991	.4991	.4992	.4992	.4992	.4992	.4993	.4993
3.2	.49931	.4993	.4994	.4994	.4994	.4994	.4994	.4995	.4995	.4995
3.3	.49952	.4995	.4995	.4996	.4996	.4996	.4996	.4996	.4996	.4997
3.4	.49966	.4997	.4997	.4997	.4997	.4997	.4997	.4997	.4997	.4998
3.5	.49977									

MATHEMATICAL TABLES

PRESENT VALUE TABLE

Present value of £1 ie $(1+r)^{-n}$ where r = interest rate; n = number of periods until payment or receipt.

Interest rates (r)

Periods (n)	1%	2%	3%	4%	5%	6%	7%	8%	9%	10%	11%	12%	13%	14%	15%	16%	17%	18%	19%	20%
1	.990	.980	.971	.962	.952	.943	.935	.926	.917	.909	.901	.893	.885	.877	.870	.862	.855	.847	.840	.833
2	.980	.961	.943	.925	.907	.890	.873	.857	.842	.826	.812	.797	.783	.769	.756	.743	.731	.718	.706	.694
3	.971	.942	.915	.889	.864	.840	.816	.794	.772	.751	.731	.712	.693	.675	.658	.641	.624	.609	.593	.579
4	.961	.924	.888	.855	.823	.792	.763	.735	.708	.683	.659	.636	.613	.592	.572	.552	.534	.516	.499	.482
5	.951	.906	.863	.822	.784	.747	.713	.681	.650	.621	.593	.567	.543	.519	.497	.476	.456	.437	.419	.402
6	.942	.888	.837	.790	.746	.705	.666	.630	.596	.564	.535	.507	.480	.456	.432	.410	.390	.370	.352	.335
7	.933	.871	.813	.760	.711	.665	.623	.583	.547	.513	.482	.452	.425	.400	.376	.354	.333	.314	.296	.279
8	.923	.853	.789	.731	.677	.627	.582	.540	.502	.467	.434	.404	.376	.351	.327	.305	.285	.266	.249	.233
9	.914	.837	.766	.703	.645	.592	.544	.500	.460	.424	.391	.361	.333	.308	.284	.263	.243	.225	.209	.194
10	.905	.820	.744	.676	.614	.558	.508	.463	.422	.386	.352	.322	.295	.270	.247	.227	.208	.191	.176	.162
11	.896	.804	.722	.650	.585	.527	.475	.429	.388	.350	.317	.287	.261	.237	.215	.195	.178	.162	.148	.135
12	.887	.788	.701	.625	.557	.497	.444	.397	.356	.319	.286	.257	.231	.208	.187	.168	.152	.137	.124	.112
13	.879	.773	.681	.601	.530	.469	.415	.368	.326	.290	.258	.229	.204	.182	.163	.145	.130	.116	.104	.093
14	.870	.758	.661	.577	.505	.442	.388	.340	.299	.263	.232	.205	.181	.160	.141	.125	.111	.099	.088	.078
15	.861	.743	.642	.555	.481	.417	.362	.315	.275	.239	.209	.183	.160	.140	.123	.108	.095	.084	.074	.065
16	.853	.728	.623	.534	.458	.394	.339	.292	.252	.218	.188	.163	.141	.123	.107	.093	.081	.071	.062	.054
17	.844	.714	.605	.513	.436	.371	.317	.270	.231	.198	.170	.146	.125	.108	.093	.080	.069	.060	.052	.045
18	.836	.700	.587	.494	.416	.350	.296	.250	.212	.180	.153	.130	.111	.095	.081	.069	.059	.051	.044	.038
19	.828	.686	.570	.475	.396	.331	.277	.232	.194	.164	.138	.116	.098	.083	.070	.060	.051	.043	.037	.031
20	.820	.673	.554	.456	.377	.312	.258	.215	.178	.149	.124	.104	.087	.073	.061	.051	.043	.037	.031	.026

CUMULATIVE PRESENT VALUE OF £1

This table shows the Present Value of £1 per annum, Receivable or Payable at the end of each year for n years $\dfrac{1-(1+r)^{-n}}{r}$.

Periods (n)	1%	2%	3%	4%	5%	6%	7%	8%	9%	10%	11%	12%	13%	14%	15%	16%	17%	18%	19%	20%
1	0.990	0.980	0.971	0.962	0.952	0.943	0.935	0.926	0.917	0.909	0.901	0.893	0.885	0.877	0.870	0.862	0.855	0.847	0.840	0.833
2	1.970	1.942	1.913	1.886	1.859	1.833	1.808	1.783	1.759	1.736	1.713	1.690	1.668	1.647	1.626	1.605	1.585	1.566	1.547	1.528
3	2.941	2.884	2.829	2.775	2.723	2.673	2.624	2.577	2.531	2.487	2.444	2.402	2.361	2.322	2.283	2.246	2.210	2.174	2.140	2.106
4	3.902	3.808	3.717	3.630	3.546	3.465	3.387	3.312	3.240	3.170	3.102	3.037	2.974	2.914	2.855	2.798	2.743	2.690	2.639	2.589
5	4.853	4.713	4.580	4.452	4.329	4.212	4.100	3.993	3.890	3.791	3.696	3.605	3.517	3.433	3.352	3.274	3.199	3.127	3.058	2.991
6	5.795	5.601	5.417	5.242	5.076	4.917	4.767	4.623	4.486	4.355	4.231	4.111	3.998	3.889	3.784	3.685	3.589	3.498	3.410	3.326
7	6.728	6.472	6.230	6.002	5.786	5.582	5.389	5.206	5.033	4.868	4.712	4.564	4.423	4.288	4.160	4.039	3.922	3.812	3.706	3.605
8	7.652	7.325	7.020	6.733	6.463	6.210	5.971	5.747	5.535	5.335	5.146	4.968	4.799	4.639	4.487	4.344	4.207	4.078	3.954	3.837
9	8.566	8.162	7.786	7.435	7.108	6.802	6.515	6.247	5.995	5.759	5.537	5.328	5.132	4.946	4.772	4.607	4.451	4.303	4.163	4.031
10	9.471	8.983	8.530	8.111	7.722	7.360	7.024	6.710	6.418	6.145	5.889	5.650	5.426	5.216	5.019	4.833	4.659	4.494	4.339	4.192
11	10.368	9.787	9.253	8.760	8.306	7.887	7.499	7.139	6.805	6.495	6.207	5.938	5.687	5.453	5.234	5.029	4.836	4.656	4.486	4.327
12	11.255	10.575	9.954	9.385	8.863	8.384	7.943	7.536	7.161	6.814	6.492	6.194	5.918	5.660	5.421	5.197	4.988	4.793	4.611	4.439
13	12.134	11.348	10.635	9.986	9.394	8.853	8.358	7.904	7.487	7.103	6.750	6.424	6.122	5.842	5.583	5.342	5.118	4.910	4.715	4.533
14	13.004	12.106	11.296	10.563	9.899	9.295	8.745	8.244	7.786	7.367	6.982	6.628	6.302	6.002	5.724	5.468	5.229	5.008	4.802	4.611
15	13.865	12.849	11.938	11.118	10.380	9.712	9.108	8.559	8.061	7.606	7.191	6.811	6.462	6.142	5.847	5.575	5.324	5.092	4.876	4.675
16	14.718	13.578	12.561	11.652	10.838	10.106	9.447	8.851	8.313	7.824	7.379	6.974	6.604	6.265	5.954	5.668	5.405	5.162	4.938	4.730
17	15.562	14.292	13.166	12.166	11.274	10.477	9.763	9.122	8.544	8.022	7.549	7.120	6.729	6.373	6.047	5.749	5.475	5.222	4.990	4.775
18	16.398	14.992	13.754	12.659	11.690	10.828	10.059	9.372	8.756	8.201	7.702	7.250	6.840	6.467	6.128	5.818	5.534	5.273	5.033	4.812
19	17.226	15.679	14.324	13.134	12.085	11.158	10.336	9.604	8.950	8.365	7.839	7.366	6.938	6.550	6.198	5.877	5.584	5.316	5.070	4.843
20	18.046	16.351	14.878	13.590	12.462	11.470	10.594	9.818	9.129	8.514	7.963	7.469	7.025	6.623	6.259	5.929	5.628	5.353	5.101	4.870

Interest rates (r)

Basic Mathematics

Basic Mathematics

> **LEARNING OUTCOMES**
>
> You will probably be familiar with the content of this chapter from your schooldays. Basic mathematics, as its name implies, underpins the rest of the subjects studied in *Business Mathematics* – and, indeed, the rest of your CIMA studies. After completing this chapter you should be able to:
>
> ▶ demonstrate the order of operations in formulae, including the use of brackets, negative numbers, powers and roots;
>
> ▶ calculate percentages and proportions;
>
> ▶ calculate answers to an appropriate number of significant figures or decimal places;
>
> ▶ solve simple equations, including two-variable simultaneous equations and quadratic equations;
>
> ▶ prepare graphs of linear and quadratic equations;
>
> ▶ manipulate inequalities.

1.1 Introduction

In this first chapter, a number of concepts are introduced that are fundamental to many areas of business mathematics. We begin by defining some key words and phrases.

1.2 Mathematical operations and brackets

The basic mathematical operations are addition, subtraction, multiplication and division; and there is a very important convention about how we write down exactly what operations are to be carried out and in what order. Brackets are used to clarify the order of operations and are essential when the normal priority of operations is to be broken. The order is:

- work out the values inside brackets first;
- powers and roots (see Section 1.5);
- multiplication and division are next in priority;
- finally, addition and subtraction.

For example, suppose you want to add 2 and 3 and then multiply by 4. You might write this as

$$2 + 3 \times 4$$

However, the above rule means that the multiplication will take priority over the addition. What you have written will be interpreted as an instruction to multiply 3 by 4 and then add 2.

It would be useful at this point to briefly digress and check your calculator. Type '2 + 3 × 4 =' into it. If the answer is 14, you have a scientific calculator that obeys mathematical priorities. If the answer is 20, your calculator is non-scientific and perhaps will not be suitable for your CIMA studies.

Returning to the main problem, if you want to add 2 to 3 and then multiply by 4, you must use brackets to give priority to the addition – to ensure that it takes place first. You should write (2 + 3) × 4. The contents of the bracket total 5, and this is then multiplied by 4 to give 20.

Example 1.2.1

Evaluate the following:

(a) $5 + 6 \times 8$
(b) $(3 + 1) \times 2$
(c) $9 - 7 \div 2$
(d) $(4 + 5)/10$
(e) $5 + 7 \times 8 - 2$
(f) $(9 - 1) \times (6 + 4)$

Solution

(a) 6×8 takes priority, then add 5, so $5 + 6 \times 8 = 48 + 5 = 53$
(b) Work out the bracket first, then multiply by 2; $3 + 1 = 4$, so $(3 + 1) \times 2 = 8$
(c) $7 \div 2$ takes priority, and is then subtracted from 9; $9 - 3.5 = 5.5$
(d) Work out the bracket first, then divide by 10; $4 + 5 = 9$, and $9/10 = 0.9$
(e) The multiplication of 7×8 takes priority, giving 56; $5 + 56 - 2 = 59$
(f) Work out the brackets first – the order is unimportant but it is usual to work from left to right; $9 - 1 = 8$, and $6 + 4 = 10$, so $8 \times 10 = 80$

1.3 Different types of numbers

A whole number such as -5, 0 or 5 is called an *integer*, whereas numbers that contain parts of a whole number are either *fractions* – such as $\frac{3}{4}$ – or *decimals* – such as 0.75.

Any type of number can be *positive* or *negative*. If you add a positive number to something, the effect is to increase it whereas, adding a negative number has the effect of reducing the value. If you add $-B$ to any number A, the effect is to subtract B from A. The rules for arithmetic with negative numbers are as follows:

- adding a negative is the same as subtracting, that is $A + (-B) = A - B$;
- subtracting a negative is the same as adding, that is $A - (-B) = A + B$;
- if you multiply or divide a positive and a negative, the result is negative, that is $(+) \times (-)$ and $(-) \times (+)$ and $(+) \div (-)$ and $(-) \div (+)$ are all negative;
- if you multiply or divide two negatives, the result is positive, that is $(-) \times (-)$ and $(-) \div (-)$ are both positive.

Notice that brackets are often used for clarity when a negative number follows one of the mathematical operators like + or ×, but they are not strictly necessary.

Example 1.3.1

Evaluate the following:

(a) $9 - 7 \times (-2)$
(b) $(5 - 8) \times (-6)$
(c) $12 - 8 \div (-4)$
(d) $(4 - 16)/(-2)$
(e) $(17 - 6) \times (8 - 3)$
(f) $7 - (2 - 20)/(6 - 4)$

Solution

(a) Multiplication takes priority; $7 \times (-2) = -14$, so $9 - 7 \times (-2) = 9 - (-14) = 9 + 14 = 23$
(b) Work out the bracket first; $(5 - 8) \times (-6) = -3 \times (-6) = 18$
(c) Division takes priority; $12 - 8 \div (-4) = 12 - (-2) = 12 + 2 = 14$
(d) Work out the bracket first; $(4 - 16)/(-2) = (-12)/(-2) = 6$
(e) $(17 - 6) \times (8 - 3) = 11 \times 5 = 55$
(f) Brackets first, then the division, and only then subtract the result from 7; $7 - (2 - 20) \div (6 - 4) = 7 - (-18) \div 2 = 7 - (-9) = 7 + 9 = 16$

1.4 Rounding

Quite often, numbers have so many digits that they become impractical to work with and hard to grasp. This problem can be dealt with by converting some of the digits to zero in a variety of ways.

1.4.1 Rounding to the nearest whole number

For example, $78.187 = 78$ to the nearest whole number. The only other nearby whole number is 79 and 78.187 is nearer to 78 than to 79. Any number from 78.0 to 78.49 will round down to 78 and any number from 78.5 to 78.99 will round up to 79.

The basic rules of rounding are that:

1. digits are discarded (i.e. turned into zero) from right to left;
2. reading from left to right, if the first digit to be discarded is in the range 0–4, then the previous retained digit is unchanged; if the first digit is in the range 5–9 then the previous digit goes up by one.

Depending on their size, numbers can be rounded to the nearest whole number, or 10 or 100 or 1,000,000, and so on. For example, $5,738 = 5,740$ to the nearest 10; 5,700 to the nearest 100; and 6,000 to the nearest 1,000.

1.4.2 Significant figures

For example, 86,531 has five digits but we might want a number with only three. The '31' will be discarded. Reading from the left the first of these is 3, which is in the 0–4 range, so the previous retained digit (i.e. the '5') is unchanged. So 86,531 = 86,500 to three significant figures (s.f.).

Suppose we want 86,531 to have only two significant digits. The '531' will be discarded and the first of these, '5', is in the 5–9 range, so the previous digit ('6') is increased by 1. So 86,531 = 87,000 to two s.f.

Zeros sometimes count as significant figures; sometimes they do not. Reading a number from the right, any zeros encountered before you meet a non-zero number do not count as significant figures. However, zeros sandwiched *between* non-zeros are significant. Hence, 87,000 has two s.f., while 80,700 has three.

1.4.3 Decimal places

The other widely used rounding technique is to discard digits so that the remaining number only has a specified number of decimal places (d.p.).

For example, round 25.7842 to two d.p. The digits to be discarded are '42', the first ('4') is in the 0–4 range and so the next digit ('8') remains unchanged. So 25.7842 = 25.78 to two d.p.

Strings of '9' can be confusing. For example, if we want to round 10.99 to one d.p., the first digit to be discarded is '9' and so the next digit, also '9', goes up to '10'. In consequence, the rounded number is written as 11.0 to one d.p.

1.4.4 Rounding up or rounding down

A number to be rounded up will be changed into the next higher whole number so, for example, 16.12 rounds up to 17.

A number to be rounded down will simply have its decimal element discarded (or truncated).

Numbers can also be rounded up or down to, say, the next 100. Rounding up, 7,645 becomes 7,700 since 645 is increased to the next hundred which is 700. Rounding down, 7,645 becomes 7,600.

Example 1.4.1

This exercise covers all the topics of this chapter so far. Evaluate the following to the accuracy specified.

(a) $89.56 - 56.4/4.3$ to two d.p.
(b) $(5.9 - 8.2) \div (3.6 - 7.1)$ to one d.p.
(c) $8,539 - 349.1 \div (32.548 - 1)$ to three s.f.
(d) $56/5 - 28$ to the nearest whole number.

Solution

In what follows, before rounding, we have not written out the full calculator display if it was plainly not going to be needed. However, note that it is good practice to retain full calculator accuracy throughout your calculation, only rounding at the final answer stage. Doing so avoids errors due to premature rounding at intermediate stages.

(a) $89.56 - 56.4/4.3 = 89.56 - 13.11627 = 89.56 - 13.12 = 76.44$ to two d.p.
(b) $(5.9 - 8.2) \div (3.6 - 7.1) = (-2.3) \div (-3.5) = 0.65714 = 0.7$ to one d.p.
(c) $8,539 - 349.1 \div (32.548 - 1) = 8,539 - 349.1 \div 31.548 = 8,539 - 11.066 = 8527.934 = 8,530$ to three s.f.
(d) $56/5 - 28 = 11.2 - 28 = -16.8 = -17$ to the nearest whole number.

Correct rounding is essential in computer-based assessments. Don't move on to the next topic until you are quite sure about this.

1.5 Powers and roots

1.5.1 Definitions

1. The nth power of a number, a, is the number multiplied by itself n times in total, and is denoted by a^n or $a\wedge n$. For example,

   2^5 or $2\wedge 5 = 2 \times 2 \times 2 \times 2 \times 2 = 32$

2. Any number to the power of zero is defined to be 1. For example,

   $7^0 = 1$

3. a^{-n} is the reciprocal of a^n, that is $a^{-n} = 1 \div a^n = 1/a^n$

   $$3^{-2} = \frac{1}{3^2} = \frac{1}{9}$$

4. The nth root of a number, a, is denoted by $a^{1/n}$ and it is the number that, when multiplied by itself n times in total, results in a. For example,

   $8^{1/3} = \sqrt[3]{8} = 2$

   Check: $2 \times 2 \times 2 = 8$

   The square root, $a^{1/2}$, is generally written as $\sqrt{a}$ without the number 2.

5. $a^{n/m}$ can be interpreted either as the mth root of a^n or as the mth root of a multiplied by itself n times. For example,

   $9^{5/2} = (\sqrt{9})^5 = 3^5 = 243$

6. The rules for arithmetic with powers are as follows:

   (i) Multiplication: $a^m \times a^n = a^{m+n}$. For example,

   $2^3 \times 2^4 = (2 \times 2 \times 2) \times (2 \times 2 \times 2 \times 2) = 2^3 \times 2^4 = 2^{3+4} = 2^7 = 128$

   (ii) Division: $a^m \div a^n = a^{m-n}$. For example:

   $3^5 \div 3^2 = (3 \times 3 \times 3 \times 3 \times 3)/(3 \times 3) = 3^{5-2} = 3^3 = 27$

   (iii) Powers of powers: $(a^m)^n = a^{m \times n}$. For example,

   $(4^2)^3 = 4^{2 \times 3} = 4^6 = 4,096$

Example 1.5.1

Simplify the following:

(a) $\dfrac{(m^2)^3}{m^5}$

(b) m^3/m^{-2}

(c) $(m^4)^{1/2}$

(d) $\dfrac{1}{m^{-3}}$

Solution

(a) $\dfrac{(m^2)^3}{m^5} = \dfrac{m^6}{m^5} = m$

(b) $m^3/m^{-2} = m^{(3-(-2))} = m^5$

(c) $(m^4)^{1/2} = m^{4 \times 1/2} = m^2$

(d) $\dfrac{1}{m^{-3}} = \dfrac{1}{1 \div m^3} = m^3$

1.6 Mathematical operations in Excel

When performing calculations in Excel the same mathematical rules that have been discussed in this chapter apply. The following examples use the data from Examples 1.2.1 and 1.3.1 and show how formulae in Excel would be created to arrive at the same results.

	A	B	C	D	E
1					
2					
3					
4		5	6	8	=B4+C4*D4
5		3	1	2	=(B5+C5)*2
6		9	7	2	=B6-C6/2
7		4	5	10	=(B7+C7)/D7
8		5	7	8	=B8+C8*D8-2
9		9	6		=(B9-1)*(C9+4)
10					
11					
12					
13					
14		9	7	-2	=B14-C14*D14
15		5	8	-6	=(B15-C15)*-6
16		12	8	-4	=B16-8/-4
17		4	16	-2	=(B17-C17)/-2
18		17	8		=(B18-6)*(C18-3)
19		7	20	6	=B19-(2-C19)/(D19-4
20					

Figure 1.1 Creating basic formulae in Excel

Notice from Figure 1.1 that most of the values have been addressed by the cell reference – but it is also possible to incorporate numbers into the formulae.

1.6.1 Rounding numbers in Excel

To accurately round numbers in Excel a built-in *function* called = ROUND() is used. This can be used to set any degree of accuracy required and once the function is incorporated into a formula any future references to the cell containing the round function will use a value rounded to the specified number of decimal places. The following example (Figure 1.2) illustrates this and uses the data from Example 1.4.1.

	A	B	C	D	E	F	G
1							
2	Rounding numbers						
3							
4		89.56	56.4	4.3		=ROUND(B4-C4/D4,2)	
5		5.9	8.2	3.6	7.1	=ROUND((B5-C5)/(D5-E5),1)	
6		8539	349.1	32.548	1	=ROUND(B6-C6/(D6-E6),3)	=ROUND(F6,3-LEN(INT(F6)))
7		56	5	28		=ROUND(B7/C7-D7,0)	
8							
9							

Figure 1.2 Rounding numbers in Excel

Notice that the third example requested the result be rounded to three significant figures, the formula is a little more complex and has been done here in two steps.

In the first step in cell F6 the arithmetic has been performed and the result rounded to three decimal places. Then in G6 the LEN and the INT functions have been applied to further round the result to three significant figures.

It is sometimes preferable to take the integer value of a number as opposed to rounding it to the nearest whole number. The difference is that the integer value is a number without any decimal places. Therefore the integer value of 9.99 is 9 and not 10 as it would be if the number had been rounded to the nearest whole number.

Figure 1.3 shows the table used in the rounding exercise but with the Excel INT function in place of the ROUND function

	A	B	C	D	E	F	G
8							
9	Taking the integer value of numbers						
10							
11		89.56	56.4	4.3		=INT(B11-C11/D11)	
12		5.9	8.2	3.6	7.1	=INT((B12-C12)/(D12-E12))	
13		8539	349.1	32.548	1	=INT(B13-C13/(D13-E13))	=ROUND(F13,3-LEN(INT(F13)))
14		56	5	28		=INT(B14/C14-D14)	
15							
16							
17							

Figure 1.3 Using the Excel INT function

Figure 1.4 shows the results of the rounding and the integer formulae used in figures 1.2 and 1.3.

	A	B	C	D	E	F	G	H	I
1									
2	Rounding numbers								
3									
4		89.56	56.4	4.3		76.44			
5		5.9	8.2	3.6	7.1	0.7			
6		8539	349.1	32.548	1	8527.934	8530		
7		56	5	28		-17			
8									
9	Taking the integer value of numb								
10									
11		89.56	56.4	4.3		76			
12		5.9	8.2	3.6	7.1	0			
13		8539	349.1	32.548	1	8527	8530		
14		56	5	28		-17			
15									
16									

Figure 1.4 The results of using =ROUND and =INT

Looking at Figure 1.4, the different result produced through the use of the INT function as opposed to the ROUND function can be seen. In each case the result has been rounded down to the integer value.

1.7 Variables and functions

A variable is something which can take different values. Variables are often denoted by letters. Thus, the set of positive whole numbers can be considered as a variable. If we denote it by x, then this variable can have many values.

$x = 1$
or $x = 2$
or $x = 3$, and so on.

Another example is the set of the major points of a compass. If this variable is denoted by c, then it can have more than one value, but only a limited number.

c = north
c = south
c = north-west, and so on.

These examples show that variables can take on non-numerical 'values' as well as numerical ones. In this text we shall concentrate on *numerical variables*, that is, those whose values are numbers, like the first case above.

A mathematical *function* is a rule or method of determining the value of one numerical variable from the values of other numerical variables. We shall concentrate on the case where one variable is determined by or depends on just *one* other variable. The first variable is called the *dependent* variable, and is usually denoted by y, while the second is called the *independent* variable, denoted by x. The relationship between them is a *function of one variable*, often referred to as a *function*, for brevity. Note that whilst functions are similar to formulae (see Section 1.8) there are specific conditions relating to the definition of a function, but these are outside the scope of this book.

A very useful way of stating a function is in terms of an *equation*, which is an expression containing an 'equals' sign. The *equation of a function* will thus take the typical form:

y = a mathematical expression containing x

If we know the value of the independent variable x, then the expression will completely determine the corresponding value of the dependent variable, y.

Example 1.7.1

The following equations represent functions with one independent variable. Evaluate the dependent variable when the independent variable has the value 2.

(a) $y = 3 + 2x$
(b) $y = x$
(c) $y = 1 + x + 3x^2$

Solution

To find the value of y, we write the known value of x (2 in this case) in place of x in the mathematical expression and perform the necessary arithmetical calculations. This is known as the substitution of the x-value into the equation.

(a) Substituting $x = 2$ gives:

$$y = 3 + 2 \times 2 = 3 + 4 = 7$$

so the dependent variable has the value 7 in this case.
(b) Clearly, this dependent variable has the value 2, the same as x.
(c) Substituting $x = 2$:

$$y = 1 + 2 + 3 \times 2^2 = 1 + 2 + 12 = 15$$

so the dependent variable has the value 15 here.

1.8 Formulae

A *formula* is a statement that is given in terms of mathematical symbols: it is a mathematical expression that enables you to calculate the value of one variable from the value(s) of one or more others. Many formulae arise in financial and business calculations, and we shall encounter several during the course of this text. In this chapter, we shall concentrate on some of the more complicated calculations that arise from the application of formulae.

Example 1.8.1

Calculate the value of A from the formula

$$A = \frac{B(C + 1)(3 - D)}{(2E - 3F)}$$

when $B = 2$, $C = 3$, $D = -1.6$, $E = -1$ and $F = -2.5$

Solution

$$(C + 1) = (3 + 1) = 4$$
$$(3 - D) = (3 - (-1.6)) = 3 + 1.6 = 4.6$$
$$(2E - 3F) = 2 \times (-1) - (3 \times (-2.5)) = -2 + 7.5 = 5.5$$
$$\text{Hence } A = \frac{2 \times 4 \times 4.6}{5.5} = 6.69 \text{ to two d.p.}$$

Example 1.8.2

The following formula occurs in calculations of interest and depreciation:

$$V = P \times (1 + r)^n$$

(a) Calculate the value of V when $P = 10{,}000$, $r = -0.06$ and $n = 4$.
(b) Calculate the value of P when $V = 1{,}000$, $r = 0.04$ and $n = 3$.

Solution

(a) We shall compute the powers from this basic definition, but you may have a calculator with an x^y or a y^x button, which will make the calculations easier.
In the first case:

$$V = 10,000 \times (1 + (-0.06))^4$$
$$= 10,000 \times (1 - 0.06)^4$$
$$= 10,000 \times 0.94^4$$
$$= 10,000 \times 0.94 \times 0.94 \times 0.94 \times 0.94$$
$$= 7807.49 \text{ (to two d.p.)}$$

(b) In the same way as above, we first calculate the expression in the bracket then the power:

$$1,000 = P \times (1 + 0.04)^3$$
$$= P \times 1.04^3$$
$$= P \times 1.04 \times 1.04 \times 1.04$$
$$= P \times 1.124864$$
$$\text{Hence } P = 1,000/1.124864$$
$$= 889.00 \text{ (to two d.p.)}$$

The example above required us to change the subject of the formula from V to P, that is, to end up with $P =$ some expression. There are various rules and techniques which help this process.

1. If something is added or subtracted at one side of an equation, then it changes its sign when you take it to the other side. For example: $P + 5 = 9$, so $P = 9 - 5 = 4$
2. If something multiplies one side of an equation, then it divides when taken to the other side. Similarly, divisions turn into multiplications. For example: $5R = 210$, so $R = 210 \div 5 = 42$; $T \div 20 = 7$, so $T = 7 \times 20 = 140$
3. If the variable you want as the subject is inside a square root, manipulate the equation into the form 'square-rooted expression = something' and then square both sides of the equation

Example 1.8.3

Rearrange the following equations to change X into the subject:

(a) $Y = a + bX$
(b) $Y = X \div (2 - X)$
(c) $Y = 2\sqrt{(abX \div c)}$

Solution

(a) If $Y = a + bX$

so $\quad Y - a = bX$ (rule 1)

thus $\quad X = \dfrac{Y - a}{b}$ (rule 2)

(b) If $Y = X \div (2 - X)$

$$Y(2 - X) = X \text{ (rule 2)}$$
$$2Y - XY = X \text{ (multiplying out the brackets)}$$

Gathering the X terms together:

$$2Y = X + XY$$
$$= X(1 + Y)$$

Finally, dividing down by (1 + Y) gives:

$$X = \frac{2Y}{1+Y}$$

(c) If $Y = 2\sqrt{(abX \div c)}$

$$\frac{Y}{2} = \sqrt{\frac{abX}{c}}$$

Squaring both sides gives:

$$\frac{Y^2}{4} = \frac{abX}{c}$$

All that remains now is to take the *a*, *b* and *c* across to the other side:

$$X = \frac{cY^2}{4ab}$$

1.9 Exponential numbers

In Excel a number is raised to a power by using the symbol referred to as a carat (^). Some practitioners refer to this symbol as being the exponential operator. Thus, for example, to cube 4 the formula required would be = 4^3. To find the square of 4, the formula required is = 4^2. The carat can also used to find the square root. In this case the formula would be = 4^(1/2), or to find the cube root the formula would be = 4^(1/3). The method is used to find the 4th root, 5th root and so on. Some examples are demonstrated in Figures 1.5 and 1.6.

	A	B	C	D	E
1					
2		3 squared	9	9	
3		3 cubed	27	27	
4		3 to the power of 4	81	81	
5		4 to the power of 4	256	256	
6					
7		Square root of 4	2		
8		Cubed root of 64	4		
9					
10					

Figure 1.5 Examples of the use of the carat (^) symbol

	A	B	C	D
1				
2		3 squared	=3*3	=3^2
3		3 cubed	=3*3*3	=3^3
4		3 to the power of 4	=3*3*3*3	=3^4
5		4 to the power of 4	=4*4*4*4	=4^4
6				
7		Square root of 4	=4^(1/2)	
8		Cubed root of 64	=64^(1/3)	
9				
10				
11				

Figure 1.6 Formulae used to produce the results

1.10 Solving equations

1.10.1 Linear equations with only one variable

An equation is linear if it has no term with powers greater than 1, that is, no squared or cubed terms, etc. The method is to use the same techniques as in changing the subject of a formula, so that the equation ends up in the form variable = something.

Example 1.10.1

(a) Solve $6 - 3X = 0$

$$6 = 3X$$
$$X = 6 \div 3 = 2$$

(b) Solve $200 = 5(X - 2) + 80$

$$200 = 5X - 10 + 80 = 5X + 70$$
$$200 - 70 = 5X = 130$$
$$X = 130 \div 5 = 26$$

(c) Solve $\dfrac{50}{X} = \dfrac{24}{X - 3}$

Multiply up by the two denominators:

$$50(X - 3) = 24X$$
$$50X - 150 = 24X$$
$$50X - 24X = 150 + 26X$$
$$X = 150 \div 26 = 5.77 \text{ to two d.p.}$$

Example 1.10.2

Solve the following equations:

(a) $10 + 3Y = 8Y - 7$

(b) $\dfrac{6.1}{Y} = \dfrac{4.9}{10 - Y}$

Solution

(a) $10 + 3Y = 8Y - 7$

$$10 + 7 = 8Y - 3Y$$
$$17 = 5Y$$
$$Y = 17 \div 5 = 3.4$$

(b) $\dfrac{6.1}{Y} = \dfrac{4.9}{10 - Y}$

$6.1(10 - Y) = 4.9Y$

$61 - 6.1Y = 4.9Y$

$61 = 4.9Y + 6.1Y = 11Y$

$Y = 61 \div 11 = 5.55$ to two d.p.

1.10.2 Quadratic equations with only one variable

A quadratic equation has the form $aX^2 + bX + c = 0$ where a, b and c are constants. The equation can be solved using a formula but if either the bX or c terms or both are missing the formula is not necessary. Examples will be used to illustrate the methods.

Example 1.10.3

Solve the following simple quadratic equations (note that the variable used is Y, but as there is only one variable used, this is fine.):

(a) $4Y^2 = 100$
(b) $Y^2 - 9 = 0$
(c) $Y^2 + 2Y = 0$
(d) $(Y - 5)^2 = 0$

Solution

(a) $Y^2 = 100 \div 4 = 25$

$Y = +\sqrt{25}$ and $-\sqrt{25} = \pm 5$

(b) $Y^2 = 9$

$Y = \pm\sqrt{9} = \pm 3$

(c) $Y(Y + 2) = 0$

Either $Y = 0$; or $Y + 2 = 0$, so $Y = -2$

(d) The only solution is that $Y - 5 = 0$, so $Y = 5$

You may have noticed that most quadratic equations have two roots, that is, two values for which the two sides of the equation are equal, but occasionally, as in (d) above, they appear to have only one. It is, in fact, a repeated (or double) root. For example, $Y^2 = -9$ has no real roots. We shall consider this again when we look at quadratic graphs in the next chapter.

For quadratic equations all of whose coefficients are non-zero, the easiest method of solution is the formula. If the equation is $aX^2 + bX + c = 0$, then the roots are given by:

$$X = \dfrac{-b \pm \sqrt{(b^2 - 4ac)}}{2a}$$

> ✎ This formula is given in your exam so you don't need to learn it.

Example 1.10.4

Solve the equation $X^2 - 50X + 600 = 0$

Solution

$a = 1; b = -50; c = 600$

$$X = \frac{-(-50) \pm \sqrt{((-50)^2 - 4 \times 1 \times 600)}}{2 \times 1}$$
$$X = \frac{50 \pm 10}{2} = \frac{60}{2} \text{ and } \frac{40}{2}$$
$$X = 30 \text{ and } 20$$

Notice that the equation has real roots only if $b^2 - 4ac$ is positive, since negative numbers do not have square roots.

Example 1.10.5

Solve the following equations:

(a) $Y^2 - 16 = 0$
(b) $2Y^2 - 5Y = 0$
(c) $Y^2 - 20Y - 800 = 0$

Solution

(a) $Y^2 = 16$ so $Y = \pm\sqrt{16} = \pm 4$.
(b) $Y(2Y - 5) = 0$, so either $Y = 0$; or $2Y - 5 = 0$, i.e. $Y = 0$ and $5 \div 2$, so $Y = 2.5$.
(c) $a = 1; b = -20; c = -800$:

$$Y = \frac{-(-20) \pm \sqrt{((-20)^2 - 4 \times (-800))}}{2 \times 1}$$
$$Y = \frac{20 \pm 60}{2} = \frac{80}{2} \text{ and } \frac{-40}{2}$$
$$Y = 40 \text{ and } -20$$

1.10.3 Simultaneous linear equations

These are equations of the type:

$$3X + 4Y = 18 \qquad \text{(i)}$$

$$5X + 2Y = 16 \qquad \text{(ii)}$$

which must both be satisfied by the roots X and Y.

Provided you multiply both sides of an equation by the same amount, it continues to be true. In the solution of these equations, one or both of the equations are multiplied by numbers chosen so that either the X or the Y terms in the two equations become numerically identical.

We have labelled the equations (i) and (ii) for clarity. Suppose we were to multiply (i) by 5 and (ii) by 3. Both equations would contain a $15X$-term that we could eliminate by subtraction, it being the case that you can add or subtract two equations and the result remains true.

In this case, however, the simplest method is to multiply equation (ii) by 2, so that both equations will contain $4Y$ and we can subtract to eliminate Y. The full solution is shown below.

$$3X + 4Y = 18 \quad \text{(i)}$$
$$5X + 2Y = 16 \quad \text{(ii)}$$

Multiply (ii) by 2:

$$10X + 4Y = 32 \quad \text{(iii)}$$

Subtract (iii) − (i):

$$7X + 0 = 14$$
$$X = 14 \div 7 = 2$$

Substitute $X = 2$ into (i)

$$6 + 4Y = 18$$
$$4Y = 18 - 6 = 12$$
$$Y = 12 \div 4 = 3$$

Check the results in (ii):

$$5 \times 2 + 2 \times 3 = 16$$

The solution is $X = 2$, $Y = 3$.

Had we chosen to substitute $X = 2$ into equation (ii) it would not have affected the result but we would then have checked in the other equation (i).

Example 1.10.4

Solve the equations:

$$2X - 3Y = 23 \quad \text{(i)}$$
$$7X + 4Y = 8 \quad \text{(ii)}$$

Solution

Multiply (i) by 4 and (ii) by 3:

$$8X - 12Y = 92 \quad \text{(iii)}$$
$$21X + 12Y = 24 \quad \text{(iv)}$$

Add the equations:

$$29X = 116$$
$$X = 116 \div 29 = 4$$

Substitute $X = 4$ in (ii):

$$28 + 4Y = 8$$
$$4Y = 8 - 28 = -20$$
$$Y = 20 \div 4 = -5$$

Check in (i):

$$2 \times 4 - 3 \times (-5) = 8 + 15 = 23$$

The solution is $X = 4$, $Y = -5$

1.11 Manipulating inequalities

Inequalities are treated in almost exactly the same way as equations. In fact an inequality says much the same thing as an equation, except that one side will be less than or greater than the other, or less than and greater than the other.

Inequalities can be manipulated in the same way as equations, except that when multiplying or dividing by a negative number it is necessary to reverse the inequality sign.

Example 1.11.1

Solve for x $3x + 10 > 40$

Solution $3x > 40 - 10$
$3x > 30$
$x > 10$

Example 1.11.2

Solve for x $5x + 20 < 60$
$5x < 60 - 20$
$5x < 40$
$x < 8$

Example 1.11.3

Solve for y $-3y + 10 > 40$

Solution $-3y > 40 - 10$
$-3y > 30$
$y < -10$

Example 1.11.4

Solve for y $5y + 20 \geq 50$

Solution $5y \geq 50 - 20$
$5y \geq 30$
$y \geq 6$

Example 1.11.5

Solve for x $x/2 + 20 \geq 30$

Solution $x/2 \geq 30 - 20$
$x/2 \geq 10$
$x \geq 20$

Example 1.11.6

Solve for y $y + 50 \geq 30$

Solution $y \geq 30 - 50$
$y \geq -20$

Example 1.11.7

Solve for y $y/3 + 20 \geq -10$

Solution $y/3 \geq -10 - 20$
$y/3 \geq -30$
$y \geq -90$

1.12 Percentages and ratios

Percentages and ratios (or proportions) occur in many financial calculations. Basically, a percentage (denoted '%' or 'per cent') is expressed out of 100, whereas a ratio is one number divided by another. A simple example will illustrate.

Example 1.12.1

(a) Express 4.6 as:

   (i) a ratio of 23.0;
   (ii) a percentage of 23.0.

(b) Evaluate 30 per cent of 450.
(c) The ratio of the earnings from a certain share to its price is 18.5. If the price is £1.50, what are the earnings?
(d) If a variable, A, increases by 8 per cent, what does it become?
(e) If a variable, B, changes to 0.945B, what percentage change has occurred?

Solution

(a) (i) A ratio is simply the two numbers expressed as a fraction

$$\frac{4.6}{23.0} \text{ or } 0.2$$

   (ii) In a basic example like this, the percentage is 100 times the ratio:

$$0.2 \times 100 = 20\%$$

(b) Thirty per cent is 30 out of 100. Thus, out of 450

$$\frac{30}{100} \times 450 = 135$$

(c) We are told that the ratio

$$\frac{\text{Earnings}}{\text{Price}} = 18.5$$

If the price is £1.50

$$\frac{\text{Earnings}}{£1.50} = 18.5$$

Earnings = £1.50 × 18.5 = £27.75

(d) An increase of 8 per cent of A is

$$\frac{8}{100} \times A \text{ or } 0.08A$$

The variable therefore becomes

$$A + 0.08A = 1.08A$$

(e) If a variable has decreased by

$$B - 0.945B = 0.055B$$

As a percentage, this is

$$\frac{0.055B}{B} \times 100 = 5.5\%$$

The next example will demonstrate the use of percentages in financial calculations.

Example 1.12.2

(a) During a certain year, a company declares a profit of £15.8 m, whereas, in the previous year, the profit had been £14.1 m. What percentage increase in profit does this represent?
(b) A consultant has forecast that the above company's profit figure will fall by 5 per cent next year. What profit figure is the consultant forecasting for the next year?
(c) If this year's profit is £6.2 m, and if the increase from last year is known to have been 7.5 per cent, what was last year's profit?

Solution

(a) The increase in profit is £1.7 m, which as a percentage of the previous year's profit is:

$$\frac{1.7m}{14.1m} \times 100\% = 12.1\% \text{ to one d.p.}$$

(b) The forecast decrease in profit is 5 per cent of £15.8 m

$$\frac{5}{100} \times 15.8 = £0.79\,m$$

Hence, the forecast profit for the following year is £15.01 m.

(c) This year's profit is 107.5 per cent of last year's

$$\text{Last year's profit} \times \frac{107.5}{100} = \text{This year's profit}$$

Last year's profit = £6.2m ÷ 1.075 = £5.77 m to three s.f.

1.13 Accuracy and approximation

All business data are subject to errors or variations. Simple human error, the rounding of a figure to the nearest hundred or thousand (or whatever), and the inevitable inaccuracies that arise when forecasting the future value of some factor, are examples of why business data may not be precise.

In certain circumstances, errors can accumulate, especially when two or more variables, each subject to error, are combined. The simplest such forms of combination are addition and subtraction.

1.14 Errors from rounding

Suppose an actual value is 826 and you round it to 830 (two s.f.). Your rounded value contains an error of 4. Someone else using the rounded figure does not know the true original value but must be aware that any rounded figure is likely to be erroneous.

The rounded value 830 could represent a true value as low as 825, or one as high as 835 (or, strictly speaking, 834.9999). There is a possible error of ±5.

In general, rounded values have a possible error given by substituting ±5 in the position of the first discarded digit. For example, with a value of 830, the first discarded digit is in the position of the '0', which is the units position. This gives a possible error of ±5 units. If the rounded figure were 82.391 (to three d.p.), the first discarded digit is immediately to the right of the '1' and the possible error is ±0.0005.

Example 1.14.1

State the maximum possible errors in the following rounded figures:

(i) 67,000
(ii) 5.63
(iii) 10.095

Solution

(i) The first discarded digit is in the '0' position immediately to the right of the '7', so the maximum possible error is ±500.
(ii) The first discarded digit is immediately to the right of the '3', so the maximum possible error is ±0.005.
(iii) The first discarded digit is to the right of the '5', so the maximum possible error is ±0.0005.

1.15 Using Excel to produce graphs of Linear and Quadratic Equations

Excel can be used to produce graphs of linear and quadratic equations. The first step is to produce a single linear equation, from which a graph can be drawn.

1.15.1 Producing a single linear equation in Excel

The form of the equation that will be used is

$$y = mx + c$$

This equation will be drawn for a given value of c (in this example we will use 20) and a range of 10 values of x (from 1 to 10), calculating corresponding values of y. Thus in this example the formula will be represented as $y = 3x + 20$.

Figure 1.7 shows the data for x and the results of entering the formula in the adjacent column.

Single linear equation	
values for x	$y = 3x + 20$
1	23
2	26
3	29
4	32
5	35
6	38
7	41
8	44
9	47
10	50

Figure 1.7 Data and formula for the equation

To show these results graphically in Excel, select the two columns and click on the Chart icon on the Standard Toolbar. This will produce a choice of graph types. Select xy and then choose the joined up line option. Click Finish to complete the chart. Figure 1.8 shows the resulting graph.

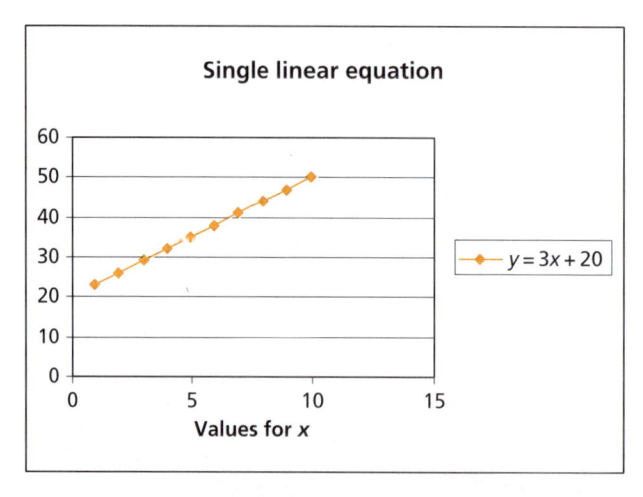

Figure 1.8 Graph showing single linear equation

1.15.2 Drawing multiple equations on a single graph

It is possible to produce multiple equations and plot the results onto a single graph, which can be useful for comparison purposes. Figure 1.9 uses the same set of data for x and the results of two different equations are shown in the adjacent two columns.

values for x	$y = 3x + 20$	$y = 6x + 1$
1	23	7
2	26	13
3	29	19
4	32	25
5	35	31
6	38	37
7	41	43
8	44	49
9	47	55
10	50	61

Figure 1.9 Data and two linear equations

The graph is produced in the same way as the first example, by selecting the three columns and clicking on the Chart icon. The results of plotting these two lines onto an *xy* line graph can be seen in Figure 1.10.

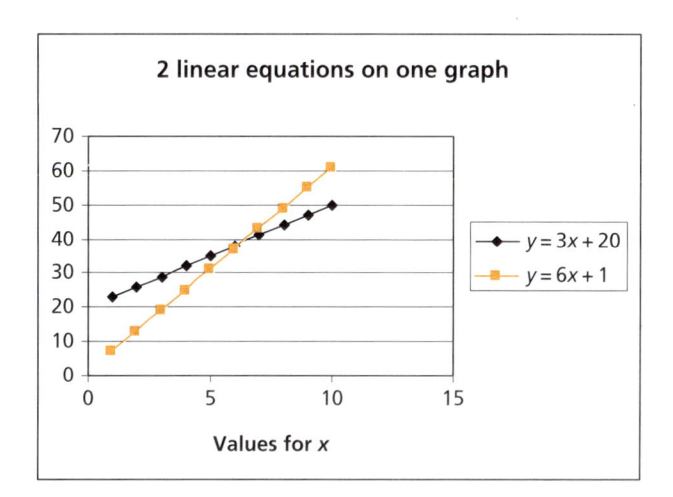

Figure 1.10 Results of 2 linear equations on one graph

1.15.3 Single quadratic equation

The form of the equation that will be used is

$$y = ax^2 + bx + c$$

This equation will be drawn for a given value of a, b and c, where in this example we will use $a = 1$, $b = 5$ and $c = 10$ and a range of 10 values of *x* (from -25 to 20), calculating corresponding values of *y*.

Thus in this example the formula will be represented as $y = x^2 + 5x + 10$. Figure 1.11 shows the data and the formula calculated in the adjacent column.

values for x	x^2 + 5x + 10
−25	510
−20	310
−15	160
−10	60
−5	10
0	10
5	60
10	160
15	310
20	510

Figure 1.11 Single quadratic equation

Using the same method as before a graph can be drawn to show these results and this is shown in Figure 1.12.

$x\char`\^2 + 5x + 10$

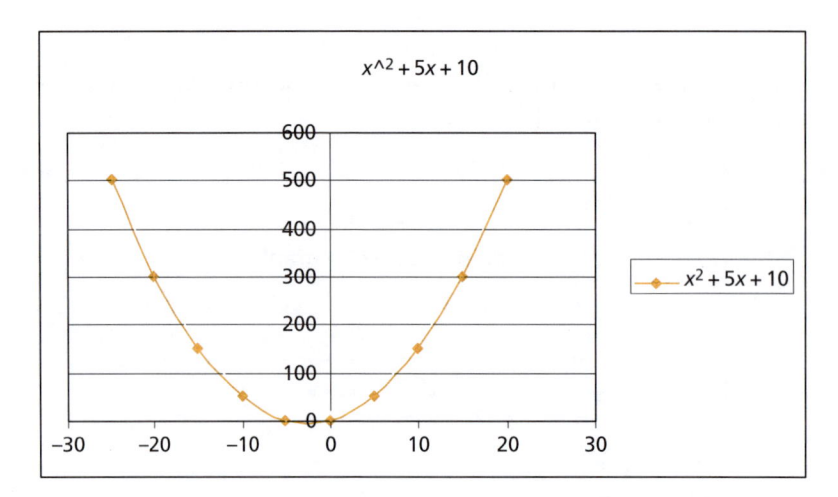

Figure 1.12 Graph showing a single quadratic equation

1.15.4 Two quadratic equations on one graph

It is possible to produce multiple quadratic equations and plot the results onto a single graph, which can be useful for comparison purposes. Figure 1.13 uses the same set of data for x and the results of two different equations are shown in the adjacent two columns.

values for X	$x\char`\^2 + 5x + 10$	$-2x\char`\^2 - x + 100$
−25	510	−1125
−20	310	−680
−15	160	−335
−10	60	−90
−5	10	55
0	10	100
5	60	45
10	160	−110
15	310	−365
20	510	−720

Figure 1.13 Two quadratic equations

The graph is produced in the same way as the previous example, by selecting the three columns and clicking on the Chart icon. The results of plotting these two lines onto an xy line graph can be seen in Figure 1.14.

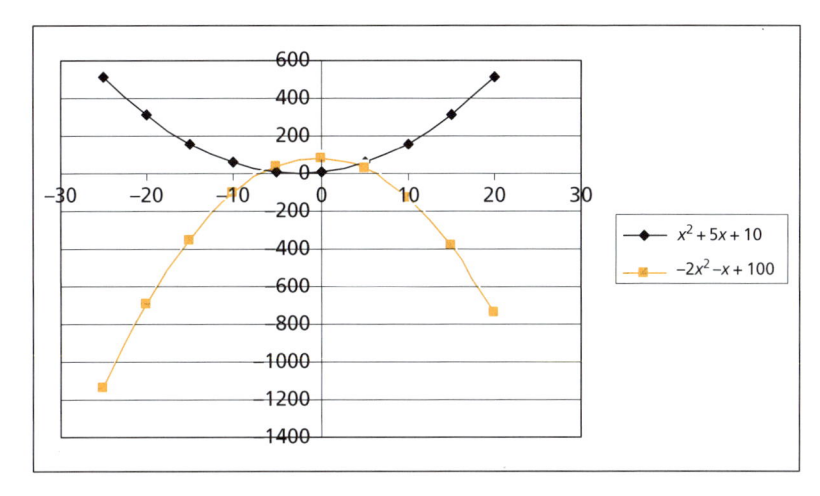

Figure 1.14 Graph of two quadratic equations

1.16 Using Excel to produce the graph of a hyperbola

The formula of a hyperbola takes the form of $y = a(1/x) + n$. In the example below values of x from 1 to 27 are used. The constant a is 10 and a value of 1 was used for n. The results are shown in Figure 1.15.

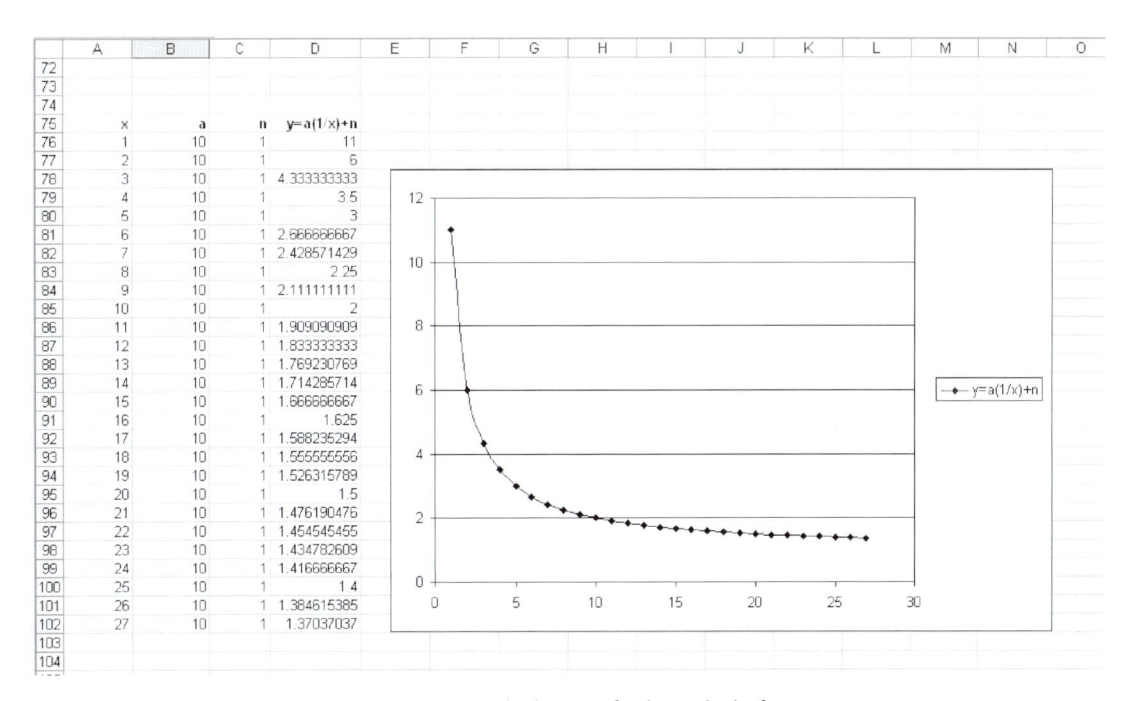

Figure 1.15 Calculation of a hyperbola function

1.17 Summary

Basic mathematics covers a wide range of topics and underlies virtually all the elements of business mathematics. The key contents of the chapter are:

- the rules for the order of mathematical operations and the use of brackets – a source of many errors in calculations;
- dealing with negative numbers;
- rounding to the nearest number or to various numbers of decimal places or significant figures;
- dealing with powers and roots;
- manipulating formulae;
- dealing with exponential numbers;
- solving equations;
- manipulating inequalities;
- dealing with percentages and ratios;
- rounding errors;
- creating graphs in a excel to draw linear and quadratic equations and graph of a hyperbola.

Revision Questions

Part 1.1 Objective testing selection

> Questions 1.1.1–1.1.10 are standard multiple-choice questions with exactly one correct answer each. Thereafter, the style of question will vary.

1.1.1 A square-ended rectangular box has a volume of 1,458 cm³. The length of the box is twice that of one side of the square end.
One side of the square end therefore measures:

(A) 6 cm
(B) 9 cm
(C) 18 cm
(D) 24 cm.

1.1.2 The expression $(x^2)^3/x^5$ equals:

(A) 0
(B) 1
(C) x
(D) x^2.

1.1.3 A buyer purchases twenty cases of Product A at £7.84 per case, ten cases of Product B at £8.20 per case, twelve cases of Product C at £8.50 per case and a number of cases of Product D at £8.60 per case. He spends £469.80 in total. If there are twelve items in each case of Product D, how many *items* of Product D does he buy?

(A) 120
(B) 144
(C) 150
(D) 180.

1.1.4 A person pays no tax on the first £3,500 of earnings and then 23 per cent tax on the remainder of earnings. If he/she wishes to have £15,000 net of tax earnings, what gross earnings (to the nearest £) does he/she need?

(A) £15,000
(B) £18,435
(C) £18,500
(D) £19,481.

1.1.5 An item priced at £90.68, including local sales tax at 19 per cent, is reduced in a sale by 20 per cent. The new price before sales tax is added is:

(A) £60.96
(B) £72.54
(C) £75.57
(D) £76.20.

1.1.6 The term x^{-1} equals:

(A) $2x$
(B) $1/x$
(C) x^2
(D) $x - 1$.

1.1.7 A buyer has spent £30,151 on 550 units of a particular item. The first 100 units cost £50 each, the next 150 units cost £8,250 in total, the next batch cost £11,200 in total and the final 100 cost £x each. The value of x is:

(A) £55
(B) £56
(C) £57.01
(D) £60.30.

1.1.8 At a value added tax (VAT) rate of 12.5 per cent, an article sells for 84p, including VAT. If the VAT rate increases to 17.5 per cent, the new selling price, to the nearest penny, will be:

(A) 87p
(B) 88p
(C) 94p
(D) 99p.

1.1.9 In the following formula substitute $Q = 100$, $C = 10$, $P = 6$ and $R = 0.2$

$$Q = \sqrt{\frac{2DC}{PR}}$$

D, to the nearest unit, is:

(A) 598
(B) 599
(C) 600
(D) 601.

1.1.10 The price, £p, of a product is planned to be £10, the planned annual demand, q, is 1,000 units and the number of trading days per year, n, is 200. If p, q and n are expected to vary by ±10 per cent, then the maximum value of pq/n, the mean revenue per trading day, will be closest to:

(A) £37
(B) £50
(C) £55
(D) £67.

1.1.11 If a number P is increased by 5 per cent, what will its new value be? Which of the following answers is/are correct?

(A) $P + 5P/100$
(B) $1.05P$
(C) $0.95P$
(D) $0.05P.$

1.1.12 The number 268.984 is to be rounded. In each case write the correct answer, to the accuracy specified.

(A) to two decimal places.
(B) to one decimal place.
(C) to the nearest whole number.
(D) to the nearest 100.
(E) to three significant figures.
(F) to four significant figures.

1.1.13 Evaluate the following *without* rounding.

(A) $7 + 2 \times 5$
(B) $(5 + 2) \times 8$
(C) $28 - 48/4$
(D) $(7 + 3)/5$
(E) $8 + 4 \times 5 - 2$
(F) $(8 - 4) \times (3 + 7).$

1.1.14 Each of the following has been algebraically simplified. Which of the answers given are correct, and which incorrect?

(A) $((a^6)^2)/a^8$ Answer: a^4
(B) $(a^6)/a^{-5}$ Answer: a
(C) $(a^8)^{1/4}$ Answer: a^2
(D) $1/a^{-7}$ Answer: a^{-6}

1.1.15 The formula $V = P \times (1 + r)^n$ occurs in compounding.
(a) Rearrange the formula to make r the subject. Which one of the following answers is correct?

(A) $r = (V/P - 1)^{1/n}$
(B) $r = (V/P)^{1/n} - 1$
(C) $r = (V - P)/n - 1$

(b) If $P = 250$, $r = 0.04$ and $n = 6$, calculate V to the nearest whole number.

1.1.16 The equation $60/Y = 25/(20 - Y)$ is to be solved to find Y correct to one decimal place. A solution comprises the following five lines, (A)–(E). Which of the lines (A)–(E) follows correctly from the line immediately prior to them (regardless of whether or not you believe the prior line to be correct)?

(A) $60(20 - Y) = 25Y$
(B) $1,200 - Y = 25Y$
(C) $1,200 = 26Y$

(D) $Y = 1,200/26$
(E) $Y = 46.15$ to two d.p.

1.1.17 Each of the following solutions of quadratic equations contains *one* line that does not follow correctly from that immediately prior to it. In each case identify the incorrect line.

(A) $Y^2 - 36 = 0$
$Y^2 = 36$
$Y = 6$

(B) $Y^2 - 5Y = 0$
$Y(2Y - 5) = 0$
$Y = 0$ or $5/2$

(C) $(Y + 6)^2 = 0$
$Y + 6 = \pm 0$
$Y = \pm 6$

(D) $Y^2 + Y - 12 = 0$

Using the standard formula:
$a = 2, b = 1, c = -12$
$Y = (-1 \pm (1 + 4 \times 2 \times 12)^{0.5})/2 \times 2$
$Y = 2.2$ or -2.7 to one d.p.

1.1.18 A price of £2,500 includes VAT at 17.5 per cent. Find the price *exclusive* of VAT correct to the nearest £.

1.1.19 For each of the following solve for x in the inequality

(A) $5x + 10 > 20$
(B) $2x - 5 < 15$
(C) $x/2 - 10 \geq 30$
(D) $-5x + 20 \leq 120$

Part 1.2 Basic mathematics

A small company produces specialised posters. The total cost is made up of three elements — materials, labour and administration — as follows:

Materials	£0.50 per poster
Labour	£15 per hour
Administration	£10 per 100, plus £50.

The set-up time for printing takes two hours, and the posters are run off at the rate of 300 per hour.

1.2.1 If the number of posters produced is denoted by N, write down the formulae for the following in £:

(A) the total cost of materials,
(B) the time taken to produce the posters,
(C) the total labour costs of production,
(D) the administration costs.

1.2.2 Calculate the solutions to Question 1.2.1 using Excel. You will first have to create a spreadsheet to represent the data for the printing company.

1.2.3 If the total cost were given by $C = 92 + 0.7N$, which of the following is the correct interpretation of the value 92?

(A) Even when no posters are produced there is a cost of £92.
(B) For every 100 posters produced there is an extra cost of £92.
(C) The cost rises by 70p for every 92 posters produced.

Which of the following is the correct interpretation of the value 0.7?

(D) The cost of producing 100 posters is £92 × 0.7.
(E) When no posters are produced there is a cost of £0.7 per hour.
(F) Costs rise by 70p for every extra poster produced.

Calculate the following:

(G) the total cost of producing 1,000 posters,
(H) the number of posters which can be produced for £500 (to the nearest whole number),
(I) the number of posters which can be produced for £N (to the nearest whole number).

Part 1.3 Accuracy and approximation

A company is preparing future production plans for a new product. Research findings suggest that next year the company could make and sell 10,000 units (±20 per cent) at a price of £50 (±10 per cent), depending on size of order, weather, quality of supply, discounts, and so on.

The variable costs of production for next year, given these data, are also uncertain but have been estimated as follows:

Type	Costs (£)	Margin of error
Materials	150,000	±2%
Wages	100,000	±5%
Marketing	50,000	±10%
Miscellaneous	50,000	±10%

1.3.1 Complete the following table showing the maximum and minimum values that might occur. The first line has been completed in order to show what is required. Answers carry 1 mark each.

	Minimum	Maximum
Number of units sold	8,000	12,000
Selling price per unit	£	£
Cost of materials	£	£
Cost of wages	£	£
Cost of marketing	£	£
Miscellaneous	£	£

Solutions to Revision Questions

✓ Solutions to Part 1.1

1.1.1 Answer: (B)

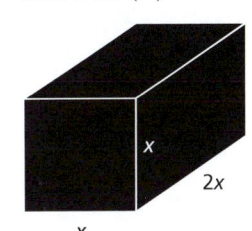

Volume = $2x^3 = 1{,}458$

$x^3 = 1{,}458/2 = 729$

$x = (729)^{1/3} = 9$.

1.1.2 Answer: (C)

$$\frac{(x^2)^3}{x^5} = \frac{x^6}{x^5} = x$$

based on rules $(x^m)^n = x^{mn}$ and $\frac{x^m}{x^n} = x^{(m-n)}$.

1.1.3 Answer: (D)

Let there be X cases of product D. Then:

$20 \times £7.84 + 10 \times £8.20 + 12 \times £8.50 + X \times £8.60 = £469.80$

i.e. $340.8 + 8.6X = 469.8$

$8.6X = 469.8 - 340.8$
$8.6X = 129$
$X = 129 \div 8.6$
$X = 15$

Number of items = $12X = 12 \times 15 = 180$.

1.1.4 Answer: (B)

£15,000 − £3,500 = £11,500, which is the taxable part of earnings, after tax at 23 per cent. Hence, taxable earnings are (£11,500 ÷ 0.77) = £14,935 before tax, and gross earnings are £14,935 + £3,500 = £18,435.

1.1.5 Answer: (A)

Reduced price, including sales tax = £90.68 × 80% = £72.54. Without sales tax: £72.54 × (100/119) = £60.96.

1.1.6 Answer: (B)

$x^{-1} = 1/x$, by definition.

1.1.7 Answer: (C)

Batch	Cost £	Cumulative cost £
100 at £50	5,000	
Next 150	8,250	13,250
Next 11,200	24,450	
Final 100 at £x	100x	24,450 + 100x

Total = 30,151 = 24,450 + 100x
30,151 − 24,450 = 100x = 5,701
x = 5701/100 = 57.01.

1.1.8 Answer: (B)

$$84p \times \frac{100}{112.5} = 74.6p = \text{price without VAT}$$
$$74.67p \times \frac{117.5}{100} = 88p.$$

1.1.9 Answer: (C)

$$Q^2 = \frac{2DC}{PR}$$
$$Q^2PR = 2DC$$
$$\frac{Q^2PR}{2C} = D = 600.$$

1.1.10 Answer: (D)

Maximum values of p and q = 11 and 1,100
Minimum value of n = 180
Therefore: 11 × (1,100/180) = 67.

1.1.11 Answers: (A), (B)

Five per cent of P is $5P/100$, so the result will be $P + 5P/100 = P + 0.05P = 1.05P$.
In answer (C), P has been reduced by 5 per cent. In D, the 5 per cent of P has been calculated but not added to the original amount.

1.1.12 The correct answers are:

(A) 268.98
(B) 269.0
(C) 269
(D) 300
(E) 269
(F) 269.0.

1.1.13 The correct answers are shown with some of the prior workings:

(A) $7 + 10 = 17$
(B) $7 \times 8 = 56$
(C) $28 - 12 = 16$
(D) $10/5 = 2$
(E) $8 + 20 - 2 = 26$
(F) $4 \times 10 = 40$.

1.1.14 The correct responses are shown with some of the workings:

(A) Correct $\quad a^{12}/a^8 = a^4$
(B) Incorrect $\quad a^{(6-(-5))} = a^{11}$
(C) Correct $\quad a^{(8/4)} = a^2$
(D) Incorrect $\quad 1/a^n = a^{-n}$, so $1/a^{-7} = a^7$.

1.1.15 (a) Answer: (B)

The steps are:
$V/P = (1 + r)^n$
$(V/P)^{1/n} = 1 + r$
$(V/P)^{1/n} - 1 = r.$

(b) $V = 250 \times 1.04^6$, so the answer is 316.

1.1.16 The correct answers are as follows:

(A) $60(20 - Y) = 25Y$ Correct
(B) $1{,}200 - Y = 25Y$ Incorrect: the Y should have been multiplied by the 60
(C) $1{,}200 = 26Y$ Correct
(D) $Y = 1{,}200/26$ Correct
(E) $Y = 46.15$ to two d.p.   Correct.

1.1.17 The incorrect lines were as follows:

(A) $Y = 6$, because $Y = \pm 6$
(B) $Y(2Y - 5) = 0$ is wrong: Y^2 is not $2 \times Y \times Y$
(C) $Y = \pm 6$ is wrong: ± 0 is the same as 0 and the correct answer is -6
(D) The line $a = 2, b = 1, c = -12$ is wrong: $a = 1$.

1.1.18 The price exclusive of VAT is £2,500/1.175 = £2,128

1.1.19

(A) $5x + 10 > 10$
    $5x > 20 - 10$
    $5x > 10$
    $x > 2.$

(B) $2x - 5 < 15$
    $2x < 15 + 5$
    $2x < 20$
    $x < 10.$

(C) $x/2 - 10 \geq 30$
    $x/2 \geq 30 + 10$
    $x/2 \geq 40$
    $x \geq 80.$

(D) $-5x + 20 \leq 120$
    $-5x \leq 120 - 20$
    $-5x \leq 100$
    $-x \leq 20$
    $x \geq 20.$

✓ Solutions to Part 1.2

1.2.1 Materials cost £0.50 per poster, that is $0.50N$ (£) (i).
Labour costs £15 per hour, and N posters take $(N/300 + 2)$ hours to produce. Thus the labour costs are $15(N/300 + 2)$
$= N/20 + 30$ (£) (ii).

Administration costs are £10 per hundred posters plus £50; that is,
$10 \times N/100 + 50$
$= N/10 + 50$ (£) (iii).

Answers:

(A) $0.5N$
(B) $2 + N/300$
(C) $15(2 + N/300)$
(D) $50 + N/10.$

1.2.2

	A	B	C
1	Revision question 1.12.2		
2			
3		Quantity required	1000
4		Materials-unit cost	0.5
5		Labour-cost per hour	15
6		Admin-basic plus £10 per 100	50
7			
8		setup time in hours	2
9		runoff rate per hour	300
10			
11		Total cost of materials	=C3*C4
12		Time taken for production	=C8+(C3/C9)
13		Total labour costs of production	=C12*C5
14		Admin costs	=C6+(C3/100*10)
15			
16			

1.2.3 (A) Is correct. When $N = 0$, $C = 92$.

(F) Is correct. If N changes to $N + 1$, C changes from $92 + 0.7N$ to $92 + 0.7(N + 1) = 92 + 0.7N + 0.7$, that is C increases by 0.7 for every extra poster.

(G) Cost $= 92 + 0.7 \times 1000 = £792$

(H) If $500 = 92 + 0.7N$, then $0.7N = 500 - 92 = 408$ and $N = 408/0.7 = 582.9 = 583$ to nearest whole number.

(I) If $N = 92 + 0.7N$, then $0.3N = 92$, so $N = 92/0.3 = 306.7 = 307$ (to the nearest whole number).

✓ Solutions to Part 1.3

1.3.1 The company can make and sell $10,000 \pm 2,000$, or 8,000 to 12,000 units in the year.

The selling price will lie in the range £50 ± £5, or £45 to £55 per unit.

Thus, the maximum revenue is $12,000 \times £55 = £660,000$; the minimum revenue is $8,000 \times £45 = £360,000$; the estimated revenue is $10,000 \times £50 = £500,000$.

Minimum and maximum values are therefore as follows:

	Minimum	Maximum
Number of units sold	8,000	12,000
Selling price per unit	£45	£55
Cost of materials	£147,000	£153,000
Cost of wages	£95,000	£105,000
Cost of marketing	£45,000	£55,000
Miscellaneous cost	£45,000	£55,000

2

Obtaining Data

Obtaining Data

Learning Outcomes

After completing this chapter you should be able to:
- explain the difference between data and information;
- explain the characteristics of good information;
- explain the difference between primary and secondary data;
- identify the sources of secondary data;
- explain the different methods of sampling and identify where each is appropriate.

2.1 Introduction

Many of the problems that accountants face require the acquisition, communication or analysis of data as part of their solution. We look at each of these aspects in turn. First of all, there is the question of how to obtain *data*, as the individual facts and figures are known.

Data can be classified in two ways: *primary* and *secondary*. Primary data is that collected specifically for the problem in hand, while secondary data is collected (by others) for some other purpose. Thus an accountant, working in the budgeting department of a manufacturing company, might get information on raw material costs by contacting the suppliers himself or herself, and so obtain primary data. Alternatively, he or she could use secondary data in the form of a list of quotations compiled for its own purposes by the company's buying department.

Primary data is the more reliable, since you have obtained it yourself (or have had it collected) and because it relates precisely to the particular problem you are facing. Its actual collection, however, does take time; obtaining it, therefore, tends to be costly, and there may be a considerable delay before the information is ready to use.

On the other hand, secondary data, if available, is relatively inexpensive and quick to obtain: often simply a reference to some relevant publication. The disadvantages here arise from the possibility that there may be no suitable sources for the information. Even if there are, the data may not match your requirements too well. In addition, although official or government statistics may be considered reliable, other secondary sources may not.

Immediately after collection, in what is often termed its raw form, data is not very informative. We cannot learn about the situation from it or draw conclusions from it. After it has been sorted and analysed, data becomes *information* that, it is to be hoped, is understandable and useful.

> In this chapter you will see many terms written in italics. These are all key terms which you might well need to be able to define in your assessment.

2.1.1 The difference between information and data

Sometimes the issue of the quality of data is raised and often there is not a clear understanding of this issue. Quality data has several characteristics including being:

- error free;
- available at the right time;
- available at the right place;
- available to the appropriate individuals.

The arrival of the Internet has made it much easier for organisations and individuals to access data at the right time and the right place. However, at the same time the Internet have opened up questions about data being error free and about who can have access to it.

As well the issue of data quality there is the question of how data, information and knowledge relate to one another. Russell Ackoff was one of the first people to speak of there being a hierarchy which he referred to as the Data Information Knowledge Wisdom (DIKW) Hierarchy. According to this model, data (which is by the way sometimes said to be a plural word as it is the actual plural for the word datum) are simple facts or figures or maybe even a photograph or an illustration. In this form data is unstructured and uninterrupted. Information comes from processing or structuring data in a meaningful way. Another way of looking at this is that information is interpreted data. An interesting story is told by Joan Magretta in her book *What Management is?* about Steve Jobs which clearly illustrates the difference between data and information.

Despite its small share of the total market for personal computers, Apple has long been a leader in sales to schools and universities. When CEO Steve Jobs learned that Apple's share of computer sales to schools was 12.5 per cent in 1999, he was dismayed, but unless you're an industry analyst who knows the numbers cold, you won't appreciate just how dismayed he was. That's because, in 1998, Apple was the segment leader with a market share of 14.6 per cent. And, while Apple slipped to the number two spot in 1999, Dell grew and took the lead with 15.1 per cent. Alone each number is meaningless. Together they spell trouble, if you're Steve Jobs, you see a trend that you'd better figure out how to reverse. This isn't number crunching, it's sense making. (Magretta, 2003, p. 123)

In this example the 12.5 per cent was data and when it was seen in conjunction with the 15.1 per cent it became information.

Knowledge is again different to data and information. Knowledge is much more personal and the presence or absence of knowledge can normally only be seen through the actions of individuals. When knowledge is written down it effectively becomes information.

Finally with respect to wisdom it is difficult to define this concept. Wisdom has something to do with understanding or insight. It is to do with achieving a good long-term outcome in relation to the circumstances you are in.

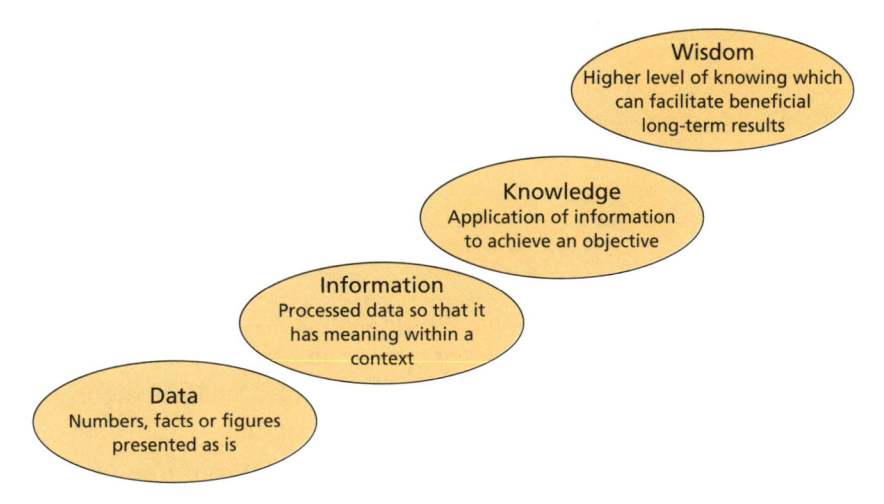

Figure 2.1 The Data Information Knowledge Wisdom (DIKW) Hierarchy

- **Wisdom**: Higher level of knowing which can facilitate beneficial long-term results
- **Knowledge**: Application of information to achieve an objective
- **Information**: Processed data so that it has meaning within a context
- **Data**: Numbers, facts or figures presented as is

The DIKW Hierarchy is often expressed graphically as shown in Figure 2.1.

2.2 Primary data: sampling

We begin by considering how primary data can be obtained. All the data relating to a problem is known as the *population*. For reasons of finance and practicability, it is rarely possible to obtain *all* the relevant data, so you normally have to use only part of the population, that is, a *sample*. It is clear that, if the sample data is to be of any use, it must be representative of the population as a whole. If a sample *is* representative of its population, it is said to be *unbiased*; otherwise it is *biased*. Another fundamental point to note is that, because a sample is only a subset – that is, some information has been omitted – any results arising from it cannot be exact representations of the whole population. This deficiency is said to constitute *sampling error*.

By careful choice of sampling method, it is possible to ensure that a sample is representative of its population, thereby avoiding bias. Since the very act of sampling omits some of the data, sampling error is inevitable. In general, if you increase its size, the sample will represent a larger proportion, and so will be 'nearer to' (or more representative of) the population. Increasing sample size thus tends to reduce sampling error.

An example will illustrate these new concepts and terms.

Example 2.2.1

You work as an assistant to the chief accountant of a company that owns a large number of retail stores across the country. The chief accountant asks you to provide him with some up-to-date information on the weekly turnover figures of the stores. Discuss how you would set about this.

Solution

Secondary financial data on the stores will no doubt be available, but it may not consist of weekly turnover figures and probably will not be up to date. Thus, provided that enough time and resources are available, you should consider obtaining primary data. We shall leave discussion of possible methods of actually collecting the information until later in this chapter and concentrate here on the meaning of the various concepts defined above, as applied to this example.

The *population* here consists of all the recent weekly turnover figures for all the stores owned by the company. Clearly it would be practically impossible to collect all this data, and so a *sample* will have to be taken. This will consist of a selection of a certain number of the weekly turnover figures, for example 100 or 1,000 of them: the exact number will depend on the time and resources available, and the level of accuracy required by the chief accountant. If the selection of 100 or 1,000 (or whatever) weekly turnover figures is representative of all the possible data, then we shall have an unbiased sample. However, because a sample consists of only part of the population (possibly just a small proportion), it will give only an approximation to the overall picture: sampling error will be present. In general, increasing the sample size from, say, 100 to 1,000 will reduce this error.

2.3 Probability sampling methods

We now look at various ways of selecting samples, beginning with *probability sampling methods* (also called *random sampling methods*): those in which there is a known chance of each member of the population appearing in the sample. Such methods eliminate the possibility of bias arising through (subjective) human selection: it can now only arise by chance. In addition, it is possible to undertake calculations concerning the effects of sample error when probability sampling methods are used.

2.3.1 Simple random sampling

Of these methods, the most basic is *simple random sampling*, in which each element of the population has an *equal* chance of being selected. Such a sample could be chosen by drawing names out of a hat, or by employing more sophisticated models using random numbers (which will be illustrated later). As we shall see in later parts of the text, random sampling is one of the most important sampling methods in statistics, since the accuracy of estimates made from the sample can be calculated.

2.3.2 Stratified random sampling

In this case, the population is divided into coherent groups or strata, and the sample is produced by sampling at random within each stratum. This process takes more time than simple random sampling, but should result in more representative samples and hence should reduce the sample error.

Example 2.3.1

How would a simple random sample and a stratified random sample be drawn in the situation described in Example 2.2.1?

Solution

To begin with, we shall need a list of the population. If, for example, the company owns 100 stores, and the investigation is confined to the last year's (50 trading weeks') trading, then the population will consist of 5,000 pieces of data. These might be arranged as follows:

Turnover of store 1	week 1	0001
Turnover of store 1	week 2	0002
. . . .	. . . .	. . . . .
Turnover of store 1	week 50	0050
Turnover of store 2	week 1	0051
. . . .	. . . .	. . . . .
Turnover of store 100	week 50	5000

The members of the population can be numbered from 1 to 5,000, using a four-digit notation, as shown in the right-hand column of the above table. The table is not set out in full for reasons of space: however, it is easy to calculate that the turnover of store 7 in, say, week 47 is represented by the number 347 (i.e. 6 × 50 + 47). The problem of selecting, say, 200 of these weekly turnover figures, each with an equal chance of being picked, can now be translated into the task of obtaining a similar sample from the digits 0001 to 5,000.

There are a number of ways of obtaining the necessary random numbers, such as computer generation or by using random number tables. The latter method consists of reading off four-digit numbers from the tables. (Because there are 5,000 elements in the population, we ensured that each one was numbered with a four-digit number: hence 0001, etc.) For example, the random numbers 0347, 4373 and 8636 would be interpreted as follows:

0347:	week 47 of store 7 is the first member of the sample
4373:	week 23 of store 88 is the second
8636:	this is bigger than 5,000, and so is ignored.

We proceed in this way until we have selected the desired sample size (200 items). Note that because each digit in the table has an equal chance of being 0, 1, 2, ..., 9, we have ensured that each element of the population has an equal chance of being sampled, that is, we have a simple random sample.

Following the above procedure, it is possible, by pure chance, that the 200 sampled weeks may come from just a few stores' figures, with many stores not being represented. If the 100 stores are similar in their trading patterns, this may not matter, but, if we wish to ensure that there is a good spread from the stores within the sample, we can stratify before sampling. By way of illustration, this can be done by taking each store's figures as a stratum and taking a sample of 2 weeks within each. Thus, the data on store 1 would form the first stratum:

Turnover, week 1	01
Turnover, week 2	02
. . . . . .	
Turnover, week 50	50

Note that we need only two-digit random numbers now. The random numbers 33, 67, 00, 98 and 09 would be interpreted as follows:

33	the turnover of week 33 is selected
67	bigger than 50, so this is ignored
00	too small (01 is the lowest in our numbering)
98	too big, so ignored
09	the turnover of week 9 is selected.

These two figures would form the contribution to the sample from the first stratum. Repeating this procedure for the 2nd to the 100th stratum (store's figure) would now produce a randomised sample in which every store was represented.

Before we leave this example, it should be noted that there are many other ways of stratifying. For example, it may be that stores number 1–10 are far bigger than the others and so should be better represented in the sample. In such a case, you might work with just two strata (larger stores' turnover figures and small stores' turnover figures) and then sample (at random) 100 values from each. In practice, situations like this demand the use of personal judgement when determining how to stratify and what proportion of the sample to include from each stratum. In other situations, it is possible to be a little more precise, as the following example illustrates.

Example 2.3.2

A market research agency is commissioned to investigate the attitudes of the adult population of a town towards a certain product. Its clients are interested only in a breakdown of the opinions by gender and by age (over or under 35). How might the agency use stratified sampling?

Solution

The agency will be able to find fairly reliable secondary data on the characteristics of the town's adult population. Suppose that this shows:

female:	51%	male:	49%
35 and over:	68%	under 35:	32%

Assuming that the age distributions of men and women are the same, a simple process of multiplication could then be used to produce the following strata:

female, 35 and over	34.68%	(0.51 × 0.68, as a percentage)
female, under 35	16.32%	(0.51 × 0.32, as a percentage)
male, 35 and over	33.32%	(0.49 × 0.68, as a percentage)
male, under 35	15.68%	(0.49 × 0.32, as a percentage)

In other words, if a sample size of 1,000 were being employed, 347 of the sample would be females aged 35 and over, 163 would be females aged under 35, 333 would be males aged 35 and over, and 157 would be males aged under 35.

2.4 Other sampling methods

If we reconsider the examples in the preceding section, we shall see that there can be great practical problems in using random methods of sampling. First of all, in order to use random number tables (or any other method of ensuring randomness), we need a list of the population. This list is often called a *sampling frame*. As we shall see, there are many instances where a sampling frame is unavailable. Even when one is, *stratified* random sampling may be impossible. For instance, in the previous example, to stratify the population it would be necessary to divide the sampling frame (possibly the town's electoral register) into the four categories shown. This would not be possible, since an individual's age could not easily be determined from the register. Note that it would not be sensible to try to find the age of every individual in the town, as one would then be contacting every member of the population – the whole idea of sampling is to avoid such an onerous task!

A second practical problem lies in the cost of random sampling. Imagine taking even a *simple* random sample of 1,000 people from a town's electoral register. This would involve counting down the register to find person number 139,103 (say), which our random number tables gave us, then contacting her or him to conduct an interview. Multiply this by 1,000 and you will appreciate the immense time and expense involved.

A number of alternative sampling methods have been devised to get round some of the problems listed above.

- *Cluster sampling* consists of taking one definable subsection of the population as the sample. Thus, you could take the inhabitants of one street as a cluster sample of the population of a town. However, such a sample is unlikely to be representative, and so a variation might be to take the inhabitants of five streets (chosen at random from an alphabetical list) as the sample. The latter example could still be unrepresentative but would be a great deal easier and cheaper to survey than a sample randomly spread all over the town. Cluster sampling is a random method provided that the clusters are randomly selected, but it does not give data as reliable as that given by either simple random or stratified random sampling. It is widely used for reasons of speed, cheapness and convenience.
- *Systematic sampling* involves taking every *n*th member of the population as the sample. This can be applied with or without a sampling frame, and so may or may not be a probability method. As an example, a sample could be drawn from an electoral register by selecting every 1,000th on the list. In a quality-control situation, we could take every 100th batch coming off a production line for testing. Note that, in this latter case, we

have only part of the sampling frame, those batches produced near the time of sampling. A complete sampling frame, consisting of all past and future batches, would be impossible to obtain. Systematic sampling from a sampling frame provides a good approximation to simple random sampling without the bother of using random numbers. Problems of bias arise only if there is a cycle in the data that coincides with the sampling cycle. For instance, if, in the quality-control situation, 100 batches were produced every two hours, then you might find yourself always sampling the last batch prior to staff taking a break: this might not be representative of the general quality of production. In general, however, systematic sampling provides random samples almost as reliable as those of simple random sampling and in a much more convenient manner.

- *Quota sampling* is essentially non-random stratified sampling. The members of the various strata are called *quotas*, which are not chosen at random but are selected by interviewers. The market research agency in the previous example could draw its sample by issuing quotas of:

    347 females, 35 and over
    163 females, under 35
    333 males, 35 and over
    157 males, under 35

The actual members of the sample would be selected by the interviewers, as they moved around the town. When the respondent's age was determined, he or she could be included as part of one of the above quotas. When a quota was complete, no more people from that category would be included. This subjective element is an obvious source of bias which can be reduced in practice by training interviewers to choose a 'spread' within each quota. For example, they would be encouraged not to choose all 40-year-olds in the '35 and over' quotas, but to try to achieve a variety of ages within the range. This method is cheap, quick and easy and, in particular, it does not require a sampling frame. It has all the advantages of stratified sampling at a much lower cost, but it is not random: information obtained from it may well be biased and there is no means of measuring its reliability.

2.5 Multistage sampling

We conclude the discussion of sampling techniques by looking at a method commonly used when a survey has to cover a wide geographical area without incurring great expense. *Multistage sampling*, as its name implies, involves splitting the process into a number of (typically three) separate steps. An example will illustrate.

Example 2.5.1

If you were organising a nationwide opinion poll, how would you set about organising the sample, using a multistage technique?

Solution

The first stage is to divide the country into easily definable regions: in the case of a political survey such as we have here, the 651 parliamentary constituencies are ideal for this. It is now a straightforward matter to select, *at random*, twenty (say) of the constituencies.

In the second stage, the regions are split into smaller, more manageable, districts. There is an ideal subdivision in this example, namely the political wards within each constituency. A random sample of (say) three wards might now be selected within each of the twenty constituencies obtained in the first stage. Note that we have now a sample of sixty wards, randomly selected, and that these could be obtained by one person in a matter of minutes, provided that a complete list of constituencies and wards and a set of random number tables are available.

The time-consuming stage is the third and final one, that of contacting and interviewing a sample of (say) thirty voters in each of the sixty wards. This could be done at random from the electoral registers of the wards, thereby ensuring that the whole process is random. A faster and less expensive alternative, albeit one that risks the introduction of bias, would be a non-random method such as quota sampling. The quotas might be by gender and age or, working with a larger budget, might be more sophisticated.

This sample involves two stages of cluster sampling and a third that may be either systematic or quota sampling.

One criticism of multistage sampling is that the regions in the first stage and the districts in the second stage will not each contain the same number of people. In the above example, one constituency may have 40,000 electors, whereas another may have 60,000. As the two are equally likely to be chosen in stage 1, an elector in the former constituency will be 1.5 times as likely to appear in the final sample than an elector in the latter constituency (one in 40,000 as opposed to one in 60,000).

A variation that redresses this imbalance is sampling with probability proportional to size. Hence, we weight the chances of choosing a region (stage 1) and then a district (stage 2) according to the number of people in the region or district; larger regions or districts having proportionately more chance of selection than smaller ones. In the above example, we would ensure that a constituency of 40,000 electors has two-thirds the chance of being selected as does a constituency of 60,000 electors, by allocating two-thirds as many random numbers to the former as compared with the latter. This proportion will then exactly compensate for the imbalance referred to in the preceding paragraph.

> You will virtually certainly have a question in your assessment which requires you to differentiate between the different types of samples.

2.6 Secondary data: sources

There are numerous potential sources of secondary data that could be used to provide the required information in a given situation. Searching out sources is usually not too problematical: the real difficulty lies in judging whether the data adequately matches the requirements or whether primary data should be sought.

Sources of secondary data can be categorised into three types. First of all, there are data collected and compiled internally by the organisation, such as its financial reports and accounts, personnel records, and so on. Second, there are business data produced by sources external to the organisation. Under this heading come the results of surveys by the CBI, the financial press and similar sources. Finally, we have the many government-produced statistics on a whole range of commercial and demographic topics, any one of which might be applicable in solving a business problem.

These publications are too numerous to list here, but the Office for National Statistics *Guide to Official Statistics* is published annually and gives a comprehensive catalogue of sources of official statistics.

2.7 Questionnaires

In many situations, data are collected by asking a sample of people a series of questions. The printed form used by interviewers to pose the questions or for respondents to complete themselves is termed a *questionnaire*. Although it is unlikely that management accountants will have to design questionnaires, they may have to commission their design, or may encounter them in some other way. It is therefore useful to be able to judge whether a questionnaire is well designed; as poor design could lead to the collection of unreliable data.

The basic ideas are to make it as easy as possible to answer the questions accurately and to encourage respondents to complete the questionnaire, if interviewers are not being used. Overall, therefore, the questionnaire needs to be as brief as possible, consistent with the data that needs to be collected: long documents can be off-putting. In addition, it should be logically structured and well laid out, otherwise errors can be introduced through confusion or, again, respondents may be discouraged from completing the forms.

The individual questions, in particular, need attention. There are a number of do's and don'ts to be considered when drafting questions, all again concerned with obtaining accurate and reliable responses from the sample. These are listed below.

- Do not ask ambiguous questions.
- Do not use leading questions.
- Do not pose questions that require technical knowledge or that use a complicated vocabulary.
- Give a brief, simple list of possible answers, whenever you can.
- Put personal or difficult questions at the end of the questionnaire.
- Do not ask questions that rely too much on memory.
- Try to avoid open-ended questions.

2.8 Contact with respondents

The following methods of making contact with respondents are all in wide use and have different advantages and disadvantages.

- Interviewers undoubtedly get the best results. The response rate is high, the questionnaire is filled in immediately and in an accurate manner, and any misunderstandings on the part of the respondent can be rectified. However, the method is not without disadvantages. It is time-consuming and costly. The interviewer needs to be well trained in order to ensure that he or she does not introduce *interviewer bias* by posing questions in such a way that respondents are inclined to give certain answers. Respondents may not be prepared to discuss certain topics in an interview, but might be prepared to complete a questionnaire privately. Finally, in interviews the respondent cannot take time to 'mull over' the questions. Indeed, they may answer quite thoughtlessly in order to speed up the interview. Notwithstanding the disadvantages, face-to-face interviews are generally regarded as the best method of contact with respondents because low response rates and poorly completed questionnaires are so devastating in surveys.
- Enumerators deliver the questionnaires and explain to the respondents what the survey is about and so on. A few days later they collect the completed questionnaires and deal with any problems that have arisen. The method secures quite good response rates, although not as good as face-to-face interviews; it gives the respondent privacy, the time to think about questions and some degree of assistance, and it reduces the likelihood of interviewer bias. Its disadvantages are that it is costly and time-consuming and that the forms may not be filled in very well.
- Telephone interviews are the other method in which there is some personal contact. It is easier to refuse an interview if you are not face-to-face, so telephone interviews

suffer from a still lower response rate. The method has most of the disadvantages of face-to-face interviews, namely interviewer bias, lack of privacy and lack of time to reflect on questions, plus the additional problem that a proportion of the population, especially among the elderly and the poor, do not have telephones. On the other hand, telephone interviews avoid the costs and problems of having to travel and are not as time-consuming or as costly as interviewing face to face.

- Postal surveys include any methods of delivering questionnaires without making personal contact with respondents, such as leaving questionnaires on desks or in pigeon-holes as well as sending them by post. They suffer from very low response rates and are frequently poorly completed. They are, however, undoubtedly the cheapest and easiest method, they are free from interviewer bias and they give the respondent privacy and the option to take time over answering. Postal surveys are the only method that can absolutely guarantee confidentiality, since in all other cases respondents cannot be certain that their names will not be associated with the completed questionnaire. However, inducements such as small gifts or entry into a lottery are often given in order to overcome the low response problem and hence confidentiality is often lost.

We saw earlier that questionnaires can typically be used in interviewer-based or postal surveys. Each type of survey has its own implications when it comes to the design of the questionnaire to be used. For example, interviewers can explain an unclear point on a form, or can (with good training) 'probe' for deeper answers. With a postal survey, therefore, even greater care is needed when drafting questions, and some types of 'probe' or follow-up question may not be possible at all.

2.9 Importing data to Excel

Having identified data to be used for an application that can be managed in Excel it is sometimes possible to import that data from its original source as opposed to having to re-enter the information directly into the spreadsheet through the keyboard. Excel has a number of importing options, some of which are described here.

2.9.1 Importing data from Word

The data shown in Figure 2.2 has been entered into Word using the Tab key to space it out. This information can be copied and pasted directly into Excel and the tabs indicate to Excel where the cell change occurs. Figure 2.3 shows the data after copying into Excel.

Month	Mon	Tues	Wed	Thurs	Fri
Jan	570	539	580	563	497
Feb	520	1480	510	1500	490
Mar	1562	588	502	516	540
Apr	568	516	550	1562	556
May	1555	562	548	548	1554
June	562	1553	560	498	554
July	562	553	1575	539	531
Aug	1586	567	509	529	587
Sept	596	577	574	555	580
Oct	569	1550	557	558	563
Nov	562	519	569	1530	560
Dec	567	553	524	501	1550

Figure 2.2 Data in Word separated with Tabs

FUNDAMENTALS OF BUSINESS MATHEMATICS

	A	B	C	D	E	F	G	H
1								
2								
3		Month	Mon	Tues	Wed	Thurs	Fri	
4		Jan	570	539	580	563	497	
5		Feb	520	1480	510	1500	490	
6		Mar	1562	588	502	516	540	
7		Apr	568	516	550	1562	556	
8		May	1555	562	548	548	1554	
9		June	562	1553	560	498	554	
10		July	562	553	1575	539	531	
11		Aug	1586	567	509	529	587	
12		Sept	596	577	574	555	580	
13		Oct	569	1550	557	558	563	
14		Nov	562	519	569	1530	560	
15		Dec	567	553	524	501	1550	
16								

Figure 2.3 Data imported into Excel using Copy and Paste.

2.9.2 Using the Excel Text to Columns feature

Sometimes it is not possible to copy and paste information from another source into Excel and have the data automatically drop into cells correctly. This might be when data is being selected from a database system or an accounting system. In such cases it is usually possible to instruct the external source to export data with a pre-defined separator, sometimes referred to as a 'delimiter'. Figure 2.4 shows some data that has been separated by commas.

```
Jones,34,car,45,finance
Brown,42,bicycle,8,sales
McDuffy,32,car,20,sales
Greggory,23,walk,2,admin
Hafeez,29,car,15,personnel
Bundi,54,bicycle,10,finance
```

Figure 2.4 Data delimited by commas

When this data is copied into Excel it appears as shown in Figure 2.5.

	A	B	C	D	E
1					
2					
3					
4		Jones,34,car,45,finance			
5		Brown,42,bicycle,8,sales			
6		McDuffy,32,car,20,sales			
7		Greggory,23,walk,2,admin			
8		Hafeez,29,car,15,personnel			
9		Bundi,54,bicycle,10,finance			
10					
11					

Figure 2.5 Delimited data in Excel

The Excel Data Text to Columns command can now be used to separate this data into different cells. First select the data in the range B4:B9 and then select Data Text to Columns. A dialogue box is displayed on the screen and in this example the delimiter should be set to comma. Click next and next again and then finish. The data appears as shown in Figure 2.6.

	A	B	C	D	E	F	G
1							
2							
3							
4		Jones	34	car	45	finance	
5		Brown	42	bicycle	8	sales	
6		McDuffy	32	car	20	sales	
7		Greggory	23	walk	2	admin	
8		Hafeez	29	car	15	personnel	
9		Bundi	54	bicycle	10	finance	
10							
11							

Figure 2.6 Data organised correctly in columns.

2.10 Summary

In obtaining data, various decisions have to be made. You should understand what the following mean and be able to discuss their relevance and advantages and disadvantages.

- What resources of staff, time and money are available?
- Will you use primary or secondary data?
- Will you sample or survey everyone?
- If sampling, is there a sampling frame?
- Can you stratify?
- Depending on the above, what sampling method will you use? You should know the relative merits of simple random, stratified random, systematic, cluster, multistage and quota sampling.
- How will you approach the respondent? You should know the advantages and disadvantages of using interviewers, enumerators, telephone interviews and postal questionnaires.
- How will you design the questionnaire? You should know the pitfalls to avoid and the features of good design to suit your chosen method of contact with respondents.
- Having obtained the data, subsequent chapters will show you how to turn it into information.

Revision Questions

Part 2.1 Objective testing selection

> Questions 1.1–1.10 are standard multiple-choice questions with exactly one correct answer each. Thereafter, the style of question will vary.

2.1.1 The essence of systematic sampling is that:

(A) each element of the population has an equal chance of being chosen.
(B) members of various strata are selected by the interviewers up to predetermined limits.
(C) every nth member of the population is selected.
(D) every element of one definable subsection of the population is selected.

2.1.2 What is meant by 'primary data'?

(A) The first data to be obtained on the subject.
(B) The most important information on the subject.
(C) Data obtained from official sources.
(D) Data obtained by conducting a survey on the subject.

2.1.3 What, if any, is the difference between data and information?

(A) They are the same.
(B) Data can only be figures, whereas information can be facts or figures.
(C) Information results from sorting and analysing data.
(D) Data results from obtaining many individual pieces of information.

2.1.4 All but one of the following are advantages of using face-to-face interviews. Which is the odd one out?

(A) The respondent gets time to think about the answer.
(B) They have a high response rate.
(C) The questionnaire is filled in correctly.
(D) The questions can be explained.

2.1.5 All but one of the following are advantages of using postal questionnaires. Which is the odd one out?

(A) They are cheap.
(B) They have high response rates.

(C) They are easy.
(D) They can guarantee confidentiality.

2.1.6 How does an enumerator differ from an interviewer?

(A) They do not meet the respondent.
(B) They do not deliver the questionnaire.
(C) They do not fill in the questionnaire.
(D) They do not take away the completed questionnaire.

2.1.7 Which of the following is a 'leading question'?

(A) The first question on the questionnaire.
(B) The most important question on the questionnaire.
(C) A question such as 'Why do you prefer margarine to butter?'
(D) A question such as 'Which do you prefer, margarine or butter?'

2.1.8 What is a sampling frame?

(A) A list of the population from which a sample is taken.
(B) The rules governing the taking of a sample.
(C) The form on which questionnaire results are initially summarised.
(D) The board provided to support a questionnaire when it is being completed.

2.1.9 A sample is taken by dividing the population into different age bands and then sampling randomly from the bands, in proportion to their size. What is such a sample called?

(A) Simple random
(B) Stratified random
(C) Quota
(D) Cluster

2.1.10 In a survey on the opinions of employees in a large company headquarters, one of the following is a cluster sample. Which is it?

(A) Staff are randomly selected from each department in proportion to departmental size.
(B) Staff are selected from the list of employees, taking every nth name.
(C) A sample, which is as representative as possible of the composition of the staff in terms of gender, age and department, is taken by stopping appropriate staff in the corridors and canteen.
(D) One department is selected and all the staff in that department are surveyed.

2.1.11 Which of the following are true, and which false?

(A) Primary data is that which is most important in a given situation.
(B) Secondary data is collected for some other purpose.
(C) Data becomes information after being sorted and analysed.

2.1.12 A mail order company is to survey customers who have placed orders at some point of the last year, by contacting one in each hundred of them. In this context, which of the following are true, and which false?

(A) The population consists of all adults living in this country last year.
(B) The population consists of everyone to whom they sent catalogues last year.
(C) The population consists of everyone who placed an order last year.
(D) The population consists of everyone with whom contact will be made.

2.1.13 Associate with each of the following sampling methods (A)–(F) the most appropriate example from the list, (P)–(U), given below.

(A) Simple random sample.
(B) Stratified random sample.
(C) Cluster sample.
(D) Systematic sample.
(E) Quota sample.
(F) Multistage sample.

Examples
(P) One city is chosen at random from all cities in the United Kingdom, then the electoral register is used to select a 1-per-1,000 sample.
(Q) Names picked from a hat.
(R) Every 10th person is chosen randomly from each ward in a hospital.
(S) One secondary school in a town is selected at random, then every pupil in that school is surveyed.
(T) One person in ten is chosen from an alphabetical list of employees.
(U) People are stopped in the street according to instructions such as 'stop equal numbers of men and women'.

2.1.14 Which of the following should be avoided as far as possible when constructing a questionnaire?

(A) Ambiguous questions.
(B) Questions requiring calculations.
(C) Leading questions.
(D) Open-ended questions.

2.1.15 Associate the following methods of contact with respondents with the most appropriate disadvantage from the list below.

Method of contact
(A) Postal questionnaires.
(B) Face-to-face interviews.
(C) Telephone interviews.

Disadvantage
(P) Omits the poorer sections of the population.
(Q) Very time consuming.
(R) Very poor response rate.

Part 2.2 Practical sampling

A local weekly newspaper sells about half a million copies a week in a region of about 100 square miles. Market research indicates that the readership profile is as follows:

Age	%	Annual income (£'000)	%	Sex	%
Under 25	10	Under 10	10	Male	50
25–34	15	10–15	10	Female	50
35–44	20	15–20	25		
45–54	20	20–25	25	*Region*	%
55–64	20	25–30	20	Rural	10
65+	15	Over 30	10	Suburban	30
Total	100	Total	100	Town	60

You are working with a marketing colleague on the design of a sample survey to find the (i) current strengths and weaknesses of the paper, and (ii) whether the introduction of colour, leisure and/or business supplements, and so on would increase sales and by how much.

2.2.1 A decision has to be made about how the data will be collected. You have to choose between a postal survey, face-to-face interviews and telephone interviews and you wish to contact at least 1,000 people.

(A) Which method is the most expensive?
(B) Which method is the least expensive?
(C) Which method is the quickest to carry out?

2.2.2 In deciding between a postal survey (P), face-to-face interviews (F) and telephone interviews (T) various advantages and disadvantages have to be considered. Associate each of the following statements with one of the three methods and say whether it is an advantage (Adv) or disadvantage (Dis). Each answer carries one mark.

(D) Questionnaires are often filled in badly.
(E) It has the best response.
(F) Not everyone in the population has a telephone.
(G) It is very time consuming.
(H) It is easy to deal with people who are not available when first contacted.
(I) The response rate is very poor.

2.2.3 It is decided that the sample will represent the various age groups, income groups, men and women and people from the different areas of the region in proportion to their numbers in the population in the region. Which of the following types of samples is/are constructed in this manner?

(J) Simple random
(K) Systematic
(L) Stratified random
(M) Quota
(N) Cluster

2.2.4 If the sample is to be constructed so that it is representative of age, gender and area but not income and so that total sample size is 1,000, how many people should be surveyed in the following categories, assuming that age, gender and location are independent?

(O) Town dwellers
(P) Rural dwellers over 65
(Q) Female suburban dwellers under 25.

Part 2.3 Surveys

A small company that sells office equipment in its local area wishes to survey its customers.

2.3.1 The company is considering the various methods it might use to contact its customers. Those under consideration are face-to-face interviews, use of an enumerator, telephoning and sending a postal questionnaire.

Match comments (A)–(F) with comparisons (G)–(L)

Comments
(A) A small section of the population cannot be reached.
(B) The questions cannot be explained.
(C) It has the best response rates.
(D) Forms are better filled in.
(E) It is cheaper.
(F) Respondents can choose the most suitable time.

Comparisons
(G) An advantage of an enumerator compared to face to face
(H) A disadvantage of postal compared to all other methods
(I) An advantage of postal compared to all other methods
(J) An advantage of face to face compared to all other methods
(K) An advantage of face to face compared to an enumerator
(L) A disadvantage of telephoning compared to all other methods.

2.3.2 The company intends to survey people chosen from an up-to-date list of customers. What is the statistical term which describes such a list?

(M) Frame of reference.
(N) Sampling frame.
(O) Standing frame.
(P) Systematic frame.

Solutions to Revision Questions

✓ Solutions to Part 2.1

2.1.1 Answer: (C)

In systematic sampling, population members are listed and members selected at regular intervals along the list.

2.1.2 Answer: (D)

Data that are already in existence (such as data from official sources) are called secondary, while that obtained by a survey are called primary. It has nothing to do with importance, nor with being the first to survey that area.

2.1.3 Answer: (C)

The two terms are frequently used synonymously but strictly speaking they mean different things. Data is obtained from a survey and is turned into information by sorting and analysis. Both data and information can comprise either facts or figures.

2.1.4 Answer: (A)

Interviews do have high response rates with correctly completed questionnaires, and the interviewer is able to clarify the questions. One snag, however, is that interviews do not allow the respondent to take time to think about the answer, since both interviewer and respondent tend to be in a hurry.

2.1.5 Answer: (B)

All the other answers are advantages of using postal questionnaires but their major disadvantage is that they have very low response rates.

2.1.6 Answer: (C)

An enumerator delivers the questionnaire and then collects the completed form but does not actually fill the form in. It is not the same as a postal survey because the enumerator must actually meet the respondent.

2.1.7 Answer: (C)

(C) is a leading question because it makes an assumption about the respondent's opinion. (D) shows how the topic can be raised without any such assumption.

Being a leading question has nothing to do with importance or position on the form.

2.1.8 Answer: (A)

The sampling frame is a list, such as the electoral register or a list of employees or clients, from which a sample is selected.

2.1.9 Answer: (B)

In simple random sampling, there is no division of the population into groups. In cluster sampling, only one group is selected and all its members are surveyed. Quota sampling and stratified random sampling are both as described in the question but quota sampling is not random.

2.1.10 Answer: (D)

(A) is a stratified random sample, (B) is systematic and (C) is a quota sample.

2.1.11 (A) False: primary data is obtained specifically for the survey in question.
(B) True.
(C) True.

2.1.12 (A) False.
(B) False.
(C) True.
(D) False.

2.1.13 The associations are as follows:

(A) Most appropriate example is (Q).
(B) Most appropriate example is (R).
(C) Most appropriate example is (S).
(D) Most appropriate example is (T).
(E) Most appropriate example is (U).
(F) Most appropriate example is (P).

2.1.14 All the answers (A)–(D) should be avoided.

2.1.15 The associations are as follows:

(A) Disadvantage (R).
(B) Disadvantage (Q).
(C) Disadvantage (P).

✓ Solutions to Part 2.2

2.2.1 One of the main factors influencing the choice of data collection method is the budget for the exercise. Closely allied to this is the 'trade-off' the newspaper proprietors are willing to make between cost of the survey and validity of the results.

As the newspaper is unlikely to have large budgets to dedicate to such an exercise (it is only operating in a small locality), this would appear to eliminate the most expensive options. The use of interviews is the most labour- and travel-intensive method available, and therefore the most costly. This possibility is eliminated.

Although relatively less expensive because more interviews per hour of interviewer time can be obtained and no travel is involved, telephone interviews do generate a bias due to non-ownership of telephones. In this case, however, the survey concerns (in part) the introduction of leisure/business supplements. These are likely to be of particular interest to middle- and upper-class households where telephone penetration is almost universal. The bias will thus be minimal.

The least expensive option is a postal survey. The response rates and bias in such surveys are often poor, even in cases where the surveyors can offer completion incentives.

Answers:

(A) face-to-face interviews.
(B) postal survey.
(C) postal survey.

2.2.2
(D) Questionnaires are often filled in badly	P: Dis
(E) It has the best response rate	F: Adv
(F) Not everyone in the population has a telephone	T/Dis
(G) It is very time consuming	F/Dis
(H) It is easy to deal with people who are not available when first contacted	T/Adv
(I) The response rate is very poor	P/Dis

2.2.3 Answers:

(L) Stratified random
(M) Quota.

2.2.4 Out of the sample of 1,000, 60 per cent are town dwellers, that is, 600 people. Ten per cent are rural dwellers, that is, 100 people in the sample and of these 15 per cent are over 65 so there must be 15 in this category. 300 must live in the suburbs of whom 150 (50 per cent) must be female and 10 per cent of these, that is, 15, must be under 25 years.

Answers:

(O) Town dwellers	600
(P) Rural dwellers over 65	15
(Q) Female suburban dwellers under 25	15

✓ Solutions to Part 2.3

2.3.1 Telephone interviews and posting out questionnaires both have several advantages and disadvantages. Telephone interviews cannot reach the small section of the population who do not possess phones, respondents find them fairly easy to refuse and they are quite expensive. Their advantages are that they have quite good response rates and they are quicker and cheaper than face-to-face interviews. Postal surveys have a very major disadvantage in being ignored by respondents but additionally questions can be misunderstood and forms are often filled in badly. Their big plus is that they are very cheap and quick.

The enumerator delivers and collects the questionnaire but does not actually remain while it is filled in. It is therefore a quicker and cheaper method than using face-to-face interviews but forms are not as well filled in and the response rate is lower. A possible advantage is that respondents can fill in the form in private, which might help if the subject was embarrassing.

Comment	Comparison
(A)	(L)

The small section of the population who do not have telephones cannot be reached.

Comment	Comparison
(B)	(H)

All the methods except postal questionnaires allow some possibility of explaining questions.

Comment	Comparison
(C)	(J)

Face-to-face interviews have the best response rates.

Comment	Comparison
(D)	(K)

Face-to-face interviews and the use of enumerators are both good methods but forms are better filled in face-to-face interviews.

Comment	Comparison
(E)	(G)

The use or enumerators is cheaper than face-to-face interviews.

Comment	Comparison
(F)	(I)

Respondents can choose the most suitable time to fill in a postal questionnaire.

2.3.2   Answer: (N) Sampling frame.

Reference

Magretta J., *What Management is?* Profile Books, 2003, New York.

3

Presentation of Data

Presentation of Data

Learning Outcomes

After completing this chapter you should be able to:

- tabulate data and explain the meaning of the results;
- prepare a frequency distribution from raw data;
- prepare and explain the following graphs and diagrams: bar charts, histograms and ogives;
- prepare graphs of linear and quadratic functions, note Chapter 1 shows how these are produced in Excel.

3.1 Introduction

Data, when first collected, are often not in a form that conveys much information. Such raw data, as they are called, may just consist of a list or table of individual data values: if the list or table is of any appreciable size then it may need some refinement before anyone can draw conclusions from it.

In this chapter we look at ways in which raw data can be collated into more meaningful formats, and then go on to see some pictorial representations of data that provides convenient ways of communicating them to others. We begin by looking at linear and other important graphs.

3.2 Linear graphs

For each function of one variable there is an associated *graph*. This is a pictorial representation in which every value of x, with its associated value of y, is shown. In order to do this, pairs of values of x and y are plotted on graph paper as illustrated in the example below.

Example 3.2.1

Calculate the values of y in the function

$$y = 3 + 2x$$

corresponding to the values: $x = 2$; $x = 1$; $x = 3$; $x = 4$; $x = -1$.
Plot the five corresponding pairs of values on a graph and hence draw the graph of the function.

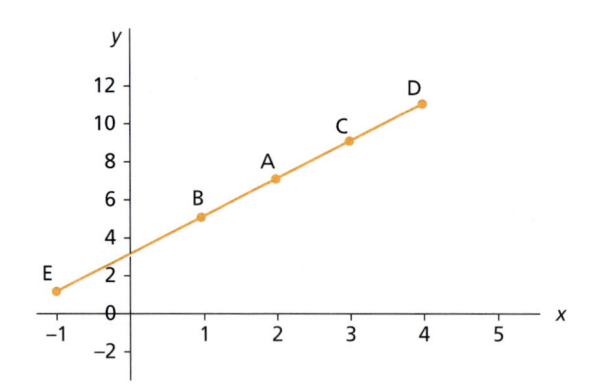

Figure 3.1 Plot of points and line

Solution

Substituting $x = 1$ gives

$$y = 3 + 2 \times 1 = 3 + 2 = 5$$

In the same way, it can be seen that $x = 3$ gives $y = 9$; and $x = 4$ gives $y = 11$.
In the final case, $x = -1$ gives

$$y = 3 + 2 \times -1 = 3 - 2 = 1$$

The five pairs of values are shown as the points A, B, C, D and E, respectively, in Figure 3.1. Two things should be noted about this figure:

1. Values of x are always measured in a horizontal direction, along the x-axis: positive values to the right, negative to the left. Values of y are measured in a vertical direction, along the y-axis: positive values upwards, negative downwards. Thus, the point A is plotted by moving from the point where the axes cross (the *origin*, where both variables have a value of zero).
   - 2 to the right (plus 2);
   - 7 upwards (plus 7).

These values are known as the x- and y-coordinates of A, respectively. Point E has a negative x-coordinate of -1 and a positive y-coordinate of 1, and so is plotted as 1 to the left and 1 upwards.
   - Note the scales on the two axes. These distances are marked off on each axis as an aid to plotting. They need not be the same as each other (indeed, they are not in this case) but they must be consistent. In other words, if you decide that one square on your graph paper equals one unit (or whatever) along the x-axis, you must keep this scale throughout the x-axis. The scales should be chosen so that the range of x and y coordinates can be displayed appropriately.

We can now join the points up, in order to form the graph of the function. In this case, the points lie *exactly* on a straight line, and so the joining up can be done best with a ruler. This is an example of a *linear graph*.

Example 3.2.2

Plot the graph of the function $y = 3 - 2x$ using the values $x = 1$ and $x = -2$. Check the accuracy of your graph.

Solution

- When $x = 1$, $y = 3 - 2 \times 1 = 3 - 2 = 1$.
- When $x = -2$, $y = 3 - 2 \times (-2) = 3 + 4 = 7$.

These coordinates are plotted in Figure 3.2.

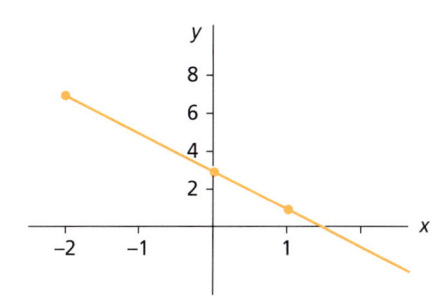

Figure 3.2 Plot of points and line

When $x = 0$, $y = 3$ which checks with the graph.
Any other values of x could have be chosen to graph the function and check it.
The next example has a more practical setting.

Example 3.2.3

A company sells a product at £10 per unit. If it sells x units daily, then its revenue (£y) is represented by the function:

$$y = 10x$$

The fixed daily costs of producing the product are £100, and the variable costs are £6 per unit. Daily costs (£) are:

$$y = 100 + 6x$$

Plot the graphs of these two functions for daily production figures (x) from 0 to 60 in steps of 10.

Solution

The question advises us to plot just seven points; so we begin by systematically calculating the necessary y-values.

Revenue calculations

x	0	10	20	30	40	50	60
$y = 10x$	0	100	200	300	400	500	600

Cost calculations

x		0	10	20	30	40	50	60
100	100	100	100	100	100	100	100	100
$6x$		0	60	120	180	240	300	360
$y = 100 + 6x$		100	160	220	280	340	400	460

Note how, in the latter, slightly more complicated, case, the calculation of y has been broken into stages, which are then added to get the total value of y.

The calculated points are plotted as dots in Figure 3.3. This has been done in the same way as before, but the origin has been placed at the bottom left, since there are no negative x- or y-values. In this instance, the scales on the axes have commercial meaning and so have been marked appropriately with the use of appropriate labels on the x and y axis.

As in the preceding example, we can see that the two sets of points lie exactly on straight lines, and so can be joined using a ruler. In fact, you can check that all the intermediate points do lie on the straight line. For instance, $x = 15$ gives revenue $= 150$ and cost $= 190$, and these two values can be seen to lie on the respective lines.

We shall shortly be using such graphs, but the reader may wish to consider now what lessons the company can draw from Figure 3.3.

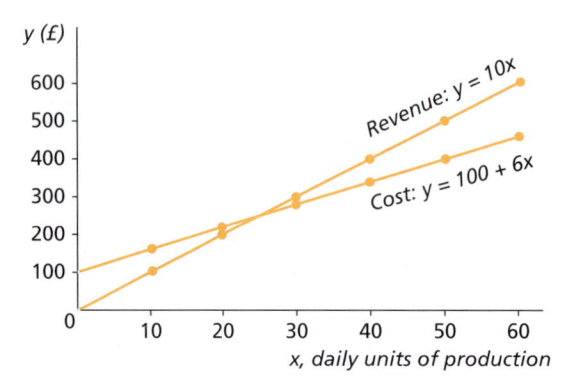

Figure 3.3 Revenue and cost functions

Functions whose graphs are straight lines are called *linear functions*. Much time could be saved if you could recognise a linear function before beginning the calculations necessary to plot its graph: only three points need then be found and a ruler used, the third being a check on accuracy of calculation and plotting. By looking at their equations, you will see that the three linear functions seen so far have the form

$$y = a + bx$$

where a and b are numbers.

In the revenue function of the previous example, $y = 10x$, so $a = 0$, $b = 10$; and in the cost function, $y = 100 + 6x$, so $a = 100$, $b = 6$.

In fact, *all* linear functions have this form and, conversely, *all* functions of this form are linear. It is, therefore, possible to recognise a linear function from its equation in the *general linear form*:

$$y = a + bx$$

The numbers a and b in this expression are given names: a, called the *intercept*, is the value of y when x is zero, and so is the length 'cut off' or intercepted on the y-axis by the line. Also, b is the *gradient* or slope of the line, representing the increase in y per unit increase in x. In the cost graph of Figure 3.3, for example, the graph cuts the y-axis at the point $y = 100$, so $a = 100$; the line rises by £6 for every extra unit of production, so $b = 6$.

Example 3.2.4

Past experience indicates that, when a factory produces x units of a certain component during a week, the costs (in £) associated with producing the component are:

$$5,000 + 200x$$

Explain what information this conveys.

Solution

It will be noted that the weekly cost function is of a linear form, $a + bx$, with a (intercept) = £5,000; b (gradient) = £200. In financial terms, this means that the weekly fixed costs, when there is no production ($x = 0$) are £5,000, and each extra unit of production, an increase in x of 1, adds the variable cost of £200.

Example 3.2.5

A small workshop manufactures just one article. From past experience, it is known that:

- if 50 units are produced weekly, the total manufacturing costs are £1,800;
- if 100 units are produced weekly, total costs are £2,800; and
- if 125 units are produced weekly, total costs are £3,300.

(a) Assuming that costs form a linear function, draw a graph and find the intercept and gradient of the corresponding line, and hence state the equation of the weekly cost function.
(b) What are the commercial meanings of the gradient and intercept of this linear cost function?

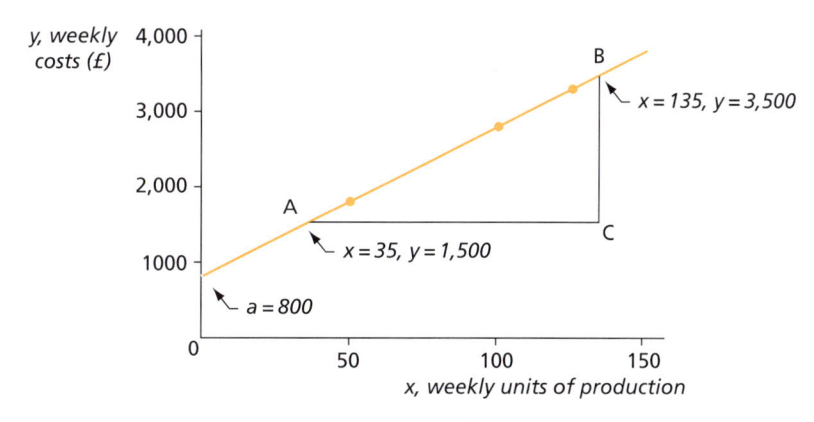

Figure 3.4 Cost function

Solution

The three given points have been plotted in Figure 3.4, with x as the number of units of production and y as the costs. The variables have been allocated this way round because costs are the *dependent* variable (depending on the number of units made) and so are denoted by y. We are told to assume a linear function, and so a straight line has been drawn.

(a) A reading from the graph shows that the intercept (on the y-axis) has value $a = 800$.
The triangle ABC has been drawn in to enable us to calculate the gradient. It shows that, as we move from A to B, x increases from 35 to 135 while y increases from 1,500 to 3,500. Thus, b is the increase in y per unit increase in x:

$$= \frac{3,500 - 1,500}{135 - 35} = 20$$

There is nothing special about the triangle we have used: any other choice of A and B on the line would give the same value for b.
The cost function therefore has the linear equation $y = 800 + 20x$.

(b) The value 800 (£) is the cost (y) incurred if there is no production ($x = 0$). It thus represents the *weekly fixed costs* of production. The value 20 (£) is the increase in costs if the level of production increases by one. Therefore, it is the *variable cost* of one unit's production.

Example 3.2.6

When a company manufactures 30 units of a product, the total manufacturing costs are £200. When 70 units are made, total costs are £400. The total cost function is known to be linear.

(a) Plot a graph of total manufacturing costs (£y) against units made (x), taking care to begin the x-axis from zero.
(b) Read off from the straight line its gradient (b) and its intercept (a). What are the practical meanings of these values?
(c) The company can sell all the units it makes for £6 each. What is the revenue function? Plot this function on the same graph as the cost function. At what production level does the company break even?

Solution

(a) When $x = 30$, $y = 200$; and when $x = 70$, $y = 400$. These points have been plotted and joined in Figure 3.5.

(b) From the graph, the intercept (a) is 50. This means that there are fixed costs of £50 that apply even if no units are produced.

When x changes from 30 to 70 (i.e. by 40 units), y increases from 200 to 400 (i.e. by £200), so the slope $(b) = 200/40 = 5$. This is the increase in y for a unit increase in x: in other words, the increase in cost for each extra unit produced is £5. We have also shown the slope on the graph paper, but it is not necessary to use both the algebraic and graphical methods.

(c) The revenue function is $y = 6x$. When $x = 0$, $y = 0$ and when $x = 70$, $y = 420$. See Figure 3.5 for the revenue function.

Breakeven occurs when revenue = cost, that is, when the graphs cross. This occurs when production is 50 units.

A check on whether or not this is accurate can be made by calculating revenue and cost when $x = 50$:

Revenue = 6×50 = £300
Cost = $50 + (5 \times 50)$ = £300

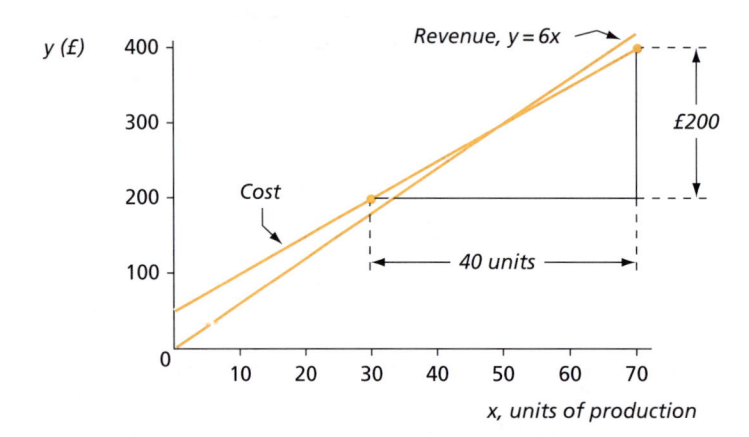

Figure 3.5 Cost and revenue functions

3.3 Solving simultaneous linear equations using graphs

We have seen that breakeven occurs when the cost and revenue graphs cross. This is the graphical interpretation of the solution of simultaneous linear equations, and a graphical method could be used instead of an algebraic method (provided that the scale was big enough to give the required accuracy).

Example 3.3.1

Solve the simultaneous equations
$2x + 3y = 8$ (i)
$5x - 2y = 1$ (ii)

by graphing the lines using the values $x = 0$ and $x = 5$.

If you feel that you need more practice solving such equations algebraically, you could do that as well.

The algebraic solution of simultaneous linear equations is often slightly easier and lends itself to greater accuracy (as you are not reading from a graph).

Solution

In (i), when $x = 0$, $3y = 8$ so $y = 8 \div 3 = 2.67$. When $x = 5$, $3y = 8 - 10 = -2$, so $y = -2/3$.
In (ii), when $x = 0$, $-2y = 1$, so $y = -1/2$. When $x = 5$, $-2y = 1 - 25 = -24$, so $y = -24 \div -2 = 12$.
These values are plotted in Figure 3.6.

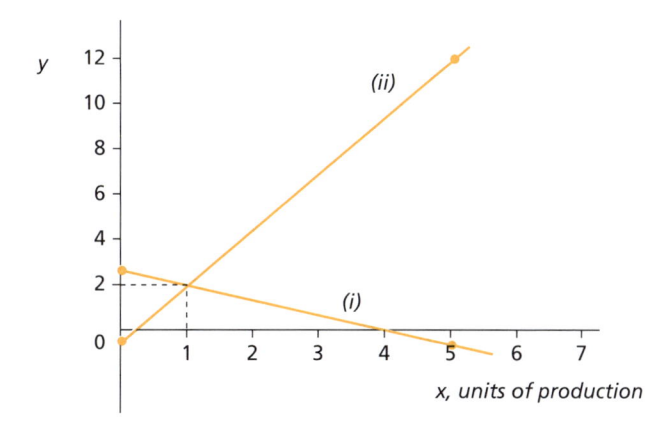

Figure 3.6 Simultaneous equations

The lines meet when $x = 1$ and $y = 2$, which is the solution of the equations.

3.4 Quadratic graphs

We saw in Section 1.10.2 that the general quadratic function is:

$$Y = aX^2 + bX + c$$

It has one of two basic graph shapes, as shown in Figure 3.7.

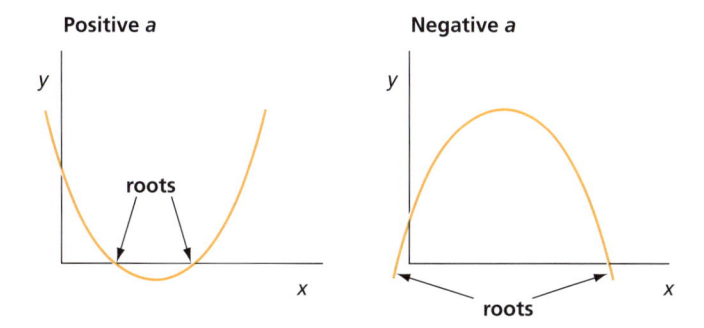

Figure 3.7 Quadratic functions

It is a symmetrical 'U'-shape or 'hump'-shape, depending on the sign of a. Another way of saying the same thing is that the y-values drop to a minimum and then rise again if a is positive, whereas they rise to a maximum and then fall if a is negative. This is of some importance in your later studies, when you may need to investigate the maximum or minimum values of functions for profits or costs, etc.

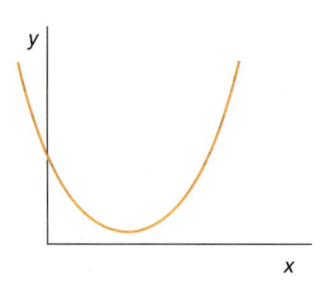

Figure 3.8 Quadratic equation with no roots

The roots or solutions of the equation

$$aX^2 + bX + c = 0$$

are given by the intercepts on the *x*-axis, and by symmetry the maximum or minimum is always halfway between them. Some quadratic equations do not have real roots, and in these cases the graph simply does not cut the *x*-axis at all — as shown in Figure 3.8.

> With computer-based assessment you cannot at present be required to actually draw graphs, so questions are likely to ask for the labels of axes, coordinates of particular points and the information given by particular points.

3.5 Tallying frequency distributions

An example will illustrate a simple way of converting raw data into a concise format.

Example 3.5.1

In order to monitor the efficiency of his department, the head of the finance section of a large company spot-checks the number of invoices left unprocessed at the end of each day. At the end of the first period of this check (26 working days), he has collected the following data:

1	5	3	3	2
3	0	4	1	4
3	3	2	1	2
1	1	0	3	6
5	0	3	4	2
3				

Collate this raw data into a more meaningful form.

Solution

By scanning the table we can see that all the values lie between 0 and 6 inclusive. It might be useful to find out how often each value in this range occurs in the table. This could be achieved simply by counting, but there are no safeguards against human error in doing this. Instead we use a *tallying* procedure, which is more accurate than counting, especially with large tables of figures. After going along the first row, the tally will look like:

Number of invoices left unprocessed	Tally
0	
1	I
2	I
3	II
4	
5	I
6	

As we go through the table, one 'notch' is put against the appropriate number each time it appears. For ease of counting, when each fifth notch is reached, it is marked thus: ||||

Number of invoices left unprocessed	Tally	Total
0					3
1						5
2						4
3									8
4					3
5				2
6			1
		26

The 'totals' in the above table are called *frequencies* and the table is called the *frequency distribution* of the sample. Thus the frequency of 0 invoices is 3 and so on.

Example 3.5.2

The daily absentee rate at a small factory is recorded for one calendar month (22 working days):

Number of employees absent:

```
          6   8
7  3  5   5   6
8  2  4   5   7
6  2  3   3   4
8  3  5   4   7
```

Tally these data into a frequency distribution.

Solution

No. of employees absent	No. of days (frequency)
2	2
3	4
4	3
5	4
6	3
7	3
8	3

The next example will demonstrate that the collation of raw data into a frequency distribution is not always as straightforward as in the case above.

Example 3.5.3

In order to assist management negotiations with the trade unions over piecework rates, the management services department of a factory is asked to obtain information on how long it takes for a certain operation to be completed. Consequently, the members of the department measure the time it takes to complete 30 repetitions of the operation, at random occasions during a month. The times are recorded to the nearest tenth of a minute.

19.8	21.3	24.6	18.7	19.1	15.3
20.6	22.1	19.9	17.2	24.1	23.0
20.1	18.3	19.8	16.5	22.8	18.0
20.0	21.6	19.7	25.9	22.2	17.9
21.1	20.8	19.5	21.6	15.6	23.1

Form the frequency distribution of this sample.

Solution

A scan of the table shows that the smallest value is 15.3 minutes and the largest 25.9 minutes. If we tallied as in the previous example

Time (minutes)	Tally
15.3	
15.4	
15.5	
...	
...	
25.9	

we should obtain a format of little more use than the original data, because most of the frequencies would be 0, interspersed by the occasional frequency of 1. A far more sensible approach is to tally the number of values in a certain range or *class*. The choice of classes is somewhat arbitrary, but should be such that they are neither too narrow, which would result in most of the frequencies being zero, as above, nor too wide, which would produce only a small number of classes and thereby tell us little. As a rough guide, between four and twelve groups are often used. Following these general guidelines, we tally as follows:

Time (minutes)	Tally	Frequency
15–under 17	III	3
17–under 19	IIII	5
19–under 21	IIII IIII	10
21–under 23	IIII II	7
23–under 25	IIII	4
25–under 27	I	1
		30

Even though some precision has been lost, this grouped frequency distribution is of considerably more use to the management services department than the raw data, because, for example, one can see at a glance where the bulk of the times lie, how often the time exceeds some target figure such as 23 minutes, say, and so on.

Example 3.5.4

At the factory mentioned in Example 3.5.2, the daily outputs, in units, of a certain article (A) are recorded during the same month as:

Daily output, units

			49	47
33	58	56	59	45
39	53	51	44	49
37	53	48	47	40
36	50	55	44	42

Tally these data into a frequency distribution using the intervals 30–under 35; 35–under 40; and so on.

Solution

Output of A units	No. of days (frequency)
30–under 35	1
35–under 40	3
40–under 45	4
45–under 50	6
50–under 55	4
55–under 60	4

3.6 Discrete and continuous variables

There is an essential difference between the variables considered in Examples 3.5.1 and 3.5.3. The former is discrete, whereas the latter is continuous. That is to say, the number of invoices can only consist of certain values:

$$0 \text{ or } 1 \text{ or } 2 \text{ or } \ldots$$
$$\text{but never} \quad 1.6, 2.3 \text{ and so on.}$$

On the other hand, the time taken to undertake a certain operation can theoretically take a value to any level of precision:

20.2 minutes
20.19 minutes
20.186 minutes
20.1864 minutes and so on.

In Example 3.5.3, the management services staff *chose* to measure to one decimal place: theoretically, they could have chosen to measure to two, three or any number of places. A number of invoices *cannot* be measured any more accurately than in whole numbers.

This distinction has a number of consequences. Here, it can affect the way we tally. Continuous variables, such as the times to undertake a certain operation, can rarely be tallied as individual values, since few of them will coincide to give meaningfully large frequencies.

Classifying is therefore almost always necessary with continuous variables. As Example 3.5.1 demonstrated discrete variables can sometimes be tallied with single values.

However, with a wider range from (0 to 100, for example), the problem of having frequencies being mostly 0, interspersed with a few 1s, could still arise: it is therefore sometimes necessary to use classes for discrete data too.

There are numerous ways of classifying when it is necessary. For instance, in Example 3.5.3, we could have used

15	to	17
17.1	to	19
19.1	to	21 and so on

or

15	to	16.95
16.95	to	18.95
18.95	to	20.95 and so on.

Both of these could be problematical if the measurements were later taken to the nearest twentieth (0.05) of a minute, as we should have difficulty placing 17.05 minutes in the former classification and 18.95 minutes in the latter. For this reason, we recommend that continuous variables are always classified:

15 to *under* 17
17 to *under* 19 and so on.

Example 3.6.1

At the factory mentioned in Example 3.5.4 the daily outputs of a different product (Q) are measured to the nearest kg and are recorded as:

Daily output, kg

			383	351
362	377	392	369	351
368	382	398	389	360
359	373	381	390	354
369	375	372	376	361

Tally these data into a frequency distribution using the intervals 350–under 360; 360–under 370 and so on.

Solution

Output of Q kg	No. of days (frequency)
350–under 360	4
360–under 370	6
370–under 380	5
380–under 390	4
390–under 400	3

3.7 Cumulative frequency distribution

It is sometimes helpful to develop the idea of frequency further and to look at *cumulative frequencies*. These are the number of data values up to – or up to and including – a certain point. They can easily be compiled as running totals from the corresponding frequency distribution, as the following will illustrate.

Example 3.7.1

Form the cumulative frequency distributions from the data given in Examples 3.5.1 and 3.5.3. Hence estimate:

(a) how often there are more than four invoices left unprocessed at the end of the day;
(b) how often the time taken beats the target of 23 minutes.

Solution

The frequency distribution of the number of unprocessed invoices can be used to obtain:

Number of invoices left unprocessed (less than or equal)	Cumulative frequency	
0	3	(simply the frequency of '0')
1	8	(i.e. 3 + 5)
2	12	(i.e. 8 + 4)
3	20	
4	23	
5	25	
6	26	

In the same way, for the distribution of times taken to undertake the operation:

Time (minutes) (less than)	Cumulative frequency	
15	0	(no values below 15 minutes)
17	3	(frequency of the first class)
19	8	(i.e. 3 + 5)
21	18	(8 + 10)
23	25	
25	29	
27	30	

In the latter example, we have to take the *upper* limit of each class to ensure that all the values in the class are definitely *less than* it. We must use 'less than' as opposed to 'less than or equal' here because it corresponds to the way the frequency table has been compiled.

It is now a simple matter to estimate:

(a) 26 − 23 = 3 occasions out of 26: that is, 11.5 per cent;
(b) 25 occasions out of 30: that is, 83.3 per cent.

How reliable these estimates are depends on how typical or representative is the period or month in which the samples are taken.

We shall see further applications of cumulative frequency in the following section.

Example 3.7.2

Form the cumulative frequency distributions for the data in Examples 3.5.2, 3.5.4 and 3.6.1.

Solution

- Example 3.5.2 data become:

No. of employees absent ($\leq$)	Cumulative frequency
2	2
3	6
4	9
5	13
6	16
7	19
8	22

- Example 3.5.4 data become:

Output of A units	Cumulative frequency
30–under 35	1
35–under 40	4
40–under 45	8
45–under 50	14
50–under 55	18
55–under 60	22

- Example 3.6.1 data become:

Output of Q kg	Cumulative frequency
350–under 360	4
360–under 370	10
370–under 380	15
380–under 390	19
390–under 400	22

3.8 Histograms and ogives

Many people find it easier to understand numerical information if it is presented in a pictorial form, rather than as a table of figures. In this section, therefore, we look at diagrammatic representations of frequency and cumulative frequency distributions.

A *histogram* is a graph of a frequency distribution. The x-axis is the variable being measured and the y-axis is the corresponding frequency. It differs from the graphs drawn earlier since, in the examples so far, the frequency is represented by the height of a block. The base of the block corresponds to the class being represented, so that it is usual to draw histograms only for continuous variables. The histogram of the cumulative frequency distribution in Example 3.5.4 is shown in Figure 3.9.

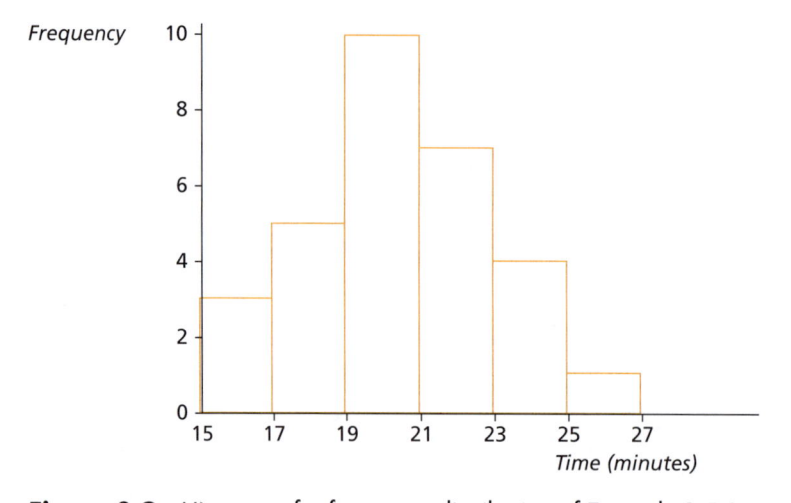

Figure 3.9 Histogram for frequency distribution of Example 3.5.3

An *ogive* is a graph of a cumulative frequency distribution. The x-axis is the variable being measured and the y-axis is the corresponding cumulative frequency, the x- and y-values being plotted in exactly the same way as we discussed earlier. With a discrete variable, intermediate x-values have no meaning in reality (recall 1.6 invoices) and so the ogive would consist of a series of discrete points. It is usual therefore not to draw it. With a continuous variable, the intermediate values *do* have a meaning, and so it makes sense to join the plotted points.

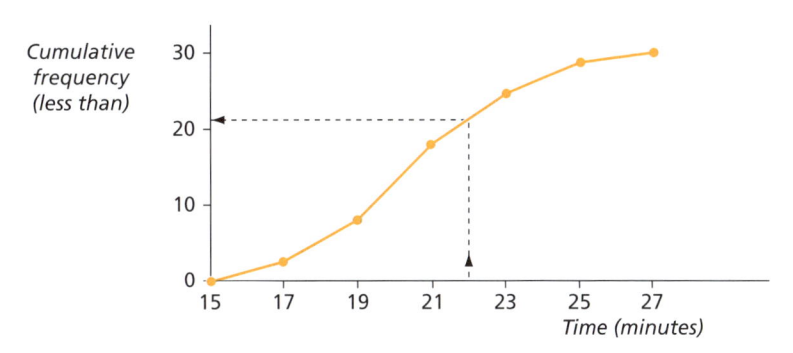

Figure 3.10 Ogive, cumulative frequency distribution, Example 3.7.1(b)

This can be done with a series of straight lines, which is tantamount to assuming that the values are evenly spread throughout their classes. The ogive of the continuous cumulative frequency distribution encountered earlier is shown in Figure 3.10.

Before leaving these graphs, we look at one simple example to show how cumulative frequency distributions and ogives can be used in practice.

Example 3.8.1

Plot the histograms and ogives to represent the data in Example 3.5.4.

Solution

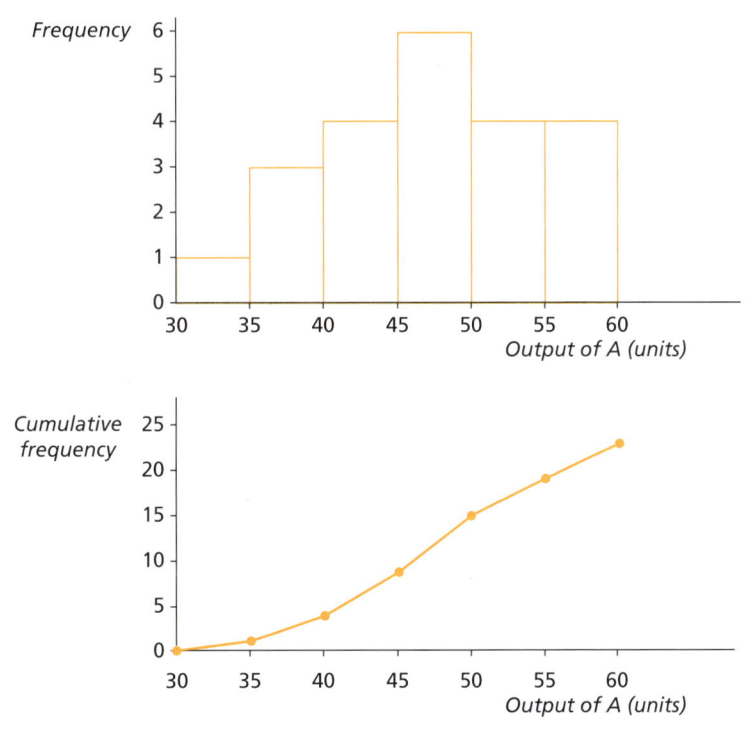

See Figure 3.11.

Figure 3.11 Histogram and ogive for Example 3.8.1

Example 3.8.2

The management of the company discussed in Example 3.5.3 wishes to reduce the target time for the operation to 22 minutes. Assuming the distribution of times remains unaltered, how often will this target be met?

Solution

First of all, it is not possible to answer this as a straight reading from the cumulative frequency distribution, as 22 minutes does not correspond to a value in the table. If we look at the ogive in Figure 3.10, however, we can estimate how many of the 30 occasions took less than 22 minutes, by reading off the graph, as shown. Thus, we estimate that the target will be met on 21.5 out of every 30 occasions: that is, 72 per cent of the time.

Example 3.8.3

Use the ogive from Example 3.8.1 to estimate:

(a) the percentage of days when output of A is less than 47 units;
(b) the percentage of days when output of A is more than 52 units.

Solution

(i) From the graph, the cumulative frequency corresponding to 47 units is 10.5, so the required percentage is $100 \times 10.5/22 = 48$ percent (approximately).
(ii) From the graph, the cumulative frequency corresponding to 52 units is 15.5, so the percentage less than 52 is $100 \times 15.5/22 = 70$ per cent and the percentage greater than 52 is 30 per cent (approximately).

We now give two examples to demonstrate problems that can arise when drawing histograms and ogives. We shall also at this point introduce a new diagram called a *frequency polygon*. For ungrouped, discrete data this consists of a simple graph of frequencies on values. For grouped data it is a graph of frequency density on interval mid-points and it may be obtained by joining the mid-points of the tops of the bars of the histogram.

The first example deals with the important topic of *unequal* class intervals.

Example 3.8.4

The compiler of a careers guide is given the following information on the initial salaries of graduates entering a certain profession during the year prior to the guide's publication.

Annual salary (£)	Number of graduate entrants
9,000–under 11,000	108
11,000–under 13,000	156
13,000–under 14,000	94
14,000–under 14,500	80
14,500–under 15,000	25

In order to convey the information in a quickly assimilated form, the compiler decides to represent it as a histogram. Draw this histogram and frequency polygon.

Solution

Before referring to the histogram, we point out that, strictly speaking, the data here are discrete. The 'gaps', however, are only of width equal to one penny, which is very small compared with thousands of pounds. We therefore effectively treat this as a continuous case.

(a) incorrect

Frequency vs Annual salary (£'000)

(b) correct

Frequency density vs Annual salary (£'000)

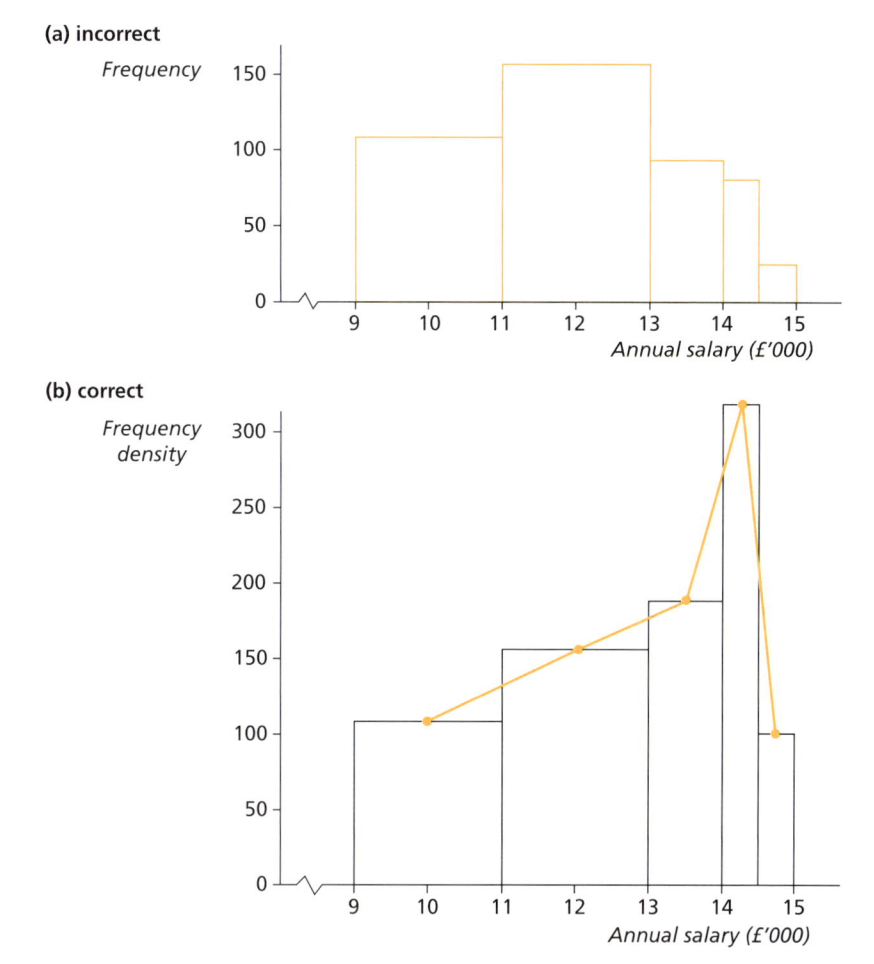

Figure 3.12 Histograms for Example 3.8.4

If we now draw the histogram as above, we obtain that shown in Figure 3.12(a). Close inspection of this will show that some discrepancies have arisen. For example, the left-hand block is supposed to represent approximately four times more graduates than the right-hand block, and yet the ratio of the size of these two blocks is nearer to 16. There are other examples of disproportion in the size of the blocks, the underlying reason being that, by drawing block heights equal to frequencies, we exaggerate those with larger class widths. Thus, in a case like this, where there are *unequal* class widths, one must compensate by adjusting the heights of some of the blocks:

13,000–under 14,000 is half the width of the first two, so	height = 94 × 2 = 188
14,000–under 14,500 is quarter the width,	height = 80 × 4 = 320
14,500–under 15,000	height = 25 × 4 = 100

(Alternatively, we could leave the frequencies of the last two classes unaltered, and divide the frequency of the first class by four and so on. This would leave the shape of the histogram as in Figure 3.12(b).)

The resulting *correct* version of the histogram is shown in Figure 3.12(b). Formally, it is the area of the block that is proportional to the frequency. It will be noted that the areas of the blocks are now in the correct proportion and that the vertical axis of the graph can no longer be labelled 'frequency', but is now 'frequency density'.

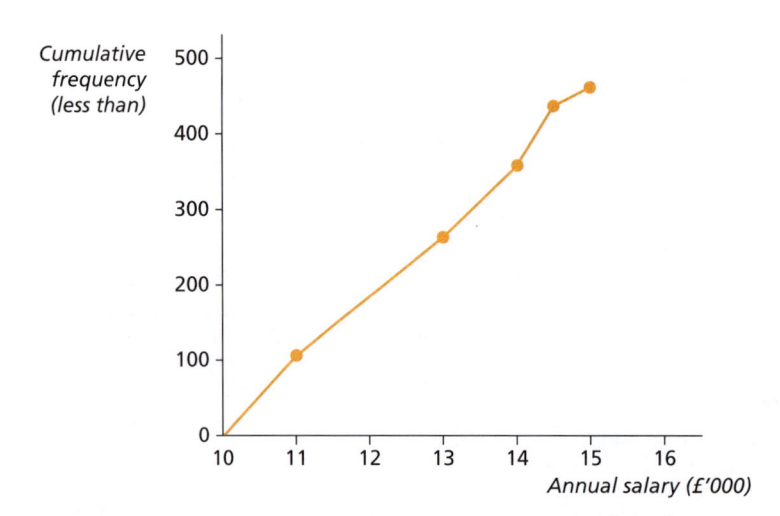

Figure 3.13 Ogive for frequency distribution of Example 3.8.4

Before leaving this example, it is worth pointing out that the ogive of this distribution (Figure 3.13) would present no extra problems. As this consists only of plotting the upper limit of each class against cumulative frequency, the unequal class intervals do not affect matters.

Example 3.8.5

Plot the histogram for the following distribution:

Time taken to complete repeated task (minutes)	Frequency
10–under 20	63
20–under 30	52
30–under 40	46
40–under 60	60
60–under 80	48
80–under 120	40

Solution

Time taken (minutes)	Class width	Frequency	Frequency density
10–20	10	63	63
20–30	10	52	52
30–40	10	46	46
40–60	20	60	60/2 = 30
60–80	20	48	48/2 = 24
80–120	40	40	40/4 = 10

We have taken the standard class width to be ten minutes. For the two classes whose widths are twice the standard, we have divided frequency by two to get the frequency density. We have divided by four for the final class, whose width is four times the standard. Figure 3.14 shows the histogram.

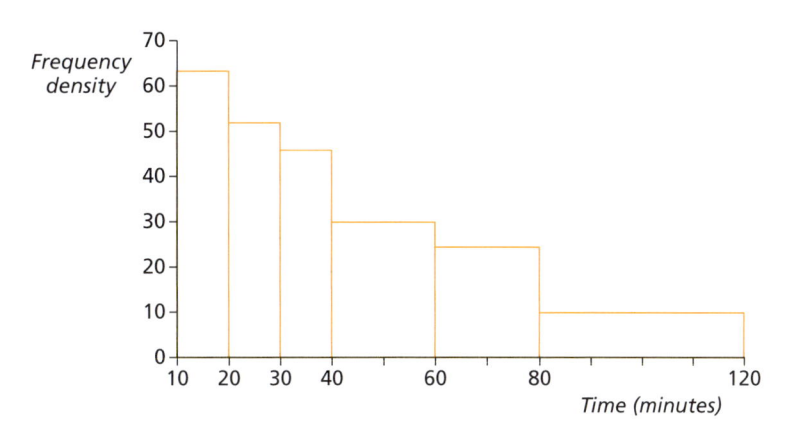

Figure 3.14 Histogram for Example 3.8.5

Example 3.8.6

The compiler of the careers guide (Example 3.8.4) also receives, from a different source, information on the graduate salaries in another profession:

Annual salary (£)	Number of graduate entrants
under 10,000	64
10,000–under 12,000	131
12,000–under 14,000	97
14,000–under 15,000	40
15,000 and over	11

What problems would the compiler have when drawing the histogram and the ogive of this distribution?

Solution

We have seen how to deal with the unequal class intervals, but here we have the extra problem of *open-ended* classes. When drawing the histogram, we can either omit the first and last class or estimate 'closing' values for these two classes. The former would leave the histogram (Figure 3.15a) looking rather sparse, and, indeed, it is often necessary to close the classes so as to make certain calculations. It might therefore be advisable to estimate values such as

9,000 under 10,000 or 15,000 under 16,000

to draw the histogram.

In the case of the ogive (Figure 3.15b), only the upper limit of each class is needed, and so it would be necessary to close only the last class in order to draw the whole ogive. It would also be possible to draw part of it from just the first four classes, omitting the last.

(a) Histogram

Frequency density vs *Annual salary (£'000)*

(b) Ogive

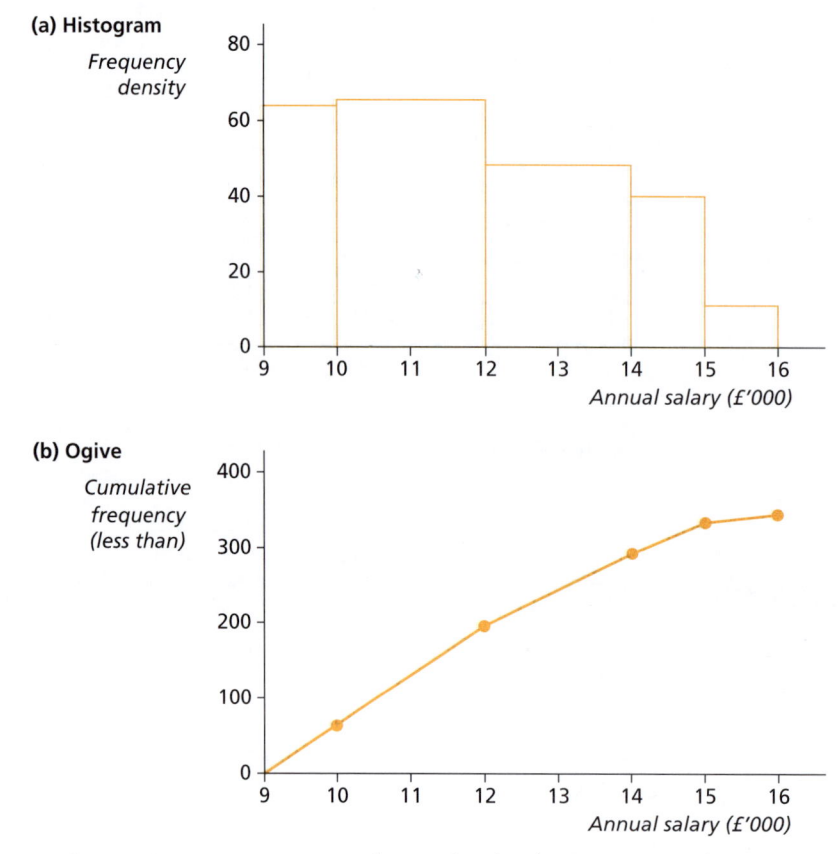

Cumulative frequency (less than) vs *Annual salary (£'000)*

Figure 3.15 Histogram and ogive for distribution in Example 3.8.6

Example 3.8.7

Plot the histogram for the following distribution:

Weekly sales (£'000)	Frequency
Under 5	8
5–under 10	23
10–under 20	98
20–under 30	80
30 and over	22

Solution

We have closed the two open intervals, taking the widths of the adjacent intervals as our guide. We have then calculated frequency densities using a standard interval width of five units.

Weekly sales (£'000)	Frequency	Frequency density
Under 5	8	8
5–under 10	23	23
10–under 20	98	98/2 = 49
20–under 30	80	40
30–under 40	22	11

The histogram is shown in Figure 3.16.

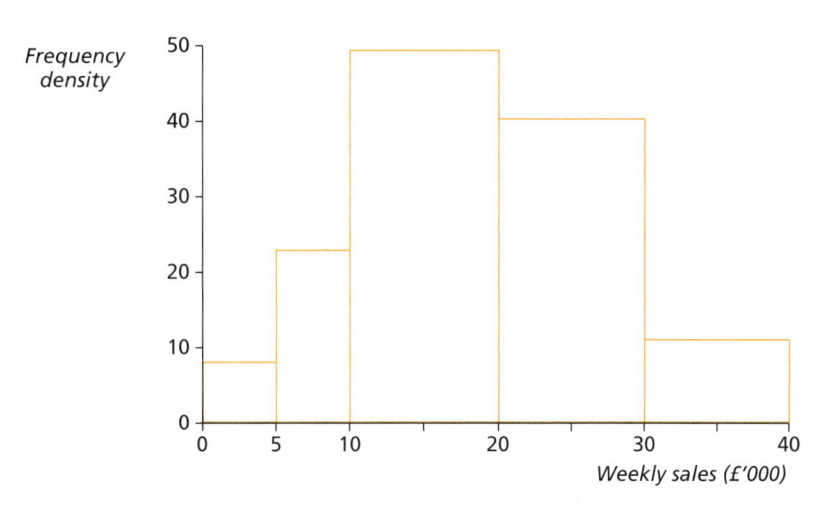

Figure 3.16 Histogram for Example 3.8.7

> It is quite a frequent exam question to work out the heights of bars where there are unequal intervals.

3.9 Pie charts

There are a number of other, more general, charts and graphs commonly used to represent business data. In this section we look at one of the most basic: pie charts.

Pie charts are a very easily understood way of depicting the percentage or proportional breakdown of a total into various categories. They are so called because the total is represented by a circle, with each component shown as a sector with area proportional to percentage. Overall, the chart looks rather like a 'pie' with 'slices' in it. Sometimes two pie charts are used to compare two totals, along with the manner in which they are broken down. In such cases the areas of the pies, in other words the squares of their radii, are proportional to the total frequencies.

Example 3.9.1

A company trades in five distinct geographical markets. In the last financial year, its turnover was:

	£m
UK	59.3
EU, outside UK	61.6
Europe, outside EU	10.3
North America	15.8
Australasia	9.9
Total	156.9

Display these turnover figures as a pie chart.

Solution

The first step is to calculate the percentage of the total turnover for each region:

	%
UK: (59.3/156.9) =	37.8
EU	39.3
Europe	6.6
North America	10.1
Australasia	6.3

Second, in order to make each 'slice' of the 'pie' proportional in area to these percentages, the whole circle (360°) has to be apportioned into five sections:

	Angle,°
UK: 37.8% of 360° =	136.1
EU	141.5
Europe	23.8
North America	36.4

Alternatively, the angles can be calculated directly as proportions of 360°, for example,

$360° \times (59.3/156.9) = 136.1°$
$360° \times (61.6/156.9) = 141.5°$, etc.

The resulting pie chart is shown in Figure 3.17.

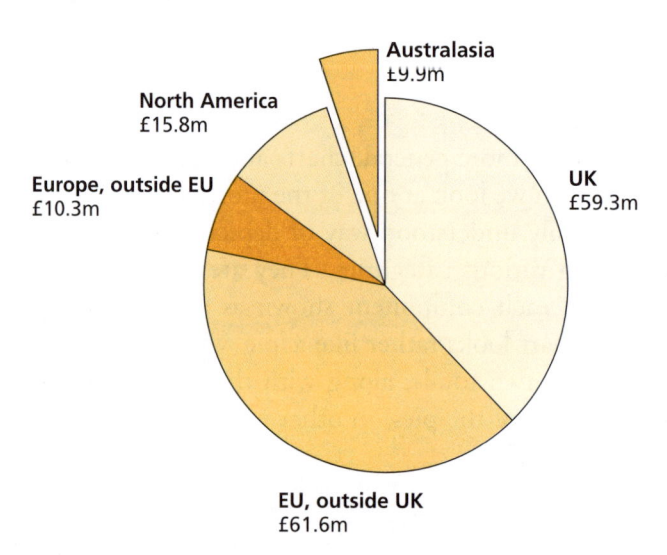

Figure 3.17 Pie chart: breakdown of company turnover, last financial year

Note how the Australasia 'slice' is pulled out for emphasis. This is easy to do when using a computer.

Example 3.9.2

Display the following data using a pie chart:

Sales of furniture	(£'000)
Settees	34
Armchairs	27
Dining sets	38
Shelving	18
Others	12

Solution

Category	Sales	Angle,°
Settees	34	95
Armchairs	27	75
Dining sets	38	106
Shelving	18	50
Others	12	34
Total	129	360

The angle is given by 360° × (sales/total sales), for example 360° × 34/129 = 95, rounded to the nearest degree. The resulting pie chart is shown in Figure 3.18.

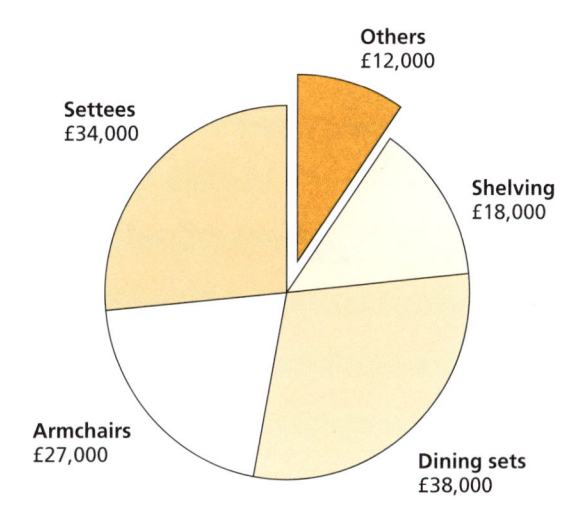

Figure 3.18 Pie chart for Example 3.9.2

3.10 Bar charts

Bar charts represent actual data (as opposed to percentage breakdowns) in a way similar to earlier graphs. They appear similar to histograms, but with one essential difference: whereas distances against the vertical axis are measurements and represent numerical data, *horizontal distances have no meaning. There is no horizontal axis or scale*, there are only labels. Other than this proviso, the construction of bar charts is straightforward, as an example will illustrate.

Example 3.10.1

Represent the data of Example 3.9.1 as a bar chart.

Solution

To draw this chart, it is simply a matter of drawing five vertical 'bars', with heights to represent the various turnover figures, and just labels in the horizontal direction (see Figure 3.19).

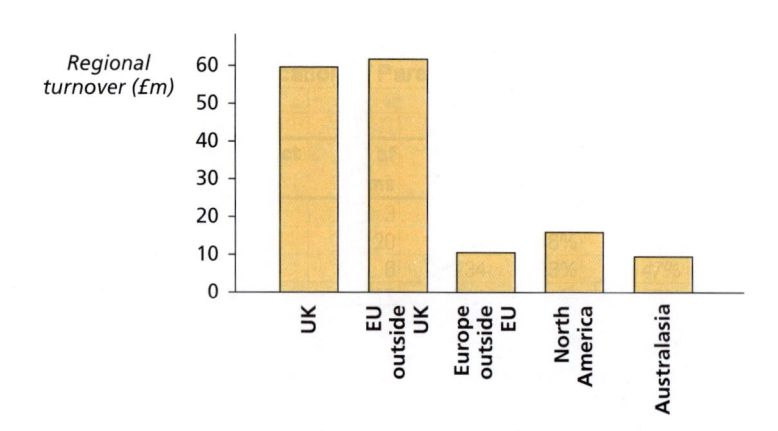

Figure 3.19 Bar chart: breakdown of company turnover, last financial year

There are a number of variations on such a basic bar chart, used to display more data or more complex data. An example will show just one.

Example 3.10.2

A rival company to the one in Examples 3.9.1 and 3.10.1 trades in the same five geographical markets. Its turnover in the last financial year was:

	£m
UK	60.2
EU, outside UK	69.0
Europe, outside EU	11.1
North America	18.0
Australasia	8.8
Total	167.1

Display the turnover figures for both companies on a single chart.

Solution

There are at least two types of bar chart which can be used here: a *multiple bar chart* and a *compound* (or *component* or *stacked*) *bar chart*. Both are shown in Figure 3.20.

The relative advantages of the two types can be seen from Figure 3.20. The multiple bar chart readily displays how well the two companies have performed in each market, but not so clearly in total. Conversely, the relative total performance of the two companies can be seen easily from the compound bar chart, but not so the breakdown by region.

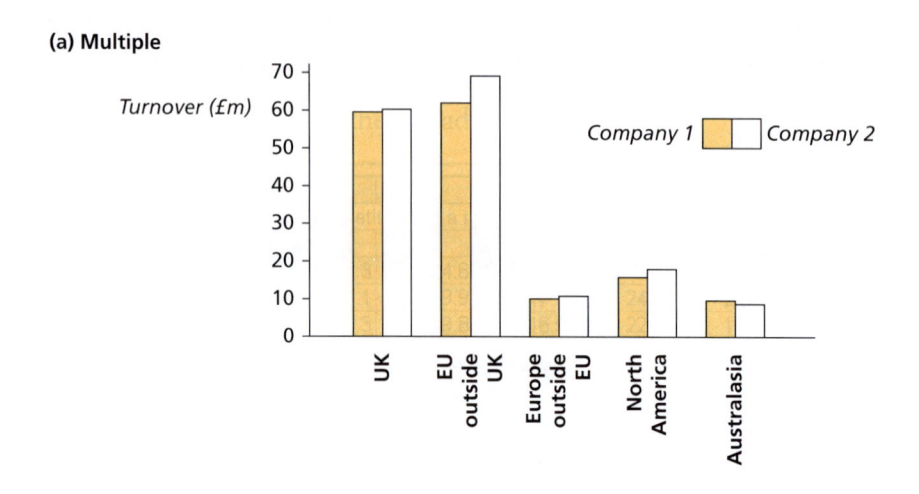

(b) Compound

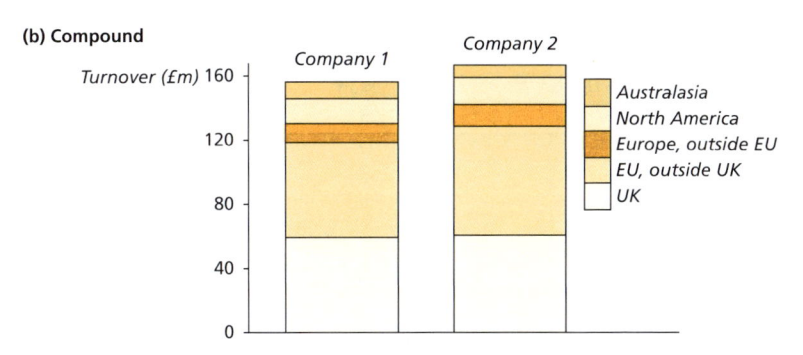

Figure 3.20 Bar charts: turnover of two companies, last financial year

Example 3.10.3

The following are percentage distributions of household income in two regions:

Income (£'000)	Region A	Region B
0–10	25	15
10–20	30	29
20–30	32	38
30–40	10	9
40 or more	3	9
Total	100	100

Display the data by the following bar charts:

(a) region A by a simple bar chart;
(b) region A by a compound bar chart;
(c) both regions by a multiple bar chart.

Solution

The bar charts are shown in Figures 3.21–3.23.

(a)

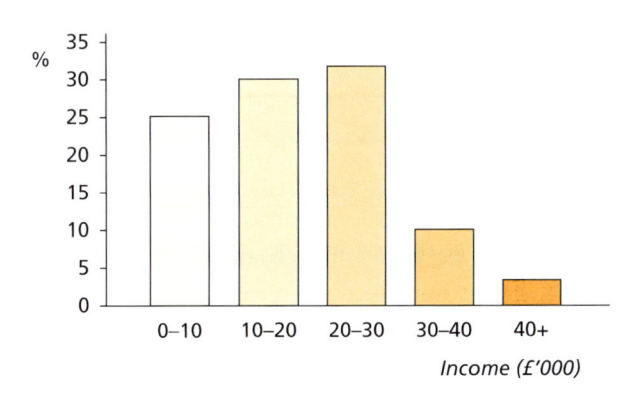

Figure 3.21 Simple bar chart for Example 3.10.3

(b) It is easiest to first calculate cumulative frequencies:

Income (£'000)	Region A	Cumulative%
0–10	25	25
10–20	30	55
20–30	32	87
30–40	10	97
40 or more	3	100
Total	100	

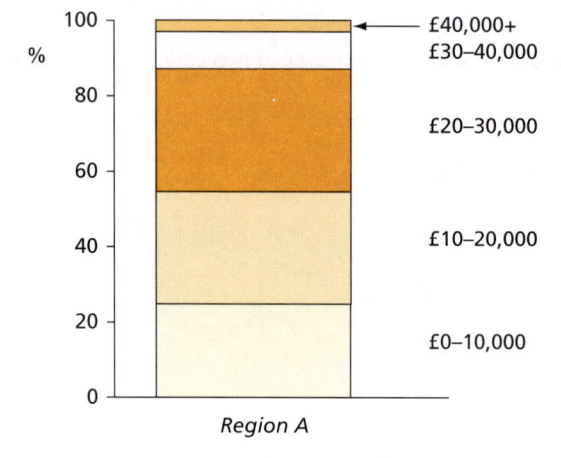

Figure 3.22 Compound bar chart for Example 3.10.3

(c)

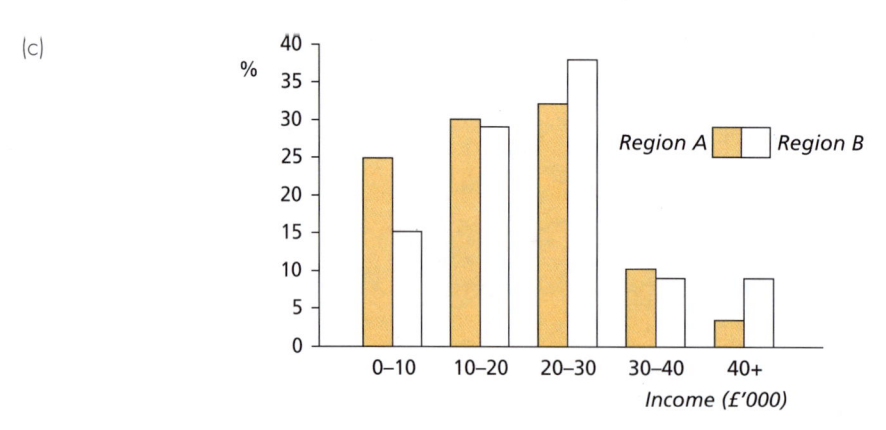

Figure 3.23 Multiple bar chart for Example 3.10.3

> At present you cannot be asked to actually draw charts during a computer-based assessment. Exam questions therefore take the form of labelling charts, calculating particular values, selecting a type of chart appropriate to particular data and drawing conclusions from charts.

3.10.1 Creating Bar charts using Excel

There are a wide range of different bar charts that can be created in Excel. Figure 3.24 shows a basic bar chart that uses the same data as Example 3.10.1.

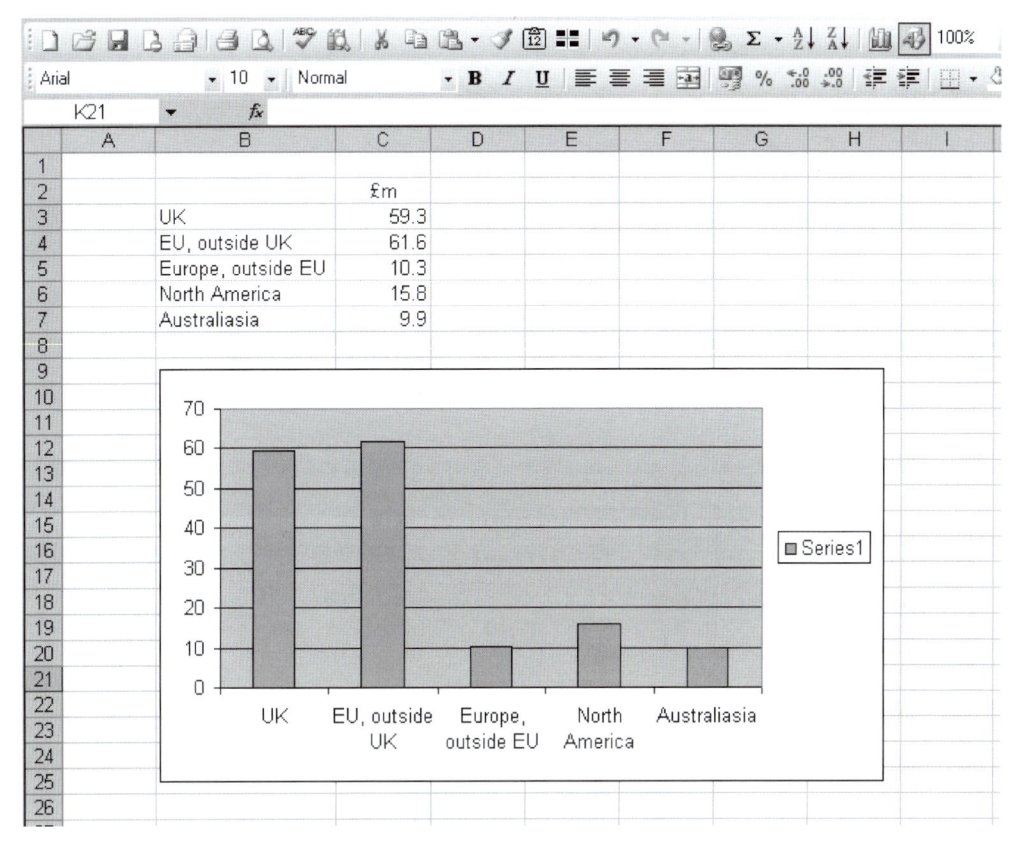

Figure 3.24 Basic Excel bar chart

The chart in Figure 3.24 is created by selecting the range B3:C7 clicking on the chart button on the toolbar and selecting the first sub-type option. This chart is representing a single set of data.

Example 3.10.2 introduced a second set of data which was represented using two different types of bar chart – a side-by-side and a stacked. Figures 3.25 and 3.26 show these charts produced in Excel.

In the case of the side-by-side bar chart the turnover for both companies for each country can easily be compared.

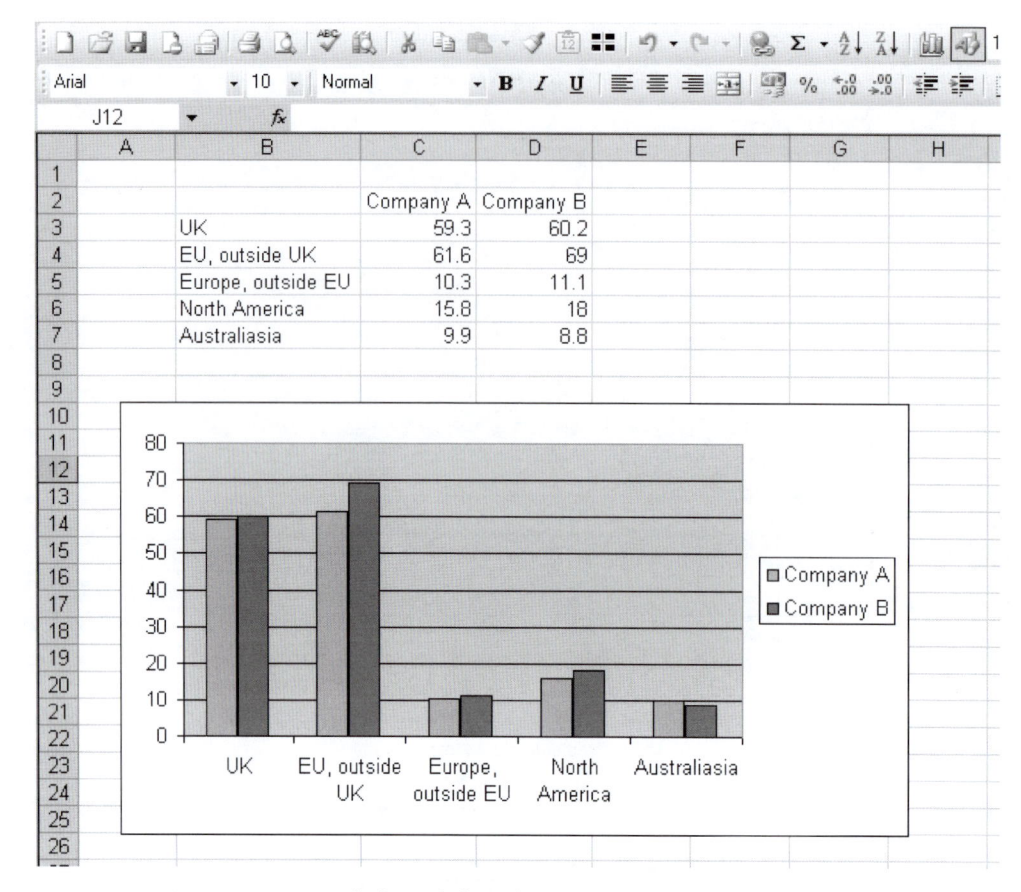

Figure 3.25 Side-by-side bar chart comparing the two companies

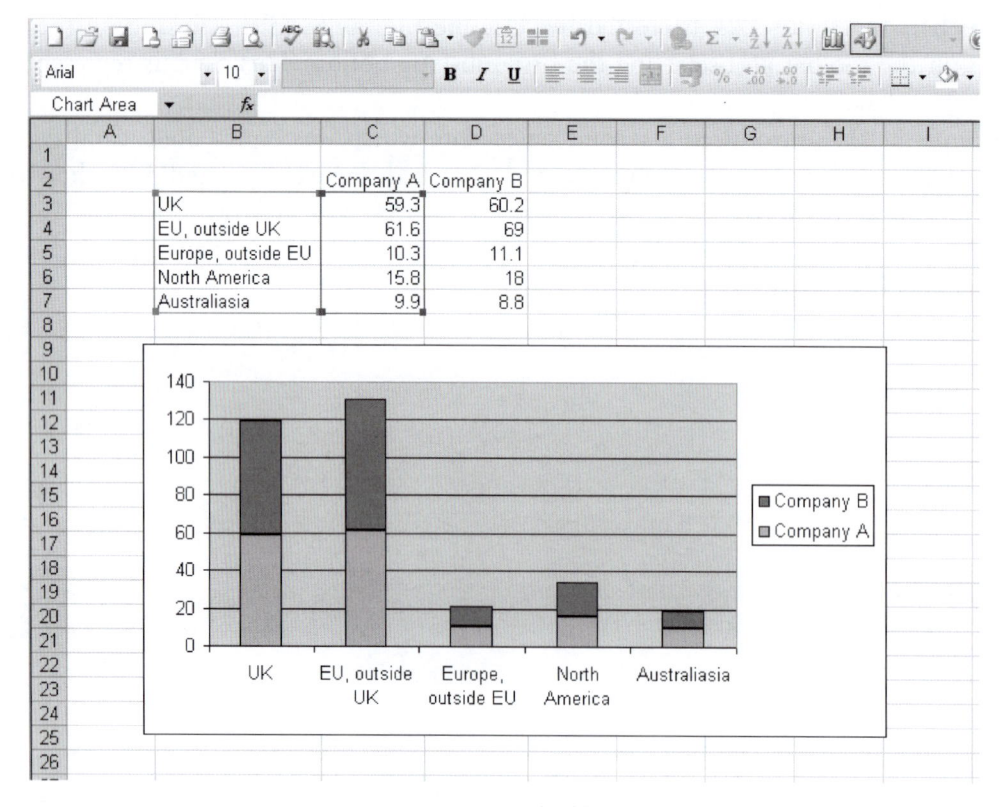

Figure 3.26 Stacked-bar chart

A slightly different version of the stacked bar is shown in Figure 3.27. This is referred to as a 100 per cent stacked bar and it compares the percentage each company contributes to the total across each country.

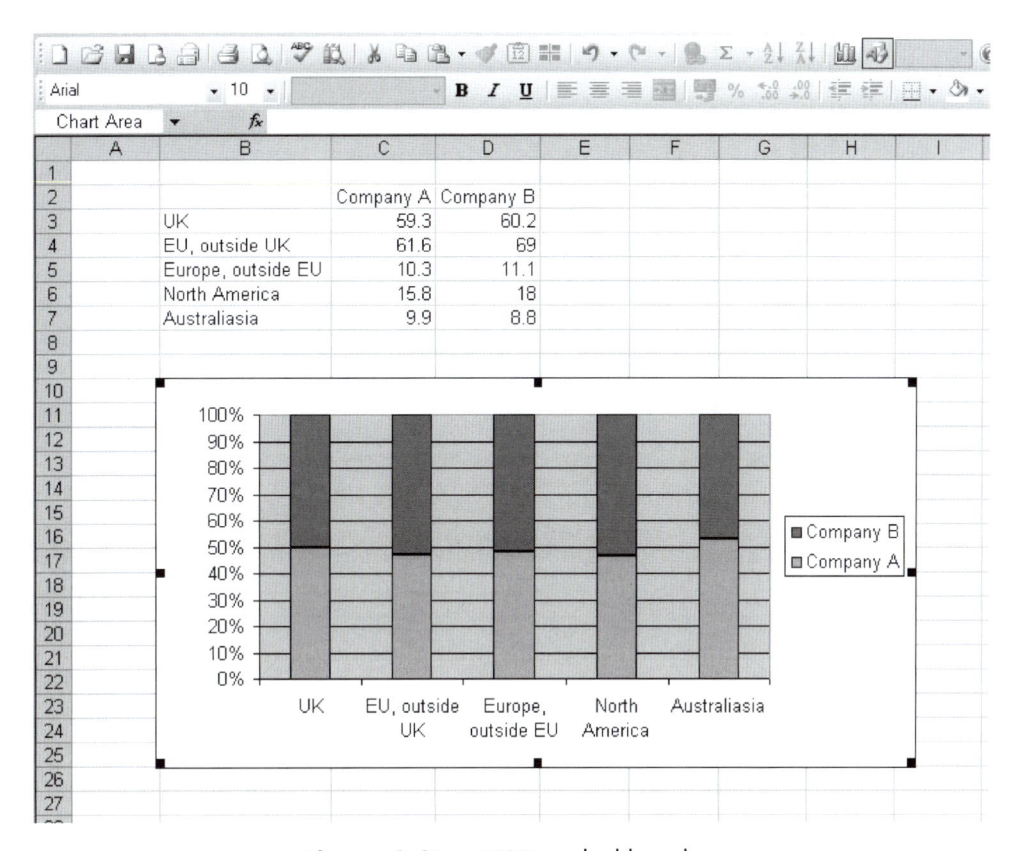

Figure 3.27 100% stacked-bar chart

The stacked bar chart compares the contribution of each company to the total across the different countries.

Excel offers a variety of options when plotting data onto charts. Bar charts do not have to be represented by upright bars, but can be pyramids, cones or cylinders. Figure 3.28a shows side-by-side bar in a pyramid shape. However, you should in each case, consider the most appropriate way is which to display date – often, the simpler methods of display are the most effective.

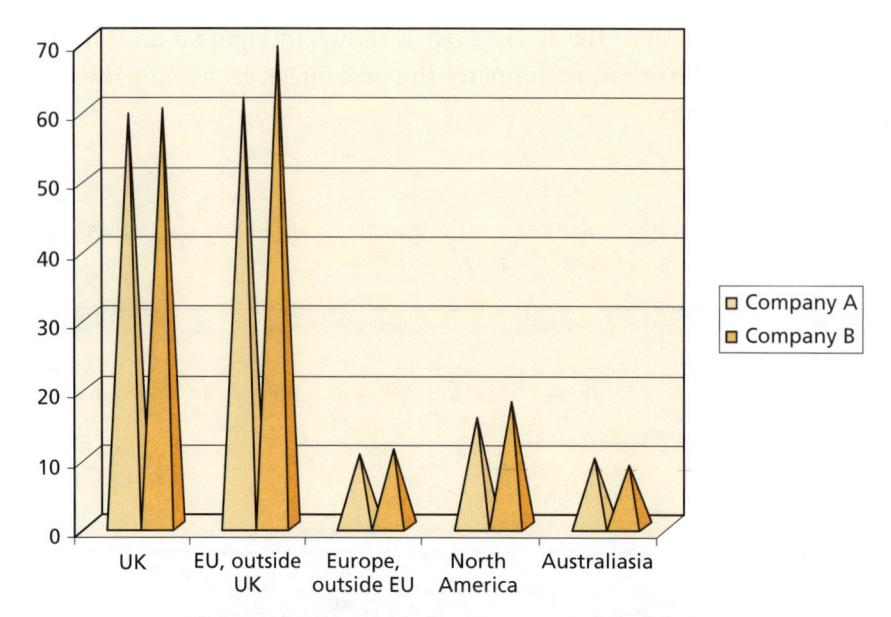

Figure 3.28a Bar chart using a pyramid shape

Furthermore bars can be positioned horizontally as opposed to vertically. This can be seen in Figure 3.28b.

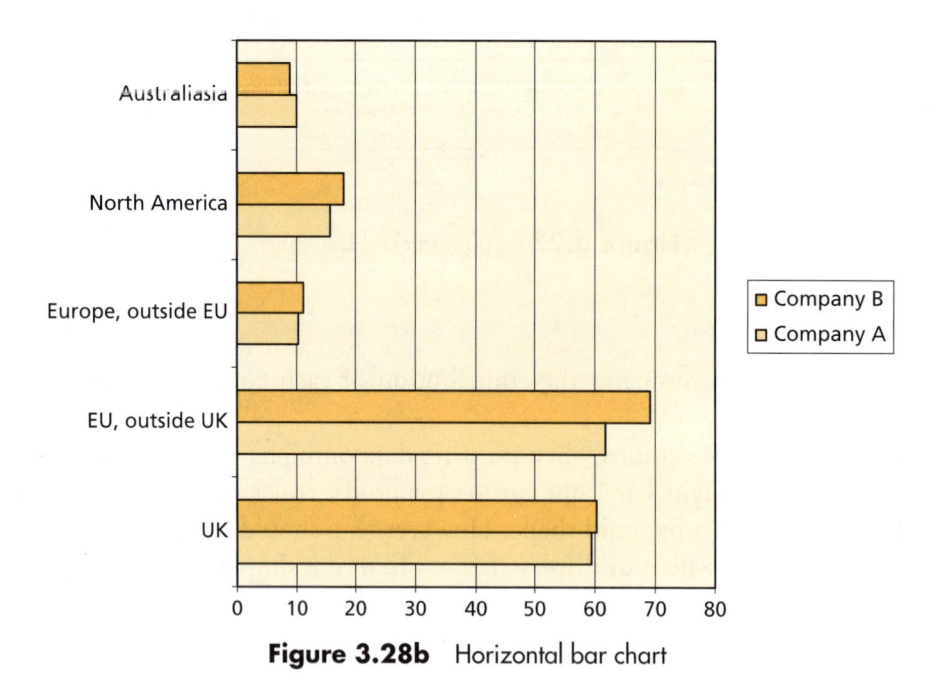

Figure 3.28b Horizontal bar chart

Another way of looking at this data is to chart the turnover of the two companies showing the contribution from each country (as shown previously in Figure 3.20). This is achieved in Excel by selecting the data as before and selecting the stacked-bar chart option from the chart sub-options. However after clicking next, change the series setting to by rows instead of by columns. The results are shown in Figure 3.28c.

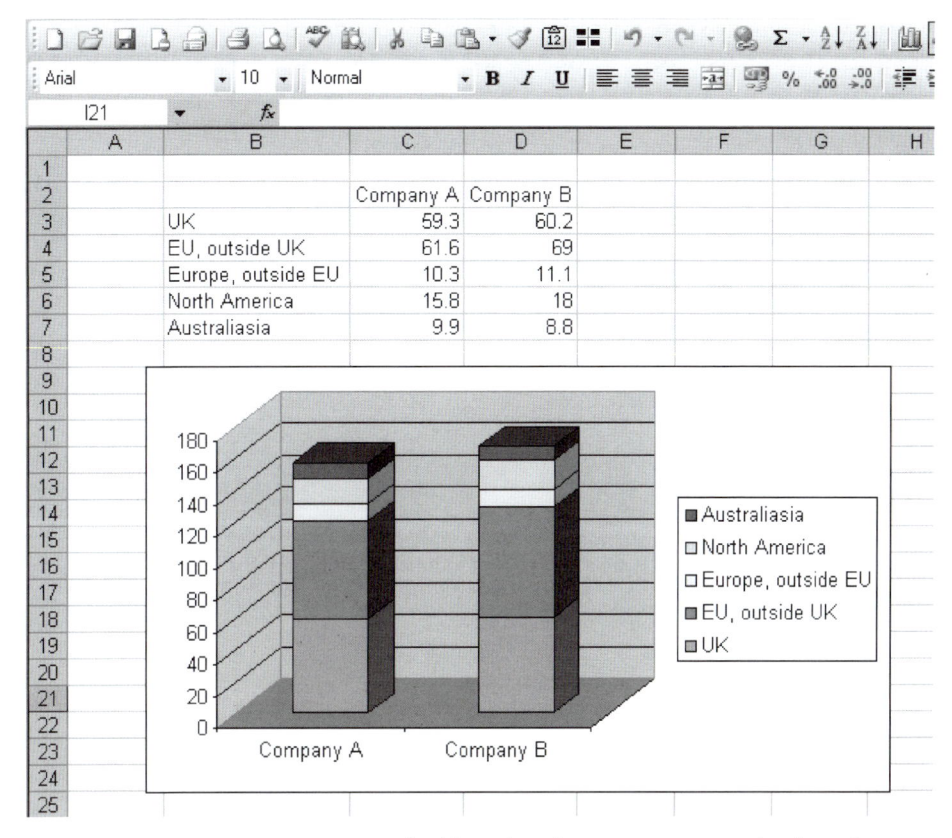

Figure 3.28c 3-D Stacked-bar chart by rows as opposed to by columns

The examples shown so far in this section have been replicating the charts produced in an earlier section of this chapter.

3.11 Tabulation

Sometimes you will need to display actual figures rather than an illustration of them, and in such cases (especially if the data is to be presented to a numerate audience) a table may be preferable to a chart.

Example 3.11.1

In country A there were 22,618,462 dwellings. Of these 9,875,380 were owner-occupied, 6,765,097 were council rentals, 3,476,907 were private rentals and the remainder were held under a variety of tenures.

In country B there were 1,846,093 in total and the numbers in the above categories were 569,043, 903,528 and 278,901, respectively.

Display this information in a table.

Solution

The first step is to realise that the figures are 'far too accurate'. The table will be too cluttered if we retain this accuracy, so we will round each to the nearest thousand. We shall also need to calculate numbers in the 'others' category.

The next step is to decide upon the basic shape of the table. It shows four categories of housing in two countries, so the basic shape of the table is one column per country and one row per category.

Were you to draw the table in rough at this point (always a good idea) you would see that another row is needed for the totals. Furthermore, you would probably realise that country A has so many more dwellings than country B that they are not really comparable. This is dealt with by turning the frequencies into percentages, which will require two more columns. Figure 3.29 shows the finished table.

	Country A		Country B	
Type of dwelling	Number		Number	
	('000)	%	('000)	%
Owner-occupied	9,875	44	569	31
Council rental	6,765	30	904	49
Private rental	3,477	15	279	15
Others	2,501	11	94	5
Total	22,618	100	1,846	100

Figure 3.29 Housing by type – Country A and Country B

By using percentages we have been able to pinpoint the way in which patterns of owner-occupation and council rental are almost directly opposite in the two countries.

The basic rules of tabulation are:

- the aim is to present the data in an orderly fashion so that patterns can be seen;
- the table, with its title and headings, should be self-explanatory;
- it should be as simple as possible;
- combine small, unimportant categories if this simplifies the table;
- eliminate unnecessary detail by rounding;
- find totals, subtotals and percentages where appropriate;
- think about who the table is aimed at – this may decide what other figures you calculate and how you position them;
- figures likely to be compared should be adjacent or at least close to one another;
- state units;
- state the source of the data if known.

3.12 Pareto analysis – The 80-20 rule

Pareto analysis was proposed by an Italian economist Vilfredo Pareto to describe how a relatively small part of a population may be so important. Pareto initially referred to wealth among individuals. He pointed out that a small number of individuals own a large portion of the wealth of any society. This idea is sometimes expressed more simply as the Pareto principle or the 80-20 rule.

In a business context the 80-20 rule states that a small number of clients will be responsible for a large proportion of the turnover, or a small number of inventory items will be responsible for a large amount of sales, or a small number of staff will present a disproportionate level of challenges to the management. When the term '80-20 rule' is used in this it does not always mean that it will actually be 20 per cent of the clients that produce 80 per cent of the profit as sometime it may be a smaller percentage like 10 which will produce the over whelming share of the profit.

In business the 80-20 rule essentially says that one should identify the really important elements of the business and focus the majority of one's time and effort on these elements.

It is possible to express the 80-20 rule in terms of a mathematical function and draw a probability density function. However, below is described a more practical approach to the 80-20 rule using simple commands in Excel.

The managing director wants to know on which of these products should the sales force concentrate. There is an understanding that the best-selling products have the most upside potential. Therefore, it has been decided to apply 80-20 rule type thinking and highlight the best-performing products.

There is a three-step process involved.

The first step is to sort the original data by the UNIT SALES. This is achieved by selecting the range C7:E27 and selecting DATA SORT. In the top box select UNIT SALES, check the Descending box and make sure that Header Row is checked and click ok to perform the sort.

Figure 3.30 shows the sorted data by UNIT SALES.

	A	B	C	D	E	F	G	H
4								
5								
6			Product Line	No of Items	Unit Sales			
7			F	3	1720			
8			U	20	1513			
9			L	6	1234			
10			T	17	1011			
11			I	4	891			
12			D	2	656			
13			A	1	598			
14			R	12	521			
15			G	3	484			
16			J	4	309			
17			B	1	267			
18			O	9	102			
19			Q	11	70			
20			N	7	55			
21			K	5	32			
22			S	13	18			
23			P	9	10			
24			H	3	5			
25			M	6	4			
26			E	2	2			
27			C	1	1			
28			Total		9502			
29								

Figure 3.30 Data sorted by UNIT SALES

The second step is to calculate the percentage of the total that each product line represents. To do this the following formula is entered into cell F7.

= E7 / $E$28

This formula can be copied to the range F8:F27

Now the third step is to calculate the cumulative sales in column G. Into cell G7 enter:

= F7

And into cell G8 enter

= G7 + F8

This formula can be copied into the range G9:G27.

Figure 3.31 shows the completed 80-20 rule table.

PRESENTATION OF DATA

	A	B	C	D	E	F	G	H
3			Application of Paretos Law to a range					
4								
5								
6			Product Line	No of Items	Unit Sales	% of total	Cum. Total	
7			F	3	1720	18%	18%	
8			U	20	1513	16%	34%	
9			L	6	1234	13%	47%	
10			T	17	1011	11%	58%	
11			I	4	891	9%	67%	
12			D	2	656	7%	74%	
13			A	1	598	6%	**80%**	
14			R	12	521	5%	86%	
15			G	3	484	5%	91%	
16			J	4	309	3%	94%	
17			B	1	267	3%	97%	
18			O	9	102	1%	98%	
19			Q	11	70	1%	99%	
20			N	7	55	1%	99%	
21			K	5	32	0%	99%	
22			S	13	18	0%	100%	
23			P	9	10	0%	100%	
24			H	3	5	0%	100%	
25			M	6	4	0%	100%	
26			E	2	2	0%	100%	
27			C	1	1	0%	100%	
28			Total		9503			
29								

Figure 3.31 Completed table showing cumulative total and 80% marker

From Figure 3.31 it may be seen that Products F, U, L, T, I, D and A are the best performers and it is on these products that most effort should be expended.

3.13 Using spreadsheets to produce histograms, ogives and pie charts

Excel is a useful tool to create professional-looking charts including histograms, ogives and pie charts.

3.13.1 Creating a histogram in Excel

In order to show how to create a histogram in Excel, the data from Example 3.5.3 will be used. Figure 3.32 shows this data in the spreadsheet.

	A	B	C	D	E	F	G	H
1	Time taken to complete 30 repetitions of a task							
2								
3		19.8	21.3	24.6	18.7	19.1	15.3	
4		20.6	22.1	19.9	17.2	24.1	23.0	
5		20.1	18.3	19.8	16.5	22.8	18.0	
6		20.0	21.6	19.7	25.9	22.2	17.9	
7		21.1	20.8	19.5	21.6	15.6	23.1	
8								

Figure 3.32 Data to be used for creation of a histogram

As previously explained in this chapter, a histogram is a graph of frequency distribution, where the x axis is the variable being measured and the y axis is the corresponding frequency. In order to calculate the frequency distribution of the time taken to complete 30 repetitions of a task the Excel FREQUENCY function is used. The format of the function is = FREQUENCY(DATARANGE,BIN), where Bin refers to the required range of to be used for the x axis – in this example, time in minutes. Figure 3.33 shows the calculated frequency table in Excel.

	A	B	C	D	E	F	G	H	I	J	K
1	Time taken to complete 30 repetitions of a task										
2									Time	Frequency	
3		19.8	21.3	24.6	18.7	19.1	15.3		15.0	0	
4		20.6	22.1	19.9	17.2	24.1	23.0		17.0	3	
5		20.1	18.3	19.8	16.5	22.8	18.0		19.0	5	
6		20.0	21.6	19.7	25.9	22.2	17.9		21.0	10	
7		21.1	20.8	19.5	21.6	15.6	23.1		23.0	8	
8									25.0	3	
9									27.0	1	
10											

Figure 3.33 Calculated frequency distribution table

Before entering the frequency formula into the spreadsheet first select the range J3:J9 and then enter:

= FREQUENCY(B3:G7,I3:I9) and hold down the CTRL key and the SHIFT key whilst pressing ENTER.

The formula is entered into all the cells in the range – this is referred to as an *array* function in Excel.

We now have the data that we want to plot onto a histogram, so select the range J2:J9 and click on the chart icon. Select Bar chart and take the first option of side-by-side bars. Click NEXT to see the current chart. The chart so far is shown in Figure 3.34.

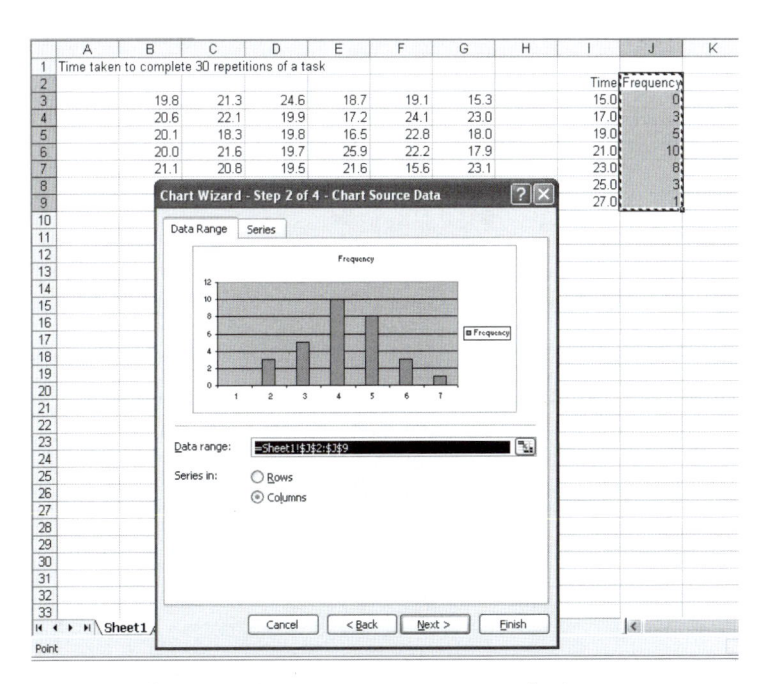

Figure 3.34 First step in creating the histogram

The next step is to take the numbers in the range I3:I9 and use them as the labels for the *x* axis on the chart. To do this, click on the SERIES tab and then click in the box next to the prompt 'Category *x*-axis labels'. Now select the range I3:I9 and then click finish. The chart is drawn as shown in Figure 3.35.

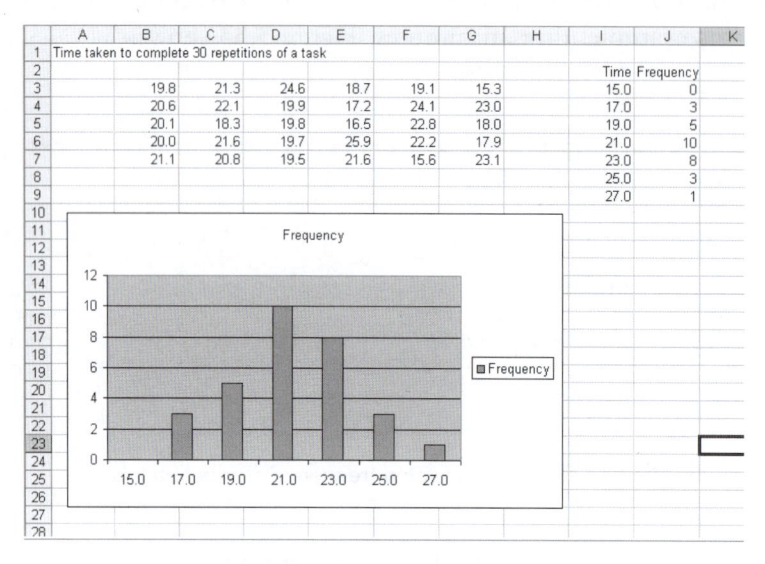

Figure 3.35 Frequency distribution chart

Histograms are generally shown with the side-by-side bars touching and using the chart formatting options in Excel this can be achieved here.

Right click on one of the bars on the chart and select FORMAT DATA SERIES. Then select the options tab. Set the *gap width* to zero and click OK. To finish off the chart it is helpful to add titles to the *x* and *y* axes. Right click on the white area surrounding the chart and select chart options, and then select the titles tab. Enter titles as prompted and the finished histogram is shown in Figure 3.36.

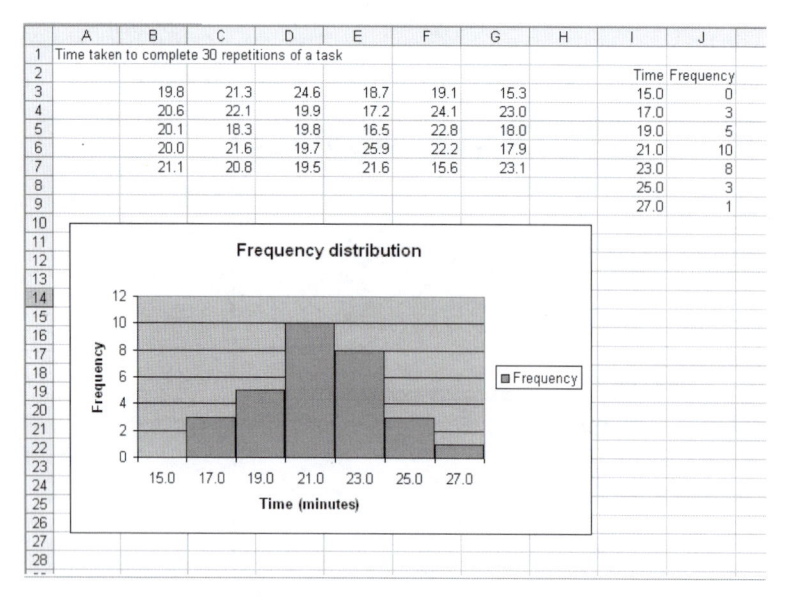

Figure 3.36 Finished histogram showing frequency distribution of time taken to complete 30 repetitions of a task

3.13.2 Creating an ogive in Excel

The data used in the above histogram example will once again be used to illustrate how we can create an ogive.

An ogive is a graph of a cumulative frequency distribution, where the x axis is the variable being measured and the y axis is the corresponding cumulative frequency. In order to calculate the cumulative frequencies for an ogive, an additional column needs to be added to the frequency distribution table used in the histogram example. Into cell K3 the following formula is required:

$= J3$

And then in K4 enter:

$= K3 + J4$

This formula can be copied through to K9.
The results of calculating the cumulative frequency are shown in Figure 3.37.

	A	B	C	D	E	F	G	H	I	J	K	L
1	Time taken to complete 30 repetitions of a task											
2									Time	Frequency	Cum Frq	
3		19.8	21.3	24.6	18.7	19.1	15.3		15.0	0	0	
4		20.6	22.1	19.9	17.2	24.1	23.0		17.0	3	3	
5		20.1	18.3	19.8	16.5	22.8	18.0		19.0	5	8	
6		20.0	21.6	19.7	25.9	22.2	17.9		21.0	10	18	
7		21.1	20.8	19.5	21.6	15.6	23.1		23.0	8	26	
8									25.0	3	29	
9									27.0	1	30	

Figure 3.37 Calculating the cumulative frequency

An ogive chart plots the cumulative frequency against the time as an x–y chart. Therefore the first step in creating the graph is to select the range I3:I9 – now hold down the CTRL key and select the range K3:K9. Click on the chart icon and select x–y and choose the option with lines. Click next and the chart will appear as shown in Figure 3.38.

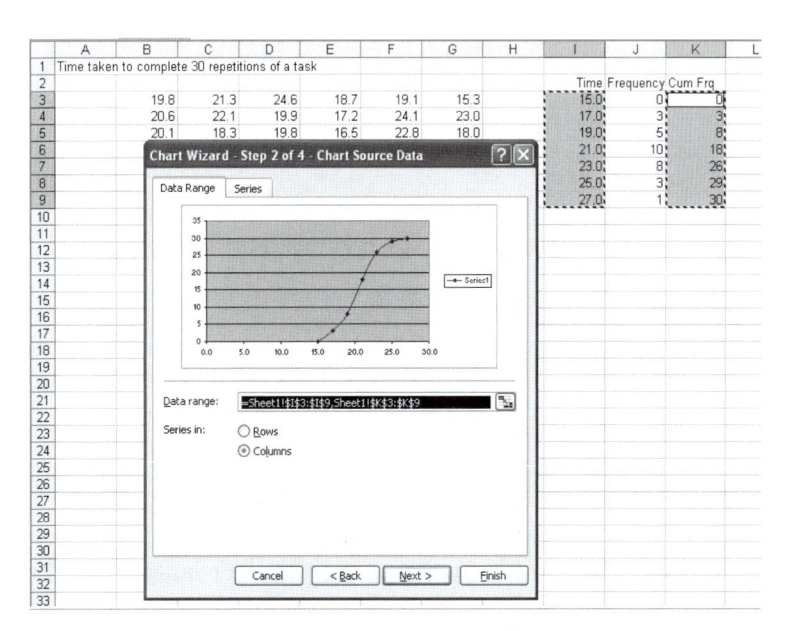

Figure 3.38 Ogive chart

To complete the chart select the SERIES tab and enter titles for the x and y axis. The completed chart is shown in Figure 3.39.

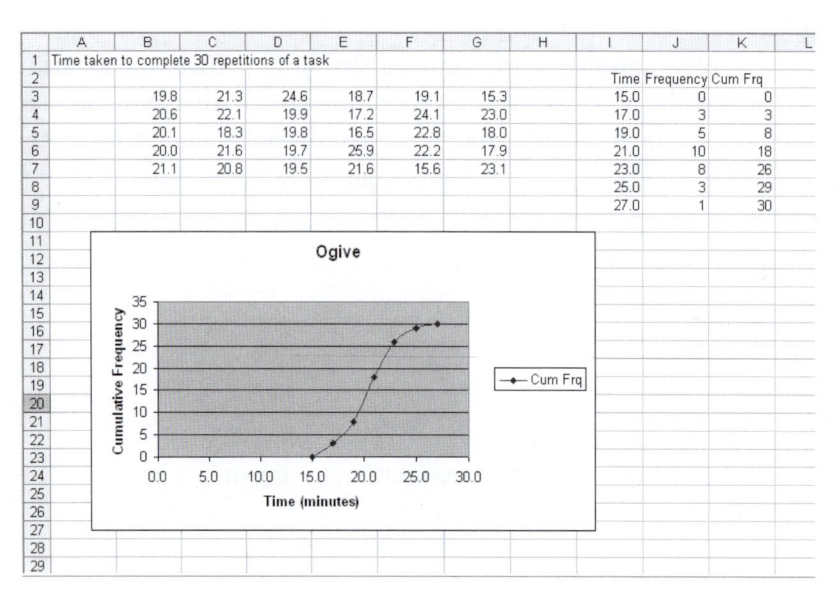

Figure 3.39 Completed ogive showing cumulative frequency

3.13.3 Creating a Pie chart in Excel

Pie charts are one of several types of chart that are useful for representing business data.

For this example that data from Example 3.9.1 will be used. The first step is to enter this into the spreadsheet, which can be seen in Figure 3.40.

Figure 3.40 Data for pie chart

To create the chart select the range B3:C7 and click on the chart icon. Select pie chart and then choose the type of pie required. For this example an exploded pie has been chosen and Figure 3.41 shows the chart so far.

To complete the chart click next and then select the data labels tab. Tick the category name and value options and then select the legend tab and remove the tick from the show legend box. The completed pie chart is shown in Figure 3.42.

You may have noticed when you were selecting the data labels that there were other options available such as showing the percentage of the total as opposed to the actual values on the chart.

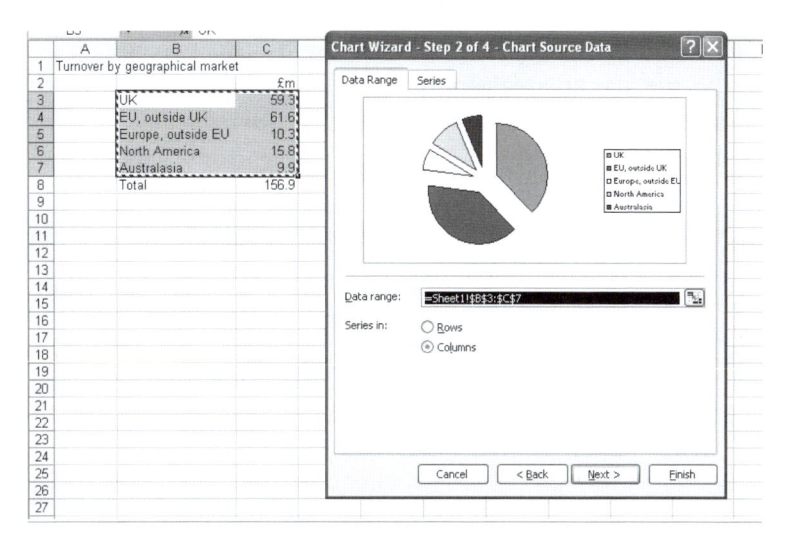

Figure 3.41 Pie chart

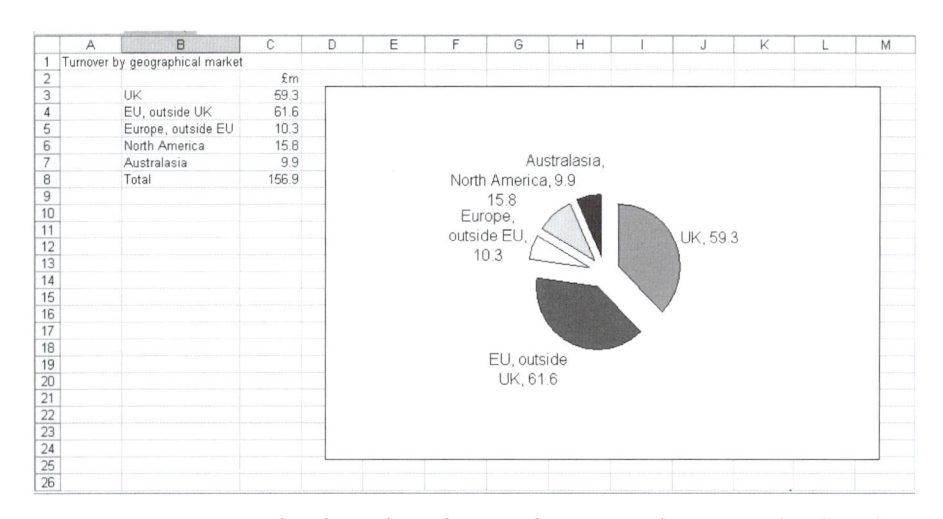

Figure 3.42 Completed pie chart showing the turnover by geographical market

3.14 Summary

- The equation $y = a + bx$ has a straight-line graph, with a giving the value of y when $x = 0$ (the intercept) and b giving the increase in y corresponding to a unit increase in x (the gradient). Simultaneous linear equations can be solved graphically, as can quadratic equations.
- *Tallying* is a more reliable method of compiling frequency distributions from raw data than is mere counting. Very often we have to tally into classes rather than individual values.
- *Continuous* variables can, in theory, be measured to any level of precision, while *discrete* variables can take only certain values e.g. integers, or whole numbers.
- The *cumulative frequency* of a value is the number of readings up to (or up to and including) that value.
- The *histogram* and the *ogive* are graphical representations of a frequency distribution and a cumulative frequency distribution respectively. If intervals are unequal, calculate frequency density before drawing the histogram.

- *Pie charts* represent the breakdown of a total figure into percentage component parts. Each sector of the 'pie' has an area proportional to the percentage it is representing.
- *Bar charts, multiple-bar charts* and *compound-bar* (or *component-bar*) *charts* represent data through vertical 'bars' whose lengths are measured against a vertical scale, as with ordinary graphs.
- Sometimes a table is to be preferred to a chart, but tables need to be kept as simple as possible.
- Pareto Analysis – The 80-20 rule is discussed and an example provided.

Readings

3

Company reports contain a mass of statistical information collected by the company, often in the form of graphs, bar charts and pie charts. A table or figures may not provide a very clear or rapid impression of company results, while graphs and diagrams can make an immediate impact and it may become obvious from them why particular decisions have been made. For example, the following graph provides a clear idea of the future of the company sales manager:

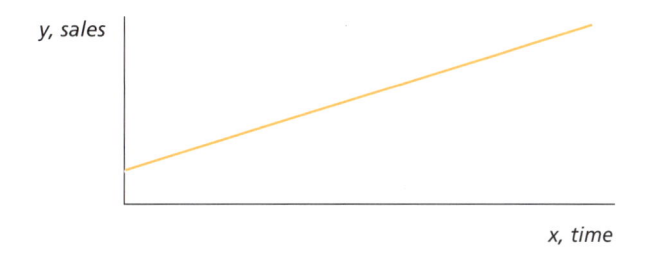

[graph: y, sales vs x, time — upward sloping line]

But pictures and diagrams are not always as illuminating as this one – particularly if the person presenting the information has a reason for preferring obscurity.

The gee-whiz graph
Darrell Huff, *How to Lie with Statistics*, Penguin 1973
© Darrell & Frances Huff Inc 1973. Reproduced by permission of Pollinger Limited and the Proprietor.

There is terror in numbers. Humpty Dumpty's confidence in telling Alice that he was master of the words he used would not be extended by many people to numbers. Perhaps we suffer from a trauma induced by early experiences with maths.

Whatever the cause, it creates a real problem for the writer who yearns to be read, the advertising man who expects his copy to sell goods, the publisher who wants his books or magazines to be popular. When numbers in tabular form are taboo and words will not do the work well, as is often the case, there is one answer left: draw a picture.

About the simplest kind of statistical picture, or graph, is the line variety. It is very useful for showing trends, something practically everybody is interested in showing or knowing about or spotting or deploring or forecasting. We'll let our graph show how national income increased 10 per cent in a year.

Begin with paper ruled into squares. Name the months along the bottom. Indicate billions of dollars up the side. Plot your points and draw your line, and your graph will look like this:

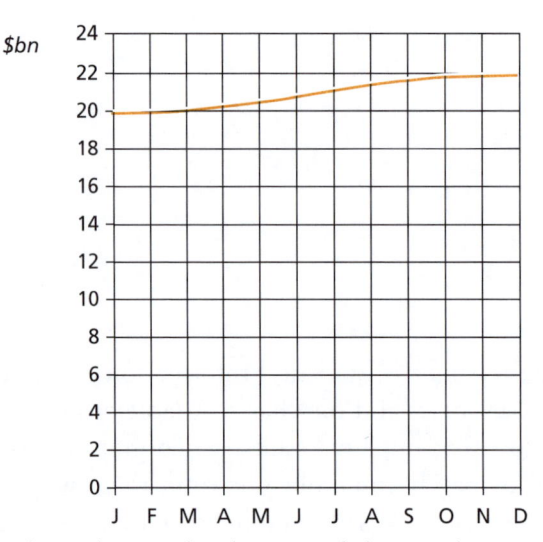

Now that's clear enough. It shows what happened during the year and it shows it month by month. He who runs may see and understand, because the whole graph is in proportion and there is a zero line at the bottom for comparison. Your 10 per cent looks like 10 per cent – an upward trend that is substantial but perhaps not overwhelming. That is very well if all you want to do is convey information. But suppose you wish to win an argument, shock a reader, move him into action, sell him something. For that, this chart lacks schmaltz. Chop off the bottom.

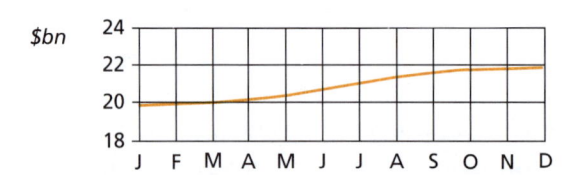

Now that's more like it. (You've saved paper too, something to point out if any carping fellow objects to your misleading graphics.) The figures are the same and so is the curve. It is the same graph. Nothing has been falsified – except the impression that it gives. But what the hasty reader sees now is a national-income line that has climbed half-way up the paper in twelve months, all because most of the chart isn't there any more. Like the missing parts of speech in sentences that you met in grammar classes, it is 'understood'. Of course, the eye doesn't 'understand' what isn't there, and a small rise has become, visually, a big one.

Now that you have practised to deceive, why stop with truncating? You have a further trick available that's worth a dozen of that. It will make your modest rise of 10 per cent look livelier than one hundred per cent is entitled to look. Simply change the proportion between the ordinate and the abscissa. There's no rule against it, and it does give your graph a prettier shape. All you have to do is let each mark up the side stand for only one-tenth as many dollars as before.

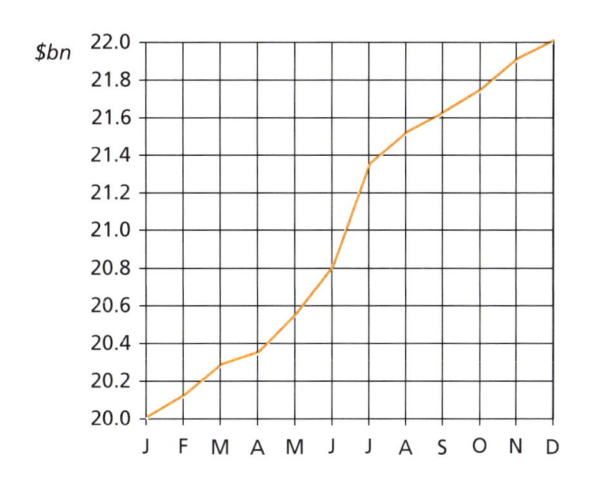

That is impressive, isn't it? Anyone looking at it can just feel prosperity throbbing in the arteries of the country. It is a subtler equivalent of editing 'National income rose 10 per cent' into '... climbed a whopping 10 per cent'. It is vastly more effective, however, because it contains no adjectives or adverbs to spoil the illusion of objectivity. There's nothing anyone can pin on you.

And you're in good, or at least respectable, company. A news magazine has used this method to show the stock market hitting a new high, the graph being so truncated as to make the climb look far more dizzying than it was. A Columbia Gas System advertisement once reproduced a chart 'from our new Annual Report'. If you read the little numbers and analysed them you found that during a ten-year period living costs went up about 60 per cent and the cost of gas dropped 4 per cent. This is a favourable picture, but it apparently was not favourable enough for Columbia Gas. They chopped off their chart at 90 per cent (with no gap or other indication to warn you) so that this was what your eye told you: living costs have more than tripled, and gas has gone down one-third!

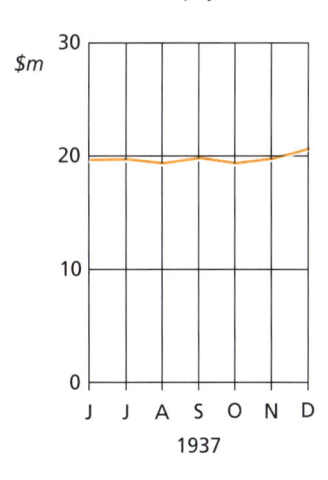

Steel companies have used similarly misleading graphic methods in attempts to line up public opinion against wage increases. Yet the method is far from new, and its impropriety was shown up long ago – not just in technical publications for statisticians either. An editorial writer in *Dun's Review* back in 1938 reproduced a chart from an advertisement advocating advertising in Washington, D.C., the argument being nicely expressed in the headline over the chart: **Government payrolls up!** The line in the graph went along with the exclamation point even though the figures behind it did not. What they showed was an increase from near the bottom of the graph clear to the top, making an increase of under 4 per cent look like more than 400. The magazine gave its own graphic version of the same figures alongside – an honest red line that rose just 4 per cent, under this caption: **Government payrolls stable!**

Postscript

Remember that if you are presenting information your objective will be to inform. Visual images can have an impact out of all proportion to the supporting detailed numbers. It is not sufficient to get the numbers right while your visual representations are slapdash – the end result may be to mislead or confuse your audience.

As a user of statistical information, remember that the pictures you see may not give the same impression as a detailed numerical analysis would reveal. It is often essential to get behind the graphics and delve into the raw statistics.

Discussion points
Discuss these within your study group before reading the outline solutions

The following data (*Social Trends 23*, 1993) show the percentage of students in various regions of the United Kingdom who obtained one or more A-level passes in 1989/90.

Region	Male	Female
North	18.6	21.5
Yorkshire & Humberside	19.4	20.1
E. Midlands	21.3	23.1
E. Anglia	22.4	25.9
S. East	27.5	28.3
S. West	23.8	25.5
W. Midlands	20.9	20.5
N. West	21.2	23.0

How would you display this data:

(a) to compare male and female results?
(b) to compare regions?
(c) to make it appear that the percentage of females in the North with at least one A-level is about twice the percentage of males?

Outline solutions

(a) The data requires a multiple bar chart and the male/female comparison will be easiest if the two bars for each region are adjacent and then there is a small gap followed by the next region with its two bars, etc. The chart will be more informative if the data is first sorted into order of magnitude for the males, say, since the order for females may be slightly different.

(b) The multiple bar chart that brings out the differences between regions will have the male bars for all regions in a block with no spaces and then a gap and a similar block of female bars. Again it will be best to sort the data into order of magnitude as far as possible. The same order must be used for females as for males.

(c) You would probably use a simple bar chart to compare the success of males and females in the North. The correct chart would have the vertical axis starting at zero. However, were you to start it at, say, 16 per cent then the male bar would have height of 2.6 and the female of 5.5 giving the visual impression that the percentage for females was twice that for males.

Revision Questions

Part 3.1 Objective testing selection

> Questions 3.1.1–3.1.10 are standard multiple-choice questions with exactly one correct answer each. Thereafter, the style of question will vary.

3.1.1 An ogive is:

(A) another name for a histogram.
(B) a chart showing any linear relationship.
(C) a chart showing a non-linear relationship.
(D) a graph of a cumulative frequency distribution.

3.1.2 In a histogram, the common class width is £10.00. For analysis purposes, the analyst has set one class width at £12.50 and the frequency recorded is 80 respondents. To maintain the accuracy of the histogram, the score that must be plotted is:

(A) 48
(B) 64
(C) 80
(D) 100.

3.1.3 In a histogram, one class is three-quarters of the width of the remaining classes. If the score in that class is 21, the correct height to plot on the histogram is:

(A) 15.75
(B) 21
(C) 28
(D) 42.

3.1.4 A pie chart shows total sales of £350,000 and a second pie chart shows total sales of £700,000. If drawn correctly to scale, the ratio of the radius of the second pie chart to the first pie chart, to two decimal places, should be:

(A) 1.41 times.
(B) 2 times.
(C) 2.82 times.
(D) 3.14 times.

3.1.5 In the equation $y = 5 + 4x$, what does the '4' tell us?

(A) y increases by 4 whenever x increases by 1.
(B) $y = 4$ when $x = 0$.

(C) 4 is the intercept on the *y*-axis.
(D) The slope is 1/4.

3.1.6 A quadratic function has a positive *x*-squared term and its graph cuts the *x*-axis at $x = 2$ and at $x = 8$. Which of the following is true?

(A) It has a maximum value when $x = 5$.
(B) It has a maximum value when $x = 3$.
(C) It has a minimum value when $x = 5$.
(D) It has a minimum value when $x = 3$.

3.1.7 A quadratic function has a maximum point. It cuts the *y*-axis at $y = -4$ and the *x*-axis at $x = 1$ and at $x = 5$. What is the *x*-coordinate of its maximum point?

(A) $x = 2$
(B) $x = 3$
(C) $x = 0.5$
(D) $x = -1.5$.

3.1.8 A pie chart is used to display the following data:

percentage voting for P 52
percentage voting for Q 32
percentage voting for R 11

What angle in degrees on the pie chart will represent R's share of the vote?

(A) 39.6
(B) 11.0
(C) 44.4
(D) 3.1.

3.1.9 Which of the following is not recommended in tabulation?

(A) Rounding.
(B) Amalgamating unimportant sections.
(C) Using percentages where necessary to make comparisons.
(D) Keeping maximum accuracy.

3.1.10 Two straight lines have been plotted on a graph. Their simultaneous solution is given by

(A) The averages of their intercepts on the respective axes.
(B) The points where they cross the line $y = x$.
(C) The point where they cross each other.
(D) No point on the graph – algebraic means must be used.

3.1.11 At what points does the line $y = 5x - 8$ cut the axes? Your answers should be correct to one decimal place.

3.1.12 What is the slope (correct to two decimal places) of the line $3x + 4y = 12$?

3.1.13 If 60 units are produced per week, total manufacturing costs are £1,200; if 80 units are produced, total costs rise to £1,900. The following is a solution to find the linear relationship between costs (*C*) and number of units (*X*). State

whether or not each line, (A)–(G), in the solution follows correctly from the lines preceding it (regardless of whether you think the preceding lines are correct).
Let the linear relationship be $C = a + bX$

(A) When $X = 60$, $C = 1{,}200$
(B) Hence $1{,}200 = a + 60b$
(C) When $X = 80$, $C = 1{,}900$
(D) Hence $1{,}900 = a + 80b$
(E) Subtracting gives $700 = 140b$
(F) Hence $b = 140/700 = 0.2$
(G) Hence $a = 1{,}200 + 60 \times 0.2 = 1{,}212$.

3.1.14 Categorise each of the following variables as either discrete or continuous:

(A) Age of 5 years.
(B) Time of 2.5 hours.
(C) Output of 12,000 kg.
(D) Output of 5,000 units.

3.1.15 Convert the following distribution of the number of employees absent per day into a cumulative frequency distribution:

Number absent	Frequency
0	10
1	15
2	7
3	4
4	2

3.1.16 A cumulative frequency distribution of weekly wages is as follows:

Weekly wage	Cumulative frequency
Less than £150	45
Less than £200	125
Less than £300	155
Less than £400	170
Less than £600	175

(A) How many were paid less than £300?
(B) How many were paid more than £200?
(C) How many were paid between £200 and £300?

3.1.17 If the following data is to be illustrated by means of a histogram and if the standard interval is taken to be 10 kg, calculate the heights of the bars of the histogram (to the nearest whole number).

Weight	Frequency
0–10	65
10–20	89
20–40	140
40–60	76
60–100	64

3.1.18 Which of the following correctly describe(s) a frequency polygon?

(A) A graph of frequency on values for ungrouped discrete data.
(B) A graph of frequency on interval mid-points for continuous data with equal width intervals.

(C) A graph of frequency on interval upper limits for continuous data with equal width intervals.

(D) A graph joining the mid-points of the top sides of the bars of a histogram.

3.1.19 The following data are to be illustrated by means of a pie chart. Calculate the angles (in degrees) that correspond to each category (to the nearest whole number).

Categories	%
A	42
B	38
C	15
D	5

3.1.20 Associate the following types of bar charts with the examples given:

Bar charts

(A) Simple
(B) Multiple
(C) Compound

Examples

(P) Two adjacent bars then a gap and two more and a further two after a final gap.
(Q) Eight separate bars.
(R) Three bars each of which is divided into four component parts.

Part 3.2 Choosing charts

	Number of pies sold			
Pie flavourings	1995	1996	1997	1998
Chocolate	240	305	290	360
Toffee	120	135	145	210
Apple	70	105	125	190
Banana	30	35	40	35

3.2.1 The following compound bar chart illustrates the 1995 section of the above data. What are the heights of the four horizontal lines in the bar?

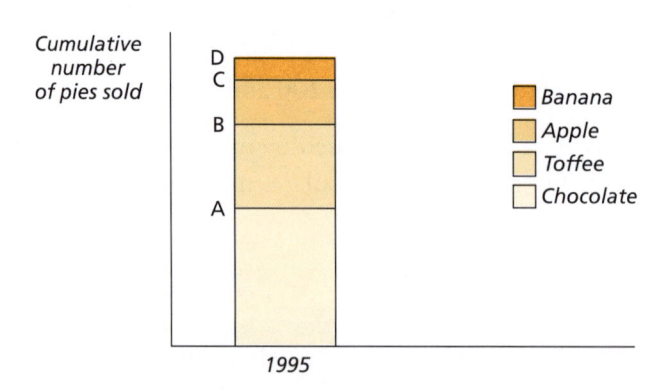

3.2.2 Which of the following statements correctly describe aspects of the data which are illustrated by the 1995 bar?

(A) In 1995, chocolate sold more than all the other flavours put together.
(B) Sales rose from 1995 to 1996.
(C) In 1995, banana was the least popular flavour.

(D) The popularity of banana increased very little over the 4 years.
(E) In 1995, toffee was less popular than apple.
(F) In 1995, chocolate was the most popular flavour.

3.2.3 The data may be illustrated by the following chart. What type of chart is it?

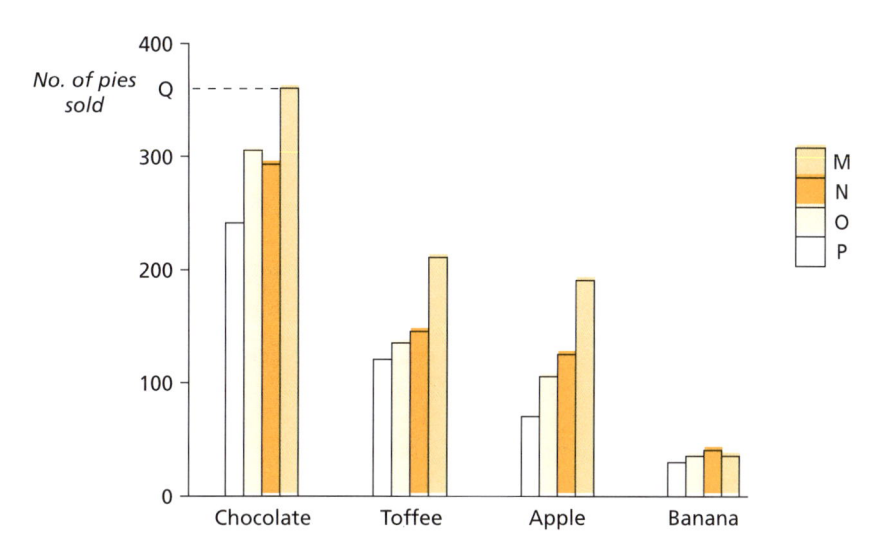

(A) Multiple bar chart.
(B) Simple bar chart.
(C) Histogram.
(D) Pictogram.
(E) Ogive.
(F) Component bar chart.

3.2.4 On the chart given in Question 2.3, replace the letters by appropriate numbers.

3.2.5 Which of the following statements correctly describe aspects of the data which are illustrated by the chart in Question 2.3?

(A) Sales of chocolate rose steadily over the 4 years.
(B) Banana was the least popular over the entire period.
(C) There was a big increase in the sales of all flavours in 1998.
(D) After 1995 sales of apple began to catch up with those of toffee.
(E) Total sales have fallen over the four-year period.

Part 3.3 Data classification/frequency diagram

The managers of a sales department have recorded the number of successful sales made by their 50 telesales persons for one week, and the raw scores are reproduced below:

20	10	17	22	35	43	29	34	12	24
24	32	34	13	40	22	34	21	39	12
10	49	32	33	29	26	33	34	34	22
24	17	18	34	37	32	17	36	32	43
12	27	43	32	35	26	38	32	20	21

Sales persons who achieve fewer than twenty sales are required to undertake further training.

3.3.1 Complete the table displaying the data as a grouped frequency distribution.

Sales	Frequency
10–14	6
15–19	4
20–24	A
25–29	B
C	14
D	6
40–44	E
45–49	F

3.3.2 Suppose the frequency distribution for the data was as follows:

Sales	Frequency	Cumulative frequency
10 and under 15	6	G
15 and under 20	12	H
20 and under 25	17	I
25 and under 30	7	J

Find the cumulative frequencies G, H, I and J.

3.3.3 Suppose the frequency distribution and cumulative frequencies were as follows:

Sales	Frequency	Cumulative frequency
10 and under 15	7	7
15 and under 20	16	23
20 and under 25	13	36
25 and under 30	4	40

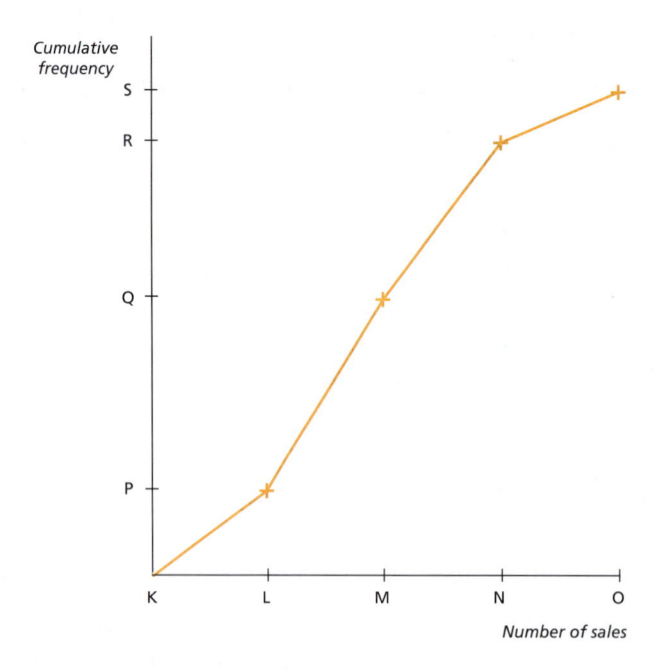

The chart is the cumulative frequency diagram illustrating this data.
Find the values corresponding to the letters K–S.

3.3.4 In the distribution given in Question 3.3, what percentage of the sales force sold less than 20?

Part 3.4 Drawing charts in Excel

3.4.1 The data below shows the number of people who passed through an airport terminal each day for a four-week period.

	A	B	C	D	E	F	G	H
1	No. of people passing through an airport terminal per day over a 4 week period							
2	All nos. in thousands							
3		Mon	Tues	Wed	Thur	Fri	Sat	Sun
4	Week 1	122	177	103	161	202	115	147
5	Week 2	178	133	109	125	106	139	164
6	Week 3	124	191	152	145	140	169	153
7	Week 4	159	154	113	144	167	128	149

(A) Using this data produce a frequency distribution table to show the variation in the volume of traffic through the terminal.
(B) Produce a histogram to graphically illustrate the frequency distribution.
(C) Calculate the cumulative frequencies.
(D) Produce an ogive chart to illustrate the cumulative frequency.

Solutions to Revision Questions

Solutions to Part 3.1

3.1.1 Answer: (D)

In an ogive, the cumulative frequency associated with each interval is graphed on the upper limit of the interval.

3.1.2 Answer: (B)

The interval is $12.50/10.00 = 1.25$ times the standard width, so the score to be plotted is $80/1.25 = 64$.

3.1.3 Answer: (C)

The correct height is $21/0.75 = 28$.

3.1.4 Answer: (A)

Step 1: Find R for the first pie chart:

$$\pi R^2 = 350{,}000$$
$$R^2 = 350{,}000/\pi$$
$$= 111{,}408.46$$
$$R = 333.779$$

Step 2: Find R for the second pie chart:

$$\pi R^2 = 700{,}000$$
$$R^2 = 700{,}000/\pi$$
$$= 222{,}816.92$$
$$R = 472.03$$

The ratio is $472.03/333.779 = 1.41$ times.

3.1.5 Answer: (A)

The Figure 4 is the slope so Y increases by 4 when X increases by 1. Answer D is not very wrong but has the reciprocal of the slope. The '5' gives the intercept that is the value of Y when $X = 0$.

3.1.6 Answer: (C)

The curve has a 'U' shape because of the positive x-squared term so it has a minimum point which, by symmetry, is halfway between its roots. This is given by $(2 + 8)/2 = 10/2 = 5$.

3.1.7 Answer: (B)

The maximum lies halfway between the roots, by symmetry, and this is given by $(1 + 5)/2 = 3$. If you selected answer (A), you have probably subtracted $(5 - 1)$ instead of adding; if you selected one of the other two answers you have probably averaged one of the roots with the intercept on the y-axis – which is actually irrelevant to this question.

3.1.8 Answer: (A)

R's angle is given by $11\% \times 360 = 39.6°$. Answer (B) is simply a repetition of the 11 per cent figure; (C) appears to replace the 11 per cent by the ratio $11/(52 + 32 + 5)$. In answer (D) it seems that 11 has been divided by 360 but then multiplied by 100 to give an answer that is hopelessly small.

3.1.9 Answer: (D)

All the others are standard procedures in tabulation. While there may be rare occasions when maximum accuracy is retained, it is unusual because it makes the table very unapproachable and hard to grasp.

3.1.10 Answer: (C)

The x- and y-coordinates where two graphs meet must satisfy both of their equations and hence give the roots of their simultaneous solution. The points where they meet the axes give the values they take when x or $y = 0$, and the points where they meet $x = y$ simply give their simultaneous solutions with that equation. (D) is incorrect – graphical solution of equations is widely used.

3.1.11 When $y = 0$ (i.e. on the x-axis), $x = 8/5 = 1.6$. When $x = 0$ (i.e. on the y-axis), $y = -8$.

3.1.12 $4y = -3x + 12$, so $y = (-3x/4) + (12/4)$ and the slope $= -3/4 = -0.75$.

3.1.13 The correct answers are as follows:

Let the linear relationship be $C = a + bX$

(A) When $X = 60$, $C = 1,200$		Correct
(B) Hence $1,200 = a + 60b$		Correct
(C) When $X = 80$, $C = 1,900$		Correct
(D) Hence $1,900 = a + 80b$		Correct
(E) Subtracting gives $700 = 140b$		Incorrect: $80b$ minus $60b$ actually gives $20b$
(F) Hence $b = 140/700 = 0.2$		Incorrect: it is upside down and should be $700/140$
(G) Hence $a = 1,200 + 60 \times 0.2 = 1,212$		Incorrect: the 60×0.2 should be subtracted

3.1.14 The correct categories are:

(A) Age of 5 years   Continuous
(B) Time of 2.5 hours   Continuous
(C) Output of 12,000 kg Continuous
(D) Output of 5,000 units Discrete

3.1.15 The cumulative frequency distribution is as follows:

Number absent	Frequency	Cumulative frequency
0	10	10
1	15	25
2	7	32
3	4	36
4	2	38

3.1.16 (A) 155 were paid less than £300.
(B) 50 were paid more than £200.
(C) 30 were paid between £200 and £300.

3.1.17 The correct heights are as follows:

Weight	Frequency	Height of bar
0–10	65	65
10–20	89	89
20–40	140	70
40–60	76	38
60–100	64	16

3.1.18 All the answers are correct *except* for (C).

3.1.19 The correct angles are given by 360° × the appropriate percentage:

Categories	%	Angle
A	42	151
B	38	137
C	15	54
D	5	18

3.1.20 The correct associations are as follows:

Bar charts	Examples
(A) Simple	Q
(B) Multiple	P
(C) Compound	R

✓ Solutions to Part 3.2

3.2.1 Chocolate on its own gives a bar height of 240. Putting a bar for toffee on top of this raises the height by a further 120, to a total of 360. The 70 added by apple raises the height to 430 and finally banana takes it up a further 30 to give an overall bar height of 460.

Answers:

(A) 240
(B) 360
(C) 430
(D) 460.

3.2.2 The bar clearly shows the total sale in 1995 and additionally enables us to see the relative importance of the various fillings. Without the bars for the other years we cannot make comparisons from one year to the next so, although statements (B) and (D) are correct they cannot be deduced from the chart. (E) is incorrect because toffee is more popular than apple. The correct answers are (A), (C) and (F).

3.2.3 Multiple bar chart showing sales of pies

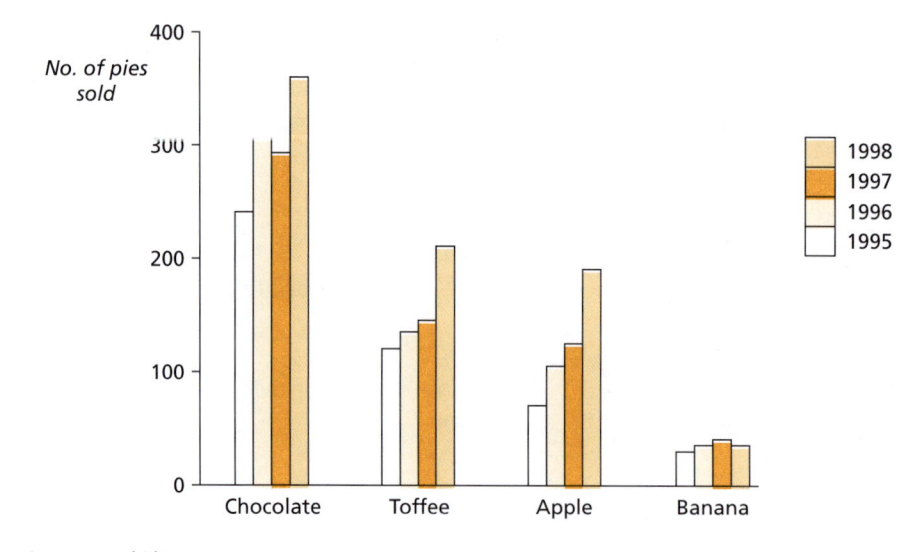

Answer: (A)

3.2.4 The key shows the various years and (E) is the sales of chocolate in 1998.

Answers:

(A) 1998
(B) 1997
(C) 1996
(D) 1995
(E) 360.

3.2.5 Sales in chocolate dipped in 1997, sales of banana fell in 1998 and total sales rose quite markedly over the period so (R), (T) and (V) are all incorrect. (S) and (U) are the correct answers.

Solutions to Part 3.3

3.3.1

Sales	Frequency
10–14	6
15–19	4
20–24	10
25–29	5
30–34	14
35–39	6
40–44	4
45–49	1

3.3.2

Sales	Frequency	Cumulative frequency
10 and under 15	6	G = 6
15 and under 20	12	H = 18
20 and under 25	17	I = 35
25 and under 30	7	J = 42

3.3.3 In a cumulative frequency diagram, cumulative frequencies are plotted (vertically) on the upper limits of the corresponding intervals (horizontally). The cumulative frequency of the very bottom limit (of 10 in this case) is always zero.

(K) 10
(L) 15
(M) 20
(N) 25
(O) 30
(P) 7
(Q) 23
(R) 36
(S) 40

3.3.4 Twenty-three people out of the sales force of 40 made less than 20 sales so the percentage is $100 \times 23/40 = 57.5$

Solutions to Part 3.4

3.4.1 (A) The first step is to calculate the minimum value in the range – use the = MIN function to do this with the formula = MIN(B4:H7). In the sample solution here this formula has been entered into cell B9.

On the assumption that we will have 10 data points (or intervals) on the chart the following formula is required in cell B10.
= B9 + (MAX($B$4:$H$7) − $B$9)*0.1
This formula should be copied through to cell B19.

The frequency function can now be applied to this range. The formula below is required in cell c9 through c19. As the frequency function is an array function the range c9:c19 must be selected before entering the formula. Then the following is put into cell c9:

= FREQUENCY(B4:H7,B9:B19)

To enter this formula hold down the CTRL key and the SHIFT key and then press ENTER. The figure below shows the results you should have.

	A	B	C	D	E	F	G	H
1	No. of people passing through an airport terminal per day over a 4 week period							
2	All nos. in thousands							
3		Mon	Tues	Wed	Thur	Fri	Sat	Sun
4	Week 1	122	177	103	161	202	115	147
5	Week 2	178	133	109	125	106	139	164
6	Week 3	124	191	152	145	140	169	153
7	Week 4	159	154	113	144	167	128	149
8								
9		103	1					
10		112.9	2					
11		122.8	3					
12		132.7	3					
13		142.6	3					
14		152.5	5					
15		162.4	4					
16		172.3	3					
17		182.2	2					
18		192.1	1					
19		202	1					

(B) A histogram chart is produced by selecting the data in the range c9:c19, clicking on the chart icon and selecting a bar chart. The data in column B can be selected as the x-axis labels and to make the bars in the chart touch each other and select FORMAT DATA SERIES and select the OPTIONS tab. Set the gap width to zero. The resulting chart is shown below.

(C) The cumulative frequency can put into the range D9 through D19. Into D9 make a reference to cell C9
= c9
In cell D10 enter the formula.
= D9 + C10
And copy this through to cell D19. The results are shown below:

	A	B	C	D	E	F	G	H
1	No. of people passing through an airport terminal per day over a 4 week period							
2	All nos. in thousands							
3		Mon	Tues	Wed	Thur	Fri	Sat	Sun
4	Week 1	122	177	103	161	202	115	147
5	Week 2	178	133	109	125	106	139	164
6	Week 3	124	191	152	145	140	169	153
7	Week 4	159	154	113	144	167	128	149
8								
9		103	1	1				
10		112.9	2	3				
11		122.8	3	6				
12		132.7	3	9				
13		142.6	3	12				
14		152.5	5	17				
15		162.4	4	21				
16		172.3	3	24				
17		182.2	2	26				
18		192.1	1	27				
19		202	1	28				

(D) To produce an ogive of the cumulative frequency the ranges B9 through B19 and D9 through D19 are plotted onto an XY chart. To select two ranges that are not adjacent select the first range and then hold down the CTRL key whilst selecting the second range. Then click on the chart icon and select XY chart. Choose an option with lines and the resulting ogive chart is shown below.

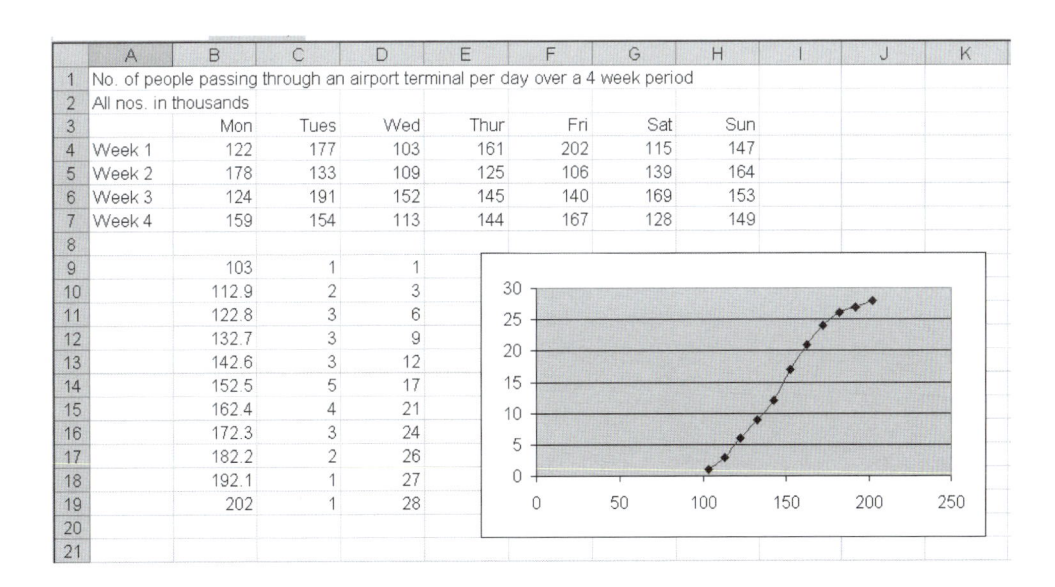

	A	B	C	D	E	F	G	H	I	J	K
1	No. of people passing through an airport terminal per day over a 4 week period										
2	All nos. in thousands										
3		Mon	Tues	Wed	Thur	Fri	Sat	Sun			
4	Week 1	122	177	103	161	202	115	147			
5	Week 2	178	133	109	125	106	139	164			
6	Week 3	124	191	152	145	140	169	153			
7	Week 4	159	154	113	144	167	128	149			
8											
9		103	1	1							
10		112.9	2	3							
11		122.8	3	6							
12		132.7	3	9							
13		142.6	3	12							
14		152.5	5	17							
15		162.4	4	21							
16		172.3	3	24							
17		182.2	2	26							
18		192.1	1	27							
19		202	1	28							
20											
21											

4

Descriptive Statistics

Descriptive Statistics

LEARNING OUTCOMES

After completing this chapter you should be able to calculate and explain the following summary statistics for grouped data:

- arithmetic mean;
- median (graphical method only);
- mode (graphical method only);
- range;
- semi-interquartile range (graphical method only);
- standard deviation;
- variance;
- coefficient of variation;
- using Excel for descriptive statistics.

4.1 Introduction

In Chapter 3 we saw how a set of raw data can be made more meaningful by forming it into a frequency distribution. Often it is advantageous to go further and to calculate values that represent or describe the whole data set; such values are called descriptive statistics. The most important are the various averages that aim to give a typical or representative value for the distribution. The other major group of descriptive statistics are the measures of spread, which tell us how variable the data are.

4.2 The arithmetic mean

Most people would understand an 'average' to be the value obtained by dividing the sum of the values in question by the number of values. This measure is the *arithmetic mean*, or, where there is no possibility of confusion, simply the *mean*. Further, if the data being considered is sample data, we refer to the *sample mean* to distinguish it from the mean of the population from which the sample is drawn.

To understand the notation, consider the following example.

Example 4.2.1

A shopkeeper is about to put his shop up for sale. As part of the details of the business, he wishes to quote the average weekly takings. The takings in each of the last 6 weeks are:

£1,120   £990   £1,040   £1,030   £1,105   £1,015

Determine the mean weekly takings that the shopkeeper could quote.

Solution

If the weekly takings are denoted by the variable x, then the sample mean value of x is written as $\bar{x}$, pronounced 'x-bar'. Thus:

$$\bar{x} = \frac{\text{Sum of the values of } x}{\text{Number of values of } x}$$

or $\bar{x} = \frac{\Sigma x}{n}$

where Σ, a Greek capital letter 'sigma', is the mathematical symbol for 'add up', and n is the number of values of x. In this example:

$$\bar{x} = \frac{1,120 + 990 + 1,040 + 1,030 + 1,105 + 1,015}{6} = \frac{6,300}{6} = 1050.$$

The shopkeeper could therefore quote a sample mean weekly takings figure of £1,050.

As we can see, this formula is very easy to apply and, as indicated above, merely reflects the arithmetical procedures most people would recognise as the determination of an average. It will, however, need some modification before it can be used to determine the mean from a frequency distribution, a form in which many data sets appear.

Example 4.2.2

A company is implementing an efficiency drive and, as part of a leaflet it is to distribute to its employees, it wishes to point out the average daily absenteeism rate. The following data is collated from the records of a sample of 200 working days: compute the sample mean number of absentees per day.

Number of absentees per day (x)	Number of days
0	9
1	28
2	51
3	43
4	29
5	18
6	10
7	7
8	5

Solution

It should be noted that the 'number of days' column simply gives the frequency of the corresponding x values, and so we shall denote this quantity by f. Now, to find the sample mean, the above formula can be applied in a straightforward manner:

$$\bar{x} = \frac{\Sigma x}{n}$$

$$= \frac{\overbrace{(0+0+0+0+0+0+0+0+0)}^{9 \text{ values of } 0} + \overbrace{(1+1+1+\cdots+1)}^{28 \text{ values of } 1} + \overbrace{(2+2+2+\cdots+2)}^{51 \text{ values of } 2} + \cdots + \overbrace{(8+8+8+8+8)}^{5 \text{ values of } 8}}{200}$$

Thus,

$$= \frac{(9 \times 0) + (28 \times 1) + (51 \times 2) + (43 \times 3) + (29 \times 4) + (18 \times 5) + (10 \times 6) + (7 \times 7) + (5 \times 8)}{200}$$

$$= \frac{614}{200} = 3.07$$

The mean number of absentees in the sample is 3.07 per day.

Note how, in general, each x-value is multiplied by its corresponding frequency, f, and the products are then summed. That is, we evaluate the product fx for each x-value and then add all the values of fx. As we are denoting addition by 'Σ', this sum can be written Σfx. The formula for the sample mean from a frequency distribution is thus:

$$\bar{x} = \frac{\Sigma fx}{\Sigma f}$$

The denominator of this expression, Σf, is simply the sum of the frequencies, which is, of course, the same as n in the earlier expression for x.

Example 4.2.3

Find the arithmetic mean for the following distribution, which shows the number of employees absent per day (originally given as Example 3.5.2 in the previous chapter):

No. of employees absent	No. of days (frequency)
2	2
3	4
4	3
5	4
6	3
7	3
8	3

Solution

x	f	fx
2	2	4
3	4	12
4	3	12
5	4	20
6	3	18
7	3	21
8	3	24
	$\Sigma f = 22$	$\Sigma fx = 111$

Mean, $\bar{x} = \dfrac{\Sigma fx}{\Sigma f} = \dfrac{111}{22} = 5.045 = 5$ employees, to nearest whole number.

This formula, which is given in the *Business Mathematics* exam, will now prove adequate for all our purposes. In order to illustrate how to deal with a minor problem that can, however, arise and to demonstrate a systematic way of performing and setting out the calculations involved, we give a further example.

Example 4.2.4

As part of its preparation for a wage negotiation, the personnel manager of a company has collated the following data from a sample of payslips. She wishes to be able to use the average weekly wage figure in the negotiations. Evaluate the mean of the sample.

Weekly wage (£)	Number of employees (f)
180–under 185	41
185–under 190	57
190–under 195	27
195–under 200	23
200–under 205	15
205–under 210	7

Solution

The extra difficulty in this problem is clear: as the data has been collated into classes, a certain amount of detail has been lost and hence the values of the variable x to be used in the calculation of are not clearly specified. Short of actually having the raw data, the actual wages of the employees in the sample, we can only approximate the value of $\bar{x}$. To do this, we adopt the obvious approach of taking x to be a representative value of each class, the most plausible being the mid-point. Doing this, we have

x	f	fx
182.50	41	7,482.5
187.50	57	10,687.5
192.50	27	5,197.5
197.50	23	4,542.5
202.50	15	3,037.5
207.50	7	1,452.5
	170	32,400.0

It is advisable to set out such statistical calculations in the way shown: very often figures have to be summed, and so they are best arranged in columns. Further, if you are using a calculator with a memory key, each '*fx*' figure can be added into the memory as it is calculated, so that the total 'Σfx' is ready for use when the memory total is recalled.

Now we have:

$$\bar{x} = \dfrac{\Sigma fx}{\Sigma f} = \dfrac{32,000}{170} = 190.58, \text{ approx.}$$

Hence, the manager can use an average weekly wage of £190.58 in the negotiations.

Before moving on, it is worth recalling that there are a number of ways of classifying data into grouped frequency distributions. Hence, a set of weekly wages expressed in whole numbers of £ sterling could be grouped:

180–under 185, 185–under 190 and so on (as in Example 4.2.4)
or 180–184, 185–189 and so on
or 179.5–184.5, 184.5–189.5 and so on

Although it has been stated earlier that the first method is recommended, other types may be encountered, and so we shall look briefly at how to deal with them when calculating means, etc.

Where there is an apparent 'gap', it can be 'closed'. Thus, with salaries, which could in fact be measured to the nearest £0.01, a class of 180–184 is actually the same as:

- either 180–under 185 (if any amounts over the £ figure have been ignored);
- or 179.5–under 184.5 (if arithmetical rounding has been used).

Where there is an overlap, such as with 184.50, 189.50, etc. in the third case, the equivalent form is

- 179.5–under 184.5

and so on, provided that 184.5, 189.5, etc. are counted in the lower class each time.

Example 4.2.5

Find the arithmetic mean for the following distribution of output levels of product Q (originally given as Example 3.6.1 in the previous chapter):

Output of Q (kg)	No. of days (frequency)
350–under 360	4
360–370	6
370–380	5
380–390	4
390–400	3

Solution

Mid-point X	Frequency f	fx
355	4	1,420
365	6	2,190
375	5	1,875
385	4	1,540
395	3	1,185
	$\Sigma f = 22$	$\Sigma fx = 8,210$

$$\text{Mean}, \bar{x} = \frac{\Sigma fx}{\Sigma f} = \frac{8,210}{22} = 373.18 \text{ kg (to two d.p.)}$$

> The formula for the arithmetic mean will be given in your exam.

4.3 The median

So far we have dealt with the most commonly used average, the mean. We now consider another widely used average, the median.

In Example 4.2.4, we computed a mean weekly wage of £190.60 which the personnel manager could quote in the wage negotiations. An impartial commentator could argue (and the manager might agree) that this is a rather high figure for a supposedly representative average. As 98 out of the sampled 170 (i.e. 58 per cent) actually earn less than £190 per week, it may well be that in excess of 60 per cent of the workforce earn less than the 'average' of £190.60 per week. If we look at this wage distribution, shown in Figure 4.1, it

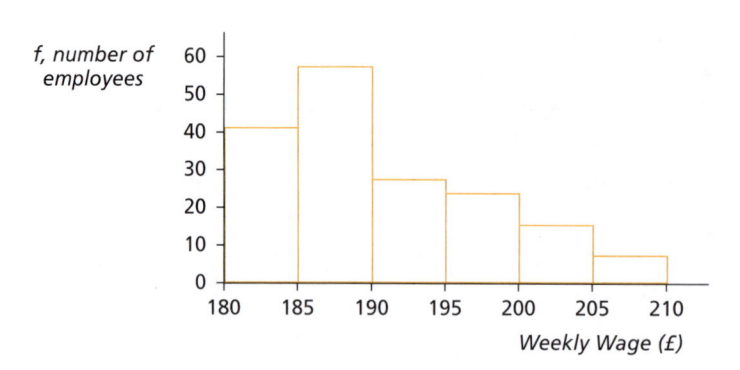

Figure 4.1 Histogram for Example 4.2.4

is easy to see the cause of this phenomenon. The two highest frequencies occur at the lowest wage classes and then the frequencies decrease slowly as the wages increase. The relatively small number of large wages has caused the mean value to be so large. Distributions of this type are said to have a long tail or to be skewed. It is a criticism of the mean as an average that very skewed distributions can have mean values that appear unrepresentative, in that they are higher or lower than a great deal of the distribution.

To address this problem, we introduce another measure of average, the *median*. This is defined as the middle of a set of values, when arranged in ascending (or descending) order. This overcomes the above problem, since the median has half the distribution above it, and half below. We leave the wage distribution for now, and look at a simpler example.

Example 4.3.1

Shop A's weekly takings are given by the following sample over six weeks. The sample has an arithmetic mean of £1,050.

£1,120   £990   £1,040   £1,030   £1,105   £1,015

A prospective purchaser of the business notices that the mean is higher than the takings in four of the 6 weeks. Calculate the median for him.

Solution

First of all, we arrange the takings figures in ascending order:

£990   £1,015   £1,030   £1,040   £1,105   £1,120

The question now is: what is the middle number of a list of six? With a little thought, you can see that there are two 'middle' values, the third and fourth. The median is thus taken to be the mean of these two values.

$$\text{Median} = \frac{(1{,}030 + 1{,}040)}{2} = 1{,}035$$

Hence, the median weekly takings figure that the prospective purchaser could quote is £1,035.

After this example, it is clear that, in the case of an odd number of values, the determination of the median is even easier, as there is a clear *single* middle item in an odd number of values. In general, if there are n observations, the position of the median is given by $(n+1)/2$. With six observations, this gives $7/2 = 3.5$, which is the position halfway between the third and fourth observations. In the case of frequency distributions, the determination of the median is not as straightforward, but can be illustrated by returning to the earlier wage distribution.

Example 4.3.2

(a) Calculate the median of the following data:

25 52 18 43 27

(b) Calculate the median of the data on staff absences (hint: use cumulative frequencies).

No. of employees absent	No. of days (f)
2	2
3	4
4	3
5	4
6	3
7	3
8	3

Solution

(a) First write the data in order of magnitude:

18 25 27 43 52

The median is in the third position [check: $(5 + 1)/2 = 3$] and is therefore 27.

(b) Find cumulative frequencies:

No. of employees absent	No. of days (f)	Cumulative frequency
2	2	2
3	4	6
4	3	9
5	4	13
6	3	16
7	3	19
8	3	22

There are 22 observations, so the position of the median is given by $(22 + 1)/2 = 11.5$, that is, the median is midway between the eleventh and twelfth observations. From the cumulative frequencies it is clear that both the eleventh and twelfth observations have value 5, so the median is 5.

Example 4.3.3

Using the data of Example 4.2.4, find the more representative median weekly wage figure that the personnel manager could argue in the wage negotiations.

Solution

It is clear that the middle wage figure in a set of 170 is halfway between the 85th and 86th. Unfortunately, we do not have the raw data from which the frequency distribution was compiled, and so cannot tell what these two wage figures are. It is therefore necessary to make an assumption about the wage distribution and to deduce an approximate value from the assumption.

If we consider the wage values to be evenly spread throughout their classes, then we can draw the ogive as in Chapter 3 and then estimate the median from a construction based on this ogive. First of all, we need the cumulative frequency distribution. Figure 4.2 shows the ogive of this cumulative frequency distribution.

Weekly wage (£): (less than)	Cumulative frequency
185	41
190	98
195	125
200	148
205	163
210	170

Now, as the median has the property that half of the wage figures lie below it, and half above it, the construction shown on the ogive, drawn at a cumulative frequency of 85 (half of 170), gives the approximate median weekly wage as £188.80. This value is arguably more representative of the sample than the earlier mean value, precisely because half the wages lie below and half above it.

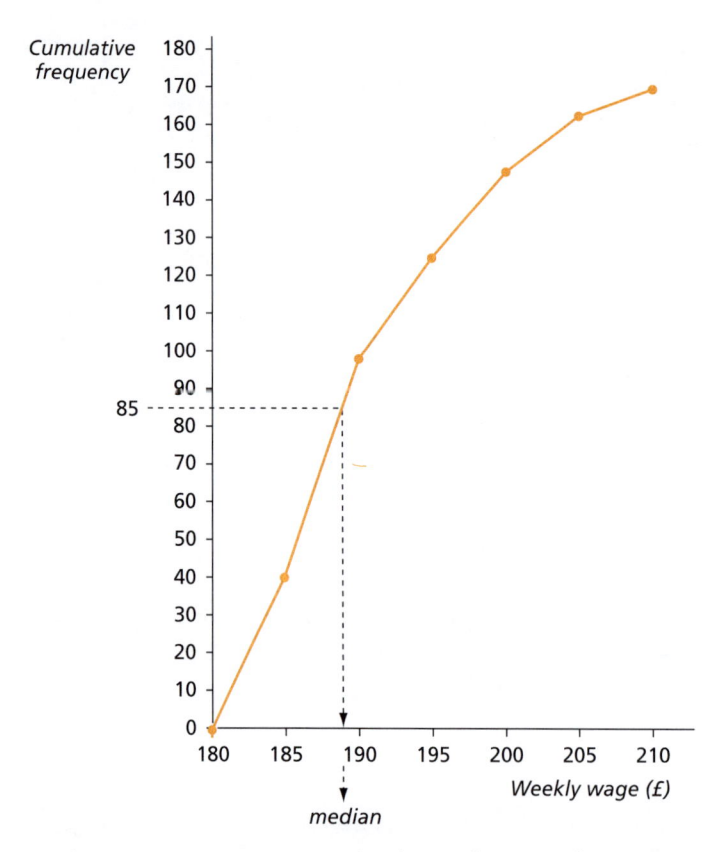

Figure 4.2 Ogive: wage distribution for Example 4.3.3

Example 4.3.4

Draw the ogive for the following data on the output of product Q and find the median from the ogive.

Output of Q (kg)	No. of days (frequency)
350–under 360	4
360–370	6
370–380	5
380–390	4
390–400	3

Solution

Output of Q (kg)	No. of days (frequency)	Cumulative frequency
350–under 360	4	4
360–370	6	10
370–380	5	15
380–390	4	19
390–400	3	22

The ogive is given in Figure 4.3.

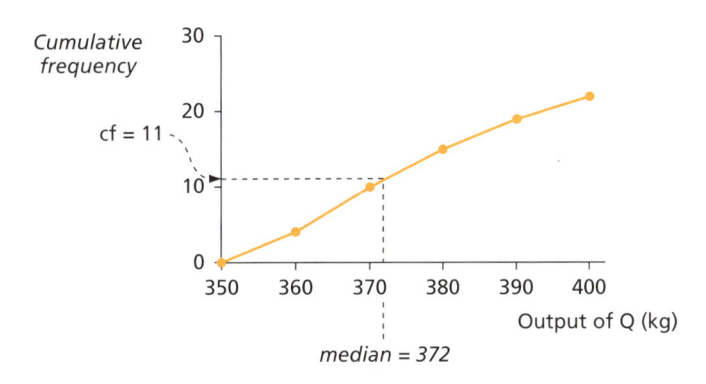

Figure 4.3 Ogive for Example 4.3.4

Total frequency is 22, so cumulative frequency of the median is $22/2 = 11$. From the ogive, the median = 372 kg.

> In your exam you cannot be asked to draw the ogive so you just have to know how to obtain the median from it. It is possible to calculate the median but this is not required in your syllabus and the formula is not given.

4.4 The mode

The *mode* or *modal value* of a data set is that value that occurs most often, and it is the remaining most widely used average. The determination of this value, when you have raw data to deal with, consists simply of a counting process to find the most frequently occurring value, and so we do not dwell on this case here, but move on to look at frequency distributions.

Example 4.4.1

Find the mode for the following distributions:

(a)

Complaints per week	No. of weeks
0	5
1	12
2	7
3	2
4	1

136 STUDY MATERIAL C3

(b)

Weekly wage (£)	No. of employees
180–under 185	41
185–190	57
190–195	27
195–200	23
200–205	15
205–210	7

Solution

(a) The mode is the value with the highest frequency, so here the mode is one complaint per week.

(b) The frequency distribution in the second case shows that the *modal class* (that one with the highest frequency) is £185 to under £190. Figure 4.4 shows a way of finding a single value to represent the mode: basically, the construction shown weights the mode towards the second most frequent class neighbouring the modal class, the one to the left in this case. The figure shows that *the modal weekly wage is approximately £186.60*.

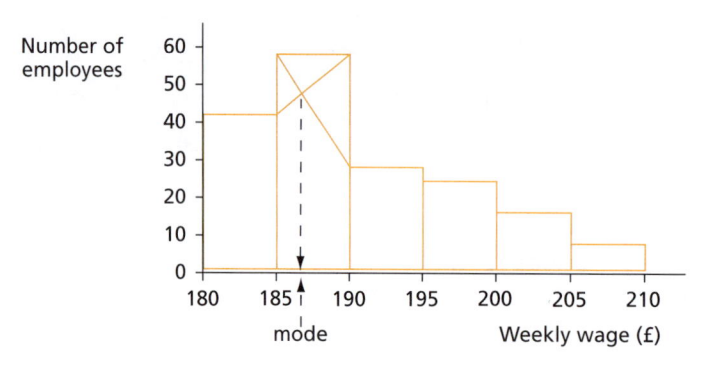

Figure 4.4 Construction to approximate the mode – Example 4.4.2

This construction can still be used when there are unequal class intervals.

Example 4.4.2

Find the mode of the following data on the output of product Q.

Output of Q (kg)	No. of days (frequency)
350–under 360	4
360–370	6
370–380	5
380–390	4
390–400	3

Solution

A histogram for the above data is shown in Figure 4.5.

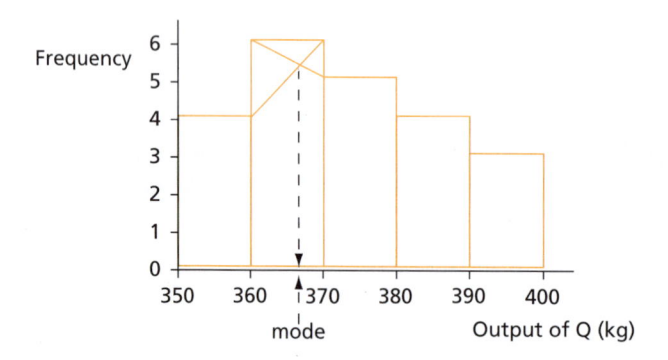

Figure 4.5 Histogram showing output of Q for Example 4.4.2

From the histogram, the mode is 366.6 kg (approximately).

> In your exam you cannot be asked to draw the histogram so you just have to know how to obtain the mode from it. It is possible to calculate the mode but this is not required in your syllabus and the formula is not given.

4.5 A comparison of the three averages

As our earlier discussion of the weekly wage distribution indicates, it is often just as important to use a measure of average appropriate to the situation as it is to evaluate the measure accurately. In this section we further discuss the relative merits and demerits of the three averages encountered in this chapter.

It is arguable that the mode is the least useful and important of the three. There are many distributions that have no definite single 'peak' in their histograms, and so it is difficult to attribute any sensible meaning to a modal value in such cases. Further, the mode is often unrepresentative of the whole data set: it may occur at one extremity of a skewed distribution or, at the very least, it takes no account of a high proportion of the data, only representing the most common value. All in all, it is fair to say that, in the vast majority of cases, the mode renders only a general description of one feature of a distribution, and is a relatively unimportant average when compared with the median or the mean.

The mean, on the other hand, has a number of features that usually make it the most appropriate and representative measure. First of all, it has the great advantage of being what most people recognise as 'the average'. It is therefore most easily communicated to non-specialists. Second, the mean is the only one of the three that takes account of all the data: like the mode, the median ignores some of a distribution by concentrating only on the middle part. The mean is thus arguably the most representative of *all* of a distribution. Finally, the mean is the measure that is most useful for further statistical analysis.

Having said that, there are some circumstances in which one might consider the median to be more appropriate than the mean. We have already encountered one important such occasion in the skewed wage distribution of Example 4.3.3.

Data is said to be positively skewed when the tail lies in the positive direction (i.e. to the right) and negatively skewed when the tail lies to the left. The mean is always pulled towards the tail, the mode towards the opposite steep slope, and the median lies between the two. So, for positively skewed data such as the wages example (and wage distributions generally) the mean will tend to overstate the average, and the mode will underestimate it.

For negatively skewed data the opposite is usually true, with the mean being too small and the mode too large.

In general, the median can often be argued to be the most representative average of a highly skewed distribution.

Another instance in which we may doubt the suitability of the mean is when we are dealing with discrete data. In Example 4.2.2 we saw an absenteeism distribution which has

Mean	3.07 absentees/day
Median	3 absentees/day
Mode	2 absentees/day

It is impossible to have 3.07 absentees, whereas the other two values are attainable. This is a common problem when dealing with means of discrete distributions, which sometimes leads to the median being used.

There is no hard and fast rule here, and each such case must be treated on its merits. Rounding the mean off to a 'possible' value of three absentees per day only represents a very small (around 2 per cent) change in its value. As this now agrees with the median, this common value can be accepted as the most appropriate measure. The decision would not be so easy with a discrete variable with a sample mean of 1.4 and median and mode both 3: rounding the mean to 1 would involve a large (almost 30 per cent) change, and so you would have to accept an unattainable mean value of 1.4 or the common median/modal value of 3 as the 'average'. A final category in which you might not use the mean is illustrated in Example 4.5.1.

Example 4.5.1

An estate agent wishing to quote the average regional house price in his advertising brochures collates the following data on the houses he has helped to sell in the last 6 months:

House price (£'000)	Number of houses
Under 40	5
40–under 45	9
45–under 50	20
50–under 60	25
60–under 80	18
80–under 120	9
120 and over	6

Solution

We have already seen that, in such grouped frequency distributions, all three measures of average are of necessity only approximations. The two open-ended classes in this distribution, however, impose an extra source of inaccuracy in the evaluation of the mean: in order to obtain x-values for use in the formula for $\bar{x}$. We have to assume closing values for these classes. Plausible examples of these values might be:

30–under 40
120–under 150

Of course, the values chosen affect the x-values (the mid-points of the various classes) and thus the value of $\bar{x}$. The estimates of the median and modal values are unaffected by this choice as they both occur towards the centre of this distribution.

Again, there is no rule for resolving this dilemma. Most people would be willing to overlook the extra inaccuracy in the mean value, provided that plausible closing values for the open-ended classes are available (as is the case here). If, however, there was some doubt or debate over the closing values, then the median would arguably be the better measure.

4.6 Measures of spread

Having obtained an average value to represent a set of data, it is natural to question the extent to which the single value is representative of the whole set. Through a simple example we shall see that part of the answer to this lies in how 'spread out' the individual values are around the average. In particular, we shall study six measures of *spread,* or *dispersion,* as it is sometimes called:

- the range;
- the interquartile range;
- the quartile deviation;
- the mean absolute deviation;
- the standard deviation;
- the coefficient of variation.

4.7 The range

The measure of spread that is most associated with the mode is the range, since both statistics are relatively quick and easy to obtain, so they are well suited to initial exploration of the data. As we shall see later, neither of them are very useful statistics in most other circumstances.

The range is defined as the highest value minus the lowest value – but this can be misleading. Where the data is arranged in classes:

Range = Upper most interval limit − Lowest interval limit

Where the data is not grouped, the range is best viewed as the number of values from the very bottom to the very top and is given by:

Range = Highest value − Lowest value + 1

These apparently different definitions amount in practice to the same thing. If we regard the highest value as being at the centre of an interval of unit width, then the uppermost interval limit is given by the highest value plus 0.5. Similarly, the lowest interval limit will be given by the lowest value minus 0.5. Consequently, the value of the range is the same whichever method is used.

The following example will illustrate the calculation of the range, and will demonstrate why such a measure may be needed.

Example 4.7.1

A recently retired couple are considering investing their pension lump sums in the purchase of a small shop. Two suitably sited premises, A and B, are discovered. The average weekly takings of the two shops are quoted as £1,050 and £1,080 for A and B, respectively. Upon further investigation, the investors discover that the averages quoted come from the following recent weekly takings figures:

Shop A:	£1,120	£990	£1,040	£1,030	£1,105	£1,015
Shop B:	£1,090	£505	£915	£1,005	£2,115	£850

Advise the couple.

Solution

You can easily check that the 'averages' quoted are, in fact, the means of the two samples. Based on these two figures alone, it might seem sensible for the couple to prefer shop B to shop A, but a glance at the actual data casts doubt on this conclusion. It is clear that the values for shop B are far more spread out than those for shop A, thereby making the mean for shop B arguably less representative. This difference is illustrated well by the ranges of the two sets:

Range of A = Highest − Lowest + 1 = 1,120 − 990 + 1 = £131
Range of B = 2,115 − 505 + 1 = £1,611

It can be seen that the much larger range in the latter case is almost entirely due to the single value '£2,115'. The retired couple would therefore be well advised to look at larger samples of weekly takings figures to see if this value is some sort of freak and whether shop B does indeed generate higher weekly takings on average.

4.8 The interquartile range; the quartile deviation

The measure of spread most associated with the median is the quartile deviation, which we shall now consider. To do this, we begin by defining:

- the *third quartile* (denoted Q_3) as the value which has 75 per cent of the data below it; and
- the *first quartile* (Q_1) as the value with 25 per cent of the data below it.

The required measure, the interquartile range, is then the range of the middle 50 per cent of the data, or $Q_3 - Q_1$.

It will be noted that, if we referred to the second quartile (Q_2), we should simply be dealing with the median.

Example 4.8.1

After receiving complaints from trade union representatives concerning the disparity between higher- and lower-paid workers in his company, the personnel manager of the company asks for information on the current wage structure. He is given the following data:

Basic weekly wage (£)	Number of employees
under 200	16
200–under 225	153
225–under 250	101
250–under 275	92
275–under 300	68
300 and over	50

The manager decides to calculate a statistical measure of the spread of these data. Perform this calculation.

Solution

If we had the raw data, it would be a relatively simple counting process to find the wage figures 25 per cent and 75 per cent the way along the list, and thus to find the range or the interquartile range. As the data is presented, however, the range is unsuitable, as there are 50 employees in the open-ended upper class, any one of which could seriously distort the measure. Also, the interquartile range cannot be found by a process of mere counting.

In fact, to determine the interquartile range, we adopt the same approach as we did for the median. First of all, we assume that the wage values are evenly spread throughout their classes, and draw the ogive. The necessary cumulative frequency distribution is:

Basic weekly wage (£) (less than)	Cumulative frequency
200	16
225	169
250	270
275	362
300	430

It will be noted that it is unnecessary to close the final class in order to draw the ogive, and so we do not do so. The ogive is shown in Figure 4.6. Alternatively, a sensible closing value, such as £325, could be selected and an extra point, with cumulative frequency 480, added to the ogive.

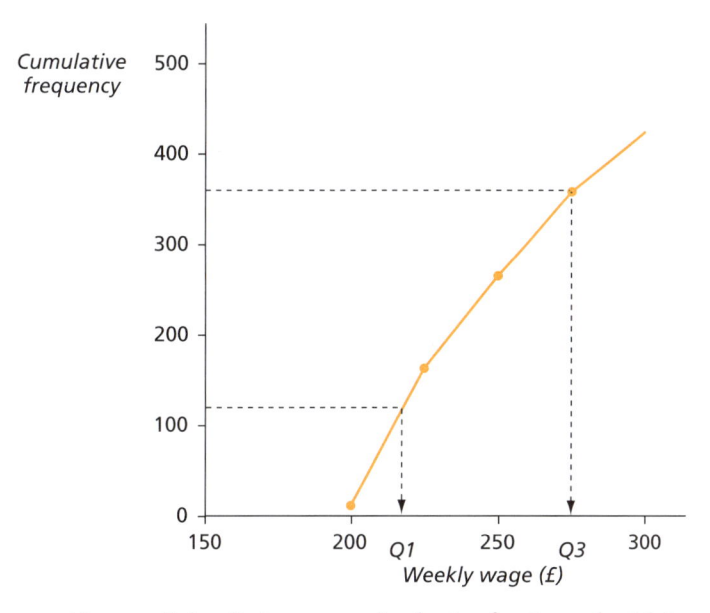

Figure 4.6 Ogive: wage distribution for Example 4.8.1.

We now note that the total frequency is 480, and so, from the constructions shown on the ogive, we have the following approximations:

Q_3 (corresponding to a cumulative frequency of $\frac{3}{4}$ of 480, or 360) = £274

Q_1 (corresponding to a cumulative frequency of $\frac{1}{4}$ of 480, or 120) = £217

and thus:

Interquartile range = £274 − £217 = £57.

Thus, the manager could use an approximate measure of the spread of wages of the middle 50 per cent of the workforce of £57.

There is a very closely related measure here, the *quartile deviation*, which is half the interquartile range. In the above example, the quartile deviation is £28.50. In practice, the quartile deviation is used rather more than the interquartile range. If you rearrange $Q_3 - Q_1$ as $(Q_3 - M) + (M - Q_1)$ you will see that the two expressions in brackets give the distances from the quartiles to the median and then dividing by two gives the average distance from the quartiles to the median. So we can say that approximately 50 per cent of the observations lie within ±one quartile deviation of the median.

Example 4.8.2

Using the data on the output of product Q (see Example 4.3.4), find the quartiles, the interquartile range and the quartile deviation from the ogive (Figure 4.3).

Solution

The total frequency = 22, so the cumulative frequency of Q_1 is $22/4 = 5.5$, and the cumulative frequency of Q_3 is $(3 \times 22/4) = 16.5$
From the ogive, $Q_1 = 362.5$ kg and $Q_3 = 383.5$ kg
Hence, the interquartile range = $383.5 - 362 = 21.5$ kg, and the quartile deviation = $21.5 \div 2 = 10.75$ kg.

4.9 Deciles

Just as quartiles divide a cumulative distribution into quarters, deciles divide a cumulative distribution into tenths. Thus:

the first decile has 10 per cent of values below it and 90 per cent above it,
the second decile has 20 per cent of values below it and 80 per cent above it and so on.

The use and evaluation of deciles can best be illustrated through an example.

Example 4.9.1

As a promotional example, a mail-order company has decided to give free gifts to its highest-spending customers. It has been suggested that the highest-spending 30 per cent get a gift, while the highest-spending 10 per cent get an additional special gift. The following distribution of a sample of spending patterns over the past year is available:

Amount spent (£)	Number of customers spending this amount
under 50	37
50–under 100	59
100–under 150	42
150–under 200	20
200–under 300	13
300 and over	9

To which customers should the gift and the additional special gift be given?

Solution

We have to determine the ninth decile (90 per cent below it) and the seventh decile (70 per cent below it). These can be found in the same way as with quartiles, by reading from an ogive.

The cumulative frequency distribution (ignoring the last open-ended class) is:

Amount spent (less than, £)	Cumulative frequency
50	37
100	96
150	138
200	158
300	171

The ogive is shown in Figure 4.7.

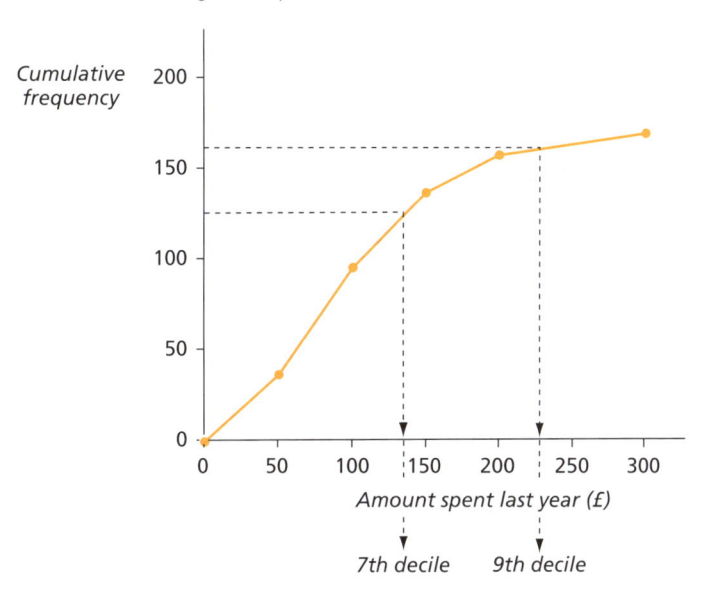

Figure 4.7 Ogive for Example 4.9.1

The ninth decile will correspond to a cumulative frequency of 162 (90 per cent of the total frequency, 180). From the ogive, this is: £230.

Similarly, the seventh decile corresponds to a cumulative frequency of 70 per cent of 180, that is 126. From the ogive, this is: £135.

Hence, in order to implement the suggestion, the company should give the free gift to those customers who have spent over £135 in the past year, and the additional free gift to those who have spent over £230.

Example 4.9.2

Using the data on the output of product Q (see Example 4.3.4), find the ninth decile from the ogive (Figure 4.3).

Solution

The cumulative frequency of the ninth decile is $0.9 \times 22 = 19.8$. From the ogive, the ninth decile is 392.5 kg (approximately).

> In your exam you cannot be asked to draw the ogive so you just have to know how to obtain the quartiles and percentiles from it. It is possible to calculate these statistics but this is not required in your syllabus and the formulae are not given.

4.10 The mean absolute deviation

If the mean is the average being used, then one very good way of measuring the amount of variability in the data is to calculate the extent to which the values differ from the mean. This is essentially the thinking behind the mean absolute deviation and the standard deviation (for which, see Section 4.11).

£1,120   £990   £1,040   £1,030   £1,105   £1,015

Example 4.10.1

Measure the spread of shop A's weekly takings (Example 4.7.1), given the following sample over 6 weeks. The sample has an arithmetic mean of £1,050.

Solution

A simple way of seeing how far a *single* value is from a (hopefully) representative average figure is to determine the difference between the two. In particular, if we are dealing with the mean, $\bar{x}$, this difference is known as the deviation from the mean or, more simply, the *deviation*. It is clear that, for a widely spread data set, the deviations of the individual values in the set will be relatively large. Similarly, narrowly spread data sets will have relatively small deviation values. We can therefore base our measure on the values of the deviations from the mean. In this case:

$$\text{Deviation} = x - \bar{x}$$

In this case, the values of $(x - \bar{x})$ are:

£70, −£60, −£10, −£20, £55, −£35

The obvious approach might now be to take the mean of these deviations as our measure. Unfortunately, it can be shown that this *always* turns out to be zero and so the mean deviation will not distinguish one distribution from another. The basic reason for this result is that the negative deviations, when summed, exactly cancel out the positive ones: we must therefore remove this cancellation effect.

One way to remove negative values is simply to ignore the signs, that is, to use the *absolute* values. In this case, the absolute deviations are:

$|(x - \bar{x})|$: £70, £60, £10, £20, £55, £35

The two vertical lines are the mathematical symbol for absolute values and are often referred to as 'modulus', or 'mod', of $(x - \bar{x})$ in this case. The mean of this list is now a measure of the spread in the data. It is known as the mean absolute deviation. Hence the mean absolute deviation of weekly takings for shop A is:

$$\frac{70 + 60 + 10 + 20 + 55 + 35}{6} = £41.67$$

Thus, our first measure of the spread of shop A's weekly takings is £41.67.

Example 4.10.2

Find the mean absolute deviation for the following data:

    2   3   5   7   8

Solution

The mean, $\bar{x}$, is $(2 + 3 + 5 + 7 + 8)/5 = 5$. So absolute deviations are given by subtracting 5 from each of the data and ignoring any negative signs. This gives values of:

    3   2   0   2   3

The mean absolute deviation is $(3 + 2 + 0 + 2 + 3)/5 = 2$.

> The mean deviation is not explicitly mentioned in your syllabus and is unlikely to be examined. We have included it as part of the theoretical build up to the standard deviation.

4.11 The standard deviation

In the preceding section, we solved the problem of negative deviations cancelling out positive ones by using absolute values. There is another way of 'removing' negative signs, namely by *squaring* the figures. If we do that, then we get another, very important, measure of spread, the *standard deviation*.

Example 4.11.1

Evaluate the measure of the spread in shop A's weekly takings (Example 4.7.1), using this new approach.

Solution

Recall that we have the deviations:

    $x - \bar{x}$: £70, −£60, −£10, −£20, £55, −£35

so, by squaring, we get:

    $(x - \bar{x})^2$: 4,900, 3,600, 100, 400, 3,025, 1,225

The mean of these squared deviations is:

$$\frac{13{,}250}{6} = 2{,}208.3$$

This is a measure of spread whose units are the square of those of the original data, because we squared the deviations. We thus take the square root to get back to the original units (£). Our measure of spread is therefore:

$$\sqrt{2208.3} = £46.99$$

This is known as the *standard deviation*, denoted by 's'. Its square, the intermediate step before square-rooting, is called the *variance*, s^2.

The formula that has been implicitly used here is:

$$s = \sqrt{\frac{\Sigma(x - \bar{x})^2}{n}}$$

Applying the same series of steps to the data in a frequency distribution will give us the corresponding formula in this case:

- square the deviations: $(x - \bar{x})^2$
- find the mean of the $(x - \bar{x})^2$ values occurring with frequencies denoted by f.

$$\frac{\Sigma f(x - \bar{x})^2}{n} \,(=s^2)$$

- Take the square root:

$$\sqrt{\frac{\Sigma(x - \bar{x})^2}{\Sigma f}} \,(=s)$$

In practice, this formula can turn out to be very tedious to apply. It can be shown that the following, more easily applicable, formula is the same as the one above:

$$s = \sqrt{\frac{\Sigma fx^2}{\Sigma f} - \left(\frac{\Sigma fx}{\Sigma f}\right)^2}$$

> This formula will be given in the *Business Mathematics* exam, with $\bar{x}$ in place of $\Sigma fx/\Sigma f$.

An example will now demonstrate a systematic way of setting out the computations involved with this formula.

Example 4.11.2

An analyst is considering two categories of company, X and Y, for possible investment. One of her assistants has compiled the following information on the price-earnings ratios of the shares of companies in the two categories over the past year.

Price-earnings ratios	Number of category X companies	Number of category Y companies
4.95–under 8.95	3	4
8.95–under 12.95	5	8
12.95–under 16.95	7	8
16.95–under 20.95	6	3
20.95–under 24.95	3	3
24.95–under 28.95	1	4

Compute the standard deviations of these two distributions and comment. (You are given that the means of the two distributions are 15.59 and 15.62, respectively.)

Solution

Concentrating first of all on category X, we see that we face the same problem as when we calculated the mean of such a distribution, namely that we have classified data, instead of individual values of x. Adopting a similar approach as before, we take the mid-point of each class:

x (mid-point)	x^2	f	fx	fx^2
6.95	48.3025	3	20.85	144.9075
10.95	119.9025	5	54.75	599.5125
14.95	223.5025	7	104.65	1,564.5175
18.95	359.1025	6	113.70	2,154.6150
22.95	526.7025	3	68.85	1,580.1075
26.95	726.3025	1	26.95	726.3025
		25	389.75	6,769.9625

Thus the standard deviation is:

$$s = \sqrt{\frac{\Sigma fx^2}{\Sigma f} - \left(\frac{\Sigma fx}{\Sigma f}\right)^2}$$

$$s = \sqrt{\frac{6{,}769.9625}{25} - \left(\frac{389.75}{25}\right)^2}$$

$$= \sqrt{270.7985 - 243.0481} = \sqrt{27.7504} = 5.27.$$

The standard deviation of the price-earnings ratios for category X is therefore 5.27. In the same way, you can verify that the standard deviation in the case of category Y is 6.29. These statistics again emphasise the wider spread in the category Y data than in the category X data. Note how a full degree of accuracy (four decimal places) is retained throughout the calculation in order to ensure an accurate final result.

The calculation for Y should be as for X above. In outline:

x (mid-point)	x^2	f	fx	fx^2
6.95	48.3025	4	27.80	193.210
...	...	...	...	...
...	...	...	...	...
26.95	726.3025	4	107.80	2,905.210
		30	468.50	8,503.075

$$s = \sqrt{(283.4358 - 243.8803)} = 6.289$$

Example 4.11.3

Using the data from Example 4.2.3 relating to absences from work, and the mean that you have already calculated, find the standard deviation.

No. of employees absent	No. of days (frequency)
2	2
3	4
4	3
5	4
6	3
7	3
8	3

It is probably easiest to calculate fx^2 by multiplying fx by x, for example, 2×4, 3×12, etc.

Solution

x	f	fx	fx²
2	2	4	8
3	4	12	36
4	3	12	48
5	4	20	100
6	3	18	108
7	3	21	147
8	3	24	192
	22	111	639

$$s = \sqrt{\frac{\Sigma fx^2}{\Sigma f} - \bar{x}^2} = \sqrt{\frac{639}{22} - \left(\frac{111}{22}\right)^2}$$

$$= \sqrt{(29.0455 - 25.4566)} = \sqrt{3.5889} = 1.89 \text{ (to two d.p.)}$$

Example 4.11.4

Using the data from Exercise 4.2.5 relating to output of product Q, and the mean that you have already calculated, find the standard deviation.

Output of Q (kg)	No. of days (frequency)
350–under 360	4
360–370	6
370–380	5
380–390	4
390–400	3

Solution

Mid-point x	Frequency f	fx	fx²
355	4	1,420	504,100
365	6	2,190	799,350
375	5	1,875	703,125
385	4	1,540	592,900
395	3	1,185	468,075
	22	8,210	3,067,550

$$s = \sqrt{\frac{\Sigma fx^2}{\Sigma f} - \bar{x}^2} = \sqrt{\frac{3,067,550}{22} - \left(\frac{8,210}{22}\right)^2}$$

$$= \sqrt{(139,434.0909 - 139,264.6694)} = \sqrt{169.4215} = 13.02 \text{ (to two d.p.)}$$

4.12 The coefficient of variation

The coefficient of variation is a statistical measure of the dispersion of data points in a data series around the mean. It is calculated as follows:

$$\text{Coefficient of variation} = \frac{\text{Standard deviation}}{\text{Expected return}}$$

The coefficient of variation is the ratio of the standard deviation to the mean, and is useful when comparing the degree of variation from one data series to another, even if the means are quite different from each other.

In a financial setting, the coefficient of variation allows you to determine how much risk you are assuming in comparison to the amount of return you can expect from an investment. The lower the ratio of standard deviation to mean return, the better your risk-return tradeoff.

Note that if the expected return in the denominator of the calculation is negative or zero, the ratio will not make sense.

In Example 4.11.2, it was relatively easy to compare the spread in two sets of data by looking at the standard deviation figures alone, because the means of the two sets were so similar. Another example will show that it is not always so straightforward.

Example 4.12.1

Government statistics on the basic weekly wages of workers in two countries show the following. (All figures converted to sterling equivalent.)

Country V: $\bar{x} = 120$ $s = £55$
Country W: $\bar{x} = 90$ $s = £50$

Can we conclude that country V has a wider spread of basic weekly wages?

Solution

By simply looking at the two standard deviation figures, we might be tempted to answer 'yes'. In doing so, however, we should be ignoring the fact that the two mean values indicate that wages in country V are inherently higher, and so the deviations from the mean and thus the standard deviation will tend to be higher. To make a comparison of like with like we must use the *coefficient of variation*:

$$\text{Coefficient of variation} = \frac{s}{\bar{x}}$$

Thus:

$$\text{Coefficient of variation of wages in country V} = \frac{55}{120} = 45.8\%$$

$$\text{Coefficient of variation of wages in country W} = \frac{50}{90} = 55.6\%$$

Hence we see that, in fact, it is country W that has the higher variability in basic weekly wages.

Example 4.12.2

Calculate the coefficients of variation for the data in Exercises 4.11.3 and 4.11.4.

Solution

- In Example 4.11.3, $\bar{x} = 5.045$ and $s = 1.8944$, so the coefficient of variation is: $100 \times 1.8944/5.045 = 37.6\%$
- In Example 4.11.4, $\bar{x} = 373.18$ and $s = 13.0162$, so the coefficient of variation is: $100 \times 13.0162/373.18 = 3.5\%$.

4.13 A comparison of the measures of spread

Like the mode, the range is little used except as a very quick initial view of the overall spread of the data. The problem is that it is totally dependent on the most extreme values in the distribution, which are the ones that are particularly liable to reflect errors or one-off situations. Furthermore, the range tells us nothing at all about how the data is spread between the extremes.

The standard deviation is undoubtedly the most important measure of spread. It has a formula that lends itself to algebraic manipulation, unlike the quartile deviation, and so, along with the mean, it is the basis of almost all advanced statistical theory. This is a pity because it does have some quite serious disadvantages. If data is skewed, the standard deviation will exaggerate the degree of spread because of the large squared deviations associated with extreme values. Similarly, if a distribution has open intervals at the ends, the choice of limits and hence of mid-points will have a marked effect on the standard deviation.

The quartile deviation, and to a lesser extent the interquartile range, is the best measure of spread to use if the data is skewed or has open intervals. In general, these measures would not be preferred to the standard deviation because they ignore much of the data and are little known.

Finally, it is often the case that data is intended to be compared with other data, perhaps nationwide figures or previous year's figures, etc. In such circumstances, unless you have access to *all* the raw data, you are obliged to compare like with like, regardless perhaps of your own better judgement.

4.14 Descriptive statistics using Excel

Many of the techniques discussed in this chapter can be facilitated through the use of Excel. This section discusses a number of these, including the *mean*, the *mode*, the *median*, the *standard deviation*, the *variance* and the *range*.

Figure 4.8 shows 100 observations that represent sample production weights of a product such as cereals, produced in grams. This data is the *sample data* from which the descriptive statistics are measured. The term *sample* is important as it implies that the data does not represent the full *population* and this affects some of the spreadsheet functions used. A population is the complete data set from which a conclusion is to be made.

	A	B	C	D	E	F	G
1	100 OBSERVATIONS PRODUCTION WEIGHTS IN GRAMS						
2							
3	525	539	580	563	497		
4	499	594	594	569	555		
5	548	588	502	516	540		
6	568	516	550	562	556		
7	555	562	548	548	546		
8	549	576	560	498	554		
9	562	553	575	539	531		
10	586	567	509	529	587		
11	596	577	574	555	580		
12	569	550	557	558	563		
13	562	519	569	530	560		
14	567	553	524	501	512		
15	558	593	558	539	588		
16	563	599	543	512	550		
17	564	579	581	546	534		
18	559	531	521	505	556		
19	559	542	587	574	533		
20	580	580	561	551	512		
21	551	523	529	548	502		
22	585	579	536	540	570		
23							

Figure 4.8 100 observations of production weights in grams

The data, has been entered into a spreadsheet and the range A3 through E22 has been named DATA. Any rectangular range of cells in Excel can be given a name, which can be easier to reference than depending cell references. To name the range, first select the area to be named (A3:E22 in this case), double-click on the name box at the top of the screen and type in the required name (DATA in this case).

The mean, median and mode are described as *measures of central tendency* and offer different ways of presenting a typical or representative value of a group of values. The range, the standard deviation and the variance are *measures of dispersion* and refer to the degree to which the observations in a given data set are spread about the arithmetic mean. The mean is the most frequently used measure of central tendency, and statisticians to describe a data set frequently use the mean together with the standard deviation. Figure 4.9 shows the result of the descriptive statistic functions. Each statistic is explained in detail below.

	A	B
1	Results of Descriptive Statistics	
2		
3	Number of Observations	100.00
4	Mean	552.30
5	Median	555.00
6	Mode	580.00
7	Minimum	497.00
8	Maximum	599.00
9	Range	102.00
10	Standard Deviation	25.14
11	Variance	631.83
12		

Figure 4.9 Results of descriptive statistics

Mean

To calculate the sample arithmetic mean of the production weights the AVERAGE function is used as follows in cell B4.

= AVERAGE(DATA)

It is important to note that the average function totals the cells containing values and divides by the number of cells that contain values. In certain situations this may not produce the required results and it might be necessary to ensure that zero has been entered in order that the function sees the cell as containing a value.

Sample median

The *sample median* is defined as the middle value when the data values are ranked in increasing, or decreasing, order of magnitude. The following formula in cell B5 uses the MEDIAN function to calculate the median value for the production weights.

= MEDIAN(DATA)

Sample mode

The sample mode is defined as the value which occurs most frequently. The following formula is required in cell B6 to calculate the mode of the production weights.

= MODE(DATA)

The mode may not be unique, as there can be more than one most frequently occurring value. Furthermore, if every value in the sample data set is different, there is no mode.

Minimum and maximum

It is useful to know the smallest and the largest value in a data series and the MINIMUM and maximum functions have been used in cells B7 and B8 to calculate this as follows:

= MIN(DATA)

= MAX(DATA)

The range

The range is defined as the difference between the largest and smallest values in a data series. The following formula can be used to calculate the range of the production weights by referencing the already calculated minimum and maximum values:

= B8 − B7

Sample standard deviation

To calculate the standard deviation for the production weights the following standard deviation function is required in cell B10:

= STDEV(DATA)

Note that the above function assume a sample population. If the data represents the entire population then in Excel the function STDEVP() would be used.

Sample variance

The sample variance is the square of the standard deviation. The formula required to calculate the sample variance of the production weights data in cell B11 is:

= VAR(DATA)

In the same way as the standard deviation, the above functions assume that sample data is being used. For the entire population the functions VARP() and VAR() respectively are required.

4.15 A practical example of descriptive statistical analysis using Excel

This section provides a worked example to further illustrate the presentation and analysis of data.

The example is based on data obtained from survey research that used a questionnaire. In order to increase the authenticity of this worked example, readers are shown how the data from the questionnaires needs to be carefully reviewed before the process of analysis begins. Thereafter, a number of different Excel functions and commands are used to provide a basis for the interpretation of the data.

4.15.1 The questionnaire

Figure 4.10 shows the questionnaire used. The objective of the survey is to obtain an assessment of the views of students studying in the Faculty of Business and Accounting Studies at a university.

The questionnaire is in three parts:

Part A is a set of 12 Likert type questions using a 9 point scale where respondents are asked to express to what extent they agree or disagree with propositions about different aspects of the educational institution. A Likert scale is a widely used scale in survey research. When responding to a Likert type question respondents specify their level of agreement to a statement. In the following questionnaire 1 means strongly disagree and 9 means strongly agree.

Part B of the questionnaire asks the respondent to indicate whether they are from the School of Business or the School of Accounting.

In Part C of the questionnaire a final Likert type question is posed, asking the respondents' overall opinion of the service delivery of the Institution.

4.15.2 Data capture

The first step is to transfer the respondents scores into the spreadsheet. This requires some planning of the spreadsheet to decide how the data will best be positioned for the analysis to be performed. Often, as in this example, rows are allocated to each respondent and if this is the case then columns are used to record the results of each question.

In this example there were 30 completed questionnaires. Figure 4.11 shows the original data, which is referred to as the 'raw data'. Notice that the responses to Part 2, which asked which School the respondent was studying in, has been entered as a 1 for School of Business and 2 for the School of Accounting.

On examination of this data it can be seen that some of the responses are invalid. For example Respondent 7's response to question 8 has been entered as 99, whereas the valid range for that question is 1 to 9.

Therefore the analyst needs to 'clean' the data. The first step is to go back to the questionnaires to see if the error was made during the transcription of the data to the spreadsheet. If this is the case a correction can be made. If there is a missing data point, where the respondent has failed to answer the question, a different approach is required. Although sometimes questionnaire results are processed in such a way as to ignore missing data points, in general it is thought to be better practice to estimate a value. One way to achieve this is to use the average or mean of the scores the respondent gave to all other questions. This approach will be taken in this exercise.

Looking at Figure 4.11 it can be seen that the first missing data point is in cell E7. The formula to calculate the mean score for the questions of respondent 4 is as follows:

= ROUND(AVERAGE(B7:D7,F7:M7),0)

Note that two separate ranges are required in the =AVERAGE function. If the current cell (E7) were included in the range this would produce a circular reference and an incorrect result. As the results have to be whole numbers, the =ROUND function has been used to round the result to the nearest whole number. After performing this calculation the formula should be replaced with the resulting value as the formula itself is no longer required.

Questionnaire

The Faculty of Business and Accounting Studies wishes to obtain an assessment of the views of the students as to the quality of the services delivered. All students are asked to complete the following questionnaire and return it to the Faculty Office.

This questionnaire should be completed anonymously and so please do not include your name, student number or any other indicator as to who you are. Your assistance is much appreciated.

Part A

Question 1
The quality of the lectures is excellent
Strongly Disagree 1. ☐ 2. ☐ 3. ☐ 4. ☐ 5. ☐ 6. ☐ 7. ☐ 8. ☐ 9. ☐ Strongly Agree

Question 2
The quality of the handouts is excellent
Strongly Disagree 1. ☐ 2. ☐ 3. ☐ 4. ☐ 5. ☐ 6. ☐ 7. ☐ 8. ☐ 9. ☐ Strongly Agree

Question 3
The quality of the class rooms is excellent
Strongly Disagree 1. ☐ 2. ☐ 3. ☐ 4. ☐ 5. ☐ 6. ☐ 7. ☐ 8. ☐ 9. ☐ Strongly Agree

Question 4
The quality of the lecturers is excellent
Strongly Disagree 1. ☐ 2. ☐ 3. ☐ 4. ☐ 5. ☐ 6. ☐ 7. ☐ 8. ☐ 9. ☐ Strongly Agree

Question 5
The quality of the library is excellent
Strongly Disagree 1. ☐ 2. ☐ 3. ☐ 4. ☐ 5. ☐ 6. ☐ 7. ☐ 8. ☐ 9. ☐ Strongly Agree

Question 6
The quality of the canteen is excellent
Strongly Disagree 1. ☐ 2. ☐ 3. ☐ 4. ☐ 5. ☐ 6. ☐ 7. ☐ 8. ☐ 9. ☐ Strongly Agree

Question 7
The quality of the projection facilities is excellent
Strongly Disagree 1. ☐ 2. ☐ 3. ☐ 4. ☐ 5. ☐ 6. ☐ 7. ☐ 8. ☐ 9. ☐ Strongly Agree

Question 8
The quality of the residence is excellent
Strongly Disagree 1. ☐ 2. ☐ 3. ☐ 4. ☐ 5. ☐ 6. ☐ 7. ☐ 8. ☐ 9. ☐ Strongly Agree

Question 9
Examinations are professionally conducted
Strongly Disagree 1. ☐ 2. ☐ 3. ☐ 4. ☐ 5. ☐ 6. ☐ 7. ☐ 8. ☐ 9. ☐ Strongly Agree

Question 10
The quality of the feedback is excellent
Strongly Disagree 1. ☐ 2. ☐ 3. ☐ 4. ☐ 5. ☐ 6. ☐ 7. ☐ 8. ☐ 9. ☐ Strongly Agree

Question 11
The quality of the ICT is excellent
Strongly Disagree 1. ☐ 2. ☐ 3. ☐ 4. ☐ 5. ☐ 6. ☐ 7. ☐ 8. ☐ 9. ☐ Strongly Agree

Question 12
The quality of the recreational facilities is excellent
Strongly Disagree 1. ☐ 2. ☐ 3. ☐ 4. ☐ 5. ☐ 6. ☐ 7. ☐ 8. ☐ 9. ☐ Strongly Agree

Part B
Which School are you a member of?
School of Business   ☐
School of Accounting   ☐

Part C
Overall I regard the service delivery to be excellent
Strongly Disagree 1. ☐ 2. ☐ 3. ☐ 4. ☐ 5. ☐ 6. ☐ 7. ☐ 8. ☐ 9. ☐ Strongly Agree

Thank you for completing this questionnaire.

Figure 4.10 The Questionnaire

	A	B	C	D	E	F	G	H	I	J	K	L	M	N	O
1	**A primary overview of the data**														
2		Scores given to the individual questions -->													
3		Q-01	Q-02	Q-03	Q-04	Q-05	Q-06	Q-07	Q-08	Q-09	Q-10	Q-11	Q-12	School	Overall Rating
4	Respondent 1	3	5	2	7	8	9	5	2	6	7	6	9	2	7
5	Respondent 2	1	6	1	6	7	8	10	3	8	6	2	9	1	6
6	Respondent 3	2	2	2	4	4	4	3	3	5	7	5	9	2	5
7	Respondent 4	8	8	6		7	9	7	7	3	6	3	9	1	6
8	Respondent 5	1	1	3	2	3	1	9	4	7	1	7	9	1	3
9	Respondent 6	3	3	3	2	5	1	8	2	4		2	9	1	4
10	Respondent 7	6	6	5	6	5	6	10	99	4	8	4	9	1	4
11	Respondent 8	2	4	5	4	3	2	15	6	6		6	9	2	5
12	Respondent 9	7	9	7	6	5	4	10	9	5	3	5	9	1	8
13	Respondent 10	1	2	3	2	5	8	9	8	8	8	8	9	2	8
14	Respondent 11	3	1	9	1	5	6	6	8	3	3	2	5	1	3
15	Respondent 12	4	1	3	4	5	4	7	2	1	8	1	5	1	7
16	Respondent 13	1	3	4	2	3	1	4	3	6	6	6	5	1	7
17	Respondent 14	3	1	5	3	3	1	5	9	4	7	9	9	2	4
18	Respondent 15	4	2	8	4	2	4	3	8	8	5	8	9	2	5
19	Respondent 16	5	3	7	3	5	1	7	2	5	5	5	9	5	6
20	Respondent 17	6	3	8	1	2	1	5	6	1	8	1	9	1	6
21	Respondent 18	2	2	5	3	5	1	5	8	7	6	9	9	2	3
22	Respondent 19	6	2	8	6	3	2	3	8	4	3	4	9	2	7
23	Respondent 20	2	1	7	3	6	2	2	2	2	4	2	9	1	5
24	Respondent 21	1	2	3	2	5	8	3	8	8	8	8	9	2	8
25	Respondent 22	2	2	9	1	5	6	6	8	3	3	2	9	1	4
26	Respondent 23	4	1	3	4	5	4	7	2	1	8	1	9	1	7
27	Respondent 24	1	3	4	2	3	1	4	3	6	6	6	9	1	7
28	Respondent 25	3	1	5	3	3	1	5	9	4	7	9	9	2	4
29	Respondent 26	4	2	8	4	2	4	3	8	8	5	8	9	2	5
30	Respondent 27	5	3	7	3	5	1	7	2	5	5	5	9	5	6
31	Respondent 28	6	3	8	1	2	1	5	6	1	8	1	9	1	6
32	Respondent 29	2	2	5	3	5	1	5	8	7	6	9	9	2	3
33	Respondent 30	6	2	8	6	3	2	3	8	4	3	4	9	2	7
34		3.47	2.87	5.37	3.38	4.30	3.47	6.03	8.70	4.80	5.71	4.93	8.60		5.53
35															

Figure 4.11 The raw data

This is achieved by selecting Edit Copy and then without moving the cursor select Edit Paste Special and tick the Values box.

Figure 4.12 shows the data after the 'cleaning up' exercise.

4.15.3 Preliminary analysis

The first piece of analysis considers whether respondents' overall rating shown in column O is greater or less than the average of the individual ratings which each of the issues were given. This involves two steps. In the first place each respondents' overall average score is calculated, that is the average of the data in columns B through M, and then the result of this is subtracted from the overall rating in column O.

Figure 4.13 shows the results.

To calculate the average score, the following formula is required in cell Q4:

$$= \text{AVERAGE}(\text{B4:M4})$$

This is then copied for the range Q5 through Q33.

To calculate how this score varies from the overall rating score the following formula is required in cell R4:

$$= \text{O4} - \text{Q4}$$

Figure 4.12 The 'cleaned' data

	A	B	C	D	E	F	G	H	I	J	K	L	M	N	O
2		Scores given to the individual questions -->													
3		Q-01	Q-02	Q-03	Q-04	Q-05	Q-06	Q-07	Q-08	Q-09	Q-10	Q-11	Q-12	School	O'all Rating
4	Respondent 1	3	5	2	7	8	9	5	2	6	7	6	9	2	7
5	Respondent 2	1	6	1	6	7	8	1	3	8	6	2	9	1	6
6	Respondent 3	2	2	2	4	4	4	3	3	5	7	5	9	2	5
7	Respondent 4	8	8	6	6	7	9	7	7	3	6	3	9	1	6
8	Respondent 5	1	1	3	2	3	1	9	4	7	1	7	9	1	3
9	Respondent 6	3	3	3	2	5	1	8	2	4	4	2	9	1	4
10	Respondent 7	6	6	5	6	5	6	1	9	4	8	4	9	1	4
11	Respondent 8	2	4	5	4	3	2	1	6	6	4	6	9	2	5
12	Respondent 9	7	9	7	6	5	4	1	9	5	3	5	9	1	8
13	Respondent 10	1	2	3	2	5	8	9	8	8	8	8	9	2	8
14	Respondent 11	3	1	9	1	5	6	6	8	3	3	2	5	1	3
15	Respondent 12	4	1	3	4	5	4	7	2	1	8	1	5	1	7
16	Respondent 13	1	3	4	2	3	1	4	3	6	6	6	5	1	7
17	Respondent 14	3	1	5	3	3	1	5	9	4	7	9	9	2	4
18	Respondent 15	4	2	8	4	2	4	3	8	8	5	8	9	2	5
19	Respondent 16	5	3	7	3	5	1	7	2	5	5	5	9	2	6
20	Respondent 17	6	3	8	1	2	1	5	6	1	8	1	9	1	6
21	Respondent 18	2	2	5	3	5	1	5	8	7	6	9	9	2	3
22	Respondent 19	6	2	8	6	3	2	3	8	4	3	4	9	2	7
23	Respondent 20	2	1	7	3	6	2	2	2	4	2	9	1	5
24	Respondent 21	1	2	3	2	5	8	3	8	8	8	8	9	2	8
25	Respondent 22	2	2	9	1	5	6	6	8	3	3	2	9	1	4
26	Respondent 23	4	1	3	4	5	4	7	2	1	8	1	9	1	7
27	Respondent 24	1	3	4	2	3	1	4	3	6	6	6	9	1	7
28	Respondent 25	3	1	5	3	3	1	5	9	4	7	9	9	2	4
29	Respondent 26	4	2	8	4	2	4	3	8	8	5	8	9	2	5
30	Respondent 27	5	3	7	3	5	1	7	2	5	5	5	9	2	6
31	Respondent 28	6	3	8	1	2	1	5	6	1	8	1	9	1	6
32	Respondent 29	2	2	5	3	5	1	5	8	7	6	9	9	2	3
33	Respondent 30	6	2	8	6	3	2	3	8	4	3	4	9	2	7

Figure 4.13 Difference between the overall score to the average score of the 12 questions

	A	B	C	D	E	F	G	H	I	J	K	L	M	N	O	Q	R	S
1	A primary statistical overview ---------------- Descriptive Statistics															Avg score	O'all rating minus	
2		Scores given to the individual questions -------------------------------------->														quest 1-12	Avg scores	
3		Q-01	Q-02	Q-03	Q-04	Q-05	Q-06	Q-07	Q-08	Q-09	Q-10	Q-11	Q-12	School	O'all Rating			
4	Respondent 1	3	5	2	7	8	9	5	2	6	7	6	9	2	7	5.75	1.25	*
5	Respondent 2	1	6	1	6	7	8	1	3	8	6	2	9	1	6	4.83	1.17	*
6	Respondent 3	2	2	2	4	4	4	3	3	5	7	5	9	2	5	4.17	0.83	*
7	Respondent 4	8	8	6	6	7	9	7	7	3	6	3	9	1	6	6.61	-0.61	
8	Respondent 5	1	1	3	2	3	1	9	4	7	1	7	9	1	3	4.00	-1.00	
9	Respondent 6	3	3	3	2	5	1	8	2	4	4	2	9	1	4	3.82	0.18	*
10	Respondent 7	6	6	5	6	5	6	1	9	4	8	4	9	1	4	5.75	-1.75	
11	Respondent 8	2	4	5	4	3	2	1	6	6	4	6	9	2	5	4.36	0.64	*
12	Respondent 9	7	9	7	6	5	4	1	9	5	3	5	9	1	8	5.83	2.17	*
13	Respondent 10	1	2	3	2	5	8	9	8	8	8	8	9	2	8	5.92	2.08	*
14	Respondent 11	3	1	9	1	5	6	6	8	3	3	2	5	1	3	4.33	-1.33	
15	Respondent 12	4	1	3	4	5	4	7	2	1	8	1	5	1	7	3.75	3.25	*
16	Respondent 13	1	3	4	2	3	1	4	3	6	6	6	5	1	7	3.67	3.33	*
17	Respondent 14	3	1	5	3	3	1	5	9	4	7	9	9	2	4	4.92	-0.92	
18	Respondent 15	4	2	8	4	2	4	3	8	8	5	8	9	2	5	5.42	-0.42	
19	Respondent 16	5	3	7	3	5	1	7	2	5	5	5	9	2	6	4.75	1.25	*
20	Respondent 17	6	3	8	1	2	1	5	6	1	8	1	9	1	6	4.25	1.75	*
21	Respondent 18	2	2	5	3	5	1	5	8	7	6	9	9	2	3	5.17	-2.17	
22	Respondent 19	6	2	8	6	3	2	3	8	4	3	4	9	2	7	4.83	2.17	*
23	Respondent 20	2	1	7	3	6	2	2	2	4	2	9	1	5	3.50	1.50	*
24	Respondent 21	1	2	3	2	5	8	3	8	8	8	8	9	2	8	5.42	2.58	*
25	Respondent 22	2	2	9	1	5	6	6	8	3	3	2	9	1	4	4.67	-0.67	
26	Respondent 23	4	1	3	4	5	4	7	2	1	8	1	9	1	7	4.08	2.92	*
27	Respondent 24	1	3	4	2	3	1	4	3	6	6	6	9	1	7	4.00	3.00	*
28	Respondent 25	3	1	5	3	3	1	5	9	4	7	9	9	2	4	4.92	-0.92	
29	Respondent 26	4	2	8	4	2	4	3	8	8	5	8	9	2	5	5.42	-0.42	
30	Respondent 27	5	3	7	3	5	1	7	2	5	5	5	9	2	6	4.75	1.25	*
31	Respondent 28	6	3	8	1	2	1	5	6	1	8	1	9	1	6	4.25	1.75	*
32	Respondent 29	2	2	5	3	5	1	5	8	7	6	9	9	2	3	5.17	-2.17	
33	Respondent 30	6	2	8	6	3	2	3	8	4	3	4	9	2	7	4.83	2.17	*

It is interesting to note how many respondents scored a higher overall rating than the average of the 12 questions in Part 1 of the questionnaire. These would be the positive values in column R. In column S a test has been performed to identify those respondents with a positive overall average. The formula in cell s4 is:

= if(R4>0,"*","")

This is interpreted as 'if R4 is greater than zero then display an asterisk, otherwise leave the cell blank'. The formula can be copied into cells s5 through s33.

Figure 4.14 is a line chart showing the difference in the overall rating score against the average score of all the questions in part one of the questionnaire.

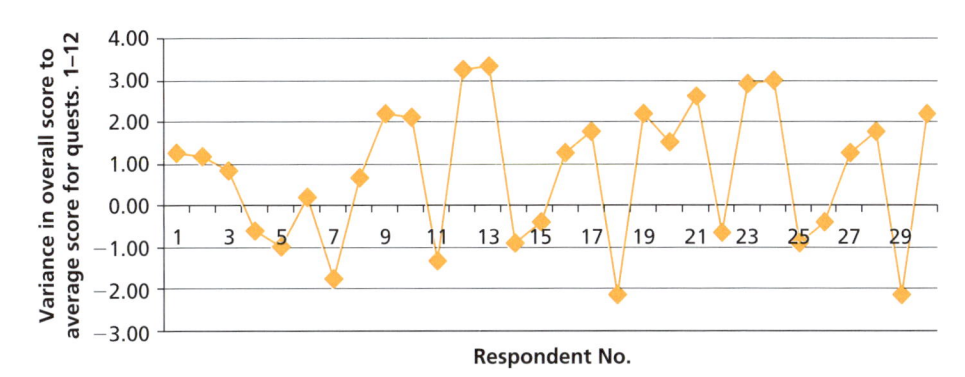

Figure 4.14 Line chart showing the difference in overall score to average score by respondent

From the chart in Figure 4.14 it can be seen inter alia that respondents 12 and 13 showed the greatest positive difference between their overall score and the average of all their scores, whist respondents 18 and 29 had the greatest negative difference between their overall score and the average of all their scores.

4.15.4 Descriptive statistics

Descriptive statistics, as the name suggests, are ways of describing what attributes a set of data is exhibiting. There are a number of different descriptive statistics functions in Excel, some of which were described in Section 4.14 of this chapter. In this worked example, in the first place, the mean, the standard deviation and the standard error are calculated.

Mean

It is interesting to see how the average responses to each question differ. The =AVERAGE function is used for this calculation. The following is entered into cell B35:

= AVERAGE(B4:B33)

This formula can be copied across to cell O34. As it is not appropriate to calculate the average of the 'which School' column the result in cell N34 has been deleted.

Figure 4.15 shows the results and Figure 4.16 shows a bar chart of the average scores for each question.

Standard deviation and standard error

In addition to the mean it is also useful to consider the standard deviation and the standard error which are measures of spread. The standard deviation is a measure of how dispersed the data is and can be used to establish whether a particular value is likely to belong to the population from which the sample has been extracted. The standard error is

	A	B	C	D	E	F	G	H	I	J	K	L	M	N	O
1	**A primary statistical overview**														
2		Scores given to the individual questions -->													
3		Q - 01	Q - 02	Q - 03	Q - 04	Q - 05	Q - 06	Q - 07	Q - 08	Q - 09	Q - 10	Q - 11	Q - 12	School	O'all Rating
4	Respondent 1	3	5	2	7	8	9	5	2	6	7	6	9	2	7
5	Respondent 2	1	6	1	6	7	8	1	3	8	6	2	9	1	6
6	Respondent 3	2	2	2	4	4	4	3	3	5	7	5	9	2	5
7	Respondent 4	8	8	6	6	7	9	7	7	3	6	3	9	1	6
8	Respondent 5	1	1	3	2	3	1	9	4	7	1	7	9	1	3
9	Respondent 6	3	3	3	2	5	1	8	2	4	4	2	9	1	4
10	Respondent 7	6	6	5	6	5	6	1	9	4	8	4	9	1	4
11	Respondent 8	2	4	5	4	3	2	1	6	6	4	6	9	2	5
12	Respondent 9	7	9	7	6	5	4	1	9	5	3	5	9	1	8
13	Respondent 10	1	2	3	2	5	8	9	8	8	8	8	9	2	8
14	Respondent 11	3	1	9	1	5	6	6	8	3	3	2	5	1	3
15	Respondent 12	4	1	3	4	5	4	7	2	1	8	1	5	1	7
16	Respondent 13	1	3	4	2	3	1	4	3	6	6	6	5	1	7
17	Respondent 14	3	1	5	3	3	1	5	9	4	7	9	9	2	4
18	Respondent 15	4	2	8	4	2	4	3	8	5	5	8	9	2	5
19	Respondent 16	5	3	7	3	5	1	7	2	5	5	5	9	2	6
20	Respondent 17	6	3	8	1	2	1	5	6	1	8	1	9	1	6
21	Respondent 18	2	2	5	3	5	1	5	8	7	6	9	9	2	3
22	Respondent 19	6	2	8	6	3	2	3	8	4	3	4	9	2	7
23	Respondent 20	2	1	7	3	6	2	2	2	2	4	2	9	1	5
24	Respondent 21	1	2	3	2	5	8	3	8	8	8	8	9	2	8
25	Respondent 22	2	2	9	1	5	6	6	8	3	3	2	9	1	4
26	Respondent 23	4	1	3	4	5	4	7	2	1	8	1	9	1	7
27	Respondent 24	1	3	4	2	3	1	4	3	6	6	6	9	1	7
28	Respondent 25	3	1	5	3	3	1	5	9	4	7	9	9	2	4
29	Respondent 26	4	2	8	4	2	4	3	8	8	5	8	9	2	5
30	Respondent 27	5	3	7	3	5	1	7	2	5	5	5	9	2	6
31	Respondent 28	6	3	8	1	2	1	5	6	1	8	1	9	1	6
32	Respondent 29	2	2	5	3	5	1	5	8	7	6	9	9	2	3
33	Respondent 30	6	2	8	6	3	2	3	8	4	3	4	9	2	7
34															
35	Mean score	3.47	2.87	5.37	3.48	4.30	3.47	4.67	5.70	4.80	5.61	4.93	8.60		5.53
36															

Figure 4.15 Average score by question

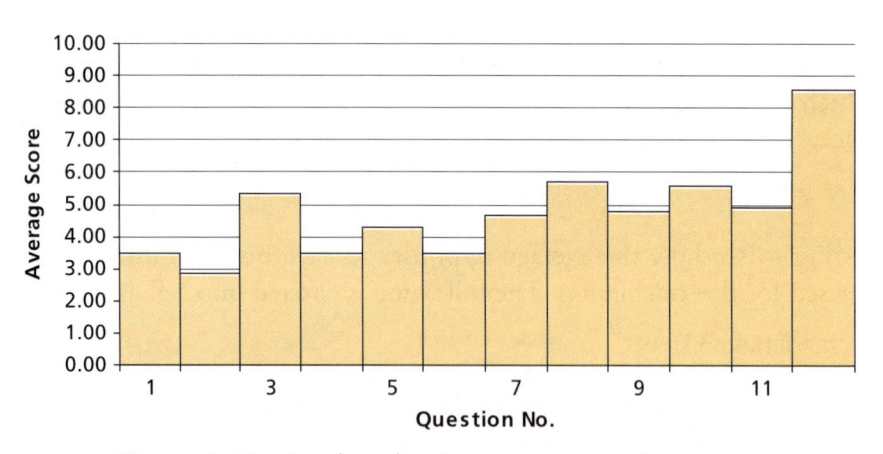

Figure 4.16 Bar chart showing average scores by question

also a measure of the dispersion of the data and is used to compare different samples to see if they are likely to have been derived from the same population.

The formula for the standard deviation that is entered into cell B36 is:

= STDEV(B4:B33)

And the formula for the standard error is standard deviation divided by the square root of the sample size. The count function has been used in row 37 to provide the data required in the formula below (= COUNT(B4:B33)), and the formula for the standard error in cell B38 is:

= B36/B37^0.5

	A	B	C	D	E	F	G	H	I	J	K	L	M	N	O	P
34																
35	Mean score	3.47	2.87	5.37	3.48	4.30	3.47	4.67	5.70	4.80	5.61	4.93	8.60		5.53	
36	Standard Deviation	2.05	2.05	2.34	1.79	1.58	2.79	2.34	2.79	2.28	1.97	2.78	1.22		1.59	
37	Count	30	30	30	30	30	30	30	30	30	30	30	30		30	
38	Standard Error	0.37	0.37	0.43	0.33	0.29	0.51	0.43	0.51	0.42	0.36	0.51	0.22		0.29	
39																

Figure 4.17 The mean, standard deviation and standard error.

Other measures of spread

The mid-point value for each question can been calculated using the median function as follows in cell B40:

= MEDIAN(B4:B33)

A measure of spread associated with the median is the quartile deviation, or inter-quartile range. The first quartile is the value with 25% of the data below it and the third quartile is the value with 75% of the data below it (the second quartile is, in fact, the median). The first and third quartiles can be calculated in Excel using the QUARTILE function as follows:

= QUARTILE(B4:B33, 1)   where 1 represents the 1st quartile.
= QUARTILE(B4:B33, 3)   where 3 represents the 3rd quartile.

The inter-quartile range is calculated as the range of the middle 50% of the data – or in the example B42–B41.

Figure 4.18 shows the results.

	A	B	C	D	E	F	G	H	I	J	K	L	M	N	O	P
39																
40	Median	3	2	5	3	5	2	5	7	5	6	5	9		6	
41	1st Quartile	2	2	3	2	3	1	3	3	3	4	2	9		4	
42	3rd Quartile	5	3	8	4	5	6	7	8	7	7	8	9		7	
43	Inter-Quartile Range	3	1	5	2	2	5	4	5	4	3	6	0		3	
44																

Figure 4.18 Other measures of spread

Two other measures sometimes used in statistical analysis are the skewness and the kurtosis.

Skewness refers to the lack of symmetry in a data distribution. The skewness of a set of data is defined as the degree to which the data congregates either to the right or to the left of the average (the measure of central tendency). If the data tends to the left (toward lower values) it is said to be skewed left (the long tail to the left); and distributions with observation reaching far out to the right (toward higher values) are said to be skewed right. If the long tail is to the left then the median will be greater than the mean and if the long tail stretches to the right then the mean will be greater than the median.

In Excel the skewness of the data set by question is calculated in cell B45 as follows:

= SKEW(B4:B33) (this formula can be copied across for the remaining questions)

Looking at the results in Figure 4.19 it can be seen that the skewness for each question does vary, but not by substantial amounts. Skewness should be between −1 and +1 otherwise the data is not symmetric.

	A	B	C	D	E	F	G	H	I	J	K	L	M	N	O	P
44																
45	Skewness	0.50	1.666	-0.06	0.43	0.311	0.81	0.069	-0.29	-0.18	-0.44	0.032	-2.81		-0.15	
46	Kurtosis	-0.81	2.503	-1.25	-0.86	-0.33	-0.72	-0.78	-1.74	-0.93	-0.69	-1.33	6.308		-1.11	
47																
48	Skewness - should be between -1 and +1 otherwise not symmetric
49	Kurtosis - should be between -1 and +1 otherwise if >1 more peaked than the normal and if < -1 less peaked
50	

Figure 4.19 Calculation of the skewness and the kurtosis

Kurtosis is a measure of the peakedness of the distribution of the data being evaluated. In Excel the kurtosis of the data set by question is calculated in cell B46 as follows:

$$= \text{KURT}(\text{B4:B33})$$

Looking at the results it can be seen that there is little variation in the kurtosis, with the exception of two data points which relate to questions 2 and 12. This analysis suggests that these two issues could be looked at more closely to see if there is any reason why they differ from the others. The kurtosis should be between −1 and +1. If it is greater than 1, it is more peaked than a normal distribution (this means that there are more observations in the tails – fat tailed) and if it is less than −1 it is less peaked than a normal distribution (this means that there are less observations in the tails).

The measures of skewness and the kurtosis are important to know if it is intended to perform hypothesis tests with the data and if modelling is going to be used.

Outliers

An outlier is an observation or data point that is numerically distant from the rest of the data set. Calculations performed on data sets that include outliers can be misleading. A data point is considered to be an outlier if it is more than one and a half times greater than the inter-quartile range. If the data point is more than one and a half times the inter-quartile range above the upper quartile, and likewise if the data point is more than one and a half times the inter-quartile range below the lower quartile, it may be regarded as an outlier.

Outliers always present a challenge to data analysis. In some cases the outlier represents an error in measurement of the phenomenon being studied or an error in the transcription of the data. If this is the case then an outlier may be amended or removed from the data set.

However sometimes an outlier is not an error, but rather represents a genuine data point. In this case it should be explained and a decision made as to how to handle the outlier. Sometimes the outlier is retained in the data set and some times the data point is adjusted or amended or removed.

In this example the outlier calculation for data points in the too high category is performed as follows:

$$= \text{ROUND}(\text{B42} + (1.5*(\text{B42} - \text{B41})),0)$$

The outlier calculation for data points in the too low category is performed as follows:

$$= \text{ROUND}(\text{B55} - (1.5*(\text{B55} - \text{B40})),0)$$

Note that the = round function has been applied in order to ensure that the results are whole numbers.

These formulae are copied across the data range for all 12 questions as well as the final overall satisfaction question and appears as shown in Figure 4.20.

	A	B	C	D	E	F	G	H	I	J	K	L	M	N	O	P
50																
51	Outliers - Upper limit	10.00	5.00	15.00	7.00	8.00	12.00	12.00	16.00	12.00	11.00	16.00	9.00		12.00	
52	Outliers - Lower limit	-3.00	1.00	-4.00	-1.00	0.00	-6.00	-3.00	-5.00	-2.00	0.00	-7.00	9.00		-1.00	
53	Potential outliers upper		*													
54	Potential outliers lower													*		
55																
56	Min	1	1	1	1	2	1	1	2	1	1	1	5		3	
57	Max	8	9	9	7	8	9	9	9	8	8	9	9		8	
58	Range	7	8	8	6	6	8	8	7	7	7	8	4		5	
59																
60																

Figure 4.20 Upper and lower outliers

The upper limit outlier now needs to be compared to the data to see if any of the data points exceed the upper limit outlier. To do this the Excel =MAX function has been used in cell B57 as follows:

= MAX(B4:B33) (and the formula is copied across for the remaining questions)

Then a test can be performed using the Excel = IF function in cell B53.

= IF(B57 > B51,"*","")

And an asterisk will be placed into the columns showing a potential outlier at the upper limit.

A similar process is required to ascertain potential outliers at the lower limit, but this time the Excel = MIN function is required in cell B56 as follows

= MIN(B4:B33)

And the test in cell B54 will be:

IF(B56 < B52,"*","")

From Figure 4.20 it can be seen that there is a potential for two outliers. The upper limit outlier for Question 2 is 5, and on examination of the data in column C it can be seen that there are data points in excess of 5. Similarly, the lower limit outlier for Question 12 is 9 and there are data points in column M that are less than 9. As mentioned above the analyst now needs to examine the original questionnaires to see if an error has been made and if so the data point needs to be corrected. If an error has not been made then a decision needs to be made as to whether the outlier is in fact a representative of the population being studied, and if not, it would have to be adjusted.

4.15.5 Worked Example Conclusions

There is a wealth of descriptive statistical analysis available to the management accountant through the use of a spreadsheet tool such as Excel. The above section has focused on a small number of Excel functions to illustrate how they may be used to describe the phenomenon being studied. For accountants wishing to go further and deeper into the interpretation of a data set there are many other Excel functions to explore.

This worked example has demonstrated that there is a pre-requisite to have a general skill of understanding data before using the Excel functions. It also shows that the results obtained by the Excel functions need to be carefully examined before any interpretations are made.

4.16 Summary

All the averages give a typical or expected value for the distribution. The mean is the total shared out equally, the median is the halfway value and the mode is the most common value.

All the measures of spread tell you how variable the data is. If the measures are relatively large, it means that the data is very variable. Both the mean deviation (directly) and the standard deviation (by a circuitous route of squaring and then square-rooting) find the average distance of the observations from the mean. In other words, they measure average variability about the mean.

The quartile deviation gives the average distance of the quartiles from the median. It is a measure of the variability of the central 50 per cent of observations, as is the interquartile range. Finally, the range itself measures the spread of the data from the very bottom to the very top.

Aside from understanding and being able to explain what the various statistics mean, there are other points of relevance to interpretation:

1. Can you rely on the data – was the sample large, representative and randomly taken?
2. Is the data skewed or open-ended? If so, are you using the right statistics?
3. Are you comparing like with like?
4. If you have to compare variability in two samples that have markedly different means, use the coefficient of variation rather than the standard deviation.
5. Finally, always remember to interpret statistics in their proper context. Give them units and do not simply interpret them in an abstract manner.
6. Think about which averages (measures of location) are used with which measures of spread, for example, the mean is used with the standard deviation (or variance).

Formulae definitions

- The mean, $\bar{x} = \Sigma x/n$ or $x = \Sigma fx/\Sigma f$ for frequency distributions.
- The median is the middle value when the data is arranged in ascending or descending order. It can be evaluated directly except in grouped frequency distributions, when it can be estimated from an ogive as the x-value corresponding to half the total frequency.
- The mode is the most commonly occurring value.
- The standard deviation,

$$s = \sqrt{\frac{\Sigma(x - \bar{x})^2}{n}}$$

or

$$s = \sqrt{\frac{\Sigma fx^2}{\Sigma f} - \left(\frac{\Sigma fx}{\Sigma f}\right)^2}$$

for frequency distributions.

- Coefficient of variation = $s/\bar{x}$
- Mean absolute deviation = $\Sigma |x - \bar{x}|/n$
- The interquartile range = $Q_3 - Q_1$
- The quartile deviation = $\frac{1}{2}(Q_3 - Q_1)$

  where Q_3 is the third quartile (which has 75 per cent of the values below it) and Q_1 is the first quartile (which has 25 per cent of the values below it).
- The values of the quartiles can be estimated from the ogive, in the case of a frequency distribution.
- Deciles divide a distribution into tenths, so that the first decile has 10 per cent of values below it, the second decile 20 per cent of values below it and so on. The values of deciles can be estimated from an ogive.
- Range = Highest interval limit − Lowest interval limit.

Readings

The well-chosen average

Darrell Huff, *How to Lie with Statistics*, Published by Penguin 1973
© Darrel & Frances Huff 1973. Reproduced by permission of Pollinger Limited and the Proprietor.

You, I trust, are not a snob, and I certainly am not an estate agent. But let's say that you are and that I am and that you are looking for property to buy along a road I know well. Having sized you up, I take pains to tell you that the average income in this neighbourhood is some £10,000 a year. Maybe that clinches your interest in living here; anyway, you buy and that handsome figure sticks in your mind. More than likely, since we have agreed that for the purposes of the moment you are a bit of a snob, you toss it in casually when telling your friends about where you live.

A year or so later we meet again. As a member of some ratepayers' committee I am circulating a petition to keep the rates down or assessments down or bus fare down. My plea is that we cannot afford the increase: after all, the average income in this neighbourhood is only £2,000 a year. Perhaps you go along with me and my committee in this – you're not only a snob, you're stingy too – but you can't help being surprised to hear about that measly £2,000. Am I lying now, or was I lying last year?

You can't pin it on me either time. That is the essential beauty of doing your lying with statistics. Both those figures are legitimate averages, legally arrived at. Both represent the same data, the same people, the same incomes. All the same, it is obvious that at least one of them must be so misleading as to rival an out-and-out lie.

My trick was to use a different kind of average each time, the word 'average' having a very loose meaning. It is a trick commonly used, sometimes in innocence but often in guilt, by fellows wishing to influence public opinion or sell advertising space. When you are told that something is an average you still don't know very much about it unless you can find out which of the common kinds of average it is – mean, median, or mode. The £10,000 figure I used when I wanted a big one is a mean, the arithmetic average of the incomes of all the families in the neighbourhood. You get it by adding up all the incomes and dividing by the number there are. The smaller figure is a median, and so it tells you that half the families in question have more than £2,000 a year and half have less. I might also have used the mode, which is the most frequently met-with figure in a series. If in this neighbourhood there are more families with incomes of £3,000 a year than with any other amount, £3,000 a year is the modal income.

In this case, as usually is true with income figures, an unqualified 'average' is virtually meaningless. One factor that adds to the confusion is that with some kinds of information all the averages fall so close together that, for casual purposes, it may not be vital to distinguish among them.

If you read that the average height of the men of some primitive tribe is only five feet, you get a fairly good idea of the stature of these people. You don't have to ask whether that average is a mean, median, or mode; it would come out about the same. The different averages come out close together when you deal with data, such as those having to do with many human characteristics, that have the grace to fall close to what is called the normal distribution. If you draw a curve to represent it you get something shaped like a bell, and mean, median, and mode fall at the same point.

Consequently, one kind of average is as good as another for describing the heights of men, but for describing their pocketbooks it is not. If you should list the annual incomes of all the families in a given city you might find that they ranged from not much to perhaps £20,000 or so, and you might find a few very large ones. More than 95 per cent of the incomes would be under £5,000, putting them way over towards the left-hand side of the curve. Instead of being symmetrical, like a bell, it would be skewed. Its shape would be a little like that of a child's slide, the ladder rising sharply to a peak, the working part sloping gradually down. The mean would be quite a distance from the median. You can see what this would do to the validity of any comparison made between the 'average' (mean) of one year and the 'average' (median) of another.

In the neighbourhood where I sold you some property the two averages are particularly far apart because the distribution is markedly skewed. It happens that most of your neighbours are small farmers or wage-earners employed in a nearby village or elderly retired people on pensions. But three of the inhabitants are millionaire weekenders and these three boost the total income, and therefore the arithmetical average, enormously. They boost it to a figure that practically everybody in the neighbourhood has a good deal less than you have in reality the case that sounds like a joke or a figure of speech nearly everybody is below average.

That's why when you read an announcement by a corporation executive of a business proprietor that the average pay of the people who work in his establishment is so much, the figure may mean something and it may not. If the average is a median, you can learn something significant from it: half the employees make more than that; half make less. But if it is a mean (and believe me it may be that if its nature is unspecified) you may be getting nothing more revealing than the average of one £25,000 income – the proprietor's – and the salaries of a crew of underpaid workers. 'Average annual pay of £3,800' may conceal both the £1,400 salaries and the owner's profits taken in the form of a whopping salary.

Discussion points

Discuss these within your study group before reading the outline solutions

If you calculate the three averages for the two small data sets that follow, you will be able to 'prove', depending upon which average you are quoting, that A and B are the same on average, that A is slightly greater than B, and that A is considerably greater than B. In fact, the only thing you won't be able to 'prove' is that B is greater than A! Try it.

	A				B	
3	6	7	8	5	5	5
5	6	7	9	6	6	6
5	6	8	9	6	7	7
6	7	8	10	7	8	9

Outline solutions

	A	B	
Mode	6.0	6.0	A and B are equal on average
Mean	6.9	6.4	A is slightly greater than B
Median	7.0	6.0	A is considerably greater than B

It is unusual for the median to be an 'extreme' average. Generally, skewness is the reason why the averages separate out and in that case the mean will be at one extreme and the mode at the other.

Revision Questions

Part 4.1 Objective testing selection

> Questions 4.1.1–4.1.10 are standard multiple-choice questions with exactly one correct answer each. Thereafter, the style of question will vary.

4.1.1 The interval between the upper quartile and the lower quartile is known as the:

(A) mean.
(B) interquartile range.
(C) standard deviation.
(D) mode.

4.1.2 A driver makes a number of deliveries in a week. In a week where his average journey was 267 miles, his individual journey distances, in miles, were 286, 192, x, 307, 185, y, 94.
When $y = 4x$, the value of x is:

(A) 161
(B) 167
(C) 267
(D) 644.

4.1.3 Sales for the first 5 months of the year averaged £8,200 per month. For the last 4 months of the year sales averaged £8,500 per month. If sales for the year totalled £102,000, the average for the sixth, seventh and eighth months must be:

(A) £8,500
(B) £9,000
(C) £9,500
(D) £10,200.

4.1.4 A group of people have the following ages in years: 21, 32, 19, 24, 31, 27, 17, 21, 26, 42. The median age of the group is:

(A) 21 years
(B) 25 years
(C) 26 years
(D) 31 years.

4.1.5 In a negatively skewed distribution:

(A) the mean is larger than the median.
(B) the mean is smaller than the median.
(C) the mean is the same as the median.
(D) the mean lies between the median and the mode.

4.1.6 The following set of data:

13, 42, x, 7, 51, 69, 28, 33, 14, 8

has a median of 29. What is the value of x?

(A) 25
(B) 29
(C) 30
(D) 32.

4.1.7 If the quartiles of a distribution are 34 and 52, what is the value of the quartile deviation?

(A) 43
(B) 18
(C) 9
(D) 4.5.

4.1.8 Which of the following would be the best measure of spread to use for a heavily skewed distribution, all other things being equal?

(A) Mean absolute deviation.
(B) Standard deviation.
(C) Quartile deviation.
(D) Range.

4.1.9 If the standard deviation of a sample of 100 people is 49, what is the value of the variance?

(A) 7
(B) 0.7
(C) 2,401
(D) 24.01.

4.1.10 All the following except one are advantages of using the standard deviation to measure spread. Which is incorrect?

(A) It is not distorted by skewed data.
(B) It is well known and widely used.
(C) It uses all the data.
(D) Its formula lends itself to mathematical manipulation.

4.1.11 Complete the missing entries in the following table and calculate the arithmetic mean (to two decimal places).

x	f	fx
0	10	?
1	15	?
2	25	?
3	5	?
Totals	?	?

4.1.12 State whether the following statements about the arithmetic mean are true or false.

(A) It measures the variability of the data.
(B) It is a measure of central tendency.
(C) It gives an average level for the data.
(D) It gives the value of the total shared out equally.

4.1.13 The arithmetic mean is given by the formula $\Sigma fx/\Sigma f$. For grouped data, which one or more of the following can constitute the x in the formula?

(A) Interval mid-points.
(B) Interval upper limits.
(C) Interval lower limits.
(D) The sum of the interval upper and lower limits divided by two.

4.1.14 State whether the following statements about the median are true or false.

(A) It is generally the best average to use when the data is skewed.
(B) When the data is grouped, it can only be estimated.
(C) For continuous data, it has a cumulative frequency of half the total frequency.
(D) It gives the middle value for the data.

4.1.15 State whether the following statements about the mode are true or false.

(A) It is the most widely used average.
(B) It is a measure of dispersion.
(C) It gives the most common value.
(D) Some distributions have several modes.

4.1.16 Which of the following are measures of spread?

(A) The upper quartile.
(B) The interquartile range.
(C) The range.
(D) The upper limit.
(E) The modal interval.
(F) The coefficient of variation.
(G) The standard deviation.

4.1.17 Associate each of the following statistics with one of the definitions.

Statistics
(A) Quartile deviation.
(B) Standard deviation.
(C) Mean deviation.

Definitions
(P) The average absolute gap between the observations and the mean.
(Q) Half the distance between the quartiles.
(R) The square root of the average squared gap between the observations and the mean.
(S) The standard deviation expressed as a percentage of the mean.

4.1.18 In country P, the coefficient of variation for the salaries of trainee accountants is 40 per cent, while in country Q it is 60 per cent. Which of the following statements can be made on the basis of this information?

(A) In P, 40 per cent of trainee accountants have a below-average salary.
(B) In Q, the lowest salary of trainee accountants is 60 per cent of the average.
(C) Salaries of trainee accountants are more variable in Q than in P.
(D) Salaries of trainee accountants are higher on average in Q than in P.

4.1.19 Which one or more of the following are advantages of using the standard deviation?

(A) It has an exact algebraic formula.
(B) It is not distorted by data being skewed.
(C) It is the most widely used measure of spread.
(D) It is not affected by open-ended intervals.

4.1.20 Match the following statistics to the charts that may be used to directly estimate them. Note that the same charts may be used for several statistics, some charts may be of no such use, and it may not be possible to estimate some statistics from charts.

Statistics
(A) The mean.
(B) The quartile deviation.
(C) The median.
(D) The mode.

Chart
(P) The frequency polygon.
(Q) The histogram.
(R) The ogive.
(S) None.

Part 4.2 Mean/SD/histogram

The managers of an import agency are investigating the length of time that customers take to pay their invoices, the normal terms for which are 30 days net.

They have checked the payment record of 100 customers chosen at random and have compiled the following table:

Payment in (days)	Interval	Mid-point (x)	frequency (f)	fx	fx²
5–9	5 and less than 10	7.5	4	30.0	225.00
10–14	A	12.5	10	125	1562.5
15–19	15 and less than 20	17.5	17	B	5,206.25
20–24	20 and less than 25	C	20	450.0	10,125.00
25–29	25 and less than 30	27.5	22	605.0	D
30–34	30 and less than 35	32.5	16	520.0	16,900.00
35–39	35 and less than 40	37.5	8	300.0	11,250.00
40–44	40 and less than 45	42.5	3	127.5	5,418.75
			100		

4.2.1 Fill in the gaps in the table, working with two decimal places (2 d.p.) where appropriate.

4.2.2 If in the above table $\Sigma fx = 2,500$. Calculate the arithmetic mean.

4.2.3 If in the above table $\Sigma fx = 2,400$ and $\Sigma fx^2 = 67,000$. Calculate the standard deviation, giving your answer to two d.p.

4.2.4 The following chart is the histogram of the original data but the scale along the horizontal axis has been omitted as has the height E of the second bar.

Fill in the scale at the ends of the bars and state the value of E.

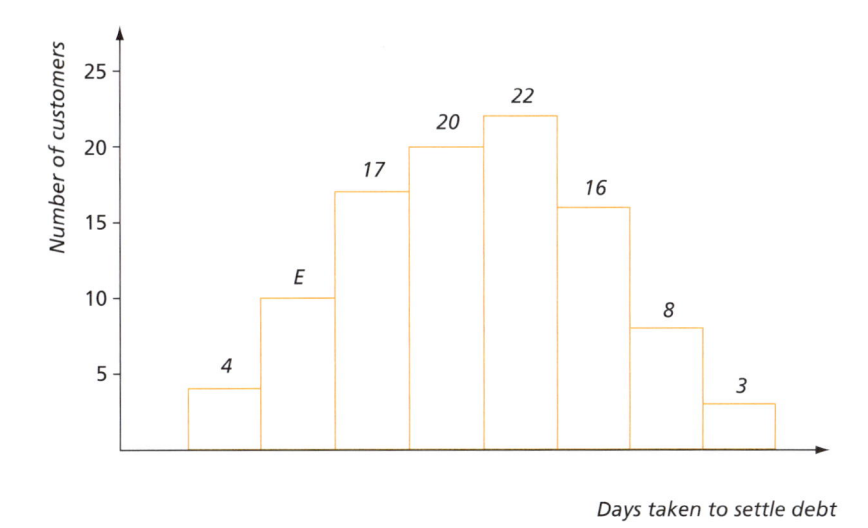

Histogram Payment record of 100 customers

4.2.5 If the intervals along the horizontal axis had limits 10, 20, 30, etc. through to 90, use the histogram given to estimate the value of the mode, clearly showing the construction you use and giving your answer to the nearest whole number.

4.2.6 From the original data estimate the probability that an invoice chosen at random will be paid in between 30 and 39 days.

Part 4.3 Ogive and interpretation

A company is investigating the cost of absenteeism within its production department. Computer records revealed the following data:

Days absent last year	Number of people
0	94
1–5	203
6–10	105
11–20	68
21–30	15
31–40	10
41+	5
Total	500

[*Source*: Internal company records]

4.3.1 Complete the following cumulative frequency distribution table:

No. of days absent	Cumulative number of people
0	94
1 and <6	297
6 and <11	402
A	470
21 and <31	B
31 and <41	495
41 and <51	C

4.3.2 The following chart is the ogive (cumulative 'less than' frequency diagram) of this data. State the y coordinates of the points labelled D, E and F.

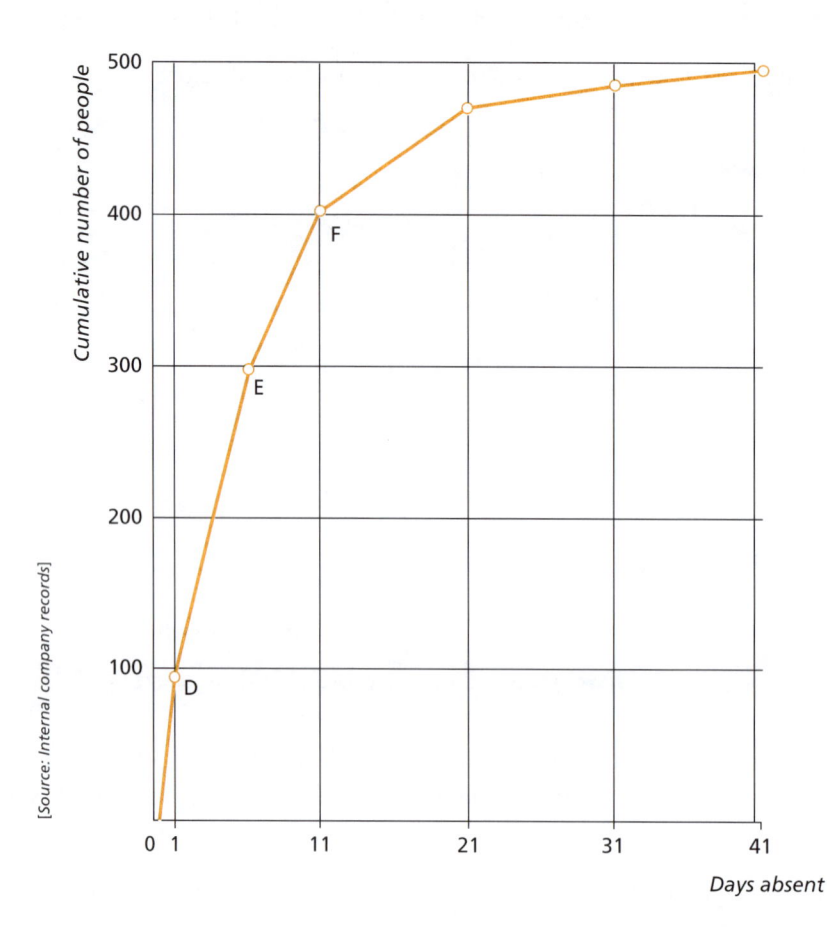

[*Source*: Internal company records]

4.3.3 Mark estimates of the following statistics on the ogive, clearly showing the constructions you have used to obtain them. You need not attempt to estimate the values of the statistics but should clearly label any cumulative frequencies you use in estimating them.

(A) median
(B) upper quartile
(C) highest decile.

4.3.4 If the median were 5 days, the lower quartile 2 days and the upper quartile 10 days, calculate the quartile deviation.

4.3.5 If the median were 5 days, lower quartile 2 days and upper quartile 10 days, which of the following comments would be correct?

(A) Only a quarter of the staff had less than 2 days absence.
(B) The high value of the upper quartile shows that absenteeism has increased.
(C) Half the staff had less than 5 days absence.
(D) The low value of the lower quartile shows that absenteeism is not very variable from one person to the next.
(E) Half the staff had more than 12 days absence.
(F) Three-quarters of the staff had less than 8 days absence.
(G) A quarter of the staff had more than 10 days absence.

Part 4.4 Descriptive statistics/charts

A firm is comparing the age structure of its workforce in the current year with that of 5 years ago, as shown in the table below:

Age group (years)	Five years ago Number in group	Current year Number in group
25 < 30	2	5
30 < 35	6	10
35 < 40	8	13
40 < 45	13	28
45 < 50	15	21
50 < 55	35	12
55 < 60	12	8
60 < 65	9	3

The mean age and standard deviation of ages 5 years ago were:

Mean age   49.05 years
Standard deviation 8.45 years

4.4.1 Complete the following table, working with two d.p. where appropriate:

Mid-point x	x^2	Score f	fx	fx^2
27.5	756.25	5	137.5	3,781.25
32.5	1,056.25	10	325.0	10,562.50
37.5	1,406.25	13	487.5	18,281.25
42.5	1,806.25	28	1190.0	50,575.00
47.5	2,256.25	21	997.5	47,381.25
52.5	2,756.25	12	630.0	33,075.00
57.5	3,306.25	8	460.0	26,450.00
62.5	3,906.25	3	187.5	11,718.75
		100	A	B

4.4.2 If in the above table $\Sigma fx = 4,400$ and $\Sigma fx^2 = 200,000$

(A) calculate the arithmetic mean.
(B) calculate the standard deviation, giving your answer to two d.p.

4.4.3 If the current mean were 40 years and the standard deviation were 8 years, which of the following comments would be correct?

(A) Over the last 5 years there has been little change in age variability from one employee to the next.
(B) The most common age group has dropped from 50 to 55 years to 40 to 45 years.
(C) Variability of ages around the mean has increased very greatly since 5 years ago.
(D) A quarter of employees are now less than 32 years old.
(E) The average recruit is now 8 years younger than 40 years.
(F) Average age of employees has fallen.
(G) A half of employees are now less than 40 years old.

4.4.4 The chart illustrates the changes in the age structure of the workforce over the 5-year period.

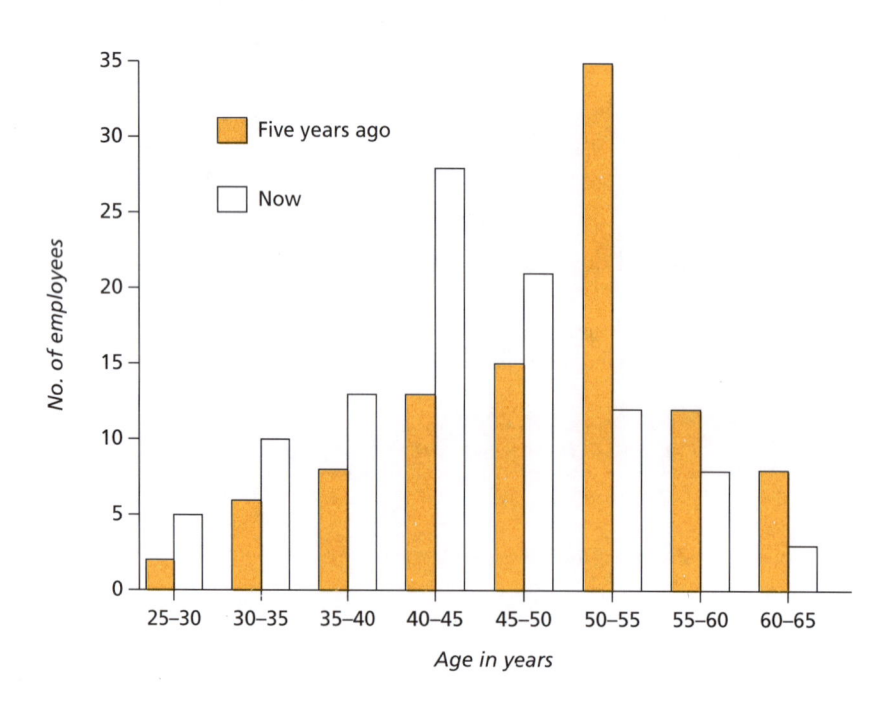

(A) What type of chart is it? Bar chart/pie chart/histogram/ogive/multiple bar chart/component bar chart.
(B) Which of the following adjectives broadly describes the shape of the distribution 5 years ago? Symmetrical/positively skewed/negatively skewed/uniform/normal.
(C) Which of the following adjectives broadly describes the shape of the distribution now? Symmetrical/positively skewed/negatively skewed/uniform/normal.

Part 4.5   Descriptive statistics with Excel

Enter the data shown below into a spreadsheet and then calculate the following:

	A	B	C	D	E	F	G
1	No. emails received by day for each month						
2							
3		Mon	Tues	Wed	Thur	Fri	
4	Jan	570	539	580	563	497	
5	Feb	520	480	510	500	490	
6	Mar	562	588	502	516	540	
7	Apr	568	516	550	562	556	
8	May	555	562	548	548	546	
9	Jun	549	576	560	498	554	
10	Jul	562	553	575	539	531	
11	Aug	586	567	509	529	587	
12	Sep	596	577	574	555	580	
13	Oct	569	550	557	558	563	
14	Nov	562	519	569	530	560	
15	Dec	567	553	524	501	550	
16	Total	6766	6580	6558	6399	6554	
17							

4.5.1 Calculate the mean number of emails received for each day of the week over the year.

4.5.2 Calculate the standard deviation of the emails received for each day of the week over the year.

Solutions to Revision Questions

✓ Solutions to Part 4.1

4.1.1 Answer: (B)

The standard deviation is another measure of variability but does not rely on the quartiles. The mean and mode are averages.

4.1.2 Answer: (A)

Average = Total/7, so total = $267 \times 7 = 1{,}064 + x + y = 1{,}064 + 5x$
Hence, $5x = 1{,}869 - 1{,}064$
Hence, $x = 805/5 = 161$

4.1.3 Answer: (B)

Let £x be the average sales for the sixth, seventh and eighth months.
$(8{,}200 \times 5) + (8{,}500 \times 4) + (x \times 3) = 102{,}000$
$x = 9{,}000$

4.1.4 Answer: (B)

$$\text{Median}$$
$$\downarrow$$
17, 19, 21, 21, 24, 26, 27, 31, 32, 42

Therefore, the median is 25.

4.1.5 Answer: (B)

In a negatively skewed distribution there is a long tail to the left and the mean is 'pulled' in the direction of the tail. Hence the mean is the smallest of the averages and is less than the median. Answer (A) would be correct for a positively skewed distribution and (C) for a perfectly symmetrical distribution. (D) could occur for a fairly symmetrical distribution.

4.1.6 Answer: (C)

In order of magnitude, without x, the values are
7, 8, 13, 14, 28, 33, 42, 51, 69

Including x, there are ten values so the median of 29 is the average of the fifth and sixth. The only possible solution is that x lies between 28 and 33 and has a value such that $(28 + x)/2 = 29$. Hence, $x = 30$.

4.1.7 Answer: (C)

The quartile deviation $= (Q_3 - Q_1)/2 = (52 - 34)/2 = 18/2 = 9$

In answer (D) you have divided by 4 instead of 2 and in (B) you have not divided by anything. In fact, you have found the interquartile range. In answer (A) you have added rather than subtracted the quartiles and hence have obtained their average.

4.1.8 Answer: (C)

The mean absolute deviation is very little known and would somewhat exaggerate the spread of a skewed distribution. The standard deviation greatly exaggerates the spread of skewed data. The range is a poor measure of spread for many reasons and it too will be greatly influenced by the data having a long tail. So the quartile deviation that measures the spread of just the central half of the data is to be preferred.

4.1.9 Answer: (C)

The variance is the square of the standard deviation $= 2{,}401$. Answers (A) and (B) have both taken the square root of 49, dividing by the square root of sample size in the case of (B), and (D) has divided the variance by the sample size.

4.1.10 Answer: (A)

The standard deviation is increased when data is skewed and this is a major disadvantage. All the others are correct.

4.1.11 The answers are as follows:

x	f	fx
0	10	0
1	15	15
2	25	50
3	5	15
Totals	55	80

Arithmetic mean $= 80/55 = 1.45$

4.1.12 All the answers except (A) are correct.

4.1.13 The correct answers are (A) and (D) since the interval mid-point is calculated by adding the limits and dividing by two.

4.1.14 All these statements about the median are true.

4.1.15 The correct answers are (C) and (D).

4.1.16 The measures of spread are (B), (C), (F) and (G).

4.1.17 The correct associations are as follows:

	Statistics	Definitions
(A)	Quartile deviation	Q
(B)	Standard deviation	R
(C)	Mean deviation	P

4.1.18 Only statement (C) can be made on the basis of the information given.

4.1.19 The correct answers are (A) and (C).
4.1.20 The correct answers are as follows:

	Statistics	Chart
(A)	The mean	S
(B)	The quartile deviation	R
(C)	The median	R
(D)	The mode	Q

✓ Solutions to Part 4.2

4.2.1 The interval A follows the same pattern as all the others; mid-point (C) is given by adding 20 and 25 and dividing the result by 2; fx is given by multiplying f (i.e. 17) by x (i.e. 17.5) and fx^2 is given by multiplying 27.5 squared by 22.

Answers:

(A) 10 and under 15
(B) 297.5
(C) 22.5
(D) 16,637.5

4.2.2 Arithmetic mean $(\bar{x}) = \dfrac{\Sigma fx}{fx} = \dfrac{2{,}500}{100} = 25$ days

4.2.3 Standard deviation $= \sqrt{\dfrac{\Sigma fx^2}{\Sigma f} - \bar{x}^2} = \sqrt{\dfrac{67{,}000}{100} - \left(\dfrac{2{,}400}{100}\right)^2}$

$= 9.70$ days (to two d.p.)

4.2.4

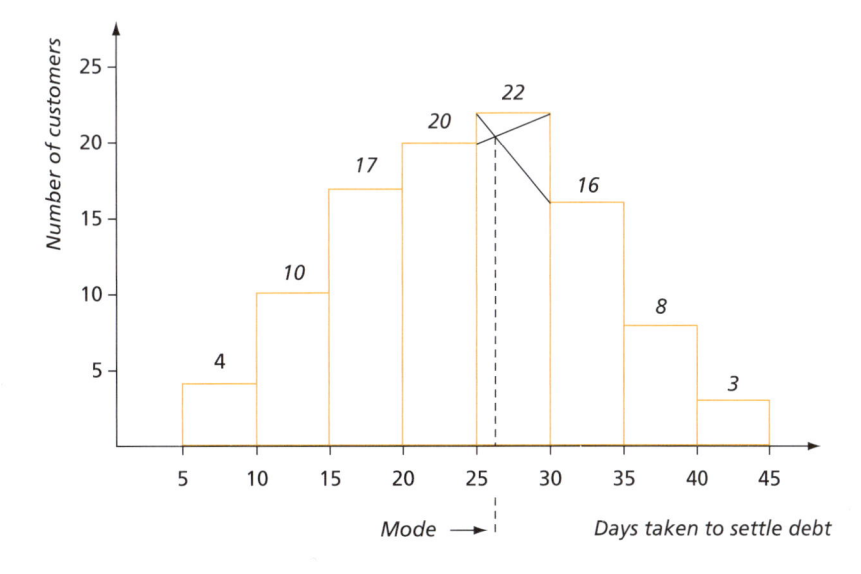

Histogram Payment record of 100 customers

4.2.5 The construction is shown on the histogram but with the new limits the mode lies between 50 and 60 in place of 25 and 30. Reading from the graph a value of 53 to the nearest whole number.

4.2.6 Of 100, sixteen lie in the class 30–34 days and eight lie in the class 35–39 days. Therefore, the best estimate that an unpaid invoice chosen at random will be between 30 and 39 days old is:

$$\frac{24}{100} = 0.24$$

✓ Solutions to Part 4.3

4.3.1 The intervals follow the previous pattern so A is 11 and less than 21. The cumulative frequency B is 470 + 15 and C is the total frequency 500.

Answers:

(A) 11 and <21
(B) 485
(C) 500.

4.3.2 D, E and F are the cumulative frequencies of 1, 6 and 11, respectively.

Answers:

(D) 94
(E) 297
(F) 402.

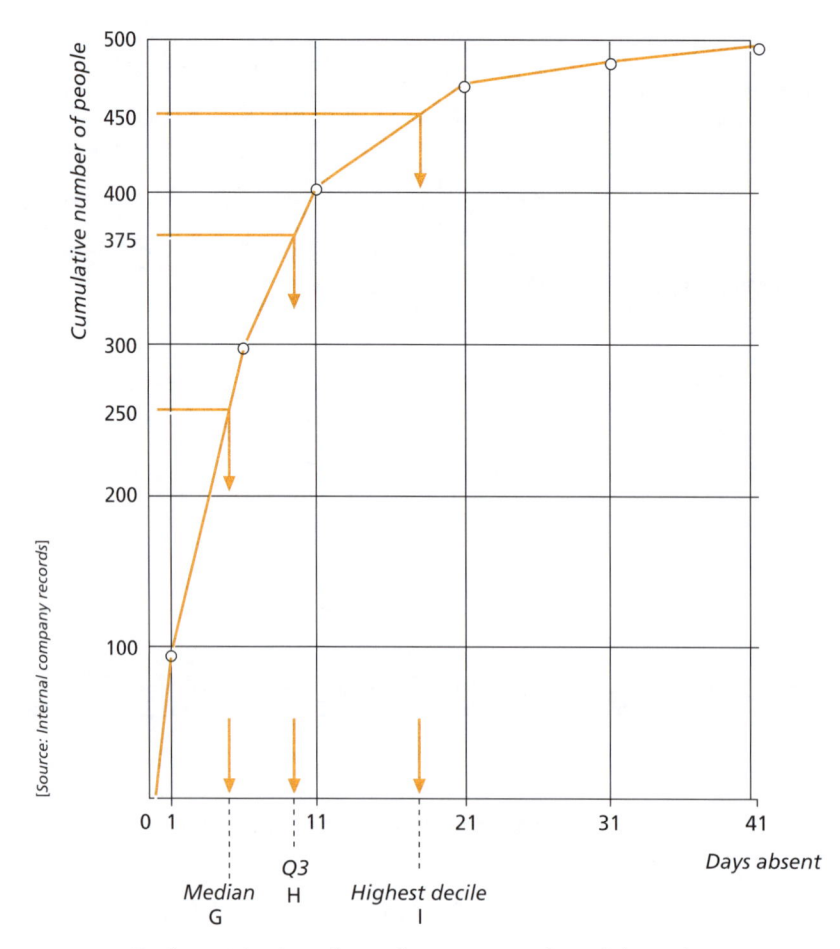

[Source: Internal company records]

Ogive Number of people against number of days absent

4.3.3 Cumulative frequencies are 500/2 = 250 for the median (A), 3 × 500/4 = 375 for the upper quartile (B) and 9 × 500/10 = 450 for the highest decile (C). The constructions required are shown on the ogive.

4.3.4 The quartile deviation = (Q3 − Q1)/2 = (10 − 2)/2 = 4
Answer:

(A) 4.

4.3.5 If the median were 5 days half the staff would have less than 5 days absence so (C) is correct. The lower quartile of 2 days tells us that only a quarter of the staff had less than 2 days absence so (A) is correct. Finally, if the upper quartile were 10 days, a quarter of the staff would have more than 10 days absence and (G) would be correct.

All the other comments are incorrect.

Answer: (A), (C) and (G).

✓ Solutions to Part 4.4

4.4.1 Answers:

(A) 4,415
(B) 201,825

4.4.2 (A) Mean $\bar{x} = \dfrac{\Sigma fx}{\Sigma f} = \dfrac{4,400}{100} = 44$ years

$$\text{Standard deviation} = \sqrt{\dfrac{\Sigma fx^2}{\Sigma f} - \left(\dfrac{\Sigma fx}{\Sigma f}\right)^2}$$

(B) Standard deviation $= \sqrt{\dfrac{200,000}{100} - \left(\dfrac{4,400}{100}\right)^2}$

$= \sqrt{(2,000 - 1,936)} = 8$ years

4.4.3 The average is given by the mean which has fallen from 49 to 40 years, so (F) is correct. Variability in age is given by the standard deviation which has changed very little so (A) is correct. It can also be seen that (B) is correct from the original data. All the other statements are incorrect or insufficient data exists to check them. (C) needs to be checked given that the mean has decreased.

Answers: (A), (B) and (C).

4.4.4 (A) Multiple bar chart
(B) The frequencies rise slowly to a peak and then drop away quickly so the data are negatively skewed.
(C) Symmetrical.

Solutions to Part 4.5

4.5.1 The AVERAGE function is used to calculate the mean. To find the mean number of emails received on each day of the week over the year the following formula is entered into cell B18:

= AVERAGE(B4:B15)

The formula is then copied into cells C18 through F18.

4.5.2 The STDEV function is used to calculate the standard deviation. To find the standard deviation of emails received on each day of the week over the year the following formula is entered into cell B19:

= STDEV(B4:B15)

The formula is then copied into cells C19 through F19.
The figure below shows the results.

	A	B	C	D	E	F
1	No. emails received by day for each month					
2						
3		Mon	Tues	Wed	Thur	Fri
4	Jan	570	539	580	563	497
5	Feb	520	480	510	500	490
6	Mar	562	588	502	516	540
7	Apr	568	516	550	562	556
8	May	555	562	548	548	546
9	Jun	549	576	580	498	554
10	Jul	562	553	575	539	531
11	Aug	586	567	509	529	587
12	Sep	596	577	574	555	580
13	Oct	569	550	557	558	563
14	Nov	562	519	569	530	560
15	Dec	567	553	524	501	550
16	Total	6766	6580	6558	6399	6554
17						
18	Mean emails	563.83	548.33	546.50	533.25	546.17
19	Standard Deviation	18.70	30.76	28.17	24.79	29.08
20						

5

Index Numbers

Index Numbers 5

LEARNING OUTCOMES

After completing this chapter you should be able to:

▸ calculate and explain a simple index number, and fixed-base and chain-base series of index numbers;

▸ use index numbers to deflate a series, and explain the results;

▸ calculate a simple weighted index number. Candidates will not have to decide whether to use base or current weights.

5.1 Introduction

We conclude the study of averages by looking at a special category, *index numbers*, which measure how a group of related commercial quantities vary, usually over time. As we shall see, most well-known index numbers are averages, but they have the extra property that they relate the quantities being measured to a fixed point or *base* period.

5.2 Definitions

If a series of values relating to different times are all expressed as a percentage of the value for a particular time, they are called *index numbers* with that time as the base.

$$\text{Index number} = \frac{\text{Value in any given year}}{\text{Value in base year}} \times 100$$

We shall generally refer to years but monthly data might have a particular month as base and so forth, so strictly speaking we should say 'time point' rather than 'year'.

Example 5.2.1

Express the following data with 1995 as the base:

Year	1995	1996	1997	1998	1999
Value	46	52	62	69	74

Solution

We have to express each value as a percentage of the value for 1995. That means we must divide each by the 1995 value (i.e. by 46) and multiply by 100.

Year	1995	1996	1997	1998	1999
1995 = 100	100	113	135	150	161

A few points of note:

- The base year did not have to be the first of the series. We could have chosen any year.
- Expressions such as '1995 = 100' tell us that the associated values are index numbers with base 1995. The index number for the base year (1995 in this case) will always be 100.
- We have rounded to the nearest whole number simply to avoid cluttering the text, while you get used to the idea of index numbers. In fact, they could be expressed to any degree of accuracy.

5.3 Interpretation of index numbers

An index of 113 tells us that there has been a 13 per cent increase since the base year.

In Example 5.2.1 we can see that values increased by 13 per cent from 1995 to 1996, by 35 per cent over the 2 years from 1995 to 1997, by 50 per cent over 3 years and by 61 per cent over the 4 years 1995–99.

It is essential to realise that the percentage changes always refer back to the base year. It is not possible to derive the percentage increase from one year to the next by subtracting index numbers.

Example 5.3.1

Find the percentage increase from 1998 to 1999 for the data in Example 5.2.1.

Solution

$$\frac{161}{150} \times 100 = 107.3$$

Therefore, the percentage increase is 7.3 per cent.

If we were to subtract the index numbers we would get $161 - 150 = 11$ points, which is clearly not the same as 11 per cent. Were the *Financial Times* 250 Share Index (which, at the time of writing, is at about 10,000) to rise by 50 points, that represents a rise of only $100 \times \frac{50}{10,000} = 2.5$ per cent. This 50 point rise must not be confused with a 50 per cent rise!

To derive the percentage increase from year A to year B, the easiest method is to index the year B figure with base year A and then subtract 100.

If values have declined, the index number will be less than 100, and when you interpret them by subtracting 100 the resulting negative tells you there has been a decline.

For example, an index of 94 means there has been a decline of 6 per cent (94 − 100 = −6) since the base year.

Finally, some index numbers become very large, like the FTSE 100 Share Index, which at the time of writing is approximately 5,300. It has a base of 1984 = 1,000 which means that share prices are approximately 5.3 times what they were in the base year.

Hence, there are two ways of interpreting an index number:

- subtracting 100 gives the percentage increase since the base year;
- dividing by 100 gives the ratio of current values to base-year values.

Example 5.3.2

Year	1991	1992	1993	1994	1995	1996	1997
Profits (£m)	1.2	1.5	1.8	1.9	1.6	1.5	1.7

(a) Express the profits figures above as index numbers with:
   (i) base 1991;
   (ii) base 1994.
(b) Interpret both the index numbers for 1995.
(c) Find the percentage increase from 1996 to 1997.
(d) Interpret the index number 2,500 with 1989 = 100.

Solution

	Year	1991	1992	1993	1994	1995	1996	1997
(a)	(i) 1991 = 100	100	125	150	158	133	125	142
	(ii) 1994 = 100	63	79	95	100	84	79	89

(b) The index of 133 means there has been a 33 per cent increase in profits from 1991 to 1995. The index of 84 means that profits in 1995 are 16 per cent below their level in 1994.
(c) 100 × (1.7/1.5) = 113 so there has been a 13 per cent increase from 1996 to 1997.
(d) An index of 2,500 means that values now are 2,500/100 = 25 times their value in the base year, 1989.

5.4 Choice of base year

Although a particular base may be satisfactory for several years, it becomes less meaningful as time passes and eventually it is necessary to shift to a new base this is called rebasing.

The only requirements of a suitable base year are, first, that it should be a fairly typical year. For example, if prices are being indexed then a year should be chosen in which prices were neither specially high nor specially low. Second, it should be sufficiently recent for comparisons with it to be meaningful. For example, it might be useful to know that production had changed by a certain percentage over the last year or two or perhaps over 10 years, but an index with base, say, 50 years ago would not be very relevant.

It is also the case, as we shall see shortly, that many index numbers span a wide range of popular goods and, reflecting what people actually buy, they are very different now from 20 or 30 years ago. The base year has to move in order to keep up with the composition of index numbers to some extent.

5.5 Change of base year

If at all possible you should return to the original data and recalculate the index numbers with the new base year. However, if only the index numbers are available, they can be indexed as if they were the original data. The only problem is that sometimes rounding errors will build up. As the following example shows, changing the base using index numbers instead of raw data can give very good results.

Example 5.5.1

(a) Express the following as index numbers with base 1990.
(b) Using the original data, change the base to 1995.
(c) Using the index with base 1990, change the base to 1995 and compare your results with those in part (b).

Express your answers to one decimal place throughout.

Year	1990	1991	1992	1993	1994	1995	1996	1997	1998
Staff	8	9	9	12	20	22	24	25	27

Solution

Year	1990	1991	1992	1993	1994	1995	1996	1997	1998
Staff	8	9	9	12	20	22	24	25	27
(a) 1990 = 100	100.0	112.5	112.5	150.0	300.0	275.0	300.0	312.5	337.5
(b) 1995 = 100	36.4	40.9	40.9	54.5	90.9	100.0	109.1	113.6	122.7
(c) 1995 = 100	36.4	40.9	40.9	54.5	90.9	100.0	109.1	113.6	122.7

The index labelled (b) has been obtained from the original data, by dividing by 22 and multiplying by 100. The index labelled (c) has been obtained from the 1990 = 100 index numbers by dividing by 275 and multiplying by 100. As you can see, the results are identical when rounded to one decimal place in this case.

Example 5.5.2

The following index numbers have base 1989. Recalculate them with base 1996.

Year	1995	1996	1997	1998	1999
1989 = 100	129.0	140.3	148.5	155.1	163.2

Interpret the two index numbers for 1999, with bases 1989 and 1996.

Solution

Divide through by 140.3 and multiply by 100:

Year	1995	1996	1997	1998	1999
1996 = 100	91.9	100	105.8	110.5	116.3

The index of 163.2 tells us that values in 1999 were 63.2 per cent higher than in 1989; the index of 116.3 tells us that they were 16.3 per cent higher than in 1996.

5.6 Combining series of index numbers

When a series of index numbers is subject to a change of base or perhaps a small change of composition, you will find in the series a year with two different index numbers, and the change of base will be shown in the series. The technique involved in combining two series into a single one is called *splicing the series together*.

Example 5.6.1

The price index below changed its base to 1983 after many years with base 1970. Recalculate it as a single series with base 1983. By how much have prices risen from 1981 to 1985?

Year	Price index
	(1970 = 100)
1980	263
1981	271
1982	277
1983	280
	(1983 = 100)
1984	104
1985	107

Solution

The index numbers from 1983 onwards already have 1983 = 100, so nothing need be done to them. What we have to do is to change the base of the original series, so it too is 1983. In this series the value for 1983 is 280, so we must divide the index numbers for 1980–82 by 280 and multiply by 100:

Year	Price index (1970 = 100)	Price index (1983 = 100)	
1980	263	94	= 100 × (263/280)
1981	271	97	= 100 × (271/280) etc.
1982	277	99	
1983	280	100	
	(1983 = 100)		
1984	104	104	
1985	107	107	

Now that we have a single series spanning both 1981 and 1985, we can compare the two:

$$100 \times \left(\frac{107}{97}\right) = 110$$

So prices have risen by 10 per cent from 1981 to 1985.

You may notice that we rounded to the nearest whole number in this example. This is because the original index numbers had plainly been rounded to the nearest whole number and at best we can hope that our results will be accurate to that same extent. You cannot acquire increased accuracy in the course of calculating.

Example 5.6.2

The following price index has undergone a change of base in 1990. Splice the two series together with base 1990 and then change the base to 1989.

Year	Price index (1980 = 100)
1987	141
1988	148
1989	155
1990	163

Year	Price index (1990 = 100)
1991	106
1992	110
1993	116

Solution

Year	Price index (1980 = 100)	Price index (1990 = 100)	Price index (1989 = 100)
1987	141	86.5	91
1988	148	90.8	95
1989	155	95.1	100
1990	163	100	105
	(1990 = 100)		
1991	106	106	111
1992	110	110	116
1993	116	116	122

The technique used in this example is quite generally applicable. Regardless of which year you eventually want as base, the first step in splicing together two index number series should always be to take as the new overall base the year in which the base changes (1990 in this example and 1983 in example 5.6.1).

5.7 Chain-base index numbers

So far we have dealt with index numbers that have the same base for several years. These are called *fixed-base index numbers* and, unless you are informed to the contrary, it is reasonable to assume that index numbers are of this type. However, it is often of more interest to know the annual increase. A *chain-base index number* (or simply a *chain index*) expresses each year's value as a percentage of the value for the previous year.

$$\text{Chain-base Index} = \frac{\text{This year's value}}{\text{Last year's value}} \times 100$$

Example 5.7.1

Express the following series as a series of chain-base index numbers:

Year	1995	1996	1997	1998	1999
Value	46	52	62	69	74

Solution

Year	1995	1996	1997	1998	1999
Value	46	52	62	69	74
Chain index	n/a	113.0	119.2	111.3	107.2

We cannot calculate the chain index for 1995 because we do not have the 1994 figure ('n/a' means 'not available').

The interpretation is the same as for fixed-base index numbers, except that the percentage change is each time over the previous year. In this example, the results tell us that values rose by 13.0 per cent from 1995 to 1996, by 19.2 per cent from 1996 to 1997, by 11.3 per cent the next year and by 7.2 per cent from 1998 to 1999.

Fixed-base index numbers can easily be changed into chain-base indices by treating them as if they were the original data. The only problem is to not pick up spurious accuracy. Try the next example.

Example 5.7.2

Convert the following fixed-base index numbers into a chain-base index and interpret your results:

Year	1995	1996	1997	1998	1999
1989 = 100	129.0	140.3	148.5	155.1	163.2

Solution

In each case we divide by the index for the previous year and multiply by 100. We cannot do this for 1995 since we do not have the 1994 figure. We shall round to the nearest whole number to try to avoid rounding errors.

Year	1995	1996	1997	1998	1999
1989 = 100	n/a	109	106	104	105

Over the period 1995–99, there were annual percentage increases of 9, 6, 4 and 5, respectively.

It can be a little harder to convert a chain-base index into a fixed-base index. Here is a fairly simple example.

Example 5.7.3

Express the following chain index as a fixed-base index with 1990 = 100:

Year	1990	1991	1992	1993	1994
Chain index	105.4	105.0	104.5	104.1	103.9

Solution

Year	1990	1991	1992	1993	1994
Chain index	105.4	105.0	104.5	104.1	103.9
1990 = 100	100	105.0	109.725	114.224	118.7

First, let 1990 = 100 as instructed. We already have the index for 1991 with 1990 as base – it is 105.0. To get the index for 1992, we start with that for 1991 (i.e. 105.0) and increase it by 4.5 per cent. We do this by multiplying by the ratio 104.5/100 = 1.045, so the index for 1992 = 105.0 × 1.045 = 109.725. For the present we shall keep the spurious accuracy. The next index is given by multiplying 109.725 by 104.1/100 = 1.041, and the last by multiplying the result by 1.039.

Rounding gives the fixed-base index with 1990 = 100 to one decimal place:

Year	1990	1991	1992	1993	1994
1990 = 100	100	105.0	109.7	114.2	118.7

If you want to change a chain index into a fixed-base index with a middle year as the base, the easiest way is probably to start by expressing it with the first year as base and then to change to the base that you want.

Example 5.7.4

Convert the following chain index into a fixed-base index: (a) with base 1986; and (b) with base 1988:

Year	1986	1987	1988	1989	1990	1991
Chain index	106.1	103.7	103.6	104.2	105.7	108.1

Solution

Year	1986	1987	1988	1989	1990	1991
Chain index	106.1	103.7	103.6	104.2	105.7	108.1
1986 = 100	100	103.7	107.4	111.9	118.3	127.9
1988 = 100	93	97	100	104	110	119

The index with 1986 = 100 is obtained by setting the 1986 figure = 100 and then multiplying consecutively by 1.037, 1.036, 1.042, 1.057 and 1.081.

The index with 1988 = 100 is then obtained from the 1986 = 100 index by dividing throughout by 107.4 and multiplying by 100.

We have only shown figures rounded to one decimal place but actually worked to about five decimal places in calculating the 1986 = 100 index. We worked from rounded figures to find the 1988 = 100 index.

5.8 Composite index numbers

In practice, most price indices cover a whole range of items and so there are two processes involved in the construction of the index number. One is indexing – comparing current values with those of the base year – and the other is averaging or somehow combining together the items under consideration.

We shall begin by using the method of combining individual price indices by means of a *weighted average*. In Chapter 4, we used the formula $\sum fx/\sum f$ for the average or arithmetic mean. The formula for a weighted average is the same as this but with weights, denoted by w, instead of frequencies. Hence:

$$\text{Weighted average} = \frac{\sum wx}{\sum w}$$

where x denotes the values being averaged and w denotes the weights.

Example 5.8.1

Average exam marks of 40 per cent, 55 per cent and 58 per cent with weights of 2, 2 and 1.

Solution

$$\text{Weighted average} = \frac{(2 \times 40) + (2 \times 55) + (1 \times 58)}{2 + 2 + 1} = \frac{248}{5} = 49.6\%$$

Weights are a measure of the importance that we allocate to each item. In the above example, the first two exams are rated as twice as important as the third one. In the arithmetic mean, values are weighted by the frequency with which they occur; in price indices, similar weighting systems operate.

Example 5.8.2

The three types of bread sold by a shop have price indices of 107.0, 103.6 and 102.9 compared with last year. Find the weighted average index for bread, using quantities as weights if the quantities sold are in the ratio 10:2:1.

Solution

$$\text{Weighted average} = \frac{(10 \times 107.0) + (2 \times 103.6) + (1 \times 102.9)}{10 + 2 + 1} = \frac{1{,}380.1}{13} = 106.2$$

Because the first type of bread has such a high weighting (10), its index (107) has had a major impact in increasing the value of the composite index.

Example 5.8.3

A manufacturer produces four items (A–D) and wishes to find an overall index of their prices compared with three years ago. The quantities sold will be used as weights. Calculate the price index using the following price indices and quantities:

Product	Price index base 3 years ago	Quantity sold per week
A	114.5	25
B	109.7	48
C	106.6	59
D	110.7	32

Solution

We need to multiply each price index by its weight, add them together and divide by the total weight. A table may help to show the method:

Product	Price index base 3 years ago	Quantity sold per week	Index × weight
A	114.5	25	2,862.5
B	109.7	48	5,265.6
C	106.6	59	6,289.4
D	110.7	32	3,542.4
		164	17,959.9

$$\text{Weighted average} = \frac{17{,}959.9}{164} = 109.5$$

5.9 Relative price indices

The notation commonly used for the construction of index numbers is as follows: the subscripts '0' and '1' are used, respectively, for the base year and the year under consideration, usually called the *current year*. Hence, for any given item:

P_0 = price in base year $\qquad$ P_1 = price in current year
Q_0 = quantity in base year $\qquad$ Q_1 = quantity in current year
$V_0 = P_0 Q_0$ = value in the base year $\qquad$ $V_1 = P_1 Q_1$ = value in current year

where value means the total expenditure on the item, and other sorts of weights are denoted by w as before.

For a given item, the price index = $100 \times (P_1/P_0)$, but quite often we work with the ratio called the *price relative* = P_1/P_0 and leave the multiplication by 100 to the end of the calculation.

The usual formula for a *relative price index* is therefore:

$$\text{Relative price index} = \frac{\sum[w \times (P_1/P_0)]}{\sum w} \times 100$$

> This formula is given in your exam.

The weights could be base-year quantities (i.e. Q_0) or values (i.e. $P_0 Q_0$), or current-year quantities or values (i.e. Q_1 or $P_1 Q_1$), or they could simply be decided on some other basis such as the weighting of exam marks.

The index will be called *base-weighted* or *current-weighted*, depending on whether it uses base or current weights.

Example 5.9.1

A grocer wishes to index the prices of four different types of tea, with base year 1990 and current year 1995. The available information is as follows:

	1990		1995	
	Price (£)	Quantity (crates)	Price (£)	Quantity (crates)
Type	P_0	Q_0	P_1	Q_1
A	0.89	65	1.03	69
B	1.43	23	1.69	28
C	1.29	37	1.49	42
D	0.49	153	0.89	157

Calculate the base-weighted relative price index using as weights (a) quantities; and (b) values (i.e. revenue for each item).

Solution

	Price relative (Rel)	Base-year quantity (Q_0)	Base-year value (V_0)	Rel × Q_0	Rel × V_0
A	1.157	65	57.85	75.22	66.95
B	1.182	23	32.89	27.19	38.88
C	1.155	37	47.73	42.74	55.13
D	1.816	153	74.97	277.85	136.15
Total		278	213.44	423.00	297.11

Base-weighted relative price indices are:

$$\text{Weighted by quantity: } \frac{\sum (Rel \times Q_0)}{\sum Q_0} \times 100 = \frac{423}{278} \times 100 = 152.2$$

$$\text{Weighted by value: } \frac{\sum (Rel \times V_0)}{\sum V_0} \times 100 = \frac{297.11}{213.44} \times 100 = 139.2$$

The first index tells us that prices have risen on average by 52 per cent; the second that they have risen by 39 per cent. Why might this be so?

The really big price rise is D's 82 per cent. The size of the index will be very strongly influenced by the weight given to D. In the first case, the quantity 153 is bigger than all the other quantities put together. D gets more than half of the total weight and so the index strongly reflects D's price rise and is very high. However, when we use value for weighting, D's value is only about one-third of the total because its price is low, so the price index is rather smaller.

Now it is your turn to see what happens if we use current quantities and values as weights.

Example 5.9.2

Using the data of Example 5.9.1, calculate the current-weighted relative price index with weights given by (a) quantities; and (b) values.

Solution

As before, we need the price relatives which have already been calculated. This time, however, they will be multiplied first by Q_1 and second by the value $Q_1 P_1$.

The calculations are as follows:

	Q_1	Rel = P_1/P_0	$V_1 = P_1 Q_1$	Q_1 × Rel	V_1 × Rel
A	69	1.157	71.07	79.85	82.25
B	28	1.182	47.32	33.09	55.92
C	42	1.155	62.58	48.51	72.28
D	157	1.816	139.73	285.16	253.80
Total	296		320.70	446.61	464.25

(a) Using Q_1 as weights, the price index is:

$$\frac{\sum (Rel \times Q_1)}{\sum Q_1} \times 100 = \frac{446.61}{296} \times 100 = 150.9$$

(b) Using V_1 as weights, the price index is:

$$\frac{\sum (Rel \times V_1)}{\sum V_1} \times 100 = \frac{464.25}{320.7} \times 100 = 144.8$$

Can you explain these further index numbers, compared with the ones we got using base weighting? Here they are in table form:

	Base-weighted	Current-weighted
Weighted by quantity	152.2	150.9
Weighted by value	139.2	144.8

Although the quantity of D purchased has dropped a little, presumably because of its high price rise, it still remains the cheapest and most popular brand. In fact, using quantities, it still accounts for over half the total weight. So its price index continues to be high, albeit slightly smaller than with base weighting.

The opposite has occurred with values. Although the quantity of D purchased has dropped, this is more than compensated by its increase in price and so it has increased its proportion of the total value (from 35 to 44 per cent). Consequently, the current-value-weighted index increasingly reflects D's big price rise and so is greater than the base-value-weighted index.

5.10 Aggregative price indices

In the previous section we indexed first (except that we did not multiply by 100) and subsequently combined the indices together in a weighted average. In this section we shall construct index numbers the other way round. We shall first combine the prices to give the total cost of a notional shopping basket and only then shall we index the cost of the basket at current prices compared with the cost at base-year prices. These indices are called 'aggregative' because the first step is to aggregate, or combine together, all the items under consideration. The first step in calculating a relative price index is to calculate all the price relatives.

If we want to compare prices now with those in the base year, we must compare like with like – the composition of the two baskets must be identical in every respect apart from price. If you buy goods with prices given by P in quantities given by Q, the total cost of the shopping basket is σPQ. The general form of an aggregative price index is therefore:

$$\frac{\sum_w P_1}{\sum_w P_0} \times 100$$

where the weights will be the quantities chosen.

> The formula for aggregative price indices is not given in your exam. It is less likely to be required than the relatives method.

Example 5.10.1

Find the aggregative price index for the following data, using the weights given:

Item	P_0	P_1	w
A	35	36	2
B	23	27	3
C	15	21	5

Solution

Item	wP_0	wP_1
A	70	72
B	69	81
C	75	105
Total	214	258

$$\text{Aggregative price index} = 100 \times \frac{\sum wP_1}{\sum wP_0}$$

$$= 100 \times \frac{258}{214}$$

$$= 120.6$$

Example 5.10.2

A company buys in just three raw materials, and its management wishes to compute a single value to reflect the average price rise of its raw materials. Calculate the aggregative price index with Year 1 = 100 using the weights given.

	Ave. price (£/ton)		Weights
	Year 1	Year 4	
Raw material X	2.50	3.00	200
Raw material Y	2.20	2.90	200
Raw material Z	2.00	2.05	400

Solution

The following table can be constructed:

	P_0	P_1	W	P_0W	P_1W
X	2.50	3.00	200	500	600
Y	2.20	2.90	200	440	580
Z	2.00	2.05	400	800	820
				1,740	2,000

The price index is $= \frac{2,000}{1,740} \times 100 = 114.9$

The company's average price rise has therefore been 14.9 per cent.

5.11 Choice of base weighting or current weighting

- In general, current weighting will seem better because it remains up to date.
- In particular, current-weighted indices reflect shifts away from goods subject to high price rises.
- Base-weighted indices do not do this and hence exaggerate inflation.
- However, current quantities can be very difficult to obtain – some considerable time may elapse after a year ends before a company knows what quantity it sold, whereas base quantities are known and remain steady for the lifetime of the index.

- So, current-weighted price indices are usually much more costly and time-consuming to calculate than are base-weighted ones.
- The stability of base weights means that the index for each year can be compared with that of every other year which, strictly speaking, a current-weighted index cannot.
- There can be no general guidance on the choice: it depends on the resources available and on the degree to which prices and quantities are changing. The only other consideration is that, as always, you must compare like with like. The retail price index (RPI), as we shall see, is a current-value-weighted relative index weighted by (almost) current values, and that method of construction should be used if at all possible if comparison with the RPI is a major function of the index being constructed.

5.12 Quantity indices

Although it is the most important and most frequently encountered, price is not the only financial factor measured by index numbers. *Quantity indices* constitute another category. They show how the amounts of certain goods and commodities vary over time or location. They are of importance when one is considering changes in sales figures, volumes of trade and so on.

When considering price indices, quantities emerged as the best weighting factor. Here, the converse is true: prices are considered the most appropriate weights when calculating quantity indices. Accordingly:

A relative quantity index will take the form:

$$\frac{\sum [w \times (Q_1/Q_0)]}{\sum w} \times 100$$

An aggregative quantity index will take the form:

$$\frac{\sum wQ_1}{\sum wQ_0} \times 100$$

where in both cases the weights could be prices, either base year or current, or values or some other measure of the importance of the items. P_0, P_1, Q_0 and Q_1 have the same meanings as earlier in this chapter.

The calculation of quantity indices and their application involve no new arithmetical techniques, as the following example illustrates.

Example 5.12.1

A company manufactures two products, A and B. The sales figures over the past 3 years have been as follows:

	A Sales '000	B Sales '000
1993	386	533
1994	397	542
1995	404	550
Weight	22	19

Using 1993 as a base, compute aggregative indices with the weights given for the combined sales of A and B in 1994 and 1995, and interpret their values.

Solution

For 1994, with 1993 as the base, we have:

Product A: $Q_0 = 386$ $Q_1 = 397$ $w = 22$
Product B: $Q_0 = 533$ $Q_1 = 542$ $w = 19$

and so the quantity index is:

$$100 \times \frac{\sum Q_1 w}{\sum Q_0 w} = 100 \times \frac{(397 \times 22 + 542 \times 19)}{(386 \times 22 + 533 \times 19)} = 102.22$$

In the same way, the quantity index for 1995 is 103.86.

These figures show that the volumes of sales in 1994 and 1995 were 2.22 and 3.86 per cent, respectively, higher than in the base year, 1993.

Example 5.12.2

A company manufactures three products, A, B and C, and the quantities sold in 1998 and 1999 were as follows:

Product	Quantity sold 1998	Quantity sold 1999	Weights
A	7	10	85
B	12	15	68
C	25	25	45

Find the index of the quantity sold in 1999 with 1998 as a base using the weights given by:

(a) using the aggregative method; and
(b) using the relatives method.

Solution

(a)

Product	wQ_0	wQ_1
A	595	850
B	816	1,020
C	1,125	1,125
Total	2,536	2,995

$$\text{Aggregative quantity index} = 100 \times \frac{2,995}{2,536} = 118.1$$

(b)

Product	Q_1/Q_0	w	$w \times (Q_1/Q_0)$
A	1.4286	85	121.4
B	1.25	68	85
C	1	45	45
Total		198	251.4

$$\text{Relative quantity index} = 100 \times \frac{251.4}{198} = 127.0$$

Notice that there is a considerable difference between these results, with the aggregative method telling us that the quantity sold has risen by 18 per cent compared with the 27 per cent given by the relative method. The choice of construction method and of weighting system will often have a major impact on the value of the resulting index number. There is, therefore, considerable scope for selecting the method that gives the results that you want!

5.13 The construction of the UK retail price index

The RPI is compiled and published monthly. It is as far as possible a relative index with current expenditures as weights. In the press it is mainly published as an annual increase, but it is in fact a fixed-base index number and currently the base is January 1987.

In the region of 130,000 price quotations are obtained monthly from a representative sample of retail outlets. It is representative in terms of geographic location within the United Kingdom, type and size of shop and timing over the month. Some 600 goods and services, called *price indicators*, are selected to be surveyed.

The selection of items for inclusion in the index and the weighting given to each item is largely determined by a massive government survey called the *Family Expenditure Survey* (FES). In the course of each year, a representative sample of households is asked to keep a diary for 2 weeks listing all their spending. They are interviewed about major items such as housing and services. Decisions about items to include as price indicators will be based on the findings of the FES, and similarly the weights, expressed as parts per £1,000, are determined by the expenditure on each item by the average household. The weights are the expenditures of the previous year, which is probably as current as is practical.

The items covered by the index are combined into 80 sections such as 'men's outerwear' and 'rail fares', which are in turn combined to give five broad groups before being averaged together in the overall index. The groups are:

- food and catering;
- alcohol and tobacco;
- housing and household expenditure;
- personal expenditure;
- travel and leisure.

There are some omissions from the RPI that may perhaps be thought important. The FES does not cover the very rich (top 4 per cent of the population) or those living on state benefits. In particular, a separate quarterly index is produced to monitor the prices of items purchased by pensioners. Life insurance, pension contributions and the capital element of mortgage repayments are not included; nor is tax. There is another index that takes taxation into account.

5.14 Using the RPI

Index numbers are widely used. The RPI, for example, is *the* measure of price inflation. Whenever you read that inflation is currently running at 3 per cent (or whatever) this means that, during the previous twelve months, the value of the RPI has increased by 3 per cent. In this section, we look at a number of applications of index numbers that, though not quoted as often in the media as the above example, are still of great commercial importance.

The first of these is *index linking*. In an attempt to protect people's savings and the incomes of some of the more vulnerable sections of society against the effects of inflation, many savings schemes, pensions and social benefits have, at various times in the past, been *linked* to the RPI in a way illustrated below.

Example 5.14.1

At the start of a year, the RPI stood at 340. At that time, a certain person's index-linked pension was £4,200 per annum and she had £360 invested in an index-linked savings bond. At the start of the following year, the RPI had increased to 360. To what level would the pension and the bond investment have risen?

Solution

First of all, the RPI has risen by 20 from 340. As a percentage, this is

$$\frac{20}{340} \times 100 = 5.88\%$$

The pension and the investment, being index-linked, would increase by the same percentage. The pension thus increases by 5.88% of £4,200 = £247 (nearest £), and the investment by 5.88% of £360 = £21.17. Hence, at the start of the year in question, the pension would be £4,447 per annum, and the investment would stand at £381.17.

Although the RPI is by far the most common index used in linking, there are others. For example, some house insurance policies have premiums and benefits that are linked to the index of house rebuilding costs, a far more suitable index than the RPI, which relates to general retail prices. At periods of low inflation, the practice of linking pay, pensions, savings and so on to the RPI is relatively harmless. When inflation is high, the automatic (and high) rises produced by linking tend to increase costs to industry and commerce, which therefore have to increase their prices. This in turn induces a rise in inflation that triggers off further index-linked rises in pay (and so on). Inflation is therefore seen to be exacerbated by this practice. Indeed, this has been observed in some countries with hyperinflation and where widespread index-linking has been introduced.

The second common use is in the *deflation of series*, or the removal of inflation from a series of figures, so that they can be compared. An example will illustrate the simple arithmetical process involved.

Example 5.14.2

Use the data given below to compare average earnings from 1978 to 1981.

	Average weekly earnings (male manual workers, 21 years+)	RPI (January 1974 = 100)
October 1978	£83.50	201.1
October 1979	£96.94	235.6
October 1980	£113.06	271.9
October 1981	£125.58	303.7

[Source: various editions, *Monthly Digest of Statistics*.]

Solution

The value of the RPI in October 1978 shows that average prices were 2.011 times higher then than in January 1974. The purchasing power of £1 will therefore have decreased by this factor in the time. An October 1978 wage of £83.50 was therefore 'worth'

$$\frac{83.50}{2.011} = £41.52$$

in January 1974. This is known as the *real* wage, at January 1974 prices. Applying this process to all the figures, we obtain:

		Real wages, January 1974 prices
October 1978		£41.52
October 1979	$\dfrac{96.94}{2.356} =$	£41.15
October 1980		£41.58
October 1981		£41.35

The average wages of this section of society can thus be seen not to have changed appreciably in real terms over this time period. The apparent rises in wages have been almost exactly cancelled out by similarly sized price rises.

To illustrate the technique further, the above example is repeated from a slightly different aspect.

Example 5.14.3

Calculate the real wages at October 1978 prices from the data in Example 5.14.2.

Solution

To convert wages to October 1978 price levels, we first need the price index based on that date. To convert the figure of 201.1 to 100, we need to multiply by:

$$\dfrac{100}{201.1}$$

Applying this to the other RPI figures:

		RPI (October 1978 = 100)
October 1978		100
October 1979	$235.6 \times \dfrac{100}{201.1} =$	117.2
October 1980		135.2
October 1981		151.0

The wages can now be expressed as real wages, based on this new index, just as above.

		Real wages, October 1978 prices
October 1978	$\dfrac{96.94}{1.172} =$	£83.50
October 1979		£82.71
October 1980	$\dfrac{113.06}{1.352} =$	£83.62
October 1981		£83.16

These figures confirm that wages have not changed appreciably in real terms.

Example 5.14.4

The following are the annual salaries of trainee accountants employed by a particular firm over the period 1988–93, and the corresponding values of the RPI with base 1987.

Year	Salary (£)	RPI
1988	18,100	106.9
1989	18,600	115.2
1990	19,200	126.1
1991	19,700	133.5
1992	20,300	138.5
1993	20,900	140.7

(a) Express the salaries at constant 1988 prices.
(b) Index the results with 1988 = 100.
(c) Comment on your results.

Solution

(a) Each value must be multiplied by

$$\frac{\text{RPI for 1988}}{\text{RPI for the year in question}}$$

(b) Each adjusted salary will then be divided by the 1988 salary and multiplied by 100. The results are:

Year	Salary (£)	RPI	Salary at 1988 prices	Index 1988 = 100
1988	18,100	106.9	18,100	100
1989	18,600	115.2	17,260	95
1990	19,200	126.1	16,277	90
1991	19,700	133.5	15,775	87
1992	20,300	138.5	15,668	87
1993	20,900	140.7	15,879	88

(c) The real salary paid to trainees, which tells us what they can purchase with their salary, has fallen steadily until 1993 when it increased a little. The decline over the entire 5-year period is 12 per cent.

We should hasten to add that this is an imaginary firm!

The RPI is not the only index used in deflation, particularly if there is a more suitable index available. For instance, an exporting company interested in its real level of profits might well deflate its actual profit figures by an index of export prices.

The main criticism of deflation, and indeed another problem of index linking, is that we are applying an average figure (for price rises or whatever) to a particular set of people who may or may not be 'average'. To illustrate the effects this could have, consider the cases of:

- an old-age pension for a single person being linked to the RPI;
- a brewery in the north of England deflating its profit figures by the RPI.

In the first instance, the single pensioner cannot be considered 'average' in at least two senses. The RPI measures price rises for the average family, which a single pensioner certainly is not, and the income of a pensioner is generally considerably below average. The effect of this latter factor is that a pensioner will spend a considerably larger portion of his/her income on heating and lighting, and on food, than most other people. Thus, at times when prices of these commodities are rising faster than others (a situation that has occurred in the past), the RPI will underestimate the average price rises in a pensioner's 'basket' of goods and so linking to this index will leave him/her worse off. Indeed, a 'pensioners' price index' has been introduced to overcome this.

The RPI measures price rises for all commodities, not just one type such as beer and related products, that might be rising in price at a different rate from the average. The brewery in the latter example would therefore be advised to deflate by the 'alcoholic drinks' section of the RPI. Even then, prices might be rising at a faster or slower rate in the north of England, compared with this average UK figure. The real profit figures would then be too high or too low, respectively.

> The technique of using the RPI to compare the purchasing power of wages etc. over several years is very important and it is a popular question with examiners.

5.15 Summary

- In general, index number:

$$\frac{\text{Current value}}{\text{Value in base year}} \times 100$$

- If we denote base-period prices by P_0; current prices by P_1; base-period quantities by Q_0; current quantities by Q_1; and weights in general by w, the two main types of price index can be expressed as:

$$\text{Relatives: } \frac{\sum [w \times (P_1/P_0)]}{\sum w} \times 100$$

$$\text{Aggregative: } \frac{\sum (w \times P_1)}{\sum (w \times P_0)} \times 100$$

- The two types of quantity index are:

$$\text{Relatives: } \frac{\sum [w \times (Q_1/Q_0)]}{\sum w} \times 100$$

$$\text{Aggregative: } \frac{\sum (w \times Q_1)}{\sum (w \times Q_0)} \times 100$$

The summation is over all items in the index.

As well as being able to calculate and interpret the above, you should also be able to:

- change the base of a series of index numbers;
- splice together two series;
- understand the factors influencing the choice of base year;
- understand the advantages and disadvantages of base weights and current weights;
- understand the construction of the RPI;
- be able to use the RPI in practice.

Readings

5

These extracts from an entertaining article from *The Economist* look at ways in which figures can be manipulated to produce the desired results.

Playing with numbers

©*The Economist* **Newspaper Limited, London, 31 May 1986**

The British science-fiction writer, H.G. Wells, had a touching faith in statistics. He predicted that statistical thinking would one day be as necessary a qualification for efficient citizenship as the ability to read and write.

That day seems to have arrived. Statistics, social and economic, abound in the press. But the world is still full of inefficient citizens. For every statistic which is used, another is abused. Few people are equipped to defend themselves against the professionals economists — as well as politicians — who manipulate figures to suit their own purposes. This brief provides a guided tour through the statistical jungle.

What should the voter make of these two contradictory assessments of the economic record of Mrs Thatcher's government? A fictitious Conservative spokesman boasts:

In four years to 1985, the British economy has grown by an average of 3 per cent a year, compared with average growth of less than 2 per cent during the Labour years of 1974 − 79. Exports are running at record levels. In 1985, Britain's exports of manufactured goods rose 15 per cent, increasing their share of world markets. This government has reduced the rate of inflation by 40 per cent since 1979.

The Labour spokesman counters:

Since the Conservative government came to power in 1979, growth has averaged a mere 1 per cent a year — only half the average rate achieved by Labour. Yet, despite their deflationary policies, the rate of inflation has fallen by a mere four percentage points. British manufacturers are being squeezed out of world markets: last year, as world trade boomed, Britain's exports grew by less than 1 per cent in volume.

Who is lying? Neither; every figure is correct. The trick is to choose from the many possible measures the one which is most favourable to your argument.

Percentages offer a fertile field for confusion. A percentage is always a percentage of something; that something is called the base. The first question to ask is, what is the base of a calculation? It can make a big difference. If it costs a company $5 to make a widget that sells for $25, its $20 profit margin is either a whopping 400 per cent or a more modest 80 per cent, according to whether it is expressed as a percentage of costs or sales.

Equal percentage increases imply bigger absolute increases as the base itself changes. If prices rise by 10 per cent a year for 10 years the total increase is not simply 100 per cent (10×10), but 159 per cent because each successive 10 per cent rise applies to a higher base.

A moving base also means that percentage increases and decreases are not symmetrical. If prices decline by 10 per cent a year, then after ten years the total fall will be only 65 per cent because the base shrinks every year. Similarly, if wages fell 50 per cent one year, but then rose 50 per cent the next, workers would find their pay packets were 25 per cent smaller than when they started: the 50 per cent fall applies to a bigger base than the 50 per cent rise (see chart 1). They need a 100 per cent pay rise to restore the 50 per cent cut.

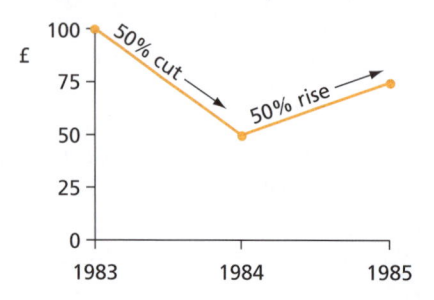

Chart 1 Unequal halves: average weekly wages

Another statistical tool is the index number. When the level of production is expressed as an index, it shows the change from a specific base year (which is usually valued at 100). So, if the index reaches a value of 150, it is easy to see that the indicator has risen by 50 per cent from its base.

An index is often used as a special kind of average to aggregate changes in different prices, e.g. the consumer price index and the share price index. Yet again there is more than one way to calculate it. The arithmetic mean, described above, is the most common method. But the FT Ordinary Share Index uses the geometric mean: individual prices are multiplied together and then the appropriate root is taken (i.e. if there are two items, the square root; if three, the cube root). Suppose there are two shares which both start at a value of 100 and one doubles in price and the other halves. Then the geometric mean will remain at 100 (i.e. the square root of 200 × 50); but the arithmetic mean is 125 [i.e. (200 + 50)/2].

Discussion points
Discuss these within your study group before reading the outline solutions

Discuss and list the measures that might be taken to ensure that an index number, such as the RPI, is less than it otherwise might be.

Outline solutions
- Change the items covered by the index.
- Change the weights given to items.
- Change the construction method – choose between relatives or aggregative, base or current weighted.
- Change the base year to one in which prices were specially high.
- In any case bring the base year as close as possible to the present.
- Calculate all possible relevant price indices and then quote the one with the best results.
- If you find yourself being given index numbers that do not seem quite to fit your expectations about a situation, start off by being suspicious!

Revision Questions

Part 5.1 Objective testing selection

> Questions 5.1.1–5.1.10 are standard multiple-choice questions with exactly one correct answer each. Thereafter, the style of question will vary.

5.1.1 In 1994, a price index based on 1980 = 100 stood at 126. In that year it was rebased at 1994 = 100. By 1996, the new index stood at 109. For a continuous estimate of price changes since 1980, the new index may be expressed, to two decimal places, in terms of the old as

(A) 85.51
(B) 137.34
(C) 135.00
(D) 135.68.

5.1.2 Profits have been as follows (£m):

1990	1991	1992	1993	1994
4.1	3.7	3.5	3.8	3.9

When converted to index numbers with base 1990, the index for 1994 is

(A) 95
(B) 105
(C) −0.2
(D) 5.

5.1.3 In general, the relative sizes of current-weighted and base-weighted price indices are as follows:

(A) more or less equal.
(B) current-weighted bigger than base-weighted.
(C) base-weighted bigger than current-weighted.
(D) no regular pattern exists.

5.1.4 In 1990, a price index based on 1980 = 100 had a value of x. During 1990, it was rebased at 1990 = 100, and in 1998 the new index stood at 112.

If the total price movement between 1980 and 1998 was an increase of 40 per cent, what was the value of x in 1990, that is, before rebasing?

(A) 125
(B) 128
(C) 136
(D) 140.

5.1.5 If an index with 1990 = 100 has values of 108 in 1995 and 128 in 1999, find the index for 1999 if the base is changed to 1995.

(A) 84.4
(B) 136
(C) 118.5
(D) 120.

5.1.6 Which of the following is an advantage of base-weighting?

(A) The index remains up to date.
(B) The index is easy to calculate.
(C) The index gives relatively high results.
(D) The index is comparable with the RPI.

5.1.7 In 1992 the retail price index was 133.5 with 1987 = 100. Convert weekly wages of £300 back to 1987 constant prices.

(A) £400.50
(B) £333.50
(C) £433.50
(D) £224.72.

5.1.8 If the base year is 1995 and the current year is 1999, find the base-weighted quantity index for 1999 given the following totals:

	wQ_0	wQ_1
Total	230	245

(A) 93.9
(B) 104.2
(C) 106.5
(D) 150.

5.1.9 How are the weights obtained for the retail price index? They are:

(A) The quantity of the item that the average household bought.
(B) The amount the average household spent on the item.
(C) The quantity of the items that were sold by a sample of retail outlets.
(D) The expenditure on the item at a sample of retail outlets.

5.1.10 Use the following data to calculate a current quantity-weighted relative price index:

Item	P_0	P_1	w
F	8	12	14
G	4	9	13

(A) 186.1
(B) 187.5
(C) 173.8
(D) 175.0.

5.1.11 In which one or more of the following ways could a price index of 235 be interpreted?

(A) There has been a 35 per cent increase since the base year.
(B) There has been a 135 per cent increase since the base year.
(C) There has been a 235 per cent increase since the base year.
(D) Prices now are 2.35 times what they were in the base year.

5.1.12 Which of the following statements about the base year is/are correct?

(A) The base year has to be changed from time to time.
(B) The base year is fixed and cannot be changed.
(C) The base year should be one in which there were important changes regarding the variable of interest.
(D) The base year should be the one in which the variable of interest took its lowest value.

5.1.13 Complete the following table which shows two index number series being spliced together to give a single series based on 1998. Give your answers correct to one decimal place.

Year	Price index (1990 = 100)	Prince index (1998 = 100)
1995	238	?
1996	242	?
1997	247	?
1998	250	100
	(1998 = 100)	
1999	104	104
2000	109	109
2001	111	111

5.1.14 Complete the following table in which values are being expressed as a chain-base index, giving your answers to the nearest whole number.

Year	1997	1998	1999	2000	2001
Value	72	75	81	84	89
Chain index		?	?	?	?

5.1.15 Complete the following table in which a chain-base index is being converted to one with fixed base 1996. Give your answers correct to the nearest whole number.

Year	1996	1997	1998	1999
Chain index	102.1	103.4	101.9	103.7
1996 = 100	100	?	?	?

5.1.16 Exam marks of 40, 58 and 65 per cent are combined as a weighted average of 51 per cent. What does this tell you about the weighting system used?

(A) The exam with the lowest mark had a relatively high weight.
(B) The exam with the highest mark had a relatively high weight.
(C) The exam marks have not been given equal weights.

5.1.17 The following table shows four items with their individual price indices and their relative weights. Calculate the weighted relative price index for the four items combined, giving your answer to the nearest whole number.

Item	Price index	Weight
A	102	42
B	130	22
C	114	30
D	107	65

5.1.18 The following table shows the prices of three items in the base year and the current year, along with their weightings. Calculate the aggregative price index for the three items. Give your answer to the nearest whole number.

Item	Base-year price (P_0)	Current-year price (P_1)	Weight (w)
A	350	367	8
B	420	480	2
C	506	520	3

5.1.19 Which of the following statements about the UK Retail Price Index (RPI) is/are correct?

(A) The RPI covers the expenditures of all households in the UK.
(B) The RPI is published annually.
(C) The weights in the RPI are derived from the *Family Expenditure Survey*.
(D) The RPI now includes tax payments.

5.1.20 Complete the table below in which annual salaries are being converted to their values at 1990 prices using the RPI. Give your answers to the nearest whole number.

Year	Salary £	RPI	Salary at 1990 prices £
1990	25,500	126.1	25,500
1991	26,900	133.5	?
1992	28,100	138.5	?
1993	28,700	140.7	?

Part 5.2 Index numbers

The managers of the catering division of a hospital wish to develop an index number series for measuring changes in food prices. As an experiment, they have chosen four items in general use that are summarised below, along with weights that reflect the quantities currently being bought.

	Prices per unit 1996	1997	Weight
Flour (kg)	0.25	0.30	10,000
Eggs (boxes)	1.00	1.25	5,000
Milk (litres)	0.30	0.35	10,000
Potatoes (kg)	0.05	0.06	10,000

5.2.1 Write the formula for the aggregative price index denoting weight by w, 1996 price by P_0 and 1997 price by P_1.

5.2.2 Calculate the aggregative price index for 1997 with base 1996, giving your answer to two decimal places.

5.2.3 Some of the following comments are advantages of current weights over base weights and some are advantages of base weights compared to current weights. Delete answers accordingly.

	Advantage of
(A) Current weights are expensive to obtain	current/base/incorrect
(B) Base-weighted indexes are preferable in times of high inflation.	current/base/incorrect
(C) Current-weighted indexes remain up to date	current/base/incorrect
(D) Current weights may be very difficult to obtain	current/base/incorrect
(E) Base weights are always out of date	current/base/incorrect
(F) Current-weighted indexes reflect changes in demand following price rises	current/base/incorrect
(G) Base weights need only be obtained once	current/base/incorrect
(H) Bases-weighted indexes can be meaningfully compared from one year to the next	current/base/incorrect

5.2.4 Which of the following are reasons why it is usual to weight the constituent parts of a price index?

(A) Weights reflect the prices of the constituent parts.
(B) Prices are always the price per some weight or other.
(C) Weights reflect the relative importance of the constituent parts.
(D) Weights must be known so that the entire 'shopping basket' will weigh 100.

Part 5.3   Price relatives and base-weighted index

A company buys and uses five different materials. Details of the actual prices and quantities used for 1995, and the budgeted figures for 1996, are as follows:

Material	Weight	Actual 1995 Unit price £	Budgeted 1996 Unit price £
A	21	11	12
B	56	22	26
C	62	18	18
D	29	20	22
E	31	22	23

5.3.1 Calculate the missing values in the following table, taking 1995 as the base year and giving your answers correct to two decimal places where appropriate.

Material	Price relative	Price relative × Weight
A	109.09	2,290.89
B	118.18	6,618.08
C	100	F
D	110	G
E	104.55	3,241.05
Total		H

5.3.2 If the total of the price relatives × weights was 21,000, calculate the relative price index for the above data with base 1995, giving your answer to the nearest whole number.

5.3.3 If the relative price index calculated in 3.2 were 105, which of the following statements would be correct?

(A) Prices are budgeted to be 1.05 times their current levels.
(B) Turnover is budgeted to rise by 5 per cent.
(C) Quantities sold are budgeted to rise by 5 per cent.
(D) Prices are budgeted to rise by 5 per cent.
(E) Prices are budgeted to rise by 105 per cent.
(F) Prices are budgeted to rise by £5 on average.

5.3.4 Would you describe the price index in Part 3.2 as base weighted or current weighted or neither?

Delete as appropriate
base/current/neither

Part 5.4 Index numbers

The data below refers to average earnings index numbers in Great Britain for different sectors of industry, 1988 = 100, and the Retail Price Index, 1987 = 100.

Date	Whole economy	Production industries	Service industries	Retail Price Index
1988	100	100	100	107
Feb 89	104.6	104.9	104.4	111.5
May 89	107.5	108.1	107.2	115.0
Aug 89	109.1	109.2	108.7	115.8
Nov 89	112.8	112.9	112.7	118.5
Feb 90	114.0	114.3	113.7	120.2
May 90	118.5	118.2	118.6	126.2
Aug 90	120.9	119.7	121.1	128.1
Nov 90	123.8	123.7	123.0	130.0
Feb 91	124.7	125.2	123.8	130.9
May 91	128.1	129.2	127.1	133.5
Aug 91	130.8	130.2	130.4	134.1
Nov 91	130.8	131.8	129.7	135.6

[Source: *Employment Gazette,* January 1992]

5.4.1 Using 1988 as the base throughout, deflate the production industries index at the points Nov 89 (A), Nov 90 (B) and Nov 91 (C), giving your answers to one decimal place.

5.4.2 Which of the following correctly states what a deflated production industries index of 105 would mean.

(A) Five per cent more goods and services can be bought by average earnings in Production Industries compared to the base year.
(B) Average earnings in Production Industries are 5 per cent more than in the base year.
(C) Real earnings in the base year were 5 per cent more than in the year in question.
(D) Average earnings in Production Industries were 5 per cent more than the average for Great Britain.

5.4.3 A retired person from the service industries had a pension of £5,000 a year starting in May 1989 and updated each November in line with the average earnings index for that sector. Find the value of the pension (to the nearest £) in Nov 1989 (A), Nov 1990 (B) and Nov 1991 (C).

5.4.4 If the answers to 4.3 were D = 5,000, E = 5,800 and F = 6,000 find the real values (in constant May 1989 prices) of the pension in Nov 89 (A), Nov 90 (B) and Nov 91 (C) to the nearest £.

5.4.5 If the answer to (C) in Question 4.4 (i.e. the real value of the pension in Nov 91) was 5,100, which of the following statements would be correct?

(A) From May 89 to Nov 91 the purchasing power of the pension has increased by 100 per cent.

(B) From May 89 to Nov 91 the purchasing power of the pension has increased by £100 at Nov 91 prices.

(C) From May 89 to Nov 91 the purchasing power of the pension has increased by £100 at May 89 prices.

Solutions to Revision Questions

✓ Solutions to Part 5.1

5.1.1 Answer: (B)

Prices in 1994 were 1.26 times those in 1980 and prices in 1996 were 1.09 times those in 1994. Hence prices in 1996 were $1.09 \times 1.26 = 1.3734$ times those in 1980. This corresponds to a price index of 137.34.

5.1.2 Answer: (A)

$$\text{Index} = \frac{3.9}{4.1} \times 100 = 95 \text{ (to the nearest whole number)}.$$

5.1.3 Answer: (C)

Base-weighted index numbers do not reflect the fact that customers buy less of items that are subject to high price rises. They subsequently exaggerate inflation and tend to be greater than current-weighted index numbers.

5.1.4 Answer: (A)

The overall increase of 40 per cent has resulted from $(x - 100)$ per cent followed by 12 per cent. Hence, using ratios, $1.12 \times (x/100) = 1.40$, giving $x = 125$.

5.1.5 Answer: (C)

The index is given by dividing the 1999 value by the base-year value and multiplying by 100, that is, $100 \times (128/108) = 118.5$. The ratio of values is upside down in A — this is the index for 1995 with 1999 as base. In B you seem to have added the 8 of the 108 to 128 and in D you seem to have translated the difference of 20 into an index of 120 without realising that the start point is 108, not 100.

5.1.6 Answer: (B)

Base-weighted indices do not remain up to date, and since the RPI is current-weighted they are not really comparable. Base-weighted indices do exaggerate inflation but this is not an advantage. However, they are easy to calculate since the same weights are used year after year and this is an advantage.

5.1.7 Answer: (D)

The value at constant 1987 prices is given by multiplying by the RPI for 1987 (i.e. 100) and dividing by the RPI for 1992. A has the correct method but the ratio is upside down. B adds the increase of 33 in the RPI to the £300 and C adds the entire RPI to it. Both are wrong. You cannot add an index to a quantity in units such as £.

5.1.8 Answer: (C)

The quantity index is given by $100 \times (\sum Q_1 w / \sum Q_0 w)$, which gives $100 \times (245/230) = 106.5$. All the other answers involved the wrong ratio or, in the case of (D), the difference between the two totals.

5.1.9 Answer: (B)

The expenditure per £1,000 spent by the average household is given by the *Family Expenditure Survey*. The quantity bought would not be applicable because the household may only have one car and lots of baked beans, but the car is more significant than the beans. (C) would not be appropriate for the same reason. It might be possible to use a system similar to (D) but this is not the method used.

5.1.10 Answer: (A)

The two price relatives 1.5 and 2.25 must be multiplied by the values of w_1, that is, 14 and 13 and totalled. Then divide by 27 and multiply by 100. B has averaged the relatives without weights. (C) is correctly calculated but uses the aggregative rather than the relatives method and (D) has simply totalled the P_1 values and expressed them as a percentage of the total of the P_0 values, without any weighting.

5.1.11 The correct answers are (B) and (D). If you subtract 100 from an index number, it gives the percentage increase since the base year. Equally, if you divide an index number by 100, it gives the ratio of current values to base-year values.

5.1.12 The correct answer is (A). A base year will be fixed for several years but will eventually have to be changed to keep it relevant. The base year should be a very typical year in which there are no big changes or specially high or low values in the variable.

5.1.13 The completed table is as follows:

Year	Price index (1990 = 100)	Price index (1998 = 100)
1995	238	95.2
1996	242	96.8
1997	247	98.8
1998	250	100
	(1998 = 100)	
1999	104	104
2000	109	109
2001	111	111

5.1.14 The completed table is as follows:

Year	1997	1998	1999	2000	2001
Value	72	75	81	84	89
Chain index		104	108	104	106

5.1.15 The completed table is as follows:

Year	1996	1997	1998	1999
Chain index	102.1	103.4	101.9	103.7
1996 = 100	100	103	105	109

5.1.16 Answers (A) and (C) are correct. The low weighted average requires the low mark to have a relatively high weight and the high mark a relatively low weight. Equal weighting would have resulted in a considerably higher average.

5.1.17 The relative index is given by $\sum \text{index} \times \text{weight}/\sum \text{weight} = 17{,}519/159$. Hence, the relative price index $= 110$.

5.1.18 The aggregative price index is given by $100 \times (\sum wP_1/\sum wP_0) = 100 \times (5{,}456/5{,}158) = 106$.

5.1.19 Only statement (C) is correct. Very rich and very poor households are not covered by the RPI, it does not include tax and it is published monthly.

5.1.20 The method is to multiply each salary by the 1990 RPI and to divide by the RPI for the year in question.

Year	Salary £	RPI	Salary at 1990 prices £
1990	25,500	126.1	25,500
1991	26,900	133.5	25,409
1992	28,100	138.5	25,584
1993	28,700	140.7	25,722

✓ Solutions to Part 5.2

5.2.1 Answer:

$100 \times \sum wP_1/\sum wP_0$.

5.2.2 Price index for *1997*

$$= \frac{(0.3 \times 10{,}000) + (1.25 \times 5{,}000) + (0.35 \times 10{,}000) + (0.06 \times 10{,}000)}{(0.25 \times 10{,}000) + (1 \times 5{,}000) + (0.3 \times 10{,}000) + (0.05 \times 10{,}000)} \times 100$$

$$= \frac{13{,}350}{11{,}000} \times 100 = 121.36.$$

Answer: 121.36.

5.2.3 With base-year quantities as weights, the denominator will remain constant from year to year. However, since current weights change each year, their denominator constantly changes.

The base-weighted index is therefore easier to calculate and enables meaningful comparisons with previous years. It is also relatively cheap because the weights need to be obtained only once. However, in volatile conditions the base weights become dated and can give misleading indices. Another disadvantage is that base-weighted price indices do not reflect the tendency of consumers to buy fewer of those items that have undergone high price rises. They consequently give unrealistically high weighting to such items and tend to overstate inflation.

Current weights are much more suitable when conditions are volatile, since they remain up to date and reflect changes in demand following price rises. Their drawback is that meaningful comparisons with previous periods may not be possible because of the continually changing weights. Additionally, it can be very difficult and costly to obtain current weights and, in practice, the most recent weights available may have to be used instead.

Answers:	Advantage of
(A) Current weights are expensive to obtain	base
(B) Base-weighted indexes are preferable in times of high inflation	incorrect
(C) Current-weighted indexes remain up to date	current
(D) Current weights may be very difficult to obtain	base
(E) Base weights are always out of date	incorrect
(F) Current-weighted indexes reflect changes in demand following price rises	current
(G) Base weights need only be obtained once	base
(H) Bases-weighted indexes can be meaningfully compared from one year to the next	base

5.2.4 Weights do not reflect prices so (A) is incorrect; (B) is basically correct but is not a reason for using weighting; (D) is simply incorrect.

Answer: (C) Weights reflect the relative importance of the constituent parts.

✓ Solutions to Part 5.3

5.3.1 The price relatives are given by expressing the current price as a percentage of the base year price. For example, the value of G is given by $100 \times 22/20 = 110$. The value of J is then given by multiplying by the weight $= 110 \times 29 = 3{,}190$. K is simply a column total.

Answers:

(F) 6,200
(G) 3,190
(H) 21,540.02

5.3.2 Relative price index $= 100 \times \dfrac{\sum[w \times (P_1 / P_0)]}{\sum w}$

Base-weighted price index $= \dfrac{21{,}000}{199} = 106$ (to nearest whole number)

Answer: 106

5.3.3 The price index cannot show changes in turnover or quantities sold nor does it relate to actual prices in £ so (B), (C) and (F) are incorrect. (E) is incorrect because the percentage increase is given by subtracting 100.

Answers:

(A) Prices are budgeted to be 1.05 times their current levels.
(D) Prices are budgeted to rise by 5 per cent.

5.3.4 Answer: Base weighting.

Solutions to Part 5.4

5.4.1 To deflate back to 1988 prices we must multiply the selected value by the Retail Price Index (RPI) for 1988 (i.e. by 107) and divide by the RPI for the year in question. Hence the value for Nov 89 is given by $112.9 \times 107/118.5 = 101.9$.

Answers:

(A) 101.9
(B) 101.8
(C) 104.0

5.4.2 Answer: (A)

Five per cent more goods and services can be bought by average earnings in Production Industries compared to the base year.

5.4.3 In May 89 the service industries average earnings index stood at 107.2. In order to update in Nov 89 we must multiply £5,000 by the index for Nov 89 (i.e. by 112.7) and divide by 107.2. Similarly, in Nov 90 we will multiply the £5,000 by 123.0 and again divide by 107.2.

Answers:

(A) 5,257
(B) 5,737
(C) 6,049

5.4.4 The real value of the pension at constant May 89 prices will be given by multiplying the value of the pension at a given point of time by the May 89 RPI (i.e. by 115) and dividing by the RPI for the particular time. For example, the real value in Nov 89 = $5,000 \times 115/118.5 = 4,852$ and that in Nov 90 is given by $5,800 \times 115/130 = 5,131$.

Answers:

(A) 4,852
(B) 5,131
(C) 5,088

5.4.5 5,100 is the value of the pension in Nov 91 at constant May 89 prices not at Nov 91 prices. The percentage change cannot be obtained by subtracting the original £5,000.

Answer: (C)

From May 89 to Nov 91 the purchasing power of the pension has increased by £100 at May 89 prices.

6

Financial Mathematics

Financial Mathematics

Learning Outcomes

After completing this chapter, which is central to: *Business Mathematics*, you should be able to:

- calculate future values of an investment using both simple and compound interest;
- calculate an annual percentage rate of interest given a quarterly or monthly rate;
- calculate the present value of a future cash sum, using both a formula and tables;
- calculate the present value of an annuity using both a formula and tables;
- calculate loan/mortgage repayments and the value of an outstanding loan/mortgage;
- calculate the present value of a perpetuity;
- calculate the future value of regular savings (sinking funds) or find the savings given the future value, if necessary, using the sum of a geometric progression;
- calculate the net present value of a project, and use this to decide whether a project should be undertaken or to choose between mutually exclusive projects;
- explain the use of the internal rate of return of a project;
- apply these techniques to financial plans in Excel.

6.1 Introduction

Perhaps the most familiar use of mathematics in finance concerns interest calculations and other topics related to investments. In this chapter we shall develop formulae involving interest payments and equivalent rates of interest, but we shall also cover highly important but less well-known concepts such as present value. The practical applications dealt with in this chapter include loans, mortgages and regular saving plans.

6.2 Simple interest

One of the most basic uses of mathematics in finance concerns calculations of *interest*, the most fundamental of which is *simple interest*. Suppose £P is invested at a fixed rate of interest of r per annum (where r is a proportion) and that interest is added just once at the end of a period of n years. The interest earned each year is calculated by multiplying the rate of interest r by the amount invested, £P, giving an amount £rP. After n years the sum of £rPn will be credited to give a total at the end of the period, £V, of:

$$V = P + rPn$$

or:

$$V = P(1 + rn)$$

This well-known formula is often referred to as the *simple interest* formula.

Example 6.2.1

An amount of £5,000 is invested at a rate of 8 per cent per annum. What will be the value of the investment in 5 years' time, if simple interest is added once at the end of the period?

Solution

The interest rate in the formula needs attention: it is assumed that r is a *proportion*, and so, in this case, we must convert $r = 8$ per cent into a proportion:

$$r = 0.08$$

Also, we have

$$P = 5,000 \text{ and } n = 5$$

So

$$V = P(1 + rn) = 5,000(1 + 0.08 \times 5) = 5,000 \times 1.4 = 7,000$$

Thus, the value of the investment will be £7,000.

Example 6.2.2

Calculate the value of the following, assuming that simple interest is added:

(a) £20,000 invested for 5 years at 5 per cent per annum;
(b) £50,000 invested for 3 years at 6 per cent per annum;
(c) £30,000 invested for 6 years with 1 per cent interest per quarter.

Solution

(a) $r = 0.05$, $n = 5$, $P = 20,000$:

$$V = P(1 + rn) = 20,000(1 + 0.25) = £25,000$$

(b) $r = 0.06$, $n = 3$, $P = 50,000$:

$$V = 50,000(1 + 0.18) = £59,000$$

(c) $r = 0.01$, $n = 6 \times 4 = 24$, $P = 30,000$:

$$V = 30,000(1 + 0.24) = £37,200$$

6.3 Compound interest

In practice, simple interest is not used as often as *compound interest*. Suppose £P is invested at a fixed rate of interest of r per annum and that interest is added at the end of each year; that is, it is compounded annually.

After 1 year, the value of the investment will be the initial investment £P, plus the interest accrued, £rP, and so will be

$$P + rP = P(1 + r)$$

During the second year, the interest accrued will be r times the amount at the end of the first year, and so will be $rP(1 + r)$. The value at the end of the second year will be

$$P(1 + r) + rP(1 + r) = P(1 + r)(1 + r) = P(1 + r)^2$$

Proceeding in this way, after n years the value, £V, will be given by

$$V = P(1 + r)^n$$

> This well-known formula is often referred to as the *compound interest* formula and is given in your exam.

As you will see, in financial mathematics we work with an *annual ratio* denoted by $1 + r$ rather than with the rate of interest.

Example 6.3.1

An amount of £5,000 is invested at a fixed rate of 8 per cent per annum. What amount will be the value of the investment in 5 years' time, if the interest is compounded:

(a) annually?
(b) every 6 months?

Solution

(a) The only part of this type of calculation that needs particular care is that concerning the interest rate. The formula assumes that r is a *proportion*, and so, in this case:

   $r = 0.08$

   In addition, we have $P = 5,000$ and $n = 5$, so:

   $V = P(1 + r)^5 = 5,000 \times (1 + 0.08)^5 = 5,000 \times 1.469328 = 7,346.64$

   Thus, the value of the investment will be £7,346.64.
   It will be noted, by comparing this answer with that of Example 6.2.1, that compound interest gives higher values to investments than simple interest.

(b) With slight modifications, the basic formula can be made to deal with compounding at intervals other than annually. Since the compounding is done at 6-monthly intervals, 4 per cent (half of 8 per cent) will be added to the value on each occasion. Hence, we use $r = 0.04$. Further, there will be ten additions of interest during the five years, and so $n = 10$. The formula now gives:

   $V = P(1 + r)^{10} = 5,000 \times (1.04)^{10} = 7,401.22$

   Thus, the value in this instance will be £7,401.22.
   In a case such as this, the 8 per cent is called a *nominal* annual rate, and we are actually referring to 4 per cent per 6 months.

Example 6.3.2

Repeat Example 6.2.2 with *compound* interest.

Solution

(a) $r = 0.05$, $n = 5$, $P = 20,000$

$$V = 20,000(1.05)^5 = £25,525.63$$

(b) $r = 0.06$, $n = 3$, $P = 50,000$

$$V = 50,000(1.06)^3 = £59,550.80$$

(c) $r = 0.01$, $n = 6 \times 4 = 24$, $P = 30,000$

$$V = 30,000(1.01)^{24} = £38,092.04$$

6.4 Equivalent rates of interest

> In Example 6.3.1 the rate of interest was stated to be 8 per cent per annum but was actually 4 per cent every 6 months. We can find the *effective annual rate of interest* by considering the impact of two 4 per cent increases on an initial value of £1:

$$\text{Value at the end of 1 year} = 1 \times 1.04 \times 1.04 = 1.0816$$

This is the annual ratio that results not from 8 per cent per annum but from 8.16 per cent. Hence, the effective annual rate of interest is 8.16 per cent in this case.

Example 6.4.1

An investor is considering two ways of investing £20,000 for a period of 10 years:

- option A offers 1.5 per cent compounded every 3 months;
- option B offers 3.2 per cent compounded every 6 months.

Which is the better option?

Solution

We have, for option A, $P = 20,000$; $n = 10 \times 4 = 40$; $r = 0.015$ and so:

$$V = 20,000(1 + 0.015)^{40} = £36,280.37$$

For option B, $P = 20,000$; $n = 10 \times 2 = 20$; $r = 0.032$ and so:

$$V = 20,000(1 + 0.032)^{20} = £37,551.21.$$

Hence, option B is the better investment.

In this case, $P = 20,000$ was given but it is not necessary to be given an initial value because £1 can be used instead.

Example 6.4.2

Find the effective annual rates of interest corresponding to the following:
(a) 3 per cent every 6 months;
(b) 2 per cent per quarter;
(c) 1 per cent per month.

Solution

(a) For £1, value at the end of 1 year = $1 \times 1.03^2 = 1.0609$. Hence, the effective annual rate is 6.09 per cent.
(b) For £1, value at the end of 1 year = $1 \times 1.02^4 = 1.0824$. Hence, the effective annual rate is 8.24 per cent.
(c) For £1, value at the end of 1 year = $1 \times 1.01^{12} = 1.1268$. Hence, the effective annual rate is 12.68 per cent.

So far, we have moved from short periods of time to longer periods and this is done by raising the monthly or quarterly ratio to the requisite power. The same mathematics apply going backwards from a longer to a shorter period, but in this situation we use roots rather than powers. Here is an example.

Example 6.4.3

Over 5 years a bond costing £1,000 increases in value to £1,250. Find the effective annual rate of interest.

Solution

The 5-year ratio = $1{,}250/1{,}000 = 1.25 =$ annual ratio^5. Hence, the annual ratio = $1.25^{1/5} = 1.0456$, giving an effective annual rate of 4.56 per cent.

Example 6.4.4

If house prices rise by 20 per cent per annum, find:

(a) the equivalent percentage rise per month;
(b) the percentage rise over 9 months.

Solution

The annual ratio = $1.2 =$ monthly ratio^{12}

(a) Monthly ratio = $1.2^{1/12} = 1.0153$, and the monthly rate is 1.53 per cent.
(b) Nine-month ratio = $1.2^{9/12} = 1.1465$, and the 9-month rate = 14.65 per cent.

Example 6.4.5

(a) Find the effective annual rate if an investment of £500 yields £600 after 4 years.
(b) If prices rise by 5.8 per cent over a year, find the percentage rise over 6 months.

Solution

(a) The 4-year ratio = $600/500 = 1.2 =$ annual ratio^4. Hence, the annual ratio is $1.2^{1/4} = 1.047$, so the effective annual rate is 4.7 per cent.
(b) The annual ratio is $1.058 =$ 6-month ratio^2. So the 6-month ratio = $\sqrt{1.058} = 1.0286$, and the 6-monthly rate is 2.86 per cent.

6.5 Depreciation

The same basic formula can be used to deal with depreciation, in which the value of an item goes down at a certain rate. We simply ensure that the rate of 'interest' is negative.

Example 6.5.1

A company buys a machine for £20,000. What will its value be after 6 years, if it is assumed to depreciate at a fixed rate of 12 per cent per annum?

Solution

We have $P = 20,000$; $n = 6$; $r = -0.12$, hence:

$$V = P(1 + r)^6 = 20,000(1 - 0.12)^6 = 20,000 \times 0.4644041 = 9,288.08$$

The machine's value in 6 years' time will therefore be £9,288.08.

Example 6.5.2

A piece of capital equipment is purchased for £120,000 and is to be scrapped after 7 years. What is the scrap value if the depreciation rate is 8 per cent per annum?

Solution

$P = 120,000$, $n = 7$, $r = -0.08$, so

$$V = 120,000(1 - 0.08)^7 = 120,000(0.92)^7 = £66,941.59$$

Example 6.5.3

In practice, rates of depreciation change over the lifetime of an item. A motor car costing £21,000 may depreciate by 15 per cent in the first year, then by 10 per cent per annum in each of the next three years, and by 5 per cent per annum thereafter. Find its value after 8 years.

Solution

$P = 21,000$, $r = 0.15$ for $n = 1$, then $r = 0.1$ for $n = 3$ and finally $r = 0.05$ for $n = 4$

$$V = 21,000 \times 0.85 \times 0.90^3 \times 0.95^4 = £10,598.88$$

Example 6.5.4

A machine depreciates by 20 per cent in the first year, then by 10 per cent per annum for the next 5 years, and by 2 per cent per annum thereafter. Find its value after 7 years if its initial price is £720,000.

Solution

$P = 720,000$, $r = 0.2$ for $n = 1$, $r = 0.1$ for $n = 5$ and $r = 0.02$ for $n = 1$

$$V = 720,000 \times 0.8^1 \times 0.9^5 \times 0.98^1 = £333,319.80$$

Example 6.5.5

The other type of problem associated with depreciation is to work out how long it will take for the value to drop to a particular level. Suppose a machine valued at £500,000 depreciates at 6 per cent per annum. How many years will it take for its value to reduce to, say, £100,000?

Solution

$P = 500,000$, $r = 0.06$, $n = ?$ and final value $= 100,000$

$$\text{Final value} = 500,000 \times 0.94^n = 100,000$$
$$\text{so } 0.94^n = 100,000/500,000 = 0.2$$

Taking logs to base 10 gives

$$n \log(0.94) = \log(0.2)$$
$$\text{so } n = \log(0.2)/\log(0.94) = 26.01$$

It will take slightly over 26 years for the value to decline to £100,000

It is worth remembering that equations of the type $A = B^n$ can be solved by taking logs, so that $\log A = n \log B$ and $n = \log A / \log B$.

Example 6.5.6

How long would it take the machine in Example 6.5.5 to reduce in value to £250,000?

Solution

Value after n years is $500,000 \times 0.94^n = 250,000$

$$0.94^n = 250,000/500,000 = 0.5$$
$$n \log(0.94) = \log(0.5)$$
$$n = \log(0.5)/\log(0.94) = 11.2$$

It will take 11.2 years.

6.6 More complex investments

We can return now to the evaluation of investments, but now considering situations where there are several different investments spread over a period of time.

Example 6.6.1

A man invests £3,000 initially and then £1,800 at the end of the first, second and third years, and finally £600 at the end of the fourth year. If interest is paid annually at 6.5 per cent, find the value of the investment at the end of the fifth year.

Solution

The diagram shows when the investments and evaluation take place.

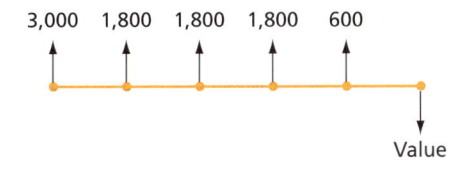

```
        3,000  1,800  1,800  1,800   600
          ↑      ↑      ↑      ↑      ↑
          •——————•——————•——————•——————•——————•
                                             ↓
                                           Value
```

The £3,000 is invested for 5 years and grows to

$$3,000(1.065^5) = 4,110.26$$

The three sums of £1,800 are invested for 4, 3 and 2 years, and grow in total to

$$1,800(1.065^4 + 1.065^3 + 1.065^2) = 6,531.55$$

Finally, the £600 is invested for just 1 year and grows to

$$600 \times 1.065 = 639$$

The total value at the end of 5 years is £11,280.81

A *sinking fund* is a special type of investment in which a constant amount is invested each year, usually with a view to reaching a specified value at a given point in the future. Questions need to be read carefully in order to be clear about exactly when the first and last instalments are paid.

Example 6.6.2

A company needs to replace a machine costing £50,000 in 6 years' time. To achieve this it will make six annual investments, starting immediately, at 5.5 per cent. Find the value of the annual payment.

Solution

The diagram shows when the investments (denoted by P) and evaluation take place.

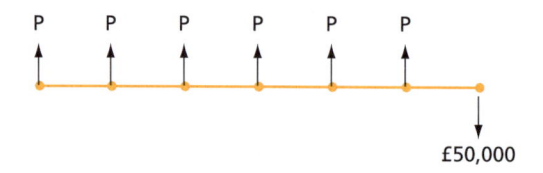

The first investment of £P lasts for 6 years and its final value is $P(1.055)^6$. The second amounts to $P(1.055)^5$, the third to $P(1.055)^4$, etc. until the sixth, which amounts to only $P(1.055)^1$.

$$50,000 = P(1.055^6 + 1.055^5 + 1.055^4 + 1.055^3 + 1.055^2 + 1.055) = 7.26689P$$

giving $P = 50,000/7.26689 = £6,881$ (to the nearest £)

Example 6.6.3

Three annual instalments of £500 are paid, starting immediately, at 4.9 per cent per annum. Find the value of the investment immediately after the third instalment.

Solution

The diagram shows when the investments and evaluation take place:

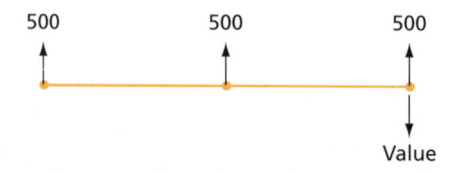

Note that the final instalment has no time to grow at all. The value is:

$$500 \times (1.049^2 + 1.049 + 1) = 500 \times 3.149401 = £1,574 \text{ (to the nearest £)}$$

6.7 Geometric progressions

We worked out the final values for the sinking fund questions simply by using calculators in the usual fashion. However, a sinking fund could easily run for 20 years or more – in fact, the endowment element of some mortgages is a very common example of a sinking fund that would typically run for 20–25 years. So it is useful to digress briefly to discuss *geometric progressions* and how they can help with all this arithmetic.

A geometric progression (GP) is a series of numbers of the form

$$A, AR, AR^2, AR^3, \ldots$$

where A and R are numbers.

The particular feature that defines a GP is that, after an initial term, A, each term in the progression is a constant multiple (R) (or ratio) of the preceding one. We shall need to know the sum of the first n terms of such a series. Denoting this by S

$$S = \frac{A(R^n - 1)}{(R - 1)}$$

Example 6.7.1

If six annual instalments of £800 are made, starting immediately, at 5 per cent per annum, the value of the investment immediately after the sixth instalment is given by the following expression. Use GP theory to evaluate it.

$$£800(1.05^5 + 1.05^4 + 1.05^3 + 1.05^2 + 1.05 + 1)$$

Solution

The series in the brackets, viewed back to front, is a GP with $A = 1$, $n = 6$ and $R = 1.05$, so its sum is:

$$S = 1 \times \frac{1.05^6 - 1}{1.05 - 1} = 6.8019$$

Hence, the value of the fund is £800 × 6.8019 = £5,442 (to the nearest £).

Notice that n is given by the number of terms, not by the greatest power of R.

Example 6.7.2

Use GPs to find the following totals:

(a) £500 $(1.042^4 + 1.042^3 + 1.042^2 + 1.042 + 1)$;
(b) £650 $(1.03^4 + 1.03^3 + 1.03^2 + 1.03)$.

Solution

(a) Inside the bracket, $A = 1$, $n = 5$, $R = 1.042$:

$$s = 500 \times \frac{1(1.042^5 - 1)}{1.042 - 1} = £2{,}719 \text{ (to the nearest £)}$$

(b) Inside the bracket, $A = 1.03$, $n = 4$, $R = 1.03$:

$$s = 650 \times \frac{1.03(1.03^4 - 1)}{1.03 - 1} = £2{,}801 \text{ (to the nearest £)}$$

6.8 Present values

The *present value* of a sum of money to be paid or received in the future is its value *at present*, in the sense that it is the sum of money that could be invested *now* (at a certain rate of interest) to reach the required value at the subsequent specified time. Some examples will make this clearer and illustrate two ways of calculating present values.

Example 6.8.1

Find the present value of:
(a) £200 payable in 2 years' time, assuming that an investment rate of 7 per cent per annum, compounded annually, is available;
(b) £350 receivable in 3 years' time, assuming that an annually compounded investment rate of 6 per cent per annum, is available.

Solution

(a) From the definition, we need to find that sum of money that would have to be invested at 7 per cent per annum and have value £200 in 2 years' time. Suppose this is £X, then the compound interest formula gives:

$$V = P(1 + r)^n$$

Thus:

$$200 = X(1 + 0.07)^2$$

$$X = \frac{200}{1.1449} = 174.69$$

Thus, the present value is £174.69: that is, with an interest rate of 7 per cent, there is no difference between paying £174.69 now and paying £200 in 2 years' time.

(b) Using the compound interest formula again:

$$350 = X(1 + 0.06)^3$$

$$X = \frac{350}{1.191016} = 293.87$$

The present value is thus £293.87.

This method of calculation is said to be from *first principles*. The present value of a quantity, £V, discounted at $100r$ per cent for n years is given by:

$$\frac{V}{(1+r)^n}$$

Alternatively, present value tables that are provided in your exam give a present value factor (or discount factor) of 0.873 for $n = 2$ years at $r = 7$ per cent. This means that the present value of £1 for this combination is £0.873; hence the present value (PV) of £200 is:

$$200 \times 0.873 = £174.60$$

Similarly, the PV factor for $n = 3$ and $r = 6$ per cent is 0.840; so the PV of £350 is:

$$350 \times 0.840 = £294$$

Before leaving the PV tables, we note that they simply give the approximate values of

$$\frac{1}{(1+r)^n}$$

thereby simplifying the calculations considerably.

It can be seen that use of the tables loses some accuracy. When there are many such calculations, however, their use is considerably faster, and so tables are generally preferred. However, their use is not always possible, since you will note that there are 'gaps' in the tables. For instance, the combination $n = 2.5$ years and $r = 4.5$ per cent does not appear in the tables, and so first principles would have to be used in an example involving these values.

Example 6.8.2

Calculate the present values of the following amounts. Use PV tables where you can, and first principles otherwise:

(a) £12,000 payable in 6 years' time at a rate of 9 per cent;
(b) £90,000 payable in 8 years' time at 14 per cent;
(c) £80,000 payable in 5 years' time at 6.3 per cent;
(d) £50,000 payable in 4 years and 3 months' time at 10 per cent.

Solution

(a) From tables, discount factor at 9 per cent for 6 years is 0.596:

$$PV = 12,000 \times 0.596 = £7,152$$

(b) Discount factor at 14 per cent for 8 years is 0.351:

$$PV = 90,000 \times 0.351 = £31,590$$

(c) The tables cannot be used for 6.3 per cent. $(1 + r) = 1.063$ and $n = 5$:

$$PV = \frac{80,000}{1.063^5} = £58,941.84 \text{ (to two d.p.)}$$

(d) The tables cannot be used for part years. To use a calculator, convert 4 years, 3 months into the decimal 4.25. So $n = 4.25$ and $(1 + r) = 1.1$:

$$PV = \frac{50,000}{1.1^{4.25}} = £33,346.56 \text{ (to two d.p.)}$$

6.9 Net present values – practical examples

In many situations, there are a number of financial inflows and outflows involved, at a variety of times. In such cases, the *net present value* (NPV) is the total of the individual present values, after discounting each, as above.

Example 6.9.1

A company can purchase a machine now for £10,000. The company accountant estimates that the machine will contribute £2,500 per annum to profits for five years, after which time it will have to be scrapped for £500. Find the NPV of the machine if the interest rate for the period is assumed to be 5 per cent. (Assume, for simplicity, that all inflows occur at year ends.)

Solution

We set out the calculations in a systematic, tabular form:

After year	Total inflow (£)	Discount factor	Present value (£)
0	−10,000	1.000	−10,000
1	2,500	0.952	2,380
2	2,500	0.907	2,267.50
3	2,500	0.864	2,160
4	2,500	0.823	2,057.50
5	3,000	0.784	2,352
			1,217

Hence, the NPV is £1,217.

The fact that the middle four inflow values are the same (£2,500) means that the cumulative present value table (provided in your exam) can be used to calculate the total pv arising from an inflow of £2,500 at a constant interest rate of 5 per cent for *each* of 4 years, starting at the end of the first year:

After year	Total inflow (£)	Discount factor	Present value (£)
0	−10,000	1.000	−10,000
1–4	2,500 per year	3.546	8,865
5	3,000	0.784	2,352
			1,217

This table gives the NPV as £1,217, exactly as before.

The fact that the NPV is positive means that the investment is more profitable than investing the original £10,000 at 5 per cent. In fact, you would need to invest £11,217 at 5 per cent in order to generate this particular set of positive cash flows, so this investment is worthwhile.

Example 6.9.2

Evaluate the net present values of the following potential purchases (figures, all in £'000, show net inflows/(outflows)):

		A r = 6%	B r = 8%
After:	Year 0	(35)	(55)
	Year 1	(10)	0
	Year 2	20	15
	Year 3	30	25
	Year 4	40	35

Are either of the above purchases worth making, on financial grounds alone?

Solution

Time	A £'000	Discount factor	PV £'000	
0	(35)	1.000	(35.00)	
1	(10)	0.943	(9.43)	
2	20	0.890	17.80	
3	30	0.840	25.20	
4	40	0.792	31.68	
Net present value:			30.25	(i.e. £30,250)

Time	B £'000	Discount factor	PV £'000	
0	(55)	1.000	(55.00)	
1	0	0.926	–	
2	15	0.857	12.86	
3	25	0.794	19.85	
4	35	0.735	25.73	
Net present value:			3.44	(i.e. £3,440)

Both investments have positive NPVs and so both are worthwhile.

The idea of NPV enables us to compare two or more options, as illustrated below.

Example 6.9.3

An investor is considering three options, only one of which she can afford. All three have the same initial outlay, but there are different income patterns available from each. Investment A pays £2,000 each year at the end of the next 5 years. Investment B pays £1,000 at the end of the first year, £1,500 at the end of the second year, and soon until the final payment of £3,000 at the end of the fifth year. Investment C pays £4,000 at the end of the first year, £3,000 at the end of the second year, and £2,000 at the end of the third.

The investor estimates a constant rate of interest of 10 per cent throughout the next 5 years: which investment should she choose?

Solution

From tables, the cumulative present value factor for a constant inflow at 10 per cent for 5 years is 3.791; hence the NPV of investment A is

$2,000 \times 3.791 = £7,582$

The other two investments do not involve constant inflows, and so the PVs for Individual years have to be summed.

		Investment B		Investment C	
		Inflow	PV	Inflow	PV
Year (end)	PV factor	(£)	(£)	(£)	(£)
1	0.909	1,000	909	4,000	3,636
2	0.826	1,500	1,239	3,000	2,478
3	0.751	2,000	1,502	2,000	1,502
4	0.683	2,500	1,707.50	–	–
5	0.621	3,000	1,863	–	–
			7,220.50		7,616

In summary, the NPVs of investments A, B and C are £7,582, £7,220.50 and £7,616, respectively. As the outlay for each is the same, the investor should choose C.

Example 6.9.4

Compare the following three potential investments, assuming the investor has a maximum of £15,000 to deploy, if the prevailing rate of interest is 11 per cent:

	Investment A £'000	Investment B £'000	Investment C £'000
Initial outlay	14	14	12
Inflow at end of:			
Year 1	0	7	10
Year 2	6	7	8
Year 3	8	7	5
Year 4	10	7	5
Year 5	10	7	5
Year 6	10	7	5

None of the investments brings any income after year 6.

Solution

Time	Discount factor	A £'000	PV £'000	B £'000	PV £'000	C £'000	PV £'000
0	1.000	(14)	(14.000)	(14)	(14.000)	(12)	(12.000)
1	0.901	0	0.000	7	–	10	9.010
2	0.812	6	4.872	7	–	8	6.496
3	0.731	8	5.848	7	–	5	–
4	0.659	10	6.590	7	–	5	–
5	0.593	10	5.930	7	–	5	–
6	0.535	10	5.350	7	29.617	5	12.590
Net present values:			14.590		15.617		16.096

In the case of B we have multiplied 7 by the cumulative PV factor for 6 years at 11 per cent, giving 7 × 4.231 = 29.617

For C we have subtracted the 2-year cumulative PV factor from the 6-year factor and then multiplied the result by 5.

All the investments are worthwhile since they have positive NPVs. Investment C costs the least initially and yet has the highest NPV and so is to be preferred.

6.10 Problems using NPV in practice

One of the major difficulties with present values is the estimation of the 'interest rates' used in the calculations. Clearly, the appropriate rate(s) at the start of the time period under consideration will be known, but future values can be only estimates. As the point in time moves further and further into the future, the rates become more and more speculative. For this reason, the NPVs of investments A and C in Example 6.9.3 are so close as to be indistinguishable, practically speaking.

Many situations in which NPV might be involved are concerned with capital investments, with the capital needing to be raised from the market. For this reason, the 'interest rate(s)' are referred to as the *cost of capital*, since they reflect the rate(s) at which the capital market is willing to provide the necessary money.

Another problem with calculating net present value is the need to estimate annual cash flows, particularly those that are several years in the future, and the fact that the method cannot easily take on board the attachment of probabilities to different estimates. Finally, it is a usual, although not an indispensable, part of the method to assume that all cash flows occur at the end of the year, and this too is a potential source of errors. With easy access to computers it is now possible to calculate a whole range of NPVs corresponding to worst-case and best-case scenarios as well as those expected, so to some extent some of the problems mentioned above can be lessened.

6.11 Annuities

> An *annuity* is an arrangement by which a person receives a series of constant annual amounts. The length of time during which the annuity is paid can either be until the death of the recipient or for a *guaranteed* minimum term of years, irrespective of whether the annuitant is alive or not. In other types of annuity, the payments are *deferred* until some time in the future, such as the retirement of the annuitant.

When two or more annuities are being compared, they can cover different time periods and so their net present values become relevant. In your exam you will be given the following formula for the NPV of a £1 annuity over t years at interest rate r, with the first payment 1 year after purchase.

$$\frac{1}{r} - \frac{1}{r(1+r)^t}$$

The cumulative present value tables can also be used.

Example 6.11.1

An investor is considering two annuities, both of which will involve the same purchase price. Annuity A pays £5,000 each year for 20 years, while annuity B pays £5,500 each year for 15 years. Both start payment 1 year after purchase and neither is affected by the death of the investor.

Assuming a constant interest rate of 8 per cent, which is the better?

Solution

Using tables, the cumulative PV factors are 9.818 for A and 8.559 for B.
Hence PV of annuity A = 5,000 × 9.818 = £49,090, and
PV of annuity B = 5,500 × 8.559 = £47,074.5

You will only be able to use the tables given in your exam if the period of the annuity is twenty years or less and if the rate of interest is a whole number. It is, therefore, essential that you learn to use the formula as well. You will notice that there is some loss of accuracy, due to rounding errors, when tables are used.

Using the above formula:

$$\text{Factor for the NPV of A} = \frac{1}{0.08} - \frac{1}{0.08(1 + 0.08)^{20}} = 9.818147$$

and so the NPV of A is:

5,000 × 9.818147 = £49,091 (to the nearest £)

Similarly:

$$\text{Annuity factor for the NPV of B} = \frac{1}{0.08} - \frac{1}{0.08(1 + 0.08)^{15}} = 8.559479$$

and so the NPV of B is:

5,500 × 8.559479 = £47,077

From the viewpoint of NPVs, therefore, *annuity A is the better* choice. As we have already seen, however, there are two further considerations the investor may have. Assuming constant interest rates for periods of 15 or 20 years is speculative, so the NPVs are only approximations: they are, however, the best that can be done and so this point is unlikely to affect the investor's decision. More importantly, although any payments after the investor's death would go to their estate, some people may prefer more income 'up front' during their lifetime. Unless the investor is confident of surviving the full 20 years of annuity A, they may prefer annuity B — especially as the two NPVs are relatively close to each other.

A further example will demonstrate an NPV being expressed as an equivalent annuity.

Example 6.11.2

An investment is due to give payoffs with an NPV calculated at £20,000 and an assumed constant interest rate of 6 per cent per annum. What annuity lasting for 10 years is equivalent to the investment, in that it has the same NPV?

Solution

If the annuity pays £x at the end of each of the next 10 years, then tables give its NPV as 7.360x. Hence:

7.360x = 20,000
x = 2,717.39

The equivalent annuity is thus £2,717.39.

Example 6.11.3

An annuity pays £12,000 at the end of each year until the death of the purchaser. Assuming a rate of interest of 6 per cent, what is the PV of the annuity if the purchaser lives for: (a) 10 years; and (b) 20 years after purchase? In order to practise both methods, use the tables in (a) and the formula in (b).

Solution

(a) If $n = 10$ and rate is 6 per cent, from tables the annuity factor is 7.360:

$$PV = 12{,}000 \times 7.360 = £88{,}320$$

(b) If $n = 20$, from the formula:

$$PV = 12{,}000 \times \left(\frac{1}{0.06} - \frac{1}{0.06 \times 1.06^{20}} \right) = £137{,}639.05$$

> 🔑 Finally, there is the concept of *perpetuity*. As the name implies, this is the same as an annuity except that payments go on for ever. It is therefore of interest to those who wish to ensure continuing payments to their descendants, or to some good cause. It must be recognised, however, that constant payments tend to have ever-decreasing value, owing to the effects of inflation, and so some alternative means of providing for the future may be preferred.

6.12 PV of a perpetuity

As t becomes very large, the second term in the formula for the PV of an annuity gets smaller and smaller, to the point where it becomes zero, and the factor for the NPV of a perpetuity simplifies considerably to:

$$\frac{1}{r}$$

Example 6.12.1

Consider the position of A and B in Example 6.11.1 if they were perpetuities.

Solution

Using the formula:

$$\text{NPV of perpetuity A} = \frac{1}{0.08} \times 5{,}000 = £62{,}500$$
$$\text{NPV of perpetuity B} = \frac{1}{0.08} \times 5{,}500 = £68{,}750$$

The NPV of annuity B is therefore higher. The assumption of a constant interest rate of 8 per cent for ever is clearly highly unlikely to materialise but, as before, it is all that can be done. In purchasing a perpetuity, an investor is not interested particularly in the income during their lifetime, so the latter consideration of Example 6.12.4 is not pertinent here: perpetuity B is unequivocally the better.

Example 6.12.2

What would the PV be in Example 6.11.3 if it were a perpetuity?

Solution

For a perpetuity of £12,000 per annum, discounted at 6 per cent, the present value is 12,000/0.06 or £200,000.

You can check this easily. At 6 per cent, the interest on £200,000 is £12,000 per annum, so the annuity can be paid indefinitely without touching the capital.

6.13 Loans and mortgages

Most people will be aware that, when a mortgage is taken out on a property over a number of years, there are several ways of repaying the loan. We shall concentrate here on *repayment mortgages*, because they are among the most popular, and because they are the only ones that involve complex mathematical calculations.

The features of a repayment mortgage are:

- a certain amount, £M, is borrowed to be repaid over n years;
- interest (at a rate r) is added to the loan retrospectively at the end of each year; and
- a constant amount, £P, is paid back each year by the borrower, usually in equal monthly instalments.

Viewed from the standpoint of the lender, a repayment mortgage is an annuity. The lender pays the initial amount (M) for it and in return receives a series of constant annual payments (P) for n years. The relationship between these variables is given by putting M equal to the present value of the annuity, using either tables or formula as appropriate.

Example 6.13.1

(a) A £30,000 mortgage is taken out on a property at a rate of 12 per cent over 25 years. What will be the gross monthly repayment?
(b) After 2 years of the mortgage, the interest rate increases to 14 per cent: recalculate the monthly repayment figure.

Solution

(a) Equating present values gives:

$$30{,}000 = P\left(\frac{1}{0.12} - \frac{1}{0.12 \times 1.12^{25}}\right) = 7.843139P$$

giving $P = 30{,}000/7.843139 = £3{,}825$ per annum (nearest £) and a monthly repayment of £318.75 (to two d.p.).

(b) After 2 years, immediately after the second annual repayment, the amount still owing is:

$$30{,}000 \times 1.12^2 - 3{,}825 \times 1.12 - 3{,}825 = £29{,}523$$

The mortgage now has 23 years to run and at 14 per cent interest we have:

$$29{,}523 = P\left(\frac{1}{0.14} - \frac{1}{0.14 \times 1.14^{23}}\right) = 6.792056P$$

giving $P = 29{,}523/6.792056 = £4{,}346.70$ per annum and a monthly repayment of £362.22 (two d.p.).

Example 6.13.2

A property is mortgaged over 20 years at a rate of 8 per cent per annum. If the mortgage is £70,000, what are the annual repayments? If, after 5 years, the rate is reduced to 7.5 per cent, to what are the annual payments reduced?

Solution

Equating PVs:

$$70{,}000 = P\left(\frac{1}{0.08} - \frac{1}{0.08 \times 1.08^{20}}\right) = 9.818147P$$

giving $P = £7{,}129.65$ per annum.
After the fifth annual payment, the amount owing is:

$$70{,}000 \times 1.08^5 - 7{,}129.65(1.08^4 + 1.08^3 + 1.08^2 + 1.08 + 1)$$
$$= 102{,}852.97 - 7{,}129.65 \times 1 \times (1.08^5 - 1) \div 0.08$$
$$= 102{,}852.97 - 41{,}826.81$$
$$= 61{,}026.16$$

At 7.5 per cent for the remaining 15 years, equating PVs gives:

$$61{,}026.16 = P\left(\frac{1}{0.075} - \frac{1}{0.075 \times 1.075^{15}}\right)$$

giving $P = £6{,}913.49$.

6.14 Internal rate of return

We have seen that if NPV is positive it means that the project is more profitable than investing at the discount rate, whereas if it is negative then the project is less profitable than a simple investment at the discount rate.

If NPV is zero the project is identical in terms of profit to investing at the discount rate, and hence this rate of interest gives us the rate of return of the project.

> The *internal rate of return* (IRR) is the discount rate at which NPV is zero. It is obtained generally by a trial and error method as follows.

1. find a discount rate at which NPV is small and positive;
2. find another (larger) discount rate at which NPV is small and negative;
3. use linear interpolation between the two to find the point at which NPV is zero.

Example 6.14.1

Find the IRR for the following project.

Time	Cash flow (£'000)
0	(80)
1	40
2	30
3	20
4	5

Solution

The question offers no guidance as to what discount rates to try, so we will select 5 per cent randomly. Since 5 per cent turns out to give a positive NPV we now randomly select 10 per cent in the hope that it will give a negative NPV.

Time	Cash flow £'000	PV (5%) £'000	PV (10%) £'000
0	(80)	(80.000)	(80.000)
1	40	38.095	36.364
2	30	27.211	24.793
3	20	17.277	15.026
4	5	4.114	3.415
Net present value:		6.697	(0.402)

We can now use either (a) a graphical method (Figure 6.1) or (b) a calculation based on proportions.

(a) *Graphical method*

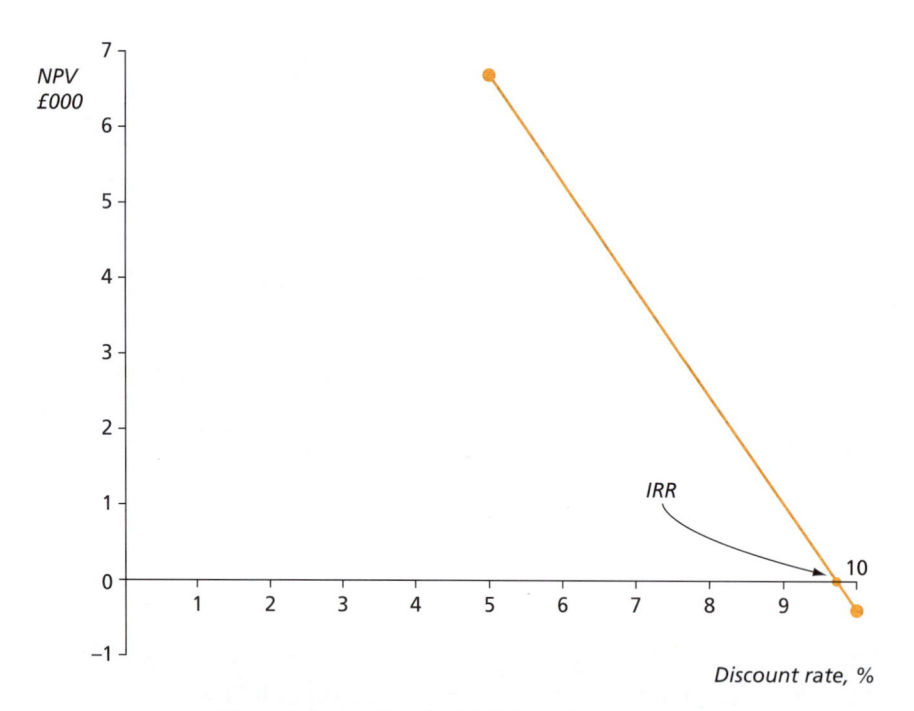

Figure 6.1 Graph of NPV on discount rate

From the graph the estimated IRR is 9.7 per cent.

(b) *Calculation method*

The NPV drops from 6.697 to −0.402, that is, a drop of 7.099, when the discount rate increases by 5 percentage points (from 5 to 10 per cent).

NPV will therefore drop by 1 when the discount rate increases by 5/7.099 = 0.7043 percentage points.

The NPV will reach zero if, starting at its 5 per cent level, it drops by 6.697. This requires an increase of 6.697 × 0.7043 = 4.7 percentage points in the discount rate. Hence, the IRR (the discount rate at which NPV is zero) is 5 + 4.7 = 9.7 per cent.

In general, if NPV drops from NPV_1 to NPV_2 when the discount rate increases from R_1 to R_2, the IRR will be given by:

$$R_1 + (R_2 - R_1) \times \frac{NPV_1}{NPV_1 - NPV_2}$$

Do not forget that if NPV_2 is negative, we effectively end up adding in the denominator.

Example 6.14.2

Use both the graphical and calculation methods to estimate the IRR for the following project, and interpret your result.

The calculation method is most likely to be useful in your assessment.

Time	Cash flow £'000
0	(100)
1	50
2	50
3	20

Solution

Time	Cash flow £'000	NPV (5%) £'000	NPV (15%) £'000
0	(100)	(100.000)	(100.000)
1	50	47.619	43.478
2	50	45.351	37.807
3	20	17.277	13.150
NPV=		10.247	(5.565)

(a) *Graphical method*

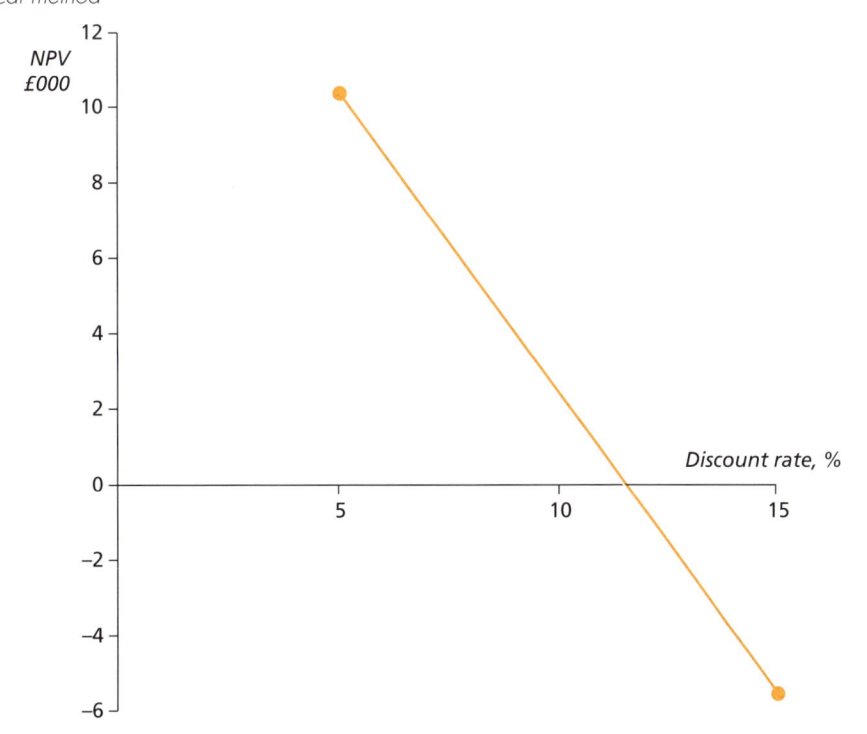

From the graph the estimate of the IRR is 11.5 per cent.

(b) NPV drops by 10.247 + 5.565 = 15.812 when discount rate increases by 10 percentage points. NPV will drop by 1 (£'000) when discount rate increases by 10/15.812 = 0.6324 percentage points. For IRR, NPV must drop by 10.247, which requires an increase in the discount rate of 10.247 × 0.6324 = 6.5 percentage points. Hence, the IRR = 5 + 6.5 = 11.5 per cent.

6.15 Financial functions in Excel

A number of the issues discussed in this chapter can be applied to the spreadsheet. Furthermore, there are a series of built-in functions in Excel that make the calculation of certain financial reports such as the net present value and the present value, the future value and the internal rate of return quite straightforward.

A capital investment appraisal example will be used to describe these features.

Figure 6.2 shows the completed capital investment appraisal plan with some sample data.

	A	B	C	D	E	F	G
1	Capital Investment Appraisal System						
2			Cash-Out	Cash-In		Net Cash Movement each year	
3	IT Investment - Cash Out		350000			-350000	
4	Net Benefits	Year 1		60000		60000	
5		Year 2		95000		95000	
6		Year 3		120000		120000	
7		Year 4		180000		180000	
8		Year 5		200000		200000	
9	Fixed Cost of Capital or Interest Rate	20.00%					
10		Y1	Y2	Y3	Y4	Y5	
11	Estimated inflation rates	3.00%	4.00%	4.00%	3.00%	2.00%	
12							
13	Investment Reports for proposed investment						
14	Payback in years & months	3	years		5	months	
15	Discounted Payback FDR in years & months	4	years		11	months	
16	Rate of return(%)	37.43%					
17	NPV Fixed Discount Rate (FDR)	2598					
18	Profitability Index FDR (PI)	1.01					
19	Internal Rate of Return (IRR)	20.28%					
20							
21	Variable Discount Rates						
22	NPV Variable Discount Rates (VDR)	-115523					
23	Profitability Index VDR (PI)	0.67					

Figure 6.2 Capital investment appraisal plan

6.15.1 The investment reports

The investment reports consist of the rate of return, the NPV, the PI and the IRR at a fixed discount rate, as well as the NPV and the PI at a variable discount rate.

Some of these reports can be calculated using built-in spreadsheet functions, but others, such as the variable discount rate reports require some additional calculations that have been grouped together in a separate area of the spreadsheet.

Rate of return

The rate of return is calculated by taking the average of the cash inflows and dividing by the original investment, expressed as a percentage. Thus the following formula is required in cell B16.

$$= \text{AVERAGE}(\text{D4}:\text{D8})/\text{C3}$$

NPV at a fixed discount rate

The NPV function is used to calculate the net present value. This function requires reference to the discount rate and the cash inflows. The following formula is required in cell B17:

= NPV(B9,D4:D8) − C3

Note that it is necessary to subtract the original investment outside of the NPV function.

Profitability index (PI)

The PI also uses the NPV function, but the result is divided by the original investment as can be seen in the formula in cell B18:

= NPV(B9,D4:D8)/C3

Internal rate of return

The IRR function is used to calculate the internal rate of return in cell B19. This function requires reference to cash inflows, but the first cell in the range must be the original investment expressed as a negative value. Furthermore the function requires a 'guess' to be entered as to what the IRR might be after the data range. Thus the formula for cell B19 is.

= IRR(F3:F8,0.3)

Note that the original investment and cash inflows were copied into column F, with the investment represented as a negative value and it is this range that has been used for the IRR calculation.

A 'guess' is entered for the IRR because the calculation of the internal rate of return is a reiterative process and the system requires a 'seed' from which to base the calculation. If no guess is entered the system will assume 0.1 or 10 per cent and this is usually sufficient for a result to be calculated within 0.00001 per cent. If IRR cannot find a result that works after 20 tries, the #NUM! error value is returned.

If IRR gives the #NUM! error value, or if the result is not close to what you expected, try again with a different value for guess.

NPV and PI at Variable Discount Rate

A separate work area is required to be able to calculate the NPV using a discount rate that varies from year to year. Figure 6.3 shows the work area required.

	A	B	C	D	E	F
49	Variable discount rate work area					
50	Year no.	1	2	3	4	5
51	Cash-Flow	60000	95000	120000	180000	200000
52	Discounted 1 period	48780	76613	96774	146341	163934
53	Discounted 2 periods	62287	61785	78044	118977	
54	Discounted 3 periods	50231	49826	62938		
55	Discounted 4 periods	40509	40182			
56	Discounted 5 periods	32669				
57						
58	Sum of Present Values	234477				
59	Net Present Value	-115523				
60	Profitability Index	0.67				

Figure 6.3 Variable discount rate work area

The NPV function assumes a constant rate of interest over the duration of the investment and therefore to accommodate an interest or discount rate that can change each year, the PV function needs to be used. In this context the PV function is used one year at a time and the discounted value is year by year picked up by a new PV function which adjusts it appropriately. In the example the cash inflows have to be discounted over the five years.

In cells B51 to F51 the nominal cash flow amounts are discounted for one year using the following formula;

$$= \text{PV}(\text{B}\$11 + \$\text{B}\$9, 1, -\text{B}50)$$

Note that the PV function assumes that the cash flow value is negative (i.e. a credit) and in the above formula this has been reversed by the negative reference to B50. The reference to B11 has the row fixed with the $ which means that the formula can be copied holding the reference to row 11 absolute but changing the column reference. Figure 6.4 shows the formulae in the first two columns.

	A	B	C
48			
49	Variable discount rate		
50	Year no.	1	2
51	Cash-Flow	=D4	=D5
52	Discounted 1 period	=PV(B$11+$B$9,1,-B51)	=PV(C$11+$B$9,1,-C51)
53	Discounted 2 periods	=PV(B$11+B9,1,-C52)	=PV(C$11+$B$9,1,-C52)
54	Discounted 3 periods	=PV(B$11+$B$9,1,-C53)	=PV(C$11+$B$9,1,-C53)
55	Discounted 4 periods	=PV(B$11+$B$9,1,-C54)	=PV(C$11+$B$9,1,-C54)
56	Discounted 5 periods	=PV(B$11+$B$9,1,-C55)	
57			
58	Sum of Present Values	=SUM(B52:B56)	
59	Net Present Value	=B58-C3	
60	Profitability Index	=B58/C3	

Figure 6.4 Formulae for calculating NPV at a variable discount rate

In rows 52 and 55 each future cash flow from year 2 to 5 is again discounted using a unique interest rate for each year until the cash flow in year 5 has been discounted 5 times and the cash flow in year has been discounted 4 times etc. The individual cash streams are then summed and in the usual way the investment is subtracted from this amount to produce the net present value.

There are clearly other financial reports that could be calculated from this capital investment plan, but those discussed here are intended to give the reader some exposure to some of the more frequently encountered issues.

6.16 Summary

The value, £V, of a sum, £P, invested for n years at a *simple* rate of r per annum is:

$$V = P(1 + rn)$$

The value, £V, of a sum, £P, invested for n years at a *compound* rate of r per annum is:

$$V = P(1 + r)^n$$

The same formula can be used to calculate the value of *depreciating* quantities by using a negative value of r.

The *present value* (PV) of a sum of money payable/receivable in the future is that sum that would have to be invested now (at a given rate of interest) to reach the target sum at the required future point in time. The PV can be calculated from the appropriate table or from first principles, using the compound interest formula:

$$V = P(1 + r)^n$$

giving the PV of X as:

$$PV = \frac{X}{(1+r)^n}$$

The *net present value* (NPV) of an investment is the total of the present values of all the inflows and outflows involved in the investment.

An annuity is a series of equal cash flows occurring at regular intervals of time. The factor giving the NPV of an annuity paying £1 per annum for t years at a rate of r is:

$$\frac{1}{r} - \frac{1}{r(1+r)^t}$$

This is equivalent to applying tables of cumulative present values of a constant amount. The factor giving the NPV of a perpetuity paying £1 per annum at a rate of r is:

$$\frac{1}{r}$$

A geometric progression is a series of numbers, each one a constant multiple of the one preceding it:

$$A, AR, AR^2, AR^3, \ldots$$

The sum, S, of the first n terms of such a progression is:

$$S = \frac{A(R^n - 1)}{R - 1}$$

Readings

6

The following extracts should help to drive home a message that has cropped up again and again in this text: numbers are not the be-all and end-all of a management accountant's role. Whether you are writing up the entries in a process account or calculating the net present value of an investment, always remember that your objective is to improve decision-making and control by analysis and interpretation of information. The accounting and statistical models you employ have limitations that you need to be aware of; and even where such limitations can be ignored in the context of a particular problem, there will invariably be other factors to consider that go beyond the purely numerical.

Money doesn't mean everything

Leslie Chadwick, *Accountant's Tax Weekly*, 12 June 1981. Reprinted by permission of Aspen Publishers.

There is a real danger for accountants to be so preoccupied with the financial aspects of capital investment appraisal that they may ignore other very important factors. Although these factors omitted may be described as non-financial and subject to qualitative decisions they could have quite a marked effect upon the firm's long-term financial performance.

Non-financial factors

In addition to the financial aspects of the capital investment decision there are also many other areas which warrant attention such as:

- *Technical*
    - (i) The need for technical superiority.
    - (ii) Flexibility and adaptability.
    - (iii) Ease of maintenance.
    - (iv) Operational considerations, e.g. need to retrain/recruit personnel.
    - (v) Servicing arrangements.
    - (vi) Manuals provided for operating and servicing.
    - (vii) Peripherals necessary for efficient operation for adding at some future date. It is not unheard of for an organisation to purchase equipment and find that it is unable to use it without first buying certain peripherals.
    - (viii) Capacity.

- *Imported equipment*
  Exchange rates may affect the position dramatically depending upon the method of payment adopted. An important question which must be answered is, 'How good is the supplier's servicing and availability of spares in the UK?' It may be first class in the supplier's own country but very poor in the UK. Other considerations under this heading involve:
  (i) The additional administration necessary to deal with the documentation and foreign exchange.
  (ii) Delays in delivery of the equipment and spares caused by air and sea transport problems and political instability.

- *Standardisation of equipment*
  The benefits of obtaining similar equipment from a tried-and-tested supplier can have profound consequences upon the financial analysis. Savings should be possible in the areas of operative training, ease of maintenance and inventory of spares, e.g. one component may fit several different machines.

- *Size and weight of equipment*
  Floors may need strengthening and walls may have to be knocked down and rebuilt to accommodate the equipment. This possibility will affect the cash flows and should not be overlooked.

- *Look before you buy*
  It may well be worth the time and expense to inspect the equipment in a working environment. The opportunity to talk with operatives and personnel involved with such equipment should certainly not be neglected.

- *Human and social factors*
  Firms which ignore such factors as safety, noise, fumes, etc. in today's complex and diverse business environment do so at their peril. The financial consequences of ignoring them could be catastrophic.

- *Organisational behaviour*
  The effects of 'people problems' upon an organisation cannot be overestimated. This area alone could jeopardise the success of the whole venture for reasons such as:
  (i) Resistance to change, e.g. introducing new technology.
  (ii) Empire-building, e.g. where subunit goals conflict with the organisation's own goal.
  (iii) Perceptions about what the management wants.
  (iv) Organisational structure, e.g. certain personnel may be in control of key information junctions or have direct access to top management.
  (v) The board room balance of power, e.g. finance *v.* engineers.

Discussion points

From your own experience or knowledge, think of decisions made on apparently sensible financial grounds that went wrong because of other factors.

Run through the list of non-financial factors given in this article and see if you can remember instances where any of them either had to be considered in making a decision or were ignored with unfortunate consequences.

Revision Questions 6

Part 6.1 Objective testing selection

> Questions 6.1.1–6.1.10 are standard multiple-choice questions with exactly one correct answer each. Thereafter, the style of question will vary.

6.1.1 A leasing agreement is for 5 years. A sum of £10,000 must be paid at the beginning of the first year, to be followed by four equal payments of £x at the beginning of years two, three, four and five. At a discount rate of 8 per cent, the present value of the four equal payments is £26,496. The total amount to be paid during the lease period is

(A) £32,000
(B) £40,000
(C) £42,000
(D) £44,000

6.1.2 A building society adds interest monthly to investors' accounts even though interest rates are expressed in annual terms. The current rate of interest is 6 per cent per annum.

An investor deposits £1,000 on 1 January. How much interest will have been earned by 30 June?

(A) £30.00
(B) £30.38
(C) £60.00
(D) £61.68

6.1.3 A company charges depreciation at the rate of 25 per cent per annum on the reducing balance method on an asset that cost £20,000.
At the end of year three the written-down value will be

(A) £5,000.00
(B) £8,437.50
(C) £11,560.50
(D) £12,500.00

6.1.4 An individual placed a sum of money in the bank and left it there for 12 years at 5 per cent per annum. The sum is now worth £1,705.56.

Using PV tables, the original principal was found (to the nearest whole £) to be

(A) £948
(B) £949
(C) £950
(D) £951

6.1.5 A firm has arranged a 10-year lease, at an annual rent of £8,000. The first rental payment has to be paid immediately, and the others are to be paid at the end of each year.

What is the present value of the lease at 12 per cent?

(A) £50,624
(B) £53,200
(C) £45,200
(D) £65,288

6.1.6 If a single sum of £12,000 is invested at 8 per cent per annum with interest compounded quarterly, the amount to which the principal will have grown by the end of year three is approximately

(A) £15,117
(B) £14,880
(C) £15,219
(D) £15,880

6.1.7 It is estimated that a particular cost will decline by 5 per cent per annum on a compound basis. If the cost now is £10,000, by the end of year four the cost will be approximately

(A) £7,500
(B) £8,000
(C) £8,145
(D) £8,500

6.1.8 A person is to receive a 10-year annuity of £5,000 per year, received at the end of each year. At what interest rate does this have a present value of £33,550?

(A) 2 per cent
(B) 4 per cent
(C) 8 per cent
(D) 16 per cent

6.1.9 An investor is to receive an annuity of £1,360 for 6 years commencing at the end of year one. It has a present value of £6,101. What is the rate of interest?

(A) 6 per cent
(B) 9 per cent
(C) 12 per cent
(D) 15 per cent

6.1.10 A bond increases in value from £400 to £500 over a 6-year period. Find the percentage increase per annum.

(A) 25 per cent
(B) 4.17 per cent
(C) 3.79 per cent
(D) 3.81 per cent

6.1.11 A sum of £40,000 is invested for 10 years at 7 per cent per annum. What is its final value (to the nearest £) if interest is (a) simple; and (b) compound?

6.1.12 A sum of £10,000 is invested at a nominal rate of 12 per cent per annum. What is its value (to the nearest £) after 4 years if interest is compounded (a) annually; (b) every 6 months; and (c) every month?

6.1.13 The following is a calculation in which a rate of interest of 2 per cent per month is converted into an effective annual rate of interest. For each line of the calculation, (A)–(D), identify whether it follows correctly from the line immediately preceding it (regardless of whether you believe the immediately preceding line to be correct).

Monthly rate is 2 per cent

(A) Monthly ratio is 1.2
(B) Annual ratio is 1.2×12
(C) 14.4
(D) Annual rate is 44 per cent

6.1.14 A bond increases from £5,000 to £8,500 over 6 years. Complete the following calculation of the effective rate of interest:

Six-year ratio = ?
Annual ratio = ?
Effective annual rate = ?% (to one decimal place)

6.1.15 Equipment costing £100,000 depreciates by 20 per cent in its first year and thereafter by 10 per cent per annum. The following calculation aims to find how many years it will take for its value to drop to £20,000. For each line of the calculation, (A)–(I), say whether or not it follows correctly from the line immediately preceding it (regardless of whether you believe the immediately preceding line to be correct).

Value of equipment at end of 1 year:
(A) $100,000 \times 0.8$
(B) 80,000
Value after a further n years
(C) $80,000 - n \times 80,000 \times (10/100)$
(D) $80,000 (1 - 0.1n)$
When value reaches £20,000, we have:
(E) $20,000 = 80,000 (1 - 0.1n)$
(F) $2/8 = 1 - 0.1n$
(G) $0.1n = 1.25$
(H) $n = 1.25/0.1 = 12.5$
The value would drop to £20,000:
(I) In 12 years.

6.1.16 Which of the following statements is/are true of a sinking fund?

(A) A sinking fund is an investment of a constant annual amount.
(B) A sinking fund is an investment of a declining annual amount.
(C) A repayment mortgage is a type of sinking fund.
(D) A sinking fund is a type of annuity.

6.1.17 Find the present value of £100,000 receivable in five years, giving your answer to the nearest £, if the discount rate is 7 per cent: (a) using the present value table and (b) by exact calculation.

6.1.18 Complete the following net present value calculation, using a 6 per cent discount rate.

Time	Cash flow £	Discount factor 6%	Present value £
0	(5,000)	1.000	(5,000)
1	3,000	0.943	?
2	1,000	0.890	?
3	2,000	?	?
Net present value			?

6.1.19 The net present value (NPV) of a project is £3,000 when the discount rate is 5 per cent. Which of the following statements is/are correct on the basis of the information given?

(A) The initial investment in this project is £3,000.
(B) If £3,000 were invested at 5 per cent, it would generate the cash flows of this project.
(C) If the discount rate were to increase to 7 per cent, the NPV would increase.
(D) The project is viable compared with investing at 5 per cent.

6.1.20 Calculate the present value of an annuity of £10,000 per annum, payable at the end of each year for 20 years at a discount rate of 5 per cent, giving your answer correct to the nearest £: (a) using the cumulative present value table and (b) by exact calculation.

6.1.21 A £50,000 repayment mortgage is taken out at 10 per cent over 20 years. Use tables to calculate the annual repayment (to the nearest £), assuming that payments are made at the end of each year.

6.1.22 Which of the following is true of the internal rate of return (IRR)?

(A) The IRR is the current cost of borrowing.
(B) The IRR is the discount rate.
(C) The IRR is the discount rate for which net present value is zero.
(D) All other things being equal, a project with a low IRR will always be preferable to one with a high IRR.

Part 6.2 Percentages and discounting

A company is planning a new product for which a 10-year life is anticipated. The product is expected to follow a typical life cycle of growth, maturity and decline with a cash flow of £56,000 in year 1. Estimates of cash flows expected from years 2 – 10 are as follows:

Year	Percentage rate of change expected on the previous year's cash flow
2	+2
3	+5
4	+10
5	+10
6	+10
7	+5
8	−1
9	−3
10	−5

Assume all cash flows arise at year ends. Work throughout to the nearest £.

6.2.1 Calculate the cash flow expected in the tenth year.

6.2.2 Supposing that the expected cash flows are as follows, complete the following table, to calculate the net present value of the expected cash flows, by filling in the appropriate numerical values in the spaces indicated by the letters. Use a discount rate of 8 per cent per annum and use CIMA tables.

Year	Cash flow (£)	Discount factor	Present value (£)
1	56,000	…	…
2	57,000	…	A
3	60,000	…	…
4	66,000	…	…
5	72,000	…	B
6	79,000	…	…
7	84,000	…	…
8	82,000	…	C
9	80,000	…	…
10	75,000	…	…
Net present value			

6.2.3 If the net present value was £450,000 what is the maximum amount that the company could invest now in the product if it is to meet a target of an 8 per cent return?

6.2.4 If the net present value was £450,000 and, if the company needs to borrow at 8 per cent in order to finance the project, which of the following statements is/are correct?

(A) £450,000 is the profit that the company expects to make if they can borrow at 8 per cent.
(B) £450,000 is the maximum profit that the company might make if they borrow at 8 per cent.
(C) £450,000 is the maximum that the company should borrow if they wish to make a profit.
(D) £450,000 is the present value of the profit that the company expects to make if they borrow at 8 per cent.

6.2.5 The following list includes three valid comments about the use of discounting in appraising investment decisions. Indicate which comments are correct.

(A) Discounting takes account of the time value of cash flows;
(B) Discounting ignores risk;
(C) Discounting is more accurate because present value tables are available;
(D) Discounting does not involve making estimates;
(E) Discounting is of use only if an appropriate discount rate can be obtained.

Part 6.3 Annual equivalent costs

To carry out identical tasks, a company uses several machines of the same type, but of varying ages. They have a maximum life of five years. Typical financial data for a machine are given below:

Time	Now	After 1 year	After 2 years	After 3 years	After 4 years	After 5 years
Initial cost	£10,000	–	–	–	–	–
Maintenance + service costs	£1,000	£1,500	£2,000	£2,500	£3,000	£5,000
Resale value if sold	–	£7,000	£5,000	£3,500	£2,500	£2,000

The rate of interest is 15 per cent.
These machines are assumed to produce flows of revenue that are constant.

6.3.1 Complete the following table, to calculate the net present value of the costs if the machine is kept for 5 years, by filling in the appropriate numerical values in the spaces indicated by the letters. Work to the nearest £ throughout.

Time (years)	Outflows (£)	Discount factor	Present value (£)
0	A	D	...
1	B	...	...
2	...	E	...
3	...	...	F
4	...	...	...
5	C	...	...

6.3.2 The present values of the costs of keeping the machine for between 1 and 4 years are given below. Convert each of these into an annual equivalent amount and write them in the final column of the table, for one mark each.

Year of scrapping	Present value of cost (£)	Annuity equivalent (£)
1	6,215	...
2	10,037	...
3	13,159	...
4	15,748	...
5	18,669	...

6.3.3 If the annual equivalent amounts calculated above were as follows, what would be the most economical age at which to replace the machines?

Year of scrapping	Annual equivalent (£)
1	7,000
2	6,000
3	5,800
4	5,500
5	5,600

Part 6.4 NPV and IRR

A company is planning capital investment for which the following cash flows have been estimated:

Time	Net cash flow (£)
Now	(10,000)
At the end of year 1	500
At the end of year 2	2,000
At the end of year 3	3,000
At the end of year 4	4,000
At the end of year 5	5,000
At the end of year 6	2,500
At the end of year 7	2,000
At the end of year 8	2,500

The company has a cost of capital of 15 per cent.

6.4.1 Complete the following table by filling in the appropriate numerical values in the spaces indicated by the letters. Work to the nearest £ throughout. Cash flows are all at the ends of years unless stated otherwise.

Year end	Net cash flow (£)	Discount factor at 15%	Present value (£)
Now	(10,000)	A	C
1	500	B	...
2	2,000	...	...
3	3,000	...	...
4	4,000	...	...
5	5,000	...	...
6	2,500	...	...
7	2,000	...	...
8	2,500	...	D

6.4.2 Which of the following defines the 'internal rate of return'.

(A) The current discount rate used by a company.
(B) The discount rate at which net present value is zero.
(C) The discount rate recommended by a trade association or similar.
(D) The discount rate at which cash flows total zero.

6.4.3 The net present value is £(543) when the discount rate is 20 per cent and is £3,802 when it is 10 per cent. Which of the following statements about the value of the internal rate of return (IRR) is correct in this case?

(A) The IRR must be below 10 per cent.
(B) The IRR must lie between 10 per cent and 15 per cent.
(C) The IRR must lie between 15 per cent and 20 per cent.
(D) The IRR must be greater than 20 per cent.
(E) None of the above statements is correct.

6.4.4 Calculate the approximate internal rate of return (to the nearest whole per cent point) of this investment without calculating any further net present values.

6.4.5 If the internal rate of return was 12 percent in this case, and ignoring any other considerations, would you recommend acceptance of the project?

Answer: Yes/No

Part 6.5   Sinking funds and mortgages

A retailer is facing increasing competition from new shops that are opening in his area. He thinks that if he does not modernise his premises, he will lose sales. A local builder has estimated that the cost of modernising the shop will be £40,000 if the work is started now. The retailer is not sure whether to borrow the money and modernise the premises now, or to save up and have the work carried out when he has suffixient funds himself. Current forecasts show that if he delays the work for 3 years, the cost of the modernisation is likely to rise by 4 per cent per annum.

Investigations have revealed that, if he borrows, he will have to pay interest at the rate of 3 per cent per quarter, but if he saves the money himself he will only earn 2 per cent per quarter.

6.5.1 Use tables to find the cumulative discount factor appropriate to quarterly payments of £1 at 3 per cent per quarter over 2 years.

6.5.2 Calculate the equal amounts that would need to be paid at the end of each quarter if the retailer borrows the £40,000 now and repays it at 3 per cent per quarter over 3 years. Give your answer to two d.p.

6.5.3 Calculate the likely cost of modernisation if it is delayed by 3 years. Give your answer to two d.p.

6.5.4 If the retailer decides to delay modernisation and to save at 2 per cent per quarter, use tables to find the present value of his savings of £x per quarter, with 12 payments in total and the first being made immediately.

6.5.5 Suppose that the likely cost of modernisation delayed for 3 years was £45,000 and that the present value of the retailer's savings as calculated in 5.4 was 11X, calculate the value of £X if there is to be sufficient in the fund to cover the amount needed for modernisation. Give your answer correct to the nearest £10.

Part 6.6 Using Excel for financial analysis

6.6.1 Create a spreadsheet to Calculate the ROI, the NPV and the IRR on the following investment.

Amount invested = 200,000
Cash flow year 1 = 70,000
Cash flow year 2 = 120,000
Cash flow year 3 = 150,000
Cash flow year 4 = 490,000
Fixed cost of capital = 20%

Solutions to Revision Questions

Solutions to Part 6.1

6.1.1 Answer: (C)

Using tables, the annuity factor of £1 over 4 years at 8 per cent = 3.312
Let x = the annual sum payable at the beginning of years two, three, four and five.
Thus:

$$3.312x = 26,496$$
$$x = 26,496 / 3.312$$
$$x = 8,000$$

Thus, the total amount payable:

$$= £10,000 + (4 \times £8,000)$$
$$= £10,000 + £32,000$$
$$= £42,000$$

6.1.2 Answer: (B)

Assuming the rate of interest stated is nominal, that is, 6 per cent per annum in this case means ½ per cent per month, monthly ratio = $1 + (0.5/100) = 1.005$
Value after 6 months = $1,000 \times 1.005^6 = 1,030.38$, that is, interest = £30.38

6.1.3 Answer: (B)

Each year, the value at the end is 0.75 times the value at the beginning. So the value after three years is $20,000 \times 0.75^3 = 8,437.5$

6.1.4 Answer: (C)

The present value of 1,705.56 discounted at 5 per cent p.a. for 12 years is $1,705.56 \times 0.557 = 949.99692 = £950$ to the nearest whole £.

6.1.5 Answer: (A)

Present value = £8,000 + present value of an annuity of £8,000 for 9 years at 12 per cent.
Present value = £50,626

6.1.6 Answer: (C)

Three years is equal to twelve quarters, at an interest rate of 2 per cent per quarter. The principal will have grown to £12,000 × 1.02^{12} = £15,219

6.1.7 Answer: (C)

Cost at end of year 4 = £10,000 × 0.95^4 = £8,145

6.1.8 Answer: (C)

Present value = annual amount × annuity factor. So, annuity factor = 33,550/5,000 = 6.71

From the 10-year row in the cumulative present value tables, 6.71 corresponds to a discount rate of 8 per cent.

6.1.9 Answer: (B)

$$\text{Present value} = \text{annual amount} \times \text{annuity factor}$$
$$6{,}101 = 1{,}360 \times \text{annuity factor}$$
$$\text{Annuity factor} = 6{,}101/1{,}360 = 4.486$$

From tables, over 6 years this factor corresponds to a rate of 9 per cent.

6.1.10 Answer: (C)

The 6-year ratio = 500/400 = 1.25, and its sixth root = the annual ratio = 1.038

Hence the rate is 3.8 per cent per annum.

A gives the 25 per cent increase over the entire period and B gives 25 per cent divided by 6. D presumably comes from raising 1.25 to the power 6 instead of taking the sixth root.

6.1.11 (a) £68,000 (= 40,000 + 10 × 40,000 × 7/100)
(b) £78,686 (= 40,000 × 1.07^{10})

6.1.12 (a) £15,735 (= 10,000 × 1.12^4)
(b) £15,938 (= 10,000 × 1.06^8)
(c) £16,122 (= 10,000 × 1.01^{48})

6.1.13 Monthly rate is 2 per cent.

(A) Monthly ratio is 1.2   Incorrect: it is 1.02
(B) Annual ratio is 1.2 × 12   Incorrect: it would be 1.2^{12}
(C) = 14.4   Correct
(D) Annual rate is 44 per cent.   Incorrect: it would be 1,340 per cent.

6.1.14 Six-year ratio = 1.7
Annual ratio = $1.7^{1/6}$ = 1.092
Effective annual rate = 9.2 per cent.

6.1.15 Value of equipment at end of 1 year:

    (A) = 100,000 × 0.8   Correct

    (B) = 80,000   Correct

Value after a further n years

    (C) = 80,000 − n × 80,000 × 10/100   Incorrect: it is 80,000 × 0.9^n

    (D) = 80,000 (1 − 0.1n)   Correct

When value reaches £20,000, we have:

    (E) 20,000 = 80,000 (1 − 0.1n)   Correct

    (F) 2/8 = 1 − 0.1n Correct

    (G) 0.1n = 1.25   Incorrect: it is 0.1n = 0.75

    (H) n = 1.25/0.1 = 12.5   Correct

The value would drop to £20,000:

    (I) In 12 years.   Incorrect: after 12 years the value would still be above £20,000 on the basis of this calculation.

6.1.16 (A) True.
    (B) False.
    (C) False.
    (D) False.

6.1.17 (a) £71,300 (= 100,000 × 0.713)
    (b) £71,299 (= 100,000/1.07^5)

6.1.18

Time	Cash flow (£)	Discount factor 6%	Present value (£)
0	(5,000)	1.000	(5,000)
1	3,000	0.943	2,829
2	1,000	0.890	890
3	2,000	0.840	1,680
Net present value			399

6.1.19 (A) Incorrect.
    (B) Correct.
    (C) Incorrect.
    (D) Correct.

6.1.20 (a) £124,620 (= 10,000 × 12.462)
    (b) £124,622 (= 10,000/0.05(1 − 1/1.05^{20}))

6.1.21 £5,873 (= 50,000/8.514)

6.1.22 (A) False.
    (B) False.
    (C) True.
    (D) False.

Solutions to Part 6.2

6.2.1 Beginning with 56,000 at the end of year one, increase by 2 per cent by multiplying by 1.02, then by 5 per cent (multiply by 1.05) and so on. To decrease by 1 per cent, multiply by 0.99 (i.e. by 1−1/100).

Year	Cash flow (£)
1	56,000
2	57,120
3	59,976
4	65,974
5	72,571
6	79,828
7	83,819
8	82,981
9	80,492
10	76,467

6.2.2 The discount factors are given by present value tables at the rate of 8 per cent and years 1–10. The present value is given by multiplying the cash flow by the appropriate discount factor and the net present value is the total of the present values.

NPV of cash flows at 8 per cent

Year	Cash flow (£)	Discount factor (£)	DCF
1	56,000		
2	57,000	0.857	48,849
3	60,000		
4	66,000		
5	72,000	0.681	49,032
6	79,000		
7	84,000		
8	82,000	0.540	44,280
9	80,000		
10	75,000		
NPV			

6.2.3 The net present value is the amount which if invested now at 8 per cent would result in the cash flows listed and hence it gives the maximum amount which should be invested if a return of 8 per cent is required.

6.2.4 Answer: (C)

£450,000 is the maximum that the company should borrow if they wish to make a profit.

6.2.5 The correct statements are (A), (B) and (E). (C) is incorrect – tables generally involve loss of accuracy due to rounding and in any case (C) does not specify which less accurate method discounting is being compared with. (D) is incorrect because all the cash flows are to one extent or another estimates, as is the future value of the discount rate.

Solutions to Part 6.3

6.3.1 The outflows are given in the question apart from the first and last which need minor arithmetic. Discount factors are given by the 15 per cent column in present value tables up to 5 years and present value is given by multiplying each outflow by the corresponding discount factor. The following table then gives the values required:

Time (years)	Outflows (£)	Discount factor	Present value (£)
0	11,000	1.000	11,000
1	1,500	0.870	1,305
2	2,000	0.756	1,512
3	2,500	0.658	1,645
4	3,000	0.572	1,716
5	3,000	0.497	1,491

6.3.2 In order to compare these five NPV figures which span five different time periods, we need to convert each of them into a regular annual payment; to do this we divide the net present value by the corresponding cumulative present value factor taken from tables.

Answers:

Year of Scrapping	Present value of cost (£)	Cum PV factor	Annuity equivalent (£)
1	6,215	0.870	7,144
2	10,037	1.626	6,173
3	13,159	2.283	5,764
4	15,748	2.855	5,516
5	18,669	3.352	5,570

6.3.3 The lowest annual cost occurs if the machines are scrapped after 4 years.

Solutions to Part 6.4

6.4.1 Discount factors are obtained from present value tables, using the 15 per cent column and the years up to 8. Present value is given by multiplying the net cash flow by the corresponding discount factor.

Year end	Net cash flow (£)	Discount factor at 15%	Present value (£)
0	−10,000	1.000	−10,000
1	500	0.870	435
2	2,000	0.756	1,512
3	3,000	0.658	1,974
4	4,000	0.572	2,288
5	5,000	0.497	2,485
6	2,500	0.432	1,080
7	2,000	0.376	752
8	2,500	0.327	818

6.4.2 Answer: (F)

It is the discount rate at which net present value is zero.

6.4.3 If the net present value is positive at 15 per cent and negative at 20 per cent, it must be zero somewhere between the two, so (C) is the correct answer.

6.4.4 At 15 per cent NPV is 1,344 and at 20 per cent it is −543, so as discount rate increases by 5 per cent the NPV drops by 1,344 + 543 = 1,887. Starting at 15 per cent, the NPV must drop by 1,344 to reach zero. A £1,887 drop corresponds to a 5 per cent increase; a £1 drop corresponds to a 5/1,887 per cent increase; and so a £1,344 drop corresponds to a 1,344 × 5/1,887 = 3.56 per cent increase.

Rounding to the nearest whole per cent point gives an IRR of 15 + 4 = 19 per cent.

6.4.5 The project is acceptable, because the IRR is greater than the cost of capital. This ignores the fact that the cash flows are almost all estimates, the applicable discount rate may change, there may be even more profitable projects available, etc.

Answer: Yes.

✓ Solutions to Part 6.5

6.5.1 Total number of payments is 8; first payment occurs at time 1; discount rate is 3 per cent. From tables the cumulative discount value is 7.020.

6.5.2 From the tables, the cumulative discount factor at 3 per cent for 12 time periods is 9.954. The present value of £x paid at the end of each of 12 quarters at 3 per cent per quarter is 9.954x and this must equal the initial debt of £40,000.
If 9.954x = 40,000, then x = 40,000/9.954 = £4,018.49

6.5.3 Likely cost is 40,000 compounded at 4 per cent for 3 years, that is 40,000 × 1.04^3 = £44,994.56.

6.5.4 From the tables, the cumulative present value of £1 at the ends of 11 time periods at 2 per cent per period is 9.787. If we include an immediate payment of £1, this PV becomes 10.787. Hence the present value required is 10.787x.

6.5.5 From present value tables, the present value of £45,000 discounted over 12 periods at 2 per cent per period = 45,000 × 0.788 = 35,460. This must equal 11X and hence X = 35,460/11 = 3,224 = £3,220 to the nearest £10.

✓ Solutions to Part 6.6

The spreadsheet below shows the data and the Excel formulae used to calculate the ROI, the NPV and the IRR of the investment. Notice that the data has been entered in a second column for the purposes of calculating the IRR as the initial investment needs to be referenced as a negative value when using the IRR function.

	A	B	C
1	Amount invested	200000	-200000
2	Cash Flow year 1	70000	=B2
3	Cash flow year 2	120000	=B3
4	Cash flow year 3	150000	=B4
5	Cash flow year 4	150000	=B5
6			
7	Fixed cost of capital	0.2	
8			
9			
10	ROI	=B1/AVERAGE(B2:B5)	
11	NPV	=NPV(B7,B2:B5)-B1	
12	IRR	=IRR(C1:C6,0.25)	
13			
14			

7

Correlation and Regression

Correlation and Regression 7

LEARNING OUTCOMES

On completing this chapter you should be able to:

- calculate the correlation coefficient between two variables, and explain the value;
- calculate the rank correlation coefficient between two sets of data, and explain the value;
- demonstrate the use of regression analysis between two variables to find the line of best fit and explain its meaning;
- calculate a forecast of the value of the dependent variable, given the value of the independent variable;
- apply correlation and regression techniques to Excel.

7.1 Introduction

In the next two chapters we look at one of the major applications of statistics, namely forecasting. Although there are a number of ways of producing forecasts that involve little or no mathematics, we shall concentrate here on two of the most important quantitative approaches, causal and extrapolative. A *causal* approach is based on the assumption that changes in the variable that we wish to forecast are *caused* by changes in one or more other variables. With an *extrapolative* approach, we examine past data on the variable that is to be forecast, in order to determine any patterns the data exhibits. It is then assumed that these patterns will continue into the future: in other words, they are *extrapolated*.

Let us begin with the causal approach, and, to simplify matters, we shall deal with the case in which the variable to be forecast (the dependent variable, y) depends on only one other variable (the independent variable, x). Such data is called bivariate because in each situation we have two pieces of information, denoted x and y. The dependent variable, y, is also referred to as the *response variable* and the independent variable, x, as the *influencing variable*. So x is assumed to influence a response in y. Before actually looking at how to produce forecasts in such situations, we must consider the question as to how we know that changes in y *are* caused by changes in x (alternatively: how we know that y depends on x). The answer to this involves the study of *correlation*.

7.2 Correlation

> There are many key terms in italics in these introductory paragraphs.

Two variables are said to be *correlated* if they are related to one another, or, more precisely, if changes in the value of one tend to accompany changes in the other. Now, we have already used the (x, y) notation of Chapter 2, and this initially suggests a graphical approach: if there are pairs of data available on the variables x and y, then these can be plotted as points against a set of x- and y-axes. The result is known as a *scatter diagram*, *scatter graph* or sometimes a *scatter plot*.

Example 7.2.1

A company is investigating the effects of its advertising on sales. Consequently, data on monthly advertising and sales in the following month are collated to obtain:

Advertising expenditure in month (£'000)	Total sales in following month (£'000)
1.3	151.6
0.9	100.1
1.8	199.3
2.1	221.2
1.5	170.0

Plot these data on a scatter diagram.

Solution

Since the company is interested in how advertising affects sales, it is clear that sales should be the dependent variable, y, and advertising the independent, x. The scatter diagram is shown in Figure 7.1.

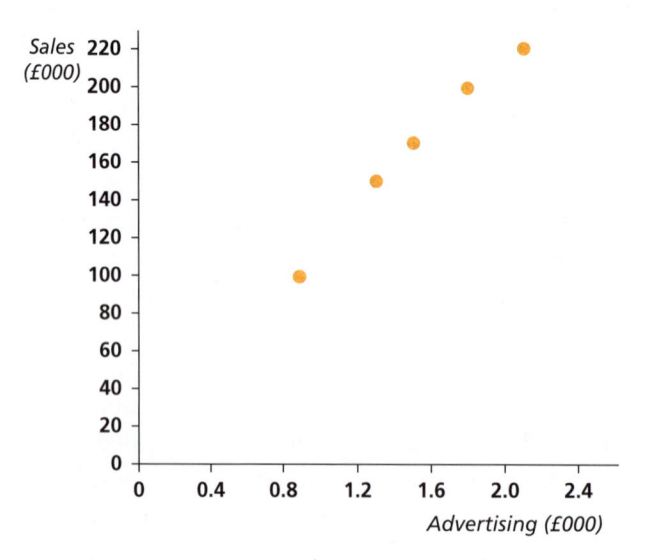

Figure 7.1 Scatter diagram (Example 7.2.1)

The five pairs of data points are marked as points on the graph.

Since, unlike in Chapter 2, we have not been told that y is a function of x here, the points have not been joined up. In particular, although the points appear to be close to lying on a straight line, they do not lie *exactly* on a line; we do not know that a linear function is involved and so none has been drawn in.

The scatter diagram in the above example seems to show a case where the two variables are related to one another. Further, the relationship seems to be of an approximately *linear* nature: it is an example of linear correlation. Since the approximation is so good, and the points are close to a straight line, we talk of *strong* linear correlation. Finally, as the gradient of the 'line' is positive, it is *positive linear* (or direct) correlation.

Scatter diagrams in Excel

The data in the above example can be plotted onto a scatter diagram in Excel.

To do this the data must first be entered into the spreadsheet. To create the chart select the range A3:B7 and click on the chart icon. Select X-Y scatter and choose the first chart option. The data and the resulting chart are shown in Figure 7.2.

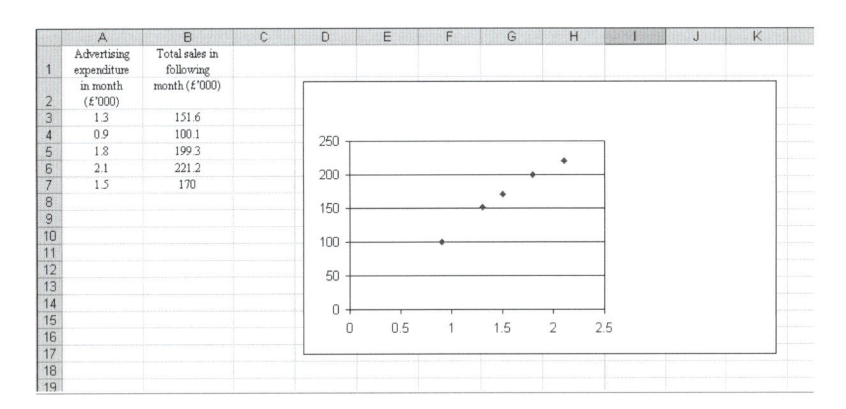

Figure 7.2 Creating a scatter diagram in Excel

Example 7.2.2

Most of the examples in this chapter relate to the following table. A company owns six sales outlets in a certain city. The sales last year of two of its key products are given below, together with the sizes of each outlet:

Outlet	Floor space m²	Sales of L '000 units	Sales of M '000 units
A	75	22.4	30.7
B	60	21.1	12.9
C	108	29.6	47.1
D	94	27.1	38.8
E	92	27.0	41.5
F	130	36.9	79.0

The company is investigating the effects of outlet size on sales.
Plot scatter diagrams of:

(a) sales of L against size;
(b) sales of M against size.

Solution

Did you plot size of outlet as x in both cases? We are investigating the effect of size on sales, so sales must be the dependent variable (see Figures 7.3 and 7.4).

Figure 7.5 shows further examples of:

- very weak positive linear correlation, in which y shows a slight tendency to increase as x does;
- strong negative linear (or inverse) correlation, in which y shows a strong tendency to decrease as x increases; and
- non-linear correlation, in which x and y are clearly related, but not in a linear fashion.

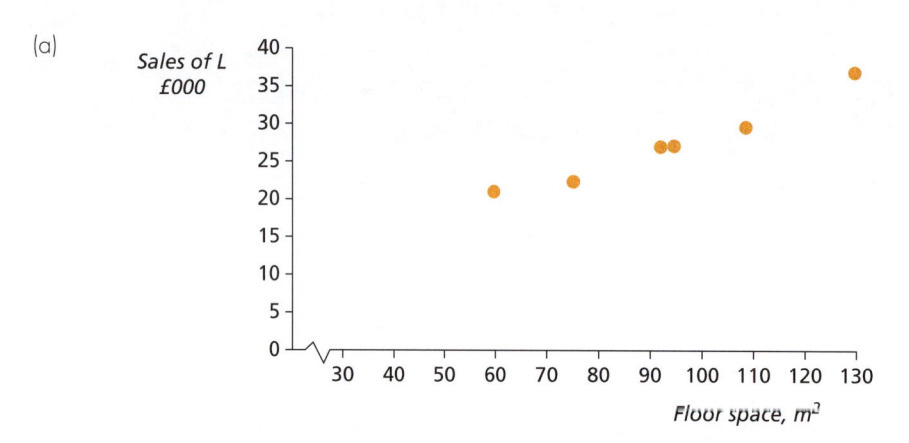

Figure 7.3 Scatter diagram (Example 7.2.2(a))

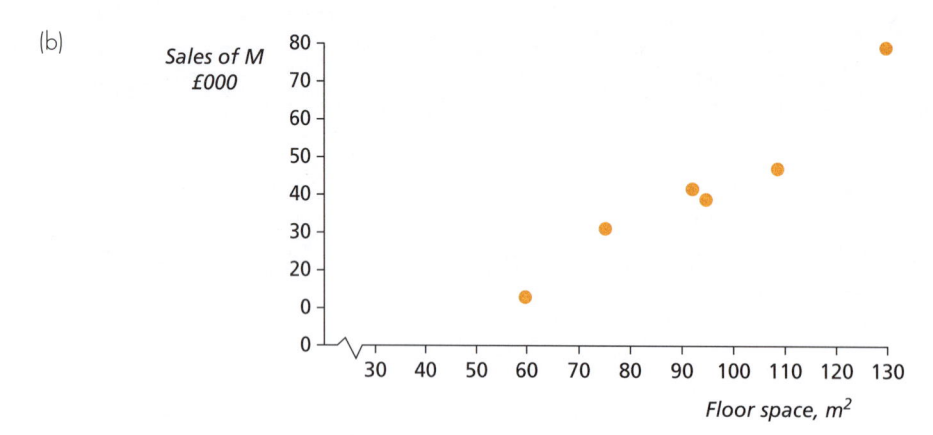

Figure 7.4 Scatter diagram (Example 7.2.2(b))

(a) Very weak positive linear

y, sales

x, number of salespersons employed

(b) Strong negative linear

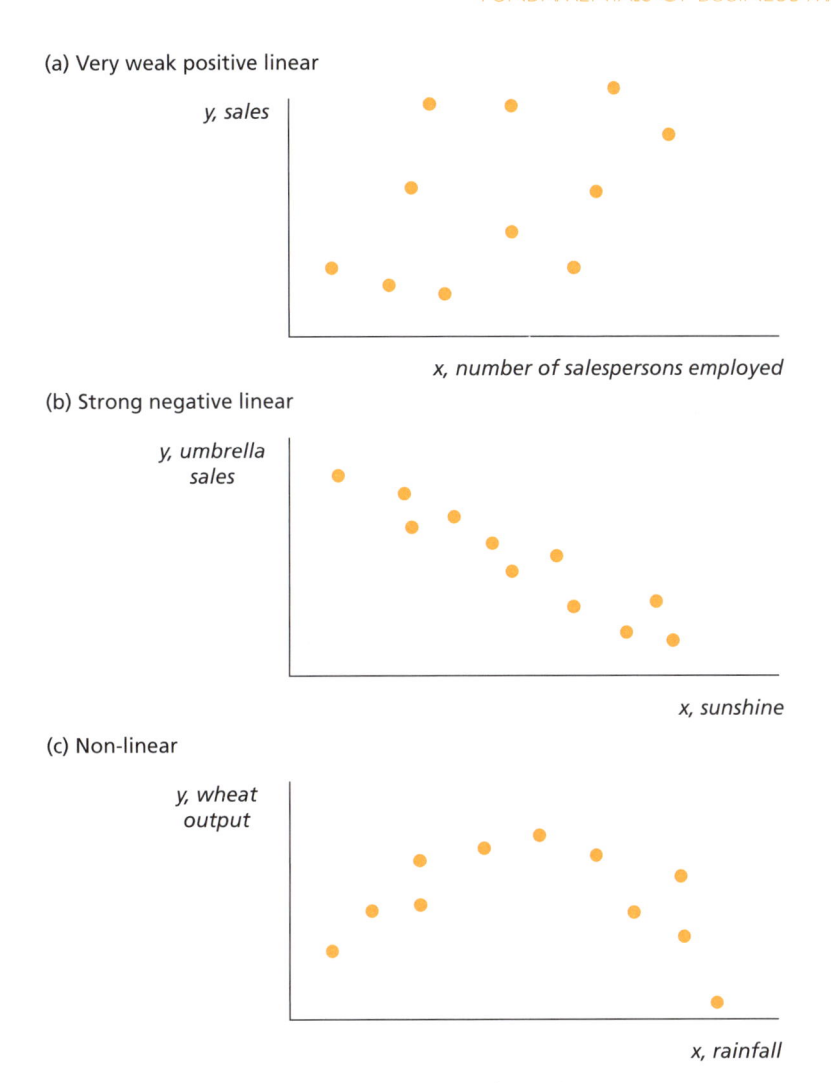

y, umbrella sales

x, sunshine

(c) Non-linear

y, wheat output

x, rainfall

Figure 7.5 Examples of correlation

Although such scatter diagrams are useful for getting a feel for the presence or otherwise of correlation, it is often difficult to judge what is 'weak' and what is 'strong', and, indeed, whether a large number of points on a diagram constitute any correlation at all. Therefore, an objective measure of correlation is needed.

Example 7.2.3

From your own experience, try to think of pairs of variables that might have the different degrees of correlation, from weak to strong and from negative to positive.

Solution

These are just some examples:

- costs probably have a strong positive correlation with the number of units produced;
- number of deaths on the roads probably has a middling positive correlation with traffic levels;
- the level of street crime is often thought to relate to the level of visible policing, so the correlation would be negative but probably not strong;
- a strong negative correlation would probably be found if almost any measure of bodily function, such as the condition of the heart, were compared with age in adults, although the graph is unlikely to be perfectly linear.

7.3 Pearson's correlation coefficient

The statistician Pearson developed a measure of the amount of linear correlation present in a set of pairs of data. Pearson's correlation coefficient, denoted r, is defined as:

$$r = \frac{n\Sigma xy - \Sigma x \Sigma y}{\sqrt{(n\Sigma x^2 - (\Sigma x)^2)(n\Sigma y^2 - (\Sigma y)^2)}}$$

where n is the number of data points.

> ❗ This formula is given in your exam so you do not need to worry about remembering it.

This measure has the property of always lying in the range -1 to $+1$, where:

- $r = +1$ denotes perfect positive linear correlation (the data points lie *exactly* on a straight line of positive gradient);
- $r = -1$ denotes *perfect* negative linear correlation (again the data points lie on a straight line but with a negative gradient); and
- $r = 0$ denotes no *linear* correlation.

The strength of a correlation can be judged by its proximity to $+1$ or -1: the nearer it is (and the further away from zero), the stronger is the linear correlation. A common error is to believe that negative values of r cannot be strong. They can be just as strong as positive values except that y is decreasing as x increases.

Example 7.3.1

Evaluate Pearson's correlation coefficient for the data on sales and advertising spend in Example 7.2.1, and interpret its value.

Solution

As with previous calculations involving summations, we facilitate the calculations by setting them out in columns:

x	y	x^2	y^2	xy
1.3	151.6	1.69	22,982.56	197.08
0.9	100.1	0.81	10,020.01	90.09
1.8	199.3	3.24	39,720.49	358.74
2.1	221.2	4.41	48,929.44	464.52
1.5	170.0	2.25	28,900.00	255.00
7.6	842.2	12.40	150,552.50	1,365.43

Thus, $r = \dfrac{(5 \times 1{,}365.43) - (7.6 \times 842.2)}{\sqrt{[(5 \times 12.4) - 7.6^2][(5 \times 150{,}552.5) - 842.2^2]}} = \dfrac{426.43}{\sqrt{4.24 \times 43{,}461.66}} = 0.993$

The value of Pearson's correlation coefficient in this case is 0.993. The arithmetic in such a calculation can be seen to be potentially very tedious. It is worthwhile investigating the availability of any computer packages or special functions on a calculator in order to ease the computation of correlation coefficients. Note that a simple check is that your calculated value for the correlation coefficient must be between -1 and 1.

The value of the coefficient in this case is clearly very close to the value 1, indicating a very strong positive linear correlation, and reflecting the close proximity of the points in Figure 7.1 to a straight line.

Example 7.3.2

Using the data on floor space and sales from Example 7.2.2, evaluate Pearson's correlation coefficients for:

(a) sales of L and size;
(b) sales of M and size.

Solution

(a) The necessary summations are $n = 6$; $\Sigma x = 559$; $\Sigma y = 164.1$; $\Sigma x^2 = 55,089$; $\Sigma y^2 = 4,648.15$; $\Sigma xy = 15,971.2$. Hence:

$$r = \frac{(6 \times 15,971.2) - (559 \times 164.1)}{\sqrt{(6 \times 55,089 - 559^2)(6 \times 4,648.15 - 164.1^2)}}$$

$$= \frac{4,095.3}{\sqrt{18,053 \times 960.09}} = \frac{4,095.3}{\sqrt{17,332,504.77}} = \frac{4,095.3}{4,163.23} = 0.984$$

This is a very strong positive correlation between outlet size and sales of L.

(b) For M, the summations are $n = 6$; $\Sigma x = 559$; $\Sigma y = 250$; $\Sigma x^2 = 55,089$; $\Sigma y^2 = 12,796$; $\Sigma xy = 25,898.5$

These result in $r = 0.974$, which similarly shows a very strong positive correlation between outlet size and sales of M.

Many students initially find these calculations very difficult. Even if you got the right answer, you may find it useful to run through the calculations once more. Correlation is a very important topic in business mathematics.

7.4 Interpreting correlation coefficients

In general, it is not always as straightforward to interpret a value of r as in the above case. Although it would be inappropriate for the purpose of this text to go into detailed theory, it must be noted that the sample size (n) has a crucial effect: the smaller the value of n, the 'easier' it is for a large value of r to arise purely by accident.

Very rough guidelines are that, with a sample of ten data points, a minimum correlation of about 0.6 is needed before you can feel confident that any sort of linear relationship holds. With twenty data points, the minimum correlation needed is about 0.4.

Extrapolation is a further danger in the interpretation of r. If your x-values range from 0.9 to 2.1, then $r = 0.993$ tells you that there is a near-perfect linear relationship between x and y in that range. However, you know nothing at all about the relationship outside that range. It may or may not continue to be linear. The process of drawing conclusions outside the range of the data is called extrapolation. It often cannot be avoided but it leads to unreliable conclusions.

It is possible that an apparently high correlation can occur *accidentally or spuriously* between two unconnected variables. There is no mathematical way of checking when this is the case, but common sense can help. In the case under discussion, it seems plausible that sales and the advertising spend *are* connected, and so it would seem reasonable to assume that this is not an accidental or spurious correlation.

More importantly here, two variables can be correlated because they are separately correlated to a *hidden third variable*. The size of the region could well be such a variable: larger regions would tend to have larger sales figures and the management of larger regions would tend to have larger advertising budgets. It is therefore *possible* that this high correlation coefficient may have arisen because the variable 'sales' is highly correlated with size of region, advertising expenditure is highly correlated with size of region, but sales and advertising spend are not themselves directly connected.

Even if this third variable effect is not present, we still cannot conclude that y depends on x. The strong correlation lends support to the *assumption* that this is so, but does not *prove* it. *Correlation cannot be used to prove causation.*

> In your assessment, interpreting correlation is as important as calculating the coefficient.

7.5 Rank correlation: Spearman's coefficient

There are occasions when the degree of correlation between two variables is to be measured but one or both of them is not in a suitable quantitative form. In such circumstances, Pearson's coefficient cannot be used, but an alternative approach – *rank* correlation – might be appropriate. The most common measure of this type is *Spearman's rank correlation coefficient, R*:

$$R = 1 - \frac{6 \Sigma d^2}{n(n^2 - 1)}$$

where d denotes the difference in ranks, and n the sample size.

> You do not need to remember this formula because it will be given in your exam.

The arithmetic involved in calculating values of this coefficient is much easier than that for Pearson's coefficient, as the following example illustrates.

Example 7.5.1

As part of its recruitment procedures, a company awards applicants ratings from A (excellent) to E (unsatisfactory) for their interview performance, and marks out of 100 for a written test. The results for five interviewees are as follows.

Interviewee	Interview grade	Test score
a	A	60
b	B	61
c	A	50
d	C	72
e	D	70

Calculate the Spearman's rank correlation coefficient for this data, and comment on its value.

Solution

In order to apply the formula, the grades and scores are ranked, with the best scores given a rank of 1. Notice how interviewees a and c share the best interview grade. They therefore share the ranks 1 and 2 to give 1.5 each.

Interviewee	Rank of interview grade	Rank of test score	d	d^2
a	1.5	4	−2.5	6.25
b	3	3	0	0.00
c	1.5	5	−3.5	12.25
d	4	1	3	9.00
e	5	2	3	9.00
				36.50

Hence:

$$R = 1 - \frac{6 \Sigma d^2}{n(n^2 - 1)} = 1 - \frac{6 \times 36.50}{5(25 - 1)} = -0.825$$

The high negative value (near to −1) indicates that interview grades and test scores almost totally disagree with each other – good interview grades go with the lowest test scores and vice versa. This should concern the company, as it may mean that one or both methods of judging applicants is faulty. The interpretation of R-values is similar to that for r. Warnings similar to those in Section 7.4 also apply when judging values of R.

Example 7.5.2

An expert was asked to rank, according to taste, eight wines costing below £4. Her rankings (with 1 being the worst taste and 8 the best) and the prices per bottle were as follows:

Sample	Rank of taste	Price £
A	1	2.49
B	2	2.99
C	3	3.49
D	4	2.99
E	5	3.59
F	6	3.99
G	7	3.99
H	8	2.99

Calculate Spearman's rank correlation coefficient for this data and interpret your result. What result would you expect if the best-tasting wine were ranked 1 and the worst 8?

Solution

Sample	Rank of taste	Rank of price	d	d^2
A	1	1	0	0
B	2	3	−1	1
C	3	5	−2	4
D	4	3	1	1
E	5	6	−1	1
F	6	7.5	−1.5	2.25
G	7	7.5	−0.5	0.25
H	8	3	5	25
				34.50

Hence, $R = 1 - \dfrac{6\Sigma d^2}{n(n^2 - 1)} = 1 - \dfrac{6 \times 34.5}{8(64 - 1)} = 1 - \dfrac{207}{504} = 1 - 0.41 = 0.59$

There seems to be some positive correlation between price and taste, with the more expensive wines tending to taste better. Given the sample size the result is not really reliable and it cannot be extrapolated to wines costing more than £4. Had the taste rankings been allocated in the opposite order, the correlation would be −0.59.

Students often find this calculation difficult and it is worth running through it again if you had problems. Probably the most common errors are either forgetting to subtract from 1 or subtracting the numerator from 1 prior to dividing by the denominator.

Tied rankings can also be difficult. B, D and H all cost £2.99. Had they been marginally different they would have been ranked 2, 3 and 4. Since they are identical, they each have the rank of 3 (the average of 2, 3 and 4). Similarly F and G share the ranks 7 and 8 by giving them an average 7.5 each.

The *d* column is obtained by subtracting rank of taste minus rank of price, but it would be equally correct the other way round.

7.6 Which correlation coefficient to use

If the data have already been ranked, there is no option but to use the rank correlation coefficient (*R*). Where actual values of *x* and *y* are given, Pearson's coefficient (*r*) should generally be used since information is lost when values are converted into their ranks. In particular, Pearson's coefficient must be used if you intend to use regression for forecasting (see later). The only advantages in converting actual data into ranks and using Spearman's coefficient are:

1. that the arithmetic is easier, but this is a minor point given computers and scientific calculators;
2. that Spearman checks for a linear relationship between the ranks rather than the actual figures. If you simply want to confirm, say, that the variables increase together but have no concern about the linearity of the relationship, you might prefer to use the rank correlation coefficient.

7.7 Regression

The preceding sections give us a way of checking on whether it may be valid to assume that one variable, *y*, depends on another, *x*. We now proceed to consider how, after making such an assumption, *y* can be forecast from *x*.

For simplicity, we restrict our attention to instances of linear correlation. Thus, we are interested in situations where the dependence is in the form of a straight line. As we saw in Chapter 2, this involves equations of the type

$$y = a + bx$$

where *a* and *b* are numbers. We are, therefore, initially concerned with determining suitable straight line(s) for the particular problem.

7.8 The least-squares criterion

The approach is illustrated through an example.

Example 7.8.1

A company has the following data on its sales during the last year in each of its regions and the corresponding number of salespersons employed during this time:

Region	Sales (units)	Salespersons
A	236	11
B	234	12
C	298	18
D	250	15
E	246	13
F	202	10

Develop a linear model for forecasting sales from the number of salespersons.

Solution

The linear correlation coefficient between these two variables can be shown to be 0.948. This high value encourages us to assume that sales, y, might depend on the number of salespersons, x, in a linear way.

The scatter diagram for the data is shown in Figure 7.6. For convenience of drawing, the scales on the axes do not start from zero. However, this has the effect of exaggerating the divergences from linearity. A truer impression would be obtained from a graph containing the origin, but this would not be so easy to draw.

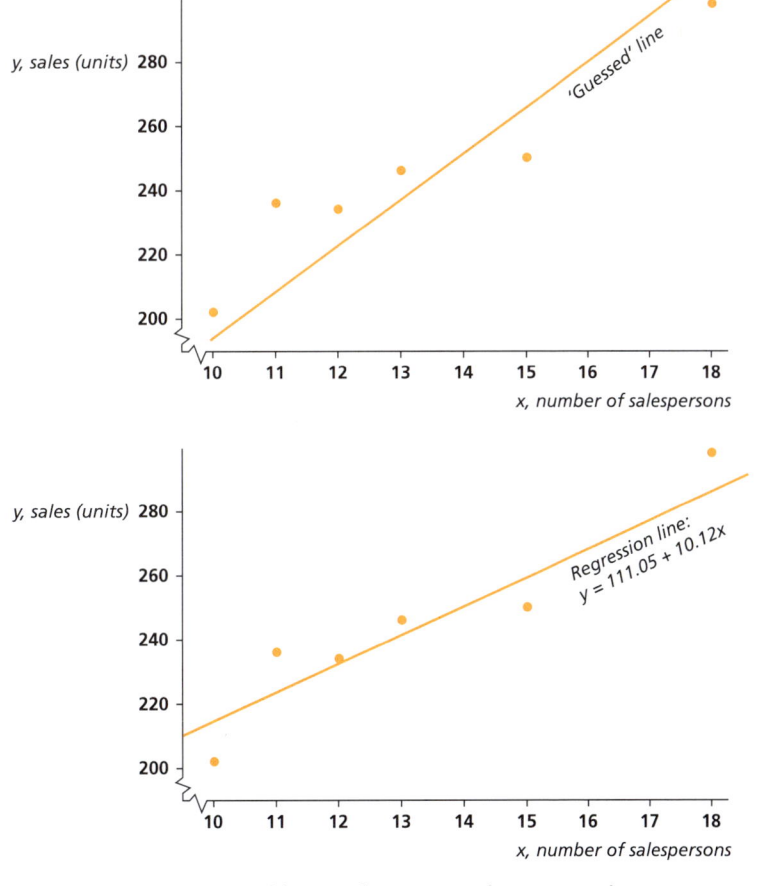

Figure 7.6 Guessed line and regression line (Example 7.8.1)

In the upper part of the figure, a straight line has been gauged or 'guessed' by using a ruler to draw a line that appears to be 'close' to all five data points. We have deliberately fitted a very poor guessed line so that the errors are clear. If you do have to fit a line 'by eye', the aim is to follow the slope of the points and to draw the line as far as possible through the centre of the points with roughly equal numbers either side. The lower part of Figure 7.5 shows the best possible fitted line.

This approximate approach may well be accurate enough in many instances, but it is certainly arbitrary. A number of different, equally plausible, lines could be drawn in: the question is, how can you judge whether one line is 'better' than another? Indeed, which is the 'best'?

If we look at the 'guessed' line, it is clear that there are discrepancies between actual y-values and those obtained from the line. There are y-errors present, and the sizes of these enable us to judge one line against another. Examples of y-errors in this instance are:

$x = 13$: actual $y = 246$
 y from line $= 239$ (approximately)
 y-error in line $= -7$
$x = 15$: actual $y = 250$
 y from line $= 266$
 y-error in line $= +16$

Some errors are positive and some negative. Simply adding the errors to judge the 'goodness' of the line, therefore, would not be a sensible idea, as positive errors would tend to be cancelled out by negative ones. To eliminate this effect, we square the errors, and deem one line 'better' than another if its sum of *squared* errors is lower. The 'best' line is thus the one with the least sum of squared errors: the so-called *least-squares* regression line of y on x. Without going through the theory, this can be shown to have equation

$$y = a + bx$$

where:

$$b = \frac{n\Sigma xy - (\Sigma x)(\Sigma y)}{n\Sigma x^2 - (\Sigma x)^2}$$

and

$a = \bar{y} - b\bar{x}$ ($\bar{y}, \bar{x}$: are the means of y and x, respectively)

> **!** These formulae are given in your exam. Note that, because $\bar{y} = a + b\bar{x}$, the regression line always passes through the point $(\bar{x}, \bar{y})$.

The calculation of *a* and *b* is set out in a familiar tabular form:

x	y	x^2	xy
11	236	121	2,596
12	234	144	2,808
18	298	324	5,364
15	250	225	3,750
13	246	169	3,198
10	202	100	2,020
79	1,466	1,083	19,736

$$b = \frac{(6 \times 19{,}736) - (79 \times 1{,}466)}{(6 \times 1{,}083) - 79^2} = \frac{2{,}602}{257} = 10.12$$

$$\bar{x} = \frac{79}{6} = 13.17$$

$$\bar{y} = \frac{1{,}466}{6} = 244.33$$

and so:

$$a = 244.33 - (10.12 \times 13.17) = 111.05$$

Thus, the least-squares regression line in this case is $y = 111.05 + 10.12x$

This line has been plotted on the lower scatter diagram of Figure 7.6 by calculating the coefficients of any two points on the line – for example:

- when $x = 10$, $y = 111.05 + 10.12 \times 10 = 212.25$
- when $x = 17$, $y = 111.05 + 10.12 \times 17 = 283.09$

These points should then be plotted on the graph and joined by a straight line.

Least-squares line in Excel

There is a built-in formula in Excel for the calculation of the least-squares line. We will illustrate this using the data from Example 7.8.1. Having entered the data into the spreadsheet the first step is to draw a scatter diagram described in the previous example. Figure 7.7 shows the data and the scatter diagram.

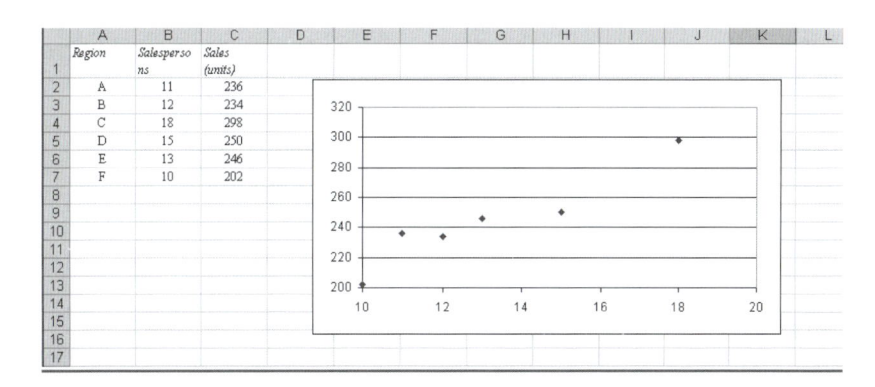

Figure 7.7 Data and scatter diagram in preparation for the least-squares line

The Excel FORECAST function can be used to calculate the least-square line. The following needs to be entered into cell D2:

= FORECAST(B2,$C$2:$C$7,$B$2:$B$7)

And the formula can then be copied through to cell D7. The range D2:D7 can then be selected, click the copy icon and then click on the chart to make it active before finally clicking the paste icon to plot the forecast data onto the chart. This will initially appear as symbols only, in the same way as the original scatter diagram was produced. However if you right click on one of the new data symbols and select FORMAT DATA SERIES, line can be set to automatic and marker can be set to none. The resulting chart and the FORECAST function formula can be seen in Figure 7.8.

	A	B	C	D
1	Region	Salespersons	Sales (units)	Least square line
2	A	11	236	=FORECAST(B2,$C$2:$C$7,$B$2:$B$7)
3	B	12	234	=FORECAST(B3,$C$2:$C$7,$B$2:$B$7)
4	C	18	298	=FORECAST(B4,$C$2:$C$7,$B$2:$B$7)
5	D	15	250	=FORECAST(B5,$C$2:$C$7,$B$2:$B$7)
6	E	13	246	=FORECAST(B6,$C$2:$C$7,$B$2:$B$7)
7	F	10	202	=FORECAST(B7,$C$2:$C$7,$B$2:$B$7)

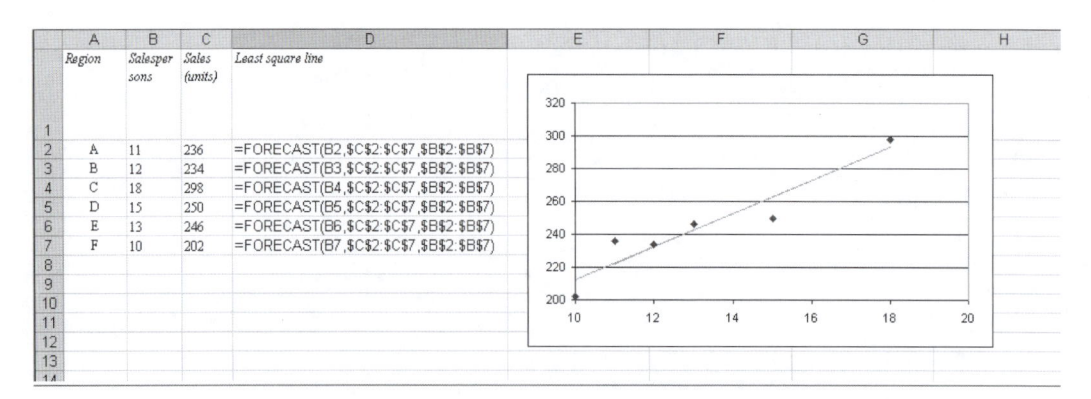

Figure 7.8 Least-squared line plotted onto scatter diagram

7.9 Interpreting *a* and *b*

You may remember from Chapter 2 that in the equation of a straight line, $y = a + bx$, a is the intercept on the y-axis and b is the gradient or slope of the line. Expressed slightly differently, that means that a is the value of y when $x = 0$, and b is the increase in y for each unit increase in x. The b-value of 10.12 tells us that each extra salesperson generates an extra 10.12 sales (on average), while the a-value of 111.05 means that 111.05 units will be sold if no salespeople are used. The latter conclusion may well be nonsensical because $x = 0$ is outside the range of the data, but we return to this later.

It should be noted that, unlike Pearson's correlation coefficient, these calculations do not use Σy^2, and so no time has been wasted evaluating it. Also, it will be appreciated that calculations such as these can involve potentially large numbers, and so it might be worthwhile to use an available computer package or statistical function on a calculator.

> ✏️ The interpretation of *a* and *b* is a frequent exam question.

Example 7.9.1

Using the data given in Example 7.2.2 on sales and floor space, find the least-squares regression lines for:

(a) sales of L against size;
(b) sales of M against size.

Interpret the values of *a* and *b* in your answers.

Solution

(a) Using the summations calculated in Example 7.3.2:

$$b = \frac{n\Sigma xy - (\Sigma x)(\Sigma y)}{n\Sigma x^2 - (\Sigma x)^2} = \frac{(6 \times 15{,}971.2) - (559 \times 164.1)}{(6 \times 55{,}089) - 559^2} = \frac{4{,}095.3}{18{,}053} = 0.2268$$

$$a = \bar{y} - b\bar{x} = \frac{164.1}{6} - 0.2268 \times \frac{559}{6} = 6.2198$$

Rounding to two decimal places gives the regression line of sales of L against floor space:

$$y = 6.22 + 0.23x$$

(b) Similarly, the regression line of sales of M against floor space can be shown to be:

$$y = -39.05 + 0.87x$$

In part (a), $b = 0.23$ means that if the floor space were increased by one square metre, sales would increase by an average of 0.23 ('000 units), that is, by 230 units. The a-value of 6.22 gives the absurd result (due to extrapolation) that an outlet with zero floor space would on average sell 6,220 units.

In part (b), the corresponding results are that sales can be expected to increase by 870 units for each extra square metre of floor space and the nonsensical sales of $-39,050$ units would occur if an outlet had zero size.

7.10 Forecasting

Once the equation of the regression line has been computed, it is a relatively straightforward process to obtain forecasts.

Example 7.10.1

In the situation of Example 7.8.1, forecast the number of sales that would be expected next year in regions that employed (a) 14 salespersons; and (b) 25 salespersons.

Solution

As we have the 'best' line representing the dependence of sales on the number of salespersons we shall use it for the forecasts. The values could be read off the line drawn on the scattergraph, but it is more accurate to use the equation of the line.

(a) The regression line is $y = 111.05 + 10.12x$ so, when $x = 14$:

$$y = 111.05 + 10.12 \times 14 = 252.73$$

Rounding this to a whole number, we are forecasting that 253 units will be sold in a region employing 14 salespersons.

(b) Substituting $x = 25$ into the formula:

$$y = 111.05 + 10.12 \times 25 = 364.05$$

Hence the forecast is sales of 364 units in a region employing 25 salespersons.

Have you noticed that $x = 25$ is well outside the range of the data? What does this tell you about the reliability of the estimated 364? If you are in any doubt about its unreliability, look back to the absurd consequences of putting $x = 0$ in Example 7.9.1.

We give one more example to illustrate the complete process of forecasting from paired samples.

Example 7.10.2

A company has the following data on its profits and advertising expenditure over the last 6 years:

Profits £m	Advertising expenditure £m
11.3	0.52
12.1	0.61
14.1	0.63
14.6	0.70
15.1	0.70
15.2	0.75

Forecast the profits for next year if an advertising budget of £800,000 is allocated.

Solution

First of all, to justify our assumption that there is a relationship between the two variables, the correlation coefficient should be computed. It is left as an exercise for you to verify that its value is 0.936. This high correlation encourages us to proceed with the regression approach.

As we wish to forecast profits, we shall make this the dependent variable, y, and advertising expenditure the independent variable, x.

The next step is to evaluate the parameters a and b:

x	y	x^2	xy
0.52	11.3	0.2704	5.876
0.61	12.1	0.3721	7.381
0.63	14.1	0.3969	8.883
0.70	14.6	0.4900	10.220
0.70	15.1	0.4900	10.570
0.75	15.2	0.5625	11.400
3.91	82.4	2.5819	54.330

Thus:

$$b = \frac{(6 \times 54.33) - (3.91 \times 82.4)}{(6 \times 2.5819) - 3.91^2} = \frac{3.796}{0.2033} = 18.67$$

$$\bar{x} = \frac{3.91}{6} = 0.652$$

$$\bar{y} = \frac{82.4}{6} = 13.73$$

and so:

$$a = 13.73 - (18.67 \times 0.652) = 1.56$$

The least-squares regression line relating profits to advertising expenditure therefore has equation

$$y = 1.56 + 18.67x$$

Hence each extra million pounds' advertising generates an extra £18.67 million profits. Also, profits would be £1.56 million without any advertising.

If advertising expenditure is to be £800,000 ($x = 0.8$), then:

$$y = 1.56 + 18.67 \times 0.8 = 16.496$$

Rounding this value off to a sensible level of apparent accuracy, we are forecasting profits of £16.5 million next year, if advertising expenditure is £800,000.

Example 7.10.3

The company in Example 7.2.2 is considering opening two further outlets in the city: G, with 85 m² of floor space; and H, with 146 m² of floor space. Use the regression lines calculated in Exercise 7.9.1 to forecast the sales of L and M at the two possible new outlets.

Solution

Outlet G

> Forecast sales of L = 6.2198 + 0.2268 × 85 = 25.4978 ('000 units)
> = 25,500 units (to three significant figures)
> Forecast sales of M = −39.052 + 0.8664 × 85 = 34.592 ('000 units)
> = 34,600 units (to 3 s.f.)

Outlet H

> Similarly, the forecast sales of L = 39,300 units and of M = 87,400 units.

> ✎ Forecasting using the regression equation is a frequent exam question.

7.11 Which variable to denote by y

When calculating the correlation coefficient it does not matter which variable you call x and which y, as the result will be the same either way. However, the regression equation and subsequent forecasts will be totally changed if you change the designation of the variables. This is because the regression line only minimises the sum of squares of the y-errors, and this is only equivalent to minimising x-errors in the case of perfect correlation, that is, when $r = \pm 1$. It is therefore essential that you stop and think about which variable to call y at the start of any exercise on regression.

Variable y is the dependent variable and sometimes it is very clear which that is. However, there are occasions when the dependency could perhaps work either way, in which case the following may be of assistance:

- if you wish to forecast a particular variable, that variable must be denoted by y;
- if the question asks for the regression of a first variable on or against a second variable, the first variable is denoted by y. This is nothing to do with the order in which the variables are tabulated in the question, which could easily have x first.

For example:

- in an investigation of the downwards trend of sales over time, the independent variable x = time and the dependent variable y = sales;
- in an investigation of the fall in cinema takings as sales of videos increase, possibly the decline in the cinema mirrors the increased use of videos (in which case cinema sales = y), but perhaps it is the other way round. Perhaps cinemas were closed, in a property boom say, and people buy videos because there is no longer a convenient local cinema (in which case video sales = y). However, if the question referred to the regression of cinema sales against video sales or asked for an estimate of cinema sales for a known level of video sales then the doubt would be removed and cinema sales would have to be denoted by y.

7.12 Judging the validity of forecasts

When we have made forecasts, obvious questions to be asked are 'how accurate are they?' and 'what validity do they have?'

Such queries can be addressed in a number of ways.

The importance of using the correlation coefficient as a check on the validity of the assumption of causality has already been stressed. In addition, you should bear in mind the caveats mentioned in earlier parts of the chapter. In particular, is there a hidden third variable in the problem? Thus, in Examples 7.8.1 and 7.10.1, sales might not depend on the number of salespersons at all, but on the size of the region, as we mentioned when first discussing this problem. If this is the case, then simply increasing the number of salespersons within a region would not in itself increase sales. Even if this is not the case, have we got the causation the right way round? In Example 7.10.2 it might be that, as profits increase, the company feels able to spend more on advertising, so that advertising expenditure depends on profits, contrary to the implicit assumption we made when forecasting profits. If this is the case, increasing the advertising would not necessarily increase profits.

> Before leaving the correlation coefficient, we mention another, closely related, measure, the *coefficient of determination*, r^2. The value of this measure, when expressed as a percentage, shows the percentage of variations in the variables that can be explained by the regression analysis. The remaining variation is due to factors omitted from the analysis.

Example 7.12.1

Evaluate the coefficients of determination for the situations in (a) Example 7.8.1 and (b) Example 7.10.2, and interpret their values.

Solution

(a) We have seen that $r = 0.948$, so $r^2 = 0.948^2 = 0.899$

Hence 89.9 per cent of the variations in sales from one region to the next can be explained by the corresponding differences in the number of salespersons. Only about 10 per cent of the differences in regional sales appear to be due to factors other than staffing levels.

(b) From $r = 0.936$ we get $r^2 = 0.936^2 = 0.876$

Thus, 87.6 per cent of the variations in profits from one year to the next can be explained by the corresponding variations in advertising expenditure, leaving a surprisingly low 12.4 per cent apparently due to other factors.

Example 7.12.2

Calculate and interpret the coefficients of determination for:

(a) sales of L and outlet size;
(b) sales of M and outlet size.

Solution

(a) For L, $r = 0.984$ so the coefficient of determination $= 0.968$. This means that 96.8 per cent of the variations in sales of L from one outlet to the next can be explained by the corresponding variations in the amount of floor space.
(b) For M, $r = 0.974$ so the coefficient of determination $= 0.949$. This means that 94.9 per cent of the variations in sales of M from one outlet to the next can be explained by the corresponding variations in the amount of floor space.

Consider now the two forecasts made in Example 7.10.1. The second one is distinctly different from the first, in that we have taken the regression line far beyond the upper data point ($x = 18$ salespersons) to twenty-five salespersons. The forecast is an *extrapolation* beyond the range of the data. This is an uncertain step to take, as the sales within a region at a certain time must have a ceiling: there must come a point where extra salespersons will generate no further sales. If this point has been passed with twenty-five salespersons, then our forecast will be an overestimate. The first case, by contrast, is an *interpolation* within the range of the data, and so can be considered more valid. In the same way, the profit forecast of Example 7.10.2 is a slight extrapolation and so should be treated with some caution.

Extreme cases of extrapolation have already been seen when interpreting values of the coefficient *a* in earlier regression equations. In doing this, we are effectively extrapolating to the *x*-value of zero, and so we should not be surprised if the result seems implausible.

The approach we have adopted is, of course, a considerable simplification of reality. Profits, sales, and so on, depend on a number of factors, not all of them quantifiable, whereas we have assumed here that they depend on just one other quantitative variable. We have studied only *simple* regression.

There is an extension to the topic, known as *multiple* regression, that enables a variable to be forecast in terms of any number of other variables. This is beyond the scope of this text.

All the forecasts made in this chapter have been for 'next year', whereas the data comes, of course, from the past. There is, therefore, an implicit assumption that conditions that obtained in the past still obtain now and, more importantly, will continue to obtain during the period of the forecast. There is no mathematical way of checking that this is so, but the forecaster will have qualitative knowledge of the particular company and its market, and so will be able to form a judgement. If, for example, a new company was known to be making a big push in the market of the company in Example 7.10.1, you might doubt the forecast of next year's profit figures.

In conclusion, this section has looked at a number of considerations that should be borne in mind when judging the validity of a regression-based forecast. We shall summarise these in the next section.

Example 7.12.3

Comment on the likely reliability of your forecasts in Example 7.10.3.

Solution

The high values of the coefficients of variation suggest reliable forecasts, with the higher value for sales of L indicating the more reliable forecasts here. Forecasts for outlet G are interpolations and so are more reliable than those for outlet H, which are extrapolations. Finally, there is the possibility of other factors that might affect sales that are not covered in the analysis (advertising budgets at the various outlets, their relatively advantageous or disadvantageous locations, etc.).

7.13 Summary

Pearson's coefficient of linear correlation, r, is

$$r = \frac{n\Sigma xy - \Sigma x \Sigma y}{\sqrt{(n\Sigma x^2 - (\Sigma x)^2)(n\Sigma y^2 - (\Sigma y)^2)}}$$

where n is the sample size (number of data points). The linear relationship between x and y is strong if r is close to $+1$ or -1 and is weak if r is close to 0.

The *coefficient of determination* is given by r^2 and it gives the percentage of the variations observed in the y-values that can be explained by the linear relationship and the corresponding variations in the x-values.

When interpreting the value of correlation coefficients or coefficients of determination, care should be taken over:

- how representative (or otherwise) is the sample;
- the sample size;
- whether the correlation is spurious or accidental;
- whether a hidden third variable is present;
- that the interpretation is not generalised beyond the range of the data.

The *least-squares y-on-x regression line* is

$$y = a + bx$$

where:

$$b = \frac{n\Sigma xy - (\Sigma x)(\Sigma y)}{n\Sigma x^2 - (\Sigma x)^2}$$

and

$$a = \bar{y} - b\bar{x}$$

In using this line to forecast values of y, the following points/questions must be considered:

- is the correlation coefficient, r (or the coefficient of determination, r^2), large enough to support the assumption that y depends on x?
- is there a hidden third variable?
- does y depend on x, or is it the case that x depends on y?
- interpolated forecasts are more reliable than extrapolated ones;
- ensure that the *y-on-x* line is used only to forecast y;
- are there any other variables that might affect y?
- have there been, or are there likely to be, any changes in background circumstances that might invalidate the forecast?
- is the sample sufficiently representative and sufficiently large for reliable results?

Revision Questions

Part 7.1 Objective testing selection

> Questions 7.1.1–7.1.10 are standard multiple-choice questions with exactly one correct answer each. Thereafter, the style of question will vary.

7.1.1 The correlation between x and y is 0.85. This means that:

  (A) x is 85 per cent of y.
  (B) y is 85 per cent of x.
  (C) there is a strong relationship between x and y.
  (D) there is a weak relationship between x and y.

7.1.2 If $\Sigma x = 440$, $\Sigma y = 330$, $\Sigma x^2 = 17,986$, $\Sigma y^2 = 10,366$, $\Sigma xy = 13,467$ and $n = 11$, then the value of r, the coefficient of correlation, to two decimal places, is:

  (A) 0.98
  (B) 0.63
  (C) 0.96
  (D) 0.59

7.1.3 In a forecasting model based on $y = a + bx$, the intercept is £234. If the value of y is £491 and x is 20, then the value of the slope, to two decimal places, is:

  (A) −24.55
  (B) −12.85
  (C) 12.85
  (D) 24.85

7.1.4 If the correlation coefficient is 0.8, what is the coefficient of determination?

  (A) 0.64
  (B) 89
  (C) −0.8
  (D) 0.4

7.1.5 If the coefficient of determination is 0.49, which of the following is correct?

  (A) $y = 0.49x$
  (B) $y = a + 0.49x$
  (C) 49 per cent of the variation in y can be explained by the corresponding variation in x.
  (D) 49 per cent of the variation in x can be explained by the corresponding variation in y.

7.1.6 Find the value of a in a regression equation if $b = 7$, $\Sigma x = 150$, $\Sigma y = 400$ and $n = 10$.

(A) 145
(B) −65
(C) $y - 7x$
(D) −650

7.1.7 If the regression equation (in £'000) linking sales (y) and advertising expenditure (x) is given by $y = 5{,}000 + 10x$, forecast the sales when £100,000 is spent on advertising.

(A) £1,005,000
(B) £501,000
(C) £4m
(D) £6m

7.1.8 If the regression equation linking costs (£m) to number of units produced ('000s) is $y = 4.3 + 0.5x$, which of the following is correct?

(A) For every extra unit produced, costs rise by £500,000.
(B) For every extra 1,000 units produced, costs rise by £500,000.
(C) For every extra 1,000 units produced, costs rise by £4.3m.
(D) For every extra unit produced, costs rise by £4,300.

7.1.9 The prices of the following items are to be ranked prior to the calculation of Spearman's rank correlation coefficient. What is the rank of item G?

Item	E	F	G	H	I	J	K	L
Price	18	24	23	23	19	23	19	25

(A) 5
(B) 4
(C) 3
(D) 3.5

7.1.10 All of the following except one will adversely affect the reliability of regression forecasts. Which is the exception?

(A) Small sample
(B) Low correlation
(C) Extrapolation
(D) Negative correlation

7.1.11 Associate each of the following scatter diagrams, (A)−(C), with one of the correlation coefficients, (P)−(R).

B

C

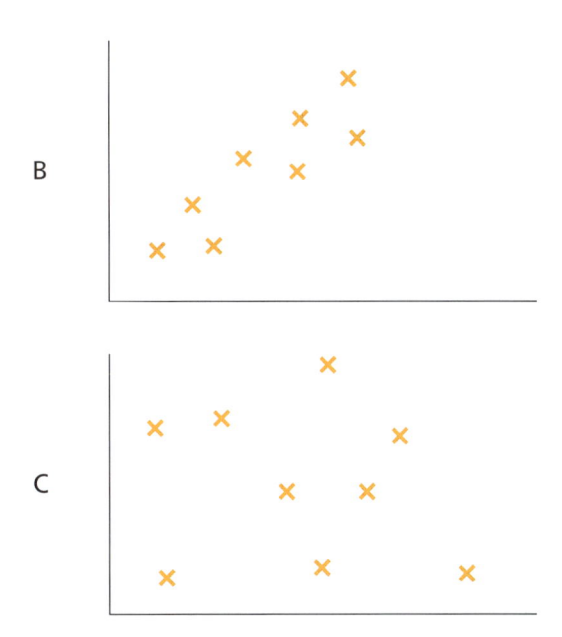

Correlation coefficients

(P) 0
(Q) −1
(R) +0.8

7.1.12 If $n = 8$, $\Sigma x = 10$, $\Sigma y = 800$, $\Sigma xy = 1{,}500$, $\Sigma x^2 = 20$ and $\Sigma y^2 = 120{,}000$, calculate the product moment correlation coefficient, giving your answer correct to three decimal places.

7.1.13 If the correlation between x and y is 0.9, which of the following is/are true?

(A) There is a strong linear relationship between x and y.
(B) y increases as x increases.
(C) Ninety per cent of the changes in y can be explained by the corresponding changes in x.
(D) The slope of the regression line of y on x is positive.

7.1.14 Over a period of 12 months, in which monthly advertising expenditure ranges from £20,000 to £50,000, the correlation between monthly advertising expenditure and monthly sales is 0.8. Which of the following is/are true on the basis of the information given?

(A) Higher sales are caused by higher expenditure on advertising.
(B) If advertising expenditure is increased to £100,000, sales will increase.
(C) Sixty-four per cent of the changes in sales from one month to the next can be explained by corresponding changes in advertising expenditure.
(D) A correlation coefficient derived from 24 months' data would be more reliable than that given above.

7.1.15 Two wine tasters ranked eight bottles of wine as follows:

Wine	A	B	C	D	E	F	G	H
Taster X	3	7	1	8	5	2	4	6
Taster Y	3	8	2	7	4	1	5	6

Find Spearman's rank correlation coefficient for this data, giving your answer to three decimal places.

7.1.16 Place the following values in rank order, with the smallest being ranked 1.

Values 3.21 3.49 3.99 4.05 3.49 4.49 4.99 4.05 3.49

7.1.17 If $n = 10$, $\Sigma x = 90$, $\Sigma y = 1{,}500$, $\Sigma x^2 = 1{,}000$ and $\Sigma xy = 20{,}000$, calculate the value of b in the regression line $y = a + bx$, giving your answer correct to three significant figures.

7.1.18 In the calculation of the regression equation $y = a + bx$ using ten pairs of x- and y-values, $\Sigma x = 80$, $\Sigma y = 500$ and $b = -1.59$. Calculate the value of a correct to three significant figures.

7.1.19 The regression equation $y = 50 - 2x$ has been obtained from fifteen pairs of x- and y-values, with the x-values ranging from 0 to 20. Which of the following is/are correct?

(A) When $x = 0$, y is estimated to be 25.
(B) y decreases by 2 whenever x increases by 1.
(C) The equation cannot be relied upon for x-values greater than 20.
(D) The correlation between x and y must be negative.

7.1.20 The correlation coefficient for ten pairs of x- and y-values, with x ranging from £500 to £700, is calculated to be 0.79, and the regression equation is $y = 620 + 4.3x$. Which of the following is/are true?

(A) When $x = £600$, the estimate of $y = 3{,}200$.
(B) When $x = £550$, the estimate of y from the regression equation is likely to be reliable.
(C) When $x = 0$, the estimate of y from the regression equation is likely to be reliable.
(D) When x increases by £1, y increases by 0.79.

Part 7.2 Scatter diagram; line of best fit

An ice-cream supplier has recorded some sales data that he believes shows a relationship between temperature and sales. The results shown below are for ten sample days in the summer:

Temperature (°C) x	Cartons sold y
13	10
16	11
17	14
19	15
20	16
21	19
23	24
26	25
27	26
28	27

7.2.1 Using the intermediate totals given below, calculate the coefficient of correlation giving your answer correct to two d.p.

$\Sigma x = 210 \quad \Sigma y = 187$
$\Sigma x^2 = 4{,}634 \quad \Sigma y^2 = 3{,}865$
$\Sigma xy = 4{,}208$

7.2.2 If the correlation coefficient was 0.95 calculate the coefficient of determination, giving your answer to the nearest whole number.

7.2.3 If the correlation coefficient was 0.95, which of the following statements would be correct?

(A) The positive sign tells us that there is a strong relationship between temperature and sales.
(B) The positive sign tells us that as temperature rises, so do sales.
(C) The value of the correlation coefficient tells us that there is a strong linear relationship between temperature and sales.
(D) The value of the correlation coefficient tells us that for each increase of 1 degree in temperature, sales increase by 0.95 cartons.
(E) The value of the correlation coefficient tells us that for each decrease of 1 degree in the temperature, sales decrease by 5 per cent.
(F) The value of correlation coefficient tells us that high temperatures cause high sales.

7.2.4 If the coefficient of determination was 85 per cent, which of the following statements would be correct?

(A) When temperature increases by 1°C, sales increase by 85 per cent.
(B) When temperature increases by 1°C, sales increase by 15 per cent.
(C) On 85 per cent of days it is possible to accurately predict sales if an accurate prediction of temperature exists.
(D) 85 per cent of the changes in sales from one day to the next can be explained by corresponding changes in temperature.

7.2.5 The following graph displays the data. What type of graph is it?

(A) Scattergram
(B) Histogram
(C) Pictogram
(D) Ogive

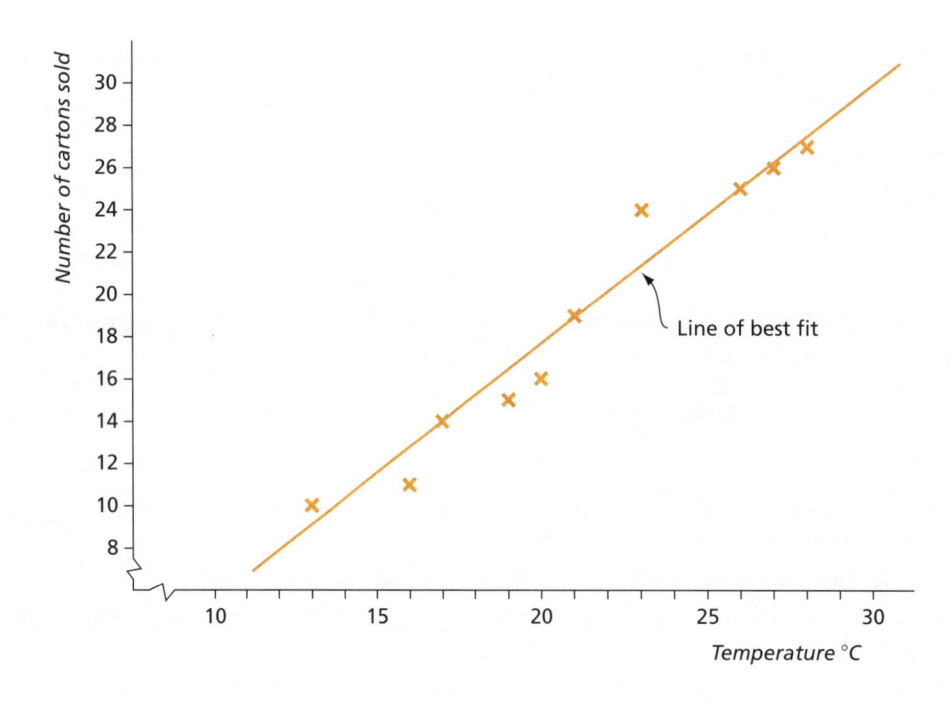

7.2.6 (A) A freehand line of best fit has been fitted to the graph of the data. Estimate the likely sales when the temperature is 15°C, giving your answer to the nearest whole number.
(B) Estimate the likely sales when the temperature is 30°C, giving your answer to the nearest whole number.

7.2.7 Which of the following statements about the reliability of the estimates made in 2.6 are correct, assuming that the correlation is 0.95.

(A) The estimate for a temperature of 15°C should be reliable because it involves interpolation.
(B) Both estimates are less reliable than they otherwise would be because the sample is small.
(C) The estimate for 30°C should be reliable because it involves extrapolation.
(D) Both estimates are more reliable than they would otherwise be because the correlation is high.

7.2.8 Using Excel, enter the data above and draw a scatter diagram to examine the relationship between the temperature and the number of cartons of ice cream sold.

Part 7.3 Least-squares analysis

A travel agency has kept records of the number of holidays booked and the number of complaints received over the past ten years. The data is as follows:

Year	1	2	3	4	5	6	7	8	9	10
Number of holidays booked	246	192	221	385	416	279	343	582	610	674
Number of complaints received	94	80	106	183	225	162	191	252	291	310

The agency suspects there is a relationship between the number of bookings and the volume of complaints and wishes to have some method of estimating the number of complaints, given the volume of bookings.

7.3.1 Denoting number of holidays by X and number of complaints by Y, the following summations are given:

$\Sigma X = 3{,}948$, $\Sigma Y = 1{,}894$, $\Sigma X^2 = 1{,}828{,}092$, $\Sigma Y^2 = 417{,}596$, $\Sigma XY = 869{,}790$.

Calculate the value of the regression coefficient 'b', giving your answer correct to three d.p.

7.3.2 If the value of b is taken to be 0.4 calculate the value of the regression coefficient 'a', giving your answer correct to two d.p.

7.3.3 If the regression equation was $y = 31 + 0.4x$ forecast the likely number of complaints if 750 holidays are booked, giving your answer to the nearest whole number.

7.3.4 Which of the following methods could be used to check whether there is in fact a linear relationship between the variables.

(A) Scatter diagram
(B) Times series analysis
(C) Coefficient of variation
(D) Regression analysis
(E) Correlation coefficient

7.3.5 Which of the following comments about the likely reliability of the estimate of complaints arising from 750 holidays is/are correct?

(A) The estimate is likely to be reliable because the value of 'a' is positive.
(B) The estimate is likely to be reliable because it lies outside the range of the data.
(C) The estimate is likely to be unreliable because the sample is small.
(D) The estimate is not likely to be reliable because the value of 'b' is not close to 1.
(E) The estimate is likely to be unreliable because it was obtained by extrapolation.

7.3.6 Using Excel, enter the data above and produce a chart to show the relationship between the number of holidays booked and the number of complaints received, and then plot the least-squared line.

Part 7.4 Correlation

A company is building a model in order to forecast total costs based on the level of output. The following data is available for last year:

Month	Output '000 units [x]	Costs £'000 [y]
January	16	170
February	20	240
March	23	260
April	25	300
May	25	280
June	19	230
July	16	200
August	12	160
September	19	240
October	25	290
November	28	350
December	12	200

7.4.1 If output is denoted by X and costs by Y, you are given that $\Sigma X = 240$, $\Sigma Y = 2{,}920$, $\Sigma XY = 61{,}500$, $\Sigma X^2 = 5{,}110$ and $\Sigma Y^2 = 745{,}200$. Calculate the correlation coefficient between output and costs, giving your answer to three d.p.

7.4.2 If the correlation coefficient was 0.9, which of the following comments are correct?

(A) The correlation coefficient shows that there is a strong linear relationship between output and costs.
(B) The correlation coefficient shows that high output causes high costs.
(C) The correlation coefficient shows that costs rise as output rises.
(D) Costs rise by 0.9 in £1000 for every extra 1000 units of output.
(E) The high value of the correlation coefficient means that estimates made using regression are likely to be reliable.

7.4.3 If the regression equation linking output and costs is $Y = 43 + 10X$, which of the following comments is/are correct?

(A) For every extra unit produced, costs will rise by £43.
(B) Even with zero output there will be costs of £43,000.
(C) For every extra 1000 units produced, costs will rise on average by £10,000.
(D) For every extra unit produced, costs are likely to increase by £53.
(E) When 1000 units are produced, costs are likely to be £10,043.

Solutions to Revision Questions

Solutions to Part 7.1

7.1.1 Answer: (C)

Correlation coefficients measure the strength of the linear relationship between two variables. They vary numerically between -1 and 1, being weak when close to 0 and strong when close to 1 or -1.

7.1.2 Answer: (B)

$$r = \frac{(11 \times 13{,}467) - (440 \times 330)}{\sqrt{((11 \times 17{,}986) - 440^2)((11 \times 10{,}366) - 330^2)}} = \frac{2{,}397}{\sqrt{4{,}246 \times 5{,}126}} = 0.63$$

7.1.3 Answer: (C)

$$Y = a + bX$$
$$491 = 234 + 20b$$
$$257 = 20b$$
$$12.85 = b$$

7.1.4 Answer: (A)

The coefficient of determination is given by squaring the correlation coefficient. Often it is also multiplied by 100.

7.1.5 Answer: (C)

The coefficient of determination gives the percentage of the variation in y which can be explained by the regression relationship with x. Answers (A) and (B) are confusing this with the actual regression equation, while answer (D) has x and y the wrong way round.

7.1.6 Answer: (B)

$$a = \frac{\Sigma y}{n} - b \frac{\Sigma x}{n} = 40 - (7 \times 15) = -65$$

Solution (A) has added instead of subtracting and (D) has failed to divide by n. Solution (C) correctly states that, since $y = a + bx$, then $a = y - bx$. However, this is an equation satisfied by a and is not the value of a.

7.1.7 Answer: (D)

$y = 5{,}000 + 10x$, and $x = 100$ when advertising is £100,000. Hence $y = 5{,}000 + 10 \times 100 = 6{,}000$ (in £'000). Hence sales forecast is £6m.
(A) is wrong because $x = 100{,}000$ has been used and the units of y ignored.
(B) In (B) $5{,}000 + 10$ has been calculated before multiplication by 100 and in
(C) the $10x$ has been wrongly subtracted.

7.1.8 Answer: (B)

In the equation $y = a + bx$, if x increases by one unit, y will increase by b units. In this case if x increases by 1 unit, y increases by 0.5 units, which translates into production increasing by 1,000 units and costs by £500,000. All the other answers have either confused a and b or confused the units of x and y.

7.1.9 Answer: (A)

Item	E	F	G	H	I	J	K	L
Price	18	24	23	23	19	23	19	25
Rank	1	7	5	5	2.5	5	2.5	8

The two 19s occupy ranks 2 and 3 with an average of 2.5, and the three 23s occupy ranks 4, 5 and 6 with an average of 5. It is essential to count both the 19s and the fact that item G happens to be the first of the 23s listed does not give it a lower rank. Answer D seems to be misled by item G's position as third in the list but adjacent to another 23.

7.1.10 Answer: (D)

It is the strength of the correlation but not its sign that influences the reliability of regression forecasts. Correlation can be negative but still very strong so (D) is the exception. Small samples, low correlation and extrapolation all tend to give unreliable forecasts.

7.1.11

Correlation coefficient	Scatter diagram
P (0)	C
Q (−1)	A
R (+0.8)	B

7.1.12

$$r = \frac{n\Sigma xy - \Sigma x \Sigma y}{\sqrt{\{(n\Sigma x^2 - (\Sigma x)^2)(n\Sigma y^2 - (\Sigma y)^2)\}}}$$

$$= \frac{8 \times 1{,}500 - 10 \times 800}{\sqrt{\{(8 \times 20 - 10^2)(8 \times 120{,}000 - 800^2)\}}}$$

$$= \frac{4{,}000}{\sqrt{(60 \times 320{,}000)}} = 0.913$$

7.1.13 (A) True: the correlation is close to 1 in value.
(B) True: the correlation is positive.
(C) Untrue: the correct percentage would be 84.
(D) True: the correlation is positive.

7.1.14 (A) Untrue on the basis of this information. Causation cannot be deduced from high correlation.
(B) Untrue on the basis of this information. We cannot be sure that the positive correlation will continue for advertising greater than £50,000.
(C) True.
(D) True.

7.1.15

	A	B	C	D	E	F	G	H
d	0	−1	−1	1	1	1	−1	0
d^2	0	1	1	1	1	1	1	0

$\Sigma d^2 = 6; n = 8$

$$\text{Rank correlation} = 1 - \frac{6 \times \Sigma d^2}{n(n^2 - 1)}$$
$$= 1 - \frac{6 \times 6}{8 \times 63} = 0.929$$

7.1.16

Values	3.21	3.49	3.99	4.05	3.49	4.49	4.99	4.05	3.49
Ranks	1	3	5	6.5	3	8	9	6.5	3

7.1.17

$$b = \frac{n\Sigma xy - (\Sigma x)(\Sigma y)}{n\Sigma x^2 - (\Sigma x)^2}$$
$$= \frac{10 \times 20{,}000 - 90 \times 1{,}500}{10 \times 1{,}000 - 90^2}$$
$$= \frac{65{,}000}{1{,}900} = 34.2$$

7.1.18

$$a = \frac{\Sigma y}{n} - b\frac{\Sigma x}{n}$$
$$= \frac{500}{10} - (-1.59) \times \frac{80}{10} = 50 + 12.72 = 62.7 \text{ to three s.f.}$$

7.1.19 (A) Incorrect: when $x = 0$, $y = 50 - 0 = 50$.
(B) Correct.
(C) Correct.
(D) Correct.

7.1.20 (A) Correct.
(B) Correct.
(C) Incorrect: $x = 0$ is outside the range of the data.
(D) Incorrect: when x increases by 1, y increases by 4.3 from the regression equation.

Solutions to Part 7.2

7.2.1
$$r = \frac{n\Sigma xy - \Sigma x \Sigma y}{\sqrt{((n\Sigma x^2 - (\Sigma x)^2)(n\Sigma y^2 - (\Sigma y)^2)}}$$

$$= \frac{(10 \times 4{,}208) - (210 \times 187)}{\sqrt{((10 \times 4{,}634) - (210)^2) \times ((10 \times 3{,}865) - (187)^2)}}$$

$$= \frac{2{,}810}{\sqrt{(2{,}240 \times 3{,}681)}} = 0.98$$

Answer: 0.98

7.2.2 Coefficient of determination = $(r^2) \times 100 = (0.95^2) \times 100 = 90$ per cent.

7.2.3 The positive sign tells us that as temperature rises, so do sales but it tells us nothing about the strength of the relationship. So (B) is correct and (A) is incorrect.

The value of the correlation coefficient tells us that there is a strong linear relationship between temperature and sales (C) but it cannot prove cause and effect, so (F) is wrong. Equally it doesn't enable us to estimate likely changes in sales corresponding to known changes in temperature and hence (D) and (E) are both incorrect.

Answers: (B), (C).

7.2.4 (A), (B) and (C) are all incorrect because predictions cannot be made on the basis of the coefficient of determination.

Answer: (D).
Eighty-five per cent of the changes in sales from one day to the next can be explained by corresponding changes in temperature.

7.2.5 Cartons sold against daily temperature

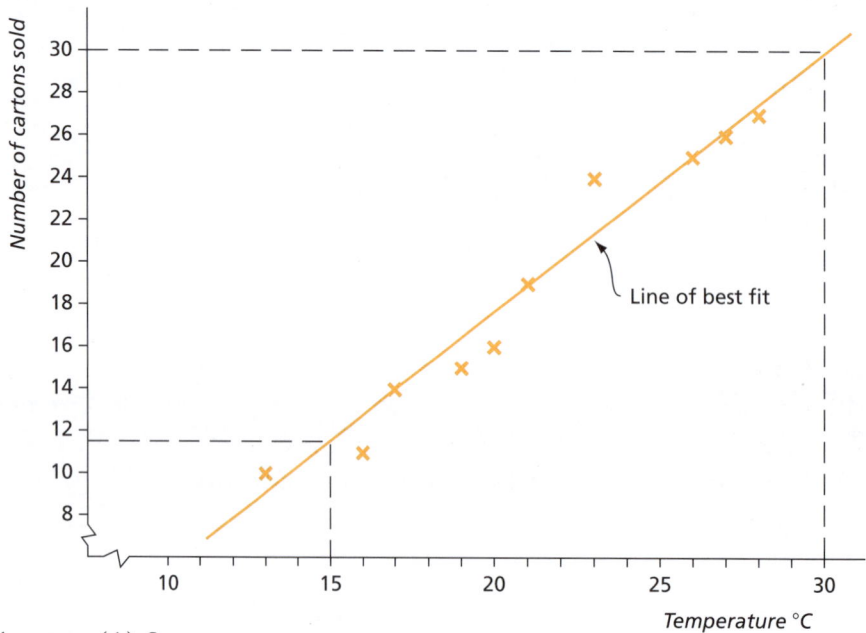

Answer: (A) Scattergram

7.2.6 (A) Answer: 11
(B) Answer: 30

7.2.7 Estimation within the range of the data is called interpolation and, all other things being equal, tends to give reliable estimates. Extrapolation – estimating outside the range of the data – is not reliable, although in this instance a temperature of 30°C is only just outside the range and would not therefore constitute so much of a problem. The high correlation coefficient will make both estimates more reliable, while the small sample of ten points will reduce the reliability of both.

The estimate for 30°C is not reliable because it involves extrapolation and the fact that correlation is high does not strictly speaking render it more reliable because it lies outside the range of the data for which the correlation has been calculated. The small sample reduces the reliability of all estimates.

Answers: (A) and (B).

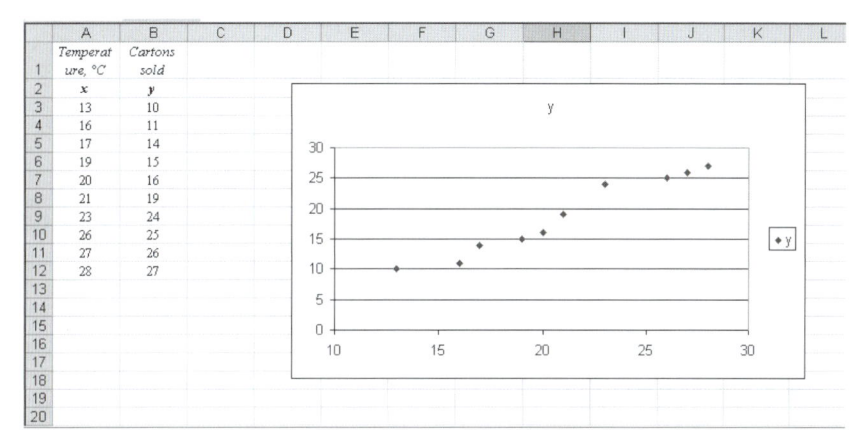

7.2.8

	A	B
1	Temperature, °C	Cartons sold
2	x	y
3	13	10
4	16	11
5	17	14
6	19	15
7	20	16
8	21	19
9	23	24
10	26	25
11	27	26
12	28	27

✓ Solutions to Part 7.3

7.3.1
$$b = \frac{n\Sigma xy - (\Sigma x)(\Sigma y)}{n\Sigma x^2 - (\Sigma x)^2}$$

$$b = \frac{(10 \times 869{,}790) - (3{,}948 \times 1{,}894)}{(10 \times 1{,}828{,}092) - 3{,}948^2} = \frac{1{,}220{,}388}{2{,}694{,}216} = 0.453$$

7.3.2 $a = \Sigma Y/n - b\Sigma X/n = 1{,}894/10 - 0.4 \times 3{,}948/10 = 31.48$

7.3.3 The number of complaints for 750 holidays booked:

$y = 31 + 0.4 \times 750 = 331$

7.3.4 Time series analysis and the coefficient of variation are not related to this question at all. Regression analysis is concerned with finding the best possible line to fit the data when it has been established that there is in fact an approximately linear relationship. Hence (B), (C) and (D) are incorrect.

Answers: (A) and (E).

7.3.5 The sample has only 10 points and the estimate was obtained by extrapolation. For both these reasons it is not likely to be reliable.

Answers: (C) and (E).

7.3.6

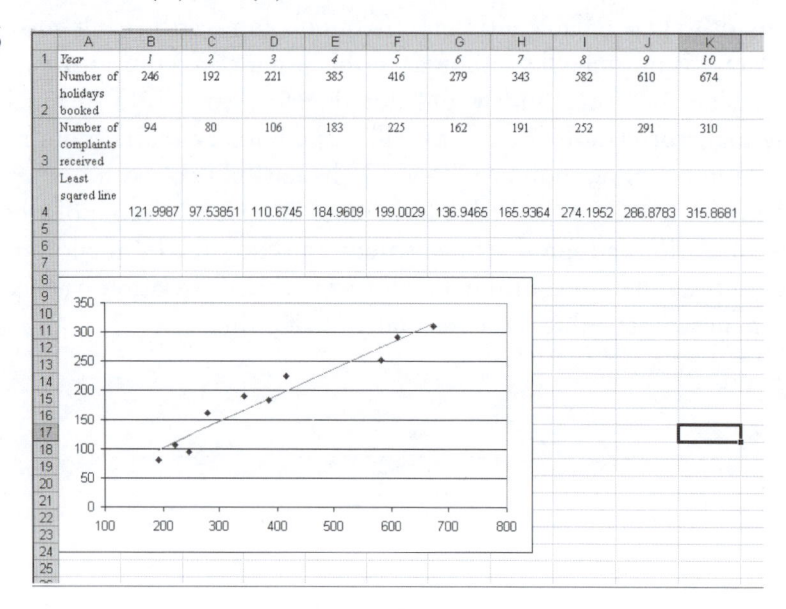

	A	B	C	D	E	F	G	H	I	J	K
1	Year	1	2	3	4	5	6	7	8	9	10
2	Number of holidays booked	246	192	221	385	416	279	343	582	610	674
3	Number of complaints received	94	80	106	183	225	162	191	252	291	310
4	Least sqared line	121.9987	97.53851	110.6745	184.9609	199.0029	136.9465	165.9364	274.1952	286.8783	315.8681

The formula in cell B4 is = FORECAST(B2,$B$3:$K$3,$B$2:$K$2) and then this is copied through to cell K4.

✓ Solutions to Part 7.4

7.4.1
$$r = \frac{12 \times 61{,}500 - 240 \times 2{,}920}{\sqrt{(12 \times 5{,}110 - 240^2)(12 \times 745{,}200 - 2{,}920^2)}} = \frac{37{,}200}{\sqrt{(3{,}720)(416{,}000)}}$$
$$= \frac{37{,}200}{39{,}338.53} = 0.946$$

7.4.2 There is a strong linear relationship because the value of the correlation coefficient is close to 1 and the positive sign means that costs rise as output rises. The high value of the correlation coefficient does means that estimates made using regression are likely to be reliable. However correlation cannot prove causation and it tells us nothing about the changes in costs resulting from particular levels of output. So (B) and (D) are incorrect.

Answers: (A), (C) and (E).

7.4.3 It is important to remember that X is 1000 units of output and Y is £1000 of costs. When $X = 0$, $Y = 43$ so costs are £43,000 and B is correct. When X increases by 1 (i.e. 1,000 units), Y increases by 10 (i.e. £10,000 in costs) so C is also correct. All the other statements are incorrect.

Answers: (B) and (C).

8

Time Series

Time Series

8

LEARNING OUTCOMES

On completing this chapter you should be able to:

- prepare a time series graph and identify trends and patterns;
- identify the components of a time series model;
- calculate the trend using a graph, moving averages or linear regression, and be able to forecast the trend;
- calculate the seasonal variations for both additive and multiplicative models;
- calculate a forecast of the actual value using either the additive or the multiplicative model;
- explain the difference between the additive and multiplicative models, and when each is appropriate;
- calculate the seasonally adjusted values in a time series;
- explain the reliability of any forecasts made.

8.1 Introduction

There are many situations in which there are no plausible or available independent variables from which a dependent variable can be forecast. In such cases, approaches alternative to regression have to be adopted. One of these consists of using past values of the variable to be forecast, a so-called *time series,* and looking for patterns in them. These patterns are then assumed to continue into the future, so that an *extrapolative* forecast is produced. The first task is thus to discuss the various patterns that time series data displays.

8.2 Components and models of time series

There are considered to be four *components of variation* in time series:

- the trend, T;
- the seasonal component, S;
- the cyclical component, C; and
- the residual (or irregular, or random) component, R.

The *trend* in a time series is the general, overall movement of the variable, with any sharp fluctuations largely smoothed out. It is often called the underlying trend, and any other components are considered to occur around this trend. There are a number of basic trend patterns that business variables tend to follow, as shown in Figure 8.1. The simplest (Figure 8.1 (a)) is a *linear* trend, in which the variable is basically growing (or declining) at a steady rate. A *logistic* trend (Figure 8.1 (b)) is typically followed by the sales figures of a product after its introduction: the level plateau is the market saturation figure that the sales eventually reach. A *compound interest* (or exponential) trend (Figure 8.1 (c)), as the name suggests, is a relatively steeply rising curve followed by variables whose values are compounded on earlier values: for instance, investments subject to compound interest.

The *seasonal* component accounts for the regular variations that certain variables show at various times of the year. Thus, a newly formed ice-cream manufacturing company may have sales figures showing a rising trend. Around that, however, the sales will tend to have peaks in the summer months and troughs in the winter months. These peaks and troughs around the trend are explained by the seasonal component. In general, if a variable is recorded weekly, monthly or quarterly, it will tend to display seasonal variations, whereas data recorded annually will not.

The *cyclical* component explains much longer-term variations caused by business cycles. For instance, when a country's economy is in a slump, most business variables will be depressed in value, whereas when a general upturn occurs, variables such as sales and profits will tend to rise. These cyclical variations cover periods of many years and so have little effect in the short term.

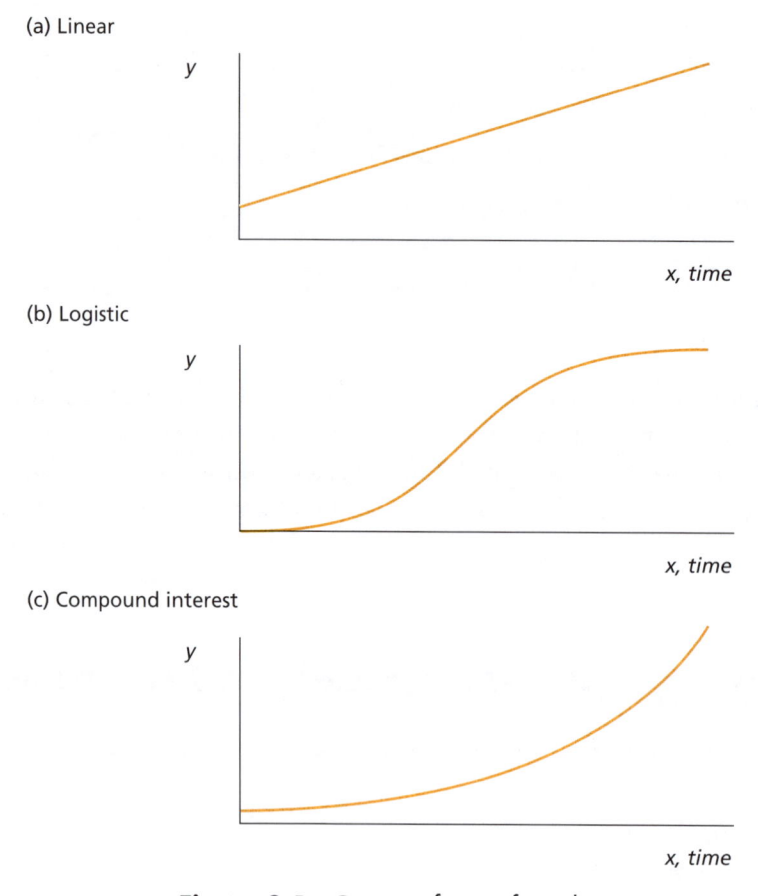

Figure 8.1 Common forms of trend

The *residual* component is that part of a variable that cannot be explained by the factors mentioned above. It is caused by random fluctuations and unpredictable or freak events, such as a major fire in a production plant. If the first three components are explaining the variable's behaviour well, then, subject to rare accidents, the irregular component will have little effect.

> The four components of variation are assumed to combine to produce the variable in one of two ways: thus we have two mathematical models of the variable. In the first case there is the *additive model,* in which the components are assumed to add together to give the variable, Y:

$$Y = T + S + C + R$$

> The second, *multiplicative,* model considers the components as multiplying to give Y:

$$Y = T \times S \times C \times R$$

Thus, under the additive model, a monthly sales figure of £21,109 might be explained as follows:

- the trend might be £20,000;
- the seasonal factor: £1,500 (the month in question is a good one for sales, expected to be £1,500 over the trend);
- the cyclical factor: £800 (a general business slump is being experienced, expected to depress sales by £800 per month); and
- the residual factor: £409 (due to unpredictable random fluctuations).

The model gives:

$$Y = T + S + C + R$$
$$21,109 = 20,000 + 1,500 + (-800) + 409$$

The multiplicative model might explain the same sales figures in a similar way:

- trend: £20,000;
- seasonal factor: 1.10 (a good month for sales, expected to be 10 per cent above the trend);
- cyclical factor: 0.95 (a business slump, expected to cause a 5 per cent reduction in sales); and
- residual factor: 1.01 (random fluctuations of +1 per cent).

The model gives:

$$Y = T \times S \times C \times R$$
$$21,109 = 20,000 \times 1.10 \times 0.95 \times 1.01$$

It will be noted that, in the additive model, all components are in the same units as the original variable (£ in the above example). In the multiplicative model, the trend is in the same units as the variable and the other three components are just multiplying factors.

8.3 Forecasting linear trends

There are many ways of forecasting time series variables. To give a flavour of extrapolative forecasting we shall concentrate here on just one. The method consists of forecasting each component separately, and then combining them through one of the models to form a forecast of the variable itself. We begin with the trend, initially by assuming the simplest case of *linear* trends. In this case, there is no need for any new theory since we can find the trend as a linear regression line.

Example 8.3.1

The following table gives the quarterly sales figures of a small company over the last 3 years. Forecast the next four values of the trend in the series.

	Time period	Sales £'000
1992	quarter 1 ($t = 1$)	42
	quarter 2 ($t = 2$)	41
	quarter 3 ($t = 3$)	52
	quarter 4 ($t = 4$)	39
1993	quarter 1 ($t = 5$)	45
	quarter 2 ($t = 6$)	48
	quarter 3 ($t = 7$)	61
	quarter 4 ($t = 8$)	46
1994	quarter 1 ($t = 9$)	52
	quarter 2 ($t = 10$)	51
	quarter 3 ($t = 11$)	60
	quarter 4 ($t = 12$)	46

Solution

The graph of these data, the *time series graph*, is shown in Figure 8.2. This shows that the company's sales are following an upward trend, of a more or less linear shape, and that there is a definite seasonal pattern: each third quarter is a peak and each fourth quarter is a trough. The approach and model being used here are therefore appropriate.

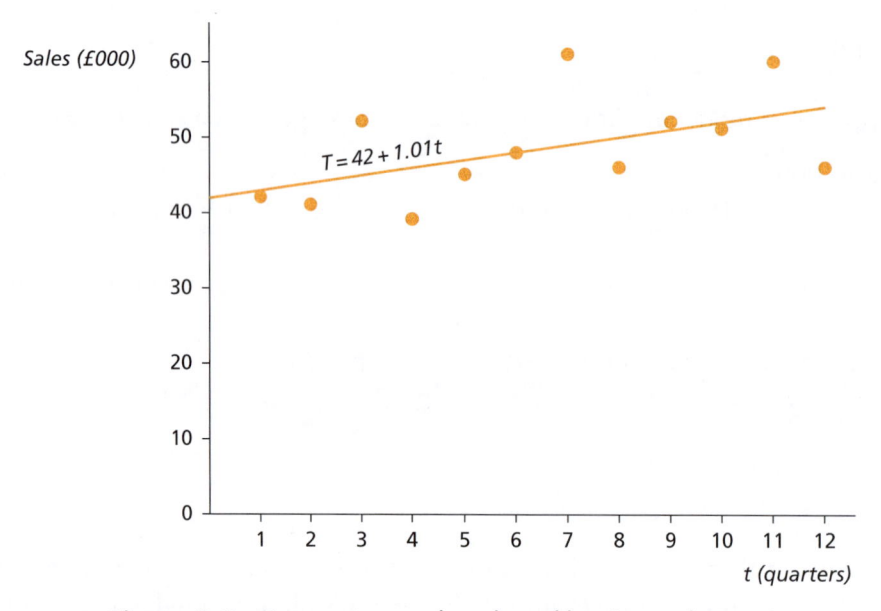

Figure 8.2 Times series graph and trend line (Example 8.3.1)

It will be noted that the twelve quarters for which we have data have been numbered from one to twelve, for ease of reference and to facilitate the computation of the regression line. It is left as an exercise for you to verify that this has equation:

$$T = 42.0 + 1.01t$$

where T is the assumed linear trend in sales (£'000) and t is the number of the quarter (1992, quarter 1: $t = 1$, and so on). This line has been superimposed on the graph in Figure 8.2. The process of calculating the trend, whether by regression or by moving averages (see later), is often described as 'smoothing the data'. As you can see from the above graph, the original ups and downs of the data have been smoothed away.

Example 8.3.2

The examples in this chapter all relate to the following table:

Sales of article B ('000 units)

	Q1	Q2	Q3	Q4	
1993	24.8	36.3	38.1	47.5	(Q = Quarter)
1994	31.2	42.0	43.4	55.9	
1995	40.0	48.8	54.0	69.1	
1996	54.7	57.8	60.3	68.9	

(a) Look at the data. What sort of trend and seasonal pattern do you expect to emerge from the analysis of this data? Plot the time series of the sales figures. Does the graph support your previous expectations regarding the trend and seasonality?
(b) Numbering 1993 Q1 as $t = 1$, through to 1996 Q4 as $t = 16$, calculate the equation of the trend (T) as a linear regression line.

Solution

(a) For every quarter, each year shows an increase in sales, so an increasing trend is expected. Also, there is a regular seasonal pattern with a steady increase in sales from Q1 to Q4. The graph (which we have omitted from this solution) supports these expectations.
(b) Letting $x = t$ and $y = T$, the necessary summations are n = 16; $\Sigma x = 136$; $\Sigma y = 772.8$; $\Sigma xy = 7,359.1$; $\Sigma x^2 = 1,496$.

$$b = \frac{n\Sigma xy - \Sigma x \Sigma y}{n\Sigma x^2 - (\Sigma x)^2} = \frac{(16 \times 7,359.1) - (136 \times 772.8)}{(16 \times 1,496) - 136^2} = 2.3244$$

$$a = \bar{y} - b\bar{x} = \frac{772.8}{16} - 2.3244 \times \frac{136}{16} = 28.54$$

The trend equation is thus:

$$T = 28.54 + 2.3244t$$

Returning to Example 8.3.1.
It is now a simple matter to forecast the trend in sales during 1995:

1995, quarter 1: $t = 13$, giving
$$\hat{T} = 42.0 + 1.01 \times 13 = 55.1 \text{ (£'000)}$$
1995, quarter 2: $t = 14$, so
$$\hat{T} = 56.1 \text{ (£'000)}$$
1995, quarter 3: $t = 15$:
$$\hat{T} = 57.2 \text{ (£'000)}$$
1995, quarter 4: $t = 16$:
$$\hat{T} = 58.2 \text{ (£'000)}$$

The notation $\hat{T}$ is used to denote a forecast value of the trend, as distinct from a historical or actual value, T. The next four trend values are therefore forecast to be £55,000, £56,000, £57,000 and £58,000 (nearest £'000), respectively.

Example 8.3.3

Use the regression equation $T = 28.54 + 2.3244t$ calculated in Example 8.3.2 to forecast the trend in sales for the four quarters of 1997.

Solution

In 1997, t takes values 17–20, giving trend forecasts as follows:

Q1	$t = 17$	$T = 28.54 + 2.3244 \times 17 = 68.0548$
Q2	$t = 18$	$T = 70.3792$
Q3	$t = 19$	$T = 72.7036$
Q4	$t = 20$	$T = 75.028$

8.4 Forecasting seasonal components

Up to now, we have not had to concern ourselves with the choice of model. Since the nature of the seasonal component is so different in the two models, we now have to make a choice. The multiplicative model is usually considered the better, because it ensures that seasonal variations are assumed to be a constant *proportion* of the sales. The additive model, in contrast, assumes that the seasonal variations are a constant *amount,* and thus would constitute a diminishing part of, say, an increasing sales trend. Because there is generally no reason to believe that seasonality does become a less important factor, the multiplicative model is adopted more frequently, as demonstrated here.

The arithmetic involved in computing seasonal components is somewhat tedious but essentially simple. Assuming a very simple model in which there are no cyclical or residual variations:

Actual value, $Y = T \times S$

so $S = \dfrac{Y}{T}$

The seasonal component, S, is therefore found as the ratio of the actual values to the trend, averaged over all available data (so as to use as much information as possible). For forecasting purposes, the same degree of seasonality is assumed to continue into the future, and so the historical seasonal components are simply projected unaltered into the future.

Example 8.4.1

Calculate the seasonal components from the sales data and trend of Example 8.3.1.

Solution

The first, tedious step is to calculate the ratio of sales trend for each of the twelve quarters given. We show the first and last here, leaving the intermediate ten calculations as exercises:

$t = 1: \quad T = 42.0 + (1.01 \times 1) = 43.01$

$S = \dfrac{Y}{T} = \dfrac{42}{43.01} = 0.9765$

$\vdots \qquad \vdots$

$\vdots \qquad \vdots$

$\vdots \qquad \vdots$

$t = 12: \quad T = 42.0 + (1.01 \times 12) = 54.12$

$S = \dfrac{Y}{T} = \dfrac{46}{54.12} = 0.8500$

The complete set of ratios, arranged by quarter, is:

	Quarter 1	Quarter 2	Quarter 3	Quarter 4
1992	0.9765	0.9314	1.1548	0.8471
1993	0.9564	0.9988	1.2431	0.9185
1994	1.0178	0.9789	1.1297	0.8500
Total	2.9507	2.9091	3.5276	2.6156
Mean	0.9836	0.9697	1.1759	0.8719

When arranged like this, the averaging process for each quarter is facilitated. The resulting values constitute the mean seasonal component for each quarter from the given data: they show that, on average in the past, quarter 1 sales have been 98 per cent (approximately) of the trend, quarter 2 sales 97 per cent of the trend, and so on. These values are now adopted as the required *forecast* seasonal components (denoted S). In this case the forecasts for the four quarters of 1995 are thus:

0.9836, 0.9697, 1.1759 and 0.8719, respectively.

As the four seasonal components under this model should, on average, cancel out over a year, an extra step is often taken here, to ensure they add up to 4 (an average of 1 each). The arithmetic is straightforward:

Total = 0.9836 + 0.9697 + 1.1759 + 0.8719 = 4.0011

To reduce this to 4, we will have to subtract from each one:

$\dfrac{4.0011 - 4}{4} = 0.0003 \text{ (to four d.p.)}$

This gives the seasonal components as:

0.9833, 0.9694, 1.1756 and 0.8716, respectively.

In this instance, the adjustment has had scarcely any effect and so can be ignored. In fact, the original data seems to have been rounded to three s.f. so giving the seasonal components to four d.p. cannot really be justified. They would be better rounded to 0.98, 0.97, 1.18 and 0.87.

We have used arithmetic averaging to find the average seasonal variation and to adjust the averages so that our estimated components add to 4. An alternative method that is more mathematically 'correct' is to use geometric means and to adjust the average ratios so they multiply to 1. However, in practice it makes virtually no difference and the arithmetic mean is easier.

Example 8.4.2

Use the data and the regression line calculated in Example 8.3.2 to find the seasonal component (S) as the arithmetic mean of $Y = T$ for each quarter, where Y denotes the actual sales and T the trend given by the regression equation. Adjust your average seasonal variations so that they add to 4.

Solution

Year	Quarter	t	T	Sales, Y	Y/T
1993	1	1	30.8669	24.8	0.8034
	2	2	33.1913	36.3	1.0937
	3	3	35.5157	38.1	1.0728
	4	4	37.8401	47.5	1.2553
1994	1	5	40.1646	31.2	0.7768
	2	6	42.4890	42.0	0.9885
	3	7	44.8134	43.4	0.9685
	4	8	47.1378	55.9	1.1859
1995	1	9	49.4622	40.0	0.8087
	2	10	51.7866	48.8	0.9423
	3	11	54.1110	54.0	0.9979
	4	12	56.4354	69.1	1.2244
1996	1	13	58.7599	54.7	0.9309
	2	14	61.0843	57.8	0.9462
	3	15	63.4087	60.3	0.9510
	4	16	65.7331	68.9	1.0482

Year	Q1	Q2	Q3	Q4	
1993	0.8034	1.0937	1.0728	1.2553	
1994	0.7768	0.9885	0.9685	1.1859	
1995	0.8087	0.9423	0.9979	1.2244	
1996	0.9309	0.9462	0.9510	1.0482	
Total	3.3198	3.9707	3.9902	4.7138	Total
Average	0.8300	0.9927	0.9976	1.1785	3.9988
+	0.0003	0.0003	0.0003	0.0003	0.0012
Comp.	0.8303	0.9930	0.9979	1.1788	4.0000

Quite a few rounding errors will have built up by now, so do not worry if your results differ a little from these. To two decimal places, the seasonal components are

	0.83	0.99	1.00	1.18

8.5 Producing the final forecast

We must now consider the final two components of variation. Isolating the *cyclical* component of time series has proved to be a controversial area in economics and statistics. There is no consensus on an approach to the problem. Also, as we have already mentioned, cyclical variations have little effect in the short term. For these reasons, we shall omit the factor C from this first treatment.

The *residual* component is by nature unpredictable. The best that we can do is to hope that any random fluctuations are small and that no freak events occur, so that the factor R has no overall effect.

For a component to be omitted or to have no effect, it must have the value 1 in the multiplicative model, since multiplying anything by 1 leaves it unchanged. We have thus simplified our model, for the purposes of forecasting, to

$$\hat{Y} = \hat{T} \times \hat{S}$$

Example 8.5.1

In the example under discussion here, forecast the sales during 1995.

Solution

We have already found values for $\hat{T}$ and $\hat{S}$, and so it is now a matter of pulling these values together to find $\hat{Y}$:

1995 quarter 1: $\hat{Y} = \hat{T} \times \hat{S}$
$= 55.1 \times 0.9833 = 54.18$
1995 quarter 2: $\hat{Y} = 56.1 \times 0.9694 = 54.38$
1995 quarter 3: $\hat{Y} = 57.2 \times 1.1756 = 67.24$
1995 quarter 4: $\hat{Y} = 58.2 \times 0.8716 = 50.73$

The forecast sales for the four quarters of 1995 are thus £54,000, £54,000, £67,000 and £51,000, respectively (to the nearest £'000).

Example 8.5.2

Use the results of Examples 8.3.3 and 8.4.2 to forecast the sales of B for the four quarters of 1997.

Solution

The model is $Y = T \times S$ so the forecast sales (Y) in '000 units are given by multiplying the trend forecasts (T) by the seasonal factors (S).

Using a regression equation and seasonal components to forecast is a very common assessment question.

Forecast trend	68.0548	70.3792	72.7036	75.028
Seasonal	0.8303	0.993	0.9979	1.1788
Forecast sales	56.5	69.9	72.6	88.4

8.6 Seasonal adjustment

Before proceeding we digress slightly to look at a closely related topic, *seasonal adjustment*. This is important, because we are often presented with a single figure for weekly revenue, monthly profit, or whatever, and it is difficult to make judgements without some idea of the extent to which the figure has been distorted by seasonal factors and consequently does not give a good indication of the trend. One approach is to *deseasonalise* or remove the seasonal effects from the figure. In the multiplicative model, in which the factor S *multiplies* with all the other components, seasonal adjustment consists of *dividing* by S. In other words, from

$$Y = T \times S$$

we estimate:

$$T = \frac{Y}{S}$$

Effectively, the seasonally adjusted figure is an estimate of the trend.

Example 8.6.1

The company of Example 8.3.1 reports sales of £50,000 during the fourth quarter of a certain year. Seasonally adjust this figure.

Solution

We saw earlier that the seasonal component for the fourth quarter in this series is 0.8716. Dividing by this:

$$\frac{50,000}{0.8716} = 57,365$$

we see that the seasonally adjusted sales for the quarter in question are £57,365.

Example 8.6.2

The company of Example 8.3.2 has sales of 60,000 in the first quarter of a certain year. Seasonally adjust this figure.

Solution

The seasonally adjusted figure is an estimate of the trend and so is given by $Y/S = 60,000/0.8303 = 72,263$ units.

Seasonal adjustment is another common exam question.

8.7 Moving average trends

The above approach is based on an assumption of a linear trend. Although this may appear plausible or 'appropriate', there are many occasions where such an assumption might not be made. An alternative approach that does not depend on linearity, but that also has some relative disadvantages discussed later, involves using *moving averages* as the trend.

The arithmetic involved in this approach is still voluminous but essentially simpler than that of regression analysis, and can just as easily be computerised. To illustrate the method, we continue to look at the example discussed above.

Example 8.7.1

In the example under discussion, compute the trend as a centred four-point moving average.

Solution

In the table below, the 'four-quarterly total' column is simply the sum of each set of four consecutive quarterly sales figures. The first is thus:

42 + 41 + 52 + 39 = 174

The second is:

41 + 52 + 39 + 45 = 177

and so on. The important question is where these totals should go. As they are to represent the four-quarterly period, the usual convention is to place them in the middle of the period, that is, between Q2 and Q3 for the first one, between Q3 and Q4 for the second, and so on. You will find that the table looks neater and is easier to read if you leave an empty line between the quarters, but there is often insufficient space to do this.

A small problem now arises because we wish each value of the trend to be eventually associated with a specific quarter. To overcome this, the figures are 'centred' – that is, each pair of values is added to give the 'centred eight-quarterly totals':

174 + 177 = 351   opposite 1992 Q3
177 + 184 = 361   opposite 1992 Q4 ... and so on

Dividing by 8 now gives the trend values shown:

		Sales (£'000)	Four-quarterly total	Centred eight-quarterly total	Moving averge (T)
1992	Q1	42			
	Q2	41			
	Q3	52	174	351	43.88
	Q4	39	177	361	45.13
1993	Q1	45	184	377	47.13
	Q2	48	193	393	49.13
	Q3	61	200	407	50.88
	Q4	46	207	417	52.13
1994	Q1	52	210	419	52.38
	Q2	51	209	418	52.25
	Q3	60	209		
	Q4	46			

We now complete the process of forecasting from *these* trend values. There are no new techniques involved, as the steps of Examples 8.4.1 and 8.5.1 are being followed with new values for $\hat{T}$.

Example 8.7.2

Using the data of Example 8.3.2, calculate the trend for the sales of article B as a centred four-point moving average.

Solution

Year	Quarter	Sales (Y)	Four-point moving total	Eight-point moving total	Four-point moving ave. trend (T)
1993	1	24.8			
	2	36.3			
	3	38.1	146.7	299.8	37.4750
	4	47.5	153.1	311.9	38.9875
1994	1	31.2	158.8	322.9	40.3625
	2	42.0	164.1	336.6	42.0750
	3	43.4	172.5	353.8	44.2250
	4	55.9	181.3	369.4	46.1750
1995	1	40.0	188.1	386.8	48.3500
	2	48.8	198.7	410.6	51.3250
	3	54.0	211.9	438.5	54.8125
	4	69.1	226.6	462.2	57.7750
1996	1	54.7	235.6	477.5	59.6875
	2	57.8	241.9	483.6	60.4500
	3	60.3	241.7		
	4	68.9			

Example 8.7.3

In this example, we use the data as presented in Example 8.3.1 and the solution to Example 8.7.1.

(a) find the seasonal components from the new trend values, assuming the multiplicative model;
(b) forecast sales for the four quarters of 1995;
(c) deseasonalise fourth-quarterly sales of £50,000.

Solution

(a) First of all, in order to find S-values, we have to compute the individual values of $Y = T$, and tabulate and average them as in Example 8.4.1.

	Quarter 1	Quarter 2	Quarter 3	Quarter 4	
1992			1.1851	0.8642	
1993	0.9548	0.9770	1.1989	0.8824	
1994	0.9927	0.9761	0.0000	0.0000	
Total	1.9475	1.9531	2.3840	1.7466	
					Total
Mean	0.9738	0.9766	1.1920	0.8733	4.0157
Adjustment	−0.0039	−0.0039	−0.0039	−0.0039	−0.0156
Seasonal component	0.9699	0.9727	1.1881	0.8694	4.0001

(b) To produce sales forecasts, we need values of $\hat{T}$. Figure 8.3 shows the sales figures with the moving average trend superimposed. We are not using a linear trend, and so an estimate of where the trend appears to be going has been included, without the benefit of a straight-line assumption. (See the next section for a discussion of this.) As before, we assume that S remains at its average values for each quarter, as computed above.

Reading values for $\hat{T}$ from Figure 8.3, we get:

$$
\begin{aligned}
&\text{1995 quarter 1:} && \hat{Y} = \hat{T} \times \hat{S} \\
&&& = 51.8 \times 0.9699 = 50.24 \\
&\text{1995 quarter 2:} && \hat{Y} = 51.6 \times 0.9727 = 50.19 \\
&\text{1995 quarter 3:} && \hat{Y} = 51.5 \times 1.1881 = 61.19 \\
&\text{1995 quarter 4:} && \hat{Y} = 51.4 \times 0.8694 = 44.69
\end{aligned}
$$

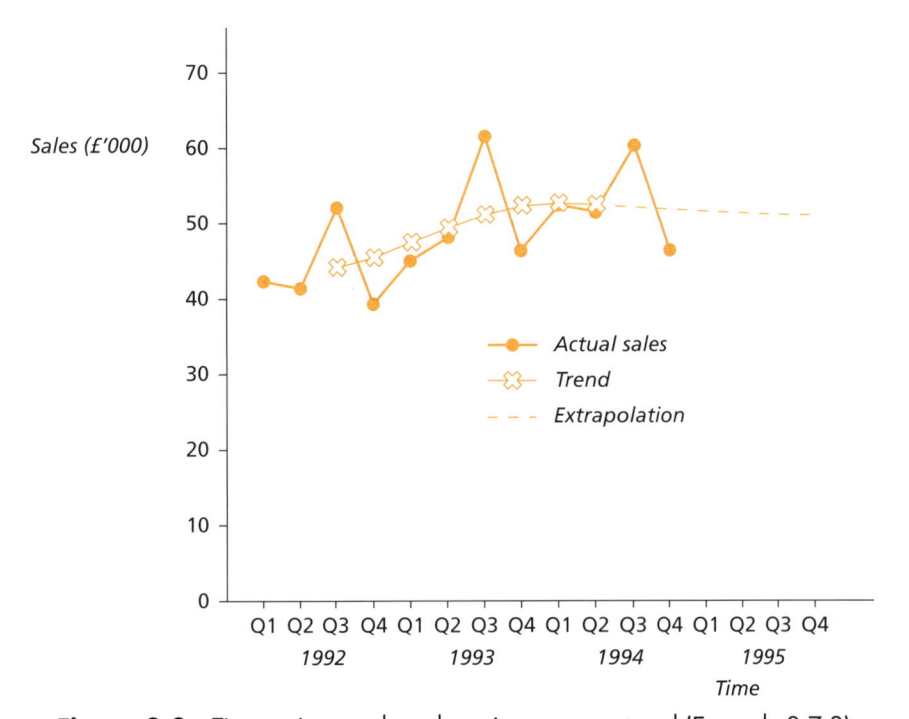

Figure 8.3 Time series graph and moving average trend (Example 8.7.3)

The forecast sales for the four quarters of 1995 are thus £50,000, £50,000, £61,000 and £45,000, respectively (to the nearest £'000). It will be noted that these figures are lower than the forecasts obtained in Example 8.5.1.

(c) As before, these seasonal components imply that, for example, quarter 4 sales are, on average, 87.33 per cent of the trend. A fourth-quarterly figure of £50,000 will therefore be deseasonalised to

$$\frac{50,000}{0.8733} = 57,254$$

With this approach to the trend, therefore, the seasonally adjusted sales figure will be £57,250 (approximately).

Example 8.7.4

Using the data introduced in Example 8.3.2:

(a) evaluate the seasonal component for each quarter based on the moving average trend obtained in Example 8.7.2;
(b) forecast the sales of B for the four quarters of 1997 using trend forecasts of 66.7, 68.8, 70.9 and 73.

Solution

(a) Calculating $Y \div T$ in the solution to Example 8.7.2 and arranging the $Y \div T$ values according to their quarters gives:

	Q1	Q2	Q3	Q4	
1993			1.017	1.218	
1994	0.773	0.998	0.981	1.211	
1995	0.827	0.951	0.985	1.196	
1996	0.916	0.956			
Total	2.516	2.905	2.983	3.625	Total
Average	0.839	0.968	0.994	1.208	4.009
−	0.002	0.002	0.002	0.002	0.008
Comp.	0.837	0.966	0.992	1.206	4.001

Rounding to two decimal places gives seasonal components of:

        0.84   0.97   0.99   1.21

(b) *Forecast for 1997*

	Q1	Q2	Q3	Q4
Trend	66.70	68.80	70.90	73.00
Comp.	0.84	0.97	0.99	1.21
Sales	56.028	66.736	70.191	88.33

Hence the sales forecasts for the four quarters of 1997 are (in '000 units):

        56   67   70   88

8.8 Other types of data

Before moving on, it will be noted that we have centred quarterly data here. In order to deal with weekly data, for example, a centred *104-point* moving average would be needed for the trend (and, incidentally, there would be fifty-two seasonal components, one for each week). Monthly data would lead to a 24-point moving average trend and twelve seasonal components.

The moving average approach can also be used for trends from annual data. If the data has a clear cycle of highs and lows spanning, say, 5 years, then non-centred five-point moving averages would be used. If there is no cyclical pattern the choice is arbitrary, but three- or five-point moving averages are often used to smooth the data because no centering is needed when an odd number of figures are averaged. Cyclical components are estimated by averaging $Y \div T$ values in the same way as seasonal components.

Example 8.8.1

The data below shows weekday attendances at a doctor's surgery in the first three weeks of a 'flu epidemic'. Carry out a time series analysis using the multiplicative model and, assuming the epidemic continues to spread at the same rate, forecast next week's attendances. Use trend forecasts of 76.4, 79.6, 82.8, 86 and 89.2.

Week	1					2					3				
Day	M	T	W	Th	F	M	T	W	Th	F	M	T	W	Th	F
Number of patients, Y	51	45	43	38	49	62	55	51	47	59	70	66	64	58	68

Solution

Week	Day	Number of patients Y	Five-point moving total	Trend T	Y/T S
1	M	51			
	T	45			
	W	43	226	45.2	0.95132
	Th	38	237	47.4	0.80168
	F	49	247	49.4	0.99190
2	M	62	255	51.0	1.21568
	T	55	264	52.8	1.04166
	W	51	274	54.8	0.93065
	Th	47	282	56.4	0.83333
	F	59	293	58.6	1.00682
3	M	70	306	61.2	1.14379
	T	66	317	63.4	1.04100
	W	64	326	65.2	0.98159
	Th	58			
	F	68			

	Mon	Tue	Wed	Thu	Fri	
			0.95132	0.80168	0.99190	
	1.21568	1.04166	0.93065	0.83333	1.00682	
	1.14379	1.04100	0.98159			
Total	2.35947	2.08266	2.86356	1.63501	1.99872	
						Total
Average	1.17973	1.04133	0.95452	0.81751	0.99936	4.99247
	0.00150	0.00150	0.00150	0.00150	0.00150	0.00752
Daily comp.	1.18124	1.04284	0.95603	0.81901	1.00086	5.00000
× trend forecast	76.4	79.6	82.8	86.0	89.2	
Forecast patients	90.2469	83.0102	79.1593	70.4352	89.2774	

As shown in the table above, the $Y \div T$ values are averaged for each day of the week, with the usual adjustment so the daily components will add to 5. The trend forecasts were obtained in the usual way by graphing the trend and extending it to cover the next week (graph not shown). The forecast patient numbers are therefore

$$90 \quad 83 \quad 79 \quad 70 \quad 89$$

The above calculation was carried out on a spreadsheet, which is why there are so many decimal places. Carrying out the calculation manually you would work to no more than three or four decimal places.

8.9 Judging the validity of forecasts

As in the preceding chapter, we now have to consider how valid are these and other extrapolative forecasts. First of all, as the name implies, they are extrapolations, and so there is the possibility of error, as discussed earlier. In particular, you should monitor background circumstances to detect any changes that might invalidate the assumption that these are constant.

Further, assumptions made about the trend can be critical. The adoption of a linear trend may appear plausible but it is sometimes difficult to check its validity. For example, the moving average trend shown in Figure 8.3 may indicate that the sales are following a logistic form (see Figure 8.1 (b)), and that the linear regression approach may be extrapolating the middle portion of the graph beyond the 'market saturation' plateau. Each such successive step into the future becomes increasingly less reliable. This 'plateauing out' is reflected in the forecasts of Example 8.7.3 but not in those of Example 8.5.1.

The moving average approach is not without its problems either. The method of calculating T meant that there were two existing quarters (1994 Q3 and Q4) through which any trend extrapolations had to extend before getting into the future. There was no guidance as to where the trend line should be extended: it had to be done 'by eye', using 'judgement', and so the additional two quarters cast further doubt on the reliability of the trend forecasts.

There are refinements to these basic methods that can remove the necessity to make such assumptions or to assert such judgements on the trend, and can deal with non-constant seasonal components. These are beyond the scope of this text.

The methods of this chapter, and any amendments to them, depend on the assumptions that a time series has a certain number of components of variation, and that these combine in a certain way ('the model'). One way of checking on these assumptions is to assess the values of the residuals from past data. To do this, we reintroduce R into our model:

$$Y = T \times S \times R$$

$$\therefore R = \frac{Y}{T \times S}$$

Thus, in 1992 quarter 1 of the time series under discussion here (linear trend):

$$Y = 42; \quad T = 43.01 \text{ (evaluated in Example 8.4.1)}; \quad S = 0.9836$$

so that:

$$\therefore R = \frac{Y}{T \times S} = \frac{42}{43.01 \times 0.9836} = 0.9928$$

Alternatively, for the other approach to the trend, using the figures of Examples 8.7.1 and 8.7.3:

$$1992 \text{ Q3}: R = \frac{Y}{T \times S} = \frac{52}{43.88 \times 1.1920} = 0.9942$$

Proceeding in this way, all past values of the residual component can be found (you might complete the calculations of these values for practice):

		R, linear regression trend	R, moving average trend
1992	Q1	0.9928	
	Q2	0.9605	
	Q3	0.9820	0.9942
	Q4	0.9715	0.9895
1993	Q1	0.9724	0.9805
	Q2	1.0300	1.0004
	Q3	1.0572	1.0058
	Q4	1.0535	1.0104
1994	Q1	1.0348	1.0195
	Q2	1.0095	0.9995
	Q3	0.9607	
	Q4	0.9748	

Ideally, the residuals should be having little effect and so should be close to 1. All the above values are fairly near to 1, which gives some support to the validity of the forecasts. Direct comparisons of the eight quarters possible, however, shows that the right-hand column is *always* closer to 1 than the left. The moving average approach therefore appears more valid, and this, in turn, possibly reflects the fact that the moving averages have dealt with a 'plateauing out' of sales, whereas the linear regression has extrapolated beyond it. Against this must be set the fact that we had to 'guess' where the moving average trend goes next, whereas it is known where a regression line goes.

Further, if we had more quarterly sales figures we could inspect the R-values for patterns: as an assumedly random component, there should not be any. If, for example, the values gradually moved away from 1, the model would be getting progressively less reliable, so casting doubts on any forecasts from it. Similarly, if there was a seasonal pattern in R, this would cast doubt on the underlying assumption of constant seasonality.

Finally, you will have noticed that there is a great amount of arithmetic involved in producing the forecasts of this chapter. It is therefore highly advantageous to use one of the many available computer packages that deal with such extrapolative models.

8.10 Computations involving the additive model

Although it has been stated that the multiplicative model is the more often applicable, the additive model may occasionally be used, and so we give an example of this latter model. As before, the computation of the trend does not depend on the model chosen, and so any form of trend can be applied. For an illustration of the method, we use the moving average type from Section 8.7.

Example 8.10.1

From the data in the example used throughout this chapter, with an additive model and a moving average trend:

(a) find the seasonal components by averaging values of $S = Y - T$, using the moving average trend calculated in Example 8.7.1;
(b) forecast sales for the four quarters of 1995 using trend estimates of 51.8, 51.6, 51.5 and 51.4, respectively;
(c) calculate the residual for 1992 quarter 3;
(d) deseasonalise fourth-quarter sales of £50,000.

Solution

(a) The trend values have been computed in Example 8.7.1. The model now being used is:

$$Y = T + S$$

and so:

$$S = Y - T$$

Rearranging the values of $Y - T$ into a familiar table:

	Quarter 1	Quarter 2	Quarter 3	Quarter 4	Total
1992			8.12	−6.13	
1993	−2.13	−1.13	10.12	−6.13	
1994	−0.38	−1.25			
Total	−2.51	−2.38	18.24	−12.26	
Mean	−1.26	−1.19	9.12	−6.13	0.54
Adjustment	−0.135	−0.135	−0.135	−0.135	−0.54
Seasonal comp.	−1.395	−1.325	8.985	−6.265	0.00

As before, the average seasonal variations have been adjusted to ensure that they have no total effect over a year: this involves making them add up to zero. The method is to find their total (0.54), divide it by 4 (0.135) and subtract that amount from each average.

The adjustment has introduced spurious accuracy and we shall take the seasonal components to be

Q_1	$Q2$	$Q3$	$Q4$
−1.4	−1.3	9.0	−6.3

(b) Using the given trend values with the above additive seasonal components, we can obtain forecasts from the model:

$$\hat{Y} = \hat{T} + \hat{S}$$

1995, quarter 1: $\hat{Y} = 51.8 + (-1.4) = 50.4$
1995, quarter 2: $\hat{Y} = 51.6 + (-1.3) = 50.3$
1995, quarter 3: $\hat{Y} = 51.5 + (+9.0) = 60.5$
1995, quarter 4: $\hat{Y} = 51.4 + (-6.3) = 45.1$

The forecast sales are thus £50,000, £50,000, £61,000 and £45,000 respectively (to the nearest £'000).

(c) As stated in Section 8.9, one way of judging the validity of these forecasts is to reintroduce the residual, R, back into the model:

$$Y = T + S + R$$

and so

$$R = Y - T - S$$

In the one case of 1992, quarter 3 asked for, this gives (in £'000):

$$R = 52 - 43.88 - 9.0 = -0.88.$$

It is left as an exercise for you to calculate the R-values for 1993 Q3 and Q4, for which the answers are 1.12 and 0.17 respectively. It should be noted that the ideal value in the additive model is zero.

(d) Now, from $Y = T + S$:

$$T = Y - S$$

Hence the deseasonalised value of fourth-quarterly sales of £50,000 is (in £'000)

$$50 - (-6.3) = 56.3$$

With this model, the seasonally adjusted sales figure is £56,300 (approximately).

Example 8.10.2

Repeat the time series analysis and forecasting exercise for the data of Example 8.3.2, using the additive model with a four-point centred moving average trend. You may assume trend forecasts of 66.7, 68.8, 70.9 and 73.0 for the four quarters of 1997.

Solution

Year	Quarter	Sales (Y)	Four-point moving total	Eight-point moving total	Trend (T)	Y − T
1993	1	24.8				
	2	36.3				
	3	38.1	146.7	299.8	37.4750	0.6250
	4	47.5	153.1	311.9	38.9875	8.5125
1994	1	31.2	158.8	322.9	40.3625	−9.1625
	2	42.0	164.1	336.6	42.0750	−0.0750
	3	43.4	172.5	353.8	44.2250	−0.8250
	4	55.9	181.3	369.4	46.1750	9.7250
1995	1	40.0	188.1	386.8	48.3500	−8.3500
	2	48.8	198.7	410.6	51.3250	−2.5250
	3	54.0	211.9	438.5	54.8125	−0.8125
	4	69.1	226.6	462.2	57.7750	11.3250
1996	1	54.7	235.6	477.5	59.6875	−4.9875
	2	57.8	241.9	483.6	60.4500	−2.6500
	3	60.3	241.7			
	4	68.9				

Y − T	Q1	Q2	Q3	Q4	
1993			0.6250	8.5125	
1994	−9.1625	−0.0750	−0.8250	9.7250	
1995	−8.3500	−2.5250	−0.8125	11.3250	
1996	−4.9875	−2.6500	0.0000	00.0000	
Total	−22.5000	−5.2500	−1.0125	29.5625	
					Total
Ave	−7.5000	−1.7500	−0.3375	9.8542	0.2667
Adj.	−0.0667	−0.0667	−0.0667	−0.0667	−0.2667
Comp.	−7.5667	−1.8167	−0.4042	9.7875	0.0000

	Q1	Q2	Q3	Q4
Forecast:				
Trend	66.7000	68.8000	70.9000	73.0000
Comp.	−7.5667	−1.8167	−0.4042	9.7875
Sales	59.1333	66.9833	70.4958	82.7875

To one decimal place, the forecast sales are ('000 units):

59.1	67.0	70.5	82.8

> You need to be able to make forecasts and to seasonally adjust using the additive model as well as the multiplicative one.

Time series with Excel

Although Excel is a useful tool for developing times series spreadsheets, an advanced knowledge of Excel is required.

A detailed explanation with a working model showing how to use Excel to develop time series forecasts is provided in the Elsevier–CIMA book Financial Planning using Excel – Forecasting, Planning and Budgeting Techniques by Sue Nugus, 2005, ISBN: 0-7506-6355-3.

8.11 Summary

We are modelling the values, Y, in a time series by

$$Y = T \times S \times C \times R$$

where T is the trend component of variation, S is the seasonal component, C is the cyclical component, and R is the residual component.

If we ignore the cyclical component and omit the unpredictable, residual component, the model becomes, for forecasting purposes:

$$\hat{Y} = \hat{T} \times \hat{S}$$

Assuming constant seasonality, $\hat{T}$ can be found from a linear regression analysis or as a centred moving average, and $\hat{S}$ can be found as the average past ratio of actual value to trend (i.e. $Y = T$). A numerical check on the validity of the model can be obtained by inspecting the past values of the residual component, found from:

$$R = \frac{Y}{T \times S}$$

In the case of the additive model:

$$Y = T \times S \times C \times R$$

For forecasting purposes:

$$\hat{Y} = \hat{T} \times \hat{S}$$

where $\hat{S}$ is found as the average past differences between actual value and trend (i.e. $Y - T$). The residuals are found from:

$$R = Y - T - S$$

Readings

8

This extract from an article by Gripaios advocates caution when using forecasts – even from so-called 'reliable' sources – and the adoption of 'think-tank' scenario planning as detailed support for forecasts. You should consider how an organisation would integrate practically 'official' forecasts with think-tank scenarios into routine forecasting.

The use and abuse of economic forecasts

Peter Gripaios, *Management Decision*, Vol. 32, No. 6, 1994. Republished with permission, Emerald Group Publishing Limited

Why firms use them

One obvious possibility is that businesses believe the results. This seems unlikely, so that more realistically it may be considered that businesses have to have something for strategic planning purposes and believe that econometric forecasts, though flawed, are better than even the best alternatives. If so, they may be wrong, for there is little evidence, certainly for some variables such as exchange rates, that complex econometric simulations are more accurate than graphical extrapolation techniques (chartism) or simple statistical models including 'random walk'. The latter work on the assumption that, as you have no idea about the future, you might as well take the present as the best guide.

Moreover, many econometric forecasters are themselves unhappy with the accuracy of their results, some so much so that they are experimenting with other types of models. One type is vector autogressive models (VAR), which do not attempt to explain how economic variables are causally related to one another. Instead, each variable is regressed on a lagged series of all the other variables in the model to form a basis for forecasting.

Perhaps many managers are comfortable with the single outcomes suggested by the individual forecasting teams and prefer them to the difficult thought processes involved in 'scenario planning' or, as practised in France, the similar 'prospective analysis'. These try to identify what fundamental economic relationships may change, the starting point for an effective consideration of sensible business strategy.

Conclusion

Though widely used in business, macroeconometric forecasts should be used with considerable caution. It may be 'comfortable' to do what others are doing in paying the economists and blaming them if they turn out to be wrong. Unfortunately, they very often are wrong, particularly at times such as turning points in the economic cycle when accurate information is most required for sensible business strategy-making. Of course, economic forecasts do have some use as an input in the strategic planning process, but the likelihood of error should be recognised from the start. One sensible approach would be to input a range of forecast output which, as individual forecasters still produce single estimates of, say, household consumption, will involve using the output of various forecasting teams. Even then, it would be prudent to carry out sensitivity analysis of the impact of different economic variables on the profits of the business in question, so that key variables can be watched with particular care.

The important point is surely that econometric forecasts should only ever be considered as one approach to formulating strategy. They should never be used as an alternative to fundamental scenario planning in which managers set up 'think tanks' to work out respective middle- and long-term scenarios on, for example, the prospects for their business in the light of such changed circumstances as the conclusion of the GATT talks, new entry into the EU, changes in European legislation, a strengthening dollar, destabilising in Russia and so on. It should also be emphasised that economic forecasts are no substitute for risk management strategies with regard to, say, movement in interest or exchange rates. Such strategies should sensibly encompass a range of operations, including holding a diversified portfolio of assets through the liquidity spectrum in a number of different currencies. Use of the forward foreign exchange markets should also be considered, as should other hedging strategies, including options. Of course, companies may not wish to hedge all of their exposure to exchange rate risk and may partially rely on economic forecasts (or guesses) of future currency movements and gamble that these will be favourable. However, this can be a very costly policy if the gamble fails, as recent evidence for Japanese motor companies in the American market demonstrates. The safest option, which is only likely to be available to large firms, is investment in foreign subsidiaries. In that way, sales can be matched with costs in a particular country or trading bloc and profits remitted to the host country at the most appropriate time.

Discussion points

Discuss these within your study group

In this chapter and the one preceding it we have considered only the most simple forecasting models, in which the variable to be forecast depends on only one other variable or simply on time. As you have seen from this article, even quite complicated models cannot guarantee accurate forecasts.

1. Try to list the reasons why forecasts are so often unreliable.
2. Spend some time evaluating how economic forecasting is (or might be) used in your organisation. Is there any laid-down system using models, etc., or is it simply guesswork?
3. On the basis of this article, does it matter if managers use only guesswork?

Revision Questions

Part 8.1 Objective testing selection

> Questions 8.1.1–8.1.10 are standard multiple-choice questions with exactly one correct answer each. Thereafter, the style of question will vary.

8.1.1 In a time series analysis, the trend equation for a particular product is given by

Trend = $(0.0004 \times \text{YEAR}^2) + (0.2 \times \text{YEAR}) + 80.2$

Owing to the cyclical factor, the forecast for 1996 is estimated at 1.87 times trend. In whole units, the forecast for 1996 is:

(A) 3,877
(B) 3,878
(C) 3,900
(D) 3,910

8.1.2 Unemployment numbers actually recorded in a town for the second quarter of 1997 were 2,200. The underlying trend at this point was 2,000 people and the seasonal factor is 0.97. Using the multiplicative model for seasonal adjustment, the seasonally adjusted figure (in whole numbers) for the quarter is:

(A) 1,940
(B) 2,061
(C) 2,134
(D) 2,268

8.1.3 Based on the last fifteen periods, the underlying trend of sales is:

$345.12 - 1.35x$

If the sixteenth period has a seasonal factor of -23.62, assuming an additive forecasting model, then the forecast for that period, in whole units, is:

(A) 300
(B) 343
(C) 347
(D) 390

8.1.4 Based on twenty past quarters, the underlying trend equation for forecasting is:

$$y = 23.87 + 2.4x$$

If quarter 21 has a seasonal factor of times 1.08, using a multiplicative model, then the forecast for the quarter, in whole units, is:

(A) 75
(B) 80
(C) 83
(D) 85

8.1.5 In December, unemployment in a region is 423,700. If the seasonal factor using an additive time series model is +81,500, find the seasonally adjusted level of unemployment to the nearest whole number.

(A) 342,200
(B) 505,200
(C) 345,316
(D) 519,877

8.1.6 In a time series analysis using the multiplicative model, at a certain time actual, trend and seasonal values are 523, 465 and 1.12. Find the residual at this point.

(A) 1.2597
(B) 56.88
(C) 1.0042
(D) 51.7857

8.1.7 In a multiplicative time series analysis, the seasonal variations given by averaging the $Y = T$ values are 1.06, 1.13, 0.92 and 0.94. They are subsequently adjusted so that their total is 4. What is the new value of the average currently valued at 1.06?

(A) 0.2975
(B) 1.01
(C) 1.0725
(D) 1.0475

8.1.8 In a time series analysis using the additive model, at a certain time actual, trend and seasonal values are 85, 91, −6.4. Find the residual at this point.

(A) −0.6
(B) 0.4
(C) −0.4
(D) −12.4

8.1.9 In an additive time series analysis, the seasonal variations given by averaging the $(Y - T)$ values are 22, 15, −8, −33. They are subsequently adjusted so that their total is 0. What is the new value of the average currently valued at −33?

(A) −34
(B) −37
(C) −29
(D) −32

8.1.10 All except one of the following are conditions that should be met if time series forecasts are to be reliable. Which is the odd one out?

(A) Residuals should be numerically small.
(B) Extrapolation should be avoided.
(C) The trend should continue as in the past.
(D) The seasonal pattern should continue as in the past.

8.1.11 The component parts of a time series model are:

(A) the trend;
(B) the cyclical component;
(C) the seasonal component;
(D) the residual component.

Associate each of the following with the appropriate component.

(P) The impact of a strike.
(Q) An economic cycle of ups and downs over 5 years.
(R) A long-term increase of 5 per cent per annum.
(S) An increase in sales over Christmas.

8.1.12 In an additive model, at a certain time point, the actual value is 32,080 while the trend is 27,076 and the seasonal factor is 4,508. If there is no cyclical variation, calculate the residual variation to the nearest whole number.

8.1.13 The regression equation of a linear trend is given by $T = 43 + 5.9t$ where the time $t = 1$ in the first quarter of 1998. Estimate the trend for the fourth quarter of 2002, giving your answer correct to three significant figures.

8.1.14 In the additive model $A = T + S + R$, which of the following is/are correct?

(A) S is estimated by averaging A/T values for the particular season.
(B) T may be estimated by a moving average.
(C) T may be estimated from an appropriate regression equation.
(D) R is estimated from $A - T$.
(E) The seasonally adjusted value is given by $A - S$.

8.1.15 In the additive model, four seasonal components initially calculated as $+25$, -54, -65 and $+90$ are to be adjusted so that they total zero. Calculate the values of the adjusted seasonal components, giving your answers to the nearest whole number.

8.1.16 If the trend is estimated to be 45.8 for a quarter with a seasonal component of 0.96, estimate the actual value using the multiplicative model and giving your answer correct to three decimal places.

8.1.17 Unemployment figures are given as 1,897,000 but after seasonal adjustment (using the multiplicative model) they are down to 1,634,000. Calculate the seasonal factor for the particular season, giving your answer to three decimal places.

8.1.18 Data showing a 5-day cycle has a trend estimated using a 5-day moving average. For how many days will it not be possible to estimate the trend?

8.1.19 The following statements all refer to time series analysis beginning with the estimation of the trend using a centred moving average. Which of the following is/are true?

(A) Centring must be used when the data has a cycle with an even number of points.
(B) When the data has a cycle with an even number of points, centring may be omitted but gives more accurate results.
(C) When the data has a four-point cycle, each centred moving average utilises five actual values.

8.1.20 Which of the following comments regarding the validity of forecasts is/are correct?

(A) Regression trends give more accurate trend forecasts than those obtained using moving averages.
(B) Forecasts depend on the previous trend continuing.
(C) Forecasts depend on the previous seasonal and cyclical patterns continuing.
(D) Forecasts made with the multiplicative model are better than those made with the additive model.
(E) Checking the fit of the model by examining the values of residuals can help in judging the validity of forecasts.
(F) Provided the model is a good fit, forecasts should be accurate even if there are unexpected events.

Part 8.2 Time series

The managers of a company have observed recent demand patterns of a particular product line in units. The original data, which has been partially analysed, is as follows:

Year	Quarter	Data	Sum of fours	Sum of twos
1993	2	31		
	3	18	94	190
	4	20	96	193
1994	1	25	97	195
	2	33	98	197
	3	19	99	198
	4	21	99	198
1995	1	26	99	199
	2	33	100	201
	3	19	101	
	4	22		
1996	1	27		

You have been commissioned to undertake the following analyses and to provide appropriate explanations. (Work to three d.p.)

8.2.1 In the following table, find the missing values of the underlying four-quarterly moving average trend.

Year	Quarter	Sum of twos	Moving average
1993	4	190	A
1994	1	193	B
	2	195	24.375
	3	197	24.625
	4	198	24.750
1995	1	198	24.750
	2	199	24.875
	3	201	C

8.2.2 Calculate the seasonally adjusted demand (to three d.p.) for the four quarters of 1994 based on the multiplicative model if the seasonal factors are as follows:

Quarter 1   1.045
Quarter 2   1.343
Quarter 3   0.765
Quarter 4   0.847

8.2.3 Which of the following statements about seasonal adjustment is/are correct?

(D) Seasonally adjusted data has had the seasonal variations removed from it.
Correct/incorrect
(E) Seasonally adjusted data has had the seasonal variations included in it.
Correct/incorrect
(F) Seasonal adjustment is the process by which seasonal components are adjusted so that they add to zero.
Correct/incorrect
(G) Seasonal adjustment is the process by which estimates of the trend can easily be obtained.
Correct/incorrect

8.2.4 If the seasonally adjusted values are increasing, which of the following would you deduce?

(H) The trend is upwards.
(I) The trend is downwards.
(J) No deductions about the trend are possible from the information given.
(K) Seasonal variability is increasing.
(L) Seasonal variability is decreasing.
(M) No deductions are possible about seasonal variability.

8.2.5 If A denotes the actual value, T the trend and S the seasonal component, write down the formula for the seasonally adjusted value if an additive model is being used.

Part 8.3 Forecasting

You are assisting the management accountant with sales forecasts of two brands – Y and Z – for the next three quarters of 1993. Brand Y has a steady, increasing trend in sales of 2 per cent a quarter and Brand Z a steadily falling trend in sales of 3 per cent a quarter. Both brands are subject to the same seasonal variations, as follows:

Quarter	Q1	Q2	Q3	Q4
Seasonality	−30%	0	−30%	+60%

The last four quarter's unit sales are shown below:

	1992 Q2	1992 Q3	1992 Q4	1993 Q1
Brand Y	331	237	552	246
Brand Z	873	593	1,314	558

8.3.1 Which of the following statements about the seasonal variations is/are correct?

(A) Actual sales are on average 30 per cent below the trend in the third quarter.
(B) Actual sales in the first and third quarters are identical on average.
(C) Average sales in the second quarter are zero.
(D) Actual sales in the fourth quarter are on average 60 per cent above the trend.
(E) Actual sales in the first quarter are 1.3 times the trend.
(F) Actual sales in the fourth quarter are 1.6 times the trend.

8.3.2 Seasonally adjust the sales figures for 1993 Q1, giving your answers to one d.p.

8.3.3 Forecast the trend for brand Y for 1993 Q4, giving your answer to one d.p.

8.3.4 If the trend forecast in 3.3 was 370, forecast the actual sales of brand Y for 1993 Q4, giving your answer to the nearest whole number.

8.3.5 Forecast the trend for brand Z for 1993 Q3, giving your answer to one d.p.

8.3.6 If the trend forecast in 3.5 was 770, forecast the actual sales of brand Z for 1993 Q3, giving your answer to the nearest whole number.

8.3.7 Which of the following are assumptions on the basis of which time series forecasts are made?

(A) That there will be no seasonal variation.
(B) That the trend will not go up or down.
(C) That there will be no change in the existing seasonal pattern of variability.
(D) That the model being used fits the data.
(E) That there will be no unforeseen events.

Part 8.4 Forecasting

The quarterly sales of a product are monitored by a multiplicative time series model. The trend in sales is described by

$$Y = 100 + 5X$$

where Y denotes sales volume and X denotes the quarterly time period.

The trend in sales for the most recent quarter (first quarter 1991, when $X = 20$) was 200 units. The average seasonal variations for the product are as follows

Quarter	First	Second	Third	Fourth
Seasonal effect	0	−20%	+40%	−20%

The price of a unit was £1,000 during the first quarter of 1991. This price is revised every quarter to allow for inflation, which is running at 2 per cent a quarter.

8.4.1 Forecast the trend in the number of units sold for the remaining three quarters of 1991.

8.4.2 Forecast the actual number of units sold (to the nearest whole number) for the remaining three quarters of 1991.

8.4.3 Forecast the price per unit for the remaining quarters of 1991, giving your answers correct to two d.p.

8.4.4 If the prior forecasts were as follows, forecast the sales revenue for the remaining quarters of 1991, giving your answers to the nearest £.

Quarter of 1991	Forecasts Numbers sold	Price per unit (£)
2	150	1010
3	300	1030
4	170	1050

Solutions to Revision Questions

✓ Solutions to Part 8.1

8.1.1 Answer: (A)

$$\text{Trend} = 0.0004 \times 1996^2 + 0.2 \times 1996 + 80.2$$
$$= 2,073.0064$$
$$\text{Forecast} = 1.87 \times \text{trend}$$
$$= 3,877 \text{ to nearest whole number}$$

8.1.2 Answer: (D)

$$\text{Actual value} = \text{trend} \times \text{seasonal factor}$$
$$\text{Seasonally adjusted figure} = \text{estimate of the trend}$$
$$= \text{actual value} \div \text{seasonal factor}$$
$$= 2,200/0.97 = 2,268$$

It seems likely that the stated trend of 2000 is incorrect.

8.1.3 Answer: (A)

For the sixteenth period, put $x = 16$:
$$\text{Trend} = 345.12 - (1.35 \times 16) = 323.52$$
Forecast is 23.62 below the trend:
$$\text{Forecast} = 323.52 - 23.62 = 299.9 = 300 \text{ (to nearest unit)}.$$

8.1.4 Answer: (B)

$$\text{Trend forecast} = 23.87 + 2.4 \times 21 = 74.27$$
$$\text{Forecast} = \text{trend} \times \text{seasonal factor}$$
$$= 74.27 \times 1.08$$
$$= 80$$

8.1.5 Answer: (A)

In the additive model, value $Y =$ trend $T +$ seasonal S. The seasonally adjusted value estimates the trend $Y - S = 423{,}700 - 81{,}500 = 342{,}200$ in this case.

The errors were: in B, adding instead of subtracting S, and in C and D, getting confused with the multiplicative model and multiplying or dividing by 0.81500.

8.1.6 Answer: (C)

In the multiplicative model $Y = T \times S \times R$, so $R = Y/(T \times S) = 523/(465 \times 1.12) = 1.0042$ (to four decimal places).

In A the $Y = T$ ratio has been multiplied by 1.12 instead of divided, while in both B and D the additive model $Y/T + S + R$ has been used.

8.1.7 Answer: (D)

Total $= 1.06 + 1.13 + 0.92 + 0.94 = 4.05$, hence we adjust by subtracting $0.05/4 = 0.0125$ from each average. The adjusted first average $= 1.06 - 0.0125 = 1.0475$.

(C) is almost correct but the excess 0.0125 has been added instead of subtracted. In (A) the averages have been adjusted to total to 1, while in (B) the entire 0.05 has been subtracted from the 1.06.

8.1.8 Answer: (B)

In the additive model $Y = T + S + R$, so $R = Y - T - S = 85 - 91 - (-6.4) = 0.4$.

(C) was almost correct but the wrong way round, while in (D) the 6.4 was subtracted rather than added, giving a very large residual. Answer (A) looks to be an arithmetical error.

8.1.9 Answer: (D)

Total $= 22 + 15 - 8 - 33 = -4$, hence we adjust by adding $4/4 = 1$ to each average. The average currently at -33 becomes $-33 + 1 = -32$.

In (A) the 1 has been subtracted rather than added; in (B) the entire 4 has been subtracted; and in (C) the entire 4 has been added.

8.1.10 Answer: (B)

It is true that extrapolation leads to unreliable forecasts but, by definition, it is totally unavoidable in time series analysis.

8.1.11 The component parts of a time series model are:

A	The trend	R
B	The cyclical component	Q
C	The seasonal component	S
D	The residual component	P

8.1.12 Residual variation $= 496$.

8.1.13 In the fourth quarter of 2002, $t = 20$, so $T = 43 + 5.9 \times 20 = 161$.

8.1.14 (A) Incorrect: S is estimated by averaging $A - T$ values and not $A = T$ values when the additive model is used.
(B) Correct.
(C) Correct.
(D) Incorrect: R is estimated from $A - T - S$.
(E) Correct.

8.1.15 $25 - 54 - 65 + 90 = -4$. So components are adjusted by adding 1 to each of them. First $= 26$; second $= -53$; third $= -64$; fourth $= 91$.

8.1.16 Estimate $= 43.968$.

8.1.17 $A = T \times S$ and the seasonally adjusted value is an estimate of T. Hence $S^{1/4}$ $1,897,000/1,634,000 = 1.161$.

8.1.18 The first trend figure will be located at time point three, so two days at the start and a similar two days at the end of the data will not be able to have their trends estimated using this method. The number of days is therefore four.

8.1.19 (A) Correct.
(B) Incorrect: centring is not optional since A and T values must be associated if seasonal components are subsequently to be estimated.
(C) Correct.

8.1.20 (A) Incorrect: regression trends would be more accurate only if the trend was linear.
(B) Correct.
(C) Correct.
(D) Incorrect: although it is generally the case that the multiplicative model gives better estimates than the additive model, one can really only tell by examining the data to see whether seasonal variation actually increases or decreases with the trend.
(E) Correct.
(F) Incorrect: forecasts cannot be expected to be accurate if there are unexpected events.

✓ Solutions to Part 8.2

8.2.1 All the moving averages are given by dividing the 'sum of twos' by 8.

Answers:
(A) 23.750
(B) 24.125
(C) 25.125

8.2.2 Seasonally adjusted demand is given by dividing the actual demand by the corresponding seasonal factor.

Quarter	Actual demand	Seasonal factor	Seasonally adjusted demand
1	25	1.045	23.923
2	33	1.343	24.572
3	19	0.765	24.837
4	21	0.847	24.793

8.2.3 The 'seasonal adjustment' described in F is used when initially calculating the seasonal components.

(D) correct
(E) incorrect
(F) incorrect
(G) correct.

8.2.4 Increasing seasonally adjusted values tell us that the trend is increasing. They provide no information about seasonal variability.

Answer: (H) The trend is upwards, and (M) No deductions are possible about seasonal variability.

8.2.5 Ignoring residuals, the model is given by $A = T + S$. Seasonal adjustment is about estimating the trend and so is given by $T = A - S$.

Answer: $A - S$

✓ Solutions to Part 8.3

8.3.1 The values of the average seasonal variations tell us that the actual values have been on average 30 per cent below the trend in the first and third quarters, identical with the trend in the second quarter and 60 per cent above it in the fourth.

Answers:
(A) Actual sales are on average 30 per cent below the trend in the third quarter.
(D) Actual sales in the fourth quarter are on average 60 per cent above the trend.
(F) Actual sales in the fourth quarter are 1.6 times the trend.

8.3.2 Answers:

Brand Y $246/0.7 = 351.4$
Brand Z $558/0.7 = 797.1$

8.3.3 The trend rises at 2 per cent per quarter and so, after three quarters, reaches the value $351.4 \times 1.02^3 = 372.9$

8.3.4 Actual sales forecast is 60 per cent greater than the trend, that is, $370 \times 1.6 = 592$ to the nearest whole number.

8.3.5 Trend forecast is given by reducing the initial trend value of 797.1 by 3 per cent a quarter over two quarters, i.e. by $797.1 \times 0.97^2 = 750.0$

8.3.6 Actual sales forecast is 30 per cent below the trend forecast, that is, $770.0 \times 0.7 = 539$.

8.3.7 The assumptions on the basis of which time series forecasts are made are really that everything will continue in the future as it has in the past. In other words the same trend and seasonal variability will apply and there will be no unforeseen events. All of this presupposes that an appropriate model is being used.

Answers:
(C) That there will be no change in the existing seasonal pattern of variability.
(D) That the model being used fits the data.
(E) That there will be no unforeseen events.

✓ Solutions to Part 8.4

8.4.1 In the first quarter of 1991, $X = 20$ and so X must take the values 21–23 in the remaining quarters. For example, the trend in the 2nd quarter will be $= 100 + 5 \times 21 = 205$ units.

Answers:
2nd quarter	205
3rd quarter	210
4th quarter	215

8.4.2 Actual forecasts are given by changing the trend by the appropriate seasonal per cent. For example, the forecast of actual numbers sold in the 2nd quarter will be $205 \times 0.8 = 164$.

Answers:
2nd quarter	164
3rd quarter	294
4th quarter	172

8.4.3 Price per unit is given by increasing 1,000 at 2 per cent per quarter, that is, by multiplying by 1.02 for each quarter.

Answers:
2nd quarter	$1,000 \times 1.02 = 1,020$
3rd quarter	$1,020 \times 1.02 = 1,040.4$
4th quarter	$1,040.4 \times 1.02 = 1,061.21$

8.4.4 Sales revenue is given by multiplying together the forecasts for unit price and sales volume.

Answers:
Quarters of 1991	Sales revenue forecast (£)
2	$150 \times 1010 = 151,500$
3	$300 \times 1030 = 309,000$
4	$170 \times 1050 = 178,500$

9

Probability

Probability

9

LEARNING OUTCOMES

On completing this chapter you should be able to:

- calculate a simple probability;
- demonstrate the use of the addition and multiplication rules of probability;
- calculate a simple conditional probability;
- calculate and explain an expected value;
- demonstrate the use of expected values to make decisions;
- explain the limitations of expected values;
- demonstrate the use of the Normal distribution and tables;
- demonstrate the application of the Normal distribution to calculate probabilities;
- use Venn diagrams.

9.1 Introduction

Most people have some intuitive conception of uncertainty or chance, as the following typical statements illustrate:

- 'On past evidence, there seems to be a 50/50 chance of this project succeeding.'
- 'I reckon that, if we stay on this course, we will have only a one in ten chance of making a profit next year.'
- 'The consultants' report says that our project launch has a 60 per cent chance of success.'

Each of the above sentences contains a term attempting to quantify the degree of uncertainty in a business situation. In this chapter we introduce the formal study of such quantification, or *probability*, initially looking at several different approaches to the subject. More detail of uncertainty and risk is given in Section 9.14.

9.2 Definitions of probability

Probability is a branch of mathematics that calculates the likelihood of a given event occurring, and is often expressed as a number between 0 and 1. It can also be expressed as a proportion or as a percentage. If an event has a probability of 1 it can be considered a certainty: for example, the probability of spinning a coin resulting in either 'heads' or 'tails' is 1, because, assuming the coin lands flat, there are no other options. So, if an event has a probability of 0.5 it can be considered to have equal odds of occurring or not occurring: for example, the probability of spinning a coin resulting in 'heads' is 0.5, because the spin is equally likely to result in 'tails.' An event with a probability of 0 can be considered an impossibility: for example, the probability that the coin will land flat without either side facing up is 0, because either 'heads' or 'tails' must be facing up. In real life, very few events are ever given a probability of zero as there is always an unknown element in human affairs.

As mentioned above one way of viewing/understanding a probability is as a proportion, as the following simple example will illustrate.

Example 9.2.1

An ordinary six-sided dice is rolled. What is the probability that it will show a number less than three?

Solution

Here it is possible to list all the possible equally likely outcomes of rolling a dice, namely the whole numbers from one to six inclusive:

1, 2, 3, 4, 5, 6

The outcomes that constitute the 'event' under consideration, that is, 'a number less than three' are:

1, 2

Hence the proportion of outcomes that constitute the event is 2/6 or 1/3, which is therefore the desired probability.

Note that this answer agrees with the intuitive statements you might make about this situation, such as 'the chances are one in three'.

In situations like this, where it is possible to compile a *complete* list of all the *equally likely* outcomes, we can define the probability of an event, denoted P(event), in a way that agrees with the above intuitive approach:

$$P(\text{event}) = \frac{\text{Total number of outcomes which constitute the event}}{\text{Total number of possible outcomes}}$$

This is known as *exact* probability because it involves having a complete list of all possible outcomes and counting the exact number that constitute the event. This definition, however, is not always practical for business purposes, as you can rarely state all the possible outcomes. To illustrate this, and to demonstrate a way of overcoming the problem, we consider the following.

Example 9.2.2

A quality controller wishes to specify the probability of a component failing within 1 year of installation. How might she proceed?

Solution

To find this probability from an exact approach would necessitate obtaining a list of the lifetimes of *all* the components, and counting those of less than 1 year. It is clearly impossible to keep such a detailed record of *every* component, after sale.

An alternative, feasible approach is to take a *sample* of components, rather than the whole population, and test them under working conditions, to see what proportion fail within one year. Probabilities produced in this way are known as *empirical* and are essentially approximations to the true, but unobtainable, exact probabilities. In this case, the quality controller may choose to sample 1,000 components. If she then finds that 16 fail within 1 year:

$$P \text{(component failing within 1 year)} = \frac{16}{1,000} \text{ or } 0.016$$

For this approximation to be valid, it is essential that the sample is representative. Further, for a more accurate approximation, a larger sample could be taken, provided that the time and money are available.

We make two comments before moving on. First of all, since we are defining probabilities as proportions, probabilities will lie in the range 0–1, with 0 denoting an impossibility and 1 denoting a certainty. Second, there are many practical instances in which a suitable sample is unavailable, so an empirical probability cannot be found. In such cases a *subjective* probability could be estimated, based on judgement and experience. Although such estimates are not entirely reliable, they can occasionally be useful, as we shall see later. The second quotation in the Introduction to this chapter is an example of the use of judgement to estimate a subjective probability.

9.3 Addition rules of probability

In principle, it is possible to find any probability by the methods discussed above. In practice, however, there are many complex cases that can be simplified by using the so-called *rules of probability*. We shall develop these via examples.

Example 9.3.1

According to personnel records, the 111 employees of an accountancy practice can be classified by their work-base (A, B or C) and by their professional qualifications thus:

	Office A	Office B	Office C	Total
Qualified	26	29	24	79
Not qualified	11	9	12	32
Total	37	38	36	111

What is the probability that a randomly selected employee will:

(a) work at office A or office B?
(b) work at office A or be professionally qualified or both?

Solution

(a) There are 37 people working in A and 38 in B, making 75 out of 111 who work in either A or B. Hence, $P(A \text{ or } B) = 75/111$.

(b) Examining the table, we can apply our earlier rule: 37 are employed at office A, and 79 are qualified, making a total of 116. It is clear, however, that we have 'double counted' the 26 employees who both work at office A and are qualified. Subtracting this double-counted amount, we see that

$$116 - 26 = 90$$

employees have the desired property. Hence:

$$P(\text{employed at office A or professionally qualified}) = \frac{90}{111}$$

We can generalise from the above results. We have:

(a) $P(A \text{ or } B) = \frac{75}{111} = \frac{37}{111} + \frac{38}{111} = P(A) + P(B)$.

This is called the *special addition rule* of probability and it holds only when A and B cannot both be true. A and B are said to be *mutually exclusive* in that, if either is true, then the other is excluded. In other words, P(A and B) = 0.

(b) $P(\text{employed at office A } or \text{ professionally qualified}) = \frac{90}{111} = \frac{37 + 79 - 26}{111}$

$$= \frac{37}{111} + \frac{79}{111} - \frac{26}{111}$$
$$= P(\text{employed at office A}) + P(\text{professionally qualified}) - P(\text{office A and qualified})$$

This is an example of the *general addition law* of probability:

$$P(X \text{ or } Y) = P(X) + P(Y) - P(X \text{ and } Y)$$

The last term in this law compensates, as we have seen, for double counting. If, however, there is no possibility of double counting – that is, if X and Y cannot occur together (i.e. P(X and Y) = 0) – then this term can be omitted and the law simplified to the 'special addition law':

$$P(X \text{ or } Y) = P(X) + P(Y)$$

These rules are given in your CIMA assessment in the forms:

$P(A \cup B) = P(A) + P(B)$ and
$P(A \cup B) = P(A) + P(B) - P(A \cap B)$.

Example 9.3.2

Several of the examples in this chapter are based on the following table, which relates to a check on the quality of all the items produced by three shifts at a factory during a certain day.

	Shift X	Shift Y	Shift Z	Total
Grade I	65	72	71	208
Grade II	56	72	33	161
Faulty	9	16	6	31
Total	130	160	110	400

If an item is selected at random from the day's production, what is the probability that:

(a) it is Grade I?
(b) it was produced by Shift X?
(c) it was produced by Shift Y or Shift Z?
(d) it was produced by Shift Y or is Grade II?
(e) it is faulty or was produced by Shift Z?

Solution

(a) $P(\text{Grade I}) = 208/400 = 0.52$
(b) $P(\text{Shift X}) = 130/400 = 0.325$
(c) $P(\text{Shift Y or Z}) = P(Y) + P(Z)$ because they are mutually exclusive
$= (160 + 110)/400 = 270/400 = 0.675$

(d) $P(\text{Shift Y or Grade II}) = P(Y) + P(\text{Grade II}) - P(\text{both})$
$= 160/400 + 161/400 - 72/400$
$= 249/400 = 0.6225$

(e) $P(\text{Faulty or Shift Z}) = P(\text{Faulty}) + P(Z) - P(\text{both})$
$= 31/400 + 110/400 - 6/400$
$= 135/400 = 0.3375$

9.4 The probability of opposites

In the example we have been using, a person is either qualified or not qualified, with probabilities 79/111 and 32/111, respectively. Not surprisingly, $P(\text{Qualified}) + P(\text{Unqualified}) = 111/111 = 1$. It is certain that a person is either qualified or unqualified and 1 is the probability of certainty.

In general:

1. If events A and B are mutually exclusive and together cover all possibilities then $P(A) + P(B) = 1$. This holds true for any number of such events.
2. $P(A \text{ is not true}) = 1 - P(A \text{ is true})$. This is in practice a remarkably useful rule. It often happens that it is easier to calculate the probability of the very opposite of the event you are interested in. It is certainly always worth thinking about if you are not sure how to proceed.

9.5 The multiplication rules of probability

Example 9.5.1

In the situation described in Example 9.3.1, what is the probability that a randomly selected employee will come from office B *and* not be qualified?

Solution

A reading from the table shows that nine of the 111 employees come under the required category. Hence:

$$P(\text{employed at office B and not qualified}) = \frac{9}{111}$$

Developing this, as above, to derive a general rule:

$$= \frac{38}{111} \times \frac{9}{38}$$
$$= P(\text{office B}) \times P(\text{not qualified, if from B})$$

This is an example of the general multiplicative law of probability:

$$P(X \text{ and } Y) = P(X) \cdot P(Y, \text{ if } X)$$

or

$$P(X \text{ and } Y) = P(X) \cdot P(Y|X)$$

In the latter form of this law we see the notation $P(Y|X)$ which is read as 'the probability of Y *if* (or *given*) X'. Such a probability is called a *conditional probability*. It is used because the fact that X occurs affects the probability that Y will occur. In the above, for example:

$$P(\text{not professionally quallified}) = \frac{32}{111}$$

Yet the value we must use in the calculation is

$$P(\text{not professionally qualified if from office B}) = \frac{9}{38}$$

On occasion, X and Y are statistically independent. That is, the fact that X occurs has no effect on the probability of Y occurring (and vice versa),

$$P(Y|X) = P(Y)$$

In this case, the rule can be simplified to the *special multiplication rule*:

$$P(X \text{ and } Y) = P(X) \cdot P(Y)$$

These rules are given in your CIMA assessment in the forms:

$$P(A \cap B) = P(A) \times P(B) \text{ and}$$
$$P(A \cap B) = P(A) \times P(B|A)$$

We now give two more worked examples to illustrate further the application of the above rules. They also serve to demonstrate typical applications of probability in finance and accountancy. The first is in the area of life assurance.

Example 9.5.2

Past data show that the probability of a married woman of age 32 being alive in 30 years' time is 0.69. Similarly, the probability of a married man of age 35 being alive in 30 years' time is 0.51. Calculate, for a married couple (woman aged 32, man aged 35), the probabilities that in 30 years' time:

(a) they are both alive;
(b) only (exactly) one is alive;
(c) neither is alive.

Solution

If we consider the woman first, there are two possibilities: she will be alive (probability 0.69) or she will not (probability 0.31). Independently of these, there are two possibilities concerning the man: alive (probability 0.51) or not (0.49). There are thus four possible combinations:

(a) woman alive and man alive; $P = 0.69 \times 0.51 = 0.3519$
(b) (i) woman not alive and man alive; $P = 0.31 \times 0.51 = 0.1581$
    (ii) woman alive and man not; $P = 0.69 \times 0.49 = 0.3381$
(c) both not alive; $P = 0.31 \times 0.49 = 0.1519$
Total   1.0000

Note that, as we are listing every possibility, there is the check that the probabilities must add to 1.

(a) This is the case A above. The probability is thus 0.3519.
(b) This possibility consists of cases B or C above. The two are mutually exclusive and so the probability is

$$P(B \text{ or } C) = P(B) + P(C) = 0.1581 + 0.3381 = 0.4962$$

The probability that only (exactly) one of the couple will be alive is 0.4962.

(c) This is simply D, so the probability that neither will be alive is 0.1519.

Before leaving this example, we point out two simplifications (and therefore two assumptions) we have made. The probabilities quoted in the question (0.69 and 0.51) are empirical, arising from the histories of many people in the past. To apply these values to the couple in the question required the assumption that the people are 'typical' of the sample from which the basic probabilities came. If, for example, either spouse had a dangerous occupation, this assumption would be invalid: in practice, actuaries would have data, and therefore empirical probabilities, to deal with such 'untypical' people.

Second, we have had to make the assumption that the life expectations of spouses are independent, which is probably not true.

Example 9.5.3

From the table on shifts and grades in Example 9.3.2, if an item is selected at random from the day's production, what is the probability that:

(a) it was produced by Shift X *and* is faulty?
(b) it was produced by Shift Y *and* is Grade II?
(c) it is faulty, given that it was produced by Shift Z? – that is, $P(\text{faulty}|\text{from Shift Z})$
(d) it is from Shift Z, given that it is Grade I? – that is, $P(\text{from Shift Z} | \text{Grade I})$
(e) it is not Grade II?

Solution

(a) $P(X \text{ and faulty}) = 9/400 = 0.0225$
(b) $P(Y \text{ and Grade II}) = 72/400 = 0.18$
(c) $P(\text{faulty}|Z) = 6/110 = 0.0545$ (to four d.p.)

Notice that in this case we only consider the 110 items produced by Shift Z because that information was given.

(d) $P(Z|\text{Grade I}) = 71/208 = 0.3413$ (to four d.p.)
(e) $P(\text{not Grade II}) = 1 - (161/400) = 0.5975$

Example 9.5.4

A manufacturing company's accountant wishes to estimate the costs arising from faults in a new product, which is soon to be launched. Tests show that:

- Two per cent of the product is faulty; and, independently of this,
- Six per cent of the packaging is faulty.

Further, it is known from past experience of similar items that customers *always* return faulty products. However, they return items with faulty packaging (product not faulty) only *half* the time.

Since costs associated with defective products differ from those relating to packaging, the accountant wishes to estimate the percentage of products that will be returned owing to:

(a) faulty product;
(b) faulty packaging, but no problems with the product itself;
(c) any fault.

Solution

Before proceeding, we point out that this is essentially a problem on probabilities. For example, 2 per cent of the product being faulty is the same as:

$P(\text{product is faulty}) = 0.02$

(a) Two per cent of products are faulty and all of these will be returned, so 2 per cent will be returned owing to the product being faulty.
(b) $P(\text{faulty package and satisfactory product}) = 0.06 \times 0.98 = 0.0588 = 5.88$ per cent. Half of these, that is, 2.94 per cent, will be returned.
(c) The two outcomes described above are mutually exclusive and cover all the circumstances in which the product might be returned, hence the percentage of products returned for any reason = 2 + 2.94 = 4.94 per cent.

It should be emphasised that these estimates are valid only if the test results are representative of the actual product performance and if this product does resemble the previous 'similar items' regarding return rates of faulty product (100 per cent) and faulty packaging (50 per cent).

Example 9.5.5

A mass-produced article can exhibit two types of fault, A or B. Past records indicate that 1 per cent of production has fault A, 2 per cent has fault B. Further, the presence of fault A has no effect on whether fault B is present or not. Find the following probabilities:

(a) $P(\text{an article has both faults})$;
(b) $P(\text{an article has no fault})$;
(c) $P(\text{an article has only fault A})$;
(d) $P(\text{an article has precisely one fault})$;
(e) $P(\text{an article has fault A, given that it does not have fault B})$.

Solution

A and B are independent and so the special multiplication rule can be used.

$P(A) = 0.01$
$P(\text{not } A) = 1 - 0.01 = 0.99$
$P(\text{not } B) = 0.98$

(a) $P(\text{both A and B}) = 0.01 \times 0.02 = 0.0002$
(b) $P(\text{neither}) = 0.99 \times 0.98 = 0.9702$
(c) $P(\text{A but not B}) = 0.01 \times 0.98 = 0.0098$
(d) $P(\text{precisely one fault}) = P(\text{A but not B}) + P(\text{B but not A})$
$= 0.0098 + 0.02 \times 0.99$
$= 0.0296$

(e) $P(A \text{ not } B) = P(A)$ since A and B are independent $= 0.01$

9.6 More conditional probabilities

Example 9.6.1

A firm produces 55 per cent of items on production line A and 45 per cent on line B. In general, 3 per cent of the products of line A and 5 per cent of that of line B are found to be defective but, once a product is packaged and sold, it is not possible to tell by which line it was manufactured. If an item is subsequently returned as faulty, what is the probability that it was made on line A?

Solution

The easiest way to calculate this type of conditional probability is to set out the information in table form, taking a total of 100 for convenience. We shall show the process in several steps, though in practice you would only produce one table:

	Defective	OK	Total
A			55
B			45
Total			100

This table shows the information about A and B having 55 per cent and 45 per cent of production respectively.

Next we shall incorporate the fact that 3 per cent of A's 55 items are defective, giving $55 \times 0.03 = 1.65$. Similarly, the percentage of defective items for B is 5 per cent of $45 = 45 \times 0.05 = 2.25$.

	Defective	OK	Total
A	1.65		55
B	2.25		45
Total			100

Finally, complete the rest of the table by addition and subtraction:

	Defective	OK	Total
A	1.65	53.35	55
B	2.25	42.75	45
Total	3.90	96.10	100

We can now find the conditional probability required:

$P(A|\text{defective}) = 1.65/3.9 = 0.42$

Example 9.6.2

Three accountancy training establishments, A, B and C, have numbers of CIMA students in the ratio 4:3:3 and their pass rates are 35, 68 and 53 per cent, respectively. What is the probability that a successful student, who is known to have been at one of these establishments, was in fact at B?

Solution

	Pass	Fail	Total
A	14.0	26.0	40
B	20.4	9.6	30
C	15.9	14.1	30
Total	50.3	49.7	100

$P(B|\text{passed}) = 20.4/50.3 = 0.4056$

9.7 Discrete probability distributions; expectations

We use the word discrete here in the same sense as in Chapter 3, namely to describe a variable that can assume only certain values, regardless of the level of precision to which it is measured. For example, the number of errors made on an invoice is a discrete variable as it can be only

   0 or 1 or 2 or ...

and never 2.3, for example.

A *discrete probability distribution* is similar to a discrete frequency distribution (see Chapter 3) in that it consists of a list of all the values the variable can have (in the case of exact probabilities) or has had (in the case of empirical probabilities), together with the appropriate corresponding probabilities. A simple example will illustrate.

Example 9.7.1

The records of a shop show that, during the previous 50 weeks' trading, the number of sales of a certain item have been:

Number of sales/week	Number of weeks
0	4
1	16
2	22
3	6
4 or more	2

Construct the corresponding probability distribution.

Solution

The variable here is clearly *discrete* (number of sales) and the probabilities are to be based on the *empirical* data given. Hence we shall have a discrete distribution of empirical probabilities. Now, using the definition of Section 9.2:

$$P(0 \text{ sales in a week}) = \frac{4}{50} = 0.08$$

Proceeding in this way, we can build up the distribution:

Number of sales/week	P(number of sales/week)
0	0.08
1	0.32
2	0.44
3	0.12
4 or more	0.04
	1.00

The *expected value* of a discrete probability distribution, $E(X)$, is defined as:

$$E(X) = \Sigma XP$$

where the summation is over all values of the variable, X, and P denotes the *exact* probability of the variable attaining the value X. At first sight, this appears to be an abstract concept, but an example will show that it has both a practical and an intuitively clear meaning.

Example 9.7.2

What is the expected number of weekly sales of the item in Example 9.7.1? What meaning does this value have?

Solution

We note that we have only empirical probabilities here, and so our answer will be an approximation. Using a familiar tabular format for the calculations:

X	P	XP
0	0.08	0.00
1	0.32	0.32
2	0.44	0.88
3	0.12	0.36
4	0.04	0.16
		1.72

(For convenience, we have taken '4 or more' as 4 in the calculation.) Thus, the expected number of sales per week is approximately 1.72.

Consider now what the probabilities in the distribution mean. In the past, the item had had weekly sales of:

0 in 8 per cent of the weeks,
1 in 32 per cent of the weeks,
2 in 44 per cent of the weeks and so on.

An intuitive approach to 'expectation' would therefore be to take

8% of 0
32% of 1 and so on

and add the resulting values. Looking at the computation above, we see that this is precisely what the formula has done.

Having shown that our definition corresponds exactly with our intuition, we can now see another meaning of an expected value. Since the empirical probabilities have been calculated simply by dividing the individual frequencies by the total frequency, that is

$$\frac{f}{\Sigma f}$$

we have in fact calculated the value of

$$\Sigma XP = \frac{\Sigma Xf}{\Sigma f} = \bar{X}, \text{ the sample mean}$$

as encountered in Chapter 4.

Hence the expected value of a probability distribution is similar to the mean of the corresponding frequency distribution. In fact, if we have *exact* probabilities to work with, the two are *precisely* the same.

Before looking at an important application, there is a special case of expected values worth mentioning. In the example above, on how many weeks would you expect there to be no sales during a trading period (4 weeks) and during a trading year (50 weeks)?

The intuitive answers to these questions are that, since the probability of no sales in any one week is 0.08, we should 'expect':

in 4 weeks, no sales to occur in $4 \times 0.08 = 0.32$ weeks and
in 50 weeks, no sales to occur in $50 \times 0.08 = 4$ weeks.

In fact, to fit in with these intuitive ideas, we extend the definition of expectation. If there are *n independent* repeats of a circumstance, and the *constant* probability of a certain outcome is P, then the expected number of times the outcome will arise in the n repeats is nP.

In the above, when we have $n = 4$ weeks, our (assumedly independent) repeated circumstances, and the constant probability $P = 0.08$ (outcome of no sales in a week), then the expected value is:

$$nP = 4 \times 0.08 = 0.32$$

as intuition told us.

Example 9.7.3

If a coin is tossed three times, the resulting number of heads is given by the following probability distribution:

No. of heads (X)	Probability (P)
0	1/8
1	3/8
2	3/8
3	1/8
Total	1

Find:

(a) the expected number of heads in three throws of a coin;
(b) the expected number of heads in 30 throws of a coin.

Solution

(a)

No. of heads (X)	Probability (P)	PX
0	1/8	0
1	3/8	3/8
2	3/8	6/8
3	1/8	3/8
Total	1	12/8 i.e. 1.5

As expected, if a coin is tossed three times the expected (or average) number of heads is 1.5.

(b) If a coin is tossed 30 times we would intuitively expect $30/2 = 15$ heads. Notice that 30 throws = 10 repeats of the three-throw trial and the expected number of heads is $10 \times 1.5 = 15$.

> Working out an expected value is a very common assessment question.

9.8 Expectation and decision-making

Many business situations require a choice between numerous courses of action whose results are uncertain. Clearly, the decision-maker's experience and judgement are important in making 'good' choices in such instances. The question does arise, however, as to whether there are objective aids to decision-making that, if not entirely replacing personal judgement, can at least assist it. In this section, we look at one such possible aid in the area of *financial* decision-making.

In order to introduce a degree of objectivity, we begin by seeking a criterion for classing one option as 'better' than another. One commonly accepted criterion is to choose the option that gives the highest expected financial return. This is called the *expected value* (EV) criterion.

Example 9.8.1

A decision has to be made between three options, A, B and C. The possible profits and losses are:

Option A: a profit of £2,000 with probability 0.5 or otherwise a loss of £500
Option B: a profit of £800 with probability 0.3 or otherwise a profit of £500
Option C: a profit of £1,000 with probability 0.8, of £500 with probability 0.1 or otherwise a loss of £400

Which option should be chosen under the EV criterion?

Solution

The expected value of each option is:

$EV(A) = (2000 \times 0.5) + (-500 \times 0.5) = £750$
$EV(B) = (800 \times 0.3) + (500 \times 0.7) = £590$
$EV(C) = (1000 \times 0.8) + (500 \times 0.1) + (-400 \times 0.1) = £810$

Thus, we would choose option C in order to maximise expected profit. However, it is arguable that a person or organisation that cannot afford a loss would opt for the 'safe' option B, which guarantees a profit in all circumstances.

Example 9.8.2

A decision-maker is faced with the following options, which can result in the profits shown:

	High sales P = 0.5	Medium sales P = 0.4	Low sales P = 0.1
Option 1	£50,000	£10,000	−£60,000
Option 2	£40,000	£10,000	−£20,000
Option 3	£30,000	£15,000	£0

If the intention is to maximise expected profit, which option should be taken?
Comment on the riskiness of the choice facing the decision-maker.

Solution

Option 1	Probability	Profit £'000	EV
	0.5	50	25
	0.4	10	4
	0.1	−60	−6
	1.0		23

Option 2	Probability	Profit £'000	EV
	0.5	40	20
	0.4	10	4
	0.1	−20	−2
	1.0		22

Option 3	Probability	Profit £'000	EV
	0.5	30	15
	0.4	15	6
	0.1	0	0
	1.0		21

Using the EV criterion, option 1 should be taken since it has the largest expected profit at £23,000.

Notice that option 1 is very risky, with a 10 per cent chance of making a loss greater than the maximum possible profit. Many decision-makers who are not specially averse to risk would nevertheless choose option 2 as having a very similar expected profit with considerably lower risk.

The next example illustrates the idea of a payoff table that assists in the application of the EV criterion in certain more complex situations.

Example 9.8.3

A storeholder has to decide how many units of the perishable commodity X to buy each day. Past demand has followed the distribution:

Demand (units)	Probability
1	0.2
2	0.4
3	0.4

Each unit is bought for £10 and sold for £20, and, at the end of each day, any unsold units must be disposed of with no financial return. Using the EV criterion, how many units should be bought daily?

Solution

If we assume that the past demand pattern will obtain in the future, we see that, logically, the store-holder has only three initial choices: buy one, two or three units per day. There are also only three possible outcomes each day, a demand of one, two or three units. We can therefore construct a payoff table showing the financial effects of the nine possible combinations (three choices by three outcomes). This is shown in Figure 9.1.

The monetary values in each case show the daily profit: we give three examples here and leave the others to be calculated as an exercise:

		Daily order number		
		1	2	3
Daily demand	1	£10	£0	−£10
	2	£10	£20	£10
	3	£10	£20	£30

Figure 9.1 Payoff table (Example 9.8.3)

- order 1, demand 1: cost = £10, revenue = £20; so profit = £10;
- order 2, demand 1: cost = £20, revenue £20; so profit = £0 (in this case, one valueless unit would be left at the end of the day);
- order 2, demand 2: cost = £20, revenue = £40; so profit = £20 (in this case, the demand for the third unit would be unsatisfied).

Using the probabilities for the various levels of demand, we can now calculate the expected daily profit for each order number:

- EV (order 1) £10 (no need for calculations here, as the profit is £10, regardless of the outcome)
- EV (order 2) $(0.2 \times 0) + (0.4 \times 20) + (0.4 \times 20) = £16$
- EV (order 3) $(0.2 \times -10) + (0.4 \times 10) + (0.4 \times 30) = £14$

Thus, in order to maximise daily profit, the storeholder should order two units per day.

It should be noted that the feature that makes the construction of the table possible is that the outcomes (demand) are independent of the decision taken (number of units ordered).

Example 9.8.4

A shopkeeper buys an item at £10 and sells it at £50 but if it is not sold by the end of the day it will be thrown away. If demand is as shown below; use the EV criterion to advise the shopkeeper on how many he should stock per day.

Demand	Probability
0	0.3
1	0.4
2	0.3

Solution

Payoff table (in £ per day)

		Probability	\multicolumn{3}{c}{Order}
			0	1	2
	0	0.3	0	−10	−20
Demand	1	0.4	0	40	30
	2	0.3	0	40	80

Expected values:

EV of order of 0 = £0
EV of order of 1 = $(-10 \times 0.3) + (40 \times 0.40) + (40 \times 0.3) = £25$
EV of order of 2 = $(-20 \times 0.3) + (30 \times 0.4) + (80 \times 0.30) = £30$

Hence, the optimal order is two units per day, on the basis of the EV criterion. The shopkeeper risks a loss of £20 a day compared with £10 a day on an order of one, but in the long term this strategy gives an improved expected profit of £5 per day.

9.9 Limitations of this approach

We are not advocating that the above approach is ideal: merely an *aid* to decision-making. Indeed, many texts that develop so-called *decision theory* further address at some length the limitations we shall discuss here. Suffice it to say, at this point, that attempts to overcome these problems meet with varying degrees of success, and so it is inconceivable that an 'objective' approach can ever replace the human decision-maker.

Another limitation that this approach shares with most other attempts to model reality is that the outcomes and probabilities need to be estimated. In Example 9.8.1 all the profits and losses are estimates, as are the probabilities attached to them. The subsequent analysis can never be more reliable than the estimations upon which it is based. There is also often a considerable degree of simplification with very limited discrete probability distributions being used when more complex ones or perhaps continuous distributions might be more appropriate. In Example 9.8.2 it is quite unbelievable that when times are good sales are exactly 50,000 – common sense tells us that they must be more variable than that.

The probabilities in Examples 9.7.1, 9.7.2 and 9.7.3 are empirical, arising from past experience, and so have some degree of reliability unless demand patterns change dramatically. In other cases (see the second quotation in Section 9.2), only subjective estimates of probabilities may be available, and their reliability may be open to question. There is therefore a doubt over this approach when *subjective* probabilities are used. Example 9.8.3 has another feature that will tend to lend some validity to this decision-making approach. It is a *repeated* decision, made every day. The expected values therefore have a commercial meaning: they are long-term *average* profits. Thus, if the storeholder orders two units per day, she/he will average £16 per day profit. As this is higher than the average profits attainable from any other choice, this is a valid and sensible decision. In many cases, however, individuals or companies are faced with *one-off* decisions. An analysis of expected values would give the best average profits over a long run of many *repeats* of the decision, a circumstance that does not obtain in a one-off situation. One must question the use of the EV criterion in the latter case.

Finally, the comment made at the end of Example 9.8.1 demonstrates a serious deficiency in this approach: it takes no account of the decision-makers' attitude to risk. In the example, option B offered the lowest EV but also the least element of risk, and so an analysis of expected values does not give the whole picture. Particularly with one-off decisions, it can only give a guide to decision-makers.

> Even with objective testing it is still important to be aware of the limitations of methods. The failure to take account of risk is a key criticism of this approach.

9.10 Characteristics of the normal distribution

In Section 9.7, the idea of a discrete probability distribution was introduced. The normal distribution is a continuous probability distribution. The values of probabilities relating to a normal distribution come from a normal distribution curve, in which *probabilities are represented by areas:* (Figure 9.2). An immediate consequence of probabilities being equated to areas is that *the total area under the normal curve is equal to 1.*

As Figure 9.2 illustrates, there are many examples of the normal distribution. Any one is completely defined by its mean (μ) and its standard deviation (σ). The curve is bell-shaped and symmetric about its mean, and, although the probability of a normal variable taking a value far away from the mean is small, it is never quite zero. The examples in the figure also demonstrate the role of the mean and standard deviation. As before, the mean determines the general position or *location* of the variable, whereas the standard deviation determines how *spread* the variable is around its mean.

(a)

(b) Higher mean than (a); same standard deviation

(c) Same mean as (a); lower standard deviation

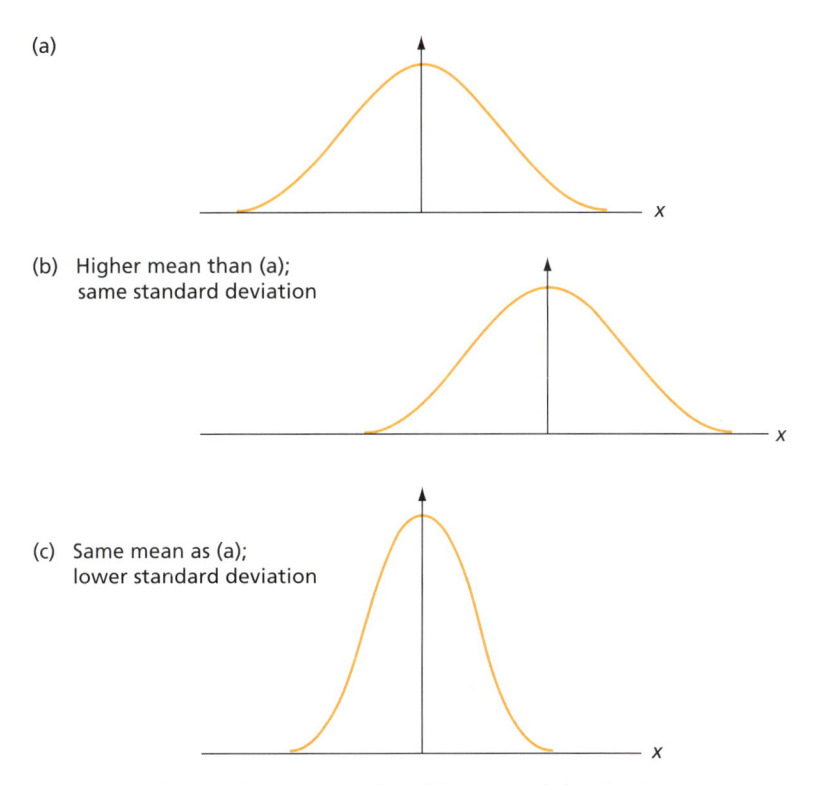

Figure 9.2 Examples of the normal distribution

9.11 Use of the tables of normal distribution

The preceding section describes the normal distribution but is insufficient to enable us to calculate probabilities based upon it, even though we know that the total area under the curve is one. To evaluate normal probabilities, we must use tables such as those given in your exam. These tables convert normal distributions with different means and standard deviations to a *standard* normal distribution, which has

a mean of 0
a standard deviation of 1

This special distribution is denoted by the variable z. Any other normal distribution denoted x, with mean μ and standard deviation σ can be converted to the standard one (or standardised) by the following formula:

$$z = \frac{x - \mu}{\sigma}$$

Example 9.11.1

Use normal distribution tables to find the following:

(a) $P(0 < z < 1)$;
(b) $P(0 < z < 1.25)$;
(c) $P(z < 2.1)$;

(d) $P(0.7 < z < 1)$;
(e) $P(z > 1.96)$;
(f) $P(z < -1.96)$;
(g) $P(-1.96 < z < 1.96)$;
(h) $P(-1.2 < z < 2.8)$;
(i) $P(z > 3)$.

Solution

We shall use the abbreviation TE to mean 'table entry' so that, for example, TE(1) means the probability given in the table corresponding to the value z = 1.00. *Please note that this is not an abbreviation in standard usage.*
 You will find it useful to look at the diagrams in Figure 9.3 while working through these solutions.

(a) $P(0 < z < 1)$ = TE(1.00) = 0.3413. In the table this is the entry in row 1.0 and column 0.00.
(b) $P(0 < z < 1.25)$ = TE(1.25) = 0.3944. In the table this is the entry in row 1.2 and column 0.05.
(c) $P(z < 2.1)$ = 0.5 + TE(2.1) = 0.5 + 0.4821 = 0.9821. This probability includes all the negative values of z, which have a probability of 0.5, as well as those between 0 and 2.1 which are covered by the table entry.
(d) $P(0.7 < z < 1)$ = TE(l) − TE(0.7) = 0.3413 − 0.2580 = 0.0833. This is given by the small area under the curve from 0 to 0.7 subtracted from the larger area from 0 to 1.
(e) $P(z > 1.96)$ = 0.5 − TE(1.96) = 0.5 − 0.475 = 0.025. This tail-end area is given by the area under half the curve (i.e. 0.5) minus the area from 0 to 1.96.
(f) $P(z < -1.96)$ = $P(z > 1.96)$ = 0.025 by symmetry.
(g) $P(-1.96 < z < 1.96)$ = 1 − 2 × 0.025 = 0.95, which is the total area of 1 minus the two tail-ends. This symmetrical interval which includes 95 per cent of normal frequencies is very important in more advanced statistics.
(h) $P(-1.2 < z < 2.8)$ = TE(1.2) + TE(2.8) = 0.3849 + 0.4974 = 0.8823. We have split this area into two. That from 0 to 2.8 is simply the table entry and that from −1.2 to 0 equals the area from 0 to +1.2 by symmetry, so it too is given by the table entry.
(i) $P(z > 3)$ = 0.5 − 0.49865 = 0.00135. The method here is the standard one for tail-end areas but we wanted to make two points. The first is that virtually all normal frequencies lie between three standard deviations either side of the mean. The second is that, for symmetrical data, the standard deviation will be approximately one-sixth of the range.

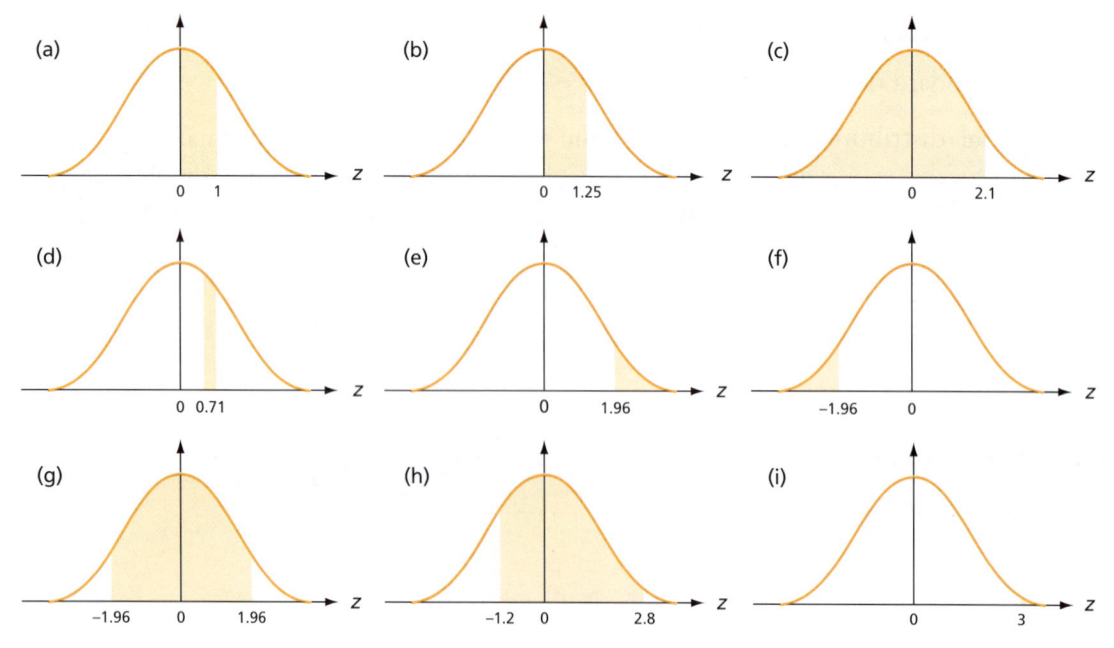

Figure 9.3 Graphs for Example 9.11.1

Example 9.11.2

Evaluate the following probabilities from the standard normal distribution (mean = 0; standard deviation = 1):
(a) $P(0 < z < 2.03)$;
(b) $P(-1.27 < z < 0)$;
(c) $P(z > 0.55)$;
(d) $P(z < -1.55)$;
(e) $P(z > -1.23)$;
(f) $P(z < 0.88)$;
(g) $P(-0.91 < z < 1.08)$;
(h) $P(0.23 < z < 0.34)$.

Solution

(a) $P(0 < z < 2.03) = TE(2.03) = 0.4788$
(b) $P(-1.27 < z < 0) = TE(1.27) = 0.3980$ by symmetry
(c) $P(z > 0.55) = 0.5 - TE(0.55) = 0.5 - 0.2088 = 0.2912$
(d) $P(z < -1.55) = P(z > 1.55) = 0.5 - TE(1.55) = 0.5 - 0.4394 = 0.0606$
(e) $P(z > -1.23) = P(z < 1.23) = 0.5 + TE(1.23) = 0.5 + 0.3907 = 0.8907$
(f) $P(z < 0.88) = 0.5 + TE(0.88) = 0.5 + 0.3106 = 0.8106$
(g) $P(-0.91 < z < 1.08) = TE(0.91) + TE(1.08) = 0.3186 + 0.3599 = 0.6785$
(h) $P(0.23 < z < 0.34) = TE(0.34) - TE(0.23) = 0.1331 - 0.0910 = 0.0421$

Example 9.11.3

A machine produces components with diameter of mean 5 cm and standard deviation 0.1 cm. Knowing that the dimensions of many such products follow a normal distribution, the production manager of the manufacturing company decides to use a normal model for the machine's production.

What proportion of the production will have diameters

(a) between 5 and 5.2 cm;
(b) between 4.9 and 5 cm;
(c) over 5.15 cm;
(d) between 4.8 and 5.1 cm;
(e) between 5.1 and 5.2 cm?

Solution

Although this question concerns proportions, it is essentially a problem on probabilities. We are dealing with a normal distribution with $\mu = 5$ and $\sigma = 0.1$.

(a) Denoting the components' diameters by x, we need

$$P(5 < x < 5.2)$$

which reads as 'the probability of 5 being less than x, and x being less than 5.2'. Standardising the x-values in this expression:

$$x = 5: z = \frac{5 - 5}{0.1} = 0$$
$$x = 5.2: z = \frac{5.2 - 5}{0.1} = 2$$

we get the equivalent probability involving z:

$(0 < z < 2)$

This probability (area) is depicted as the shaded area in Figure 9.4(a). This is a direct reading from the tables, giving 0.4772.

Hence 0.4772 (47.72 per cent) of components produced will have diameters between 5 and 5.2 cm

(b) The probability involved here is:

$$P(4.9 < x < 5)$$

Standardising:

$$x = 4.9: z = \frac{4.9 - 5}{0.1} = -1$$
$$x = 5: z = 0 \text{ (see above)}$$

we get:

$$P(-1 < z < 0)$$

This is the area shown in Figure 9.4(b). However, we recall that the normal curve is *symmetric* about its mean; hence the shaded area is the same as the corresponding area to the *right* of the central dividing line, between the z-values 0 and 1. Tables give this area to be 0.3413.

Thus, 0.3413 (34.13 per cent) of components produced will have diameters between 4.9 and 5 cm

(c) We want:

$$P(x > 5.15)$$

which standardises, as before, to:

$$P(z > (5.15 - 5)/0.1) = P(z > 1.5)$$

This area, shown in Figure 9.4(c), cannot be read directly from the table of probabilities. However, the area immediately to its left (between z-values 0 and 1.5) can: it is 0.4332. Now, as the total area under the curve is 1, and the central dividing line splits the area into two symmetrical halves, the area to the right of the dividing line is 0.5. Hence the area required is

$$0.5 - 0.4332 = 0.0668$$

and so 0.0668 (6.68 per cent) of components produced will have diameters over 5.15 cm

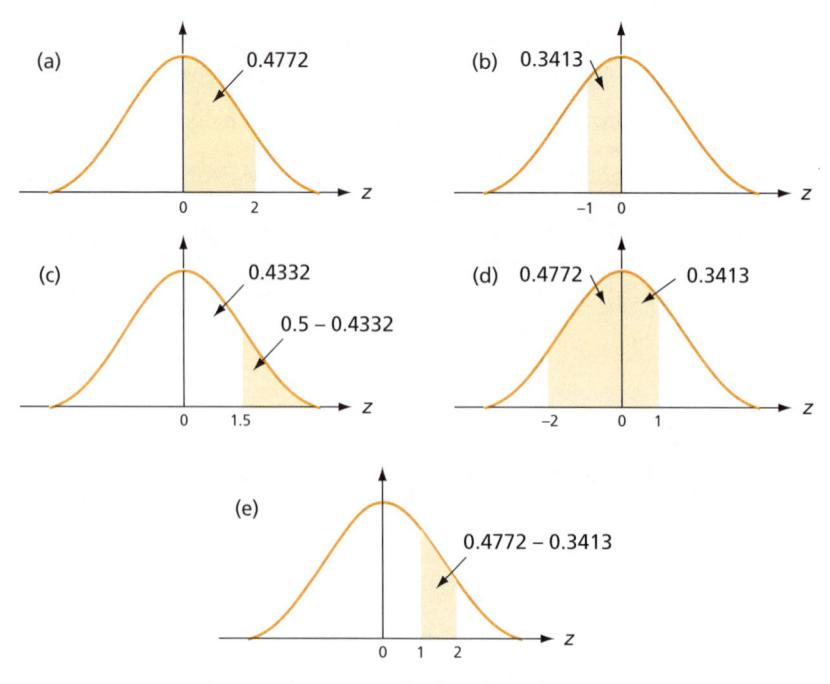

Figure 9.4 Graphs for Example 9.11.3

(d) In this case, the probability is:

$$P(4.8 < x < 5.1)$$

which standardises to:

$$P\left(\frac{4.8 - 5}{0.1} < z < \frac{5.1 - 5}{0.1}\right) = P(-2 < z < 1)$$

which is the shaded area in Figure 9.4(d). The central dividing line splits this area into two parts, convenient for direct readings from the table:

z from −2 to 0 = 0.4772 (the symmetry property has been used here, as in part (b) of this example)
z from 0 to 1 = 0.3413
total = 0.8185

That is, 0.8185 (81.85 per cent) of components produced will have diameters between 4.8 and 5.1 cm
(e) The final case is:

$$P(5.1 < x < 5.2)$$

or:

$$P(1 < z < 2).$$

The tables show that the area between:

z-values 0 and 1 = 0.3413
z-values 0 and 2 = 0.4772

Now, the shaded area in Figure 9.4(e) can be seen to be the difference between these:

0.4772 − 0.3413 = 0.1359

So 0.1359 (13.59 per cent) of components produced will have diameters between 5.1 and 5.2 cm.

The crucial role of the diagrams in Figures 9.3 and 9.4 should be noted. Such graphs need not be drawn very accurately, but their use is strongly advised in order to make correct use of the probabilities taken from the table.

Example 9.11.4

Evaluate the following probabilities from the normal distribution stated:
(a) $P(2 < x < 3)$ when $\mu = 2$, $\sigma = 4$;
(b) $P(x < 6)$ when $\mu = 10$, $\sigma = 5$;
(c) $P(2 < x < 6)$ when $\mu = 3$, $\sigma = 4$;
(d) $P(2 < x < 6)$ when $\mu = 1$, $\sigma = 4$;
(e) $P(2 < x < 6)$ when $\mu = 8$, $\sigma = 5$.

Solution

(a) $P(2 < x < 3) = P[(2 - 2)/4 < z < (3 - 2)/4] = P(0 < z < 0.25) = TE(0.25) = 0.0987$
(b) $P(x < 6) = P[z < (6 - 10)/5] = P(z < -0.8) = P(z > 0.8) = 0.5 - TE(0.8) = 0.5 - 0.2881 = 0.2119$
(c) $P(2 < x < 6) = P[(2 - 3)/4 < z < (6 - 3)/4] = P(-0.25 < z < 0.75) = TE(0.25) + TE(0.75) = 0.0987 + 0.2734 = 0.3721$
(d) $P(2 < x < 6) = P[(2 - 1)/4 < z < (6 - 1)/4] = P(0.25 < z < 1.25) = TE(1.25) - TE(0.25) = 0.3944 - 0.0987 = 0.2957$
(e) $P(2 < x < 6) = P[(2 - 8)/5 < z < (6 - 8)/5] = P(-1.2 < z < -0.4) = P(0.4 < z < 1.2) = TE(1.2) - TE(0.4) = 0.3849 - 0.1554 = 0.2295$

> You are virtually certain to encounter a simple Normal problem like those above in your assessment.

9.12 Further normal distribution examples

Example 9.12.1

The finance department of a pharmaceutical company is concerned that the ageing machinery on its production line is causing losses by putting too much on average of a certain product into each container. A check on the line shows that the mean amount being put into a container is 499.5 ml, with a standard deviation of 0.8 ml

(a) Adopting a normal distribution, what percentage of containers will contain more than the notional contents of 500 ml?
(b) There are two courses of remedial action available: one would reduce the mean amount inserted (leaving the standard deviation unaltered), while the other would reduce the standard deviation (mean unaltered). If the manager wishes to reduce the percentage of containers containing over 500 ml to 10 percent, how could this be achieved by reducing (i) the mean; and (ii) the standard deviation amount inserted?

Solution

(a) Initially, we are working with a normal distribution having $\mu = 499.5$ and $\sigma = 0.8$, and we want:

$$P(x > 500)$$

Standardising, we get:

$$P(z < 0.63)$$

which is the shaded area in Figure 9.5(a) and equals:

$$0.5 - 0.2357 = 0.2643$$

Thus, 26.43 per cent of containers have contents over 500 ml

(b) This problem is different from the earlier ones: we now know the probability (10 per cent or 0.1) and we need to 'work backwards' to find a new value for μ and σ.

Figure 9.5(b) shows the standard normal distribution, with the upper 10 per cent of area shaded. To find the unknown z-value marked, we must look through the body of the table to find the z-value corresponding to an area of 0.4. The nearest to this is $z = 1.28$.

Before moving on, we point out that all we have done is use the table 'backwards' to see that

$$P(z > 1.28) = 0.5 - 0.4 = 0.1$$

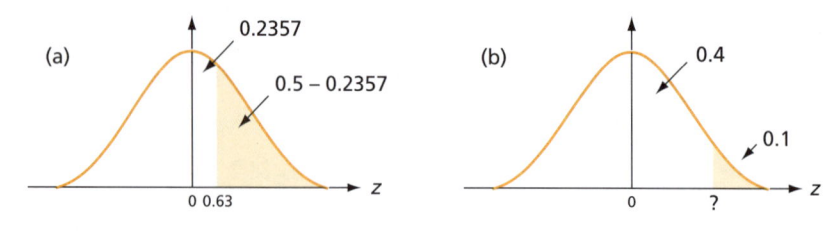

Figure 9.5 Graphs for Example 9.12.1

(i) Now we have:

$$z = \frac{x - \mu}{\sigma}$$

So, using the value of z we have found:

$$1.28 = \frac{500 - \mu}{0.8}$$

Therefore:

$$1.28 \times 0.8 = 500 - \mu$$
$$\mu = 499.0 \text{ (to one d.p.)}$$

Hence, reducing the mean input to 499.0 ml would reduce the percentage of containers with over 500 ml to 10 per cent.

(ii) Similarly, if we regard μ as fixed and change σ:

$$1.28 = \frac{500 - 499.5}{\sigma}$$

so:

$$1.28\sigma = 0.5$$

$$\sigma = 0.39 \text{ (to two d.p.)}$$

Thus, the standard deviation input must be reduced to 0.39 ml to achieve the reduction to 10 per cent of containers with contents over 500 ml.

> Part (b) of Example 9.12.1 shows how, for a given probability, the normal tables can be used to work 'backwards' through the usual steps to find a revised value of the mean or standard deviation. In other words, use the value of the probability (or area) to find z from the tables; then use the standardisation formula to calculate μ or σ.

Example 9.12.2

The weights of a certain mass-produced item are known, over a long period of time, to be normally distributed with a mean of 8 kg and a standard deviation of 0.02 kg

(a) Any item whose weight lies outside the range 7.985–8.035 kg is deemed to be faulty. What percentage of products will be faulty?
(b) If it is required to reduce the percentage that is too heavy (i.e. with weight over 8.035 kg) to 2 per cent, to what value must the mean weight be decreased, leaving all other factors unchanged?
(c) If it is required to reduce the percentage that is too light (i.e. with weight below 7.985 kg) to 2 per cent, to what value must the standard deviation be decreased, leaving other factors unchanged?

Solution

(a) $P(7.985 < W < 8.035) = P[(7.985 - 8)/0.02 < z < (8.035 - 8)/0.02] = P(-0.75 < z < 1.75) =$ TE(0.75) + TE(1.75) = 0.2734 + 0.4599 = 0.7333
Faulty items are outside this range so the probability that an item is faulty is $1 - 0.7333 = 0.2667$. Hence 26.67 per cent of products will be faulty.
(b) The tail-end probability of 2 per cent corresponds to the table entry 48% = 0.48, and so to the z-value 2.05. Hence $z = 2.05 = (8.035 - \text{mean})/0.02$, giving mean $= 8.035 - 2.05 \times 0.02 = 7.994$. So the mean weight must be decreased to 7.994 kg
(c) The z-value must now be $-2.05 = (7.985 - 8)/\sigma$ giving $\sigma = -0.015/-2.05 = 0.0073$ (to four d.p.). Hence, the standard deviation must fall to 0.0073 kg.

9.13 Venn diagrams

Venn diagrams were first developed in the 19th century by John Venn. They are a graphic device useful for illustrating the relationships between different elements or objects in a set. A Venn diagram is a picture that is used to illustrate intersections, unions and other operations on sets. Venn diagrams belong to a branch of mathematics called *set theory*. They are sometimes used to enable people to organise thoughts prior to a variety of activities. Using Venn diagrams enables students to organise similarities and differences in a visual way.

A set of elements is a group which has something in common. Such a group could be all the children in a school. Such a Venn diagram is shown in Figure 9.6.

Figure 9.6   Venn Diagram representing the set of all the children in a Village School

A second Venn diagram (Figure 9.7) shows all the boys and the girls at the school.

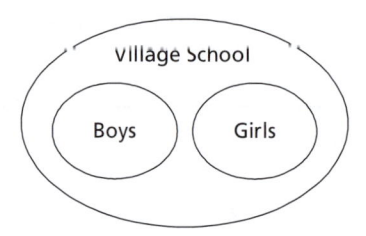

Figure 9.7   Venn Diagram representing the boys and girls in a Village School

A third Venn diagram (Figure 9.8) could be the children who play for the village football team.

Figure 9.8   Venn diagram representing the children from the village who play in the football team

So, if we want to represent the children in a village school who also play football for the village team we would draw the following Venn diagram (Figure 9.9). Then the area of intersection between the two ellipses is a pictorial representation of the children from the Village School who are in the Village football team.

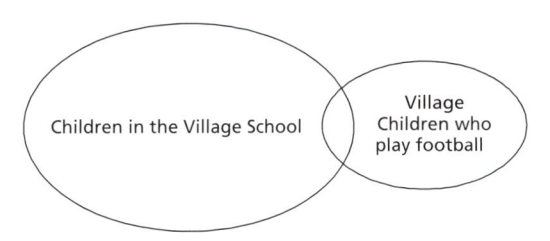

Figure 9.9 The intersection of the Venn diagrams represents the children from the Village School who play in the football team

9.13.1 Using Venn diagrams to assist with probability

Venn diagrams can be a useful way of understanding calculations of probability. This will be explained through the use of an example.

Example 9.13.1

The probability that a woman drinks wine is 0.4.
   The probability that a woman drinks gin and tonic is 0.7.
   The probability that a woman does drink wine and does not drink gin and tonic is 0.1.
   This example will show how a Venn diagram will assist in obtaining the probability that a woman selected at random drinks wine, and gin and tonic.
   The first step is to draw a Venn diagram showing the two sets of women, that is those that drink wine and those that drink gin and tonic (Figure 9.10). The group that drink wine will be referred to as set W and the set that drink gin and tonic will be referred to as G&T.

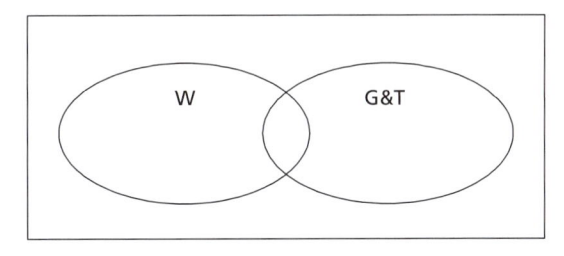

Figure 9.10 Two sets of women who drink wine, and gin and tonic

The next step in the process is to insert the probabilities in the Venn diagram and to start the calculations. Let x be the probability that a woman drinks both wine and gin and tonic. This is represented by the intersection of the two ellipses. This assumption now allows us to say that the area of the set W, which represents the women who only drink wine and not gin and tonic is 0.4−x. In the same way we can say that the area of the set G&T, which represents women who only drink G&T and not wine is 0.7−x. We also know from our data that the probability of a woman not drinking wine and not drinking gin and tonic is 0.1. These are all represented in Figure 9.11.

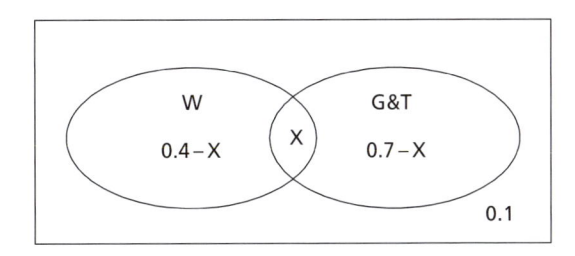

Figure 9.11 Venn diagram showing the sum of all the probabilities

It is known that the sum of all the probabilities in Figure 9.11 equals 1. Therefore the following equation can be constructed.

$$(0.4 - x) + x + (0.7 - x) + 0.1 = 1$$
$$1.2 - x = 1$$
$$-x = -0.2$$
$$x = 0.2$$

From this calculation it is possible to ascribe the probabilities to each part of the Venn diagram which is shown in Figure 9.12.

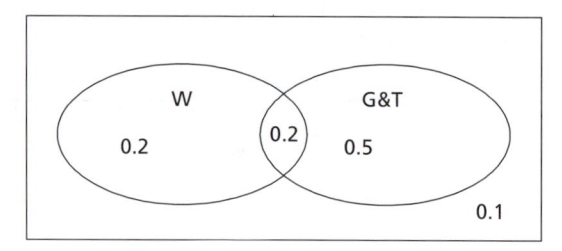

Figure 9.12 Venn diagram showing the final results

9.14 Uncertainty and risk

This section gives some background to the concepts of uncertainty and risk, and in particular, how probability can be used as a measure of risk. Although uncertainty and risk are connected concepts, they are sufficiently different to require separate explanations. Whilst a detailed understanding of uncertainty and risk is not required for your exam, it is useful to have an appreciation of these terms, and also the practical role that probability plays when assessing risks.

The terms uncertainty and risk are used in different ways by different commentators, researchers and professional practitioners in the business world, and it is useful to start with a discussion of what these words or terms mean.

Starting with risks, every business is said to face a series of risks, and as a result of these risks it is difficult to be able to say how the business will actually perform. These risks have a number of different origins or drivers and can include risks relating to marketing, production, technology, personnel, information systems and financial. (Note that this is not intended to be an exhaustive list of the sources of business risk.)

For example, the marketing risks which a business faces may include the chance that the product which they are selling going out of fashion. It may include the chance that a large and powerful competitor may enter the market and take traditional customers away. Another risk might be that due to a recession and the corresponding reduction in buying power, clients, and as a result sales decline. There may also be the risk of new government legislation being aimed at market controls which make the product too expensive for its traditional customers. Thus, from these examples, it may be seen that a risk can be a threat to the business.

If we considered production risks, there would be a similar list of issues, which may, for example, include the risk of a disruption in the supply of raw materials, or the risk of substantial price increases in essential services such as electricity and gas costs. Another risk could be that new legislation might require a much more costly regime of waste disposal in order to protect the environment.

It is not difficult to list similar types of risks for technology, personnel and information aspects of the business and the reader may do that for himself/herself. The category of risks referred to as financial risks are sometimes perceived to be different. Financial risks include the availability of credit, the cost of borrowing, the value (price) of the business' shares if they are quoted on the stock market. The issues which are discussed under this heading are often thought to be more volatile than those under the other more general business risks. But financial risks pose essentially the same sort of problems as other risks.

It is important for every organisation to be aware of the risks which it faces and there are no organisations which do not have a set of business and financial risks which directly affect them. Businesses need to assess the risks which they face and to take appropriate action. The assessment of risk is not a trivial matter and it requires considerable skill. The first step is to list all the possible risks, preferable by the major activities and functions of the business. Once this list is complete then an assessment needs to be made to estimate the likelihood of the risk occurring, as well as the amount of damage which the business could sustain if the risk materialises. The likelihood of the risk occurring is normally expressed on a scale from 0 (zero) to 1 where 0 means the risk will not actually occur and 1 means the risk will certainly occur[1]. You will recognise this as the description of probability, which was introduced in Section 9.2. Thus, a score of 0.50 suggest that there is a 50% chance that the risk will occur. However, there is no rigorous way of assessing the likelihood of a risk. It is simply a question of management judgement.

With regard to the question of how much damage a risk could do to the business, it is possible to make a more detailed and objective assessment of this and the use of financial estimates play a large role in this activity.

Once these numbers have been estimated then they may be used to calculate the expected value of a given risk. The expected value (EV) of a risk is the product of the chance (probability) of it happening multiplied by the size of the damage it will do to the organisation if the risk occurs. The expected value combines the probability and the damage of the result of the risk to give a figure which represents the relative importance of the risk to the business.

The calculation of expected value is for each item in the list of marketing risks is shown in Figure 9.13. Note that the expected value of the individual risks may be summed to give a total expected value of the risks emanating out of the marketing activity of the business.

---

[1] The zero and 1 positions are theoretically limits on a spectrum. If the possible threat is rated at 0 then it need not be included in risk analysis as it will not occur. If the possible threat is rated at 1 then it need not be included in risk analysis as it has either occurred or will certainly occur and therefore there is not the element of chance which is inherent in the definition of risk.

Marketing risks

Type of risk	Probability of occurrence	Estimate of financial damage	Expected value
Product out of fashion	0.30	1,200,000	360,000
Entry of big competitor	0.25	1,500,000	375,000
Recession	0.10	2,000,000	200,000
Legislation changes	0.05	3,000,000	150,000
Total Marketing risks			1,085,000

Figure 9.13 Individual marketing risks and their total expected value

From Figure 9.13 it may be seen that the most damaging risk which the business faces is the possibility of the entry of big competitor. If this occurs then the loss to the business is expected to be £375,000. The second greatest risk is the possibility that the product could go out of fashion. If this occurs then the loss to the business is expected to be £360,000. The size of the other risks may be read from Figure 9.13.

In a similar way, analyses may be undertaken for other risks; production, technology, personnel, information systems and financial.

There are two courses of action which management may take in the face of these risks. The first is to initiate risk avoidance measures, and the second is to establish a programme which will mitigate the impact of the risk if it should occur. However, a detailed discussion of this is beyond the scope of this book.

The technique described above whereby the expected values are calculated, may also be applied to other business calculations in which it is appropriate to include risk assessments. There are two major approaches to this. Both approaches call for the use of a range of estimates of the projected values of cost and benefits for the production of budgets. These techniques are frequently used in capital investment appraisal or assessment. By using the maximum estimated and the minimum estimated values, a range of possible outcomes for the investment are calculated. The results of these calculations which will be a range of values themselves will show the result of the investment if the impact of the risks are minimal i.e. few of the threats materialise, and also the result of the investment if the impact of the risks are large i.e. most of the threats materialise. Management judgement is then required to decide which of these scenarios is the most plausible.

There are sophisticated variations of this approach which use a technique known as Monte Carlo simulation, although this is beyond the scope of this book.

Before concluding this section it is appropriate to more comprehensively define risk in broad terms. The risk of a project is the inherent propensity of the estimates concerning the cost, time or benefits for the project not to be achieved in practice, due to foreseeable and unforeseeable circumstances.

Although risk is often spoken of in a negative context i.e. the project will cost more than budgeted for, or take longer than originally believed, it is obviously the case that sometimes projects are completed below budget and before their deadlines. Thus risk may enhance the potential of a project as well as detract from it.

It is clear that risk is based on the fact that the future is always unknowable or uncertain in the sense that we are unable to be sure of anything before it happens.

With regard to the concept of uncertainty when it is not possible to make any estimate of the probability or the impact of a future event or threat we do refer to its risk – rather we refer to *uncertainty*. For example, we cannot state with any degree of confidence about the risk that any large banks will become insolvent. This is because we have neither a way of estimating the chance nor a probability of that happening (nor the ability of estimating the impact that such an event would have on our society). However, we can safely say is that at present, the future of banks is uncertain.

Thus uncertainty may be thought of as a sort of risk about which nothing may be estimated. While risk is a concept which is used extensively by business and management practitioners, the concept of uncertainty is employed by economists when they are referring more generally about business affairs in the economy.

9.15 Summary

Probability can be defined from a complete list of equally like outcomes as

$$P(\text{event}) = \frac{\text{Total number of outcomes that constitute the event}}{\text{Total number of possible outcomes}}$$

This can be used in an *exact* sense when applied to the population of outcomes, or in an empirical, approximate sense when applied to a sample. *Subjective* probabilities arise from individuals' or a group's judgement.

The *additive law* of probability states that

$$P(X \text{ or } Y) = P(X) + P(Y) - P(X \text{ and } Y)$$

which becomes:

$$P(X \text{ or } Y) = P(X) + P(Y)$$

when X and Y are *mutually exclusive*.

The *multiplicative law* of probability states that:

$$P(X \text{ and } Y) = P(X) \times P(Y|X)$$

which becomes:

$$P(X \text{ and } Y) = P(X) \times P(Y)$$

when X and Y are *independent*.

Further, we saw the concept of a *discrete probability distribution* with its associated expected value:

$$E(X) = \Sigma XP$$

If, further, the probability of a certain outcome in a certain circumstance is P, then, in n independent repeats of the circumstance, the expected number of times the outcome will occur is nP.

The *expected value* (EV) criterion of decision-making consists of choosing the option giving the maximum expected return.

A *payoff table* is a method of setting out financial returns when faced with choosing between a number of options with a number of outcomes that are not dependent on the option chosen. A rectangular table can then be drawn to show the financial results of each combination of option and outcome.

A *normal distribution* is a bell-shaped continuous distribution, symmetric about its mean. It is completely defined by its mean, μ, and standard deviation, σ, and can be transformed to the standard normal distribution (mean 0 and standard deviation 1) by:

$$z = \frac{x - \mu}{\sigma}$$

If you know the variance of a distribution, the standard deviation can be found by taking its square root.

Venn diagrams may be used to assist in the calculation of probabilities.

Revision Questions

Part 9.1 Objective testing selection

> Questions 9.1.1–9.1.10 are standard multiple-choice questions with exactly one correct answer each. Thereafter, the style of question will vary.

9.1.1 A sample of 100 companies has been analysed by size and whether they pay invoices promptly.
   The sample has been cross-tabulated into *large/small* against *fast payers/slow payers*. Sixty of the companies are classified as *large*, of which forty are *slow payers*. In total, thirty of all the companies are *fast payers*.
   The probability that a company chosen at random is a *fast paying, small* company is:

   (A) 0.10
   (B) 0.20
   (C) 0.30
   (D) 0.40

9.1.2 In a group of 100 CIMA students, thirty are male, fifty-five are studying Foundation level, and six of the male students are not studying Foundation level. A student chosen at random is female. What is the probability that she is not studying Foundation level?

   (A) 0.80
   (B) 0.56
   (C) 0.44
   (D) 0.20

9.1.3 A sales representative makes calls to three separate unrelated customers. The chance of making a sale at any one of them is 60 per cent. The probability that a sale is made on the third call only is:

   (A) 0.096
   (B) 0.216
   (C) 0.36
   (D) 0.4

9.1.4 A normal distribution has a mean of 55 and a variance of 14.44. The probability of a score of 59 or more is approximately:

(A) 0.15
(B) 0.35
(C) 0.50
(D) 0.65

9.1.5 In a normally distributed population with a mean score of 850 and a standard deviation of 74.63, the lower quartile score will be approximately:

(A) 700
(B) 750
(C) 800
(D) 900

9.1.6 A company has a normally distributed sales pattern for one of its products, with a mean of £110. The probability of a sale worth more than £120 is 0.0119. Using normal tables, the standard deviation, to two decimal places, associated with sales is:

(A) 4.41
(B) 4.42
(C) 4.43
(D) 4.44

9.1.7 From past records it is known that 10 per cent of items from a production line are defective. If two items are selected at random, what is the probability that only one is defective?

(A) 0.09
(B) 0.10
(C) 0.18
(D) 0.20

9.1.8 A project may result in profits of £20,000 or £12,000, or in a loss of £5,000, with probabilities 0.3, 0.5 and 0.2, respectively. What is the expected profit?

(A) £11,000
(B) £27,000
(C) £9,000
(D) £12,000

9.1.9 Project S will result in profits of £2 m or £1.3 m, with probabilities 0.3 and 0.7, respectively. If Project T results in £1.5 m with probability p or alternatively £2.1 m, what is the value of p for which the projects are equally attractive under the expected value criterion?

(A) 0.3933
(B) 0.9167
(C) 0.9833
(D) 0.7

9.1.10 If weights are normally distributed with mean 65 kg and standard deviation 8 kg, what is the probability of a weight being less than 70 kg?

(A) 0.2357
(B) 0.7357
(C) 0.7643
(D) 0.2643

9.1.11 Associate each of the following rules of probability with one of the qualifying statements:

(A) $P(\text{not } A) = 1 - P(A)$
(B) $P(A \text{ or } B) = P(A) + P(B)$
(C) $P(A \text{ and } B) = P(A) \cdot P(B)$
(D) $P(A + B + C) = 1$

Qualifying statements:

(P) provided that the events are mutually exclusive.
(Q) for all such events.
(R) provided that the events cover all possible outcomes.
(S) provided that the events are independent.

9.1.12 Which of the following events is/are likely to be independent?

(A) Successive tosses of a coin.
(B) Successive selections of a card from a pack without replacement.
(C) Gender and shoe size.
(D) Breakdown of machines of different types and ages.

9.1.13 Use the data about the production of faulty or acceptable items in three departments to answer the probability questions. All items referred to in the questions are randomly selected from this sample of 361 items. Give all answers correct to four decimal places.

	\multicolumn{3}{c}{Department}		
	P	Q	R	Total
Faulty	6	13	3	22
Acceptable	94	195	50	339
Total	100	208	53	361

(a) What is the probability that an item is faulty?
(b) What is the probability that an item is from either department P or Q?
(c) What is the probability that an item is either from P or is faulty or both?
(d) What is the probability that two items are both faulty?
(e) What is the probability that, of two items, one is faulty and the other is acceptable?
(f) If an item is known to be from department P, what is the probability that it is faulty?
(g) If an item is faulty, what is the probability that it is from department P?

9.1.14 A firm produces 62 per cent of items in department A and the rest in department B. In A, 4 per cent of production is faulty whereas in B the proportion is 5 per cent. Complete the following table, giving answers correct to two decimal places.

	Department A	Department B	Total
Faulty	?	?	?
Acceptable	?	?	?
Total	?	?	100

9.1.15 A project may result in the following profits with the probabilities stated.

Profit	Probability
£50,000	0.2
£22,000	0.5
(£10,000)	0.3

Calculate the expected profit.

9.1.16 A decision-maker must choose between three projects with profit distributions and expected values (EV) as shown below:

Profits (£'000)	Good	State of the economy Average	Poor	EV
Probabilities	0.5	0.4	0.1	
Project P	26.0	6.0	(29.0)	12.5
Project Q	21.0	6.0	(9.0)	12.0
Project R	16.0	8.5	0.0	11.4

Which of the following comments is/are correct, if the decision-maker broadly follows the EV criterion?

(A) Using the EV criterion, project P should be chosen.
(B) A risk-averse decision-maker would probably choose option R.
(C) Option Q is much less risky than P and has only slightly less expected profit. It would be a good compromise choice.
(D) Project R should be chosen because it shows the highest profit when the economic situation is average.

9.1.17 Which of the following is/are limitations of the expected value criterion for decision-making, as compared with other decision criteria or methods?

(A) Virtually no decisions can be based only on financial considerations.
(B) All the profits and probabilities need to be estimated.
(C) It does not take account of the fact that circumstances may change.
(D) The method takes no account of the decision-maker's attitude to risk.

9.1.18 A variable, X, is normally distributed with mean 65 kg and standard deviation 8 kg. Find the following probabilities:

(A) $P(X > 69)$
(B) $P(X < 81)$
(C) $P(59 < X < 75)$

9.1.19 If a normal distribution has a standard deviation of 10 kg and it is known that 20 per cent of the items concerned weigh more than 50 kg, what is the value of the mean?

9.1.20 If 88.6 per cent of certain normally distributed items must have weights within 8 kg either side of the mean, what is the maximum allowable value of the standard deviation? (Give your answer correct to two decimal places.)

Part 9.2 Expected values and decision-making

A wholesaler buys a perishable commodity at £30 per case and sells it at £60 per case. Daily demand is uncertain, and any unsold cases at the end of the day are given without charge to a local charity and so represent a loss to the wholesaler.

Past records suggest that the pattern of demand is as follows:

Daily demand

Number of cases	Probability
20	0.20
21	0.40
22	0.30
23	0.10

The wholesaler wishes to know the amounts of stock to be purchased each day in order to maximise long-run profitability.

9.2.1 Complete the following table showing profit for each quantity bought and each level of demand by filling in the appropriate numerical values in the spaces indicated by the letters.

Conditional profit (£)

Sales demand (cases)	Quantity of stock bought (cases)			
	20	21	22	23
20	A	B	…	…
21	…	…	C	…
22	…	…	D	…
23	…	…	…	…

9.2.2 If 23 cases are bought, the conditional profits are as follows. Calculate the expected profit in this case.

Sales demand (cases)	23 cases bought conditional profit
20	510
21	570
22	630
23	690

9.2.3 If expected profits associated with the various numbers of cases bought per day were as follows, what number of cases should be bought daily?

	Number of cases bought			
	20	21	22	23
Expected profit	600	618	612	590

9.2.4 Which of the following most closely describes the distribution of demand?

(A) Slightly skewed
(B) Approximately normal
(C) Approximately uniform.

9.2.5 Which of the following describes the distribution of demand?

(A) Discrete
(B) Continuous

Part 9.3 Conditional and simple probabilities

A pharmaceutical company has developed a new headache treatment that is being field-tested on 1,000 volunteers. In a test, some volunteers have received the treatment and some a placebo (a harmless neutral substance). The results of the test are as follows:

	Treatment received	Placebo received
Some improvement	600	125
No improvement	150	125

Calculate the probabilities required in 9.3.1–9.3.4, giving your answers correct to three d.p.

9.3.1 The probability that a volunteer has shown some improvement.

9.3.2 The conditional probability that the volunteer has shown some improvement, given that he or she has received the treatment.

9.3.3 The conditional probability that the volunteer has received the treatment, given that no improvement has been observed.

9.3.4 The conditional probability that the volunteer has received the placebo, given that some improvement has been observed.

9.3.5 On the basis of this survey, does the treatment appear to be effective?

Part 9.4 Normal distribution; stock control

The Bell Curve Company carries out repair work on a variety of electronic equipment for its customers. It regularly uses a circuit board, Part Number X216. To replenish its stock of Part Number X216 takes 3 weeks (lead time) and during this time the average demand is 950 boards with a standard deviation of eighty boards.

Evidence suggests that the distribution of usage is normal. It has been company policy to keep a safety stock of 100 boards, so they order new stocks when existing stock reaches 1,050 boards.

9.4.1 Fill in the numerical values indicated by letters in the following calculation, giving your answers correct to two d.p. The standard normal variable is denoted by z.

The probability of not running out of stock of Part Number X216 during lead time
$= P(\text{demand in lead time} < A)$
$= P(z < B)$
$= C$

9.4.2 If the company wishes to improve the probability of not running out of stock to 99 per cent, they will need a higher level of safety stock. Fill in the numerical values indicated by letters in the following calculation of the necessary level of safety stock. Answers should be given correct to two d.p.

From Normal tables, the z-value which is greater than 99 per cent of Normal values is D. This corresponds to a demand level of E.

So safety stock = F

9.4.3 If the standard deviation of the distribution of usage were to increase, would the company need to hold more or less safety stock in order to satisfy the same level of service?

Part 9.5 Using venn diagrams

9.5.1 Given a probability of 0.2 that a man has trained as an accountant, and a probability of 0.3 that a man has trained as a salesperson, and a probability of 0.3 that a man has trained neither as an accountant nor as a salesman, what is the probability that he is both an accountant and a salesman?

Solutions to Revision Questions

9

✓ Solutions to Part 9.1

9.1.1 Answer: (A)

	Fast	Slow	Total
Large	20	40	60
Small	10	30	40
	30	70	100

$P(\text{fast and small}) = 10/100 = 0.1$

9.1.2 Answer: (B)

	Male	Female	Total
Foundation level	24	31	55
Not Foundation level	6	39	45
Total	30	70	100

$P(\text{not Foundation level}|\text{female}) = 39/70 = 0.56$
Answer (C) is on the right lines but $P(\text{Foundation level}|\text{female})$ and the other two answers have wrongly been obtained from the male column.

9.1.3 Answer: (A)
If $P(\text{sale}) = 0.6$ then $P(\text{no sale}) = 1 - 0.6 = 0.4$. Thus:
$P(\text{two no sales then one sale}) = 0.4 \times 0.4 \times 0.6 = 0.096$

9.1.4 Answer: (A)
Standard deviation $= \sqrt{14.44} = 3.8$
$$P(score > 59) = P\left(z > \frac{59 - 55}{3.8}\right) = P(z > 1.05)$$
$$= 0.5 - \text{normal table entry for } 1.05$$
$$= 0.5 - 0.3531$$
$$= 0.15 \text{ (two d.p.)}$$

9.1.5 Answer: (C)

In a normal population, the lower quartile will have 25 per cent of frequencies between itself and the mean. From tables, this corresponds to $z = 0.67$. Hence the lower quartile score is:

mean $- 0.67 \times$ standard deviation
$850 - 0.67 \times 74.63 = 800$

9.1.6 Answer: (B)

$$P(sale > 120) = 0.0119$$
$$P(110 < sale < 120) = 0.5 - 0.0119$$
$$= 0.4881$$

which corresponds to $z = 2.26$ from normal tables. Hence the gap of £10 between £110 and £120 corresponds to 2.26 standard deviations.

Standard deviation $= 10/2.26$
$= £4.42$

9.1.7 Answer: (C)

$$P(\text{defective}) = 0.1$$
$$P(\text{satisfactory}) = 0.9$$
$$P(\text{first defective, second not}) = 0.1 \times 0.9 = 0.09$$
$$P(\text{second defective, first not}) = 0.9 \times 0.1 = 0.09$$
$$\therefore P(\text{only one defective}) = 0.18$$

9.1.8 Answer: (A)

Expected profit $= 20 \times 0.3 + 12 \times 0.5 - 5 \times 0.2 = 11$ (£'000)

Answer (B) has simply totalled all possible profits, whereas (C) has averaged them without reference to their probabilities. (D) has selected the profit with the highest probability.

9.1.9 Answer: (C)

$$EV(S) = 2 \times 0.3 + 1.3 \times 0.7 = 1.51 \text{ (£m)}$$
$$EV(T) = 1.5P + 2.1(1 - P) = 2.1 - 0.6P$$

so the projects are equally attractive when $1.51 = 2.1 - 0.6P$, that is, when $P = 0.9833$ (four d.p.). In answer (A), the probability 1 has been taken instead of $(1 \times P)$. Answer (B) divided the profits of S by those of T, while answer (D) selected the higher of the two probabilities of S.

9.1.10 Answer: (B)

$$P(W < 70) = P[z < (70 - 65)/8] = P(z < 0.63) = 0.5 + \text{TE}(0.63)$$
$$= 0.5 + 0.2357 = 0.7357$$

The other answers have all correctly arrived at 0.2357 but have not added the 0.5 that covers all the negative z-values.

9.1.11 Associate each of the following rules of probability with one of the qualifying statements:

(A) $P(\text{not } A) = 1 - P(A)$ Q
(B) $P(A \text{ or } B) = P(A) + P(B)$ P
(C) $P(A \text{ and } B) = P(A) \cdot P(B)$ S
(D) $P(A + B + C) = 1$ R

9.1.12 The events that are likely to be independent are (A) and (D).

Successive selections of a card from a pack without replacement will involve probabilities changing as the number of cards is reduced and, in general, gender and shoe sizes tend to be related.

9.1.13 (a) $P(\text{faulty}) = 22/361 = 0.0609$
(b) $P(P \text{ or } Q) = (100 + 208)/361 = 0.8532$
(c) $P(P \text{ or faulty or both}) = (100 + 22 - 6)/361 = 0.3213$
(d) $P(\text{two items both faulty}) = P(\text{1st faulty}) \times P(\text{2nd faulty}) = (22/361) \times (21/360) = 0.0036$
(e) $P(\text{one faulty and other OK}) = 2 \times P(\text{1st faulty}) \times P(\text{2nd OK}) = 2 \times (22/361) \times (339/360) = 0.1148$
(f) $P(\text{faulty/from P}) = 6/100 = 0.06$
(g) $P(\text{from P/faulty}) = 6/22 = 0.2727$

9.1.14 The table should look as follows:

	Department A	Department B	Total
Faulty	2.48	1.90	4.38
Acceptable	59.52	36.10	95.62
Total	62.00	38.00	100.00

9.1.15 Expected profit $= 50 \times 0.2 + 22 \times 0.5 + (-10) \times 0.3 = 18$ (£'000).

9.1.16 (A) Correct.
(B) Correct.
(C) Correct.
(D) Incorrect: there is no commonly used decision criterion that would argue as in option (D), and the EV criterion would not do so.

9.1.17 (A) Yes.
(B),(C) No: both would be limitations regardless of which decision criterion or method was used.
(D) Yes.

9.1.18 (a) $P(X > 69) = P[Z > (69 - 65)/8] = P(Z > 0.5) = 0.5 - 0.1915 = 0.3085$

(b) $P(X < 81) = P[Z < (81 - 65)/8] = P(Z < 2) = 0.5 + 0.4772 = 0.9772$

(c) $P(59 < X < 75) = P[(59 - 65)/8 < Z < (75 - 65)/8] = P(-0.75 < Z < 1.25)$
$$= 0.2734 + 0.3944 = 0.6678$$

9.1.19 A total of 29.95 per cent of Z-values lie between 0 and 0.84, so 20 per cent of Z-values exceed 0.84. Hence 50 = mean + 0.84 standard deviations. Therefore, mean = $50 - 0.84 \times 10 = 41.6$.

9.1.20 A total of 44.3 per cent of Z-values lie between 0 and 1.58, so 88.6 per cent of weights are within 1.58 standard deviations either side of the mean. Hence 8 = 1.58 standard deviations.

Maximum standard deviation = $8/1.58 = 5.06$

✓ Solutions to Part 9.2

9.2.1 Consider the column headed '20'. This means that 20 cases are bought and all 20 will be sold, regardless of the level of demand. The sales revenue will be $20 \times £60$ and costs will be $20 \times £30$ giving profit of £600. If 21 items are bought, the profit will mostly be $21 \times £60 - 21 \times £30 = 630$ but not if demand is only 20. In this case profit = $20 \times £60 - 21 \times £30 = 570$. The rest of the table can be completed in a similar fashion and the results are shown below.

Conditional profit (£)

	Quantity of stock bought (cases)			
Sales demand (cases)	20	21	22	23
20	600	570	540	510
21	600	630	600	570
22	600	630	660	630
23	600	630	660	690

9.2.2 The expected profit is given by multiplying each conditional profit by its probability and then totalling. So, 510 is multiplied by 0.2 to give 102, 570 by 0.4 giving 228 and so on. The total of the expected values in the 23 column is the expected profit of £588 if the order is for 23 cases.

Expected profit (£)

Sales demand (cases)	Prob.	Expected profit
20	0.2	102
21	0.4	228
22	0.3	189
23	0.1	69
		588

9.2.3 The best choice is that which will return the highest expected profit.

Answer: 21

9.2.4 The probabilities are not all equal (i.e. uniform) nor are they symmetrical (i.e. approximately normal). They do reach their peak quite quickly and then tail away, which is the defining characteristic of a positively skewed distribution.

Answer: (A)

9.2.5 The variable in this case is the number of cases. It can only take whole number values and is therefore discrete.

Answer: (A)

✓ Solutions to Part 9.3

Initial workings

	Treatment received	Placebo received	Total
Some improvement	600	125	725
No improvement	150	125	275
Total	750	250	1,000

9.3.1 Prob. (some improvement) = 725/1,000 = 0.725

9.3.2 Prob. (some improvement/treatment received) = 600 improved/750 treated = 0.8

9.3.3 Prob. (treatment received/no improvement observed) = 150 treated/275 no improvement = 0.545

9.3.4 Prob. (placebo received/improvement observed) = 125 had placebo/725 improved = 0.172

9.3.5 Answer: Yes

✓ Solutions to Part 9.4

9.4.1 The probability of not running out of stock during lead time

$$= P(\text{demand in lead time} < 1{,}050)$$
$$= P(z < [1{,}050 - 950]/80)$$
$$= P(z < 1.25)$$
$$= 0.5 + \text{Normal table entry for } z = 1.25$$
$$= 0.5 + 0.3944$$
$$= 0.8944$$

Answers:

(A) 1,050
(B) 1.25
(C) 0.89

9.4.2 From Normal tables, the z-value which is greater than 99 per cent of Normal values is 2.33. This corresponds to a demand level of $950 + 2.33 \times 80 = 1{,}136.4$. So safety stock $= 1{,}136.4 - 950 = 186.4$

Answers:

(D) 2.33
(E) 1,136.4
(F) 186.4

9.4.3 If the standard deviation of demand gets larger it means that demand will become more variable and, specifically, that there will be higher levels of demand. Safety stock will have to be increased to cover these increased levels. Another way of looking at it is to say that safety stock $= 2.33 \times$ standard deviation (see Question 4.2) and so must increase as standard deviation increases.

Answer: More.

✓ Solutions to Part 9.5

9.5.1 Draw a Venn diagram showing the two sets of men, i.e. those who have trained as accountants (A) and those who have trained as salesmen (S).

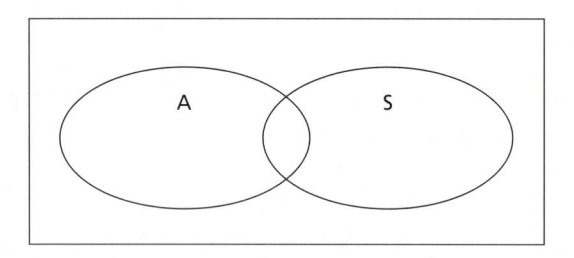

Insert the probabilities in the Venn diagram and begin calculations.

Let x be the probability that a man is trained as both an accountant and a salesman. This is represented by the intersection of the two ellipses.

Therefore A, which represents the men who are only trained as accountants is $0.2-x$ and S, which represents the mean who are only trained as salesmen is $0.3-x$.

We also know from our data that the probability of a man not being trained as an accountant nor as a salesman is 0.3.

This information can be added to the Venn Diagram.

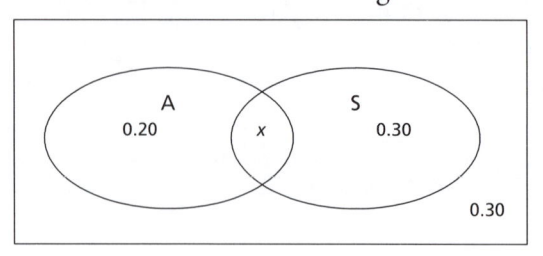

It is known that the sum of all the probabilities in the example is 1. Therefore the following equation can be constructed.

$$(0.2 - x) + x + (0.3 - x) + 0.3 = 1$$
$$0.8 - x = 1$$
$$-x = -0.2$$
$$x = 0.2$$

From this calculation the Venn diagram can be completed.

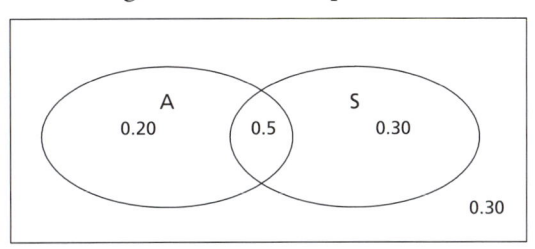

```
┌─────────────────────────────────────┐
│      ╭───A───╮ ╭───S───╮            │
│      │ 0.20  │ 0.5 │ 0.30 │         │
│      ╰───────╯ ╰───────╯            │
│                          0.30       │
└─────────────────────────────────────┘
```

10

Spreadsheet Skills using Excel

Spreadsheet Skills using Excel 10

LEARNING OUTCOMES

The objective of this chapter is to help you improve your understanding of how to use a spreadsheet in the business environment, especially with regards to financial forecasting and planning. This chapter assumes that you are familiar with the more basic operation of Excel and focuses on how to produce professional spreadsheets that minimise the amount of potential error that can occur.

After completing this chapter you should be able to:

- produce well-designed and robust spreadsheets;
- produce spreadsheets that can support management decision-making;
- understand how management accountants may make better use of a spreadsheet.

Please note that this chapter takes a different approach to the other chapters. In previous sections of the book, where appropriate we discussed the detailed use of Excel to perform specific tasks. In this chapter we look at how to design and maintain a higher standard of spreadsheet. Concepts in this chapter are addressed without using examples and solutions. Instead by working through this chapter you can develop a spreadsheet which incorporates all the good practices highlighted here.

10.1 Introduction

A spreadsheet is a multipurpose piece of software which may be used for calculations, drawing graphs or handling data in a way similar to a database program. All these functions are available in most spreadsheets at both an elementary level and a highly sophisticated level. In a spreadsheet like Excel, complex problems may be handled by using macros.

A spreadsheet may also be described as a computer program that allows data to be entered and formulae to be created in a tabular format. It was designed to mimic a large paper-based worksheet with many rows and columns. Spreadsheet information is stored in *cells* and the power of this technology lies in the way each cells can store numerical or alphabetical data or a formula for operating on other cells. A cell can also hold references to other spreadsheets or objects (such as graphics).

The first spreadsheet program was called VisiCalc (standing for Visible Calculator). The program was created by two American Computer Science researchers called Dan Bricklin and Bob Frankston and was first released through Software Arts in 1979. It was in 1982 that the next improvement in spreadsheet technology came about with the release of Lotus 1-2-3. A much faster running program and increased functionality helped Lotus 1-2-3 to become the market leader – a place it kept until 1989 when Excel arrived as part of Microsoft's Office suite of programs to run on its Windows operating system. Although Lotus produced a Windows version of 1-2-3, it did not stand up against the popularity of the Office suite and thus Excel has become the de facto spreadsheet in use today.

For any readers using an alternative, the basic functionality of most spreadsheets is pretty similar and the exercises and examples used in this book can still largely be followed.

> In your exam, it is important that you input your answer exactly how you would enter it into Excel, for example, including the leading = sign. It is, of course, possible to enter alternative, but equivalent correct formulae; the assessment software will handle this.

10.2 Spreadsheet terminology

It is worth clarifying the different application areas within the spreadsheet.

10.2.1 Workbooks and Worksheets

An Excel file is referred to as a *workbook*. A workbook can consist of a single *worksheet* or can be a combination of multiple worksheets, charts, databases etc. An Excel file is saved on disk with a .xls file extension.

10.2.2 Cells

A worksheet is described by column letters and row numbers and each row/column co-ordinate is referred to as a *cell*. In Excel there are 256 columns labelled A through IV and 65,536 rows. This in theory provides 16,777,216 cells into which information can be placed! In actual fact the number of cells that can really be used is restricted by the specification of the computer and the complexity of the data and formulae being worked on.

10.3 A note on macros and application development

It is possible in Excel to *record* a series of keystrokes and/or mouse clicks which can be stored in a *macro*. The macro can then be *run* whenever that series of keystrokes and/or mouse clicks is required. For example, to print a specific area of a spreadsheet, or to save a file with a particular name.

In addition to recordable macros, Excel has a powerful computer language called Visual Basic for Applications (VBA). With VBA it is possible to program the spreadsheet to perform in very individualistic ways.

The development and use of macros requires a substantial understanding of the spreadsheet and is thus beyond the scope of this book.

10.4 Getting started with Excel

When the Excel program is launched a blank spreadsheet is displayed. Figure 10.1 shows what this looks like and highlights some of the main features of the system.

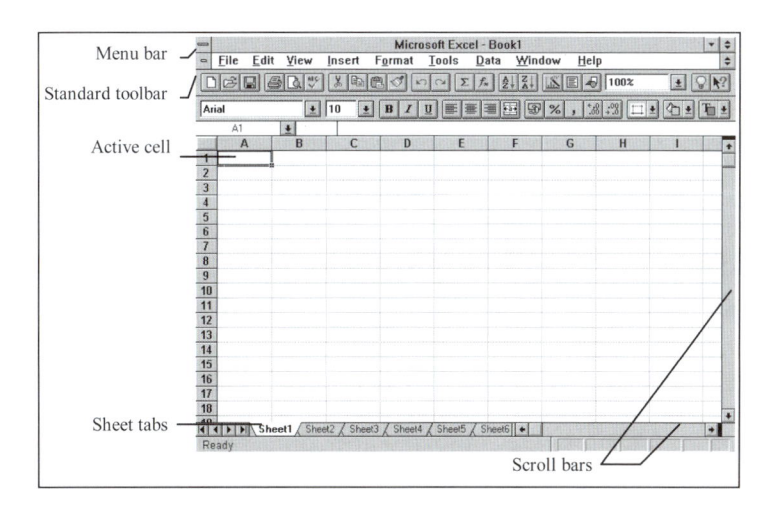

Figure 10.1 The Excel spreadsheet

Note: *This figure assumes that Excel has not been customised in any way. If your system has been installed with customised toolbars the screen may not look the same. It would be preferable to re-install Excel without customisation for the purposes of working with this book.*

10.4.1 Workbooks of files

When Excel is loaded a new, blank *workbook* is displayed as shown in Figure 10.1. This workbook is called BOOK1 and consists of a number of blank *worksheets*. Each worksheet is labelled on a tab at the bottom of the workbook. You will be able to customise the name of these worksheets as you use them, but at this stage they are labelled *Sheet 1, Sheet 2* etc. Sheets can be moved or copied between workbooks, and you can reorganise sheets within a workbook. In addition you can have several workbooks open at the same time, each in its own window.

10.4.2 Worksheets

Most of the work you do will use worksheets. As you can see in Figure 10.1 a worksheet is a grid of rows and columns, forming a series of *cells*. Each cell has a unique address. For example, the cell where column C and row 8 intersect is referred to as cell C8. You use cell references when you create formulae or reference cells in command instructions.

The *active* cell is the one into which data will be placed when you start typing. You can determine the active cell by the bold border it has around it. When you open a new workbook this will be cell A1 on Sheet1.

To change the active cell you can either use the directional arrow keys on the keyboard to move one cell at a time to the left, right, up or down, or you can use the mouse to move the pointer into the required cell and then click once on the left mouse button.

10.4.3 Scroll bars

To the right and the bottom right of the screen there are scroll bars which allow you to scroll up and down and left and right around the active window.

Click on the down arrow in the vertical scroll bar which will scroll the worksheet down by one row.

10.4.4 Status bar

At the bottom of the screen are the horizontal scroll bar and the status bar which display information about the current document or the task you are working on. The exact information displayed will vary according to what you are doing. When you open a new workbook there are indicators to the right of the status bar that are highlighted if the CAPS LOCK key, NUM LOCK key or SCROLL LOCK key is activated.

10.4.5 Toolbars

As in all Windows applications the toolbars allow quick access to commonly used commands. On starting Excel the Standard and Formatting toolbars are displayed.

Move the pointer over one of the toolbar buttons and notice the name is displayed in a small box below the selected button. This is called a *ToolTip*. A brief description of what the button does is displayed.

10.5 Good spreadsheet design

Whether a spreadsheet is being developed for specific business mathematical calculations or as a forecasting plan, a profit and loss account or a marketing plan it is essential that duecare and attention be given to its design and structure. Establishing some rules as to how all the spreadsheets in a department or organisation are developed enables different people to look at different plans and feel familiar with the layout, style, reports, charts, etc. This is in much the same way as users feel familiar with software applications that have a similar interface such as those in the Microsoft Office suite of products.

The objectives of good design in spreadsheet terms are exactly the same as those required for any other software development:

1. to ensure that the spreadsheet is as error free as possible;
2. to ensure that the spreadsheet can be used without much training or control;
3. to minimise the work required to enhance or change the spreadsheet.

If care is taken to ensure sound structure and good design a spreadsheet will be straightforward to develop, easy to read, simple to use, not difficult to change and will produce the required results.

The plan developed over a number of stages in this chapter illustrates a variety of aspects of the principles of spreadsheet design and development. The series begins with a plan that has had little or no thought put into its design and layout and as the chapter proceeds ways of improving and enhancing the plan are identified and explained.

FUNDAMENTALS OF BUSINESS MATHEMATICS

10.6 Getting started

The spreadsheet in Figure 10.2 is a simple profit projection that may be of use to the author, but is unlikely to be helpful to anyone else. This is clearly a quick one-off plan which has been prepared with very little care and which may well not even be saved on the disk.

	A	B	C	D	E
1	sales	150	173	198	228
2	price	12.55	12.55	12.55	12.55
3	revenue	1883	2165	2490	2863
4	costs	1185	1362	1567	1802
5	profit	698	803	923	1061
6					

Figure 10.2 Simple profit projection

10.6.1 Problems with this spreadsheet

The immediately obvious problems with this spreadsheet are that it has no title, it is not clear what the columns represent, i.e. are they different periods or perhaps different products, and the author is unknown.

With regards the data itself, the figures are hard to read as there are varying numbers of decimal places. Whilst perhaps there has been a growth in sales and price, the percentage has not been indicated. The costs line could be misleading as no indication of where the costs have been derived is supplied.

10.6.2 Positive aspects of this spreadsheet

If the author of the spreadsheet required a quick profit estimation based on known data and growth rates for sales units, price and costs then the spreadsheet has supplied that information quickly and in a more concise form than would have been achievable using a calculator and recording the results on paper.

10.7 Ownership and version

In Figure 10.3 the three major shortfalls of the first spreadsheet have been remedied. The plan has also been given a title and author details have been included. It is important that

	A	B	C	D	E	F	G	H	I
1	Profit Projection for Widget Division for 20XX						Last updated:	Jan 20XX	
2		Written by P.A. Jones							
3		pajones@business.com							
4		0118 999 9999							
5									
6									
7			Qtr 1	Qtr 2	Qtr 3	Qtr 4			
8	sales		150	175	195	220			
9	price		12.55	12.55	12.55	12.55			
10	revenue		1882.5	2196.25	2447.25	2761			
11	costs		1184.55	1381.975	1539.915	1737.34			
12	profit		697.95	814.275	907.335	1023.66			
13									
14									
15									
16									

Figure 10.3 Incorporating some annotation

every business plan have a clear owner who is responsible for overseeing the accuracy and maintenance of the system. A name plus some form of contact details should always be included.

10.7.1 Problems with this spreadsheet

The construction of the data and results is still unclear and the lack of formatting makes the figures hard to read. The costs remain grouped together.

10.7.2 Positive aspects of this spreadsheet

In addition to the owner details having been added to the plan, the date when the plan was written is a useful feature. The date becomes particularly important when the question of spreadsheet versions arise. Note that the date has been entered here as text. If a DATE function had been used it would be continually updated each time the file is retrieved, whereas here it is the date of the last update that is required. The ruling lines above and below specific sections of the spreadsheet are also quite helpful. This can be quickly achieved using the automatic formatting features. These are accessed via the Format Autoformat command.

10.8 Formatting

In Figure 10.4 the data for the four quarters is totalled and reported as an annual figure. The values in the plan have also been formatted with the majority of figures being formatted to zero decimal places and the price line to two decimal places.

One of the automatic formatting options has been selected to shade and outline the plan.

10.8.1 Problems with this spreadsheet

By looking at the plan in Figure 10.4 it can be seen that the sales and the costs both increase over time. However it is not clear by how much because the sales growth factor and the increase in costs have been incorporated into the formulae as absolute references.

The inclusion of absolute values in formulae is not recommended and can lead to GIGO. To change the sales growth factor in Figure 10.4 two processes are required. First, cell c5 is

	A	B	C	D	E	F	G	H	I
1		Profit Projection for Widget Division for 20XX					Last updated:	Jan 20XX	
2		Written by P.A. Jones							
3		pajones@business.com							
4		0118 999 9999							
5									
6		Qtr 1	Qtr 2	Qtr 3	Qtr 4	Total			
7	sales	150	173	198	228	749			
8	price	12.55	12.55	12.55	12.55				
9	revenue	1883	2165	2490	2863	9400			
10	costs	1185	1362	1567	1802	5915			
11	profit	698	803	923	1061	3485			
12									
13									
14	Report Printed		22-Mar-05	12:29:57					

Figure 10.4 Formatting the plan

accessed and the edit key pressed. The growth factor is changed and enter is pressed. This has changed the formula in this one cell, but only once the formula has been extrapolated across into cells D5 and D6 is the amendment complete. It is not difficult to see that there is room for error here in a number of different ways.

10.8.2 Positive aspects of this spreadsheet

Having a current date and time indicator displayed on the spreadsheet ensures that a hard copy report will reflect the date, and perhaps more importantly the time it was printed. This is achieved through the NOW( ) function, which can be formatted with a range of different display options. Because it is likely that a spreadsheet will be recalculated, even if it is set to manual calculation, before printing, the date and time will always be up to date. It is of course possible to include the date and time in headers and footers, but during the development phase of a system the page layout is less relevant than printing the section being worked on and so thought should be given to the positioning of the NOW function.

The cells in this plan have now been formatted, which makes the data easier to read. When formatting a spreadsheet it is important to consider the entire plan and not just the cells that are currently being worked on. The entire spreadsheet should be formatted to the degree of accuracy required for the majority of the plan then those cells that need to be different, such as percentages, can be reformatted accordingly. This is quickly achieved by right clicking on the top left corner of the spreadsheet at the intersection between the column letters and row numbers and then select format cells. Whatever formatting is now applied will affect the entire worksheet.

It is important to understand that formatting cells only changes the display and does not affect the results of calculations that are still performed to the full degree of accuracy, which is usually 16 significant decimal places. This is why a cell containing the sum of a range of cells might display an answer that does not agree with the result of visually adding the values in the range.

The only safe way to ensure that the results of a calculation are actually rounded to a given number of decimal places the ROUND function is required. Figure 10.5 shows two

	A	B	C	D	E	F
14	Costs					
15	Administration	1500	1576	1656	1739	6471
16	Depreciation	1500	1553	1607	1663	6322
17	Finance Charges	1200	1288	1382	1482	5352
18	Maintenance	600	630	662	696	2588
19	Salary Expenses	13000	13858	14773	15748	57378
20	Total Other Costs	17800	18904	20079	21328	78112
21						
22	Net Profit B.T.	200	1102	2060	3076	6438
23						

Table A

	A	B	C	D	E	F
14	Costs					
15	Administration	1500	1576	1656	1739	6471
16	Depreciation	1500	1553	1607	1663	6322
17	Finance Charges	1200	1288	1382	1482	5352
18	Maintenance	600	630	662	696	2588
19	Salary Expenses	13000	13858	14773	15748	57378
20	Total Other Costs	17800	18904	20079	21328	78111
21						
22	Net Profit B.T.	200	1102	2060	3076	6438
23						

Table B

Figure 10.5 Difference between rounding and formatting cells

tables representing the same extract from a profit and loss account. In both cases all the cells have been formatted to zero decimal places, but in Table B the ROUND function has been incorporated in the formulae for cells F15 through F20.

The formula entered into cell F15, which can then be copied for the other line items is: = ROUND(SUM(B15:E15),0)

The effect of the ROUND function can be seen in cell F20. By visually adding up the numbers in the range F15 through F19 the result is 78111 whereas the formatting of these cells without the use of the ROUND function in Table A returns a value of 78112 in cell F20. Having applied the ROUND function to a cell any future reference made to that cell will use the rounded value.

Excel does offer an alternative to the ROUND function in the Precision as displayed option within TOOLS:OPTIONS:CALCULATION. This command assumes that calculations will be performed to the level of accuracy currently displayed. The danger of using this command is that when data is changed or added to the spreadsheet the command is no longer valid and it is then necessary to repeat the command to update the spreadsheet – this is another invitation to GIGO.

10.9 Documentation

Spreadsheet developers are notoriously bad at supplying documentation and other supporting information about the plan. There are a number of features offered by Excel to assist in the documenting of plans including the INSERT COMMENT command. Figure 10.6 shows a comment being entered onto a plan – notice how the user name of the comment author is included. This is useful when a team of people are working on a system. The presence of a comment is indicated by a small red triangle on the cell – to read the comment move the cursor over the cell and it will automatically be displayed. A word of caution concerning the use of comment boxes – they take up a considerable amount of space and if used widely they can make a noticeable difference to the size of a file. To clear all the comments use the EDIT CLEAR COMMENTS command.

The provision of a hard copy report showing the logic used to create a plan is also helpful as this is the ultimate reference point if a formula has been overwritten and needs to be reconstructed.

In Excel there is a shortcut key to display the formulae which is CTRL + (accent grave). Alternatively this can be achieved through the TOOLS OPTIONS VIEW command and then check the Formulas box.

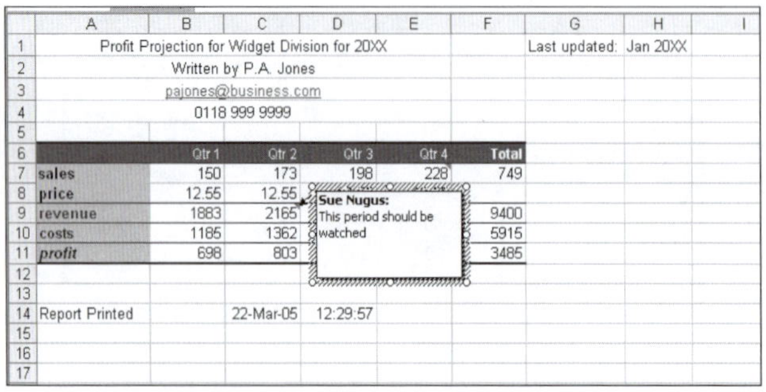

Figure 10.6 Inserting comments

	A	B	C	D	E	F
1						
2			Written by P.A. Jones			
3			pajones@business.com			
4			0118 999 9999			
5						
6		Qtr 1	Qtr 2	Qtr 3	Qtr 4	Total
7	sales	150	=B7*1.15	=C7*1.15	=D7*1.15	=SUM(B7:E7)
8	price	12.55	12.55	12.55	12.55	
9	revenue	=B7*B8	=C7*C8	=D7*D8	=E7*E8	=SUM(B9:E9)
10	costs	=B7*7.897	=C7*7.897	=D7*7.897	=E7*7.897	=SUM(B10:E10)
11	profit	=B9-B10	=C9-C10	=D9-D10	=E9-E10	=SUM(B11:E11)
12						
13						
14	Report Printed		=NOW()	=NOW()		
15						
16						
17						
18						
19						

Figure 10.7 Report showing formulae

In addition to providing documentation for a spreadsheet system, looking at the contents of the cells as opposed to the results can also be a helpful auditing tool. For example, Figure 10.7 highlights the fact that there are still values embedded in formulae which is not good practice and is addressed in the next version of the plan.

A third form of documentation which can be particularly useful for large systems is the 'sentence at the end of the row' technique. Requiring less file space than comment boxes, and always on view it can be useful to have a brief description of the activity taking place in each row of a plan.

10.10 Minimising absolute values

One of the reasons that spreadsheets have become such an integral part of the way we do business is the fact that they facilitate quick, easy and inexpensive what-if analysis. What-if analysis may be defined as the process of investigating the effect of changes to assumptions on the objective function of a business plan.

Performing what-if analysis on the opening sales assumption or the opening price assumption is quite straightforward, involving placing the cursor on the figure and entering the new value. On pressing ENTER the spreadsheet is re-evaluated and all cells which refer to the changed values, either directly or indirectly are updated.

The success of performing even the simplest what-if analysis is dependent on the spreadsheet having been developed with the correct series of relationships. For example, changing the opening sales value in Figure 10.8 would automatically cause the other quarter sales values to recalculate, as well as the revenue, costs and profit lines, because they relate, through the cell references in the formulae, either directly or indirectly to the sales value in cell B5.

	A	B	C	D	E	F
1						
2			Written by P.A. Jones			
3			pajones@business.com			
4			0118 999 9999			
5						
6		Qtr 1	Qtr 2	Qtr 3	Qtr 4	Total
7	sales	150	=B7*1.15	=C7*1.15	=D7*1.15	=SUM(B7:E7)
8	price	12.55	12.55	12.55	12.55	
9	revenue	=B7*B8	=C7*C8	=D7*D8	=E7*E8	=SUM(B9:E9)
10	costs	=B7*7.897	=C7*7.897	=D7*7.897	=E7*7.897	=SUM(B10:E10)
11	profit	=B9-B10	=C9-C10	=D9-D10	=E9-E10	=SUM(B11:E11)
12						
13						
14	Report Printed		=NOW()	=NOW()		
15						
16						
17						
18						
19						

Figure 10.8 Absolute values restricting what-if analysis

However, as already mentioned this plan incorporates absolute values in the formulae for sales and costs growth. Furthermore, the price is a fixed value and has been entered once into cell B6 and the value has then been copied into the other periods. This presents problems when what-if analysis is required on any of these factors.

10.10.1 Problems with this spreadsheet

Because no growth in the price is required the opening value of 12.55 has been copied for the four quarters. Whilst this is fine all the time a price of 12.55 is required, it presents a problem when the price requires changing. With this spreadsheet it would be necessary to overwrite the price in the first quarter and then copy the new value for the remaining three quarters. The same applies if the sales growth or the cost factors required changing.

To prevent these problems arising, a different approach to the development of the plan needs to be taken.

In the first instance all growth and cost factors should be represented in a separate area of the spreadsheet – even on a different sheet altogether in the case of a large system with a lot of input. The factors can then be referenced from within the plan as and when they are required. Figure 10.9 shows the adapted layout for this plan after extracting the sales growth and costs factors.

	A	B	C	D	E	F	G	H
1		Profit Projection for Widget Division for 20XX					Last updated:	Jan 20XX
2		Written by P.A. Jones						
3		pajones@business.com						
4		0118 999 9999						
5								
6								
7		Qtr 1	Qtr 2	Qtr 3	Qtr 4	Total		
8	sales	150	152	153	155	609		
9	price	12.55	12.61	12.68	12.74			
10	revenue	1883	1911	1940	1969	7703		
11	costs	1125	1136	1148	1159	4569		
12	profit	758	775	792	810	3134		
13								
14								
15	Growth in Sales Volume as %			1.01%				
16	Growth in Price as %			0.5%				
17	Cost per unit of production			7.50				
18								
19	Report Printed	22-Mar-05	13:00:00					
20								
21								
22								

Figure 10.9 Using cell references for non-changing values

Having the growth and cost factors in separate cells means that the formulae need to be changed to pick up this information. Figure 10.10 shows the amended formulae for this plan.

Note that the references to cells D15, D16 and D17 are fixed references. This is achieved by placing the $ symbol before the column letter and row number, i.e. $D$15, and means that when the formula is copied the reference to cell D15 remains fixed. A shortcut key to add the $ symbols to a cell reference is F4.

	A	B	C	D	E	F
1		Profit Projection for Widget Division for 20XX				Last
2		Written by P.A. Jones				
3		pajones@business.com				
4		0118 999 9999				
5						
6						
7		Qtr 1	Qtr 2	Qtr 3	Qtr 4	Total
8	sales	150	=B8*(1+$D$15)	=C8*(1+$D$15)	=D8*(1+$D$15)	=SUM(B8:E8)
9	price	12.55	=B9*(1+$D$16)	=C9*(1+$D$16)	=D9*(1+$D$16)	
10	revenue	=B8*B9	=C8*C9	=D8*D9	=E8*E9	=SUM(B10:E10)
11	costs	=B8*$D$17	=C8*$D$17	=D8*$D$17	=E8*$D$17	=SUM(B11:E11)
12	profit	=B10-B11	=C10-C11	=D10-D11	=E10-E11	=SUM(B12:E12)
13						
14						
15	Growth in Sales Volume as %			0.01		
16	Growth in Price as %			0		
17	Cost per unit of production			7.5		
18						
19	Report Printed	=NOW()	=NOW()			
20						
21						

Figure 10.10 Amended formulae to take account of extracted growth and cost factors

In this plan an option in the growth factors has been included for the price, despite the fact that in this plan the price does not change. It is important to always think ahead when developing any plan and although the price does not currently change, it might be necessary to include a percentage increase in the future. Having the facility for change built-in to the plan could save time later – and for the time being the growth factor is simply set to zero.

Removing the growth and cost factors from the main body of a business plan is the first step in developing a data input form which will ultimately separate all the input data from the actual logic of the spreadsheet. This separation of the data allows the logic cells to be protected from accidental damage. This is discussed further in the Template section of this chapter.

10.11 Control checks for auditing

As already mentioned, spreadsheet users are not inherently good at auditing plans as thoroughly as perhaps they should, and therefore an important aspect of spreadsheet design is to build into the system checks on the arithmetical accuracy that will raise the alarm if things begin to go wrong. This might include validating input data through the use of an IF function, or performing a cross-check on a calculation.

When creating calculation checks the first step is to select a number of key items from the model, whose result can be calculated using a different arithmetic reference. A separate sheet can be allocated for data validation and arithmetic checks. For example, in Figure 10.11 below the Year End Gross Profit has been calculated by referencing the individual total values in column F and then by totalling the values in the Gross Profit row. An if function is then applied to compare the two results and if they are not the same the word 'error' is displayed in cell D8.

	A	B	C	D	E	F
1						
2						
3						
4		Arithmetic Check on Year End Gross Profit				
5						
6		Vertical total		37925		
7		Horizontal total		37925		
8		Difference		OK		

Figure 10.11 Cross-check control box

The formulae required in cells D6 and D7, which calculate the year-end gross profit from the plan illustrated in Figure 10.11 are:

For the vertical total

= 'P&L Account'!F10-'P&L Account'!F17-'P&L Account'!F19

and for the horizontal total

= sum('P&L Account'!B23:E24)

The formula in cell 8 is an if function that compares the two cells as follows:

= IF(D6 < > D7,"error","OK")

A macro could also be created that alerts the user if the arithmetic does not balance, probably by sounding a beep and going to a suitable message screen.

10.12 Charts

It is useful to support the information supplied in business plans with charts. In the profit and loss account used in this chapter various charts might be useful, for example to show the relative impact of price and sales volume figures. Although charts can be placed on the same worksheet as the plan, it is usually preferable to keep graphs on separate *chart sheets*. The exception might be if it is appropriate to view changes on a chart at the same time data in the plan is changed, or if a spreadsheet is to be copied into a management report being created in Word. Figure 10.12 is an example of the type of chart that might be produced from the plan used in this chapter.

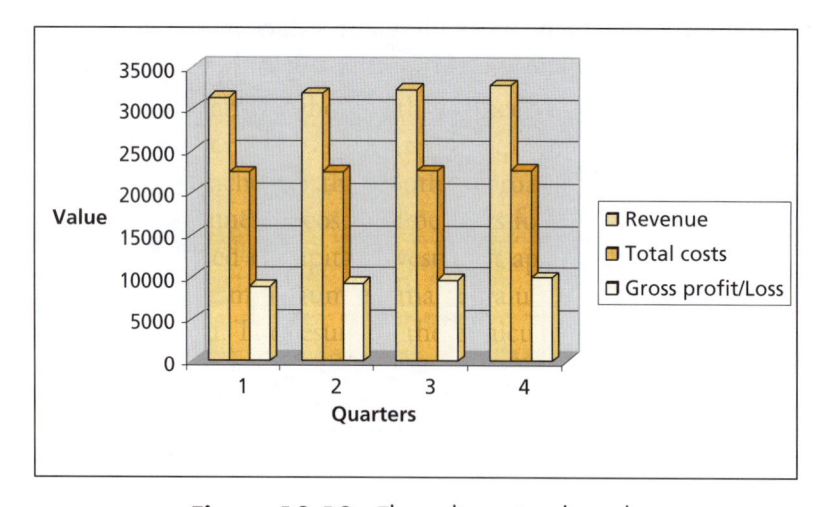

Figure 10.12 Three-dimensional graph

10.13 Tips for larger plans

The plan used in this chapter has been a simple quarterly plan, but in many cases business plans will be larger and more complex. Figure 10.13 is an extract from a five-year quarterly plan. Although it is not obvious by looking at Figure 10.13, each year in this report has been formatted with a different colour font. This is a useful technique when working with large models because it enables the user to quickly know which part of the plan is being viewed or worked on, without having to scroll around the spreadsheet to see the titles.

	A	B	C	D	E	F	G	H	I	J	K
1	Five Year Profit Projection for Widget Division for 1998										
2	Written by P.A. Jones 31 July 1997										
3											
4		Y1 Qtr 1	Y1 Qtr 2	Y1 Qtr 3	Y2 Qtr 4	Y1 Total	Y2 Qtr 1	Y2 Qtr 2	Y2 Qtr 3	Y2 Qtr 4	Y2 Total
5	Sales Volume	8000	8080	8161	8242	32483	12000	12000	12000	12000	48000
6	Price	50.00	50.75	51.51	52.28		67.00	67.00	67.00	67.00	
7	Revenue	400000	410060	420373	430945	1661378	804000	804000	804000	804000	3216000
8											
9	Raw Materials	96000	96960	97930	98909	389798	180000	180000	180000	180000	720000
10	Labour	12000	12060	12120	12181	48361	15000	15150	15302	15455	60906
11	Energy	9600	9792	9988	10188	39567	10000	10050	10100	10151	40301
12	Depreciation	2000	2020	2040	2061	8121	2500	2519	2538	2557	10113
13	Total Direct Costs	119600	120832	122078	123338	485848	207500	207719	207939	208162	831320
14											
15	Gross Profit	280400	289228	298295	307607	1175530	596500	596281	596061	595838	2384680
16	Overheads	20000	20300	20605	20914	81818	22000	22220	22442	22667	89329
17											
18	Net Profit	260400	268928	277691	286694	1093712	574500	574061	573618	573171	2295351

Figure 10.13 Five-year extended plan

This colour coding can then be carried over to summary reports, and other reports pertaining to the different parts of the plan.

From a design point of view it is preferable to place different reports associated with a plan on separate worksheets. The report in Figure 10.14, which has been placed on a separate sheet called *Summary* is created by referencing the cells from the yearly totals in the main plan.

	A	B	C	D	E	F	G
1	Five Year Summary Profit Projection for Widget Division for 1998						
2	Written by P.A. Jones 31 July 1997						
3							
4		Y1 Total	Y2 Total	Y3 Total	Y4 Total	Y5 Total	5 yr Total
5	Sales Volume	32483	48000	60452	72542	90675	304152
6	Average Annual Price	51.14	67.00	70.97	71.06	71.06	
7	Revenue	1661378	3216000	4290334	5154924	6444709	20767344
8							
9	Raw Materials	389798	720000	1027676	1233211	1813508	5184192
10	Labour	48361	60906	64966	68000	70067	312301
11	Energy	39567	40301	40301	48361	113750	282281
12	Depreciation	8121	10113	10113	12090	12945	53382
13	Total Direct Costs	485848	831320	1143056	1361662	2010270	5832156
14							
15	Gross Profit	1175530	2384680	3147278	3793262	4434439	14935189
16	Overheads	81818	89329	89329	89329	97816	447621
17							
18	Net Profit	1093712	2295351	3057949	3703933	4336623	14487568

Figure 10.14 Summary report

10.14 Templates

A business plan that requires time and effort to design and implement is likely to be in regular use for some time. In addition, the data in the plan will almost certainly change, either as situations within the business change, or on a periodic basis. In such circumstances it is advisable to convert the developed plan into a template, into which different data can be entered whenever necessary.

A template is a plan that contains the logic required, i.e the formulae, but from which the data has been removed. When new data is entered so the formulae will be calculated. Figure 10.15 shows the simplest approach to creating a template. Taking the one-year

	A	B	C	D	E	F	G	H
1	Profit Projection for Widget Division for 20XX						Last Updated	31 July 20XX
2	Written by P.A. Jones 31 July 20XX							
3	pajones@business.com							
4	0118 999 9999							
5								
6								
7		Qtr 1	Qtr 2	Qtr 3	Qtr 4	Total		
8	Sales volume		0	0	0	0		
9	Unit price		0.00	0.00	0.00			
10	Revenue	0	0	0	0	0		
11								
12	Costs							
13	Raw Materials	0	0	0	0	0		
14	Labour		0	0	0	0		
15	Energy		0	0	0	0		
16	Depreciation		0	0	0	0		
17	Total direct costs	0	0	0	0	0		
18								
19	Overheads		0	0	0	0		
20								
21	Total Costs	0	0	0	0	0		
22								
23	Gross Profit/Loss	0	0	0	0	0		
24								
25	*Factors*							
26	Growth in sales volume as %							
27	Growth in Price as %							
28	Cost of raw materials							
29	Labour cost increase							
30	Energy cost increase							
31								
32								

Figure 10.15 Plan converted to a template

quarterly plan used in this chapter the input data and growth factors have been removed and these cells have been highlighted by shading the cells.

When the input cells are set to zero, all other cells that are directly or indirectly related to those cells should also display zero. The only exception to this is if there are division formulae in which case a division by zero error will be displayed. The act of removing the data is in itself a useful auditing tool, because if values are found in any cells this indicates that there is an error in the way that the plan was developed which can be rectified.

When the template is complete the spreadsheet should be protected and then only the input cells unprotected in order that the user can only enter data into the designated cells. This is a two-step process. First, the cells into which data can be entered are unprotected using the FORMAT CELLS PROTECTION command and removing the tick on the Locked box. The second step is to then enable protection by selecting Tools Protection Protect Sheet.

It is also important to save the file now as a Template file as opposed to a Worksheet file. This is achieved by selecting FILE SAVE AS TEMPLATE (.XLT) in the FILE TYPE box. The location of the template file defaults to the directory where other Microsoft Office template files are located. To use the template FILE NEW is selected which accesses the Template directory and when a file is selected a copy of it is opened, leaving the original template unchanged on the disk.

10.14.1 Data input forms

A further enhancement that makes working with templates easier to control is to remove all the data from the main plan and place it on one or more data input forms which will normally be located on separate worksheets. Figure 10.16 is a data input form for the quarterly plan, and Figure 10.17 shows the amended formulae in the plan which picks up the data from the input form.

	A	B	C	D
1	Profit Projection for Widget Division for 20XX			
2	Data Input Form			
3		Opening input	Growth or cost factor	
4	Sales volume	0.00	0.00%	
5	Unit price	0.00	0.00%	
6				
7	Costs			
8	Labour	0.00	0.00%	
9	Cost of raw materials	n/a	0.00	
10	Energy	0.00	0.00%	
11	Depreciation	0.00	0.00%	
12				
13	Overheads	0.00	0.00%	
14				
15				
16				

Figure 10.16 Data input form

	A	B	C	D	E	F	
1			Profit Projection for Widget Division for 20XX				Last Update
2			Written by P.A. Jones 31 July 20XX				
3			pajones@business.com				
4			0118 999 9999				
5							
6							
7		Qtr 1	Qtr 2	Qtr 3	Qtr 4	Total	
8	Sales volume	='Input form'!B4	=B8*(1+'Input form'!$C$4)	=C8*(1+'Input form'!$C$4)	=D8*(1+'Input form'!$C$4)	=SUM(B8:E8)	
9	Unit price	='Input form'!B5	=B9*(1+'Input form'!$C$5)	=C9*(1+'Input form'!$C$5)	=D9*(1+'Input form'!$C$5)		
10	Revenue	=B8*B9	=C8*C9	=D8*D9	=E8*E9	=SUM(B10:E10)	
11							
12	Costs						
13	Labour	='Input form'!B8	=B13*(1+'Input form'!$C$8)	=C13*(1+'Input form'!$C$8)	=D13*(1+'Input form'!$C$8)	=SUM(B13:E13)	
14	Raw Materials	=B8*'Input form'!$C$9	=C8*'Input form'!$C$9	=D8*'Input form'!$C$9	=E8*'Input form'!$C$9	=SUM(B14:E14)	
15	Energy	='Input form'!B10	=B15*(1+'Input form'!$C$10)	=C15*(1+'Input form'!$C$10)	=D15*(1+'Input form'!$C$10)	=SUM(B15:E15)	
16	Depreciation	='Input form'!B11	=B16*(1+'Input form'!$C$11)	=C16*(1+'Input form'!$C$11)	=D16*(1+'Input form'!$C$11)	=SUM(B16:E16)	
17	Total direct costs	=SUM(B13:B16)	=SUM(C13:C16)	=SUM(D13:D16)	=SUM(E13:E16)	=SUM(F14:F16)	
18							
19	Overheads	='Input form'!B13	=B19*(1+'Input form'!$C$13)	=C19*(1+'Input form'!$C$13)	=D19*(1+'Input form'!$C$13)	=SUM(B19:E19)	
20							
21	Total Costs	=B17+B19	=C17+C19	=D17+D19	=E17+E19	=F17+F19	
22							
23	Gross Profit/Loss	=B10-B21	=C10-C21	=D10-D21	=E10-E21	=F10-F21	
24							

Figure 10.17 Amended formulae to reference data input form

There are many benefits to be derived from using data input forms including the fact that the data can be checked more easily. Sometimes it might be possible to design an input form that is compatible with a forecasting or accounting system so that the data can be electronically picked up from the other system without having to type it in again. Even if this is not possible, the order of items in the data input form does not have to be the same as the order in which they are referenced in the logic, which means that the data input form can be created to be as compatible with the source of the input data as possible. Furthermore, the worksheet containing the logic for the plan can be protected, and if necessary made read-only in order to maintain the integrity of the system.

It is not a trivial task to change existing systems to be templates with data input forms, and it will also take a little longer to develop a new system in this way, as opposed to incorporating the data with the logic. However, the ease of data input and ongoing maintenance should make the additional effort worthwhile.

10.15 The use of spreadsheets by management accountants

There are a number of different ways in which the management accountant can use a spreadsheet in his or her work. In the first place, spreadsheets are especially useful in the performance of calculations. In addition to the basic mathematical operators discussed such as addition, subtraction, division, multiplication etc., there are many other functions which will be of direct use. These include NPV, IRR, PV to mention only three. There are in fact more than 350 built-in functions in Excel. When it comes to repetitive calculation the management accountant can set up templates that can be used again and again.

There are many different aspects to the way that Excel can be used for planning and those who are interested in more detail should consult the Elsevier Cima Publication, Financial Planning Using Excel – Forecasting, Planning and Budgeting Techniques, by Sue Nugus, 2005.

In addition to the calculation side of the spreadsheet the management accountant will find useful the ease with which graphs and charts can quickly be created in Excel.

10.16 Summary

This chapter has considered some of the principal design elements that should be considered when embarking on the creation of any business model or plan, be it a financial statement, a budgetary control system, a marketing model or a forecast. A small plan has been used for demonstration purposes, and many of the techniques illustrated become essential when working with larger plans. Taking time to consider the layout and design of a system before embarking on its development has been proven by many users to pay considerable dividends in the long term. In addition, it is worth talking with colleagues who might find a plan useful before starting development to see whether some additional lines need to be incorporated, as it is always more difficult to add to a spreadsheet later. As the use of information and communications technology has spread, being competent in the use of a spreadsheet has become a pre-requisite for being an efficient and effective management accountant.

Preparing for the Assessment

Preparing for the Assessment

> This chapter is intended for use when you are ready to start revising for your assessment. It contains:
> - a summary of useful revision techniques;
> - details of the format of the assessment;
> - a bank of examination-standard revision questions and suggested solutions.

Revision technique

Planning

The first thing to say about revision is that it is an addition to your initial studies, not a substitute for them. In other words, do not coast along early in your course in the hope of catching up during the revision phase. On the contrary, you should be studying and revising concurrently from the outset. At the end of each week, and at the end of each month, get into the habit of summarising the material you have covered to refresh your memory of it.

As with your initial studies, planning is important to maximise the value of your revision work. You need to balance the demands for study, professional work, family life and other commitments. To make this work, you will need to think carefully about how to make best use of your time.

Begin as before by comparing the estimated hours you will need to devote to revision with the hours available to you in the weeks leading up to the assessment. Prepare a written schedule setting out the areas you intend to cover during particular weeks, and break that down further into topics for each day's revision. To help focus on the key areas, try to establish which areas you are weakest on, so that you can concentrate on the topics where effort is particularly needed.

Do not forget the need for relaxation, and for family commitments. Sustained intellectual effort is only possible for limited periods, and must be broken up at intervals by lighter activities. And do not continue your revision timetable right up to the moment when you enter the exam hall: you should aim to stop work a day or even two days before the assessment. Beyond this point, the most you should attempt is an occasional brief look at your notes to refresh your memory.

Getting down to work

By the time you begin your revision you should already have settled into a fixed work pattern: a regular time of day for doing the work, a particular place where you sit, particular equipment that you assemble before you begin and so on. If this is not already a matter of routine for you, think carefully about it now in the last vital weeks before the assessment.

You should have notes summarising the main points of each topic you have covered. Begin each session by reading through the relevant notes and trying to commit the important points to memory.

Usually this will be just your starting point. Unless the area is one where you already feel very confident, you will need to track back from your notes to the relevant chapter(s) in the *Learning System*. This will refresh your memory on points not covered by your notes and fill in the detail that inevitably gets lost in the process of summarisation.

When you think you have understood and memorised the main principles and techniques, attempt an exam-standard question. At this stage of your studies you should normally be expecting to complete such questions in something close to the actual time allocation allowed in the assessment. After completing your effort, check the solution provided and add to your notes any extra points it reveals.

Tips for the final revision phase

As the assessment comes closer, consider the following list of techniques and make use of those that work for you:

- Summarise your notes into more concise form, perhaps on index cards that you can carry with you for revision on the way into work.
- Go through your notes with a highlighter pen, marking key concepts and definitions.
- Summarise the main points in a key area by producing a wordlist, mind map or other mnemonic device.
- On areas that you find difficult, rework questions that you have already attempted, and compare your answers in detail with those provided in the *Learning System*.
- Rework questions you attempted earlier in your studies with a view to completing them within the time limits.

Format of the assessment

Structures of the paper

The assessment for *Business Mathematics* is a two hours computer-based assessment comprising approximately 45 questions, with one or more parts. Single part questions are generally worth 2 marks each, but two and three part questions may be worth 4 or 6 marks. There will be no choice and all questions should be attempted if time permits. CIMA are continuously developing the question styles within the CBA system and you are advised to try the on-line website demo, to both gain familiarity with the assessment software and examine the latest style of questions being used.

Weighting of subjects

The current weightings for the syllabus sections are:

- Basic mathematics – 15%
- Probability – 15%
- Summarising and analysing data – 15%

- Inter-relationships between variables – 15%
- Forecasting – 15%
- Financial mathematics – 15%
- Spreadsheets – 10%.

In broad terms, the entire syllabus will be covered in each assessment. Please note that the weightings of the syllabus and of the assessment are not exactly reflected by the space allocated to the various topics in the book. Some subjects involve tables, graphs and charts that take up a lot of space but do not require specially large amounts of time or effort to study. In revision and in the assessment, the relative importance of the various topic areas is given by the percentages shown above and not by the space they occupy in this book.

Revision Questions

Syllabus area (%)	Questions	Pages
Basic Mathematics (15%)	1–15	417–421
Summarising and Analysing Data (15%)		
Obtaining data	16–23	421–423
Presentation of data	24–32	423–427
Descriptive statistics	33–44	427–430
Index numbers	45–55	430–435
Financial Mathematics (15%)	56–68	435–438
Inter-relationships between variables (15%)		
Correlation and Regression	69–78	439–441
Forecasting (15%)		
Time series	79–90	441–444
Probability (15%)	91–109	445–449
Spreadsheet (15%)	110–114	449–451

Basic mathematics

Question 1

An item sells for £3.99 when it includes value added tax (VAT) at 17.5 per cent. Were VAT to be reduced to 15 per cent, what would the new selling price be, correct to the nearest penny?

(A) £3.79
(B) £4.08
(C) £3.91
(D) £3.40

Question 2

The number 2,490.742 is to be rounded. In each case write the correct answer in the space provided, to the accuracy specified.

(A) to two d.p.
(B) to one d.p.
(C) to the nearest whole number
(D) to the nearest 1,000
(E) to three s.f.
(F) to four s.f.

Question 3

The equation $20/(40 - Y) = 85/Y$ is to be solved to find Y correct to two decimal places. A solution comprises the following five lines, (A)–(E). In each case, identify whether the line follows correctly from the line immediately preceding it (regardless of whether or not you believe the preceding line to be correct).

(A) $20Y = 85(40 - Y)$
(B) $20Y = 3,400 - Y$
(C) $19Y = 3,400$
(D) $Y = 3,400/19$
(E) $Y = 178.94$ (two d.p.).

Question 4

A chartered management accountant has established the cost of materials for a particular component as £20.00 to the nearest £1.

(a) Calculate the maximum absolute error in the cost.
(b) Calculate the maximum percentage error in the cost.

Question 5

The manager of an electronics component manufacturing company has estimated the following costs for a component for the year ahead:

Direct materials   £4.00 but could rise or fall by 4 per cent over the next year
Direct labour   £2.00 but could rise or fall by 5 per cent over the next year
Direct overheads   £1.20 but could rise or fall by 6 per cent over the next year

(a) Complete the following table showing the maximum, minimum and expected cost per unit by filling in the appropriate numerical values in the spaces indicated by letters. Give your answers to two d.p.

Costs per unit (£)	Minimum	Expected	Maximum
Materials	A	...	...
Labour	...	...	C
Overheads	...	B	...
Totals	6.87	7.20	7.53

(b) Calculate the maximum percentage error in the total cost per unit, giving your answer correct to one d.p.
(c) At a production level of 50,000 units, calculate the maximum absolute error in the total cost, giving your answer correct to the nearest £.

Question 6

A company has recently set up a mail-order operation to sell direct to the public. As an experiment, two different prices have been tried for a particular product, each for one week, with the following results:

Price per unit	£7	£9
Units sold per week	1050	950

Assuming that the relationship between price (P) and demand (D) is of the form $P = aD + b$, find the values of a and b.

Question 7

If price $= 30 - 0.03D$ where D is demand, find an expression for revenue as a function of demand.

Question 8

The fixed costs of part of the mail-order operation are £2,000 per week. Variable costs of production are £4 per unit plus insurance costs given by 2 per cent of the square of the quantity sold. Find an expression for total cost as a function of demand.

Question 9

If Revenue $= 25D - 0.01D^2$ and Costs $= 1500 + 4D + 0.03D^2$ find an expression for profit as a function of demand (D).

Question 10

Find the two levels of demand at which breakeven occurs, if profit $= -2000 + 24D - 0.04D^2$.

Question 11

If Price $= 30 - 0.03D$ and if breakeven occurs when D is 200 and 400, find the two prices at which breakeven occurs.

Scenario common to Questions 12–15

A company produces a car anti-theft device consisting of *one* control unit made in India and *two* reinforced aluminium linkages made in the United States. Instrumentation and assembly are carried out at the company's home factory in the United Kingdom. The following information is available:

Question 12

India to UK factory. The company buys in consignments of 100 units. The control unit price is 500 rupees (Rs), subject to a quantity discount of 20 per cent for orders of at least 100.

Freight charges for a consignment of 100 units are Rs 60,000. Insurance is payable at the rate of 2 per cent of the gross sum insured: the gross sum insured equals the cost of units plus freight. After landing in the United Kingdom, transport costs to the company's factory are £200, plus £5 per unit carried.

Exchange rate: £1 = Rs 47.

Complete the following table to calculate the total cost for 100 units, India to UK

Costs for 100 units, India to UK	
Cost in rupees of 100 units	...
Freight	...
Subtotal	...
Subtotal plus insurance	...
Total in £ (to two d.p.)	...
Plus transport in UK	...
Total cost in £ for 100 units (to two d.p.)	A

Question 13

USA to UK factory. The company buys in consignments of 500 aluminium linkages whose unit price is $20, with a discount of 10 per cent per 500. Carriage, insurance and freight equals $1,000 plus 5 per cent of the cost of linkages.

Exchange rate: £1 = $1.8.

Complete the following table by filling in the appropriate numerical values in the spaces indicated by the letters.

Costs for 500 units, USA to UK	
Cost in $ of 500 units	...
Carriage etc.	...
Total cost in $	...
Total cost in £ (to two d.p.)	B

Question 14

At the UK factory. Other materials from UK suppliers cost £10 per device. Within the factory, each production run of 100 devices requires 500 hours in instrumentation at £6 per hour; 200 hours in production at £5 per hour; and 50 hours in inspection at £8 per hour.

At the current planned production levels, fixed costs are absorbed into production by adding 50 per cent to the overall cost of UK labour and UK materials.

Complete the following table by filling in the appropriate numerical values in the spaces indicated by the letters.

Costs in UK per 100 devices	
Other materials	...
Instrumentation	...
Production	...
Inspection	...
Subtotal	...
Subtotal including fixed costs	C

Question 15

On average, inspection (which is the final stage) rejects 20 per cent of the devices as defective. These are worthless. The selling price to the trade is set so that the gross profit is 25 per cent of the total amount invoiced to customers. If the costs are as follows, calculate the unit price giving your answer to two d.p.

India to UK for 100 units	£3,000
USA to UK for 500 units	£6,000
In UK for 100 units	£8,000

Obtaining data

Question 16

A sample is taken by randomly selecting a name from a list and thereafter selecting every 100th name. What is such a sample called?

(A) Quota sample
(B) Systematic sample
(C) Simple random sample
(D) Stratified sample.

Question 17

One or more of the following result in cluster samples. Which are they?

(A) In a college, three classes are selected randomly and then all the students in those classes are surveyed.
(B) In a workplace, all the staff in one randomly selected department are surveyed.
(C) In a randomly selected street, every third house is surveyed.
(D) In a village, 5 per cent of men and 5 per cent of women are randomly selected and surveyed.

Question 18

Associate with each of the following sampling methods the most appropriate example from the list given below.

Methods

(A) Simple random sample
(B) Stratified random sample
(C) Cluster sample
(D) Systematic sample
(E) Quota sample
(F) Multistage sample.

Examples

(P) Every 50th person is chosen from an alphabetic list of students.
(Q) People are stopped in the street according to instructions such as 'stop equal numbers of young and old'.
(R) One school is chosen at random from all schools in a city then the registers are used to select a one in ten sample.

(S) One ward in a hospital is selected at random then every patient in that ward is surveyed.
(T) One person in ten is chosen randomly from each ward in a hospital.
(U) Names are picked from a numbered list using random numbers.

Question 19

Which of the following defines what is meant by a census?

(A) A survey associating people with their places of birth
(B) A survey of the entire population of interest
(C) A survey asking households about their composition
(D) A survey asking household about their expenditure.

Question 20

Which of the following defines what is meant by a sample in the context of a statistical survey?

(A) A list of people who are to be surveyed
(B) A number of people stopped in the street
(C) A subgroup of the population of interest
(D) A group of people who are typical of the population as a whole.

Question 21

A small travel agency that operates in only its local area wishes to conduct a survey of its customers to assess whether it is offering the best balance of holidays in the United Kingdom and overseas, and whether there is a demand for coach tours, which it has so far never offered.

Company records indicate that the profile of adult clients is as follows:

Age	%	Gender	%
Under 20	10	Male	45
20–34	20	Female	55
35–49	35		
50–64	20		
65 and over	15		

Home address	%	Destination	%
Town	30	UK	25
Suburban	60	Overseas	75
Rural	10		

Assuming that men and women are represented pro rata in all group's of the company's clients, how many suburban women aged 34 years or less should be included in a stratified random sample of total size 1000?

Question 22

A company decides to select a stratified random sample from among its clients over the last 3 years. Which of the following statements are in general true of such samples?

(A) They are relatively cheap.
(B) They tend to be representative of the population.
(C) They require access to quite detailed information about the population.
(D) They tend to provide reliable estimates.

Question 23

A company has to decide between posting out questionnaires, conducting a telephone survey and conducting face-to-face interviews.

(A) Which of the above methods is cheapest?
(B) Which of the above methods is dearest?
(C) Which of the above methods results in the highest quality of completed questionnaires?
(D) Which of the above methods results in the lowest quality of completed questionnaires?
(E) Which of the above methods results in the highest response rate?
(F) Which of the above methods results in the lowest response rate?

Presentation of data

Question 24

A quadratic function has a negative x-squared term, its graph cuts the x-axis at -1 and $+3$ and the y-axis at 30. Answer the following:

(a) Does it have a maximum or a minimum value?
(b) For what value of x does its maximum or minimum value occur?
(c) Substitute the correct numbers into the following calculation of the quadratic equation:

$$y = k(? - x)(? + x)$$
$$y = k(? + ?x - x^2)$$

When $x = 0$, $y = ?k$, so k must $= ?$

Question 25

If the following data is to be illustrated by means of a histogram and if the standard interval is taken to be 5 kg, complete the column showing heights of the bars of the histogram (to the nearest whole number):

Weight	Frequency	Height of bar
0–5	83	?
5–10	105	?
10–20	160	?
20–40	96	?
40–100	108	?

Question 26

The following data is to be illustrated by means of a pie chart. Complete the table showing the angles that correspond to each category (to the nearest whole number):

Categories	%	Angle
A	8	?
B	43	?
C	37	?
D	12	?

Question 27

A mail-order company has kept records of the value of orders received over a period. These are given in the following table:

Value of orders £	Number of orders
5 and under 15	36
15 and under 20	48
20 and under 25	53
25 and under 30	84
30 and under 35	126
35 and under 40	171
40 and under 45	155
45 and under 50	112
50 and under 55	70
55 and under 65	60
65 and under 85	54
	969

Complete the table, showing frequency densities with a standard interval width of 5 units, by filling in the appropriate numerical values in the spaces indicated by the letters.

Value of orders	Frequency density
5–15	A
15–20	B
20–25	…
25–30	…
30–35	…
35–40	…
40–45	…
45–50	…
50–55	…
55–65	C
65–85	D

Question 28

What information is provided by frequency densities?

(A) The points which must be plotted for an ogive.
(B) The heights of the bars in a histogram.
(C) The areas of the bars in a histogram.
(D) The area under a frequency polygon.

Question 29

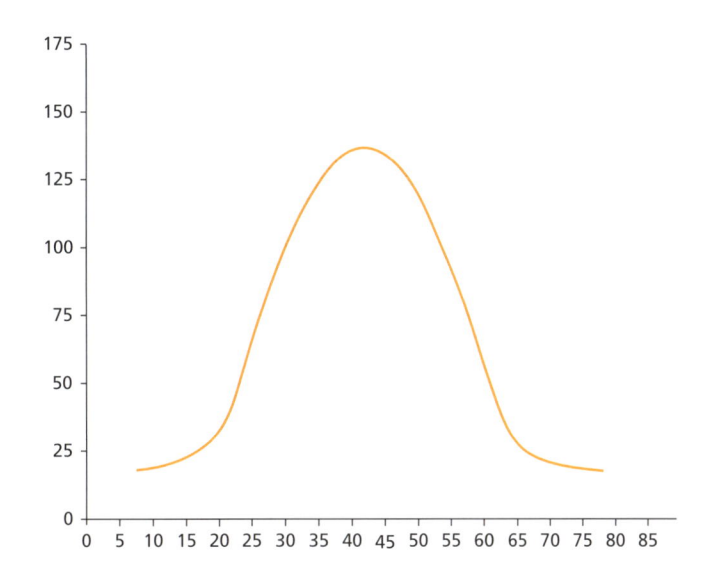

(E)

(F)

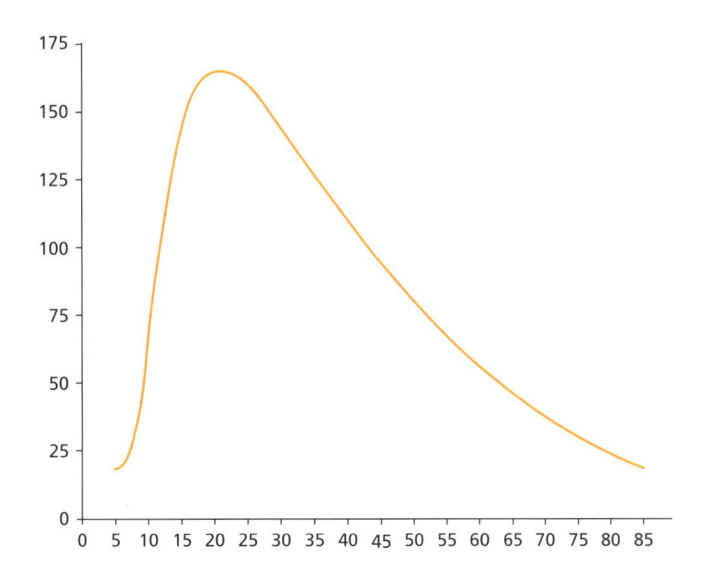

What types of frequency curves are shown in charts (E) and (F)? Allocate one or more of the following titles to each chart.

(G) Normal
(H) Symmetrical
(I) Negatively skewed
(J) Positively skewed
(K) Uniform.

Scenario common to Questions 30–32

The data used for the charts in Questions 30–32 are UK trade balances in £ hundred millions spanning the years 1990–99 and broken down to show visible oil, visible non-oil and invisibles separately.

Balance of payments, 1990

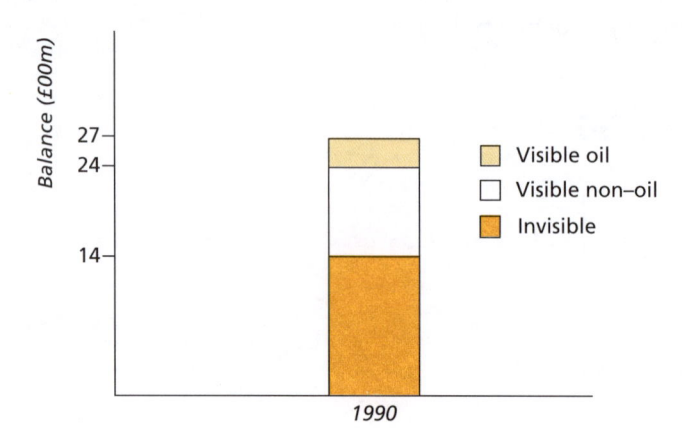

Question 30

What type of chart is shown in the scenario?

(A) Multiple bar chart
(B) Simple bar chart
(C) Component bar chart
(D) Pictogram.

Question 31

Which of the following statements can be correctly deduced from the chart given in the scenario?

(A) In 1990 the United Kingdom had a positive balance of trade.
(B) In 1990 the invisible balance accounted for over half of the total balance.
(C) In 1990 oil was already declining as a major contributor to the balance of trade.
(D) In 1990 the visible non-oil balance was considerably greater than the visible oil balance.
(E) From 1990 onwards the balance of trade began to decline.

Question 32

UK trade balances 1990–99

[Chart showing UK trade balances 1990–99 with four lines: Visible oil, Visible non-oil, Invisibles, Overall balance of payments. Y-axis: Balance (£00m) from (250) to 100. X-axis: Year from 1990 to 1999.]

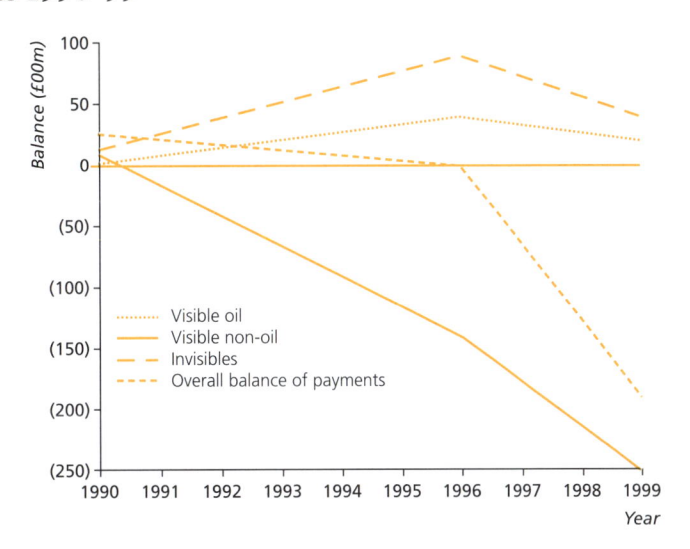

Which of the following statements can be correctly deduced from the above chart showing UK trade balances 1990–99?

(A) From 1990 onwards the overall balance of payments declined.
(B) Since 1990 the invisible balance has climbed steadily.
(C) By 1999 the balance on visible oil was greater than that on invisibles.
(D) By 1999 the deficit on visible non-oil was so great as to more than offset the two positive balances.

Descriptive statistics

Question 33

In a positively skewed distribution, which of the following is/are generally true?

(A) The mean is larger than the median.
(B) The mode is larger than the mean.
(C) The median is smaller than the mode.
(D) The mode is the smallest of the three commonly used averages.

Question 34

A group of people have the following weekly rents (£): 60, 130, 250, 200, 85, 75, 125, 225. Calculate the following, giving your answers correct to two d.p.:

(a) The mean
(b) The median
(c) The lower quartile
(d) The upper quartile
(e) The quartile deviation.

Question 35

A distribution has $\Sigma f = 100$, $\Sigma fx = 550$ and $\Sigma fx^2 = 12{,}050$. Calculate the standard deviation, giving your answer to one d.p.

Question 36

The director of a medium-sized company has decided to analyse the salaries that are paid to staff. The frequency distribution of salaries that are currently being paid is as follows. Calculate the cumulative frequencies.

Salary £'000	Number of staff	Cumulative frequency
Under 10	16	–
10–under 20	28	–
20–under 30	36	–
30–under 40	20	–
40–under 50	12	–
50–under 70	4	–
70 and over	4	–

Question 37

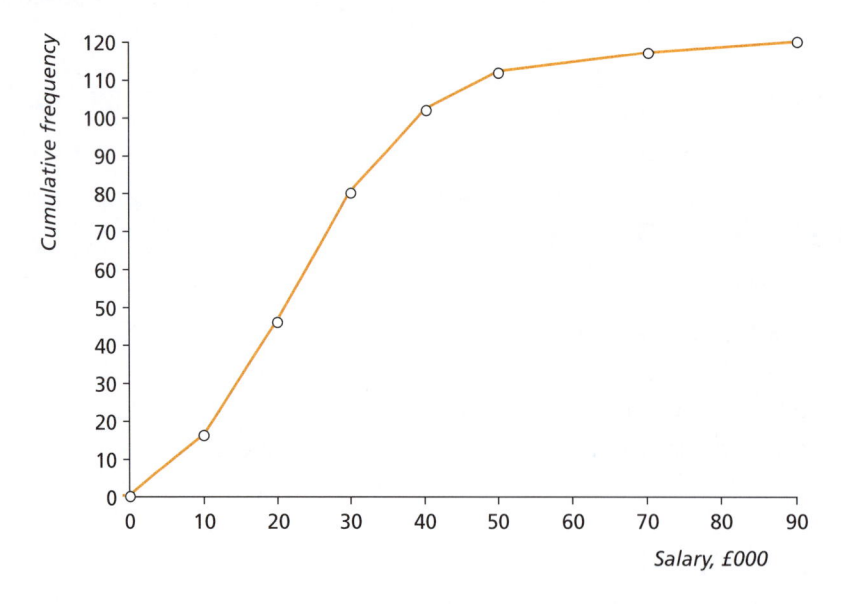

The ogive shows the salary distribution for 120 staff. From the ogive, obtain the following statistics, giving your answers to the nearest £5,000.

(A) the median
(B) the lower quartile
(C) the upper quartile.

Question 38

Calculate the quartile deviation, if Q_1 = £892 and Q_3 = £1,242.

Question 39

Given that Σf = 120, Σfx = 3,140 and Σfx^2 = 112,800, calculate the following:

(A) the mean (to the nearest £)
(B) the standard deviation (to the nearest £100).

Question 40

If the mean and standard deviation salaries now and 5 years ago are as follows

	5 years ago	Now
Mean	£18,950	£25,000
Standard deviation	£10,600	£15,000

Which of the following statements is/are correct?

(A) The standard deviations show that salaries are now more variable than 5 years ago.
(B) The standard deviations show that the average salary has increased.
(C) The means show that the average salary has increased.
(D) The means show that variability in salaries has increased.

Question 41

In a distribution showing the values of 400 invoices, the median value is £2,500, the lower quartile is £1,500 and the upper quartile is £4,000.

(a) Calculate the quartile deviation.
(b) Which of the following statements is/are true?

   (A) A quarter of the invoices have values above £4,000.
   (B) Half the invoices have values below £2,500.
   (C) A quarter of the invoices are greater than £1,500.
   (D) Three quarters of the invoices are greater than £1,500.
   (E) A half of the invoices have values in the range £1,500–£4,000.
   (F) Two-thirds of invoices have values within approximately one quartile deviation either side of the median.

Question 42

For what type of data should the median be used in preference to the mean as an average?

(A) Symmetrical
(B) Discrete
(C) Skewed
(D) Secondary.

Question 43

The number of telephone support calls given each day during the last 64-day quarter, which is representative, is shown below in the table and the chart

Telephone support calls

Number of calls:	0–9	10–19	20–29	30–39	40–49	50–59	60–69	70+	Total
Frequency:	Nil	5	10	20	15	20	4	Nil	64

Number of telephone calls

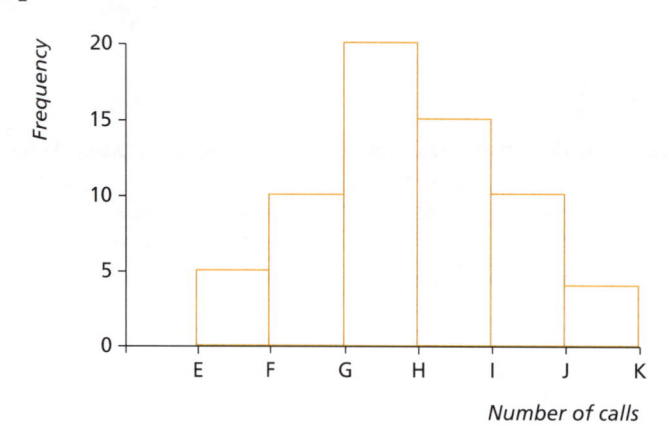

(a) What type of chart is being used?

- (A) Bar chart
- (B) Ogive
- (C) Multiple bar chart
- (D) Histogram

(b) What are the values represented by the letters E–K?

Question 44

If $\Sigma fx = 2{,}478$, $\Sigma f = 64$ and $\Sigma fx^2 = 106{,}906$, calculate the following:

- (A) the mean (to two d.p.).
- (B) the standard deviation (to one d.p.).
- (C) the average daily cost of calls, to the nearest £, if the average call costs £20.

Index numbers

Question 45

In 2000, a retail price index was 178 with 1990 = 100. Convert a weekly wage of £400 back to 1990 constant prices, giving your answer correct to the nearest penny.

Question 46

Complete the following table which shows two index number series being spliced together to give a single series based in 1997. Give your answers correct to one d.p.

Year	Price index (1991 = 100)	Price index (1997 = 100)
1994	138	?
1995	142	?
1996	147	?
1997	150	100
	(1997 = 100)	
1998	109	109
1999	113	113
2000	119	119

Question 47

Complete the following table in which a chain-base index is being converted to one with fixed base 1997. Give your answers correct to one decimal place.

Year	1997	1998	1999	2000
Chain index	105.4	104.8	103.9	104.2
1997 = 100	100	?	?	?

Question 48

You are assisting with the work on a maintenance department's budget for the next quarter of 2000. The maintenance department's budget for the current quarter (just ending) is £200,000. Its use of materials, and their respective prices, are shown below.

	Quantity used in current quarter Units	Average price payable per unit Current quarter £	Next quarter £
Material A	9	10	10.20
Material B	13	12	12.50
Material C	8	9	9.00
Material D	20	25	26.00

(a) You require an all-items price index for materials for the next quarter, using the current quarter as base and the current quantities as weights.

Complete the table by filling in the appropriate numerical value in the spaces indicated by the letters.

Material	w	P_0	P_1	P_{1w}	P_{0w}
A	...	10	10.2	...	...
B	...	12	12.5	E	F
C	...	9	9	...	...
D	...	25	26	...	...
Totals	...	...	...	846.3	818

(b) Calculate the required index, using the formula $100 \times (\Sigma wP_1 / \Sigma wP_0)$ giving your answer to one d.p.

(c) If the price index calculated above was 104, estimate the budget for the next quarter, giving your answer to the nearest £000.

Question 49

If a price index is 104, which of the following statements is/are correct about average prices?

(A) Prices have risen by 104 per cent.
(B) Prices are now 1.04 times their base year value.
(C) Prices have risen by 4 per cent.
(D) Prices have risen by 96 per cent.

Question 50

Which of the following statements about the method of index number construction used in Q48 is/are correct?

(A) It is an unweighted method.
(B) It is a current weighted method.
(C) It is a relatives method.
(D) It is a base weighted method.
(E) It is an aggregative method.

Question 51

This question will examine your understanding of the principles and methods involved in the compilation, construction and use of the UK General Index of Retail Prices.

(a) Which of the following statements about the base time is/are correct?

   (A) The base time is always January of a particular year.
   (B) The base time changes annually.
   (C) The base time is a year when price inflation was specially high.
   (D) The base time is updated from time to time.
   (E) The index does not have a fixed base time.

(b) Which of the following statements about the weighting used is/are correct?

   (A) The index is unweighted.
   (B) The weights reflect the quantities of goods bought.
   (C) The weights reflect the expenditure on goods.
   (D) The weights are updated annually.
   (E) The weights are derived from the Family Expenditure Survey.

(c) Which of the following statements about items included in the index is/are correct?

   (A) Life insurance is not included.
   (B) The items to be included change from time to time.
   (C) Income tax is now included.
   (D) Approximately 80 price indicators are used.
   (E) The index covers services as well as goods.

(d) Which of the following statements about data collection for the index is/are correct?

 (A) Prices are obtained from the Family Expenditure Survey.
 (B) Prices are obtained from a survey conducted by the Department of Employment.
 (C) Prices are obtained once a month.
 (D) Providers of services are asked to provide prices.
 (E) A representative sample of consumers are asked to provide prices.

Question 52

The following table shows data for gross domestic product (GDP), gross earnings and retail prices for the United Kingdom, 1980–89:

	GDP (market prices, £bn)	Ave. gross earnings (1985 = 100)	Retail prices (1985 = 100)
1980	231	65	71
1981	255	73	79
1982	278	80	86
1983	303	87	90
1984	323	92	94
1985	354	100	100
1986	379	108	103
1987	414	116	108
1988	430	126	113
1989	436*	136*	122*

*provisional
[Source: *British Business*, 1 Sept. 1989 and *Economic Trends* (various)]

(a) Complete the table expressing the GDP series as index numbers with 1985 = 100, by filling in the appropriate numerical values in the spaces indicated by the letters. Answers should be rounded to one d.p.

Year	GDP 85 = 100
80	A
81	…
82	…
83	…
84	…
85	100
86	…
87	…
89	B

(b) Calculate the index for average earnings at constant 1985 prices. Complete the table by filling in the appropriate numerical values in the spaces indicated by the letters. Answers should be rounded to one d.p.:

Year	Index at constant 1985 prices Average gross earnings
80	C
81	…
82	…
83	…
84	…
85	100
86	…
87	D
89	…

Question 53

If an index of average gross earnings with base year 1995 and at constant 1995 prices is calculated to be 107 by 2000, which of the following is/are correct about changes in average gross earnings over this 5-year period?

(A) A total of 1.07 per cent more goods and services can be bought by average earnings.
(B) A total of 7 per cent more goods and services can be bought by average earnings.
(C) Earnings have risen by 1.07 per cent.
(D) The average price of goods and services has risen by 7 per cent.

Question 54

A manufacturer of domestic freezers has produced the following sales figures for the last six months:

	Last quarter 1997		First quarter 1998	
	Units sold	Sales value £'000	Units sold	Sales value £'000
Small	800	80	1,100	110
Medium	500	70	700	105
Large	200	40	300	60

[*Source*: Statlab Research, internal data]

(a) Calculate the index of total sales revenue for the first quarter of 1998, with base the last quarter of 1997. Give your answer to one d.p.
(b) It is possible that what the manufacturer wants is an index showing the quantity of freezers sold. Calculate an unweighted index of the number of units sold.

Question 55

The following table is to be used to calculate a relative index of quantity sold with base revenues as weights.

Items	Q_0	R_0	Q_1	R_0Q_1/Q_0
Small	800	80	1,100	110
Medium	500	70	700	98
Large	200	40	300	60
Totals	1,500	190	2,100	268

Calculate the relative index of quantity sold with base revenues as weights to one d.p.

Financial mathematics

Question 56

A building society adds interest monthly to accounts even though interest rates are expressed in annual terms. The current rate is stated as 4.8 per cent per annum. If an investor deposits £2,500 on 1 January, calculate the value of the account on 31 August, giving your answer correct to the nearest penny.

Question 57

A bond increases from £3,500 to £4,000 over 3 years. Complete the following calculation of the effective annual rate of interest:

- Three-year ratio = ?
- Annual ratio = ?
- Effective annual rate = ? per cent (giving your answer to one d.p.).

Question 58

Complete the following calculation of net present value (NPV) at a 5 per cent discount rate (working to the nearest whole number):

Time	Cash flow £	Discount factor 5%	Present value £
0	(10,000)	1.000	?
1	4,000	?	?
2	5,000	?	?
3	4,000	?	?
NPV			?

Question 59

All answers should be given correct to two d.p.

An amount of £500 was invested at the start of each of 60 consecutive months. Compound interest at a nominal annual rate of 12 per cent is payable.

(a) If interest is compounded annually, what will be the value of the first year's £6,000 by the end of the 5-year period?

(b) If interest is compounded annually, what total sum will have accumulated after five complete years?

(c) If interest is compounded monthly, what total sum will have accumulated after five complete years?

Question 60

A 25-year mortgage of £50,000 is to be repaid by 100 equal quarterly payments in arrears. Interest at a nominal annual rate of 16 per cent is charged each quarter on the outstanding part of the debt.

Note: The sum, S, of a geometric progression of N terms, with first term A, and common ratio R, is:

$$S = \frac{A(R^N - 1)}{(R - 1)}$$

(a) Viewing the repayments as an annuity of £A running for 100 quarters at 4 per cent per quarter, use the formula for the present value of an annuity to calculate the present value of the repayments as a function of £A.

(b) How much are the quarterly repayments?

(c) What is the effective annual rate of interest?

Question 61

The building services department of a hospital has estimated that the maintenance costs over the next 8 years (payable at the beginning of each year) for an existing air conditioner will be as follows:

Year	Estimated cost £	Year	Estimated cost £
1	3,000	5	4,000
2	3,500	6	4,500
3	4,000	7	5,000
4	12,000	8	13,000

(a) Given that the discount factor is 6 per cent, complete the following table by filling in the appropriate numerical values in the spaces indicated by the letters.

Beginning of year	Discount factor	cash flow	Discounted cash flow
1	...	3,000	B
2	A	3,500	...
3	...	4,000	C
4	...	12,000	...
5	...	4,000	...
6	...	4,500	...
7	...	5,000	...
8	...	13,000	...
Total			

(b) Based on the estimated costs, a contract maintenance company has offered to take over the maintenance for the hospital for a fixed annual charge £X payable at the start of each of the 8 years. Find the present value of the payments as a function of X.

(c) If the present value of the estimated maintenance costs is £38,640 and that of the annual payments were 6.8X, calculate the maximum annual amount that the hospital might be prepared to pay to the contractor to two d.p.

Question 62

A company will carry out its own maintenance of a new boiler with a life of 7 years estimated at £10,000 per annum now, rising at 5 per cent per annum with a major overhaul at the end of year 4 costing an additional £25,000.

The discount rate is 10 per cent, and all payments are assumed to be made at year ends.

Complete the following table (showing the annual maintenance costs and corresponding present values) by filling in the appropriate numerical values in the spaces indicated by the letters A–E. Throughout this question you should work to the nearest £.

Year	Annual cost	Discount factor	Present
1	A	…	
2	…	C	
3	…	…	D
4	25,000 + B	…	
5	…	…	E
6	…	…	
7	…	…	

Question 63

A boiler supplier offers a 7-year contract with an annual charge of £13,000 at each year end. If the discount rate is 10 per cent, calculate the present value of the contract, giving your answer to the nearest £.

Question 64

Given two projects of which you know the net present values and ignoring all other factors, which project would you select?

(A) The one with the larger net present value.
(B) The one with the smaller net present value.
(C) Present value is not relevant to such a decision.

Question 65

In exactly 3 years from now, a company will have to replace capital equipment that will then cost £0.5 m. The managers have decided to set up a reserve fund into which twelve equal sums will be put at quarterly intervals, with the first being made *now*. The rate of compound interest is 2 per cent per quarter.

(a) If the quarterly sum invested is £A, find an expression for the final value of the fund as a function of A. Do not attempt to simplify it.
(b) Use the formula for the sum of a geometric progression to evaluate the expression $1.035 + 1.035^2 + 1.035^3 + \cdots + 1.035^{10}$. You should work to four d.p.

Question 66

A fixed-interest, 10-year £100,000 mortgage is to be repaid by 40 equal quarterly payments in arrears. Interest is charged at 3 per cent per quarter on the outstanding part of the debt.

(a) Viewing the mortgage as an annuity, use the PV of an annuity formula to calculate its present value as a function of the quarterly repayment £B. You should work to four d.p.
(b) If the present value calculated in (a) was 24B, calculate the value of B to two d.p.

Question 67

Find the effective annual rate of interest to two d.p. if interest is charged at 3 per cent per quarter.

Question 68

A company is considering the purchase of one of two machines, A or B, for £180,000. The terms of payment for each machine are £90,000 on delivery and £90,000 a year later. The machines are expected to produce year-end net cash flows as follows:

	End of year				
Net cash flows (£'000)	1	2	3	4	5
Machine A	60	50	40	30	20
Machine B	40	40	40	40	40

At the end of year 5, either machine would be sold for £20,000. The annual cost of capital is 9 per cent for each year.

(a) Complete the following table, to obtain the net present value for machine A, by filling in the appropriate numerical values in the spaces indicated by the letters. Give present values to two d.p.

Year	Net cash inflow (£'000)	Discount factor	Present value (£'000)
0	C	F	...
1	D	...	...
2	...	...	G
3	...	...	...
4	...	...	...
5	E	...	...
NPV			2.71

(b) Complete the following table, to obtain the net present value for machine B, by filling in the appropriate numerical values in the spaces indicated by the letters. Give present values to two d.p.

Year	Net cash inflow (£'000)	Discount factor	Present value (£'000)
0	...	...	...
1	H	...	...
2	...	...	J
3	...	...	...
4	...	...	...
5	I	...	...
NPV			3.97

(c) Which machine should be purchased?

Correlation and regression

Question 69

You are working with a marketing colleague, trying to establish the relationship, if any, between expenditure on local newspaper advertising and sales revenue of restaurants. The annual data for a random sample of ten restaurants are as follows:

Restaurant code	Expenditure (£'000) on advertising, A	Sales, S (£'000)
B	1.0	55
C	1.5	55
D	1.0	45
E	2.0	50
F	2.0	65
G	2.5	60
H	2.5	55
I	3.0	70
J	3.5	65
K	4.0	80

$\Sigma(A^2) = 62$ $\Sigma(S^2) = 36{,}950$ $n = 10$
$\Sigma(A) = 23$ $\Sigma(S) = 600$ $\Sigma(AS) = 1457.5$

(a) Calculate the regression coefficient 'b' for the regression line of sales on advertising, giving your answer to three d.p.
(b) If the value of 'b' was 8.691, calculate the regression coefficient 'a' for the regression line of sales on advertising, giving your answer to two d.p.
(c) Calculate the correlation coefficient (r) between sales and advertising, giving your-answer correct to two d.p.

Question 70

A company operates ten factories. Its expenditure on training in accident prevention and safety (TAPS) and the number of minor accidents there last quarter are shown below. Any accidents were judged by nursing staff as either 'minor' and treated on site, or 'major' and referred to the local hospital.

Site:	A	B	C	D	E	F	G	H	I	J
Minor accidents	17	9	10	4	12	21	25	8	6	3
TAPS spending (£'000)	6	15	10	22	8	9	5	8	16	30

Complete the following table which ranks the number of minor accidents and the level of TAPS spending in order of magnitude as well as calculating d = accidents rank minus spending rank. Fill in the appropriate numerical values in the spaces indicated by the letters.

Site	Accidents rank	Spending rank	d
A	P	...	...
B	Q	...	...
C	...	R	...
D	...	...	...
E	...	S	...
F	...	...	...
G	...	...	...
H	...	T	...
I	...	...	U
J	...	...	...
Total			

Question 71

If data comprising 10 pairs of corresponding ranks has $\Sigma d^2 = 304.5$ where d represents the difference between corresponding ranks, calculate Spearman's rank correlation coefficient, giving your answer correct to three d.p.

Question 72

If the rank correlation coefficient between variables X and Y is 0.85, which of the following comments is/are correct?

(A) Values of Y increase as values of X increase
(B) Y decreases by 0.15 for every increase of 1 in X
(C) Y increases by 0.85 for every increase of 1 in X
(D) The link between X and Y values is very strong
(E) The link between X and Y values is linear
(F) Increases in X causes corresponding increases in Y.

Question 73

Over a period of 10 months a factory's monthly production costs [Y, £000] range from 5 to 16 whilst output [X, units] ranges from 50 to 500. If the regression equation is $Y = 5.0913 + 0.2119X$.

(a) Which of the following statements is/are correct?

 (A) When X increases by 1, Y increases by 0.2119
 (B) Fixed costs are £5.0913
 (C) When $X = 0$, $Y = 5.11249$
 (D) Fixed costs are £5,091.3
 (E) Fixed costs are £211.9

(b) If the planned output for the next month is 300 units, estimate production costs, giving your answer to the nearest £.

Question 74

If the coefficient of determination between output and production costs over a number of months is 89 per cent, which of the following comments is/are correct?

(A) Eighty-nine per cent of the variation in production costs from one month to the next can be explained by corresponding variation in output.
(B) Costs increase as output increases.
(C) The linear relationship between output and costs is very strong.
(D) An increase of 100 per cent in output is associated with an increase of 89 per cent in costs.

Question 75

A standard regression equation $Y = a + bX$ is to be used for making estimates. Which of the following is/are correct?

(A) Y can be estimated if X is known.
(B) X can be estimated if Y is known.

Question 76

If the correlation coefficient is 0.95, what is the coefficient of determination?

(A) -0.95
(B) 0.475
(C) 0.9025
(D) 0.9747

Question 77

If $n = 10$, $\Sigma x = 8$, $\Sigma y = 650$, $\Sigma xy = 525$, $\Sigma x^2 = 18$ and $\Sigma y^2 = 43{,}000$, calculate the product moment correlation coefficient, giving your answer correct to three d.p.

Question 78

The regression equation $Y = 45 + 3.6X$ has been obtained from 25 pairs of X- and Y-values, with the X-values ranging from 50 to 150. Which of the following is/are correct?

(A) When $X = 0$, Y is estimated to be 12.5.
(B) Y increases by 45 whenever X increases by 1.
(C) The equation cannot produce reliable estimates of Y if X is less than 50.
(D) The product moment correlation coefficient is 3.6.

Time series

Question 79

The actual value at a certain point is 1,500 and the seasonal factor is 1.17. Using the multiplicative model, the seasonally adjusted figure (to the nearest whole number) is:

(A) 1,501
(B) 1,755
(C) 1,282
(D) 1,499

Question 80

In the multiplicative model $A = T \times S \times R$, which of the following is/are correct?

(A) S is estimated by averaging $A - T$ values for the particular season.
(B) T may be estimated by a moving average.

(C) *T* may be estimated from an appropriate regression equation.
(D) *R* is estimated from *A/T*.
(E) The seasonally adjusted value is given by $A - S$.

Question 81

If the trend is estimated to be 2,308 for a quarter with a seasonal component of 1.06, estimate the actual value using the multiplicative model and giving your answer correct to four significant figures.

Question 82

The managers of a company are preparing revenue plans for the last quarter of 1993–94, and for the first three quarters of 1994–95.

(a) The table below is being used for part of the calculations to obtain a centred four-point moving average trend.

Year	Qtr	Actual revenue	Sum of 4 qtrs	Sum of 8 qtrs	Trend	Actual/Trend
90/91	1	49				
	2	37				
			A			
	3	58		C	D	
			B			
	4	67			53.125	E
91/92	1	50				
	2	38				
	3	59				
	4	68				

Calculate the values in the spaces denoted by the letters, giving your answers correct to three d.p. where appropriate.

Question 83

In a time series showing sales in £000, the quarterly values of actual sales divided by trend in sales are as follows:

Year	Quarter	Actual/trend
2000	1	0.937
	2	0.709
	3	1.095
	4	1.253
2001	1	0.934
	2	0.727
	3	1.088
	4	1.267

Calculate the average seasonal ratios correct to four d.p. using the multiplicative method. Do not adjust the ratios to make them total four.

Question 84

Adjust the following average seasonal ratios so that they total 4.

1st quarter   0.8
2nd quarter   0.6
3rd quarter   1.0
4th quarter   1.2

Question 85

Annual sales of Brand Y over an 11-year period were as follows:

Unit sales, Brand Y: 1983-93 ('000)

1983	1984	1985	1986	1987	1988	1989	1990	1991	1992	1993
50	59	46	54	65	51	60	70	56	66	76

Complete the following table by filling in appropriate numerical values in the spaces indicated by letters in order to find the 3-year moving average trend in sales. Each answer should be correct to one d.p.

Year	Sales ('000)	Three-year moving total	Trend
1983	50		
1984	59	A	…
1985	46	…	C
1986	54	…	…
1987	65	…	…
1988	51	…	B
1989	60	…	
1990	70	…	…
1991	56	…	…
1992	66		…
1993	76		

Question 86

Suppose the actual minus trend values in a time series analysis with a 3-year cycle are as follows:

1990	1991	1992	1993	1994	1995	1996	1997	1998
7.3	−1	−1	8.3	−1.1	−0.3	8	−8	0

Designating 1990 as year 1 of a cycle, calculate the cyclical components for the 3 years of the cycle, using an additive model and giving your answers correct to the nearest whole number.

Question 87

In data with a 4-year cycle, the cyclical components using the additive model are given to be:

Year 1	Year 2	Year 3	Year 4
10	15	−5	−20

If 2000 is year 1 of a cycle and if the trend for 2004 is predicted to be 70, predict the actual value for 2004.

Question 88

What is the formula for seasonally adjusted data in a multiplicative model? Use the symbols A for actual value, T for trend, S for seasonal component and R for residual.

Question 89

Which of the following correctly describes the purpose of seasonal adjustment?

(A) It adjusts the trend to give an estimate of the actual value.
(B) It adjusts the seasonal components to add to zero in an additive model.
(C) It adjusts the actual value to give an estimate of the trend.

Question 90

The quarterly sales of Brand X for a 2-year period are given below:

	Q_1	Q_2	Q_3	Q_4
1997	45	66	79	40
1998	64	99	105	60
1999	90			

Past experience has shown that the average seasonal variations for this product field are as follows:

Q_1	Q_2	Q_3	Q_4
−10%	+20%	+30%	−40%

A multiplicative model is assumed to apply: Sales = Trend × Seasonal × Residual.

(a) Seasonally adjust the sales of brand X for the four quarters of 1997, giving your answers to one d.p.
(b) Which of the following correctly describes the seasonal variation shown above for the 3rd quarter?

(A) Actual sales are 30 per cent above the trend.
(B) The trend is 30 per cent above the actual sales.
(C) Actual sales are 30 per cent more than the annual average.
(D) The trend is 30 per cent more than that of the previous quarter.

Probability

Question 91

A sales representative calls on three unrelated customers. There is an 80 per cent chance of making a sale at any one of them. The probability of making exactly two sales is:

(A) 0.128
(B) 0.64
(C) 1.92
(D) 0.384

Question 92

A project may result in the following profits with the probabilities stated.

Profit	Probability
£40,000	0.32
£35,000	0.54
(£12,000)	0.14

Calculate the expected profit.

Question 93

A variable X is normally distributed with mean 45 kg and standard deviation 5 kg. Find the following probabilities:

(a) $P(X > 50)$
(b) $P(X < 58)$
(c) $P(38 < X < 50)$

Question 94

A porcelain manufacturer has three assembly lines (X, Y and Z) producing decorative plates. An inspector samples finished plates from the assembly lines in the ratio 1:2:3 respectively.
 During a shift the inspector examines 240 plates.
 Calculate how many plates the inspector examines per shift from each assembly line.

Question 95

During a shift an inspector examines 50, 100 and 150 items from three production lines X, Y and Z respectively. Analysis of past inspection records suggests that the defective rates from the assembly lines are:

X	Y	Z
8%	10%	30%

Complete the following table by filling in the appropriate numerical values in the spaces indicated by the letters:

	X	Y	Z	Total
Good	...	...	...	C
Defective	A	B	...	...
Total	50	100	150	300

Question 96

In a typical shift, the numbers of good or defective items examined from three production lines (X, Y and Z) are as follows:

	X	Y	Z	Totals
Good	45	70	120	235
Defective	5	25	45	75
Totals	50	95	165	310

(a) Calculate the probability that a plate sampled is defective, giving your answer to three d.p.
(b) Calculate the probability that a plate sampled comes from Assembly line Z, given that it is defective, giving your answer to three d.p.

Question 97

A travel agent keeps a stock of holiday brochures. Currently there is a total of 500 brochures in stock, as follows: 285 for European holidays, 90 for American holidays, 110 for Asian holidays and 15 for African holidays. A brochure is selected at random. Calculate the following probabilities (to two d.p.):

(A) that a European brochure is selected;
(B) that an African brochure is not selected;
(C) that neither an American nor an Asian brochure is selected;
(D) that either a European or an Asian brochure is selected.

Question 98

What is meant by 'mutually exclusive events'?

(A) Events which can only occur together
(B) Events for which the occurrence of one has no effect on the probability of the occurrence of the other
(C) Events which cannot occur together
(D) Events for which the occurrence of one makes the probability of the occurrence of the other equal zero.

Question 99

A die is rolled twice and first shows a 3 and then a 5. Are these two events

(a) Independent
(b) Mutually exclusive
(c) Neither?

Question 100

A travel agent decides to use expected profits as an aid to deciding which holidays to offer. Which of the following statements about the use of expected profits is/are correct?

(A) Options are selected on the basis of how high their expected profits are
(B) An advantage of the method is that it takes no account of subjective factors such as attitude to risk
(C) A disadvantage of the method is that it fails to take account of the probabilities of various outcomes
(D) A disadvantage of the method is that it requires substantial prediction of profits and probabilities.

Question 101

In a forthcoming sales promotion each pack of cigarettes is to contain a leaflet with eight 'scratch-off square patches, randomly arranged. The purchaser will scratch off one patch to reveal the value of a small prize. The value of the eight patches on the leaflet is to be as follows:

Value of prize	£0.20	£0.50	£1
Number of patches	5	2	1

(a) The company has to decide on the number of packs in which to put leaflets, given a budget of £75,000. Calculate the average value of prizes per leaflet, giving your answer to three d.p.
(b) If the mean cost per leaflet were 40p, calculate the number of leaflets that would on average be appropriate to a budget of £75,000.

Question 102

In a promotion for cigarettes, a leaflet pictures a roulette wheel with thirty-seven numbers, seven of which are randomly arranged winning numbers. The purchaser is allowed to scratch off seven of the thirty-seven numbers in the hope of winning a prize. It is therefore possible to select 0, 1, 2, 3, 4, 5, 6 or 7 winning numbers on each leaflet.

(a) What is the probability, to three d.p., that the first number scratched does not win a prize?
(b) What is the probability, to four d.p., that all seven numbers scratched do not win prizes?
(c) If there are one million purchases during the promotion and if the probability that all seven numbers do not win a prize were 0.2, what is the expected number of purchasers who will win no prizes at all?

Question 103

The specification for the length of an engine part is a minimum of 99 mm and a maximum of 104.4 mm. A batch of parts is produced that is normally distributed with a mean of 102 mm and a standard deviation of 2 mm.

(a) Calculate the percentage of undersized parts.
(b) Calculate the percentage of oversized parts.

Question 104

If 7 per cent of parts are defective, calculate the average number of parts that must be produced in order to obtain 1,000 usable parts, giving your answer to the nearest whole number.

Question 105

A golf club has to decide how many programmes to produce for a charity golf tournament.

The best quotation from a local printer is £2,000 plus 10p per copy. Advertising revenue totals £1,500. Programmes are sold for 60p each. Unsold programmes are worthless. Throughout this question, work to the nearest £.

(a) Complete the table showing the cost of producing various numbers of leaflets by filling in appropriate numerical values in the spaces indicated by letters:

Number produced	Cost (£)
1,000	A
2,000	B
3,000	...
4,000	...
5,000	C

(b) Complete the table showing the revenue from selling various numbers of leaflets by filling in appropriate numerical values in the spaces indicated by letters:

Number sold	Revenue (£)
1,000	...
2,000	...
3,000	D
4,000	E
5,000	F

Question 106

Suppose the profit table at various production and sales levels and the probabilities of the various levels of demand were as follows:

Profit table (£)

Demand (probability)	Production levels				
	1,000	2,000	3,000	4,000	5,000
1,000 ($p = 0.1$)	0	(100)	(200)	(300)	(400)
2,000 ($p = 0.4$)	0	500	400	300	200
3,000 ($p = 0.2$)	0	500	1,000	900	800
4,000 ($p = 0.2$)	0	500	1,000	1,500	1,400
5,000 ($p = 0.1$)	0	500	1,000	1,500	2,000

Calculate the expected profit resulting from each production level.

Question 107

A company manufactures automatic vending machines. One of the simplest machines is operated by a £1 coin. Inside the machine, a photoelectric cell is used to assess whether a coin is genuine or counterfeit by measuring the time (t) it takes to roll a fixed distance down a slope. Since coins and machines vary a little in size and wear, there is some small variation in time t.

From extensive testing it has been found that the time t taken by genuine £1 coins follows a normal distribution with a mean of 300 units of time and a standard deviation of 20.

For commonly used counterfeit coins the tests revealed a normally distributed time with a mean of 150 units of time and a standard deviation of 50.

The manufacturer sets the limits of acceptability at a minimum of 260 units of time.

(a) Calculate the percentage of counterfeit coins that take more than 260 units of time.
(b) Calculate the percentage of genuine coins taking less than 260 time units.
(c) Find the value N such that the probability $P(z < N) = 0.01$, where z is the standard normal variable. Give your answer to two d.p.

Question 108

(a) Solve for y where
$8x + 4y \geq 100$
(b) Solve for y where
$-10x + 20y \leq -80$.

Question 109

The probability that a student speaks French fluently is 0.20. The probability that a student speaks Greek is 0.10. The probability that a student speaks neither languages is 0.75.

Using Venn Diagrams calculate the probability that a student speaks both.

Spreadsheet skills using Excel

Question 110

Write down the formula required to perform the following calculations.

(a) A group of 8 people share the cost of a birthday celebration for 34 friends. The price of the meal per person is £25 plus £6 for wine and £4 for coffee. Calculate the amount each of the 8 will need to pay – enter all the variables into your calculation and use only one Excel cell.
(b) The cost per head of new football shirt and shorts for the village team is £25 plus £6 for socks, and £10 for the goalkeeper's gloves. How much will it cost to kit out the full team of 11 players? Enter all the variables into your calculation and use only one Excel cell.

(c) Perform these calculations to the specified number of decimal places

$= 34/5 \times 6.37$ (to 2 d.p.)
$= 1126 \times 14.2^2$ (to nearest whole number)
$= (199 + 45) \times 1.177 + 78.43$ (to 1 d.p.).

Question 111

(a) Given the following spreadsheet give the formula that would required in cell B4 through B8 to calculate the compound interest rate.

	A	B	C	D	E
1	Investment amount	2000			
2	Interest rate	10%			
3					
4	Year no.	1			
5		2			
6		3			
7		4			
8		5			
9					
10					

(b) Given that the cost of buying boxes of your favourite breakfast cereal from a supermarket website is £3.45 per box for 1 to 10 units and that there is a discount if 7.5 per cent for purchases of more than 10 units calculate the cost of 15 units. There is also a delivery charge of £5.99. Enter the Excel formula for calculating the cost of 15 boxes.

Question 112

Given the data below show the Excel functions and formulae required to calculate the ROI and the NPV on the following investment

	A	B	C	D	E	F
1	Amount invested	80000				
2	Cash Flow year 1	60000				
3	Cash flow year 2	15000				
4	Cash flow year 3	21000				
5	Cash flow year 4	25000				
6						
7	Fixed cost of capital	15%				
8						
9						
10	ROI					
11	NPV					
12						
13						

Question 113

Given the data in the spreadsheet below, show the linear regression formula required in cell c2 to forecast the sale of drinks at a given temperature.

	A	B
1	Temperature	Litre of cold drinks sold
2	15	120
3	17	125
4	19	125
5	15	120
6	21	130
7	25	130
8	22	125
9	19	125
10	18	100
11	20	115

Question 114

State three important principles of spreadsheet design.

Solutions to Revision Questions

Basic mathematics

✓ Solution 1

Answer: (C)

The selling price without VAT would be £3.99 × 100/117.5 = 3.395745. Hence the price with 15 per cent VAT would be 3.395745 × 1.15 = £3.91.

(A) is incorrect because the price has been reduced by 17.5 per cent prior to increasing by 15 per cent. (B) cannot be correct because it shows an increase – it results from getting the 17.5 per cent and 15 per cent interchanged. (D) is the price with no VAT at all.

✓ Solution 2

(A)	To two d.p.	2,490.74
(B)	To one d.p.	2,490.7
(C)	To the nearest whole number	2,491
(D)	To the nearest 1,000	2,000
(E)	To three s.f.	2,490
(F)	To four s.f.	2,491

✓ Solution 3

(A)	$20Y = 85(40 - Y)$	Correct.
(B)	$20Y = 3,400 - Y$?	Incorrect: the Y should also have been multiplied by 85.
(C)	$19Y = 3,400$	Incorrect: the $-Y$ should become $+Y$ when taken across to the other side of the equation.
(D)	$Y = 3,400/19$	Correct.
(E)	$Y = 178.94$ (two d.p.)	Incorrect: 178.947 rounds to 178.95.

✓ Solution 4

(a) Working to the nearest £, the maximum possible difference between the true figure and the rounded figure is 50p.

(b) The maximum absolute error as a percentage of the rounded figure = 100 × 0.5/20 = 2.5 per cent.

Solution 5

(a)

	Minimum cost per unit £	Expected cost per unit £	Maximum cost per unit £
Direct materials	3.84	4.00	4.16
Direct labour	1.90	2.00	2.10
Direct overheads	1.13	1.20	1.27
	6.87	7.20	7.53

(b) Maximum absolute error = 0.33
Maximum percentage error = $100 \times 0.33/7.20 = 4.6$ per cent

(c) For 50,000 units the maximum absolute error in total cost is $50,000 \times 0.33 =$ £16,500.

Solution 6

If $P = aD + b$

where $P = 7, D = 1,050$ so $7 = 1,050a + b$ (1)
where $P = 9, D = 950$ so $9 = 950a + b$ (2)

(2) minus (1) gives
$$2 = -100a$$
so $a = -0.02$

substituting into (1) gives
$$7 = -0.02 \times 1,050 + b$$
so $b = 7 + 21 = 28$
hence $P = 28 - 0.02D$

Answer: $a = -0.02$; $b = 28$

Solution 7

Revenue = Price $\times$ Demand
$= (30 - 0.03D)D$
$= 30D - 0.03D^2$

Solution 8

Costs per week consist of:
    Fixed costs: £2,000
    Variable costs £4 per unit + 2% of D^2

Answer: $C = 2,000 + 4D + 0.02D^2$

Solution 9

Profit = Revenue − Costs
$$= (25D - 0.01D^2) - (1,500 + 4D + 0.03D^2)$$
$$= -1,500 + 21D - 0.04D^2$$

Solution 10

Breakeven occurs where profit = 0

The solution is given by $D = \dfrac{-b \pm \sqrt{b^2 - 4ac}}{2a}$

where $a = -0.04$, $b = 24$, $c = -2000$

$$D = \dfrac{-24 \pm \sqrt{576 - 320}}{-0.08} = \dfrac{-24 \pm 16}{-0.08}$$
$$= 500 \text{ or } 100$$

Solution 11

The corresponding prices are
$$P = 30 - 0.03 \times 200 = £24$$
$$\text{or } P = 30 - 0.03 \times 400 = £18$$

Solution 12

Costs for 100 units, India to UK

Cost of 100 units: 100 × Rs 500 × 0.8	Rs 40,000
Freight	Rs 60,000
Subtotal	Rs 100,000
Plus 2% insurance: subtotal × 1.02	Rs 102,000
Total in £ = 102,000/47	£2,170.21
Plus transport in UK = £200 + £5 × 100	£700
Total cost for 100 units from India to UK	£2,870.21

Solution 13

Costs for 500 units, USA to UK

Cost of 500 units: 500× $20 × 0.9	$9,000
Carriage etc. = 1,000 + 0.05 × 9,000	$1,450
Total cost	$10,450
Total cost in £: 10,450/1.8	£5,805.56

Solution 14

Costs in UK per 100 devices

	£
Other materials: £10 × 100	1,000
Instrumentation: £6 × 500	3,000
Production: £5 × 200	1,000
Inspection: £8 × 50	400
Subtotal	5,400
Plus 50% for fixed costs: 5,400 × 1.5	8,100

Solution 15

Total cost for 100 units

$$3,000 + 6,000 \times 2/5 + 8,000 = 13,400$$

After inspection only 80 devices remain per 100

$$\text{Unit cost} = 13,400/80 = 167.50$$

In order to give profit at 25 per cent of trade price, the unit cost must equal 75 per cent of the trade price per unit and hence

$$\text{Unit price} = 167.50/0.75 = £223.33$$

Obtaining data

Solution 16

Answer: (B)

Solution 17

The methods that result in cluster samples are (A) and (B). (C) gives a multistage sample, and (D) gives a stratified sample.

Solution 18

Method	Example
A Simple random sample	U
B Stratified random sample	T
C Cluster sample	S
D Systematic sample	P
E Quota sample	Q
F Multi-stage sample	R

Solution 19

The census in the United Kingdom does generally ask households about their composition and expenditure but these features do not define what is meant by a census. It is a survey of the entire population of interest which might not even comprise people.

Answer: (B)

Solution 20

A sample is a subgroup of the population of interest. All the other groups described were types of samples but none of them were general enough to constitute a definition.

Answer: (C)

Solution 21

If the required total sample size is 1,000, of these, 450 will be men and 550 women. Sixty per cent of the 550 women, that is, 330 women, will live in the suburbs. Thirty per cent of these women will be aged 34 or less, which amounts to 99 women.

Solution 22

The company presumably has quite detailed records of its clients of recent years and so it should be possible to select a representative sample from, say, clients spanning the last 2 years. Stratified random sampling is the method that most ensures representative samples and accurate estimates, and the company possesses sufficient information to make this method possible. Stratification has the additional benefit of providing information about people in the different strata. It will also be possible to compare the responses of different types of clients.

Answers: (B), (C) and (D) are correct

Solution 23

Visiting people at home and conducting face-to-face interviews is the best survey method in terms of percentage response and high-quality completion of questionnaires. However, it is also the most expensive option due to labour and travel costs and, if the company is small with only a small budget to devote to the survey, this method would probably not be used.

Telephone interviews seem to be quite a good alternative to face to face in this case. The response rate is not as good as with face-to-face interviews but is a great deal better than that obtained from simply posting out questionnaires, and the quality of completion of questionnaires remains high. It is considerably cheaper than travel costs and far more interviews can be carried out per hour since no time is lost in travelling. There may be slight bias in telephone surveys due to a small proportion of the population not having telephones.

Posting out questionnaires is the cheapest option, even if some prize is offered to encourage response. It is, however, a poor method in terms both of response rate and the standard of completion of questionnaires and should be avoided unless the survey has a really very low budget.

Answers:
(A) posting questionnaires;
(B) face-to-face interviews;
(C) face-to-face interviews;
(D) postal questionnaires;
(E) face-to-face interviews;
(F) postal questionnaires.

Presentation of data

✓ Solution 24

(a) Maximum
(b) $x = (-1 + 3)/2 = 1$
(c) $y = k(3 - x)(1 + x)$
   $y = k(3 + 2x - x^2)$
   When $x = 0$, $y = 3k = 30$, so $k = 10$

✓ Solution 25

Weight	Frequency	Height of bar
0–5	83	83
5–10	105	105
10–20	160	80
20–40	96	24
40–100	108	9

✓ Solution 26

Categories	%	Angle
A	8	29
B	43	155
C	37	133
D	12	43

Solution 27

Value of orders £	Frequency	Interval width	Freq. density
5–15	36	10	18
15–20	48	5	48
20–25	53	5	53
25–30	84	5	84
30–35	126	5	126
35–40	171	5	171
40–45	155	5	155
45–50	112	5	112
50–55	70	5	70
55–65	60	10	30
65–85	54	20	13.5

Solution 28

Answer: (B)
The heights of the bars in a histogram.

Solution 29

Chart E is symmetrical or normal
Answers: (G), (H)

Chart F is positively skewed
Answer: (J)

Solution 30

Answer: (C)
Component bar chart.

Solution 31

Although it is evident from the next graph that from 1990 onwards the balance of trade began to decline, this was not shown by the component bar chart. The statement that oil was declining was incorrect in 1990 and also could not possibly be deduced from the chart. The other three conclusions could correctly be drawn from the chart.

Answers: (A), (B) and (D)

Solution 32

The invisible balance peaked in 1996 and then fell, so it has not climbed steadily. Also by 1999 the balance on visible oil was not greater then that on invisibles. The other statements are correct

Answers: (A) and (D)

Descriptive statistics

✅ Solution 33

(A) and (D) are true. In general the averages are mode, median and mean in order of increasing magnitude.

✅ Solution 34

(a) The mean = 1,150/8 = 143.75
Putting the data into order of magnitude: 60, 75, 85, 125, 130, 200, 225, 250
(b) The median = (125 + 130)/2 = 127.5
(c) The lower quartile = (75 + 85)/2 = 80
(d) The upper quartile = (200 + 225)/2 = 212.5
(e) The quartile deviation = (212.5 − 80)/2 = 66.25

✅ Solution 35

Standard deviation = 9.5 $\left(\text{as } s = \sqrt{\dfrac{\Sigma fx^2}{\Sigma f} - \dfrac{\Sigma fx}{\Sigma f}} = \sqrt{\dfrac{12{,}050}{100} - \left(\dfrac{550}{100}\right)^2} \right)$

✅ Solution 36

Salary (£000)	Frequency	Cumulative frequency
Under 10	16	16
10–under 20	28	44
20–under 30	36	80
30–under 40	20	100
40–under 50	12	112
50–under 70	4	116
70 and over	4	120

✅ Solution 37

Ogive of salaries

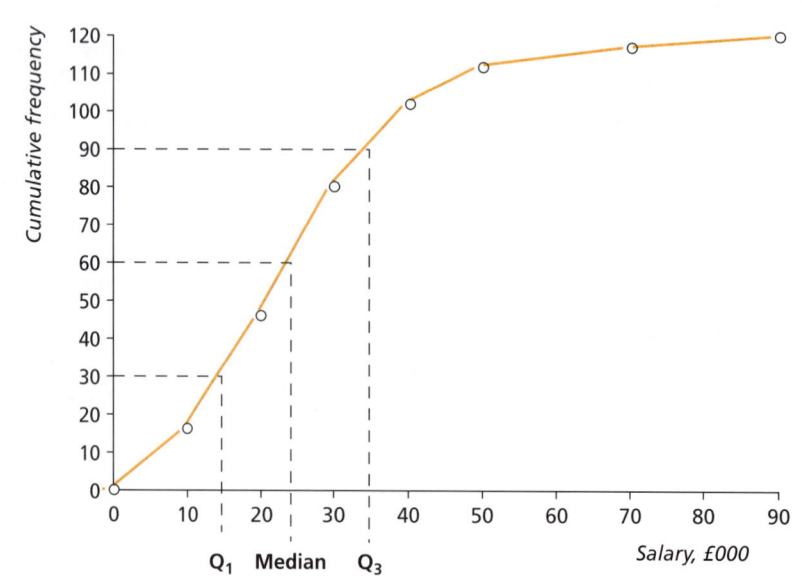

$$\text{Cumulative frequency of median} = \frac{120}{2} = 60$$

From ogive, median = £24,000

$$\text{Cumulative frequency of Q1} = \frac{120}{4} = 30$$

From ogive, Q1 = £15,000

$$\text{Cumulative frequency of Q3} = 3 \times \frac{120}{4} = 90$$

From ogive, Q3 = £35,000

Answers to the nearest £5000:
(A) £25,000
(B) £15,000
(C) £35,000

✓ Solution 38

$$\text{Quartile deviation} = \frac{1,242 - 892}{2} = £175$$

✓ Solution 39

$$\bar{x} = \frac{3,140}{120} = 26.167$$

The mean salary is £26,167

$$\sigma = \sqrt{\frac{112,800}{120} - \left(\frac{3,140}{120}\right)^2} = 15.978$$

The standard deviation of salary is £15,978

Answers:
(A) £26,167
(B) £16,000

✓ Solution 40

Both the mean and the standard deviation have increased. The mean measures the average level whilst the standard deviation measures variability so statements (A) and (C) are correct.

✓ Solution 41

(a) Quartile deviation = (4,000 − 1,500)/2 = 1,250

Answer: 1,250

(b) The quartiles and the median lie at the quarter, half and three quarter points of the data so statements (A), (B), (D) and E are all correct. For symmetrical data we would expect approximately two-thirds of invoices have values within one standard deviation either side of the mean but this does not apply to quartiles and the median.

Answers: (A), (B), (D) and (E)

✓ Solution 42

When the data are skewed the mean either underestimates or exaggerates the average level and the median is preferable.

Answer: (C)

✓ Solution 43
Number of telephone calls

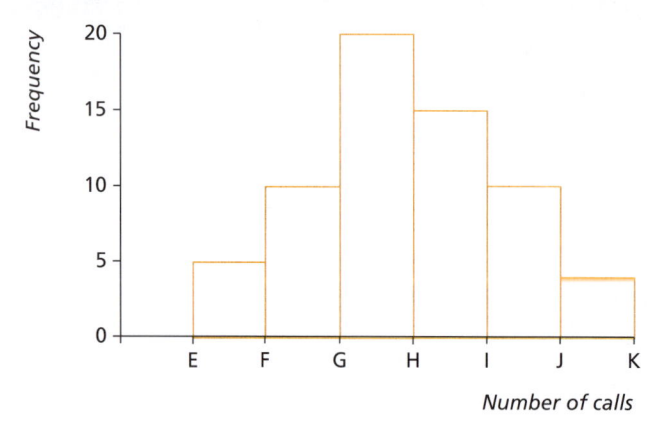

(a) The chart is a histogram
Answer: (D)

(b) (E)   9.5
(F) 19.5
(G) 29.5
(H) 39.5
(I)   49.5
(J)   59.5
(K) 69.5

✓ Solution 44

The mean number of calls is:

$$\frac{\Sigma fx}{\Sigma f} = \frac{2,478}{64} = 38.72 \text{ calls.}$$

The standard deviation, s, is given by:

$$s^2 = \frac{\Sigma fx^2}{\Sigma f} - \bar{x}^2 = \frac{106,906}{64} - 38.72^2 = 171.17$$

hence, $s = 13.08$ calls $= 13.1$ calls (to one d.p.).

Average daily cost is £20 × 38.72 = 774.4.

Answers:
(A) 38.72
(B) 13.1
(C) 774

Index numbers

✓ Solution 45

Answer: 400 × 100/178 = £224.72

✓ Solution 46

Year	Price index (1991 = 100)	Price index (1997 = 100)
1994	138	92
1995	142	94.7
1996	147	98
1997	150	100
	(1997 = 100)	
1998	109	109
1999	113	113
2000	119	119

✓ Solution 47

Year	1997	1998	1999	2000
Chain index	105.4	104.8	103.9	104.2
1997 = 100	100.0	104.8	108.9	113.5

✓ Solution 48

(a)

	w	P_0	P_1	$P_1 w$	$P_0 w$
A	9	10	10.2	91.8	90
B	13	12	12.5	162.5	156
C	8	9	9	72	72
D	20	25	26	520.0	500
Totals				846.3	818

(b) Price index = $100 \times \dfrac{\Sigma P_1 w}{\Sigma P_0 w} = 100 \times \dfrac{846.3}{818} = 103.5$ (one d.p.)

(c) If the quantities remain the same but prices increase by 4 per cent, the current budget of £200,000 will increase to 200,000 × 1.04 = £208,000.

✓ Solution 49

An index of 104 means that prices have risen by 4 per cent, which in turn means that current values are 1.04 times their values in the base year, on average.

Answers: (B), (C)

✓ Solution 50

It is a current weighted aggregative index, so B and E are correct.

Answers: (B) and (E)

✓ Solution 51

(a) *Base year*

The current base time is January 1987, so all subsequent values of the retail price index (RPI) must be related back to that date. In order that the index will be meaningful and useful, the base time has to be updated from time to time, depending on the extent to which prices and consumer preferences are changing. The most recent previous base times were January 1962 and 1974.

Answers: (A), (D)

(b) *Weights*

The weights used in the construction of the RPI are given by the average household's expenditure on each particular item, out of every £1,000 spent. So if the typical household spends £5 out of every £1,000 on margarine, then the weighting for margarine will be 5. The weights are obtained from a massive annual government survey called the Family Expenditure Survey (FES). The sample of households used is distributed in a representative fashion across the United Kingdom, in terms of the type of area in which they live (rural, urban, etc.) and of their region, and the survey is conducted throughout the year. Every member of selected households keeps a diary of all their expenditure for two weeks and one member of the household is interviewed about larger expenditures. Very rich (top 4 per cent) and very poor people (14 per cent, mainly dependent on state benefits) are not included in the survey and so the weights used in the RPI will not reflect their purchasing habits. Finally, the weights used come from the previous year's survey since it is not possible to use absolutely current weights.

Answers: (C), (D), (E)

(c) *Items included*

From time to time items are removed from the RPI and replaced by new ones. The information necessary to make this sort of decision is largely derived from the FES and items will be removed when their weights become very low. Some 600 'price indicators' are currently included. They are combined together into 80 sections which in turn are combined into the following five broad groups:

- food and catering;
- alcohol and tobacco;
- housing and household expenditure;

- personal expenditure;
- travel and leisure.

Certain things on which households spend money are not in the index. Among these are savings, including pension contributions, and the capital part of mortgage repayments, life insurance, betting payments, cash gifts and income tax.

Answers: (A), (B), (E)

(d) *Data collection*

Each month approximately 130,000 price quotations are collected for the 600 price indicators. Department of Employment staff from some 180 offices throughout the country, on a Tuesday in the middle of each month, visit a representative sample of outlets – supermarkets, corner shops, etc.

Answers: (B), (C), (D)

✓ Solution 52

(a) GDP index (1985 = 100)

$$1980 \quad \frac{231}{354} \times 100 = 65.3 = A$$

$$1989 \quad \frac{436}{354} \times 100 = 123.2 = B$$

(b) $C = 65 \times 100/71 = 91.5$
$D = 116 \times 100/108 = 107.4$

Answers: $C = 91.5$, $D = 107.4$

✓ Solution 53

If an index of average gross earnings with base year 1995 and at constant 1995 prices is calculated to be 107 by 2000, it means that 7 per cent more goods and services can be bought by average earnings over a 5 year period.

Answer: (B)

✓ Solution 54

(a) Index comparing total revenues

$= 100 \times \Sigma R_1 / \Sigma R_0$
$= 100 \times 275/190$
$= 144.7$

(b) Unweighted index of numbers sold $= 100 \times 2,100/1,500 = 140$

Solution 55

Relative index of quantity sold with base revenues as weights

$= 100 \times (SR_0 Q_1 / Q_0) \div SR_0$
$= 100 \times 268/190$
$= 141.1$

Financial mathematics

Solution 56

Answer: $2{,}500 \times 1.004^8 = 2{,}581.13$

Solution 57

- Three-year ratio $= 4{,}000/3{,}500 = 1.142857$
- Annual ratio $= 1.0455$
- Effective annual rate $= 4.6$ per cent

Solution 58

Time	Cash flow £	Discount factor 5%	Present value £
0	(10,000)	1.000	(10,000)
1	4,000	0.952	3,808
2	5,000	0.907	4,535
3	4,000	0.864	3,456
NPV			(1,799)

Solution 59

(a) If interest is compounded annually with £6,000 being invested per year, the first year's £6,000 will be invested for four years and will grow to $6{,}000 \times 1.12^4$.

Answer: 9,441.12

(b) The second year's £6,000 will grow to $6{,}000 \times 1.12^3$ and so on to the fifth year's £6,000, which will not have grown at all.

$Total = 6{,}000(1.12^4 + 1.12^3 + 1.12^2 + 1.12 + 1) = £38{,}117.08$

(b) If interest is compounded monthly, the first of the 60 payments will be invested for 60 months and will grow to 500×1.01^{60}; the second will grow to 500×1.01^{59} and so on. The final payment will be invested for just one month and so will grow to 500×1.01.

$Total = 500(1.01^{60} + 1.01^{59} + \cdots + 1.01)$
$= 500 \times \dfrac{1.01(1.01^{60} - 1)}{0.01} = £41{,}243.18$

Solution 60

(a) The mortgage can be viewed as an annuity of £A running for 100 quarters at a rate of 4 per cent. We can equate the present value of the annuity to the initial cost of £50,000 using the formula for the PV of an annuity:

$$50,000 = A \times \left(\frac{1}{0.04} - \frac{1}{0.04 \times 1.04^{100}} \right) = 24.505A$$

(b) $50,000 = 24.505A$

$A = 50,000/24.505 = £2,040.40$ payment per quarter

(c) The annual ratio is $1.04^4 = 1.16986$, so the effective annual rate is 16.99 per cent (to two d.p.).

Solution 61

(a)

Beginning of year	Discount factor	Cash flow £	Discounted cash flow £
1	1.000	3,000	3,000
2	0.943	3,500	3,300.5
3	0.890	4,000	3,560
4	0.840	12,000	10,080
5	0.792	4,000	3,168
6	0.747	4,500	3,361.5
7	0.705	5,000	3,525
8	0.665	13,000	8,645
			38,640

(b) The discount factor for £1 at the *start* of each of 8 years is 1 (for the immediate payment) plus the cumulative discount factor given by tables for the *end* of the first 7 years. So if the hospital pays £X at the start of each of the 8 years, its present value = $X(1 + \text{cumulative discount factor for 7 years at 6 per cent}) = 5.582X$.

(c) The maximum is given by $6.8X = 38,640$

hence $X = 38,640/6.8 = 5,682.35$

Solution 62

Present value

	Cash flow £	Discount factor 10%	Present value £
Year 1	10,500	0.909	9,545
Year 2	11,025	0.826	9,107
Year 3	11,576	0.751	8,694
Year 4	25,000 + 12,155	0.683	25,377
Year 5	12,763	0.621	7,926
Year 6	13,401	0.564	7,558
Year 7	14,071	0.513	7,218

Answers:

(A) 10,500
(B) 12,155
(C) 0.826
(D) 8,694
(E) 7,926

Solution 63

The supplier's maintenance contract is a year-end annuity of £13,000 per year. Discounting at 10 per cent and using the cumulative discount factor table gives a present value of $13{,}000 \times 4.868 = 63{,}284$.

Solution 64

All things being equal, the project with the larger net present value would be selected.

Answer: (A)

Solution 65

(a) The first payment £A is invested for 12 quarters at 2 per cent and achieves a value of $A \times 1.02^{12}$. The second achieves a value of $A \times 1.02^{11}$ and so on until the twelfth payment achieves a value of $1.02A$. Hence the final value of the fund is $A[1.02^{12} + 1.02^{11} + \cdots + 1.02]$.

(b) The expression is a GP with first term 1.035, common ratio 1.035 and $n = 10$. Sum $= 1.035(1.035^{10} - 1)/0.035 = 12.1420$

Solution 66

(a) It is easiest to consider a mortgage as an annuity with, in this case, $n = 40$, $r = 0.03$ and quarterly repayment B. Hence:

$$100{,}000 = B\left(\frac{1}{0.03} - \frac{1}{0.03 \times 1.03^{40}}\right) = 23.11477B$$

(b) $24B = 100{,}000$
$B = 100{,}000/24 = £4{,}166.67$

✅ Solution 67

Annual ratio = quarterly ratio^4 = 1.03^4 = 1.1255

Hence the effective annual rate is 12.55 per cent.

✅ Solution 68

(a)

Year	Net cash inflow (£'000)	Discount factor	Present value (£'000)
0	(90)	1.000	(90)
1	(30)	0.917	(27.51)
2	50	0.842	42.10
3	40	0.772	30.88
4	30	0.708	21.24
5	40	0.650	26.00
			NPV = 2.71

(b)

Year	Net cash inflow (£'000)	Discount factor	Present value (£'000)
0	(90)	1.000	(90)
1	(50)	0.917	(45.85)
2	40	0.842	33.68
3	40	0.772	30.88
4	40	0.708	28.32
5	60	0.650	39.00
			NPV = (3.97)

(c) Answer: Machine A.

Correlation and regression

✅ Solution 69

(a) Denoting sales by y and advertising expenditure by x,

$$b = \frac{n\Sigma xy - \Sigma x \Sigma y}{n\Sigma x^2 - (\Sigma x)^2} = \frac{10 \times 1{,}457.5 - 23 \times 600}{10 \times 62 - (23)^2} = 8.516$$

(b) $a = 60 - (8.516 \times 2.3) = 40.41$

(c) The correlation coefficient is given by:

$$r = \frac{n\Sigma xy - \Sigma x \Sigma y}{\sqrt{(n\Sigma x^2 - (\Sigma x)^2)(n\Sigma y^2 - (\Sigma y)^2)}} = \frac{10 \times 1{,}457.5 - 23 \times 600}{\sqrt{(10 \times 62 - 23^2)(10 \times 36{,}950 - 600^2)}}$$
$$= 0.83$$

Solution 70

Site	Accidents rank	Spending rank	D
A	8	2	6
B	5	7	−2
C	6	6	0
D	2	9	−7
E	7	3.5	3.5
F	9	5	4
G	10	1	9
H	4	3.5	0.5
I	3	8	−5
J	1	10	−9

Solution 71

$$R = 1 - \frac{6 \times 304.5}{10 \times 99} = 1 - 1.8455 = -0.8455$$

Solution 72

The rank correlation is positive and hence values of Y increase as values of X increase. Numerically its value is close to 1 and hence the link between X and Y values is very strong. We can never deduce cause and effect from any correlation coefficient, however large, so (F) is incorrect as are the numerical comments in (B) and (C). (E) is incorrect because a linear relationship between ranks of values does not necessarily imply one between the values themselves.

Answers: (A), (D)

Solution 73

(a) $Y = 5.0913 + 0.2119X$

When X increases by 1, Y increases by 0.2119 and since Y is measured in £000 this means that marginal cost is £21.19 per unit. When $X = 0$, $Y = 5.0913$ which means that fixed costs are £5,091.3

Answers: (A) & (D)

(b) $Y = 5.0913 + 0.2119 \times 300 = 11.488$ (£'000)

Solution 74

A coefficient of determination between output and production costs, tells us that 89 per cent of the variation in production costs from one month to the next can be explained by corresponding variation in output. It also tells us that the linear relationship between output and costs is very strong.

Only a positive correlation can tell us that costs increase as output increases and we cannot assume this from the coefficient of determination.

Answers: (A), (C)

✓ Solution 75

A standard regression equation $Y = a + bX$ can only be used to estimate Y for a known X. It cannot be used to estimate X if Y is known.

Answer: (A)

✓ Solution 76

Answer: (C)
The coefficient of determination is given by squaring the correlation coefficient.

✓ Solution 77

Answer: 0.054

✓ Solution 78

(a) False: $Y = 45$ when $X = 0$.
(b) False: Y increases by 3.6 whenever X increases by 1.
(c) True.
(d) False: it is not possible to deduce the correlation coefficient from the regression equation.

Time Series

✓ Solution 79

Answer: (C)
The seasonally adjusted figure is given by $A/S = 1,500/1.17$

✓ Solution 80

(A) False: S is estimated by averaging A/T, not $A - T$.
(B) True.
(C) True.
(D) False: R is estimated from $A/(T \times S)$.
(E) False: the seasonally adjusted value is given by A/S.

Solution 81

Answer: Estimate = 2,446

Solution 82

The value of A is given by 49 + 37 + 58 + 67; B is the four quarters starting with 37 and reading downwards and C = A + B = 211 + 212 and the trend D = 423/8 = 52.875.

Year	Qtr	Actual revenue	Sum of 4 qtrs	Sum of 8 qtrs	Trend	Actual trend
90/91	1	49				
	2	37				
			211			
	3	58		423	52.875	
			212			
	4	67			53.125	1.261
			213			
91/92	1	50				
	2	38				
	3	59				
	4	68				

Solution 83

		Quarter		
	1	2	3	4
	0.937	0.709	1.095	1.253
	0.934	0.727	1.088	1.267
Total	1.871	1.436	2.183	2.52
Average	0.9355	0.718	1.0915	1.26

Solution 84

1st quarter	0.8 + 0.1 = 0.9
2nd quarter	0.6 + 0.1 = 0.7
3rd quarter	1.0 + 0.1 = 1.1
4th quarter	1.2 + 0.1 = 1.3
Total	3.6 + 0.4 = 4

Solution 85

Year	Sales ('000)	Three-year moving total	Trend
1983	50		
1984	59	155	51.7
1985	46	159	53
1986	54	165	55
1987	65	170	56.7
1988	51	176	58.7
1989	60	181	60.3
1990	70	186	62
1991	56	192	64
1992	66	198	66
1993	76		

Solution 86

$A - T$ values	Year one	Year two	Year three
	7.3	−7	−1
	8.3	−7.7	−0.3
	8	−8	0
Average	7.87	−7.57	−0.43

Rounding to nearest whole number gives cyclical components that total to zero:

Year one	Year two	Year three
+8	−8	0

Solution 87

The year 2004 will be year 1 of a cycle, with cyclical component = +10
Predicted value = predicted trend + seasonal component = 70 + 10 = 80

Solution 88

The formula for multiplicative model is $A = T \times S \times R$. Seasonal adjustment gives an instant estimate of the trend and hence its formula is $T = A/S$. Note that R is not involved because it can only be calculated when all of the other variables are known. In the multiplicative model we have to assume $R = 1$ for the purposes of seasonal adjustment.

Answer: *A/S*

Solution 89

Seasonal adjustment adjusts the actual value to give an estimate of the trend

Answer: (C)

Solution 90

(a) The actual seasonal factors are 0.9, 1.2, 1.3 and 0.6, respectively. The seasonally adjusted values are therefore 45/0.9, 66/1.2, 79/1.3 and 40/0.6.

Answers:
1st quarter   50
2nd quarter   55
3rd quarter   60.8
4th quarter   66.7

(b) If the seasonal variation is given as +30% it means that actual sales are 30% above the trend

Answer: (A)

Probability

✓ Solution 91

Answer: (D)
The probability is $3 \times 0.2 \times 0.8^2$.

✓ Solution 92

Expected profit = £30,020. This is given by $40 \times 0.32 + 35 \times 0.54 - 12 \times 0.14$ (£'000).

✓ Solution 93

(a) $P(X > 50) = P(Z > (50 - 45)/5) = P(Z > 1) = 0.5 - 0.3413 = 0.1587$
(b) $P(X < 58) = P(Z < (58 - 45)/5) = P(Z < 2.6) = 0.5 + 0.4953 = 0.9953$
(c) $P(38 < X < 54) = P(38 - 45)/5 < Z (54 - 45)/5)$

$$= P(-1.4 < Z < 1.8)$$
$$= 0.4192 + 0.4641 = 0.8833$$

✓ Solution 94

The ratio to apply is 1:2:3 = a total of 6. Therefore, the number of plates examined from each production line =

X	240/6 × 1	40
Y	240/6 × 2	80
Z	240/6 × 3	120
		240

✓ Solution 95

Good/defective table

	X	Y	Z	Total
Good	46	90	105	241
Defective	4	10	45	59
	50	100	150	300

✓ Solution 96

(a) The probability of a plate sampled being defective is therefore 75/310 = 0.242
(b) From the table there are 75 defective items and of these 45 come from Z. The probability is therefore 45/75 = 0.6

✓ Solution 97

Probability that a European brochure is selected:

  285/500 = 0.57

Probability that an African brochure is not selected:

  485/500 = 0.97

Probability that neither an American nor an Asian brochure is selected:

  300/500 = 0.60

Probability that either a European or an Asian brochure is selected:

  395/500 = 0.79

✓ Solution 98

Mutually exclusive events are those which cannot occur together. Another way of saying this is that the occurrence of one makes the probability of the occurrence of the other equal zero.

Answer(s): (C), (D)

✓ Solution 99

The result of the second roll of a die should not be affected in any way by the result of the first roll. So the events are independent.

Answer: (A)

✓ Solution 100

The method requires the expected profit to be calculated for each decision and then decisions are selected on the basis of how high their expected profits are.

Using expected values in decision-making introduces an objective tool to counter any personal bias of the decision-maker. Expected value analysis can be very useful where decisions have to be made on a repeated basis (e.g. how much stock to produce each day) since, in the long run, the outcomes will tend to average out in accordance with the probabilities set. One-off decisions do not have this attribute and therefore are less predictable.

Expected value analysis, however, restricts the benefits of one choice over another to purely financial considerations and cannot account for factors not directly related to short-term financial gain. For example, decision (A) may have a higher expected value than decision (B), but decision (B) may be preferred for strategic or marketing reasons.

Also, expected value theory does not account for the decision-maker's attitude towards risk. Decision (A) may be more profitable than (B) under expected value rules, but it may involve much more risk of a loss than decision (B). (B) may therefore be chosen on the basis that it will at least return a profit, even though this may not be as high as that possible or probable under decision (A).

Expected values are only as reliable as the data on which they are based. Much of this data may only be obtainable in a subjective way, for examples estimates of probabilities and potential cash flows.

Answers: (A), (D)

✓ Solution 101

(a) The mean value of the prize paid can be found:

Value of prize, x(£)	Number of patches (f)	xf
0.20	5	1.00
0.50	2	1.00
1.00	1	1.00
	8	3.00

The mean $= \dfrac{\Sigma fx}{\Sigma f} = £0.375$ per leaflet

(b) To attain a total budgeted payout of £75,000 at an average payout of £0.4 per leaflet, the number of leaflets should be:

$$\dfrac{75{,}000}{0.4} = 187{,}500$$

✓ Solution 102

(a) The probability of the first number scratched not winning a prize is 30/37.

Answer: 0.811.

(b) Once the first number is not a prize winner, there are twenty-nine non-prize-winning numbers left of the thirty-six on the card. The probability of the second number not winning a prize is thus 29/36.

Continuing this process, the probability of all seven numbers not winning is:

$(30/37) \times (29/36) \times (28/35) \times (27/34) \times (26/33) \times (25/32) \times (24/31) = 0.1977$

(c) The expected number is $1{,}000{,}000 \times 0.2 = 200{,}000$ purchasers

✓ Solution 103

(a) P (length < 99)

$= P(z < (99 - 102)/2 = -1.5)$
$=$ tail-end area associated with 1.5
$= 0.5 -$ table entry for 1.5
$= 0.5 - 0.4332$
$= 0.0668$, that is 6.68%

(b) $P(\text{length} > 104.4)$

$\quad = P(z < (104.4 - 102)/2 = -1.2)$
$\quad = \text{tail-end area associated with } 1.2$
$\quad = 0.5 - \text{table entry for } 1.2$
$\quad = 0.5 - 0.3849$
$\quad = 0.1151, \text{ that is } 11.51\%$

✓ Solution 104

In order to end up with 1,000 usable parts we need to produce N parts, of which $0.07N$ will be too small and will be scrapped. Hence:

$$N(1 - 0.7) = 1,000$$
$$N = 1,000/0.93 = 1,075$$

✓ Solution 105

(a)

Number produced	Cost (£)
1,000	2,100
2,000	2,200
3,000	2,300
4,000	2,400
5,000	2,500

(b)

Number sold	Revenue (£)
1,000	2,100
2,000	2,700
3,000	3,300
4,000	3,900
5,000	4,500

✓ Solution 106

For each decision (i.e. production level), the expected profit is given by multiplying profits by the their probabilities and totalling. For example, the expected profit if 5,000 items were produced is given by $-400 \times 0.1 + 200 \times 0.4 + 800 \times 0.2 + 1,400 \times 0.2 + 2,000 \times 0.1$.

Answers:
Production of 1,000, expected profit = 0
Production of 2,000, expected profit = 440
Production of 3,000, expected profit = 640
Production of 4,000, expected profit = 720
Production of 5,000, expected profit = 680

Solution 107

(a) For counterfeit coins:

$P(t > 260)$
  $= P(z > (260 - 150)/50 = 2.2)$
  $=$ tail-end area associated with 2.2
  $= 0.5 -$ table entry for 2.2
  $= 0.5 - 0.4861$
  $= 0.0139$ or 1.39%

(b) For genuine coins:

$P(t < 260)$
  $= P(z < (260 - 300)/20 = -2)$
  $=$ tail-end area associated with 2
  $= 0.5 -$ table entry for 2
  $= 0.5 - 0.4772$
  $= 0.0228$ or 2.28%

(c) We want a tail-end probability of 0.01 but CIMA tables give the probability between the mean and the z-value. The tail-end value 0.01 therefore corresponds to a table probability of $0.5 - 0.01 = 0.49$ and this in turn corresponds to a z-value of 2.33. Hence $P(z > 2.33) = 0.01 = P(z < -2.33)$.

Solution 108

(a) $8x + 4y \geq 100$
   $4y \geq 100 - 8x$
   $y \geq 25 - 2x$

(b) $-10x + 20y \leq -80$
   $20y \leq -80 + 10x$
   $y \leq 4 + 0.5x$

Solution 109

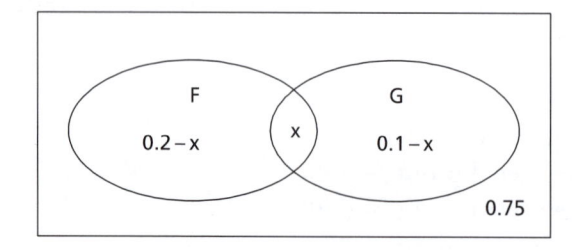

F: $0.2 - x$
x
G: $0.1 - x$
0.75

Using a Venn diagram we can easily see that

$X + 0.2 - X + 0.10 - X + 0.75 = 1$
$-X + 1.05 = 1$
$-X = -0.05$
$X = 0.05$

Spreadsheet skills using Excel

✓ Solution 110

(a) $= 34 \times (4 + 6 + 25)/8$

The answer is 148.75

(b) $= 11 \times 25 + 11 \times 6 + 10$ or $= (25 + 6) \times 11 + 10$

The answer is 351

(c) $= \text{ROUND}(34/5 \times 6.37, 2)$
The answer is 43.14

$= \text{ROUND}(112.6 \times 14.2^2, 0)$
The answer is 22,705

$= \text{ROUND}((199 + 45) \times 1.177 + 78.43, 1)$
The answer is 365.6

✓ Solution 111

(a)

	A	B	C	D	E
1	Investment amount	2000			
2	Interest rate	0.1			
3					
4	Year no.	1	=$B$1*(1+$B$2)^B4		
5		2	=$B$1*(1+$B$2)^B5		
6		3	=$B$1*(1+$B$2)^B6		
7		4	=$B$1*(1+$B$2)^B7		
8		5	=$B$1*(1+$B$2)^B8		
9					
10					

The answers are 2200.00, 2420.00, 2662.00, 2928.20 and 3221.02

(b)

	A	B	C
1	price per box	3.49	
2	no of boxes	15	
3	discount	0.1	
4	delivery	5.99	
5	total	=((B1*B2)*(1-B3)+B4)	
6			
7			
8			

The answer is £53.11

Solution 112

	A	B	C
1	Amount invested	80000	
2	Cash Flow year 1	60000	
3	Cash flow year 2	15000	
4	Cash flow year 3	21000	
5	Cash flow year 4	25000	
6			
7	Fixed cost of capital	0.15	
8			
9			
10	ROI	=AVERAGE(B2:B5)/B1	
11	NPV	=NPV(B7,B2:B5)-B1	
12			
13			

The ROI is 38 per cent and the NPV is 11,617.74

Solution 113

	A	B	C	D
1	Temparature	Litre of cold drinks sold	Formula	Answer
2	15	120	=FORECAST(A2,$B$2:$B$11,$A$2:$A$11)	116.85
3	17	125	=FORECAST(A3,$B$2:$B$11,$A$2:$A$11)	119.12
4	19	125	=FORECAST(A4,$B$2:$B$11,$A$2:$A$11)	121.39
5	15	120	=FORECAST(A5,$B$2:$B$11,$A$2:$A$11)	116.85
6	21	130	=FORECAST(A6,$B$2:$B$11,$A$2:$A$11)	123.65
7	25	130	=FORECAST(A7,$B$2:$B$11,$A$2:$A$11)	128.19
8	22	125	=FORECAST(A8,$B$2:$B$11,$A$2:$A$11)	124.79
9	19	125	=FORECAST(A9,$B$2:$B$11,$A$2:$A$11)	121.39
10	18	100	=FORECAST(A10,$B$2:$B$11,$A$2:$A$11)	120.26
11	20	115	=FORECAST(A11,$B$2:$B$11,$A$2:$A$11)	122.52
12				
13				
14				

Solution 114

There are many principles of good spreadsheet design, but perhaps five of the most important are:

1. Take time to collect all the information you can about the issue to be planned or analysed before entering anything into the spreadsheet.
2. Do produce monster-sized spreadsheets. Modularise a system into multiple spreadsheets and multiple files where appropriate.
3. Minimise the use of absolute values (numbers) in formulae and use cell references wherever possible. Remember to use absolute values where appropriate.
4. Be consistent with formatting and do not over-use different fonts.
5. Build in cross-checks to validate data/calculations.

Mock Assessment 1

Mock Assessment 1

**Certificate Level
Fundamentals of Business Mathematics**

Instructions to students

You have 2 hours in which to complete this assessment.

You may attempt all questions. Mathematical tables and formulae are available.

Do not turn the page until you are ready to attempt the assessment under timed conditions.

Question 1

Use the following data about the production of faulty or acceptable items in three departments to answer the probability questions. All items referred to in the questions are randomly selected from this sample of 250. Give all answers correct to four d.p.

	Department			
	P	Q	R	Total
Faulty	7	10	15	32
Acceptable	46	78	94	218
Total	53	88	109	250

(A) What is the probability that an item is faulty?
Answer [ ]

(B) What is the probability that an item from department P is faulty?
Answer [ ]

(C) What is the probability that an item found to be faulty comes from department P?
Answer [ ]   **(6 marks)**

Question 2

In an additive model, the seasonal variations given by averaging $Y - T$ values are 25, 18, -5 and -30. They have to be adjusted so that their total is 0. What is the value after adjustment of the average currently valued at -30?

Answer [ ]   **(2 marks)**

Question 3

Which of the following examples would constitute a multiple bar chart?

(A) Three adjacent bars then a gap then another three bars.
(B) Six separate bars.
(C) Two bars with a gap between them, each divided into three sections.
(D) Any bar chart which displays more than one variable.

Answer [ ]   **(2 marks)**

Question 4

If $\Sigma x = 500$, $\Sigma y = 200$, $\Sigma x^2 = 35{,}000$, $\Sigma y^2 = 9{,}000$, $\Sigma xy = 12{,}000$ and $n = 10$, calculate the product moment correlation coefficient to three d.p.

Answer [ ]   **(2 marks)**

Question 5

Which of the following statements about standard deviation is incorrect?

(A) It measures variability.
(B) It uses all the data.
(C) It is not distorted by skewed data.
(D) Its formula lends itself to mathematical manipulation.

Answer ☐ (2 marks)

Question 6

An investment rises in value from £12,000 to £250,000 over 15 years. Calculate the percentage increase per year, to one d.p.

Answer ☐ (2 marks)

Question 7

Events P and Q are said to be independent. What does this mean?

(A) If P occurs, Q cannot occur
(B) If P occurs the probability of Q occurring is unchanged
(C) If P occurs the probability of Q occurring is 0
(D) If P occurs the probability of Q occurring is 1.

Answer ☐ (2 marks)

Question 8

A wages distribution is as follows

Weekly wages (£)	Frequency	cf
100 and less than 200	5	..
200 and less than 300	20	..
300 and less than 400	55	..
400 and less than 500	18	..
500 or more	2	..

(A) Write the cumulative (less than) frequencies in the cf column.
(B) What is the cumulative frequency of the upper quartile?

Answer ☐ (4 marks)

Question 9

Sales figures are given as 547,000 but after seasonal adjustment using a multiplicative model they are only 495,000. Calculate the seasonal component for the particular season, to 3 d.p.

Answer ☐ (2 marks)

Question 10

A sample is taken by randomly selecting from the staff in each department, with sample numbers in proportion to the numbers employed in the various departments. What is such a sample called?

(A) Systematic
(B) Simple random
(C) Stratified random
(D) Quota.

Answer _____ (2 marks)

Question 11

If a sum of £15,000 is invested at 4.6 per cent per annum, find its value after 5 years, to the nearest £.

Answer _____ (2 marks)

Question 12

(A) Express the following average weekly wages as index numbers with base 1998, to 1 d.p.

Year	97	98	99	2000	2001	2002
RPI	166	172	178	184	190	197
Wages	414	426	440	450	468	480
Index	…	…	…	…	…	…

(B) If the index for 2003 were to be 116 and the RPI 204, express the index for 2003 at constant 1998 prices.

(C) If the average wages index for 2003 at constant 1998 prices were to be 96, which of the following comments would be correct?

(A) Average wages in 2003 could buy 4 per cent less than in 1998
(B) Average wages in 2003 could buy 4 per cent more than in 1998
(C) Average wages in 2003 were 4 per cent more than in 1998
(D) Average prices in 2003 were 4 per cent less than in 1998

Answer _____ (6 marks)

Question 13

The expression $(x^3)^2/x^4$ equals

(A) $1/x$
(B) 1
(C) x
(D) x^2

Answer _____ (2 marks)

Question 14

If Q is given as 34 with a possible error of $\pm 2\%$ and R is given as 6.5 with a possible error of $\pm 4\%$, find the largest possible true value of Q/R to 3 d.p.

Answer [ ]   (2 marks)

Question 15

The pass rate for a particular exam is 48 per cent. In a randomly selected group of three students, find the probabilities (to 4 d.p.) that

(A) No one passes
     Answer [ ]

(B) All three pass
     Answer [ ]   (4 marks)

Question 16

A company has to choose between borrowing £100,000 at 3 per cent a quarter in order to modernise now or saving at 2 per cent a quarter in order to modernise in 4 years time, at an estimated cost of £117,000. Throughout this question, use tables whenever possible.

(A) Find the cumulative discount factor appropriate to quarter end payments of £1 per quarter at 3 per cent per quarter over 5 years.
     Answer [ ]

(B) Calculate the amount £X which must be paid per quarter if the company borrows £100,000 now repayable at the end of each quarter over 4 years. Give your answer correct to the nearest £.
     Answer [ ]

(C) Calculate the amount £Y which must be saved at the end of each quarter if the company wishes to cover the cost of modernisation in 4 years time. Give your answer to the nearest £.
     Answer [ ]   (6 marks)

Question 17

Eight samples of wine have been listed in order of taste (with the best taste being ranked number one) and their prices are also listed.

Sample taste	1	2	3	4	5	6	7	8
Price (£)	6.99	4.95	5.99	5.99	4.99	3.99	2.99	2.99
Rank of price	..	..	..	..	..	..	..	..

(A) Rank the prices of the wines with the lowest price being ranked number one.
(B) If the differences in corresponding ranks are denoted by 'd' and if $\Sigma d^2 = 150$, calculate Spearman's rank correlation coefficient to 3 d.p.
   Answer [   ]
(C) If the rank correlation coefficient was -0.9, which of the following statements would be correct?
(D) There is a strong link between price and taste.
(E) There is a strong linear relationship between price and taste.
(F) Taste rank increases as price gets higher.
(G) Ninety per cent of the differences in price from one sample to the next can be explained by corresponding differences in taste.

Answer(s) [   ]   (6 marks)

Question 18

Calculate the present value of an annuity of £2,800 per annum, payable at the end of each year for 10 years at a discount rate of 4 per cent. Use tables and give your answer to the nearest £.

Answer [   ]   (2 marks)

Question 19

An asset originally worth £80,000 depreciates at 28 per cent per annum. Find its value to the nearest £ at the end of 3 years.

Answer [   ]   (2 marks)

Question 20

If the following data are to be illustrated by means of a histogram and if the standard interval is taken to be 5 seconds, calculate the heights of the bars of the histogram (to the nearest whole number).

Time taken (seconds)	Frequency	Height of bar
0–5	47	
5–10	62	
10–20	104	
20–40	96	

(4 marks)

Question 21

In an additive time series model, at a certain point of time, the actual value is 32,000 while the trend is 26,000 and the seasonal component is 6,200. If there is no cyclical variation, calculate the residual variation.

Answer [ ] (2 marks)

Question 22

Solve the equation $2x^2 - 5x - 7 = 0$ giving your answers correct to 1 d.p.

Answer [ ] (2 marks)

Question 23

A project may result in the following profits with the probabilities stated.

Profit	Probability
£40,000	0.2
£25,000	0.4
(£12,000)	0.4

Calculate the expected profit to the nearest £.

Answer [ ] (2 marks)

Question 24

If weights are normally distributed with mean 43 kg and standard deviation 6 kg, what is the probability of a weight being less than 50 kg?

Answer [ ] (2 marks)

Question 25

A sum of £30,000 is invested at a nominal rate of 12 per cent per annum. Find its value after 3 years if interest is compounded every month. Give your answer to the nearest £.

Answer [ ] (2 marks)

Question 26

Which one of the following is a disadvantage of using postal questionnaires as a method of contact with respondents in a survey?

(A) It omits the poorer sections of the population
(B) It is very expensive
(C) It gets very poor response rates
(D) It is subject to interviewer bias.

Answer [ ] (2 marks)

Question 27

If $\Sigma x = 400$, $\Sigma y = 300$, $\Sigma x^2 = 18{,}000$, $\Sigma y^2 = 10{,}000$, $\Sigma xy = 13{,}000$ and $n = 10$,

(A) Calculate the value of 'b' in the regression equation, to 1 d.p.
(B) If the value of b were 0.9, calculate the value of 'a' in the regression equation to 1 d.p.

Answers
A [ ]
B [ ] (4 marks)

Question 28

In a time series analysis, the trend Y is given by the regression equation $Y = 462 + 0.34t$ where t denotes the quarters of years with 1st quarter of 2000 as $t = 1$.

(A) Predict the trend for the first quarter of 2004 to one d.p.
   Answer [ ]

(B) If the average seasonal variations are as follow

Quarter	Q1	Q2	Q3	Q4
Variation	−20%	0	−20%	+40%

Use the multiplicative model to predict the actual value for a 3rd quarter in which the trend prediction is 500.
Answer [ ] (4 marks)

Question 29

A sales representative calls on three separate, unrelated customers and the chance of making a sale at any one of them is 0.7. Find the probability that a sale is made on the third call only, to 3 d.p.

Answer [ ] (2 marks)

Question 30

Rearrange the formula $V = P \times (1 + r)^n$ to make r the subject.

Answer [ ] (2 marks)

Question 31

In November, unemployment in a region is 238,500. If the seasonal component using an additive time series model is −82,000, find the seasonally adjusted level of unemployment to the nearest whole number.

Answer ☐ (2 marks)

Question 32

A company is planning capital investment for which the following year end cash flows have been estimated.

Year end	Net cash flow
Now	(10,000)
1	5,000
2	5,000

(A) Use tables to calculate the net present value (NPV) of the project using tables if the company has a cost of capital of 15 per cent.
Answer ☐

(B) If the NPV is £928 when the discount rate is 10 per cent and −£628 when it is 20 per cent, calculate the internal rate of return to two d.p.
Answer ☐ (4 marks)

Question 33

If the regression equation (in £'000) linking sales (Y) to advertising expenditure (X) is given by $Y = 4,000 + 12X$, forecast the sales when £150,000 is spent on advertising, to the nearest £.

Answer ☐ (2 marks)

Question 34

An item sells for £4.39 including value added tax at 17.5 per cent. If tax were reduced to 16 per cent, the new selling price to the nearest penny will be

(A) £4.33
(B) £4.01
(C) £4.32
(D) £5.09

Answer ☐ (2 marks)

Question 35

If $\Sigma f = 50$, $\Sigma fx = 120$ and $\Sigma fx^2 = 400$, calculate

(A) The mean (to 1 d.p.)
   Answer [ ]

(B) The standard deviation (to 1 d.p.)
   Answer [ ] (4 marks)

Question 36

The Economic Order Quantity (EOQ) for a particular stock item is given by the expression:

$$\text{EOQ} = \sqrt{\frac{2C_o D}{C_h}}$$

(A) If $C_o = £2$ per order, $D = 1{,}000$ items and $C_h = £0.25$ per item, then EOQ (rounded to the nearest whole number) will be

   (A) 400
   (B) 320
   (C) 160
   (D) 126

   Answer [ ]

(B) If, for a different stock item, EOQ = 200 items, $C_o = £4$ per order and $D = 1{,}000$ items, then C_h (in £ per item) will be

   (A) 0.05
   (B) 0.10
   (C) 0.15
   (D) 0.20

   Answer [ ] (4 marks)

Question 37

A graphical presentation of classified data in which the number of items in each class is represented by the area of the bar is called

   (A) an ogive.
   (B) a histogram.
   (C) a bar chart.
   (D) a compound bar chart.

   Answer [ ] (2 marks)

Question 38

The following table shows the index of prices (1995 = 100) for a certain commodity over the period 2000–2005:

2000	2001	2002	2003	2004	2005
100	105	115	127	140	152

(A) The percentage increase in the price between 2002 and 2004 is nearest to

(A) 25.0
(B) 22.3
(C) 21.7
(D) none of these.

Answer

(B) It has been decided to rebase the index so that 2005 = 100. The index for 2003 will now be nearest to

(A) 193.1
(B) 139.4
(C) 125.0
(D) 119.7

Answer

Question 39

The cost of an office desk is £263 plus value added tax of 17.5 per cent. Using the numbers given what Excel formula is required to calculate the total price to 2 d.p.

Answer

Question 40

Given the scenario in the spreadsheet above, what Excel formulae are required in

	A	B	C	D	E
1	IT Investment - Cash Out		250000		
2	Net IT Benefits	Year 1		66000	
3		Year 2		87000	
4		Year 3		98000	
5		Year 4		120000	
6		Year 5		110000	
7					
8	Fixed Cost of Capital or Interest Rate			24%	
9					
10	ROI				
11	NPV				
12					

(A) Cell D10 to calculate the ROI

Answer

(B) Cell D11 to calculate the NPV

Answer

Question 41

	A	B	C	D	E
1	INTEREST RATES AND CASH DEPOSITS				
2					
3	Interest rate	Deposit		Forecast	
4	10.00%	11550			
5	10.25%	11900			
6	10.50%	12500			
7	10.50%	11990			
8	10.75%	12900			
9	11.00%	13000			
10	11.25%	14000			
11	11.25%	13020			
12	11.25%	14000			
13	11.25%	14100			
14	11.50%	13380			
15	11.50%	14200			
16	11.75%	13500			
17	11.75%	14050			
18	12.00%	14500			
19	12.00%	14100			
20	12.25%	14500			
21	12.25%	14600			
22					

Given the scenario above, what Excel formula is required in cell D4 to calculate the forecast (using a least squared line approach). Write your answer so that the formula can be copied into cells D5 through D21.

Answer [   ]

Question 42

	A	B	C	D	E	F	G
1			Average weight of pallets				
2	73	62	66	75	70	71	
3	83	69	74	79	78	82	
4	65	72	66	79	82	77	
5	69	61	63	80	82	66	
6	82	82	65	75	71	80	
7	74	84	72	78	67	84	
8							
9	Weight in kg.						
10	60						
11	65						
12	70						
13	75						
14	80						
15	85						
16							

Given the scenario above, what Excel formula is required in the range B10:B15 to calculate the frequency distribution of the pallet weights.

Answer [   ]

Question 43

	A	B	C	D	E
1	Average daily temperature in degrees centigrade				
2		29	25	22	29
3		24	26	25	28
4		28	27	20	22
5		21	20	24	24
6		21	22	27	26
7		23	26	21	24
8		25	25	24	25
9					
10	Median				
11	Mode				
12	Mean				
13					

Given the scenario above, what Excel formulae are required to calculate:

(A) The median (to 1 d.p.)

Answer ☐

(B) The mode (to 0 d.p.)

Answer ☐

(C) The mean (to 2 d.p.)

Answer ☐

Question 44

Solve for y in the following inequalities.

(A) $-5x + 10y + 120 \geq 25x + 5y + 320$

Answer ☐

(B) $240 + 8x \leq 12x + 10y + 140$

Answer ☐

Question 45

(a) Describe the shaded area in the following Venn diagram.

  (A) Even numbers which begin with 3
  (B) Numbers that are even but do not have a 3 in them
  (C) The numbers 6, 12, 24, 30, 36
  (D) None of the above

Answer ☐

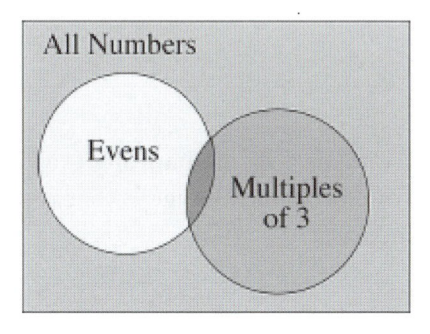

(b) If 50 people were asked whether they liked apples or oranges or both, 38 liked apples and 32 liked oranges. Use a Venn diagram to help you calculate how many people liked both?

  (A) 10
  (B) 15
  (C) 20
  (D) 25

Mock Assessment 1 – Solutions

✓ Solution 1

(A) 32 out of 250 items are faulty
Answer = 32/250 = 0.1280

(B) 7 of the 53 items from P are faulty
Answer = 7/53 = 0.1321 (4 d.p.).

(C) 7 out of the 32 faulty items come from P
Answer = 7/32 = 0.2188 (4 d.p.).

✓ Solution 2

Total = 25 + 18 − 5 − 30 = 8
If we subtract 2 from each of the four averages they will add up to zero.

Answer: −30 − 2 = − 32

✓ Solution 3

(B) describes a simple bar chart and (C) describes a compound or component bar chart. (D) is incorrect because a compound bar also shows several variables.

Answer: (A)

✓ Solution 4

$$r = [n\Sigma xy - \Sigma x \Sigma y]/\sqrt{\{[n\Sigma x^2 - (\Sigma x)^2] \times [n\Sigma y^2 - (\Sigma y)^2]\}}$$
$$= [10 \times 12{,}000 - 500 \times 200]/\sqrt{\{[10 \times 35{,}000 - 500^2][10 \times 9{,}000 - 200^2]\}}$$
$$= 20{,}000/\sqrt{\{100{,}000 \times 50{,}000\}} = 0.283 \text{ (3 d.p.)}$$

Answer: 0.283

✓ Solution 5

Standard deviation uses all the data in a mathematically exact formula as a means of measuring variability. However, its one big disadvantage is that is greatly exaggerates the dispersion of skewed data so (C) is incorrect.

Answer: (C)

✓ Solution 6

15 year ratio = 250/12 = 20.83333
1 year ratio = $20.83333^{(1/15)}$ = 1.2244
Annual % increase = 22.4%

Answer: 22.4

Solution 7

Events are independent if the occurrence of one does not alter the probability of the other, so (B) is correct. (A) and (C) are both definitions of mutually exclusive events.

Answer: (B)

Solution 8

(A) Answer

Cf
5
25
80
98
100

(B) The upper quartile is at the three quarters point and its cf = 100 × 3/4 = 75
    Answer: 75

Solution 9

Seasonally adjusted value = actual value/seasonal component. So seasonal component = actual value divided by seasonally adjusted value = 547/495 = 1.105

Answer: 1.105

Solution 10

Answer: (C)

that is, it is a stratified random sample.

Solution 11

Value = $15{,}000 \times 1.046^5$ = £18,782

Answer: 18,782

Solution 12

(A) Wages are indexed with base 98 by dividing each year's wages figure by the '98 figure. (i.e. by 426) and multiplying by 100.

   Answers

97	98	99	00	01	02
97.2	100	103.3	105.6	109.9	112.7

(B) Value at '98 prices = 116 × 98 RPI/'03 RPI = 116 × 172/204 = 97.8
    Answer: 97.8

Solution 13

$(x^3)^2/x^4 = x^6/x^4 = x^{(6-4)} = x^2$

Answer: (D)

Solution 14

Maximum Q/R = Maximum Q/Minimum R
$= 34 \times 1.02/6.5 \times 0.96$
$= 5.558$ (3 d.p.)

Answer: 5.558

Solution 15

(A) Probability of failing is $1 - 0.48 = 0.52$
Probability of all three failing $= 0.52^3 = 0.1406$
Answer: 0.1406

(B) Probability of all three passing $= 0.48^3 = 0.1106$
Answer: 0.1106

Solution 16

(A) There are 20 quarterly payments in 5 years, so the discount factor required is that corresponding to 3 per cent and 20 periods.
Answer: 14.878

(B) The method is to equate the present value of the repayments with the 100,000 borrowed. The cumulative discount factor at 3 per cent for 16 periods is 12.561 so $100,000 = 12.561X$

$X = 100,000/12.561 = £7,961$ (to the nearest £)
Answer: 7,961

(C) The present value of the saving scheme must be equated to that of £117,000 discounted at 2 per cent for 16 periods. The cumulative discount factor is 13.578 whilst the single discount factor is 0.728. Hence $13.578Y = 117,000 \times 0.728$ and $Y = £6,273$ (to nearest £).
Answer: 6,273

✓ Solution 17

(A) **Answer:** 8 4 6.5 6.5 5 3 1.5 1.5

(B) $R = 1 - 6\Sigma d^2/n(n^2 - 1) = 1 - 6 \times 150/8 \times 63 = -0.786$ (to 3 d.p.)
Answer: -0.786

(C) The value -0.9 means that there is a strong link between taste and price but it need not be linear. Because of the strange way in which taste is ranked, with the lowest rank being the best taste, rank of taste actually declines as price increases.
Answer: (D)

✓ Solution 18

The cumulative discount factor for 10 years at 4 per cent is 8.111, so the present value is $2,800 \times 8.111 = £22,711$ (to the nearest £)

Answer: 22,711

✓ Solution 19

If something declines at 28% per year, its value at the end of each year is only 72 per cent of its value at the start, so year-end value is start value times 0.72.
Value after 3 years $= 80,000 \times 0.72^3 = £29,860$ (to the nearest £)

Answer: 29,860

✓ Solution 20

If the width of an interval is n times the standard width, then the height of its bar is frequency/n.
Heights are 47, 62, 104/2 = 52 and 96/4 = 24.

Answers: 47, 62, 52, 24

✓ Solution 21

The formula for an additive time series is $A = T + S + R$ and hence residual = $A - T - S = 32,000 - 26,000 - 6,200 = -200$

Answer: -200

✓ Solution 22

Using the formula for the roots of a quadratic, $a = 2$, $b = -5$ and $c = -7$. Alternately, factorisation gives $(2x - 7)(x + 1) = 0$ and hence $x = -1$ or 3.5

Answers: $-1, 3.5$

✓ Solution 23

Expected profit (£'000) $= 40 \times 0.2 + 25 \times 0.4 - 12 \times 0.4 = 13.2$

Answer: 13,200

✓ Solution 24

$P(W < 50) = P(z < [50 - 43]/6)\ P(z < 1.17)$
$= 0.5 + \text{Normal table entry for } 1.17 = 0.5 + 0.3790$
$= 0.8790$

Answer: 0.8790

✓ Solution 25

A nominal 12 per cent per annum means 1 per cent per month and in 3 years there are 36 months. Value $= 30{,}000 \times 1.01^{36} = £42{,}923$ (to the nearest £).

Answer: 42,923

✓ Solution 26

Only (C) is a disadvantage of postal questionnaires. The other comments are not true.

Answer: (C)

✓ Solution 27

(A) $b = [n\Sigma xy - \Sigma x \Sigma y]/[n\Sigma x^2 - (\Sigma x)^2]$
$= 10 \times 13{,}000 - 400 \times 300]/[10 \times 18{,}000 - 400^2] = 10{,}000/20{,}000$
$= 0.5$

Answer: 0.5

(B) $A = \Sigma y/n - b \times \Sigma x/n = [300 - 0.9 \times 400]/10 = -6$
Answer: -6

✓ Solution 28

(A) For the 1st quarter of 2004, $t = 17$ and trend $Y = 462 + 0.34 \times 17 = 467.8$ (to 1 d.p.)
Answer: 467.8

(B) Prediction = trend prediction reduced by 20% = 500×0.8
Answer: 400

✓ Solution 29

$P(\text{not making a sale}) = 1 - P(\text{making a sale}) = 1 - 0.7 = 0.3$
$P(\text{sale at 3rd call only}) = P(\text{not at 1st}) \times P(\text{not at 2nd}) \times P(\text{sale at 3rd}) = 0.3 \times 0.3 \times 0.7$
$= 0.063$

Answer: 0.063

Solution 30

$(1 + r)^n = V/P$ so $1 + r = (V/P)^{(1/n)}$ and $r = (V/P)^{(1/n)} - 1$

Answer: $(V/P)^{(1/n)} - 1$

Solution 31

The additive model is $A = T + S$ and seasonal adjustment provides an estimate of $T = A - S = 238{,}500 - (-82{,}000) = 238{,}500 + 82{,}000$

Answer: 320,500

Solution 32

(A)

Year	Cash flow	Discount factor	Present value
0	(10,000)	1	(10,000)
1	5,000	0.87	4,350
2	5,000	0.756	3,780
3	3,000	0.658	1,974
			NPV = 104

Answer: 104

(B) The IRR is the rate at which NPV is zero. NPV drops by £928 + £628 = £1,556 as the percentage rises from 10 per cent to 20 per cent that is by 10 per cent points. The drop per point is therefore 1,556/10 = £155.6. Since it starts at £928, the NPV will reach zero after an increase in the rate of 928/155.6 = 5.96% points. This occurs when the rate = 10 + 5.96 = 15.96% (to 2 d.p.)

Answer: 15.96

Solution 33

When £150,000 is spent on advertising, $X = 150$ and $Y = 4{,}000 + 12 \times 150 = 5{,}800$. Forecast sales = 5,800 (£'000).

Answer: £5,800,000

Solution 34

Price with VAT at 17.5% = 1.175 × Price without VAT
So price without VAT = 4.39/1.175
Price with VAT at 16% = 1.16 × Price without VAT = 1.16 × 4.39/1.175 = £4.33

Answer: (A)

Solution 35

(A) Mean = $\Sigma fx/\Sigma f = 120/50 = 2.4$
Answer: 2.4

(B) Standard deviation = $\sqrt{[\Sigma fx^2/\Sigma f - (\Sigma fx/\Sigma f)^2]} = \sqrt{[400/50 - (120/50)^2]}$
$= \sqrt{2.24} = 1.5$ (to 1 d.p.)

Answer: 1.5

Solution 36

(A) $EOQ = \dfrac{\sqrt{2C_0 D}}{C_h}$

$C_0 = 2, D = 1,000, C_h = 0.25$

$\therefore EOQ = \sqrt{\dfrac{2 \times 2 \times 1,000}{0.25}} = \sqrt{\dfrac{4,000}{0.25}} = \sqrt{16,000}$

$\therefore EOQ = 126.49 = 126$ (to the nearest whole number)

Answer: (D)

(B) $EOQ = 200, C_0 = 4, D = 1000$

$\therefore 200 = \sqrt{\dfrac{2 \times 4 \times 1,000}{C_h}} = \sqrt{\dfrac{8,000}{C_h}}$

$\therefore 200^2 = \dfrac{8,000}{C_h}$

$\therefore C_h = \dfrac{8,000}{40,000} = 0.20$

Answer: (D)

Solution 37

An ogive doesn't have bars. A bar chart looks similar to a histogram but in a bar chart the height of the bar represents the frequency. In a histogram this is only the case if the classes are of equal width. In general the area of the bar in a histogram represents class frequency.
Answer: (B)

Solution 38

(A) % increase between 2002 and 2004:

$\left(\dfrac{140 - 115}{115}\right) \times 100 = \dfrac{25}{115} \times 100 = 21.74$

Answer: (C)

(B) Rebased price

$$\frac{152}{127} \times 100 = 119.69$$

Answer: (D)

✓ Solution 39
Answer: = ROUND(263 × 1.175,2)

✓ Solution 40
(A) **Answer:** = AVERAGE(D2:D6)/C1
(B) **Answer:** = NPV(D8,D2:D6) − C1

✓ Solution 41
Answer: FORECAST(A4,$B$4:$B$21,$A$4:$A$21)

✓ Solution 42
Answer: = FREQUENCY(A2:F7,A10:A14)

✓ Solution 43
(A) **Answer:** = ROUND(MEDIAN(A2:D8),1)
(B) **Answer:** = ROUND(MODE(A2:D8),0)
(C) **Answer:** = ROUND(AVERAGE(A2:D8),2)

✓ Solution 44
(A) $10y - 5y \geq 25x + 5x + 200$
    $5y \geq 30x + 200$
    $y \geq 6x + 40$
(B) $-10y \leq 12x - 8x + 140 - 240$
    $-10y \leq 4x - 100$
    $-y \leq 0.4x - 10$
    $y \geq -0.4x + 10$

✓ Solution 45
(A) **Answer:** (D)
(B) **Answer:** (C)

Mock Assessment 2

Mock Assessment 2

Question 1

When a = 4 and x = 3, $(3a^3x)^2$ is equal to:

(A) 1,728
(B) 82,944
(C) 331,776
(D) 5,184.

Answer

Question 2

The coefficient of determination measures:

(A) the percentage of variation in the variables that cannot be explained by regression analysis;
(B) the strength of the correlation between the variables;
(C) the percentage of the variation in the variables that can be explained by regression analysis;
(D) the proximity of the observations to a straight line.

Answer

Question 3

In a histogram, one class interval is twice the width of the others. For that class, the height to be plotted in relation to the frequency is

(A) ×2
(B) ×0.5
(C) ×1
(D) ×0.25.

Answer

Question 4

A market research project has identified that for a particular product, a price of £12 will sell 2,500 units/month and a price of £10 will sell 3,300 units/month.

If the relationship between price (P) and demand (D) is given by P = aD + b, what are the values of a and b?

(A) a = 18.25   b = −0.0025
(B) a = 0.0025   b = −18.25
(C) a = −0.0025   b = 18.25
(D) a = −18.25   b = 0.0025.

Answer

Question 5

Which of the following are advantages of the median

(i) It is not affected by extreme values.
(ii) It can be used in mathematical tables.
(iii) Data can be taken in any order which speeds calculation.
(iv) It is unaffected by unequal class intervals.

(A) (i) and (iii)
(B) (i), (ii), (iii) and (iv)
(C) (ii) and (iii)
(D) (i) and (iv).

Answer

Question 6

At what two levels of demand will X Ltd breakeven if their profitability can be represented by the equation:

Profit = −2,400 + 30D − 0.06D^2

(A) 67 units and 567 units
(B) 100 units and 400 units
(C) 10 units and 40 units
(D) 167 units and 467 units.

Answer

Question 7

A company has calculated the least squares regression line for the relationship between staff numbers and unit sales in its national branches, where y = sales units and x = number of staff on duty.

The equation is y = 156.98 + 14.38x

From this equation it can be stated that:

(A) 156.98 is the maximum number of units that can be sold;
(B) unit sales fall by 14.38 for each additional member of staff employed;
(C) an additional 14.38 staff members are needed to sell one more unit;
(D) unit sales rise by 14.38 for each additional member of staff employed.

Answer

Question 8

A product sells for £4.36 inclusive of VAT at 17.5%. What would be the new price (rounded to the nearest penny) if the rate of VAT were reduced to 10.5%?

(A) £3.71
(B) £4.09
(C) £4.10
(D) £4.64.

Answer

Question 9

A credit card company is charging an annual percentage rate of 26.8%. What three monthly rate is it equivalent to?

(A) 6.70%
(B) 8.93%
(C) 6.10%
(D) 8.24%.

Answer

Question 10

When using Excel, a macro is:

(A) the name given to a group of named cells;
(B) the name for a group of worksheets;
(C) a series of keystrokes or mouse clicks;
(D) a cross check designed to validate calculations.

Answer

Question 11

Factorising the following expression:

$9a^3b^2 - 15ab^3 + 6a^2b$ gives the following

(A) $3ab(3a^2b - 5b^2 + 2a)$
(B) $3a^2b(3ab - 5ab^2 + 2a)$
(C) $3ab^2(3a^2b - 5b + 2ab)$
(D) $3ab(3ab - 5b^2 + 2ab)$.

Answer

Question 12

A company has calculated the Net Present Value of four mutually exclusive projects and the associated probabilities as follows:

Project A		Project B		Project C		Project D	
NPV £	Probability	NPV £	Probability	NPV £	Probability	NPV £	Probability
10,000	0.6	20,000	0.2	8,000	0.9	7,000	0.5
5,000	0.4	2,000	0.8	3,000	0.1	6,000	0.5

If the projects were ranked in terms of expected values, with the highest first, the order would be:

(A) B, A, C, D
(B) A, C, D, B
(C) D, A and C equal, B
(D) C, A, D, B.

Answer

Question 13

A number of animals were tested for immunity to a virus

Type of animal	Number tested	Number immune
Dog	1,500	1,200
Cat	750	450

If an animal is selected at random what is the probability of selecting a cat that is immune to the virus?

(A) 1 in 2
(B) 1 in 8
(C) 1 in 3
(D) 1 in 5.

Answer

Question 14

A down-turn in the size of the population is an example of:

(A) long-term trend
(B) cyclical variation
(C) seasonal variation
(D) random variation.

Answer [   ]

Question 15

A bag contains nine balls, four are red, three are yellow and two are green. If three balls are selected and not replaced, what is the probability that one ball of each colour will have been selected?

(A) 0.26
(B) 0.29
(C) 0.16
(D) 0.33.

Answer [   ]

Question 16

An investor has the following four investment options available but has the cash only to take up one.
    Which one would maximise her wealth assuming an interest rate of 10%?

Project	Initial outlay	Return
A	£7,000	£3,000 each year, payable in arrears, for five years
B	£4,500	£1,000 at the end of the first year, £2,500 at the end of the next two years and £4,000 for the last two years
C	£5,500	£2,000 payable every year in advance for five years
D	£11,000	£1,500 in perpetuity

(A) Project A
(B) Project B
(C) Project C
(D) Project D.

Answer [   ]

Question 17

Solve $7{,}467 - 356.1 \div (44.846 - 2)$ to 3 significant figures (s.f):

(A) 7,461.023
(B) 7,460
(C) 7,458.689
(D) 7,459.

Answer

Question 18

A £50,000 mortgage is taken out on a property at a rate of 6% over 20 years. What will be the gross monthly repayment?

(A) £208.33
(B) £363.25
(C) £220.83
(D) £414.67.

Answer

Question 19

A property worth $750,000 is insured against fire. The probability of a fire occurring on the premises has been assessed at 1.5 in 1,000. If the insurance company is paid a premium of £1,500 per year, what is the expected value of the insurance policy to the insurance company?

(A) £1,500
(B) −£9,750
(C) £375
(D) £1,125.

Answer

Question 20

Which of the following statements are true?

(i) In the equation $y = mx + c$, y is the independent variable.
(ii) A quadratic equation plotted on a graph will have a maximum and a minimum point.
(iii) If $b^2 - 4ac$ is zero in a quadratic equation, there are no real solutions.
(iv) Multiple quadratic equations can be plotted on one graph.

(A) (i), (ii) and (iii)
(B) (iv) only
(C) (i) and (ii) only
(D) (i) and (iii) only.

Answer

Question 21

A baker knows that the demand for white rolls follows the following probability distribution:

Demand	Probability
500	0.1
600	0.2
700	0.3
800	0.4

Rolls are baked first thing in the morning before demand for the day is known. The cost of a roll is 10p, the selling price is 50p and all unsold rolls are scrapped at the end of the day.

To maximise her expected value, how many rolls should the baker bake each morning?

(A) 500
(B) 600
(C) 700
(D) 800.

Answer

Question 22

The figures below relate to the number of customers buying a particular product in a week, aggregated by quarter:

	Quarter 1	Quarter 2	Quarter 3	Quarter 4
2003	–	–	–	72
2004	79	84	90	45
2005	52	63	66	36
2006	47	51	88	–

The first figure to go in the 4th quarter total is:

(A) 325
(B) 298
(C) 312
(D) 64.

Answer

Question 23

A company is investigating the effect of outdoor temperature on their sales of heating products. The recorded data has been plotted on a scatter diagram.

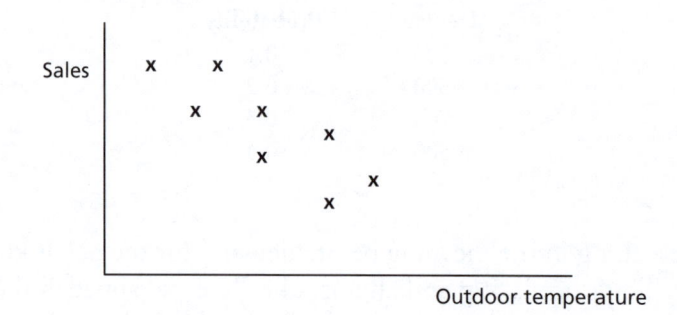

Based on analysis of the diagram, which of the following conclusions may be drawn?

(i) The relationship between sales and outdoor temperature appears to be correlated.
(ii) The relationship between sales and outdoor temperature appears to be non-linear.
(iii) The relationship between sales and outdoor temperature appears to be positively correlated.
(iv) Sales would be considered the independent variable.

(A) (i) only
(B) (i) and (iii)
(C) (i), (iii) and (iv)
(D) (i), (ii) and (iii).

Answer

Question 24

The Net Present Value of a planned investment project has been calculated at interest rates of 12% and 8%. The NPVs are £1,090 and –£960 respectively. What is the Internal Rate of Return of the project to one decimal place?

(A) 10.1%
(B) 11.7%
(C) 10.8%
(D) 11.5%.

Answer

Question 25

Four products have the same mean weight of 550 grams but different standard deviations as shown below:

Product WW   34 grams
Product XX   21 grams
Product YY   18 grams
Product ZZ   28 grams

Which has the highest co-efficient of variation?

(A) Product WW
(B) Product XX
(C) Product YY
(D) Product ZZ.

Answer

Question 26

A factory regularly tests its product X for defects. Two types of defects may be found, either F_1 or F_2.

Past data shows that 2% of production shows defect F_1 whilst 3% has defect F_2. Having one defect has no impact on whether or not the product has the other.

What is the probability that a selected unit has precisely one defect?

(A) 0.9506
(B) 0.9512
(C) 0.0488
(D) 0.0494.

Answer

Question 27

A frequency distribution of a sample of weekly takings is as follows:

£	Frequency
4,500 and less than 8,500	7
8,500 and less than 10,500	16
10,500 and less than 12,500	28
12,500 and less than 13,500	21
13,500 and less than 14,500	8
	80

If the area between £8,500 and less than £10,500 has a height of 4 cm, what is the height of the rectangle £10,500 and less than £12,500?

(A) 28 cm
(B) 8 cm
(C) 14 cm
(D) 7 cm.

Answers

Question 28

A distribution $\Sigma f = 150$, $\Sigma fx = 4,200$ and $\Sigma fx^2 = 156,300$
What is the standard deviation?

(A) 258
(B) 18.5
(C) 16.1
(D) 342.25.

Answer

Question 29

You have been supplied with the following data regarding the grades of candidates in an interview presentation and their written exam scores:

Candidate	Grade awarded	Exam score
Mr A	A	70
Ms B	B	76
Mrs C	A	58
Mr D	C	88
Mr E	D	81

What is the Spearman's rank correlation co-efficient?

(A) 0.825
(B) −0.825
(C) 0.548
(D) −0.548.

Answer

Question 30

The regression line of y on x is calculated using the following data:

$$n = 14, \Sigma x = 590, \Sigma y = 84, \Sigma xy = 15{,}390, \Sigma x^2 = 87{,}400$$

It will be equal to:

(A) $-0.189 + 1.96x$
(B) $1.96 + 0.189x$
(C) $0.189 + 1.96x$
(D) $-1.96 + 0.189x$.

Answer

Question 31

In a time series analysis, the trend equation for a particular product is given by:

$$\text{Trend} = (0.0021 \times \text{YEAR}^2) + (0.5 \times \text{YEAR}) + 42.8$$

Owing to the cyclical factor, the forecast for 2008 is estimated at 1.78 times trend. In whole units, what is the forecast for 2008?

(A) 9,514
(B) 5,345
(C) 12,856
(D) 16,935.

Answer

Question 32

When analysing decisions using decision trees, a decision point represents:

(A) A point where various probable outcomes may now occur.
(B) A point where random events render a decision impossible.
(C) A point where a decision about options is taken.
(D) The highest expected value of the possible decisions is calculated.

Answer

Question 33

The figures for December's sales in an additive model for the trend in monthly sales figures has the following values:

T = £25,000
S = £2,300
C = −£500
R = £207.

The predicted value of sales in December is given by:

(A) 27,007
(B) 27,593
(C) 27,300
(D) 25,000.

Answer ☐

Question 34

In a forecasting model based on y = a + bx, the intercept is £467. If the value of y is £875 and x = 35, then b is equal to

(A) 38.34
(B) 8.58
(C) 11.66
(D) 22.98.

Answer ☐

Question 35

Based on 20 quarters, the underlying trend equation for forecasting is y = 42.81 + 8.7x. Quarter 21 has a seasonal factor of 2.21.

Using the multiplicative model, what would be the forecast for the quarter in whole units?

(A) 226
(B) 102
(C) 498
(D) 62.

Answer ☐

Question 36

A pie chart is to be used to display the following data:

Percentage of passengers flying from airport A	25
Percentage of passengers flying from airport B	36
Percentage of passengers flying from airport C	16
Percentage of passengers flying from airport D	23

What angle in degrees on the pie chart will represent airport C's share of the passengers?

(A) 16.0
(B) 57.6
(C) 16.8
(D) 4.44

Answer

Question 37

What is the value of Pearson's correlation co-efficient based on the following data:

$$n = 5, \Sigma x = 7.2, \Sigma y = 877, \Sigma xy = 1,360, \Sigma x^2 = 11.7 \text{ and } \Sigma y^2 = 164,766.42$$

(A) 0.64
(B) 0.80
(C) 0.13
(D) 0.17.

Answer

Question 38

An inflation index and a sales index of a company's sales for the last year are as follows:

Quarter	1	2	3	4
Sales index	108	113	119	125
Inflation index	100	105	110	116

What is the real value of sales for quarter 4?

(A) 119
(B) 116
(C) 99
(D) 108.

Answer

Question 39

An investor wishes to have a pension of £6,000 per annum in perpetuity, with the first payment in one year's time. How much would need to be invested now if interest rates are 3.5%?

(A) £171,429
(B) £17,143
(C) £210,000
(D) £21,000.

Answer

Question 40

Prices of land have been rising by 18% per annum. What does that equate to as a rise over 9 months?

(A) 13.50%
(B) 1.13%
(C) 13.22%
(D) 24.69%.

Answer

Question 41

A product is found to have a mean weight of 10 kg and a standard deviation of 5 kg. What percentage of items will have a weight of under 6 kg?

(A) 28.81%
(B) 0.07%
(C) 49.93%
(D) 21.19%.

Answer

Question 42

A cell in an Excel spreadsheet has been formatted to three decimal places. The impact of this is to:

(A) Change the display to show 3 decimal places but leave the data held unrounded.
(B) Display data in the cell to 3 decimal places and round the data held.
(C) Display the data in the cell to 2 decimal places as usual, but round the data held to 3 decimal places.
(D) Cells cannot be formatted to 3 decimal places.

Answer

Question 43

An annuity pays £15,000 per year every year for 15 years starting in one year's time. The rate of interest is 4.5%. What is the present value of the annuity?

(A) £50,000
(B) £29,029
(C) £161,093
(D) £100,739.

Answer

Question 44

The figures for December's sales in an additive model for the trend in monthly sales figures has the following values:

T = £25,000
S = £2,300
C = −£500
R = £207.

Which of the following comments explain the values given:

(A) There is an economic boom increasing sales levels throughout the industry.
(B) Sales are often higher in December.
(C) Sales are entirely dependent on the time of year and the economic cycle of the business.
(D) Sales are usually lower around year end.

Answer

Question 45

The formula in cell B10 below calculates the ROI on the investment.
    Two parts of the formula have been omitted here. Identify the blanks
    = ROUND(■ (B3:B6)/B2, ■)

	A	B	C	D	E
1					
2	Amount invested	166700			
3	Cash Flow year 1	69550			
4	Cash flow year 2	65550			
5	Cash flow year 3	45000			
6	Cash flow year 4	35000	215100		
7					
8	Fixed cost of capital	8%			
9					
10	ROI	0.30			
11					

(A) IRR   1
(B) AVERAGE   1
(C) NPV   2
(D) ROI   2

Answer

Mock Assessment 2 – Solutions

✓ Solution 1

$(3a^3x^2) = (3 \times 4^3 \times 3)^2 = (3 \times 64 \times 3)^2 = 331{,}776$

Answer: (C).

✓ Solution 2

If the coefficient of determination is 0.899 for example, this tells us that 89.9% of the variations between the observations would be predicted by the regression analysis. The remaining 1.01% is caused by other factors.

Answer: (C).

✓ Solution 3

If one side is multiplied by 2 then the other must be divided by 2 which is ×0.5.

Answer: (B).

✓ Solution 4

If $P = aD + b$

Where $P = 12$, $D = 2{,}500$ so $12 = 2{,}500a + b$ (1)
Where $P = 10$, $D = 3{,}300$ so $10 = 3{,}300a + b$ (2)

(1) minus (2) gives:

$$2 = -800a$$
$$\text{so} \quad a = -0.0025$$

substituting into (1) gives:

$$12 = 2{,}500 \times (-0.0025) + b$$
$$\text{so} \quad b = 6.25 + 12 = 18.25$$
$$\text{hence} \quad P = 18.25 - 0.0025D$$

Therefore $a = -0.0025$ and $b = 18.25$.

Answer: (C).

✓ Solution 5

(ii) is not true as it is not suitable for use in mathematical tables.
(iii) is not true as data must be arranged in order of size which can be time consuming.

Answer: (D).

✅ Solution 6

Breakeven occurs where profit = 0
(i.e.) where $-2,400 + 30D - 0.06D^2 = 0$

The Solution is given by $D = \dfrac{-b \pm \sqrt{b^2 - 4ac}}{2a}$

Where a = -0.06, b = 30 and c = $-2,400$

$$D = \frac{-30 \pm \sqrt{30^2 - 4 \times -0.06 \times -2,400}}{2 \times -0.06}$$

$$D = \frac{-30 \pm \sqrt{900 - 576}}{-0.12}$$

$$D = \frac{-30 \pm 18}{-0.12}$$

$$D = 100 \text{ or } 400 \text{ units}$$

Answer: (B).

✅ Solution 7

156.98 units is the number that would be sold if no sales staff are employed. The correlation is positive so sales units are increased as more staff are employed.

Answer: (D).

✅ Solution 8

The price excluding VAT is currently:

$$\frac{4.36}{1.175} = 3.71$$

If VAT were 10.5%, the price would become £3.71 × 1.105 = £4.10 to the nearest penny.

Answer: (C).

✅ Solution 9

Three months is a quarter of a year.

There are four querters in a year so $(1 + r)^4 = 1.268$

$$(1 + r) = \sqrt[4]{1.268}$$

$$r = \sqrt[4]{1.268} - 1 = 0.61$$

Answer: (C).

Solution 10

A group of worksheets is called a workbook.

A named group of cells does not have a specific name although is often referred to as a range.

Answer: (C).

Solution 11

3ab is common to all three of the terms. Dividing each term by 3ab gives the figures inside the brackets.

Answer: (A).

Solution 12

Project A = [0.6 × 10,000] + [0.4 × 5,000] = 8,000

Project B = [0.2 × 20,000] + [0.8 × 2,000] = 5,600

Project C = [0.9 × 8,000] + [0.1 × 3,000] = 7,500

Project D = [0.5 × 7,000] + [0.5 × 6,000] = 6,500

Therefore project A is best, followed by C, then D then B.

Answers: (B).

Solution 13

Probability of selecting a cat: $\dfrac{750}{(750+1{,}500)}$

Probability of the cat selected being immune: $\dfrac{450}{750}$

Probability of selecting an immune cat: $\dfrac{750}{(750+1{,}500)} \times \dfrac{450}{750} = \dfrac{450}{2{,}250} = 1$ in 5.

Answer: (D).

Solution 14

Cyclical variation is caused by business cycles resulting from changes in the economy. Seasonal variations account for the regular variations that occur at certain times of year. Random variation is caused by unpredictable factors.

Answer: (A).

Solution 15

A ball of each colour can be selected in one of six different ways:

Ball 1	Ball 2	Ball 3
Red p(4/9)	Yellow p(3/8)	Green p(2/7)
Red p(4/9)	Green p(2/8)	Yellow p(3/7)
Green p(2/9)	Red p(4/8)	Yellow p(3/7)
Green p(2/9)	Yellow p(3/8)	Red p(4/7)
Yellow p(3/9)	Red p(4/8)	Green(2/7)
Yellow p(3/9)	Green p(2/8)	Red p(4/7)

The probability of each selection occurring is $\dfrac{4 \times 3 \times 2}{9 \times 8 \times 7} = \dfrac{24}{504} = 0.048$

So the probability of selecting one of each colour is 6×0.048 = 0.29.

Answer: (B).

Solution 16

Project A has the highest Net Present Value

	PV	Return
A	−£7,000 + (£3,000 × 3.791) = 4,373	£3,000 each year, payable in arrears, for five years
B	−£4,500 + [(£1,000 × 0.909) + (£2,500 × 0.826) + (£2,500 × 0.751) + (£1,500 × 0.683) + (£1,500 × 0.621)] = £2,286	£1,000 at the end of the first year, £2,500 at the end of the next two years and £1,500 for the last two years
C	−£5,500 + [£2,000 × (1 + 3.17)] = £2,840	£2,000 payable every year in advance for five years
D	−£11,000 + (1500 ÷ 0.1) = £4,000	£1,500 in perpetuity

Answer: (A).

Solution 17

$7,467 - 356.1 \div (44.846 - 2)$
$= 7,467 - 356.1 \div 42.846$
$= 7,467 - 8.311$
$= 7,458.689$
$= 7,460$ to 3 s.f.

Answer: (B).

Solution 18

£50,000 = Repayment × 20 yr factor

$$AF = \frac{1}{r}\left[1 - \frac{1}{(1+r)^n}\right] \text{ or } \frac{1-(1+r)^{-n}}{r}$$

$$AF = \frac{1}{0.06}\left[1 - \frac{1}{(1+0.06)^{20}}\right] \text{ or } \frac{1-(1+0.06)^{-20}}{0.06}$$

AF = 11.4699

£50,000 = Repayment × 11.4699

$$\text{Repayment} = \frac{50,000}{11.4699} = £4{,}359 \text{ per annum to the nearest £}$$

$$\text{Gross monthly payment} = \frac{£4{,}359}{12} = £363.25 \ .$$

Answer: (B).

Solution 19

The insurer receives	£1,500
Less: 0.0015 × 750,000	£1,125
Value of the policy	£375

Answer: (C).

Solution 20

(i) False — y is the dependent variable
(ii) False — Quadratic equations have one turning point — either a minimum or a maximum depending on the equation
(iii) False — If $b^2 - 4ac$ is zero there is one solution
(iv) True — any number of equations can be plotted on the same graph

Answers: (B).

Solution 21

Probability	0.1	0.2	0.4	0.3	Expected value
Demand	500	600	700	800	
Bake					
500	500 × 0.4 = 200	200	200	200	0.1 × 200 + 0.2 × 200 + 0.4 × 200 + 0.3 × 200 = 200
600	500 × 0.5 − 600 × 0.1 = 190	600 × 0.4 = 240	240	240	0.1 × 190 + 0.2 × 240 + 0.4 × 240 + 0.3 × 240 = 235
700	500 × 0.5 − 700 × 0.1 = 180	600 × 0.5 − 700 × 0.1 = 230	700 × 0.4 = 280	280	0.1 × 180 + 0.2 × 230 + 0.4 × 280 + 0.3 × 280 = 260
800	500 × 0.5 − 800 × 0.1 = 170	600 × 0.5 − 800 × 0.1 = 220	700 × 0.5 − 800 × 0.1 = 270	800 × 0.4 = 320	0.1 × 170 + 0.2 × 220 + 0.4 × 270 + 0.3 × 320 = 265

Answer: (D).

Solution 22

$72 + 79 + 84 + 90 = 325$

Answers: (A).

Solution 23

The correlation is approximately linear as the data roughly follows a straight line, but the correlation is negative as the line is downward sloping. Since sales depend on the temperature, sales would be considered to be the dependent variable.

Answer: (A).

Solution 24

$$IRR = A + \left(\frac{NA}{NA - NB}\right) \times (B - A)$$

$$IRR = 8 + \left(\frac{1,090}{1,090 - (-960)}\right) \times (12 - 8)$$

$$IRR = 8 + \frac{1,090}{2,050}(4)$$

$$IRR = 10.13\%$$

Answer: (A).

Solution 25

Co-efficient of variation = $\dfrac{\sigma}{X}$

Product WW	34/550 = 6.18%
Product XX	21/550 = 3.82%
Product YY	18/550 = 3.27%
Product ZZ	28/550 = 5.09%

So product WW has the highest co-efficient of variation.

Answer: (A).

Solution 26

$P(F_1) = 0.02$
$P(\text{not } F_1) = 1 - 0.02 = 0.98$
$P(F_2) = 0.03$
$P(\text{not } F_2) = 1 - 0.03 = 0.97$

$P(\text{one defect only}) = P(F_1 \text{ but not } F_2) + P(F_2 \text{ but not } F_1)$
$= [0.02 \times 0.97] + [0.03 \times 0.98] = 0.0488$

Answer: (C).

Solution 27

The scale is 1 cm = 4 frequencies, so 28 should have a height of 7 cm.

Answer: (D).

Solution 28

The standard deviation is calculated as follows:

$$\sigma = \sqrt{\left(\dfrac{\sum fx^2}{\sum f}\right) - \left(\dfrac{\sum fx}{\sum f}\right)^2}$$

$$\sigma = \sqrt{\dfrac{156{,}300}{150} - \left(\dfrac{4{,}200}{150}\right)^2}$$

$$\sigma = \sqrt{1{,}042 - 28^2}$$

$$\sigma = \sqrt{1{,}042 - 784} = \sqrt{258} = 16.1$$

Answer: (C).

Solution 29

Candidate	Rank of grade	Rank of exam score	d (difference)	d²
Mr A	1.5*	4	−2.5	6.25
Ms B	3	3	0	0.00
Mrs C	1.5*	5	−3.5	12.25
Mr D	4	1	3	9.00
Mr E	5	2	3	9.00
				36.5

* Since Mr A and Mrs C share the 1st position, ranks 1 and 2 are split to give them 1.5 each

$$R = 1 - \frac{6 \sum d^2}{n(n^2 - 1)} = 1 - \frac{6 \times 36.5}{5(25 - 1)} = -0.825$$

Answer: (B).

Solution 30

The equation of the line is $y = a + bx$

where $b = \dfrac{n \sum xy - (\sum x)(\sum y)}{n \sum x^2 - (\sum x)^2}$

$$b = \frac{(14 \times 15{,}390) - (590 \times 84)}{14 \times 87{,}400 - 590^2}$$

$$b = \frac{165{,}900}{875{,}500}$$

$$b = 0.189$$

$a = \bar{y} - b\bar{x}$ ($\bar{y}, \bar{x}$: means of y and x, respectively)

Therefore

$$a = \frac{84}{14} - 0.189 \times \frac{590}{14} = -1.965$$

Regression line is therefore:

$$Y = -1.96 + 0.189x$$

Answer: (D).

Solution 31

Trend = $0.0021 \times 2008^2 + 0.5 \times 2008 + 42.8 = 9{,}514.13$
Forecast = $1.78 \times$ Trend = $16{,}935$ to nearest whole number.

Answer: (D).

Solution 32

Answer: (C).

Solution 33

$$Y = T + S + C + R$$

Where T = trend, S = seasonal component, C = cyclical component and R = random component

$$Y = 25,000 + 2,300 - 500 + 207$$
$$Y = 27,007$$

Answer: (A).

Solution 34

$$875 = 467 + 35b$$

$$b = \frac{875 - 467}{35} = 11.66$$

Answer: (C).

Solution 35

Trend forecast = $42.81 + 8.7 \times 21 = 225.51$

Forecast = trend × seasonal factor
= $225.51 \times 2.21 = 498.38 = 498$ to the nearest whole number.

Answer: (C).

Solution 36

Since the data is given in percentages already, the angle is simply 16% × 360°.

Answer: (B).

✓ Solution 37

$$r = \frac{n\sum xy - \sum x \sum y}{\sqrt{\left(\left(n\sum x^2 - \left(\sum x\right)^2\right)\left(n\sum y^2 - \left(\sum y\right)^2\right)\right)}}$$

$$r = \frac{5 \times 1,360 - 7.2 \times 877}{\sqrt{((5 \times 11.7 - 7.2^2)(5 \times 164,776.42 - 877^2))}}$$

$$r = \frac{485.6}{\sqrt{(6.66 \times 54,753.1)}}$$

$$r = \frac{485.6}{603.87}$$

$$r = 0.80$$

Answer: (B).

✓ Solution 38

$$\frac{125}{116} \times 100 = 108$$

Answer: (D).

✓ Solution 39

$$\text{Present Value} = \frac{\text{Annual payment}}{r}$$

$$\frac{£6,000}{0.035} = £171,429$$

Answer: (A).

✓ Solution 40

Nine month ratio = $1.18^{\frac{9}{12}} = 1.1322$

The nine month rate is therefore 13.22%.

Answer: (C).

Solution 41

$$z = \frac{x - \mu}{\sigma}$$

$$z = \frac{6 - 10}{5} = -0.8$$

From the tables, the shaded area is p = 0.2881
The area below 6 kg is 0.5 − 0.2881 = 0.2119

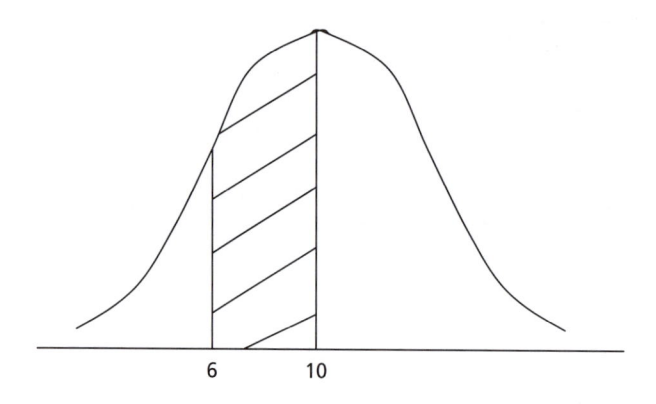

Answer: (D).

Solution 42

Formatting only changes the display, the full number is still the one used for any further calculations. To round the actual data, the = ROUND function must be used.

Answer: (A).

Solution 43

$$AF = \frac{1}{r}\left[1 - \frac{1}{(1+r)^n}\right] \text{ or } \frac{1 - (1+r)^{-n}}{r}$$

$$AF = \frac{1}{0.045}\left[1 - \frac{1}{(1+0.045)^{15}}\right] \text{ or } \frac{1 - (1+0.045)^{-15}}{0.045}$$

AF = 10.74

PV = 15,000 × 10.74 = 161,093

Answer: (C).

✓ Solution 44

The cycle factor is negative suggesting less than normal sales activity. The existence of a random factor shows that sales are dependent on more than just the season and the cycle. Since the seasonal factor is positive, sales usually rise at this time of year.

Answer: (B).

✓ Solution 45

Average is the Excel term used to calculate the ROI. Neither NPV nor IRR would require the figures to be divided by a cell contents as in the formula here. The answer is rounded to one decimal places so the second blank must be 1.

Answer: (B).

Index

Index

A
Accountant's Tax Weekly, 251
Accuracy considerations, 20
Acquisition processes, data, 41
Addition:
   concepts, 3–4
   data variations, 20
   probability rules, 349–51
Additive models, time series, 325–8
Aggregative price index:
   concepts, 198–9
   formulae, 198
Aggregative quantity index:
   concepts, 200–1
   formulae, 200
Annual ratio, interest calculations, 227
Annuities, 239–41
Approximations, 20
Arithmetic mean:
   classes, 127–31
   coefficient of variation, 148–9
   comparisons, 137
   concepts, 127–31
   deviation concepts, 140–2, 144, 145–8
   discrete variables, 138
   formulae, 128
   frequency distributions, 128, 129
   mean absolute deviation, 144–5
   normal distributions, 166, 362–9
   skewed distributions, 132, 137
   standard deviation, 145–8
   see also Averages; Sample mean
Assessment:
   format, 414–15
   mock assessments, 483–533
   preparation, 413–14
   questions, 417–51
   solutions, 453–80
   tips, 414
   weightings, 414–15
Averages:
   comparisons, 137
   concepts, 127
   frequency distributions, 76–8
   index numbers, 187–206, 212–13, 214–15, 463–6
   moving averages, 319–22
   skewed distributions, 132, 137
   standard deviation, 145–8
   weighted averages, 194–5
   see also Arithmetic mean; Median; Mode; Normal distributions

B
Bar charts, 87–90
   using Excel, 90–5
Base-weighted indices, 196
Base years, index numbers, 196
Basic mathematics, 3–37, 414, 417, 453
Behavioural considerations, decision-making, 358–61
Bias:
   interviews, 49–50
   sampling, 43
Bivariate data, 273
Brackets, 3–4
Breakeven level, 70

C
Calculators, 4
   formulae, 11–13
Capital investments:
   costs, 239
   decision-making, 240
   see also Investments

Causal approaches, forecasting, 287
CBI surveys, 48
Chadwick, Leslie, 251
Chain-base index numbers:
    concepts, 192–4
    formulae, 192
Classes:
    arithmetic mean, 127–31
    frequency distributions, 72–4, 76, 78, 79, 99, 101, 129, 356
    mid-points, 138, 150
    mode, 135
    open-ended classes, 138, 143
    standard deviation, 145–8
    unequal intervals, 80, 82, 85, 103, 136
Cluster sampling, 46
Coefficient of determination, 290, 292
Coefficient of variation, 148–9
Components, time series, 309–11
Composite index numbers, 194–5
Compound bar charts, 88, 104, 112
Compound interest:
    concepts, 227–8
    formulae, 227
Conditional probabilities, 355
Continuous probability distributions, 362
Continuous variables, 75–6
Correlation, 274–91, 300, 439, 469
    coefficient of determination, 290, 292
    concepts, 274–82
    formulae, 278, 280
    interpretation, 279
    Pearson's coefficient, 280, 282, 292
    rank correlation, 280–2
    Spearman's coefficient, 280–2
    types, 280–2
Cost of capital, 239
Cumulative frequency distributions:
    concepts, 76–8
    deciles, 142–3
    median, 131–5
    ogives, 78–9, 98–103
    quartile deviation, 140–2
Current-weighted indices, 199–200
Cyclical components, time series, 310, 317, 322

D

Data:
    accuracy, 20
    acquisition processes, 41
    bar charts, 87–90
    bivariate data, 273
    capture, 153–5
    classification types, 41–2
    concepts, 41–2
    importing to Excel, 50–2
    obtaining data, 41–52, 421–3, 456–8
    pie charts, 85–7
    presentation, 65–103, 423–7, 458–9
    primary data, 41, 43
    questionnaires, 48–9
    raw data concepts, 65
    sampling, 43–4
    secondary data, 48
    tabulation, 95–6
    time series, 309–28
    variations, 20
    see also Graphs
Deciles, 142–3
Decimals, 6
Decision-making:
    behavioural considerations, 358–9
    capital investments, 239, 246, 248, 251
    expected value, 376, 381, 475
    financial, 359
    non-financial considerations, 251–2
    probabilities, 358–61
    risk, 362
Deflation of series, 203
Dependent variables:
    concepts, 10, 273, 309
    graphs, 78
    regression analysis, 290
Depreciation, 11, 230–1
Descriptive statistics, 129–55, 157, 175, 177, 427
    mean, 157
    measures of spread, 159–60
    outliers, 160–1
    standard deviation and standard error, 157–9
Deseasonalise concept, 318
Deviation concepts, 144, 145–8
Discount factors *see* Present values
Discrete probability distributions:
    concepts, 356–8
    formulae, 357
Discrete variables:
    averages, 137
    concepts, 356
Dispersion *see* Spread
Division:
    concepts, 3–5
    data variations, 20
    powers, 7

E

Economic forecasts, 329–30
Economist, 207
Effective annual rates of interest, 229
Empirical probabilities, 353, 356, 357
Enumerators, questionnaires, 49
Equals sign, equations, 10
Equations:
    concepts, 14–25
    linear graphs, 65–70
    quadratic graphs, 71–2
    regression analysis, 290
    solving, 14–17
    types, 22–6
    see also Formulae
Equivalent rates of interest, 228
Errors:
    data, 20
    rounding, 20–1
    sampling, 43
    see also Variations
EV *see* Expected value
Exact probabilities, 349, 356
Examination *see* Assessment
Expected value (EV):
    decision-making, 358–61
    discrete probability distributions, 356–8
    limitations, 361–2
    risk, 373
Exponential number, 13
Extrapolative approaches, 273, 309, 312, 324, 325

F

Family Expenditure Survey (FES), 202
Financial mathematics, 225–49
    Accountant's Tax Weekly article, 251–2
    annuities, 239–41
    capital investment decisions, 251
    concepts, 227–49
    decision-making, 358–61
    geometric progressions, 223
    internal rate of return, 243–6
    limitations, 251
    loans, 242–3
    mortgages, 242–3
    perpetuities, 241–2
    present values, 234–5
    see also Interest calculations; Investments
Financial Times, 188
Fixed-base index numbers, 192, 193
Forecasting:
    correlation, 274–7, 300, 439, 469
    economic forecasts, 329–30
    extrapolative approaches, 273, 309, 312, 324, 325
    linear trends, 312–14
    moving averages, 313, 319, 322, 325
    regression analysis, 290
    seasonal components, 314–16
    time series, 309–28
    validity, 324–5
Formulae, 11–13
    aggregative price index, 198
    aggregative quantity index, 200
    annuities, 239
    arithmetic mean, 128
    chain-base index numbers, 192
    compound interest, 227
    concepts, 11–13
    correlation, 274–7, 300, 439, 469
    correlation coefficients, 278–9
    discrete probability distributions, 356–8
    general linear form, 68
    geometric progressions, 223
    index numbers, 189, 192
    internal rate of return, 243
    least-squares regression lines, 286
    mean absolute deviation, 144–5
    median, 131–5
    normal distributions, 166, 362–9
    Pearson's correlation coefficient, 278–9
    perpetuities, 241–2
    present values, 234–5
    probability, 349–51
    quadratic equations, 15–16
    regression analysis, 290
    relative price indices, 196–8
    relative quantity index, 200
    simple interest, 225–6
    Spearman's rank correlation coefficient, 280–2
    standard deviation, 145–8
    see also Equations
Fractions:
    concepts, 4–5
    ratios concept, 19–20
Frequency density, 81
Frequency distributions:
    arithmetic mean, 127–31
    classes, 72–4, 76, 78, 79, 99, 101, 129, 356
    concepts, 72
    continuous/discrete variables, 76

Frequency distributions: (*Continued*)
    cumulative frequency distributions, 76–8
    discrete probability distributions, 356–8
    histograms, 78–85
    median, 131–5
    mode, 135–7
    ogives, 78–85, 98–103
    open-ended classes, 138, 140, 143
    ranges, 139–40
    skewed distributions, 132, 137, 138
    tallying, 72–4
    unequal class intervals, 80, 82, 83
Frequency polygons, 80
Functions:
    concepts, 10–11
    general linear form, 68
    linear graphs, 65–70
    quadratic graphs, 71–2

G

General addition rules, probability, 349–51
General linear form, formulae, 68
General multiplicative rules, probability, 352
Geometric progressions (GP), 233–4
Gradients:
    concepts, 68
    least-squares regression lines, 284, 275, 288
Gradients Solving equations, 14–17
Graphs:
    frequency polygons, 80
    gradients concept, 68
    histograms, 78–85
    of hyperbola, using Excel to produce, 25
    intercept concepts, 68, 72, 286
    internal rate of return, 243
    linear graphs, 65–70
    normal distributions, 166, 362–9
    ogives, 78–85, 98–102
    quadratic graphs, 71–2
    scales, 87
    scatter diagrams, 275
    simultaneous linear equations, 70–1
    time series, 312, 321
    unequal class intervals, 80, 82, 83
    x/y-co-ordinates, 66
Gripaios, Peter, 329
Guide to Official Statistics (Office for National Statistics), 48

H

Histograms:
    concepts, 78–85
    mode, 135–6

How to Lie with Statistics (Huff, 1973), 105–8, 165–6
Huff, Darrell, 105–8, 165–6

I

Independent variables, 10, 273, 288, 289, 309
Index linking, RPI, 202, 203, 205
Index numbers, 187–206
    aggregative price index, 198–9
    aggregative quantity index, 200
    chain-base index numbers, 192–4
    composite index numbers, 194–5
    concepts, 187–206
    Economist article, 207–8
    formulae, 187, 192, 194
    index linking, 202, 203, 205
    interpretation, 188–9
    notation, 196
    quantity indices, 200–1
    relative price indices, 196–8
    relative quantity index, 200–1
    RPI, 202–6
    series splicing, 191
    weighted averages, 194–5
Inflation, 202
    deflation of series, 203
    index linking, 202, 203, 205
    see also Retail price index
Influencing variable, 273
Information, 42–3
    analysed data, 42
    see also Data
Integers, 4
Intercept:
    concepts, 68
    least-squares regression lines, 284, 285, 292
Interest calculations:
    annuities, 239–41
    complex investments, 231–2
    compound interest, 227–8
    depreciation, 11, 230–1
    effective annual rates of interest, 229
    equivalent rates of interest, 228–9
    internal rate of return, 243–6
    loans, 242–3
    net present values, 240–1
    perpetuities, 241–2
    present values, 234–5
    simple interest, 225–8
Internal rate of return (IRR), 243–6
    formulae, 245
    graphs, 244

Interpolation, forecasting, 291
Interquartile range concept, 140–2
Interviews, 49–50
Investments:
    cost of capital, 239
    evaluations, 231–2
    present values, 234–5
    sinking funds, 260
    see also Interest calculations
IRR *see* Internal rate of return

K
Kurtosis, 160

L
Least-squares regression lines, 284, 285, 292
Linear correlation, 275, 276, 278, 282, 283, 292
Linear equations:
    graphs, 70–1
    solving, 14–17
Linear trends:
    concepts, 312–14
    forecasting, 312–14
Loans, 242–3
Logistic trends, 310

M
Management Decision, 329–30
Market research, 45, 47, 56
Marketing risks, 374
Maxima, quadratic graphs, 71–2
Mean *see* Arithmetic mean; Median
    comparisons, 137
    concepts, 127–31, 157
    cumulative frequency distributions, 76–8
    formulae, 128
    ogives, 78–85, 98–101
    quartile deviation, 140–2
    skewed distributions, 132, 137
    see also Averages
Mean absolute deviation, 144–5
Median, 131–4
Mid-points, classes, 138, 150
Minima, quadratic graphs, 71–2
Mock assessments, 483–503, 507–33
Mode:
    comparisons, 137
    concepts, 135–6
    range, 139–40
    skewed distributions, 132, 137
    see also Averages

Models, time series, 309–11, 325–8
Mortgages, 242–3
Moving averages, 313, 319, 322, 325
Multiple bar charts, 88, 90
Multiple regression, 291
Multiplication:
    concepts, 3, 351–4
    data variations, 20
    powers, 7–8
Multiplicative models, time series, 311, 314, 317, 325
Multiplicative rules, probability, 352, 375
Multistage sampling, 47–8

N
Negative linear correlation, 276, 278
Negative numbers, 4
Net present values (NPV):
    concepts, 236–9
    problems, 239
Non-financial considerations, decision-making, 251–2
Non-linear correlation, 276
Normal distributions, 166, 362–9
    concepts, 362–3
    formulae, 363
    graphs, 363, 364
    tables, 363–7
NPV *see* Net present values
Numbers:
    powers, 7–8
    roots, 7–8
    rounding concepts, 5–6
    types, 4–5
    whole numbers, 4
    see also Operations

O
Obtaining data, 41–57
Office for National Statistics, 48
Ogives:
    concepts, 78–85, 98–103
    deciles, 142–4
    median, 131–5
    quartile deviation, 140–2
Open-ended classes, frequency distributions, 138, 143
Operations:
    concepts, 3–4
    positive/negative numbers, 4–5
    priorities, 4
    see also Numbers

P

Payoff tables, 376
Pearson's correlation coefficient, 278–9
Percentages concept, 19–20
Perpetuities, 241–2
Pie charts, 85–7
Population sampling, 46
Positive linear correlation, 276, 278–9
Positive numbers, 4
Postal surveys, 50
Powers, numbers, 7–8
Preliminary analysis, 155–7
Preparing for the assessment, 413–15
Present values (PV), 234–5
    calculation, 235
    concepts, 234–5
    formulae, 235
    perpetuities, 241–2
    tables, 235
Presenting data, 65–103, 423–7, 458–9
Prices:
    relative ratio, 196
    RPI indicators, 202
Primary data:
    concepts, 41
    sampling, 43–4
Priorities, operations, 3–4
Probability:
    addition rules, 349–51
    concepts, 348–9
    decision-making, 358–61
    discrete probability distributions, 356–8
    empirical probabilities, 353, 356
    expected value, 356
    formulae, 348, 351, 353
    multiplicative rules, 352, 375
    normal distributions, 166, 362–9
    opposites, 351
    payoff tables, 360, 376
    random number tables, 45, 46, 48
    rules, 349–51
    sampling, 44–6
Probability sampling methods:
    concepts, 44–6
    costs, 46
Profitability, NPV calculation, 247
Proportions, 19
Public statistics, 42, 46, 48
PV see Present values

Q

Quadratic equations:
    roots, 7
    solving, 14–17
Quadratic graphs, 71–2
Quantity indices, 200–1
Quartile deviation, 140–2
Questionnaires, 48–9, 153
    see also Sampling
Quota sampling, 47

R

Random number tables, 45, 46, 48
Random sampling methods see Probability
Range:
    concepts, 139–40
    frequency distributions, 72–4, 76, 78, 79, 99, 101, 129, 132, 135, 162, 163, 350
Rank correlation, 280–2
Ratios:
    interest calculations, 225
    price relative, 196, 198, 213–14
Raw data concepts, 65, 72, 73, 103, 127, 135, 165, 190
Real wages, 204
Regression analysis:
    concepts, 282
    forecasting, 312–14
    formulae, 282
    least-squares criteria, 283–6
    linear trends, 312–14
    multiple regression concepts, 291
    validity, 290–1
    variable selection, 282
Relative price indices, 196–8
Relative quantity index, 200–1
Repayment mortgages, 242
Residual components, time series, 311, 317, 325
Response variable, 273
Retail price index (RPI):
    concepts, 202
    deflation of series, 203
    index linking, 202, 203, 205
    omissions, 202
    real wages, 204
    usage, 382, 383
Revision see Assessment
Risk and uncertainty, 372–5
Roots:
    numbers, 7
    quadratic equations, 15–16

Opposites, probability, 351
Outliers, 160–1

Rounding:
    concepts, 5
    decimal places, 6
    errors, 21
    index numbers, 187–206
    significant figures, 5–6
RPI *see* Retail price index
Rules of probability, 349–51

S
Sample mean, 128
Sampling:
    cluster sampling, 46
    concepts, 41–2
    errors, 43
    frames, 46
    methods, 46–7
    multistages, 47–8
    primary data, 43–4
    probability, 44–6
    quota sampling, 47
    stratified sampling, 47
    systematic sampling, 46–7
Scales, graphs, 68
Scatter diagrams, 275
Seasonal adjustments, 318
Seasonal components:
    forecasting, 314–16
    time series, 303–5
Secondary data:
    concepts, 41
    sources, 48
Series:
    geometric progressions, 233–4
    splicing, 191
    time series, 309, 334–5, 441–9, 471–80
Significant figures, rounding, 5–6
Simple interest, 225–6
Simple random sampling, 44
Simple regression, 291
Simultaneous linear equations:
    graphs, 21–5, 70–1
    solving, 16–17
Sinking funds, 232, 260
Skewed distributions, 132, 137
Skewness, 159
Slopes *see* Gradients Solving equations
Spearman's rank correlation coefficient, 280
Special addition rules, probability, 349
Special multiplication rules, probability, 351, 354
Splicing, index numbers, 191, 192

Spread:
    coefficient of variation, 148–9
    comparisons, 150
    deciles, 142–4
    mean absolute deviation, 144–5
    quartile deviation, 140–2
    range, 139–40
    standard deviation, 145–8
Stacked bar charts, 88
Standard deviation:
    classes, 75
    coefficient of variation, 148–9
    concepts, 145–8
    normal distributions, 166, 362–9
    skewed distributions, 132, 137
    and standard error, 157–9
Statistical analysis using Excel, 152
    data capture, 153–5
    descriptive statistics, 157
    mean, 157
    standard deviation and standard error, 157–9
    measures of spread, 159–60
    outliers, 160–1
    preliminary analysis, 155–7
    questionnaire, 153
Statistics:
    descriptive statistics, 127
    Economist article, 207–8
Stratified random sampling, 44–6
Subject-change rules, equations, 14
Subjective probabilities, 362
Subtraction:
    concepts, 3
    data variations, 20
Systematic sampling, 46–7

T
Tables:
    mathematical, 3–4, 8–9
    normal distributions, 166, 362–9
    payoff tables, 376
Tallying:
    concepts, 72–4
    frequency distributions, 72–4
Telephone interviews, 49–50
Thatcher, Margaret, 207
Time series:
    additive models, 311, 325–8
    components, 309–11
    concepts, 309

Time series: (*Continued*)
  graphs, 312, 321
  models, 309–11
  moving averages, 313, 319, 322, 325
  multiplicative models, 311
  seasonal adjustments, 318
  validity, 290
Trends, time series, 310, 312–14

U
Unbiased sampling, 44
Uncertainty, 347
  and risk, 372–5
  see also Probability
Underlying trend, time series, 310
Unequal class intervals, frequency distributions, 80, 81, 83, 136

V
VAR *see* Vector autogressive models
Variables:
  concepts, 10–11
  continuous variables, 75–6
  correlation, 274–9
  discrete variables, 75–6
  equation solving, 14–15, 70–1
  formulae concept, 11
  functions, 10–11
  regression analysis, 290, 319, 328
  simultaneous linear equations, 16–17
Variance concepts, 145, 150, 151, 152
Variations:
  coefficient of determination, 290, 292
  coefficient of variation, 148–9
  data, 20
  time series, 309–10
  see also Errors
Vector autogressive models (VAR), 329

W
Weighted averages, 194
Weightings, assessment, 414–15
Wells, H.G. 207
Whole numbers, 10, 75

X
X-co-ordinates concept, 66

Y
Y-co-ordinates concept, 66